matt kindt   tyler jenkins   hilary jenkins

GRASS KINGS

volume two

BOOM! STUDIOS

GRASS KINGS Volume Two, June 2018. Published by BOOM! Studios, a division of Boom Entertainment, Inc. Grass Kings is ™ & © 2018 Matt Kindt & Tyler Jenkins. Originally published in single magazine form as GRASS KINGS No. 7-11. ™ & © 2017, 2018 Matt Kindt & Tyler Jenkins. All rights reserved. BOOM! Studios™ and the BOOM! Studios logo are trademarks of Boom Entertainment, Inc, registered in various countries and categories. All characters, events, and institutions depicted herein are fictional. Any similarity between any of the names, characters, persons, events, and/or institutions in this publication to actual names, characters, and persons, whether living or dead, events, and/or institutions is unintended and purely coincidental. BOOM! Studios does not read or accept unsolicited submissions of ideas, stories, or artwork.

BOOM! Studios, 5670 Wilshire Boulevard, Suite 400, Los Angeles, CA, 90036-5679. Published in China. First Printing.

ISBN: 978-1-68415-181-3, eISBN: 978-1-61398-996-8

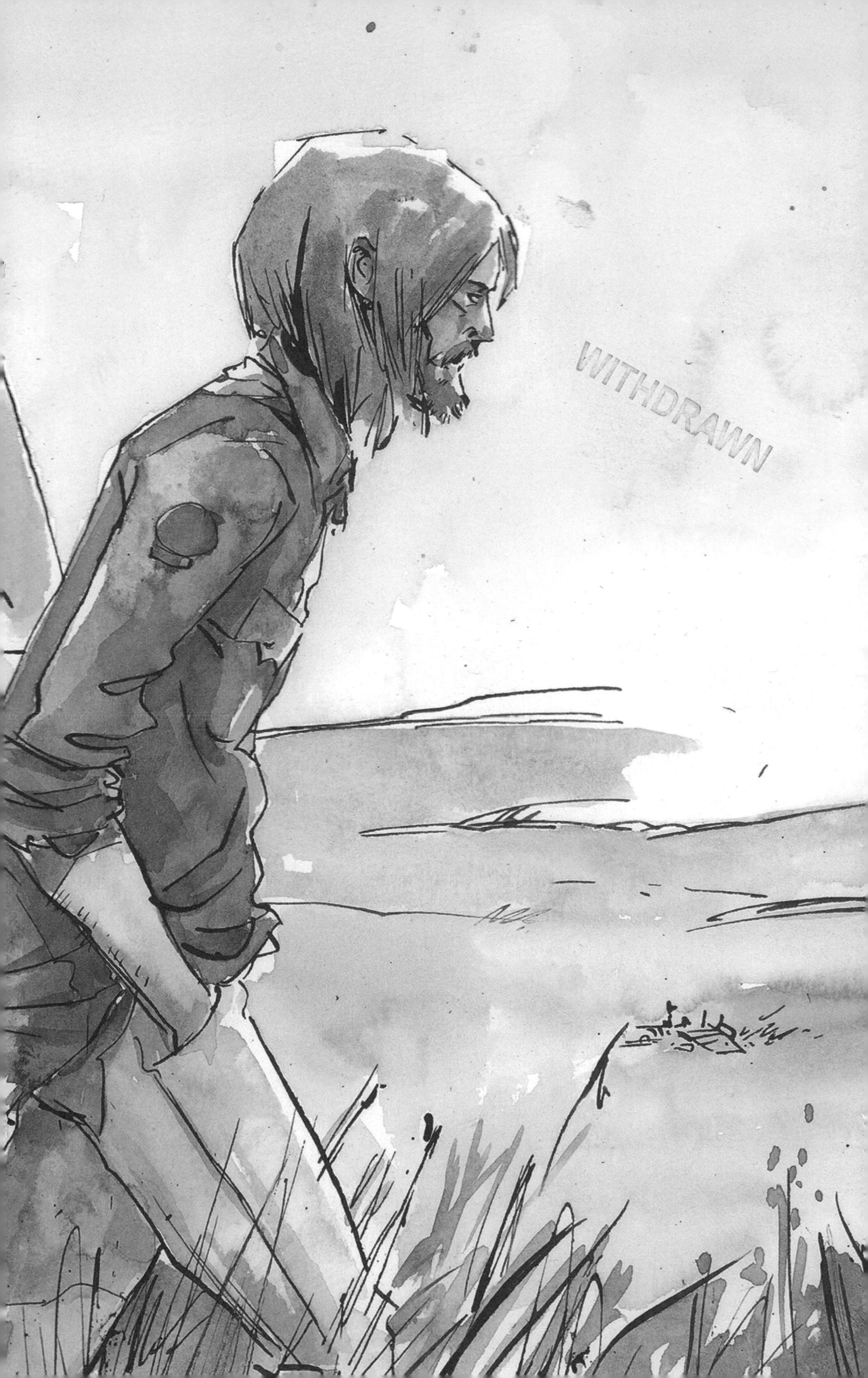

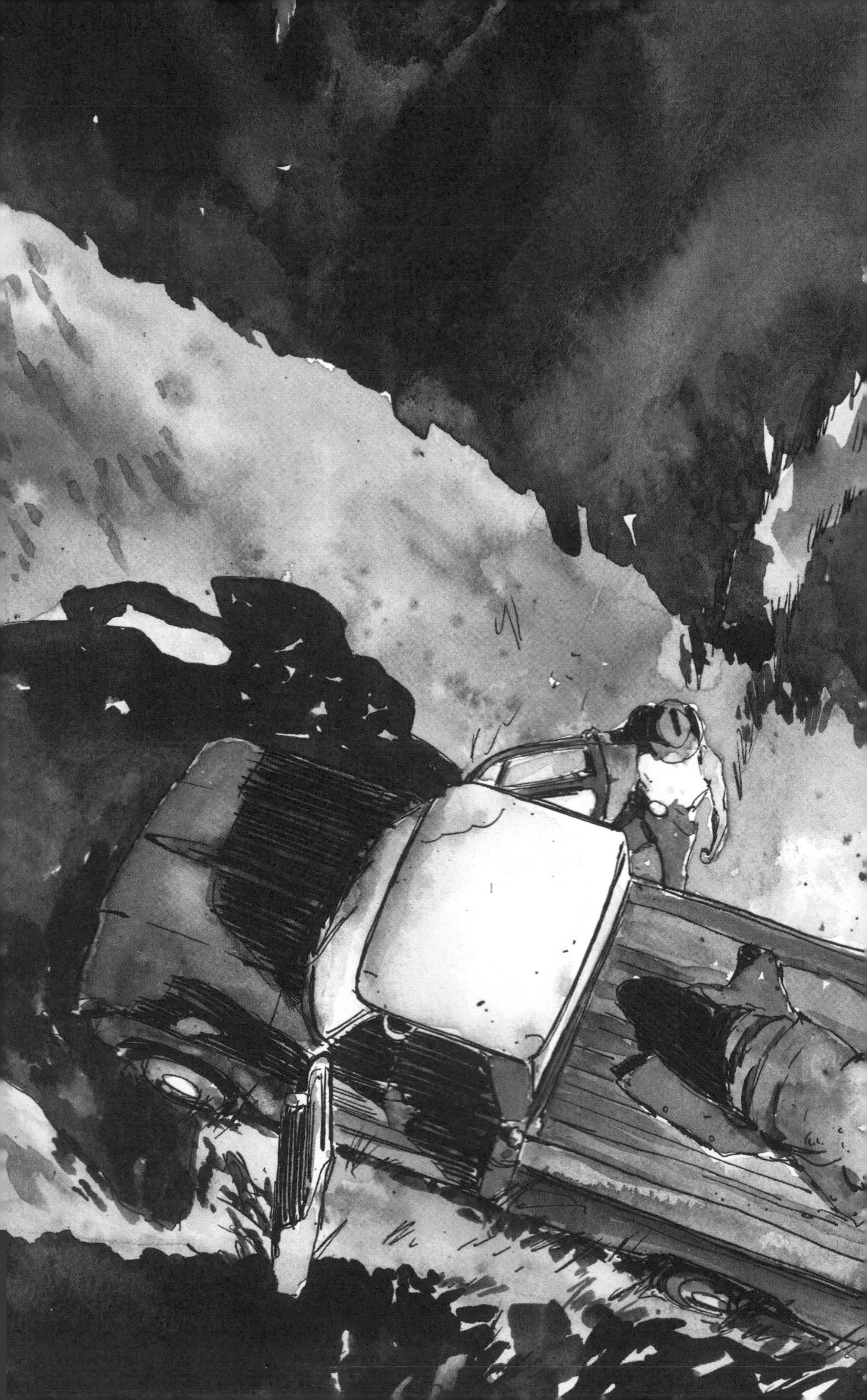

GRASS ⌂ KINGS

created by **matt kindt** + **tyler jenkins**

written by **matt kindt**
illustrated by **tyler jenkins**
with colors by **hilary jenkins**
lettered by **jim campbell**
cover by **tyler jenkins**

designer **scott newman**
editors **jasmine amiri** + **eric harburn**

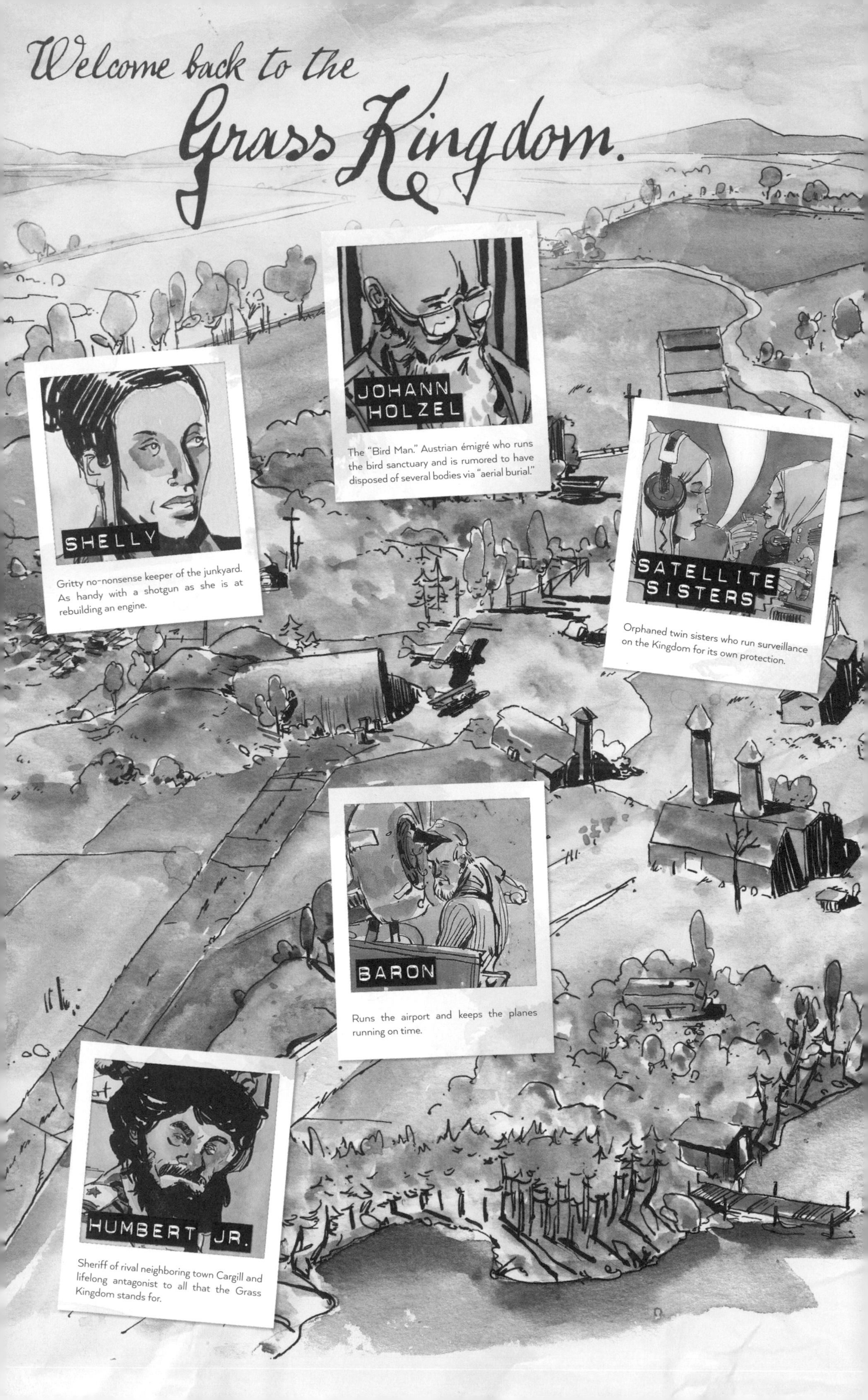
Welcome back to the
Grass Kingdom.
JOHANN HOLZEL
The "Bird Man." Austrian émigré who runs the bird sanctuary and is rumored to have disposed of several bodies via "aerial burial."
SHELLY
Gritty no-nonsense keeper of the junkyard. As handy with a shotgun as she is at rebuilding an engine.
SATELLITE SISTERS
Orphaned twin sisters who run surveillance on the Kingdom for its own protection.
BARON
Runs the airport and keeps the planes running on time.
HUMBERT JR.
Sheriff of rival neighboring town Cargill and lifelong antagonist to all that the Grass Kingdom stands for.

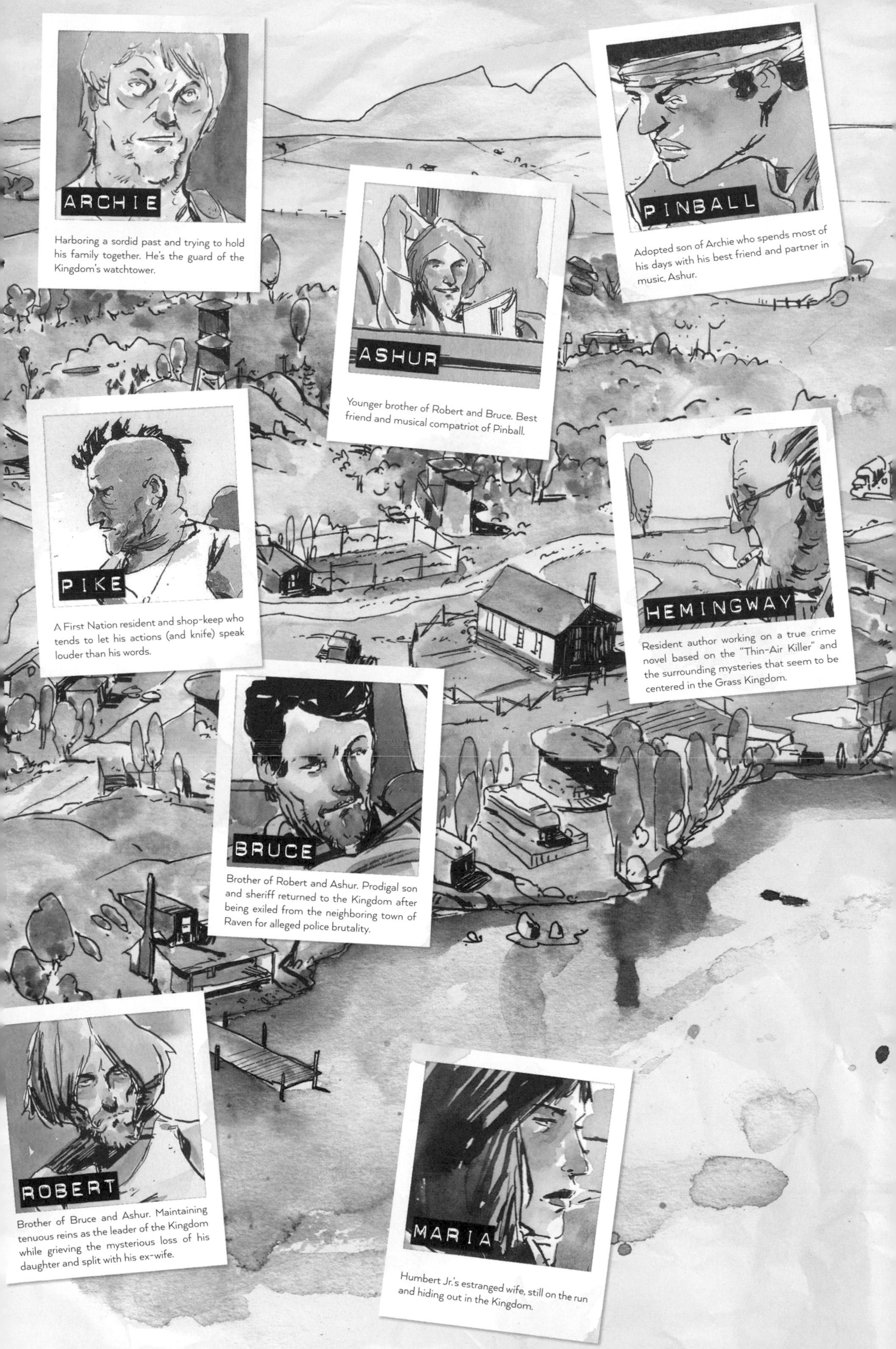
ARCHIE
Harboring a sordid past and trying to hold his family together. He's the guard of the Kingdom's watchtower.
ASHUR
Younger brother of Robert and Bruce. Best friend and musical compatriot of Pinball.
PINBALL
Adopted son of Archie who spends most of his days with his best friend and partner in music, Ashur.
PIKE
A First Nation resident and shop-keep who tends to let his actions (and knife) speak louder than his words.
HEMINGWAY
Resident author working on a true crime novel based on the "Thin-Air Killer" and the surrounding mysteries that seem to be centered in the Grass Kingdom.
BRUCE
Brother of Robert and Ashur. Prodigal son and sheriff returned to the Kingdom after being exiled from the neighboring town of Raven for alleged police brutality.
ROBERT
Brother of Bruce and Ashur. Maintaining tenuous reins as the leader of the Kingdom while grieving the mysterious loss of his daughter and split with his ex-wife.
MARIA
Humbert Jr.'s estranged wife, still on the run and hiding out in the Kingdom.

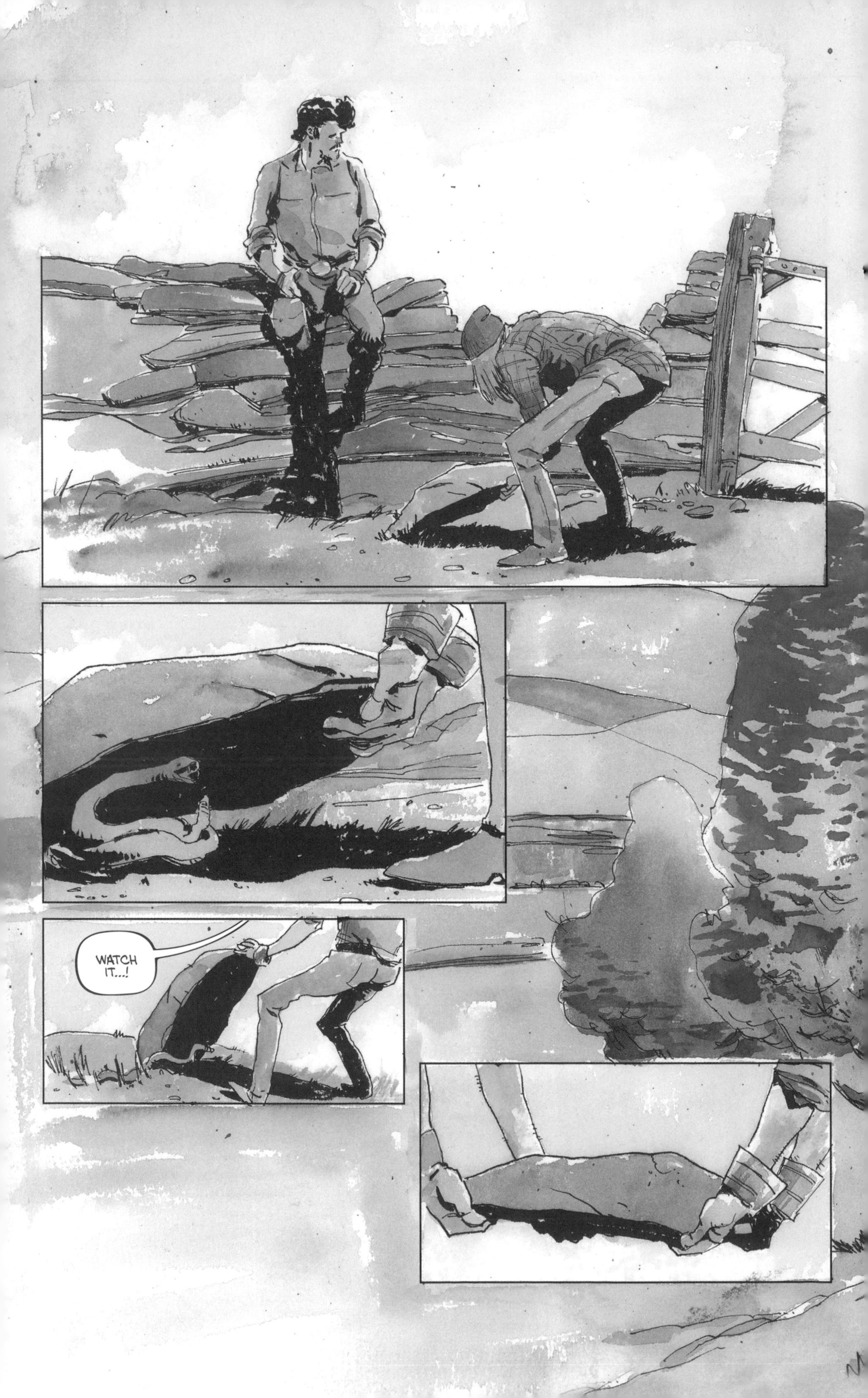
WATCH IT...!

chapter seven

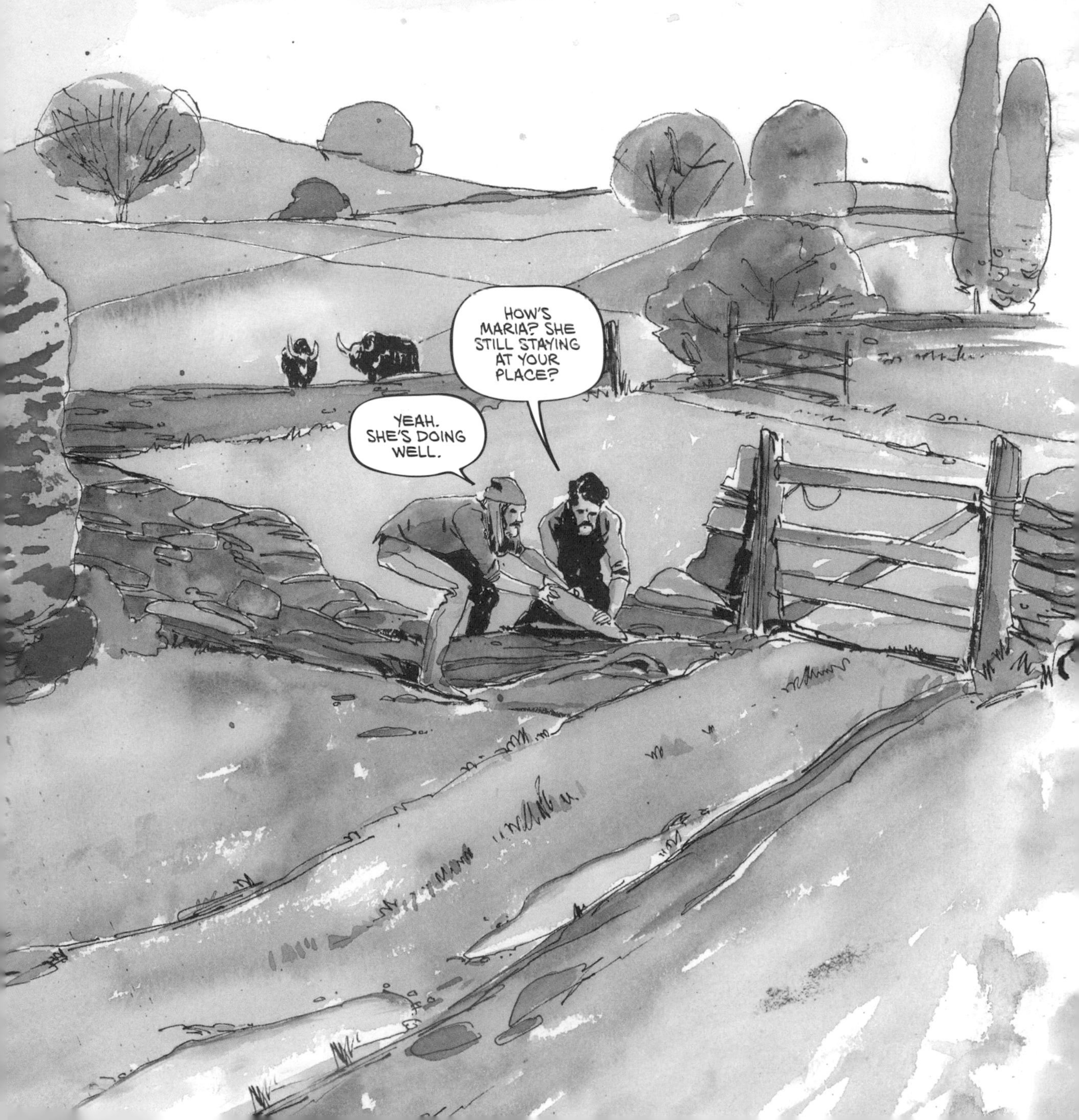
HOW'S MARIA? SHE STILL STAYING AT YOUR PLACE?
YEAH. SHE'S DOING WELL.

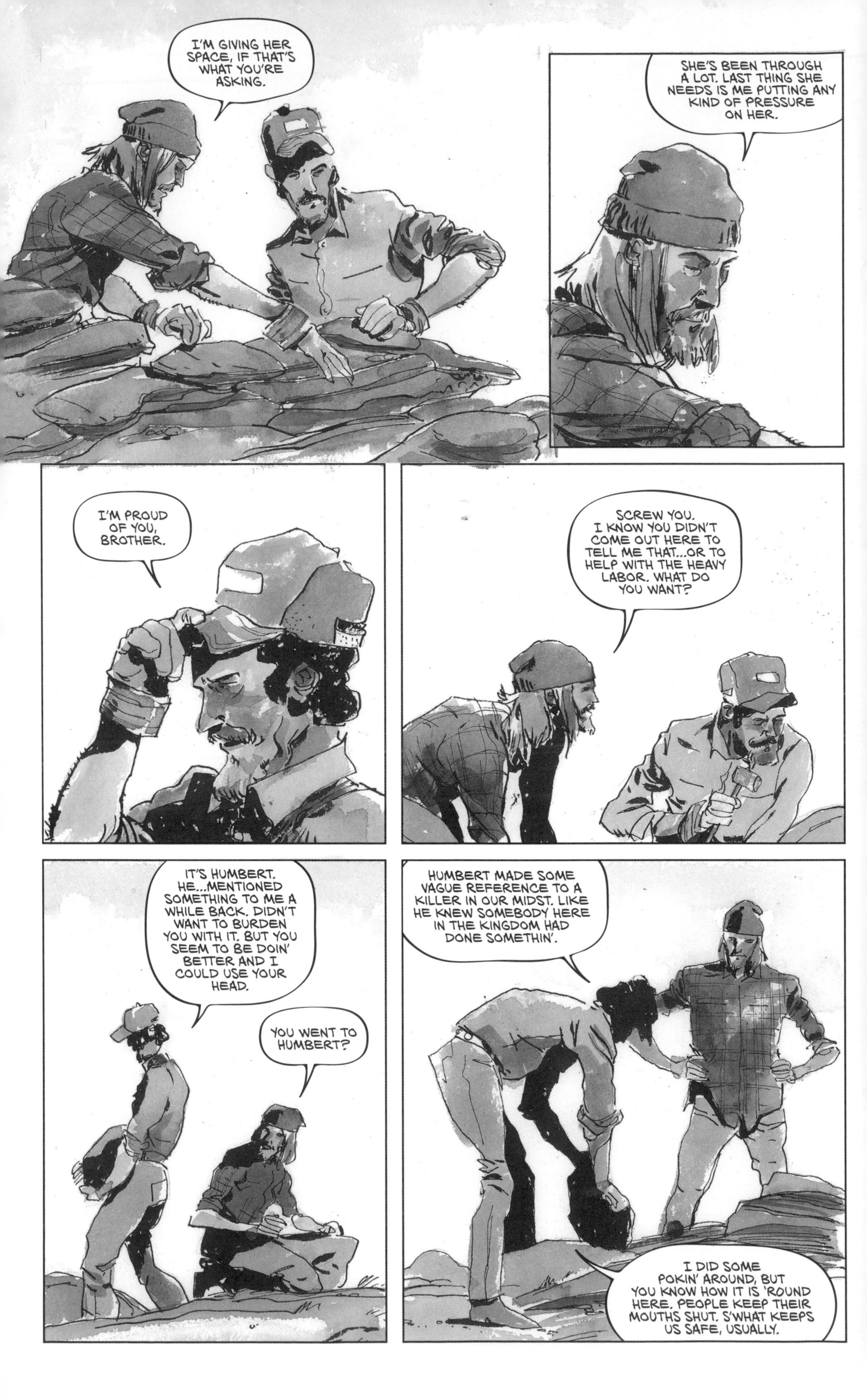
I'M GIVING HER SPACE, IF THAT'S WHAT YOU'RE ASKING.
SHE'S BEEN THROUGH A LOT. LAST THING SHE NEEDS IS ME PUTTING ANY KIND OF PRESSURE ON HER.
I'M PROUD OF YOU, BROTHER.
SCREW YOU. I KNOW YOU DIDN'T COME OUT HERE TO TELL ME THAT...OR TO HELP WITH THE HEAVY LABOR. WHAT DO YOU WANT?
IT'S HUMBERT. HE...MENTIONED SOMETHING TO ME A WHILE BACK. DIDN'T WANT TO BURDEN YOU WITH IT. BUT YOU SEEM TO BE DOIN' BETTER AND I COULD USE YOUR HEAD.
YOU WENT TO HUMBERT?
HUMBERT MADE SOME VAGUE REFERENCE TO A KILLER IN OUR MIDST. LIKE HE KNEW SOMEBODY HERE IN THE KINGDOM HAD DONE SOMETHIN'.
I DID SOME POKIN' AROUND, BUT YOU KNOW HOW IT IS 'ROUND HERE. PEOPLE KEEP THEIR MOUTHS SHUT. S'WHAT KEEPS US SAFE, USUALLY.

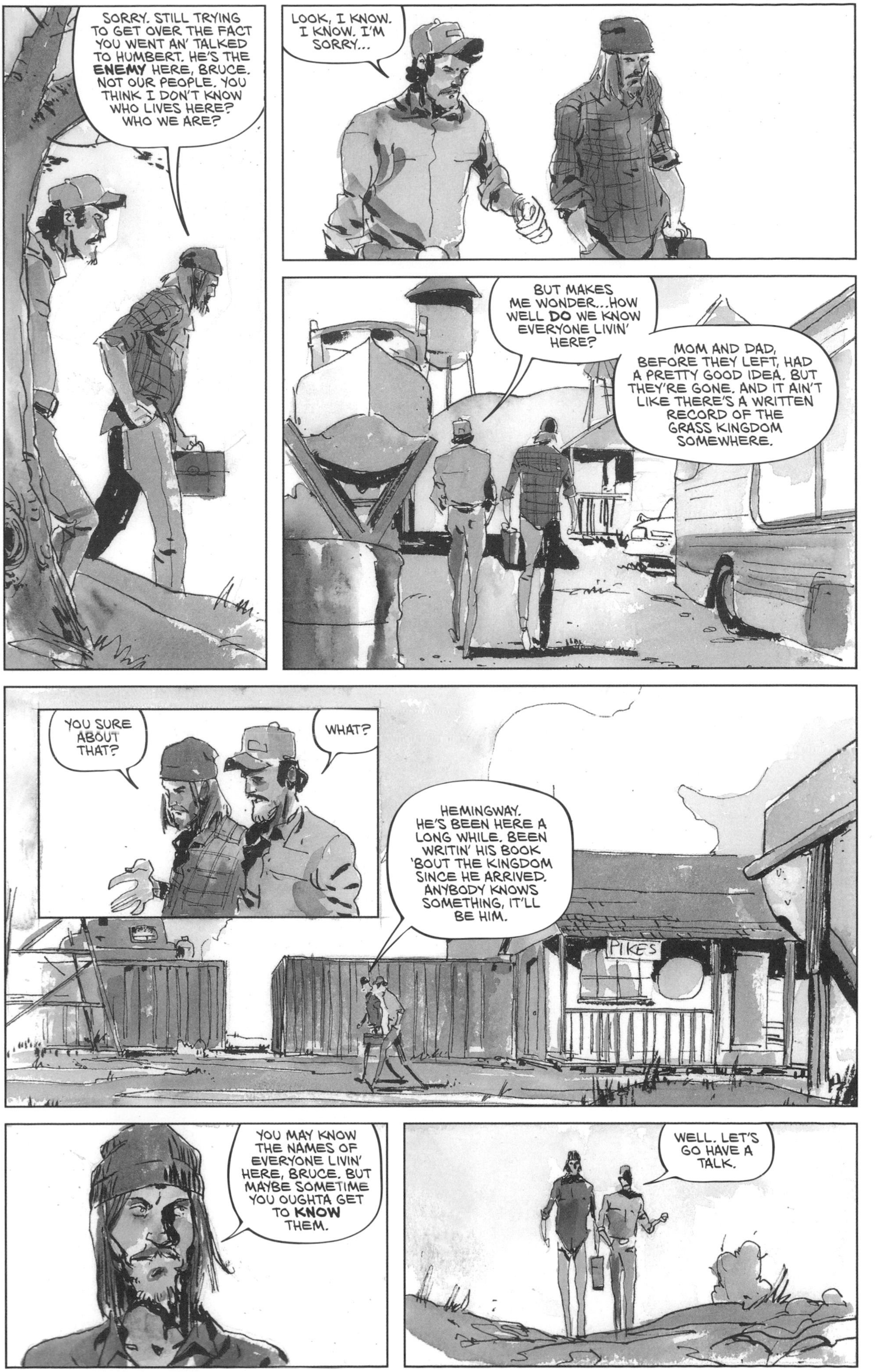

SORRY. STILL TRYING TO GET OVER THE FACT YOU WENT AN' TALKED TO HUMBERT. HE'S THE **ENEMY** HERE, BRUCE. NOT OUR PEOPLE. YOU THINK I DON'T KNOW WHO LIVES HERE? WHO WE ARE?
LOOK, I KNOW. I KNOW. I'M SORRY...
BUT MAKES ME WONDER...HOW WELL **DO** WE KNOW EVERYONE LIVIN' HERE?
MOM AND DAD, BEFORE THEY LEFT, HAD A PRETTY GOOD IDEA. BUT THEY'RE GONE. AND IT AIN'T LIKE THERE'S A WRITTEN RECORD OF THE GRASS KINGDOM SOMEWHERE.
YOU SURE ABOUT THAT?
WHAT?
HEMINGWAY. HE'S BEEN HERE A LONG WHILE. BEEN WRITIN' HIS BOOK 'BOUT THE KINGDOM SINCE HE ARRIVED. ANYBODY KNOWS SOMETHING, IT'LL BE HIM.
PIKES
YOU MAY KNOW THE NAMES OF EVERYONE LIVIN' HERE, BRUCE. BUT MAYBE SOMETIME YOU OUGHTA GET TO **KNOW** THEM.
WELL. LET'S GO HAVE A TALK.

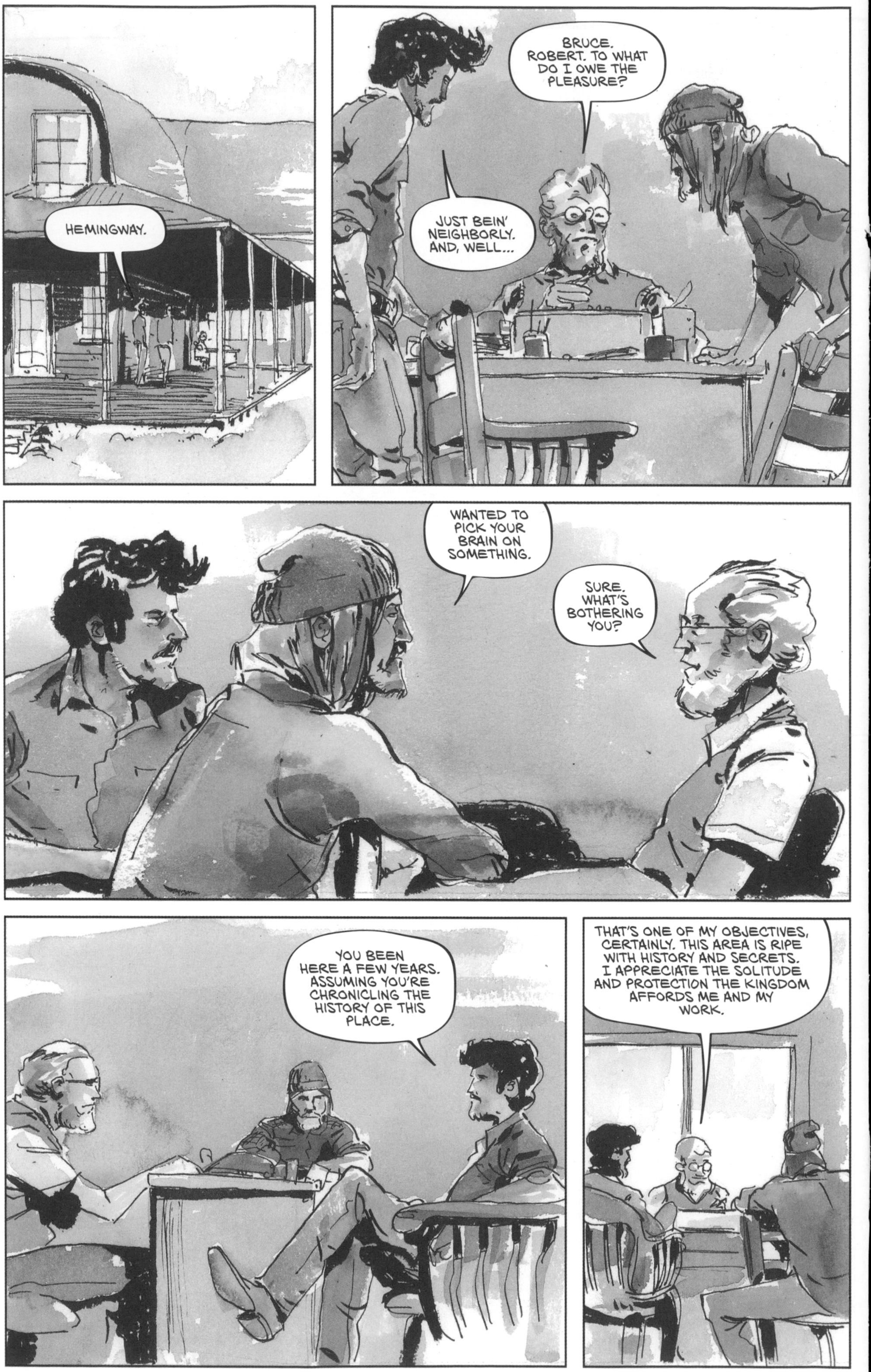
HEMINGWAY.
BRUCE. ROBERT. TO WHAT DO I OWE THE PLEASURE?
JUST BEIN' NEIGHBORLY. AND, WELL...
WANTED TO PICK YOUR BRAIN ON SOMETHING.
SURE. WHAT'S BOTHERING YOU?
YOU BEEN HERE A FEW YEARS. ASSUMING YOU'RE CHRONICLING THE HISTORY OF THIS PLACE.
THAT'S ONE OF MY OBJECTIVES, CERTAINLY. THIS AREA IS RIPE WITH HISTORY AND SECRETS. I APPRECIATE THE SOLITUDE AND PROTECTION THE KINGDOM AFFORDS ME AND MY WORK.

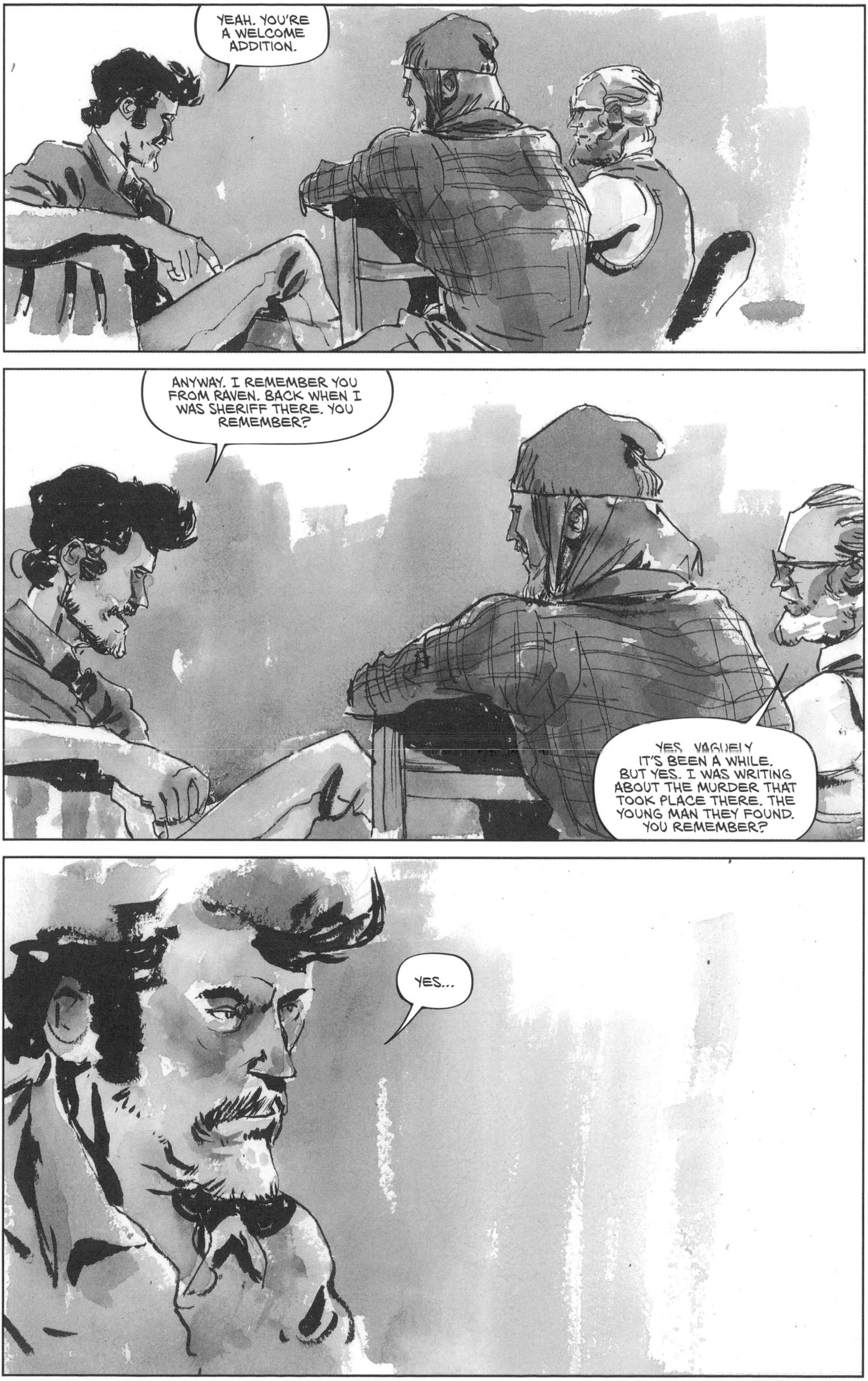
YEAH. YOU'RE A WELCOME ADDITION.
ANYWAY. I REMEMBER YOU FROM RAVEN. BACK WHEN I WAS SHERIFF THERE. YOU REMEMBER?
YES. VAGUELY. IT'S BEEN A WHILE. BUT YES. I WAS WRITING ABOUT THE MURDER THAT TOOK PLACE THERE. THE YOUNG MAN THEY FOUND. YOU REMEMBER?
YES...

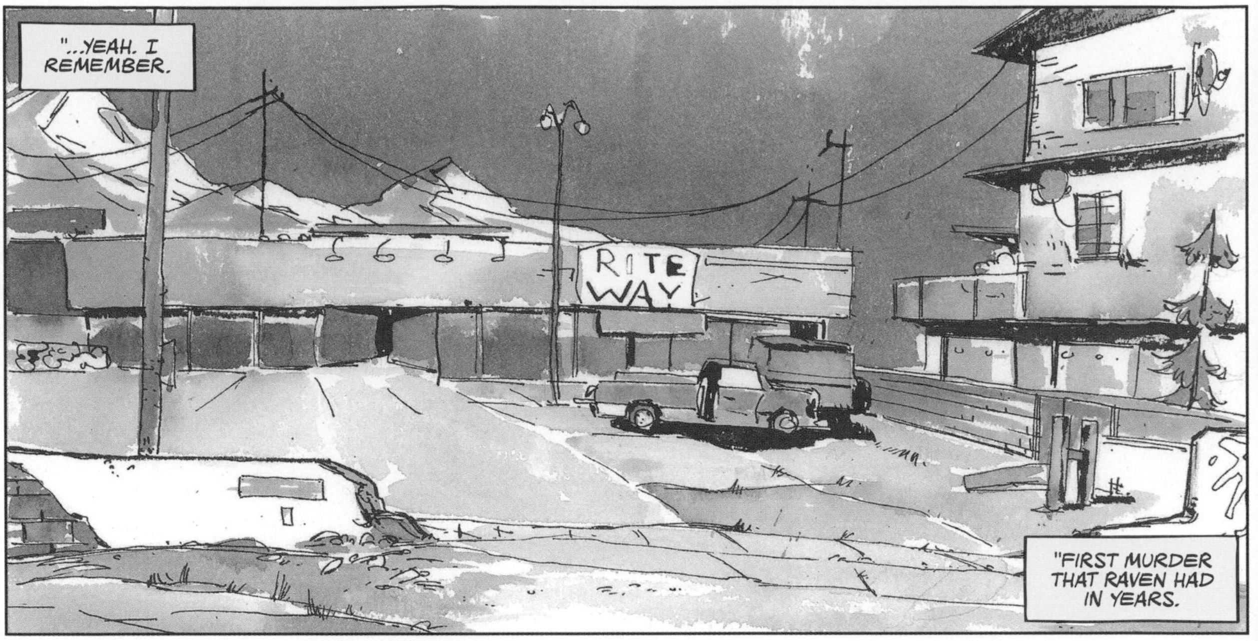
"...YEAH. I REMEMBER.
RITE WAY
"FIRST MURDER THAT RAVEN HAD IN YEARS.

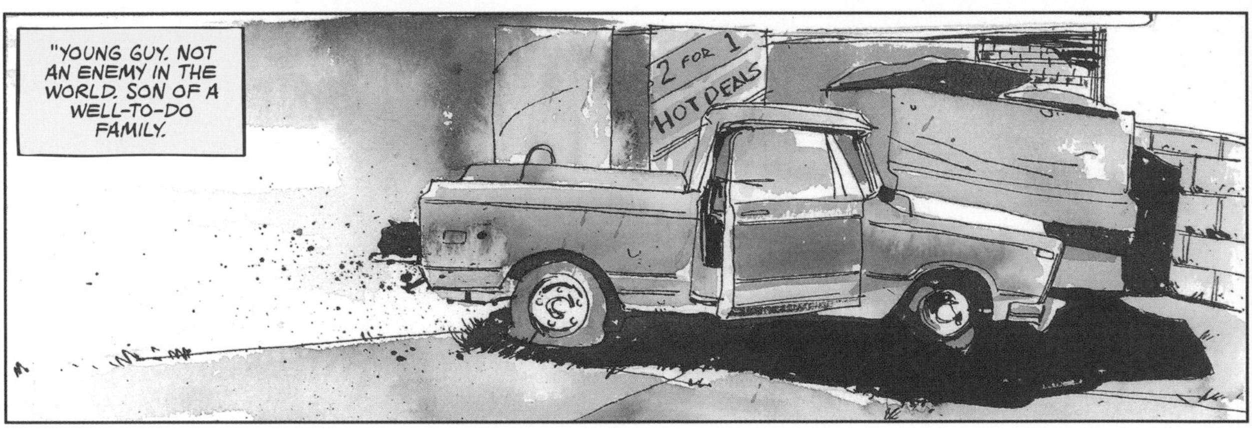
"YOUNG GUY. NOT AN ENEMY IN THE WORLD. SON OF A WELL-TO-DO FAMILY.
2 FOR 1
HOT DEALS

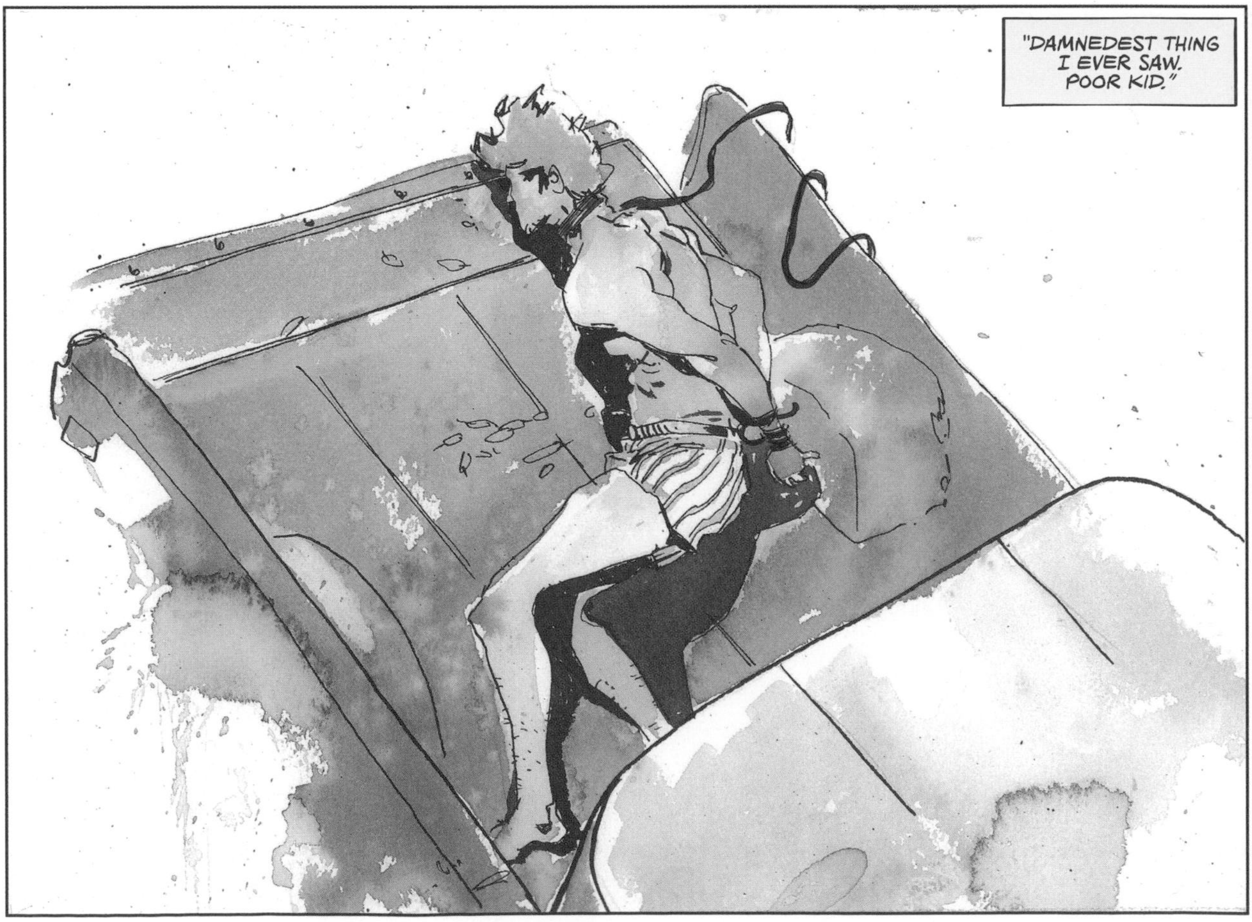
"DAMNEDEST THING I EVER SAW. POOR KID."

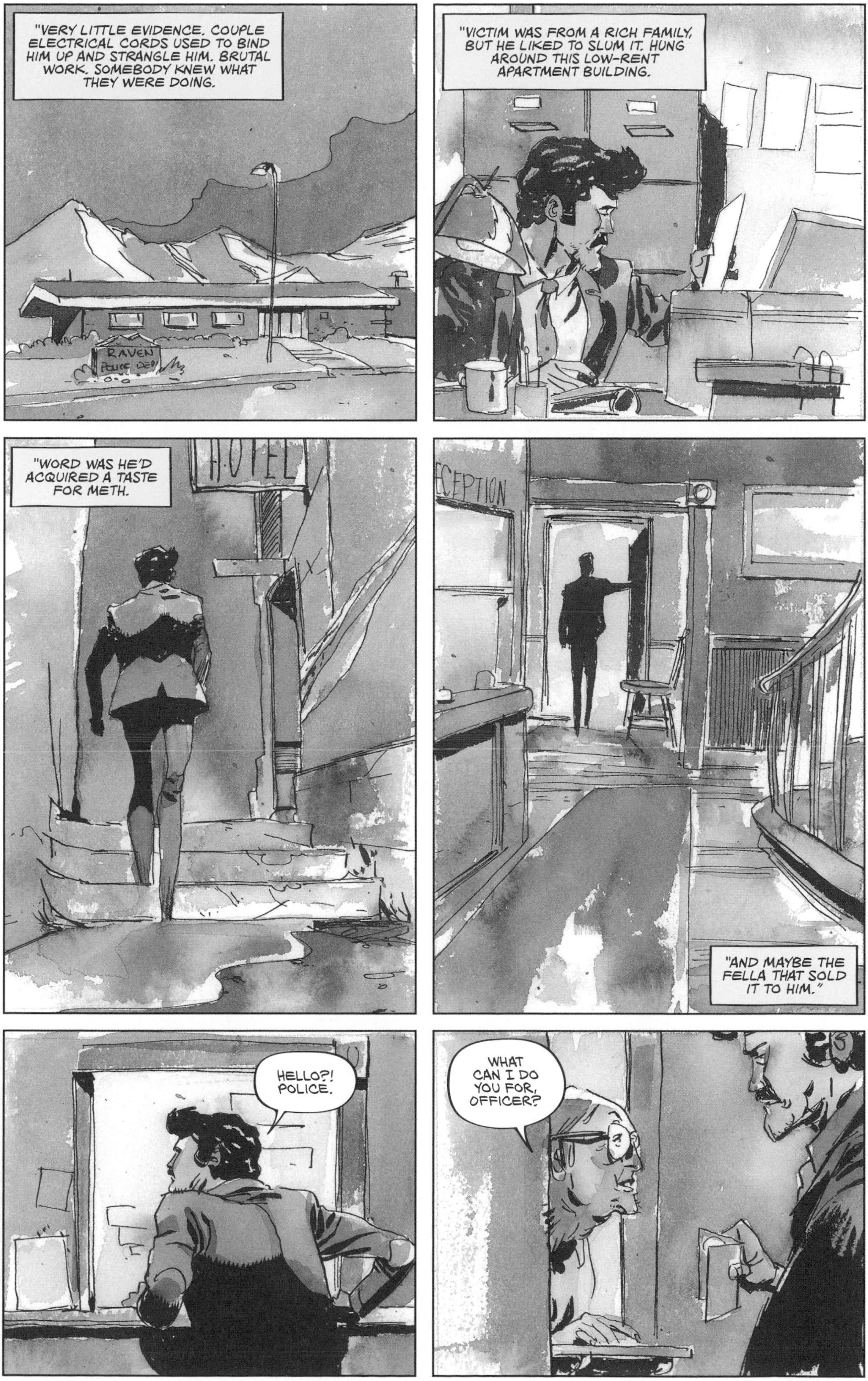
"VERY LITTLE EVIDENCE. COUPLE ELECTRICAL CORDS USED TO BIND HIM UP AND STRANGLE HIM. BRUTAL WORK. SOMEBODY KNEW WHAT THEY WERE DOING.
RAVEN POLICE DEPT
"VICTIM WAS FROM A RICH FAMILY, BUT HE LIKED TO SLUM IT. HUNG AROUND THIS LOW-RENT APARTMENT BUILDING.
"WORD WAS HE'D ACQUIRED A TASTE FOR METH.
HOTEL
ECEPTION
"AND MAYBE THE FELLA THAT SOLD IT TO HIM."
HELLO?! POLICE.
WHAT CAN I DO YOU FOR, OFFICER?

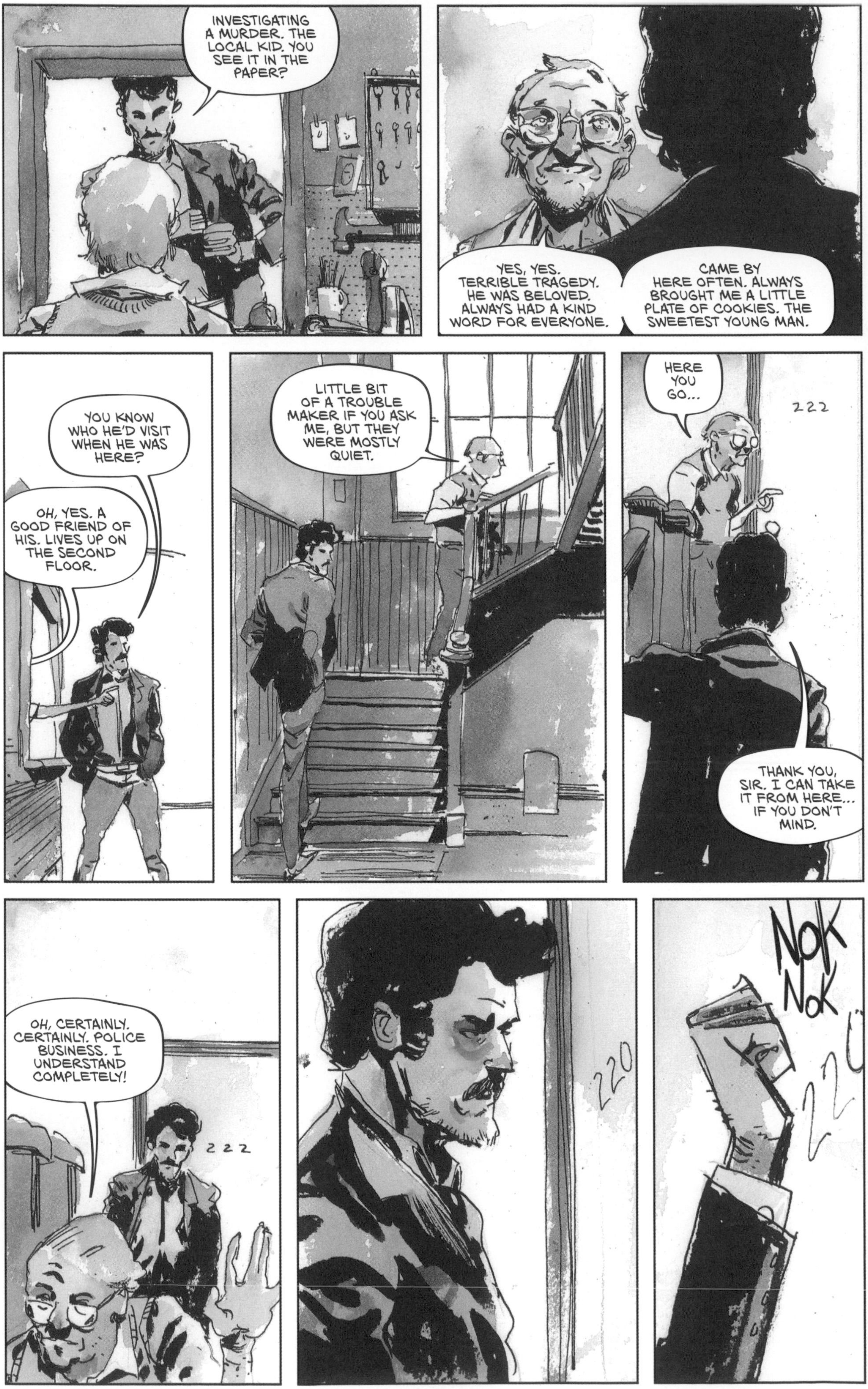
INVESTIGATING A MURDER. THE LOCAL KID. YOU SEE IT IN THE PAPER?
YES, YES. TERRIBLE TRAGEDY. HE WAS BELOVED. ALWAYS HAD A KIND WORD FOR EVERYONE.
CAME BY HERE OFTEN. ALWAYS BROUGHT ME A LITTLE PLATE OF COOKIES. THE SWEETEST YOUNG MAN.
YOU KNOW WHO HE'D VISIT WHEN HE WAS HERE?
OH, YES. A GOOD FRIEND OF HIS. LIVES UP ON THE SECOND FLOOR.
LITTLE BIT OF A TROUBLE MAKER IF YOU ASK ME, BUT THEY WERE MOSTLY QUIET.
HERE YOU GO...
222
THANK YOU, SIR. I CAN TAKE IT FROM HERE... IF YOU DON'T MIND.
OH, CERTAINLY. CERTAINLY. POLICE BUSINESS. I UNDERSTAND COMPLETELY!
222
220
NOK
NOK
220

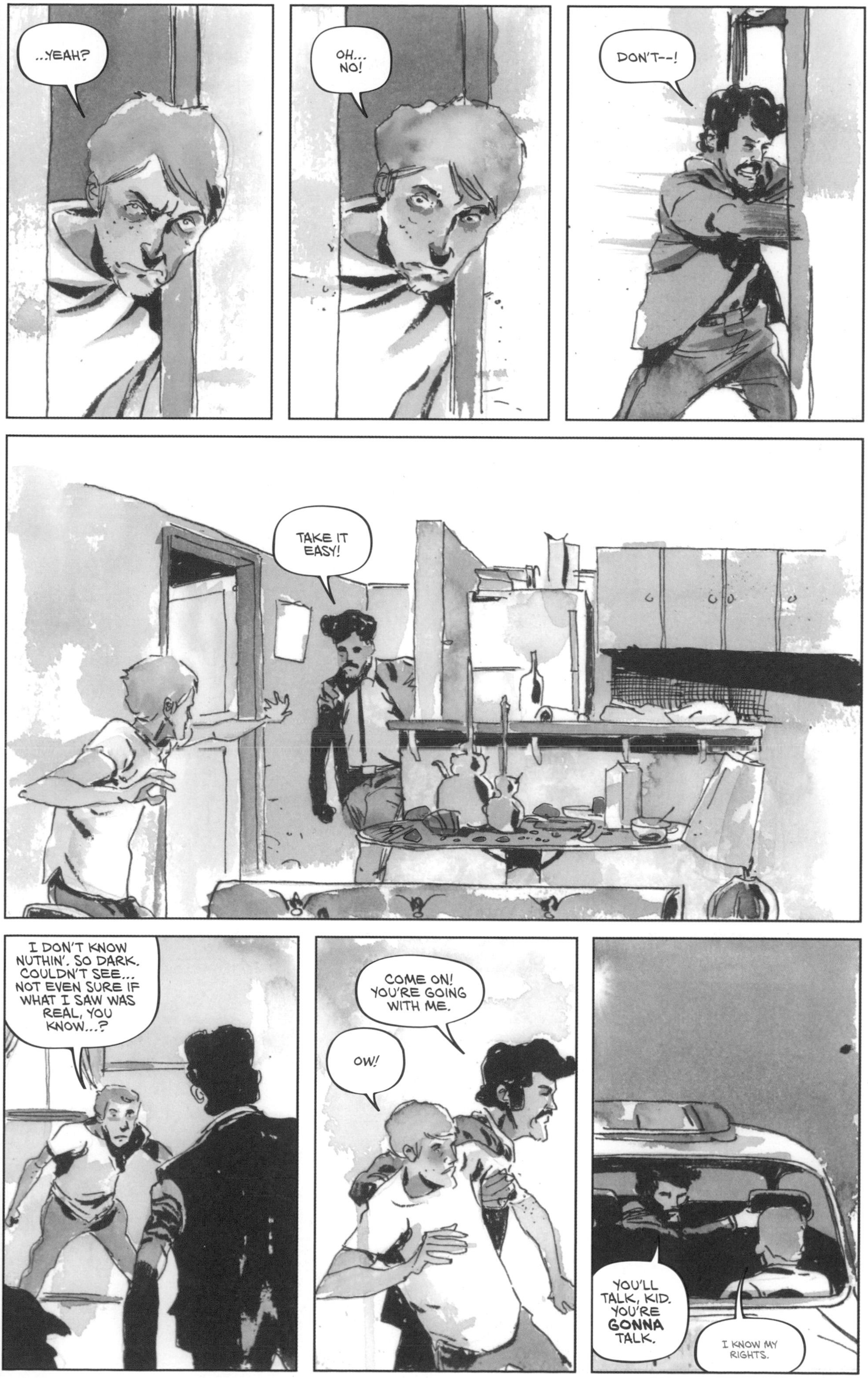

...YEAH?
OH... NO!
DON'T--!
TAKE IT EASY!
I DON'T KNOW NUTHIN'. SO DARK. COULDN'T SEE... NOT EVEN SURE IF WHAT I SAW WAS REAL, YOU KNOW...?
COME ON! YOU'RE GOING WITH ME.
OW!
YOU'LL TALK, KID. YOU'RE GONNA TALK.
I KNOW MY RIGHTS.

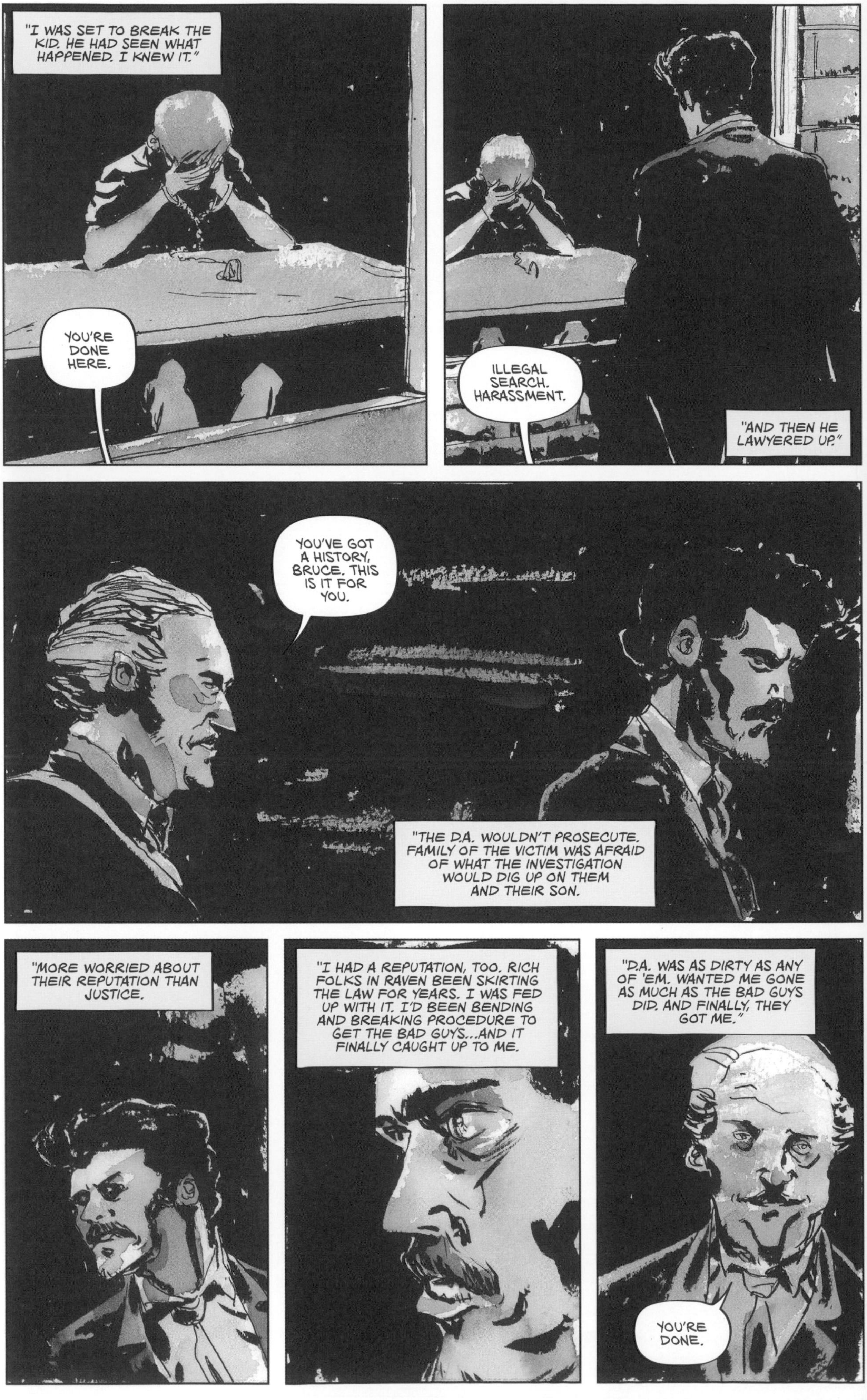
"I WAS SET TO BREAK THE KID. HE HAD SEEN WHAT HAPPENED. I KNEW IT."
YOU'RE DONE HERE.
ILLEGAL SEARCH. HARASSMENT.
"AND THEN HE LAWYERED UP."
YOU'VE GOT A HISTORY, BRUCE. THIS IS IT FOR YOU.
"THE D.A. WOULDN'T PROSECUTE. FAMILY OF THE VICTIM WAS AFRAID OF WHAT THE INVESTIGATION WOULD DIG UP ON THEM AND THEIR SON.
"MORE WORRIED ABOUT THEIR REPUTATION THAN JUSTICE.
"I HAD A REPUTATION, TOO. RICH FOLKS IN RAVEN BEEN SKIRTING THE LAW FOR YEARS. I WAS FED UP WITH IT. I'D BEEN BENDING AND BREAKING PROCEDURE TO GET THE BAD GUYS...AND IT FINALLY CAUGHT UP TO ME.
"D.A. WAS AS DIRTY AS ANY OF 'EM. WANTED ME GONE AS MUCH AS THE BAD GUYS DID. AND FINALLY, THEY GOT ME."
YOU'RE DONE.

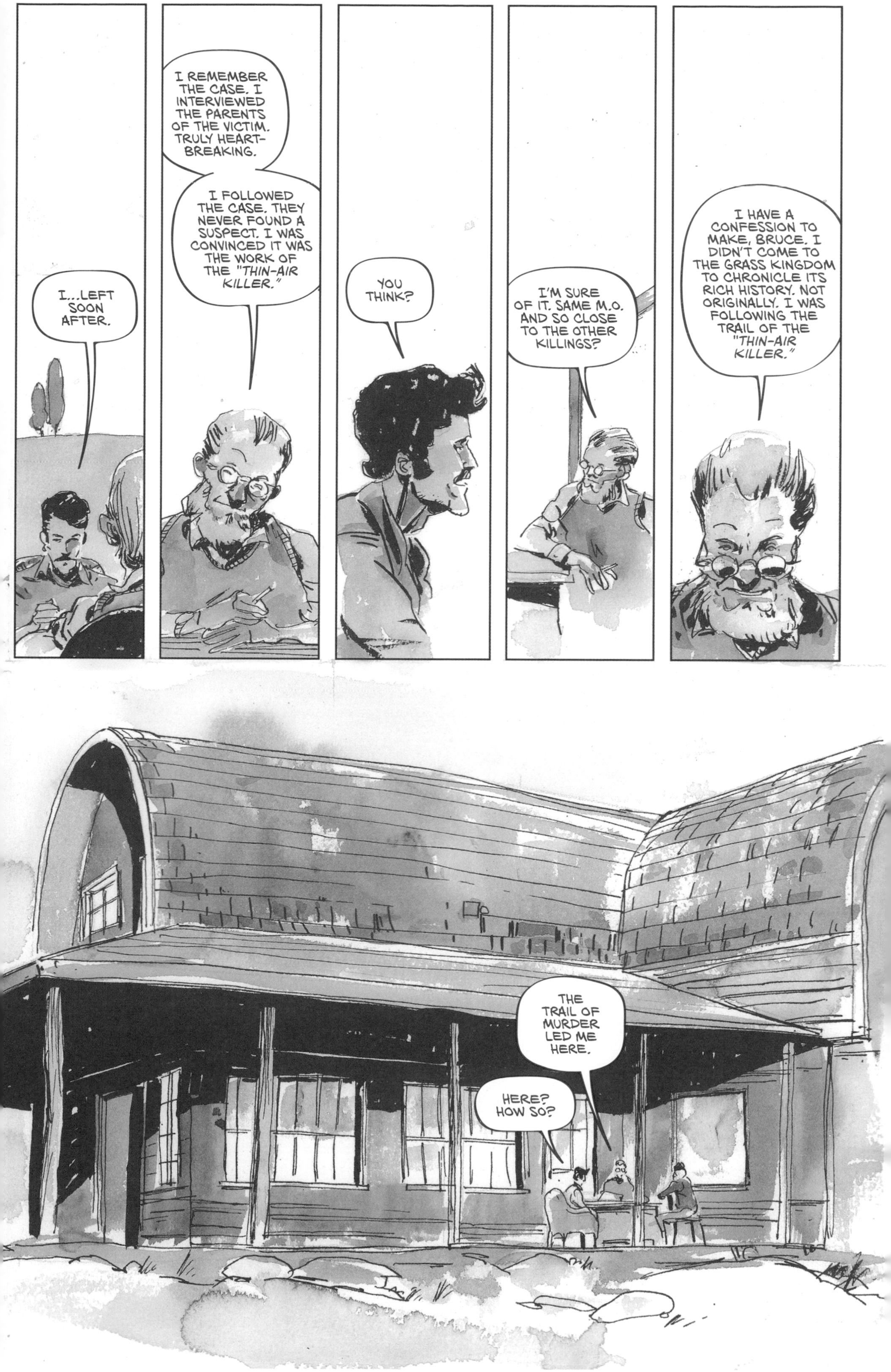
I...LEFT SOON AFTER.
I REMEMBER THE CASE. I INTERVIEWED THE PARENTS OF THE VICTIM. TRULY HEART-BREAKING.
I FOLLOWED THE CASE. THEY NEVER FOUND A SUSPECT. I WAS CONVINCED IT WAS THE WORK OF THE "THIN-AIR KILLER."
YOU THINK?
I'M SURE OF IT. SAME M.O. AND SO CLOSE TO THE OTHER KILLINGS?
I HAVE A CONFESSION TO MAKE, BRUCE. I DIDN'T COME TO THE GRASS KINGDOM TO CHRONICLE ITS RICH HISTORY. NOT ORIGINALLY. I WAS FOLLOWING THE TRAIL OF THE "THIN-AIR KILLER."
THE TRAIL OF MURDER LED ME HERE.
HERE? HOW SO?

A MURDER THAT WAS SIMILAR TO THE OTHERS. WHILE I WAS IN RAVEN...NEWS OF A DEATH HERE PROVOKED MY INTEREST.

YEAH... THAT BLOODY TRAILER MYSTERY WE HAD A WHILE BACK? THAT WAS A DRUG DEAL GONE BAD, HEMINGWAY. OPEN AND SHUT.

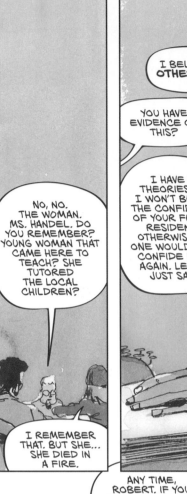

NO, NO. THE WOMAN. MS. HANDEL. DO YOU REMEMBER? YOUNG WOMAN THAT CAME HERE TO TEACH? SHE TUTORED THE LOCAL CHILDREN?

I REMEMBER THAT. BUT SHE... SHE DIED IN A FIRE.

I BELIEVE... OTHERWISE.

YOU HAVE EVIDENCE OF THIS?

I HAVE MY THEORIES BUT I WON'T BETRAY THE CONFIDENCE OF YOUR FELLOW RESIDENTS. OTHERWISE, NO ONE WOULD EVER CONFIDE IN ME AGAIN. LET ME JUST SAY...

...THE SECRET OF HER DEATH IS HIDING HERE IN YOUR KINGDOM. AND IF I HAD THE ANSWER...I WOULD HAVE PUBLISHED MY BOOK BY NOW.

THANKS FOR THE TIME, HEMINGWAY.

ANY TIME, ROBERT. IF YOU CARE TO PERUSE MY MANUSCRIPTS, THEY ARE EVER AT YOUR DISPOSAL.

THANKS. MAYBE NEXT TIME.

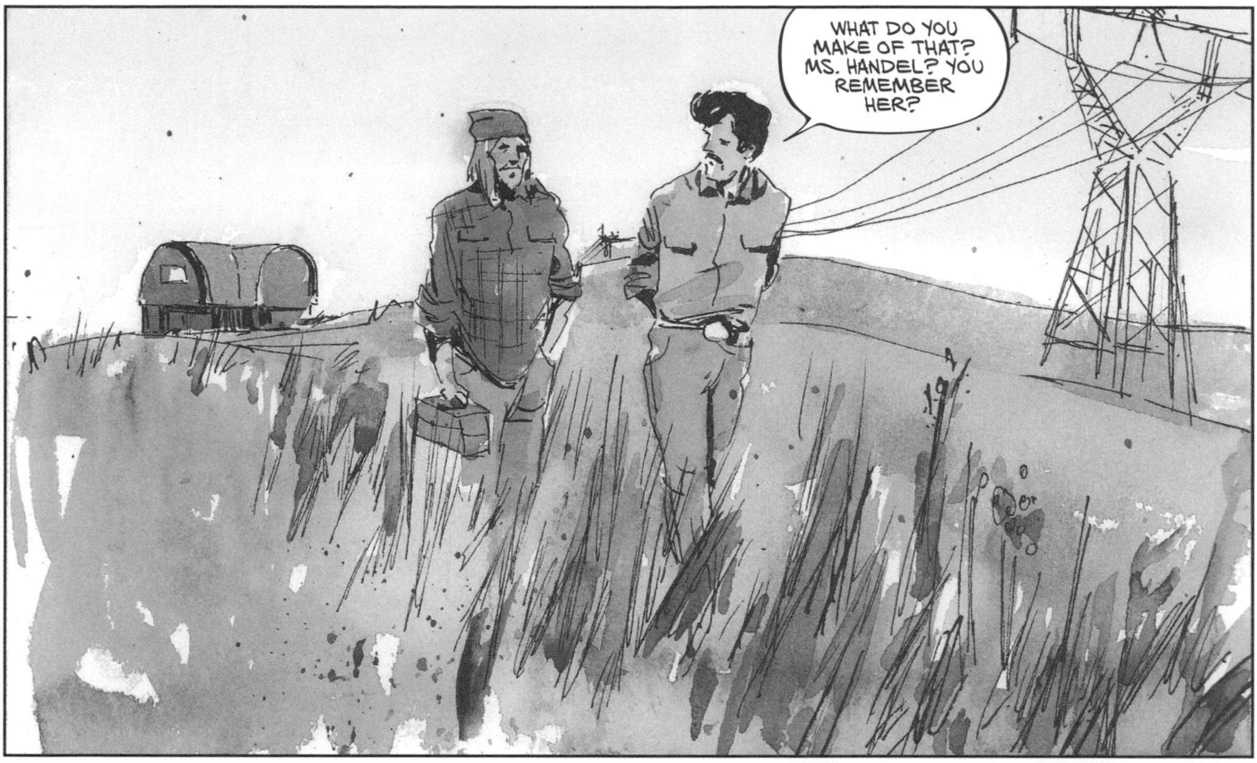
WHAT DO YOU MAKE OF THAT? MS. HANDEL? YOU REMEMBER HER?

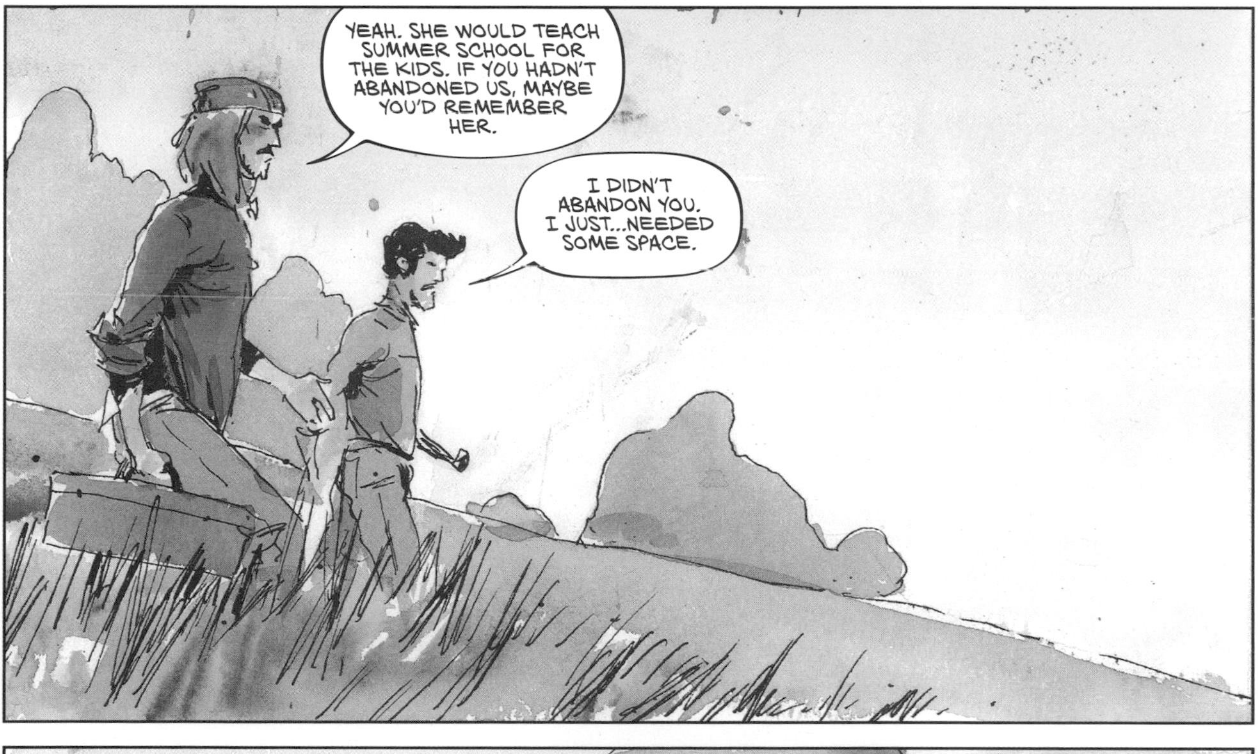
YEAH. SHE WOULD TEACH SUMMER SCHOOL FOR THE KIDS. IF YOU HADN'T ABANDONED US, MAYBE YOU'D REMEMBER HER.
I DIDN'T ABANDON YOU. I JUST...NEEDED SOME SPACE.

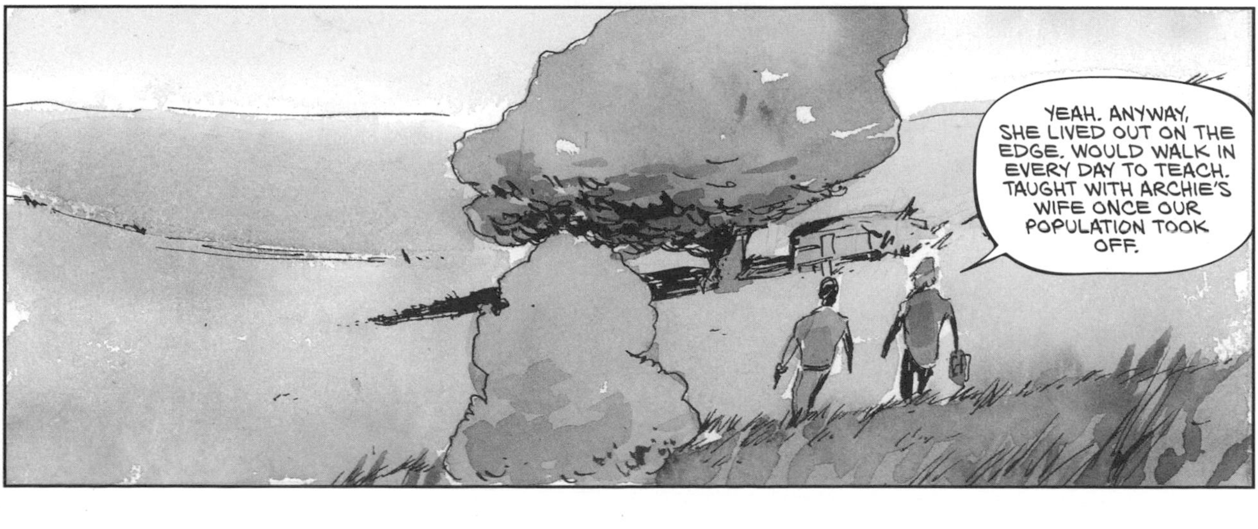
YEAH. ANYWAY, SHE LIVED OUT ON THE EDGE. WOULD WALK IN EVERY DAY TO TEACH. TAUGHT WITH ARCHIE'S WIFE ONCE OUR POPULATION TOOK OFF.

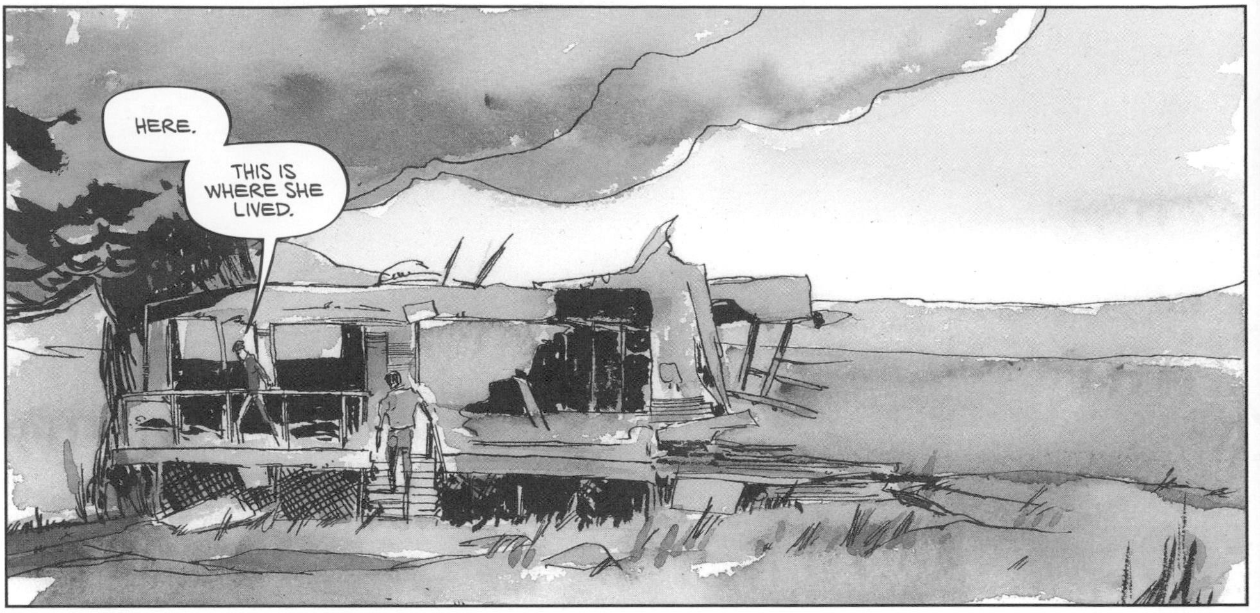
HERE.
THIS IS WHERE SHE LIVED.

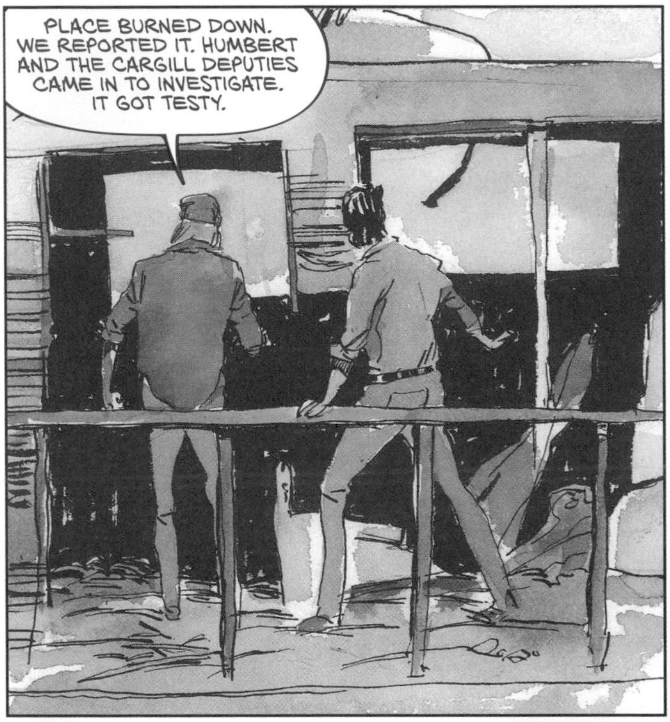
PLACE BURNED DOWN. WE REPORTED IT. HUMBERT AND THE CARGILL DEPUTIES CAME IN TO INVESTIGATE. IT GOT TESTY.

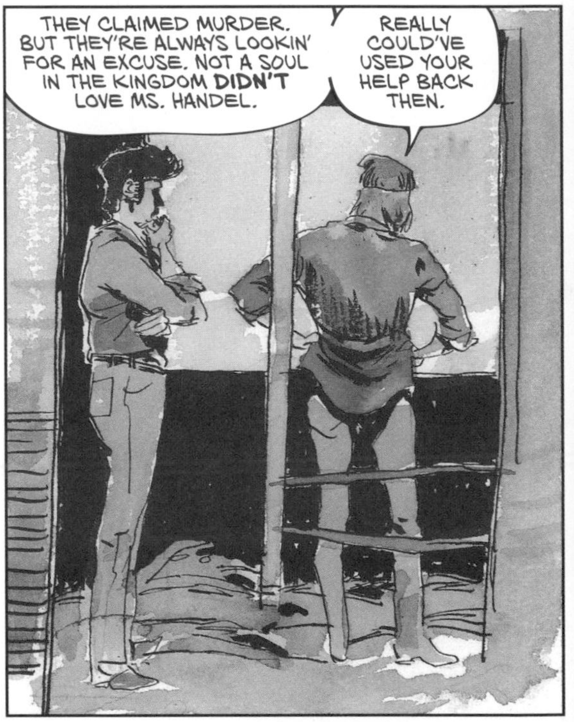
THEY CLAIMED MURDER. BUT THEY'RE ALWAYS LOOKIN' FOR AN EXCUSE. NOT A SOUL IN THE KINGDOM **DIDN'T** LOVE MS. HANDEL.
REALLY COULD'VE USED YOUR HELP BACK THEN.

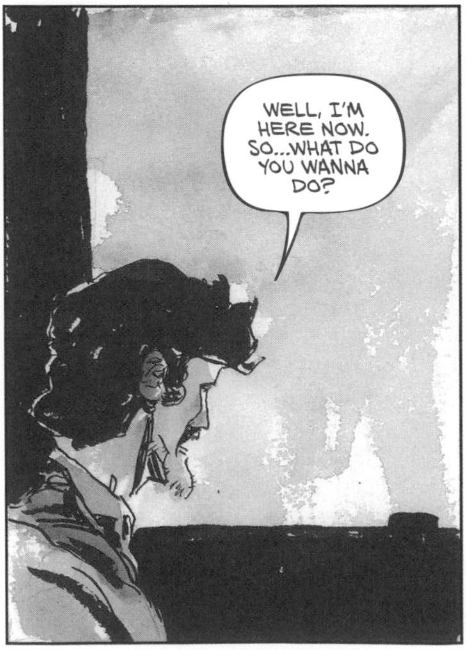
WELL, I'M HERE NOW. SO...WHAT DO YOU WANNA DO?

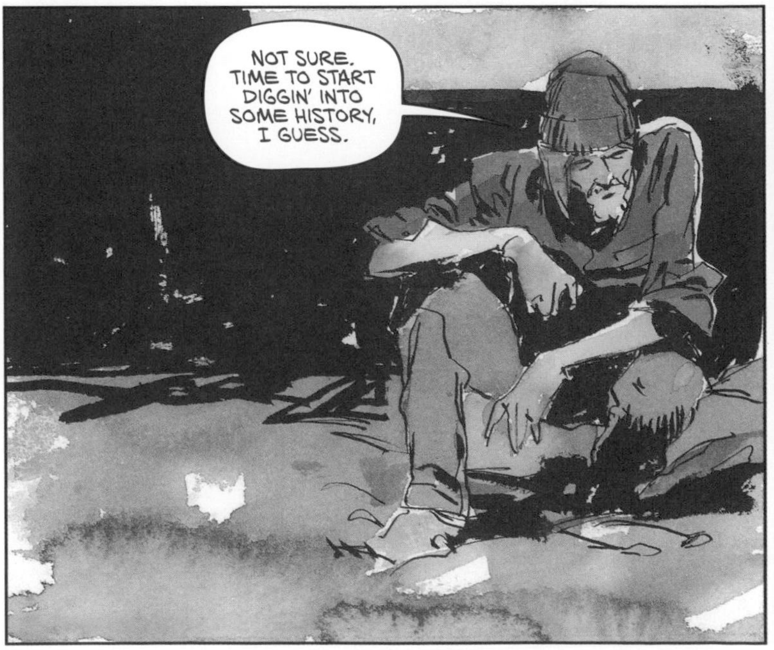
NOT SURE. TIME TO START DIGGIN' INTO SOME HISTORY, I GUESS.

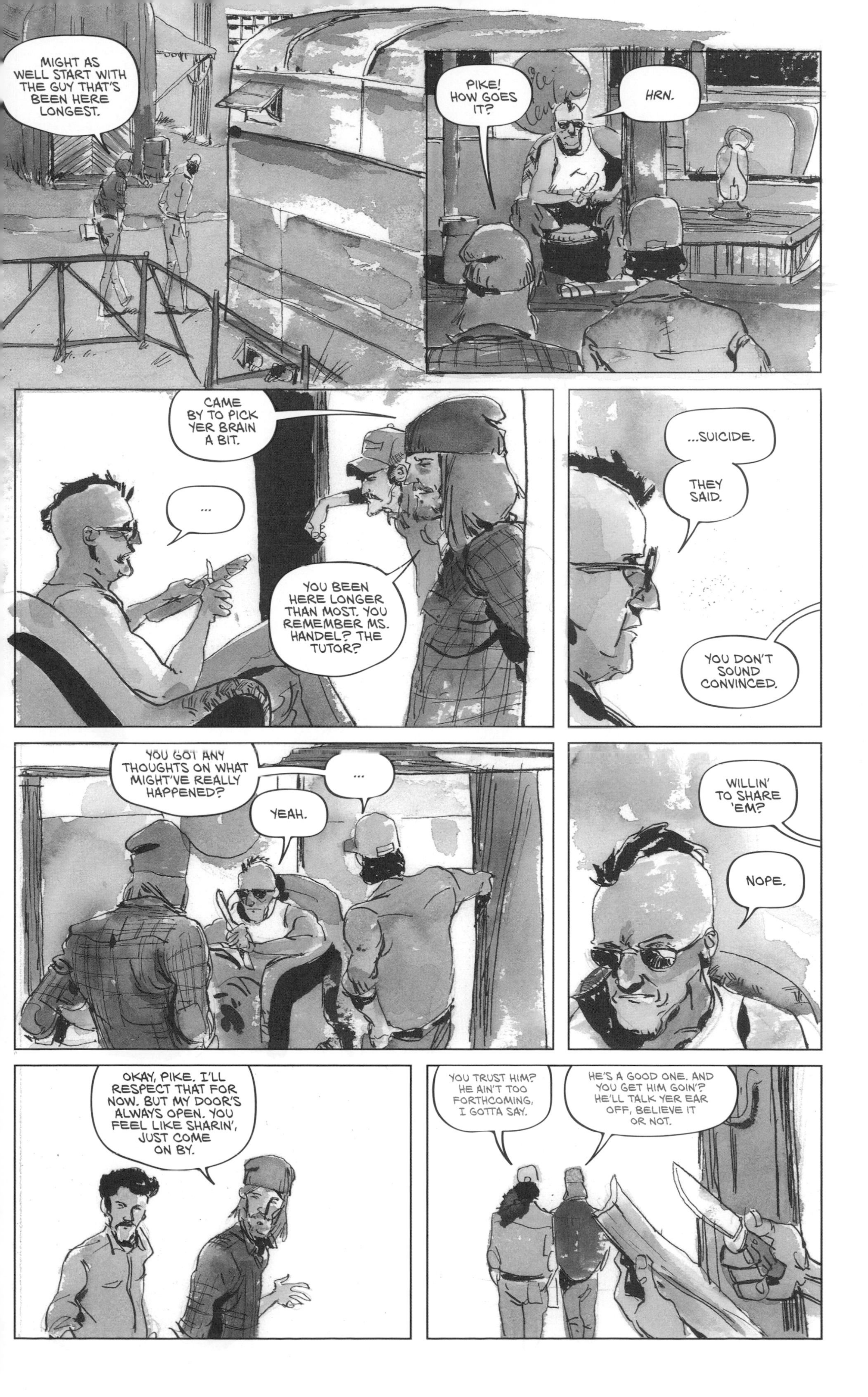
MIGHT AS WELL START WITH THE GUY THAT'S BEEN HERE LONGEST.
PIKE! HOW GOES IT?
HRN.
CAME BY TO PICK YER BRAIN A BIT.
...
YOU BEEN HERE LONGER THAN MOST. YOU REMEMBER MS. HANDEL? THE TUTOR?
...SUICIDE.
THEY SAID.
YOU DON'T SOUND CONVINCED.
YOU GOT ANY THOUGHTS ON WHAT MIGHT'VE REALLY HAPPENED?
...
YEAH.
WILLIN' TO SHARE 'EM?
NOPE.
OKAY, PIKE. I'LL RESPECT THAT FOR NOW. BUT MY DOOR'S ALWAYS OPEN. YOU FEEL LIKE SHARIN', JUST COME ON BY.
YOU TRUST HIM? HE AIN'T TOO FORTHCOMING, I GOTTA SAY.
HE'S A GOOD ONE. AND YOU GET HIM GOIN'? HE'LL TALK YER EAR OFF, BELIEVE IT OR NOT.

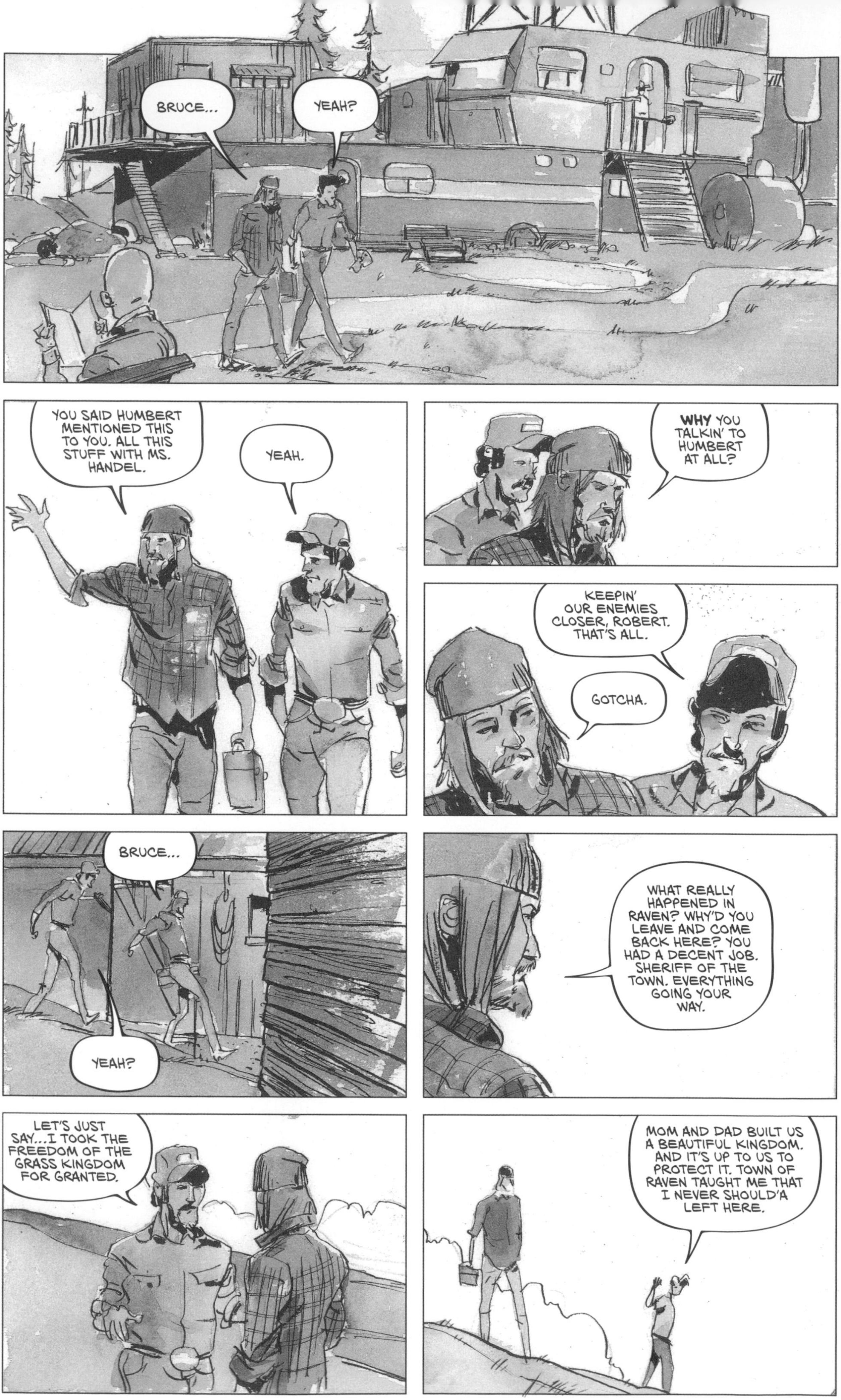
BRUCE...
YEAH?
YOU SAID HUMBERT MENTIONED THIS TO YOU. ALL THIS STUFF WITH MS. HANDEL.
YEAH.
WHY YOU TALKIN' TO HUMBERT AT ALL?
KEEPIN' OUR ENEMIES CLOSER, ROBERT. THAT'S ALL.
GOTCHA.
BRUCE...
YEAH?
WHAT REALLY HAPPENED IN RAVEN? WHY'D YOU LEAVE AND COME BACK HERE? YOU HAD A DECENT JOB. SHERIFF OF THE TOWN. EVERYTHING GOING YOUR WAY.
LET'S JUST SAY...I TOOK THE FREEDOM OF THE GRASS KINGDOM FOR GRANTED.
MOM AND DAD BUILT US A BEAUTIFUL KINGDOM. AND IT'S UP TO US TO PROTECT IT. TOWN OF RAVEN TAUGHT ME THAT I NEVER SHOULD'A LEFT HERE.

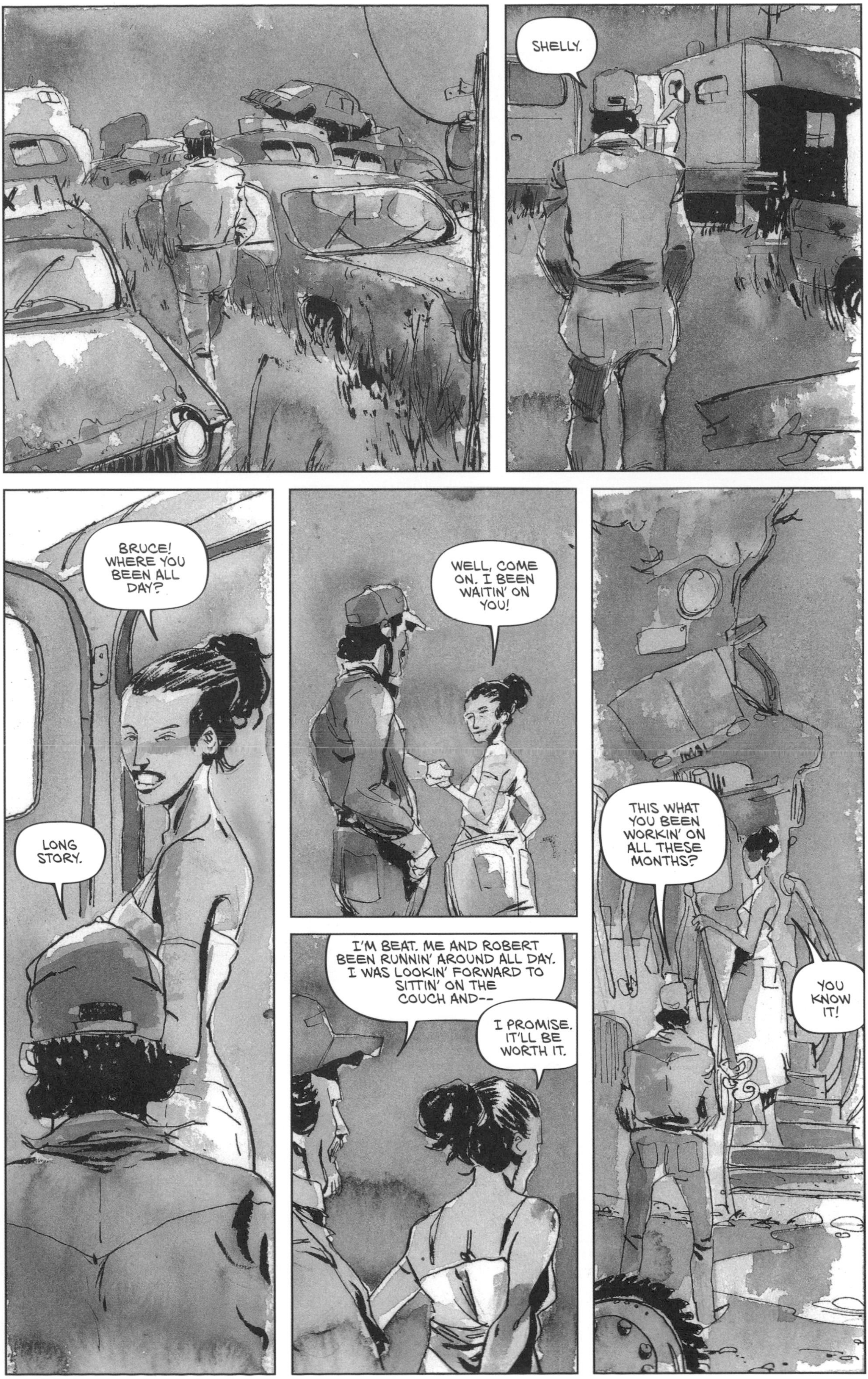
SHELLY.
BRUCE! WHERE YOU BEEN ALL DAY?
LONG STORY.
WELL, COME ON. I BEEN WAITIN' ON YOU!
I'M BEAT. ME AND ROBERT BEEN RUNNIN' AROUND ALL DAY. I WAS LOOKIN' FORWARD TO SITTIN' ON THE COUCH AND--
I PROMISE. IT'LL BE WORTH IT.
THIS WHAT YOU BEEN WORKIN' ON ALL THESE MONTHS?
YOU KNOW IT!

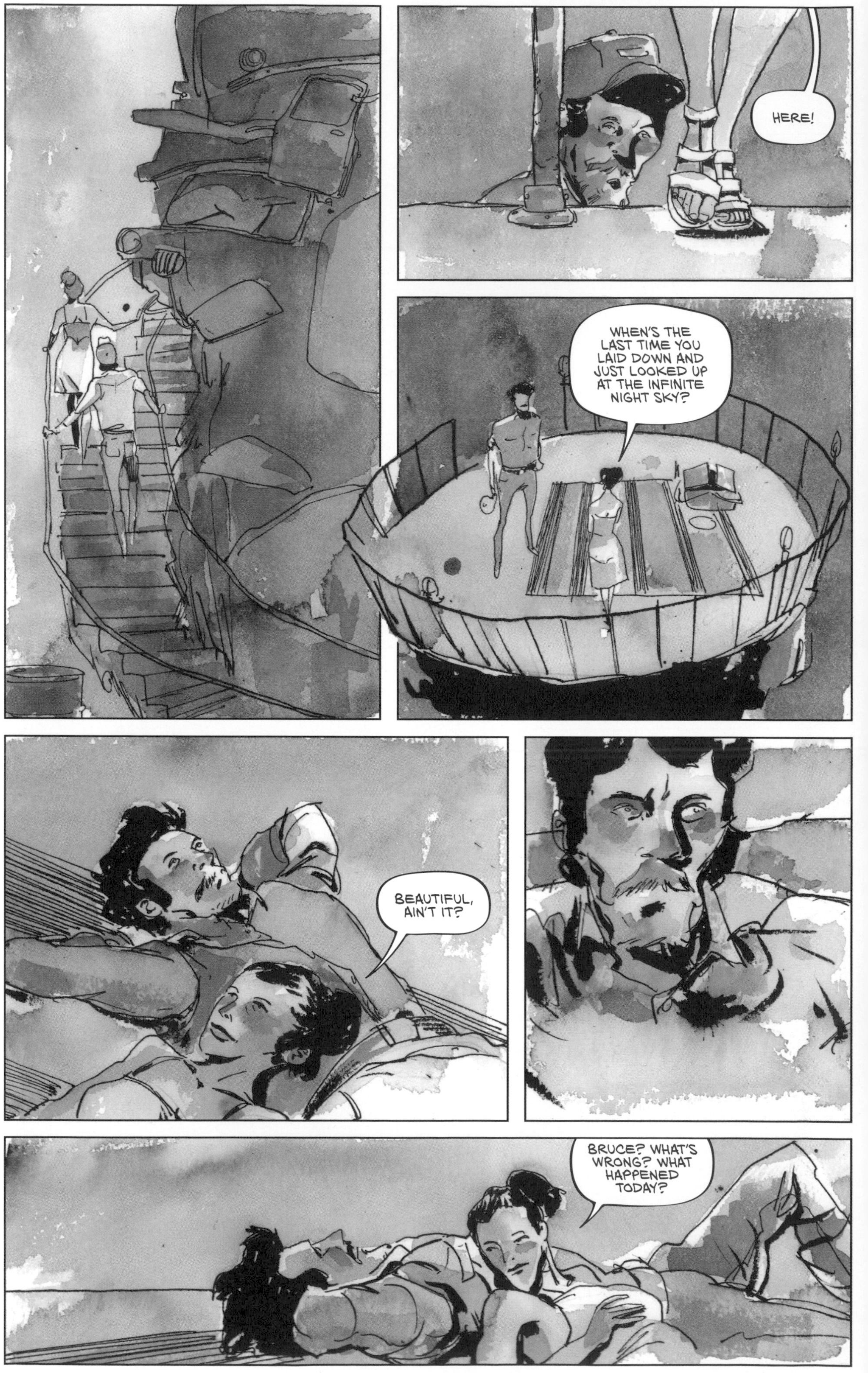
HERE!
WHEN'S THE LAST TIME YOU LAID DOWN AND JUST LOOKED UP AT THE INFINITE NIGHT SKY?
BEAUTIFUL, AIN'T IT?
BRUCE? WHAT'S WRONG? WHAT HAPPENED TODAY?

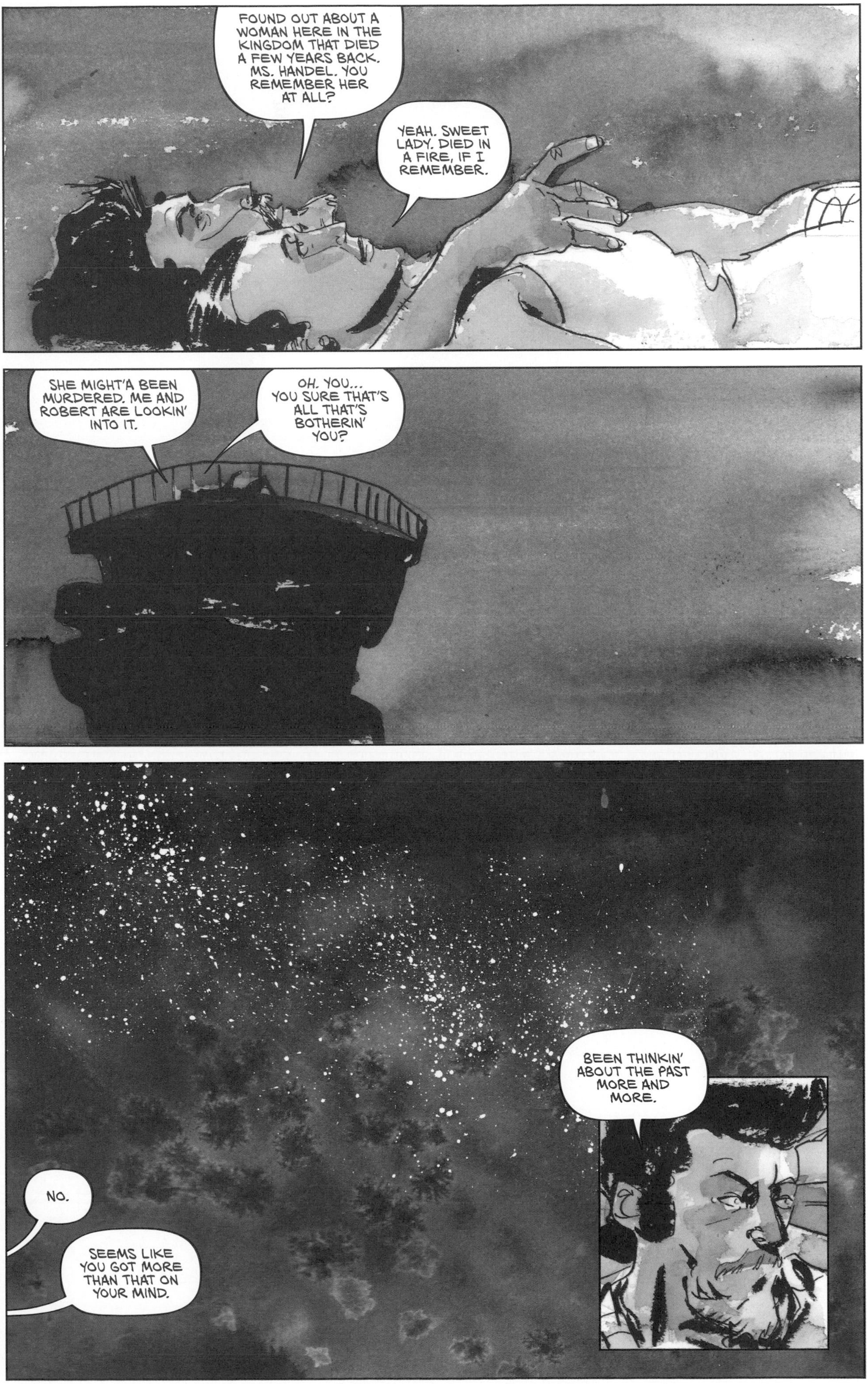
FOUND OUT ABOUT A WOMAN HERE IN THE KINGDOM THAT DIED A FEW YEARS BACK. MS. HANDEL. YOU REMEMBER HER AT ALL?
YEAH. SWEET LADY. DIED IN A FIRE, IF I REMEMBER.
SHE MIGHT'A BEEN MURDERED. ME AND ROBERT ARE LOOKIN' INTO IT.
OH. YOU... YOU SURE THAT'S ALL THAT'S BOTHERIN' YOU?
BEEN THINKIN' ABOUT THE PAST MORE AND MORE.
NO.
SEEMS LIKE YOU GOT MORE THAN THAT ON YOUR MIND.

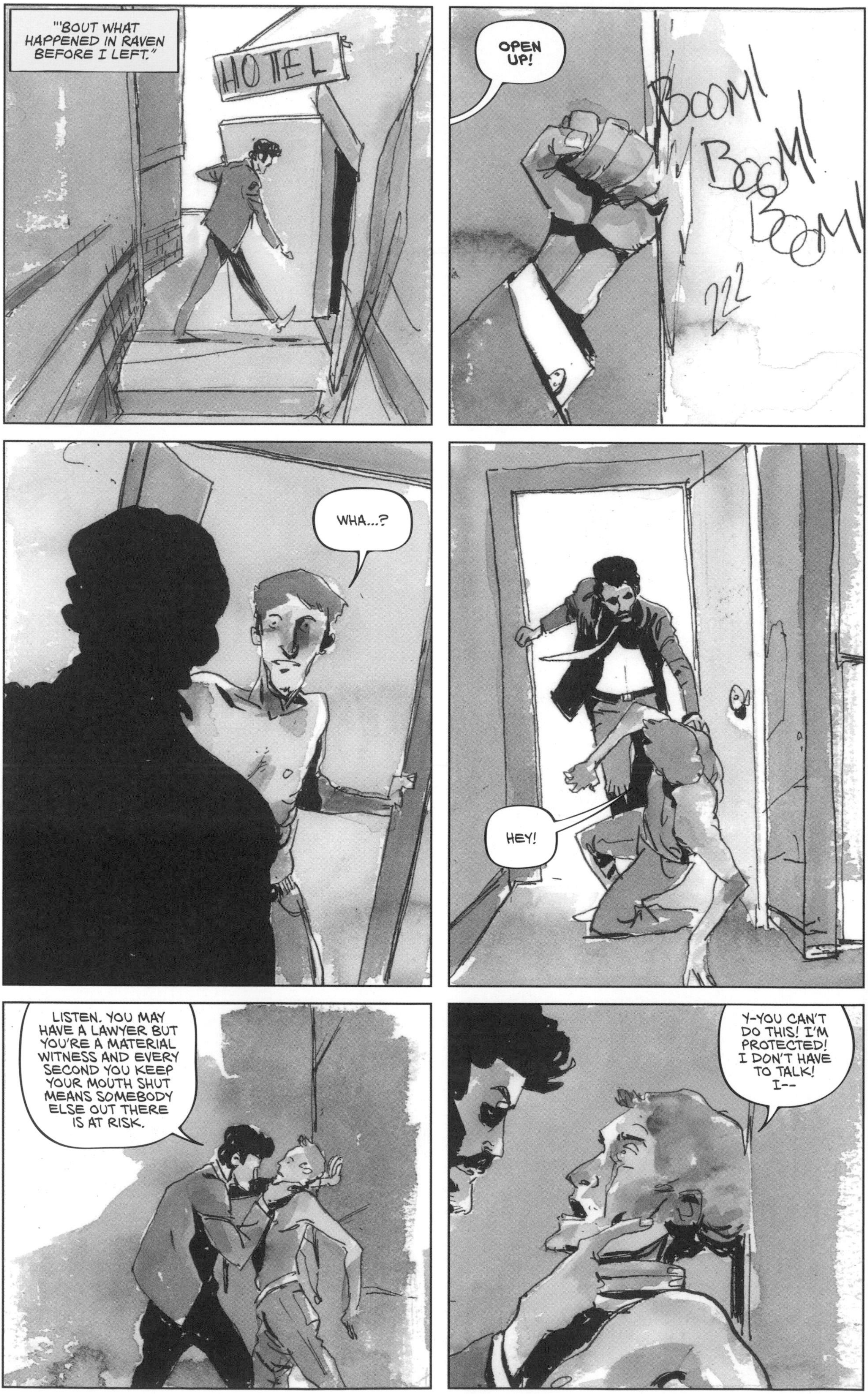
"'BOUT WHAT HAPPENED IN RAVEN BEFORE I LEFT."
HOTEL
OPEN UP!
BOOM! BOOM! BOOM!
222
WHA...?
HEY!
LISTEN. YOU MAY HAVE A LAWYER BUT YOU'RE A MATERIAL WITNESS AND EVERY SECOND YOU KEEP YOUR MOUTH SHUT MEANS SOMEBODY ELSE OUT THERE IS AT RISK.
Y-YOU CAN'T DO THIS! I'M PROTECTED! I DON'T HAVE TO TALK! I--

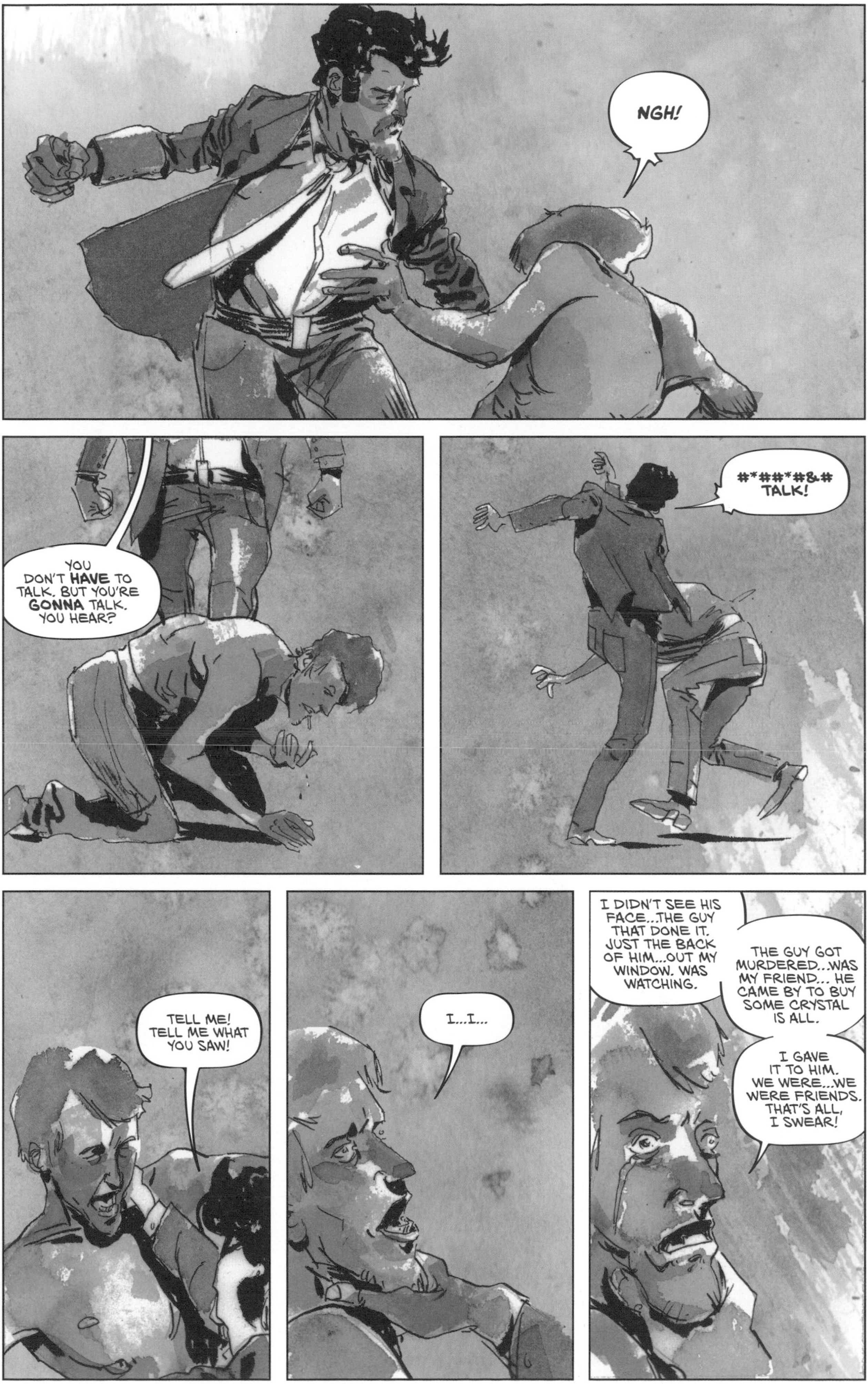
NGH!
YOU DON'T HAVE TO TALK. BUT YOU'RE GONNA TALK. YOU HEAR?
#*##*#&# TALK!
TELL ME! TELL ME WHAT YOU SAW!
I...I...
I DIDN'T SEE HIS FACE...THE GUY THAT DONE IT. JUST THE BACK OF HIM...OUT MY WINDOW. WAS WATCHING.
THE GUY GOT MURDERED...WAS MY FRIEND... HE CAME BY TO BUY SOME CRYSTAL IS ALL.
I GAVE IT TO HIM. WE WERE...WE WERE FRIENDS. THAT'S ALL, I SWEAR!

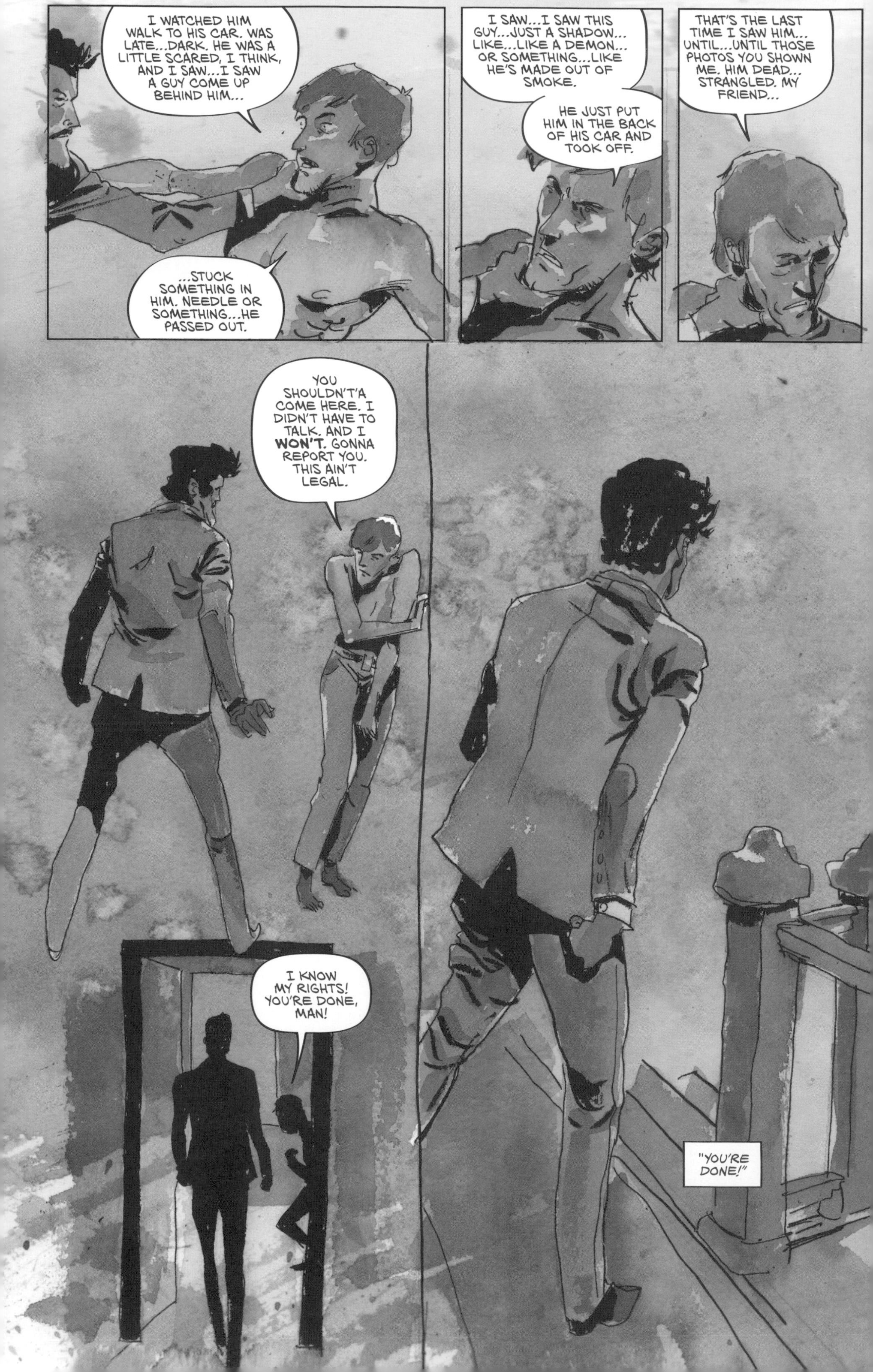
I WATCHED HIM WALK TO HIS CAR. WAS LATE...DARK. HE WAS A LITTLE SCARED, I THINK, AND I SAW...I SAW A GUY COME UP BEHIND HIM...
...STUCK SOMETHING IN HIM. NEEDLE OR SOMETHING...HE PASSED OUT.
I SAW...I SAW THIS GUY...JUST A SHADOW... LIKE...LIKE A DEMON... OR SOMETHING...LIKE HE'S MADE OUT OF SMOKE.
HE JUST PUT HIM IN THE BACK OF HIS CAR AND TOOK OFF.
THAT'S THE LAST TIME I SAW HIM... UNTIL...UNTIL THOSE PHOTOS YOU SHOWN ME. HIM DEAD... STRANGLED. MY FRIEND...
YOU SHOULDN'T'A COME HERE. I DIDN'T HAVE TO TALK. AND I **WON'T.** GONNA REPORT YOU. THIS AIN'T LEGAL.
I KNOW MY RIGHTS! YOU'RE DONE, MAN!
"YOU'RE DONE!"

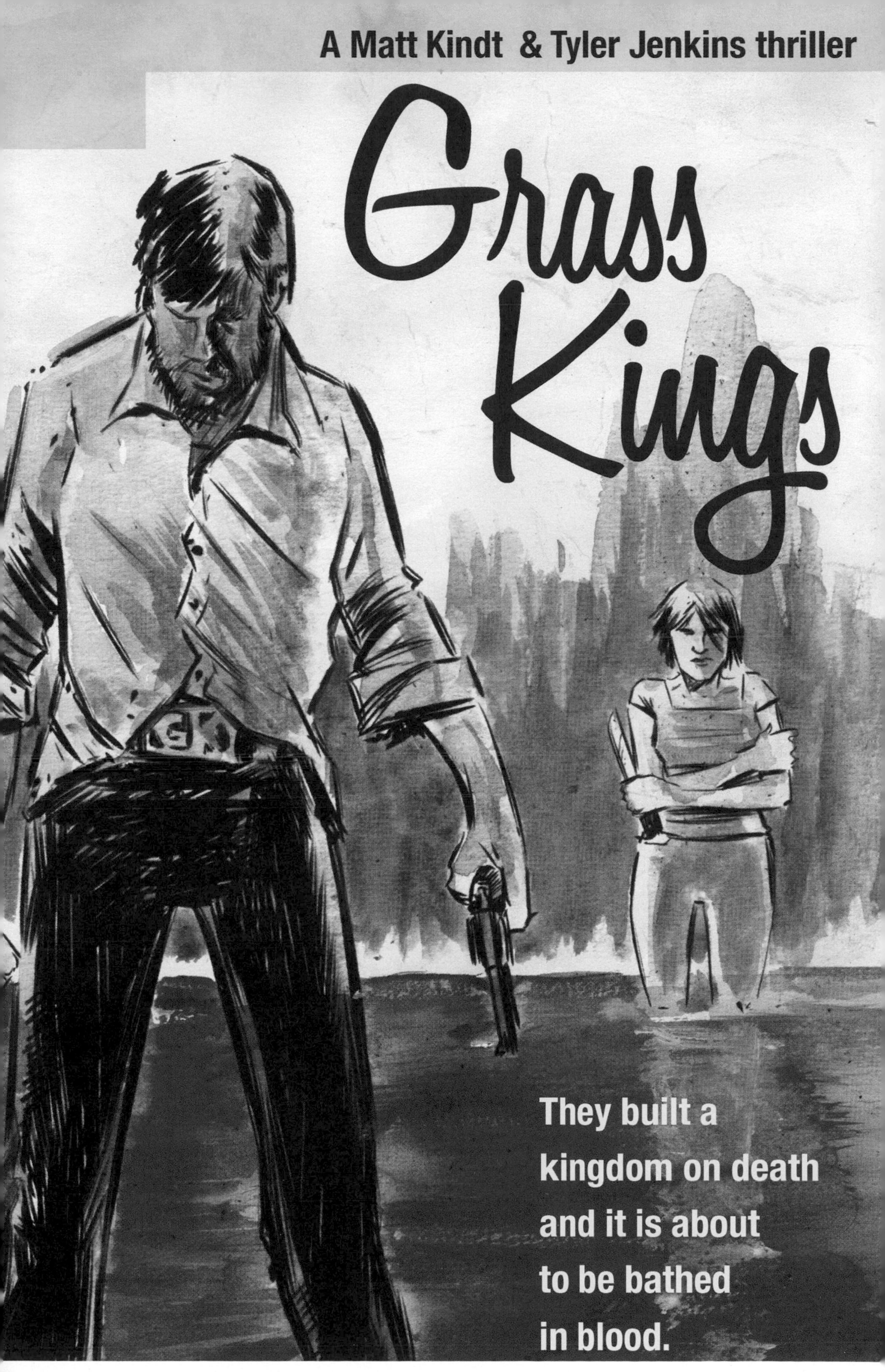
A Matt Kindt & Tyler Jenkins thriller
Grass Kings
They built a kingdom on death and it is about to be bathed in blood.

issue #7 cover by matt kindt

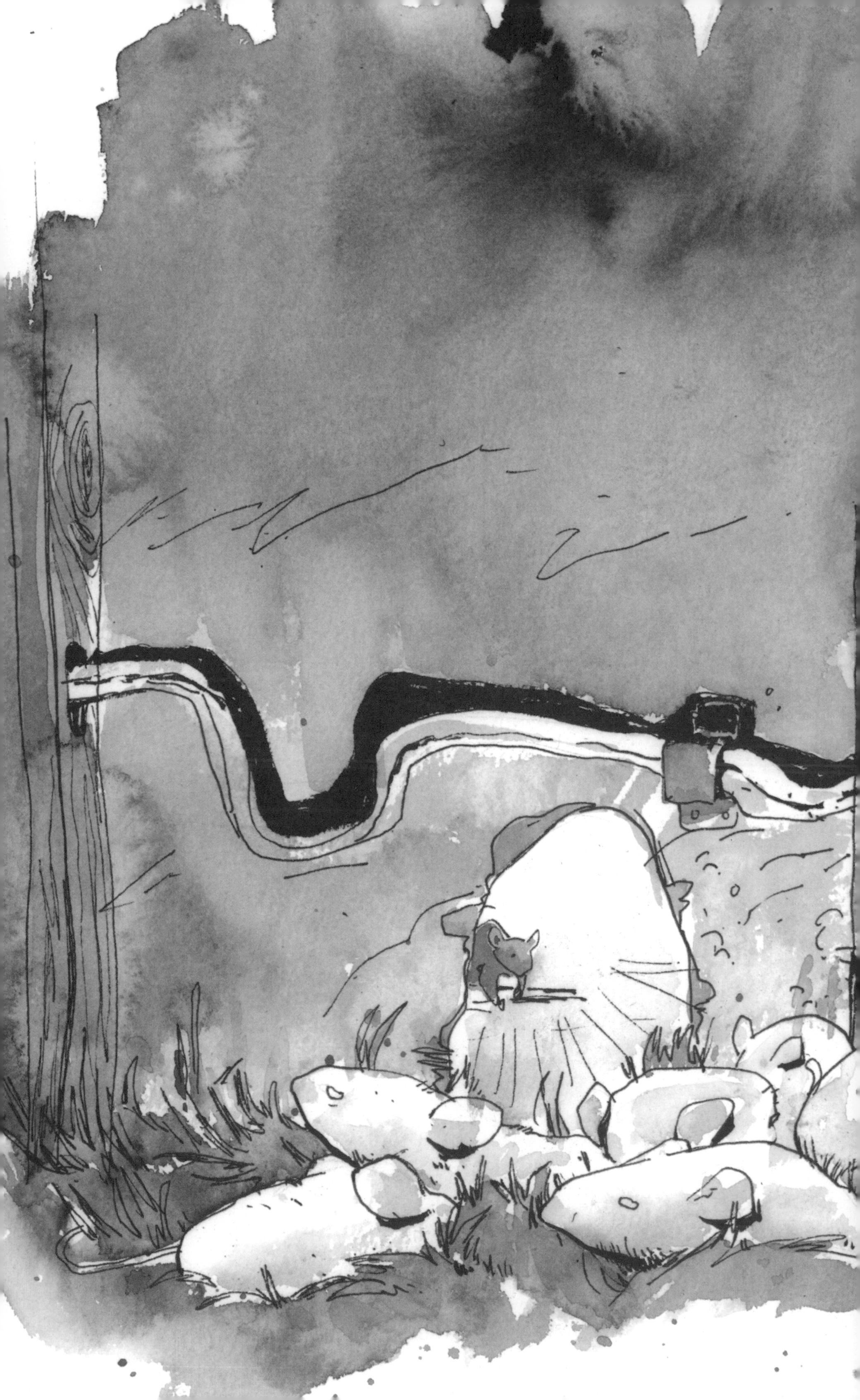

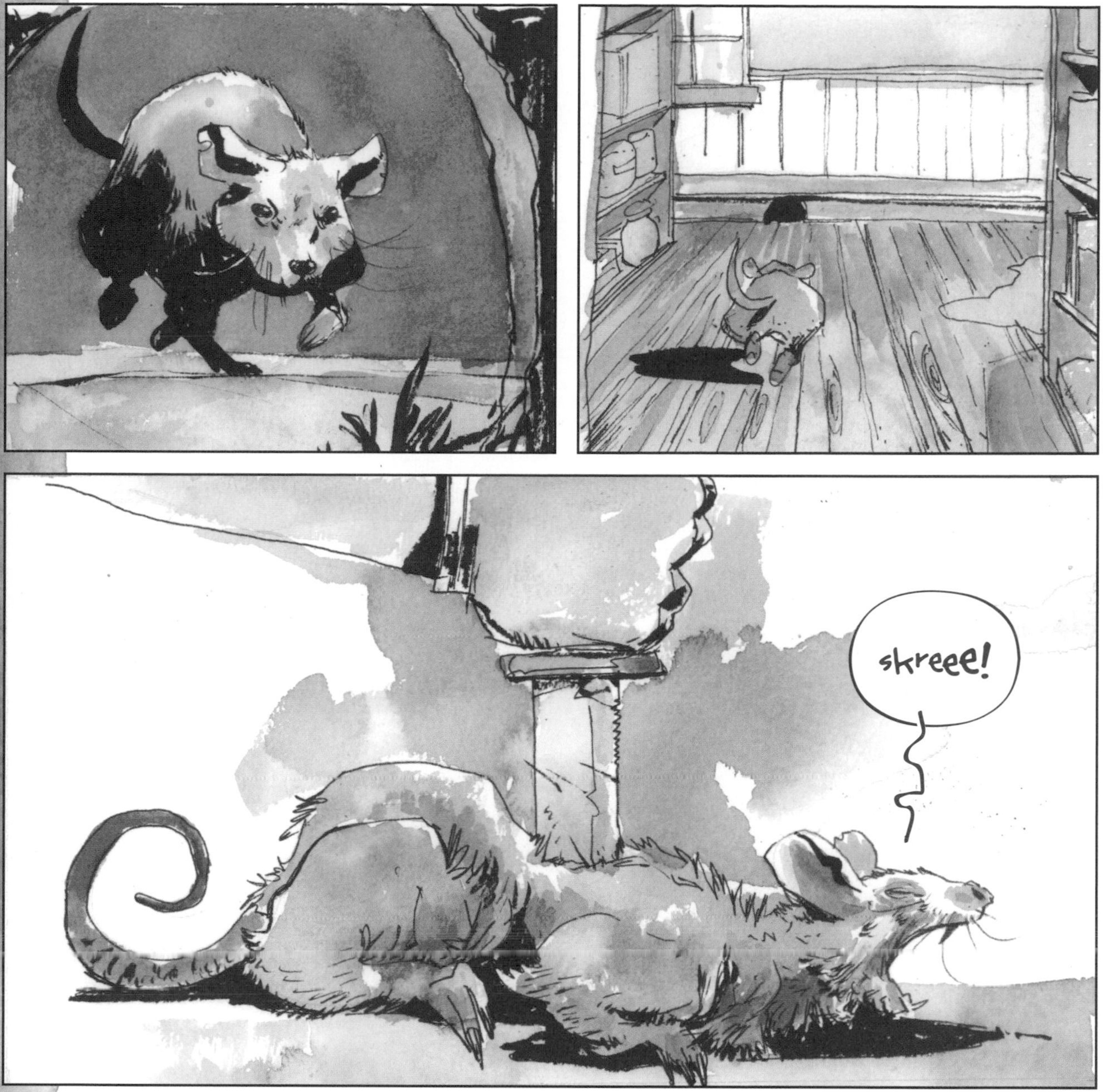
skreee!

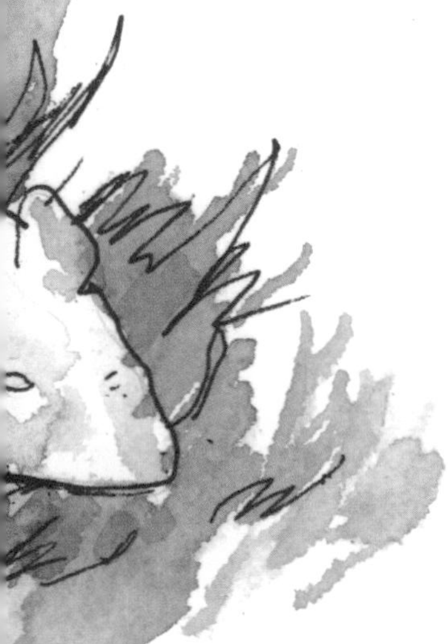

chapter eight

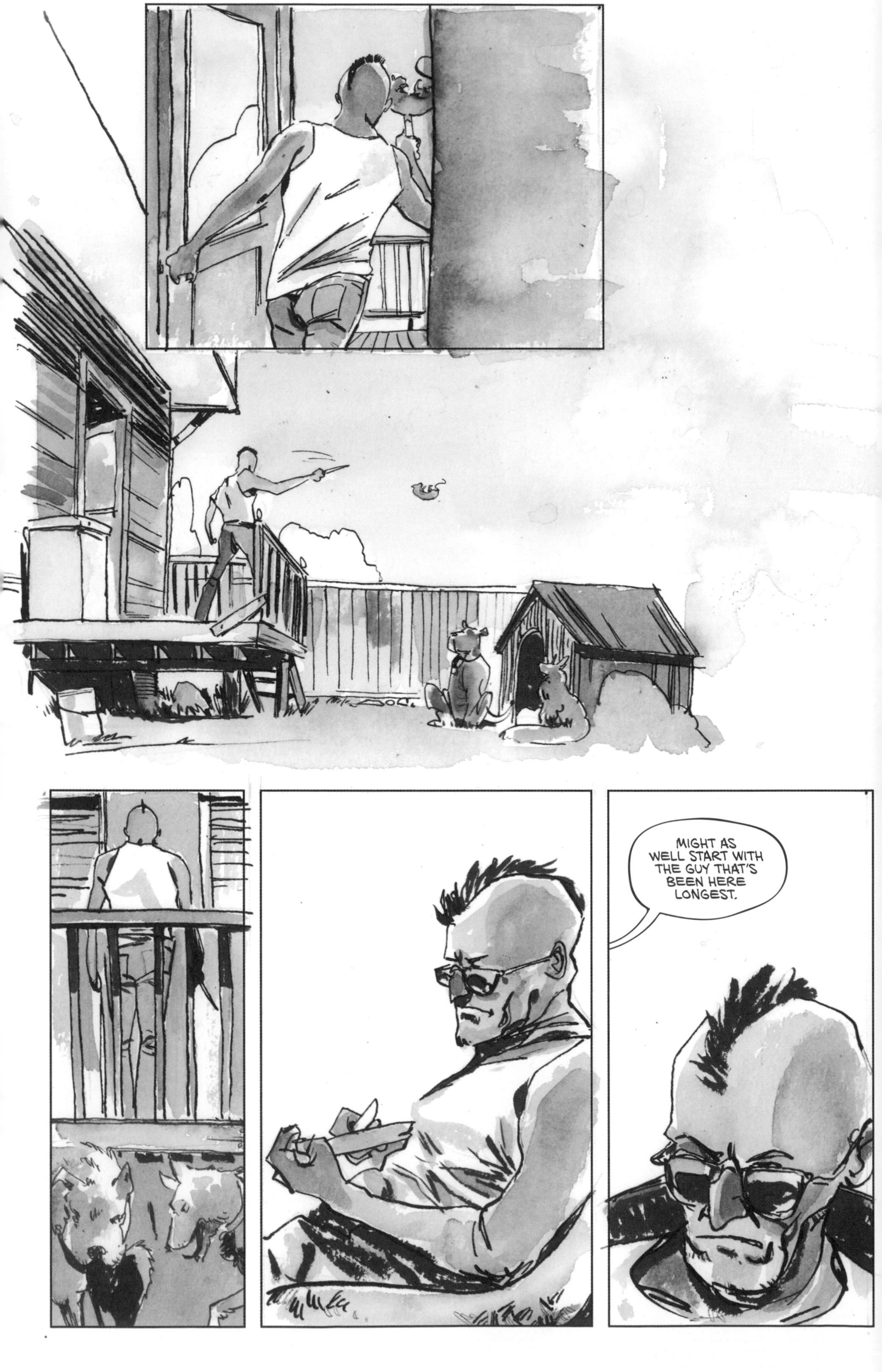
MIGHT AS
WELL START WITH
THE GUY THAT'S
BEEN HERE
LONGEST.

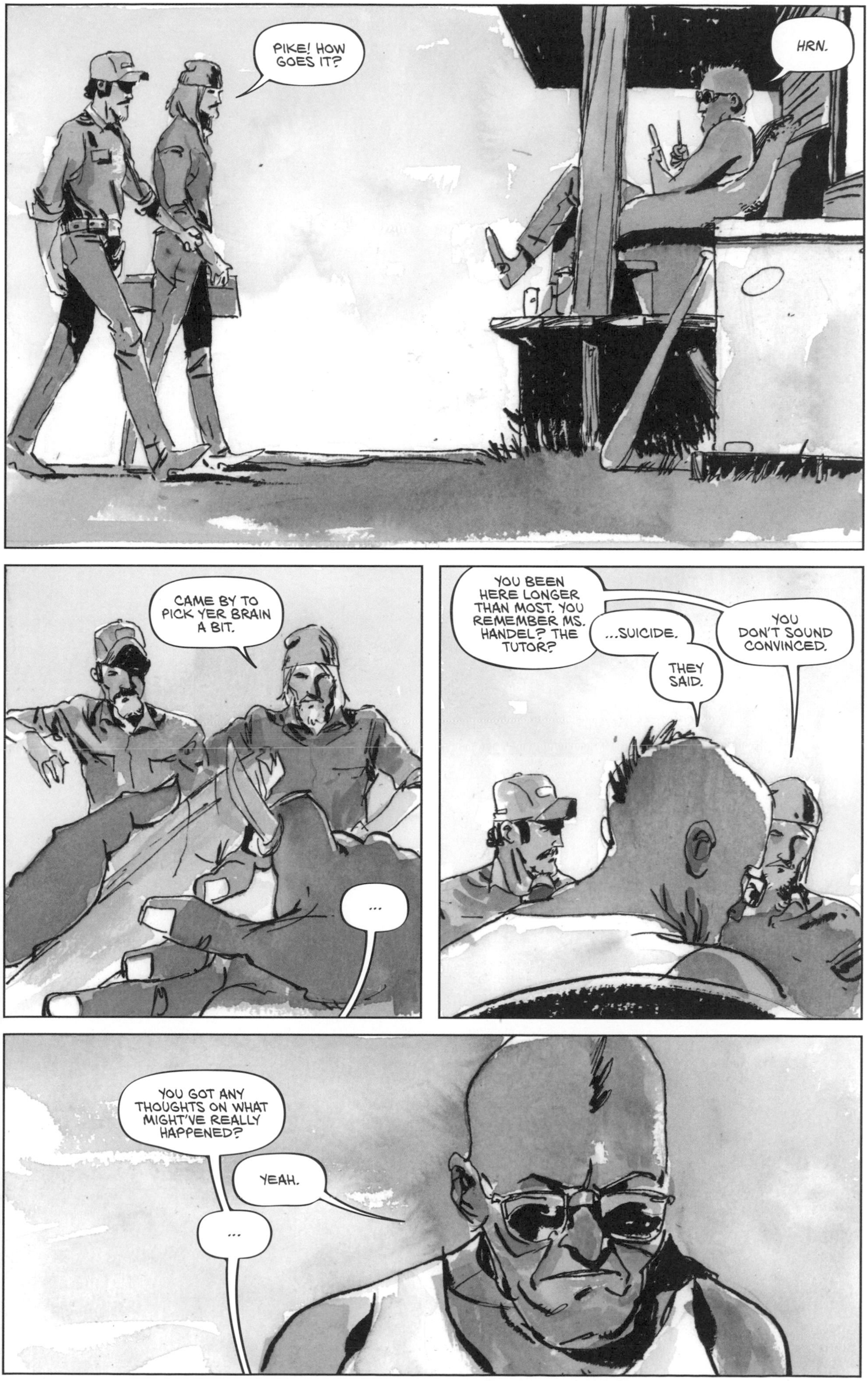

PIKE! HOW GOES IT?
HRN.
CAME BY TO PICK YER BRAIN A BIT.
...
YOU BEEN HERE LONGER THAN MOST. YOU REMEMBER MS. HANDEL? THE TUTOR?
...SUICIDE.
THEY SAID.
YOU DON'T SOUND CONVINCED.
YOU GOT ANY THOUGHTS ON WHAT MIGHT'VE REALLY HAPPENED?
YEAH.
...

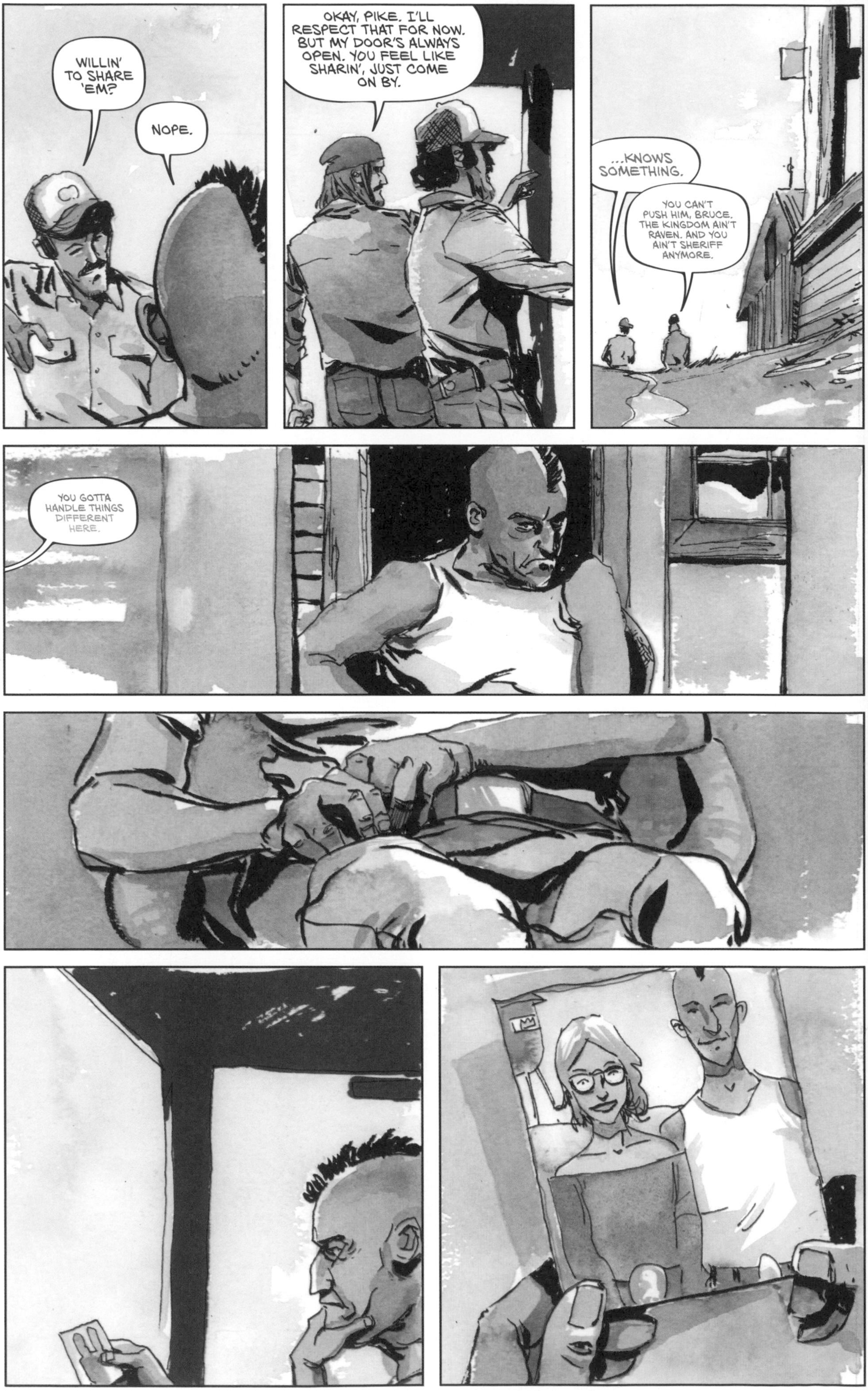
WILLIN' TO SHARE 'EM?
NOPE.
OKAY, PIKE. I'LL RESPECT THAT FOR NOW. BUT MY DOOR'S ALWAYS OPEN. YOU FEEL LIKE SHARIN', JUST COME ON BY.
...KNOWS SOMETHING.
YOU CAN'T PUSH HIM, BRUCE. THE KINGDOM AIN'T RAVEN. AND YOU AIN'T SHERIFF ANYMORE.
YOU GOTTA HANDLE THINGS DIFFERENT HERE.

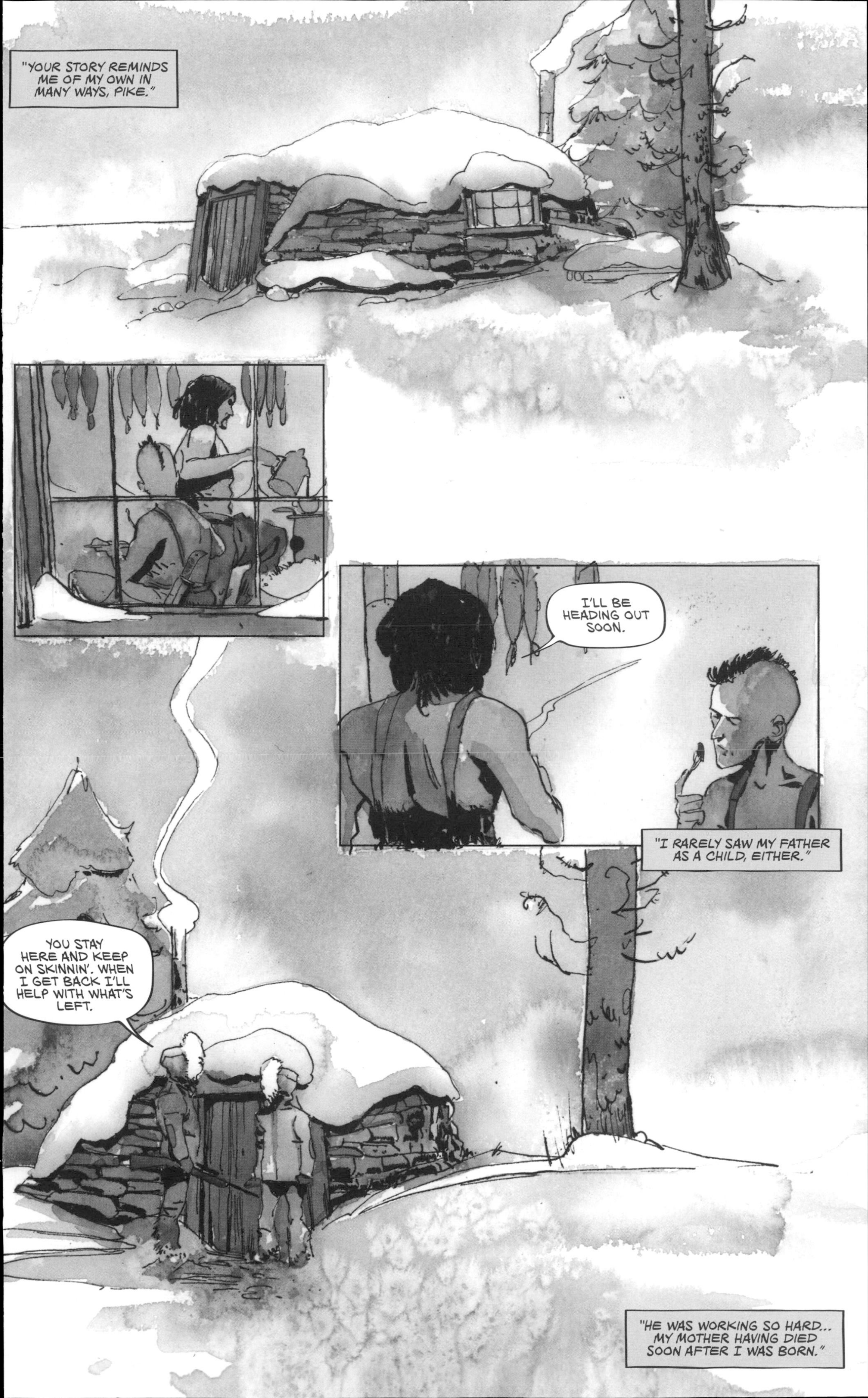
"YOUR STORY REMINDS ME OF MY OWN IN MANY WAYS, PIKE."
I'LL BE HEADING OUT SOON.
"I RARELY SAW MY FATHER AS A CHILD, EITHER."
YOU STAY HERE AND KEEP ON SKINNIN'. WHEN I GET BACK I'LL HELP WITH WHAT'S LEFT.
"HE WAS WORKING SO HARD... MY MOTHER HAVING DIED SOON AFTER I WAS BORN."

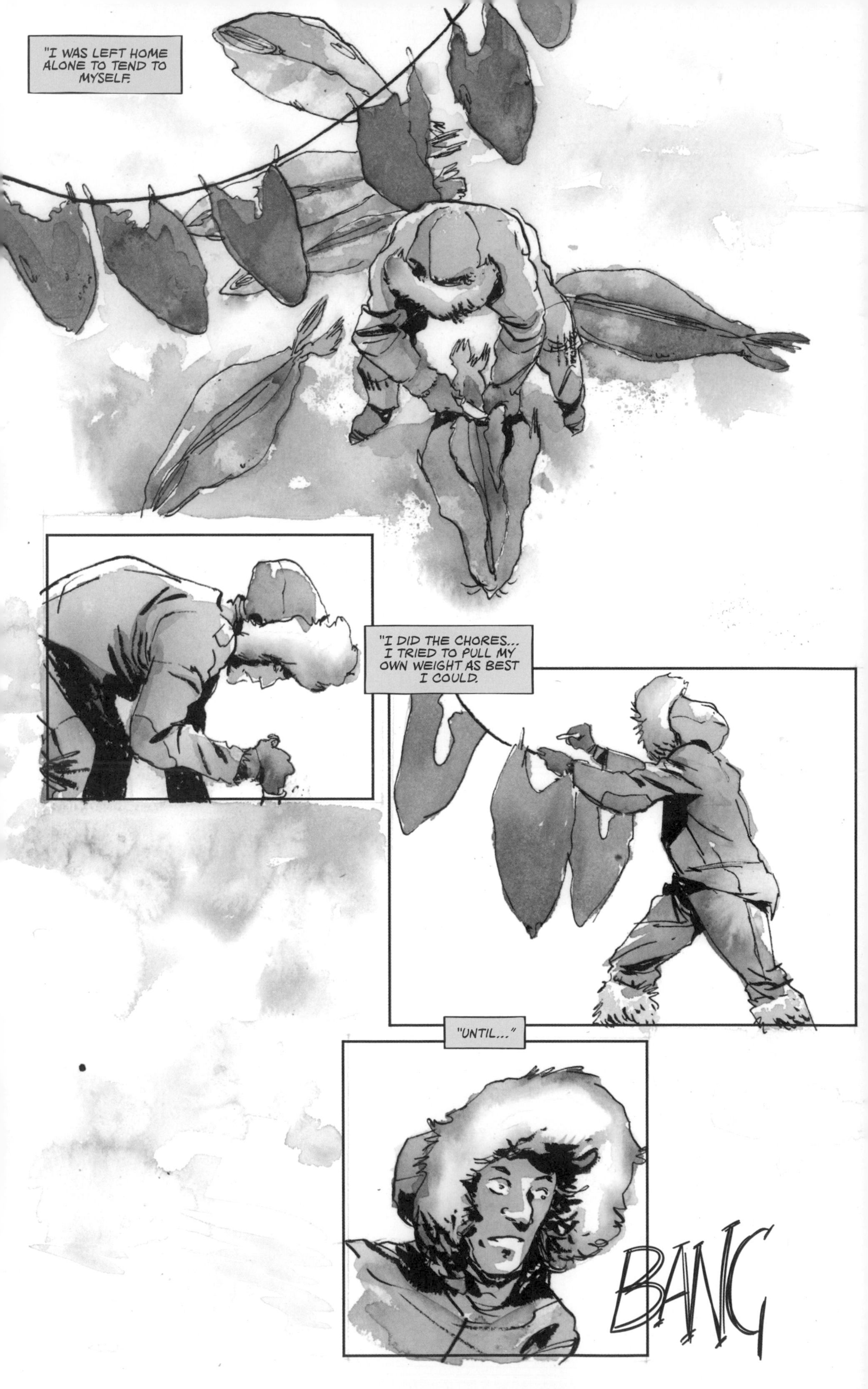
"I WAS LEFT HOME ALONE TO TEND TO MYSELF.
"I DID THE CHORES... I TRIED TO PULL MY OWN WEIGHT AS BEST I COULD.
"UNTIL..."
BANG

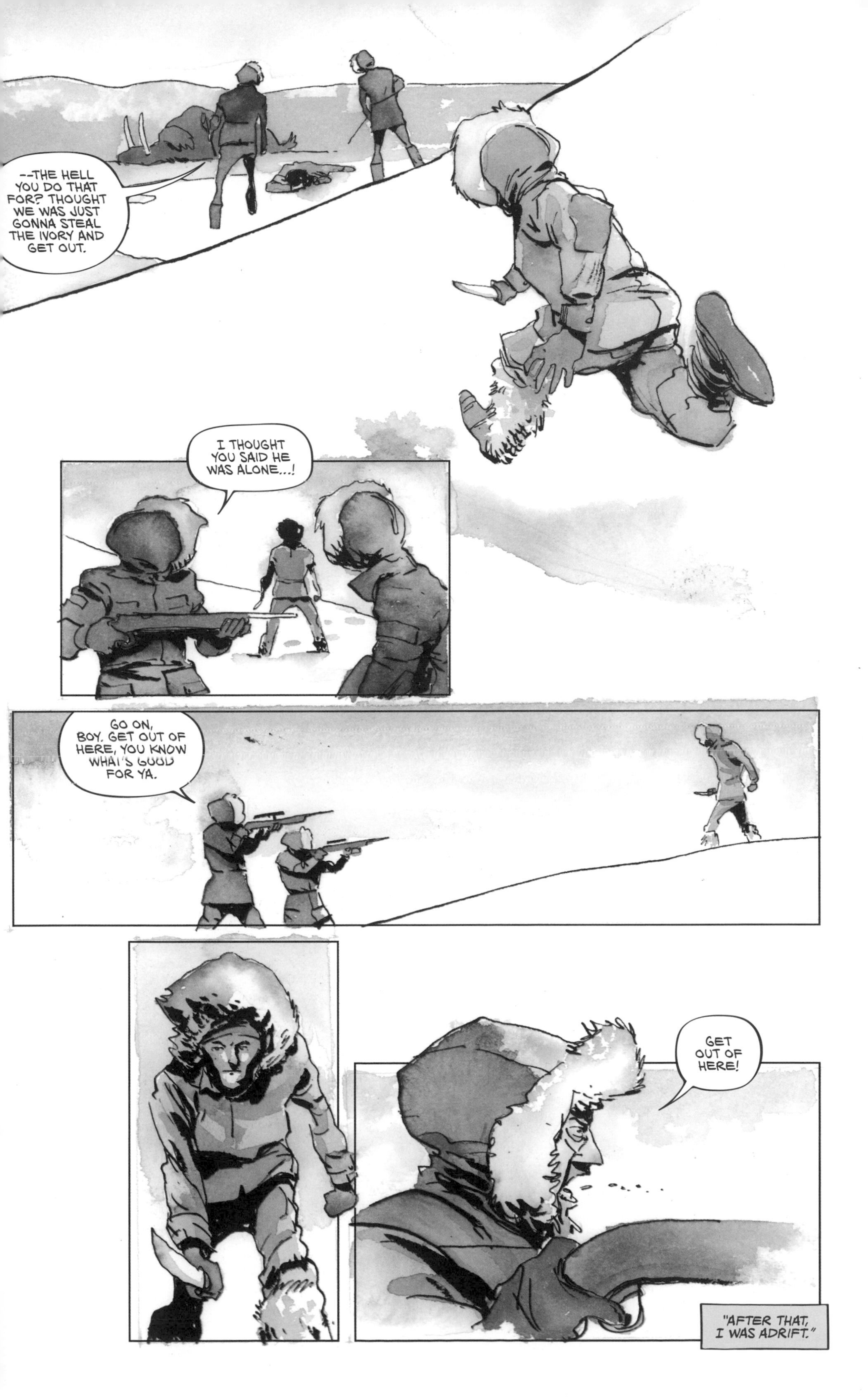
--THE HELL YOU DO THAT FOR? THOUGHT WE WAS JUST GONNA STEAL THE IVORY AND GET OUT.
I THOUGHT YOU SAID HE WAS ALONE...!
GO ON, BOY. GET OUT OF HERE, YOU KNOW WHAT'S GOOD FOR YA.
GET OUT OF HERE!
"AFTER THAT, I WAS ADRIFT."

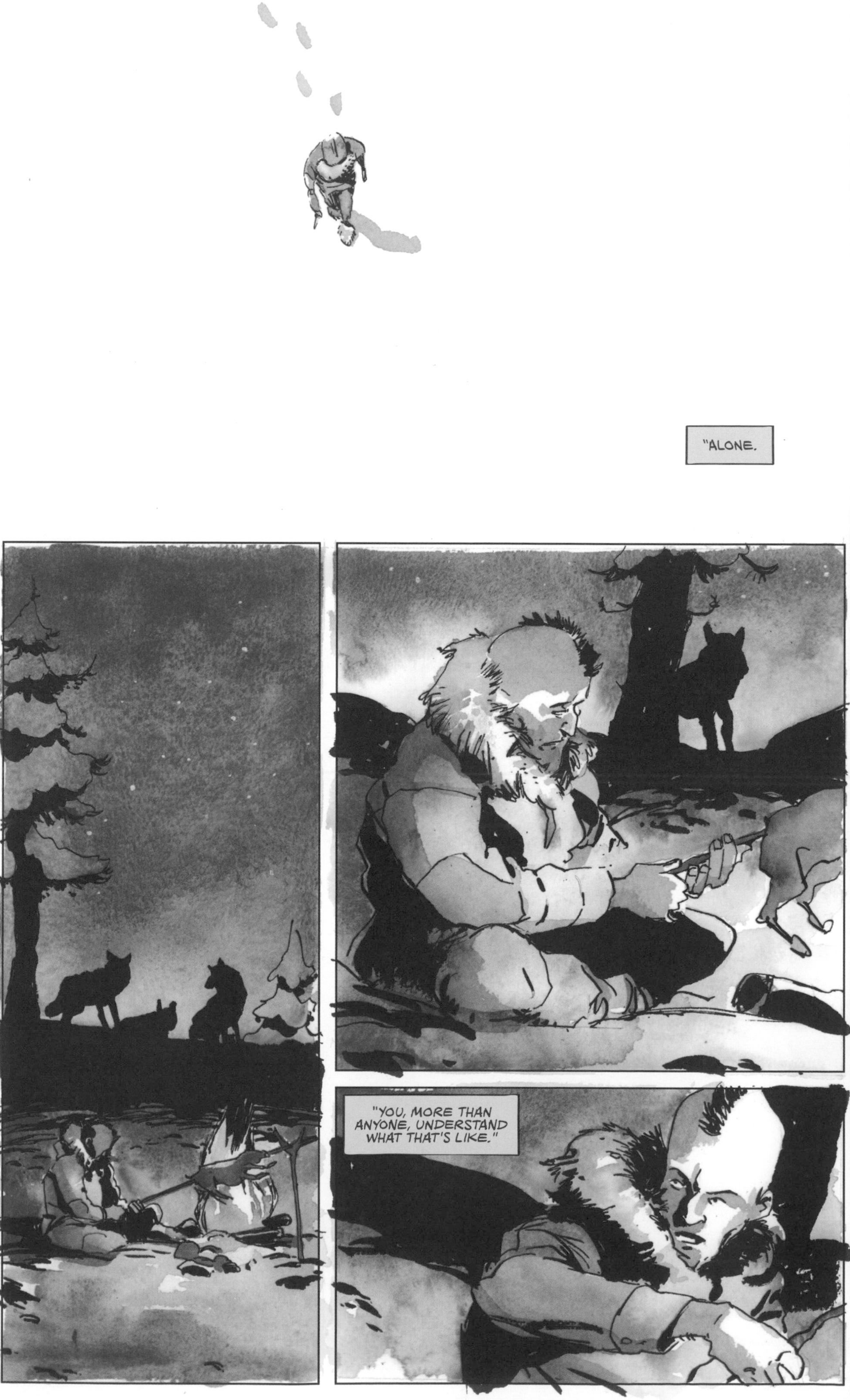
"ALONE.
"YOU, MORE THAN ANYONE, UNDERSTAND WHAT THAT'S LIKE."

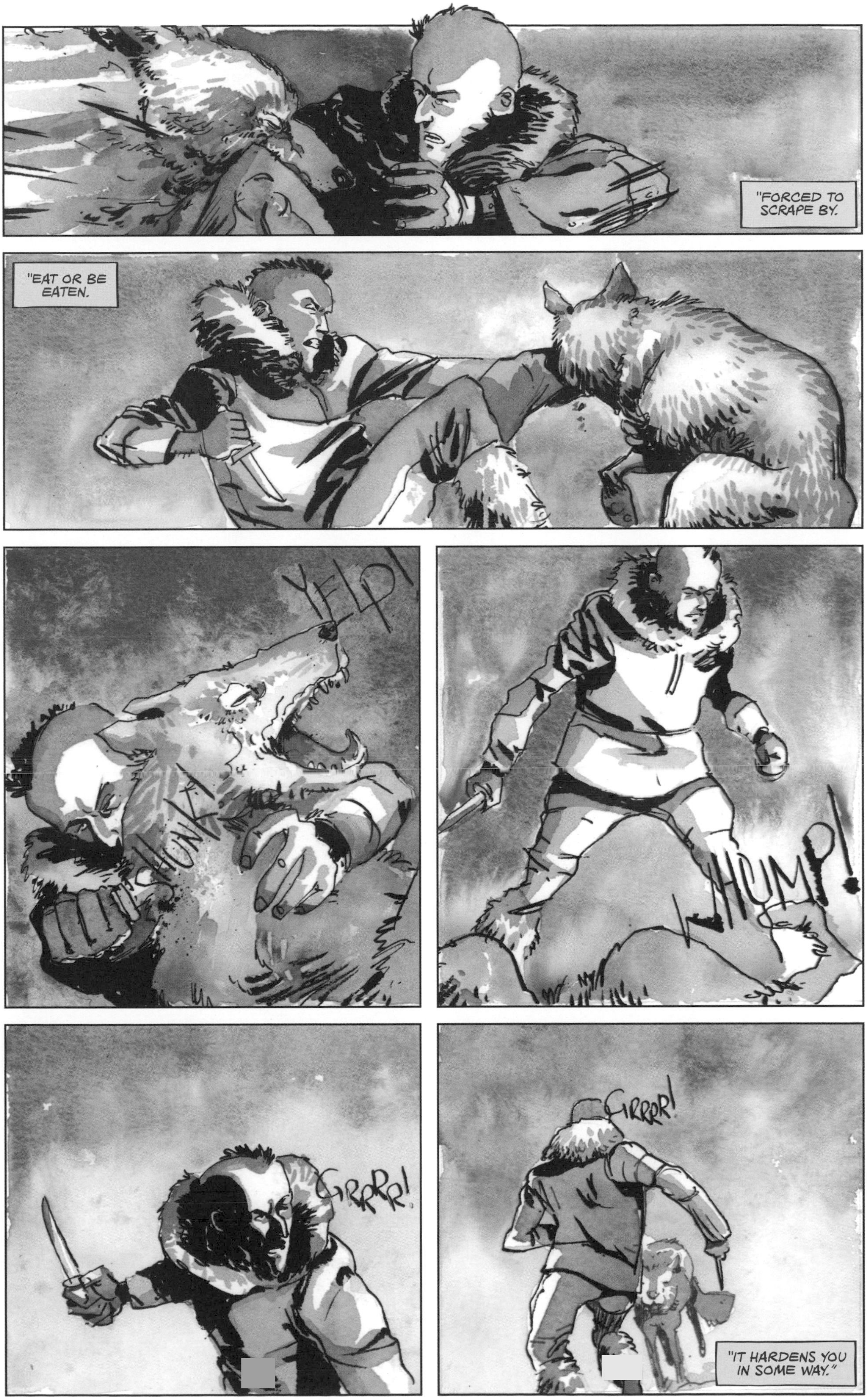
"FORCED TO SCRAPE BY.
"EAT OR BE EATEN.
YELP!
SHUNK!
WHUMP!
GRRRR!
GRRR!
"IT HARDENS YOU IN SOME WAY."

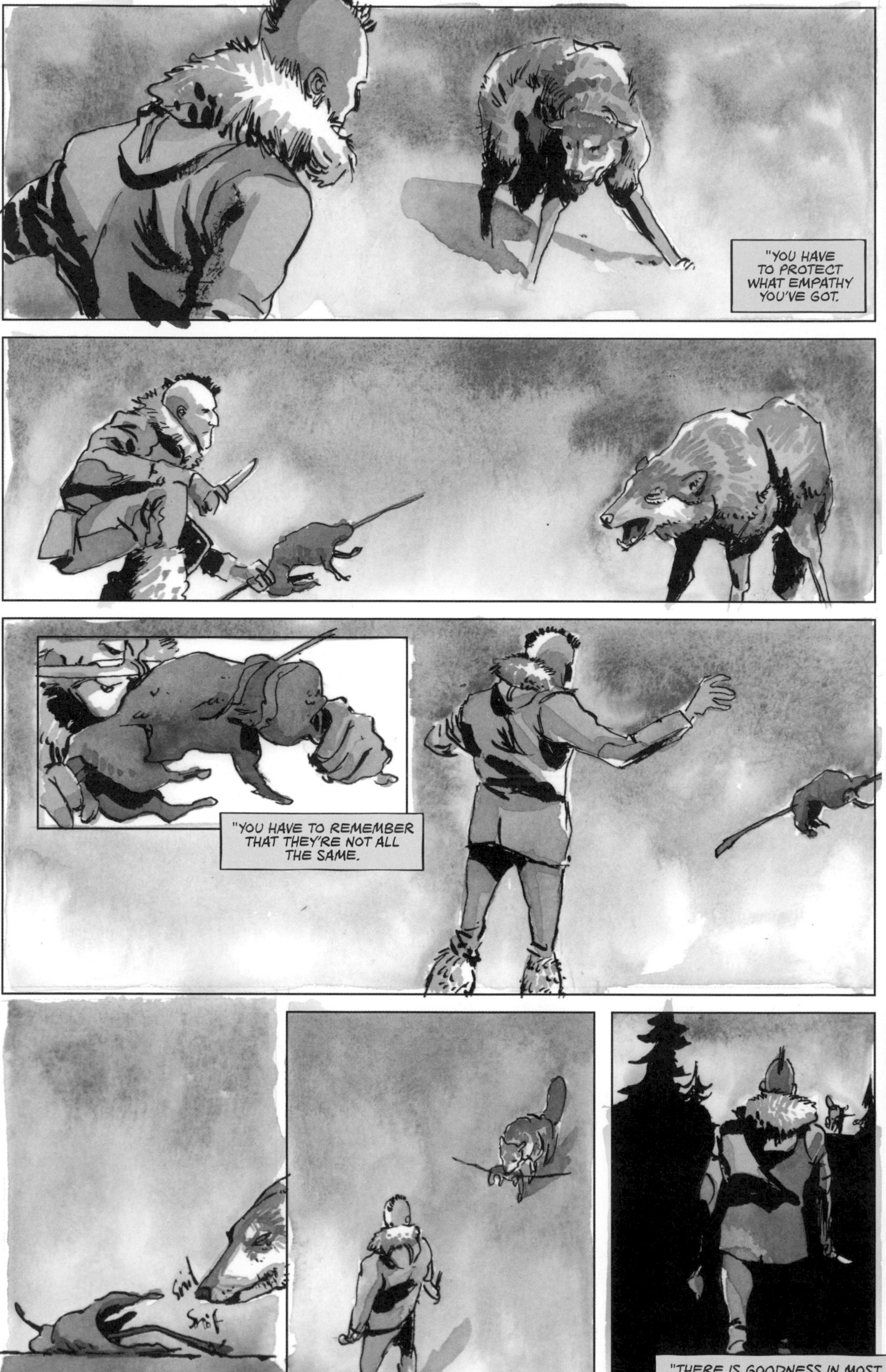
"YOU HAVE TO PROTECT WHAT EMPATHY YOU'VE GOT.
"YOU HAVE TO REMEMBER THAT THEY'RE NOT ALL THE SAME.
Snif
Snif
"THERE IS GOODNESS IN MOST PEOPLE. SOMETIMES YOU JUST HAVE TO FIND OUT HOW TO BRING IT OUT IN THEM."

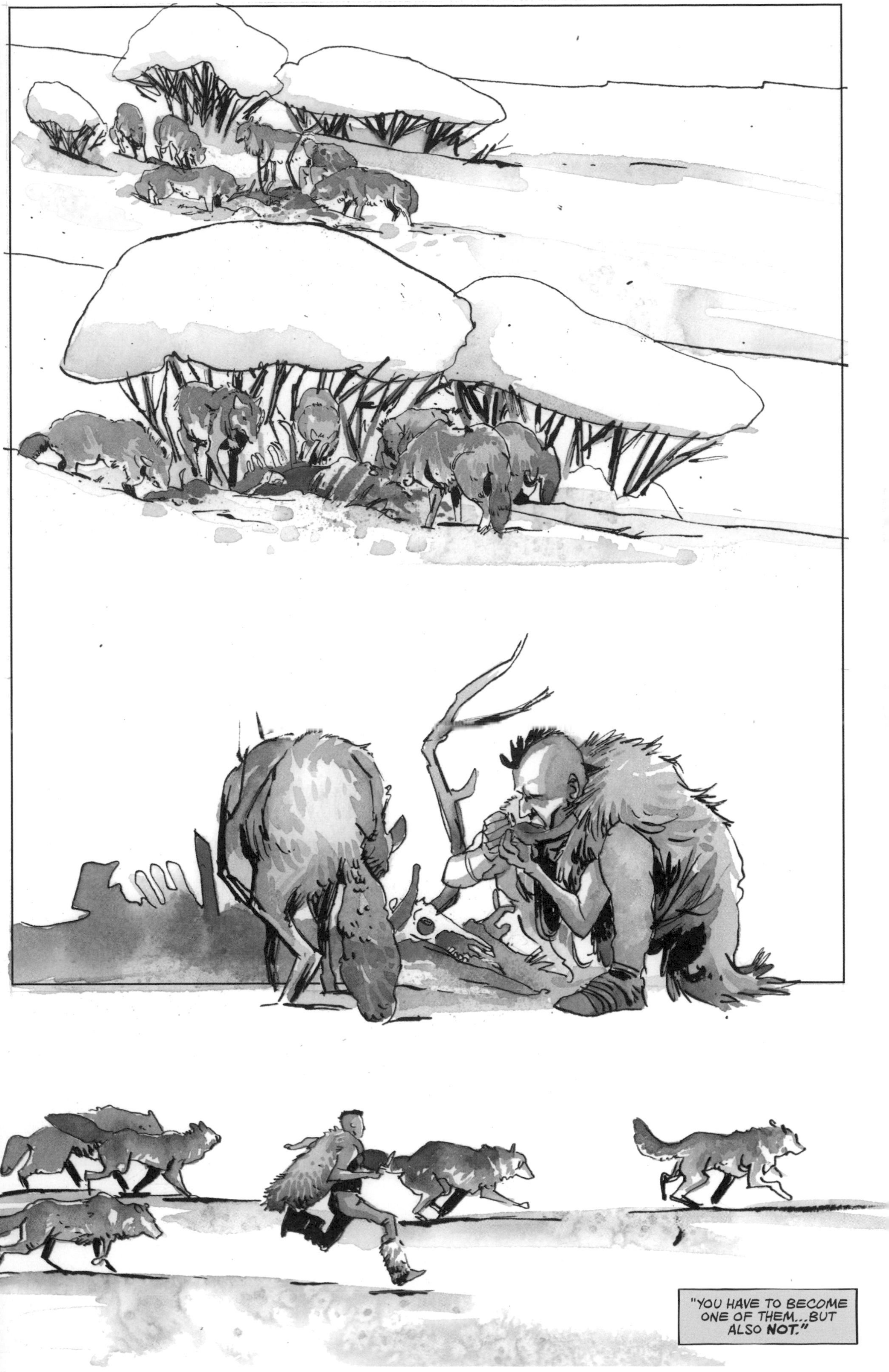
"YOU HAVE TO BECOME ONE OF THEM...BUT ALSO NOT."

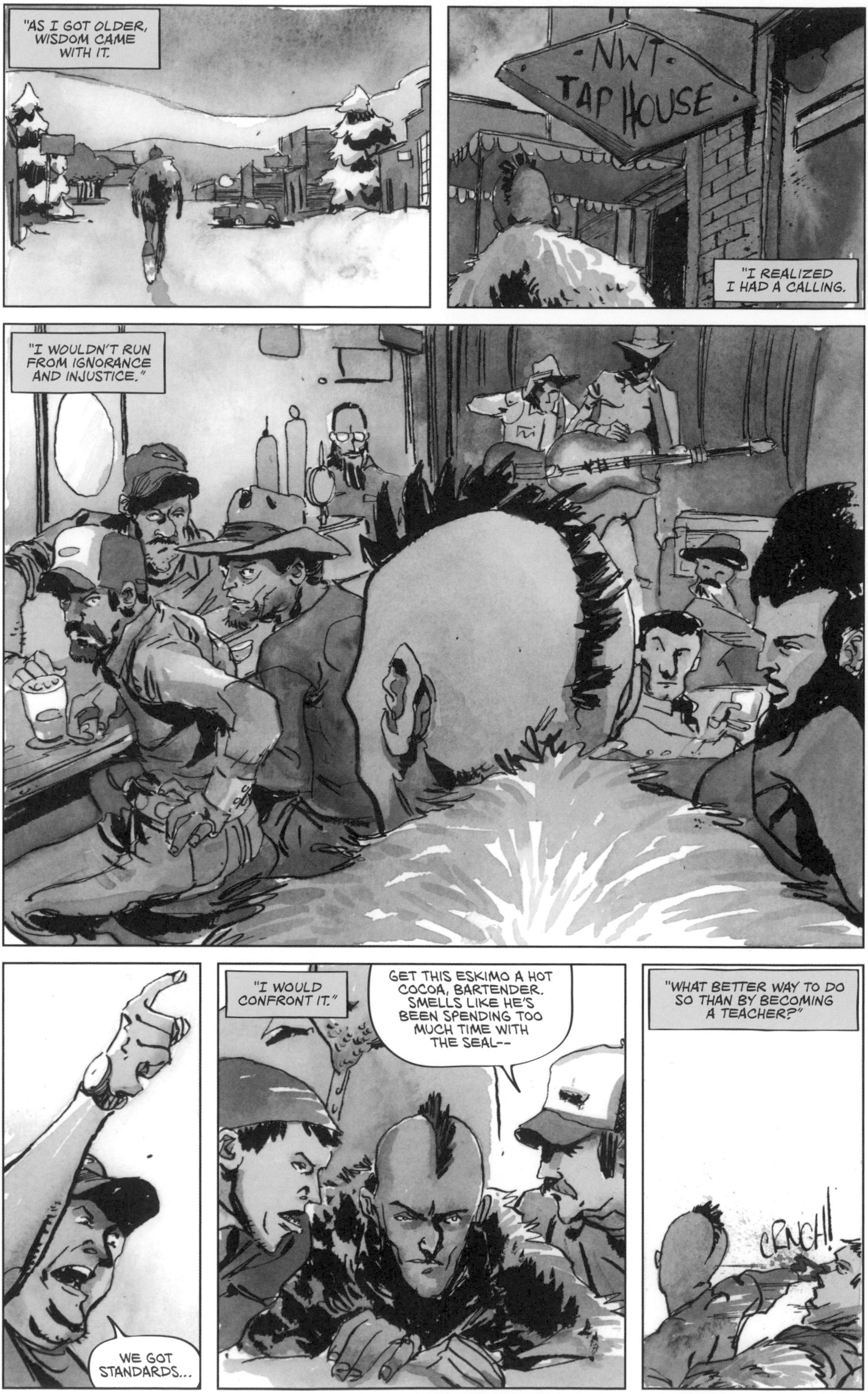
"AS I GOT OLDER, WISDOM CAME WITH IT.
NWT TAP HOUSE
"I REALIZED I HAD A CALLING.
"I WOULDN'T RUN FROM IGNORANCE AND INJUSTICE."
WE GOT STANDARDS...
"I WOULD CONFRONT IT."
GET THIS ESKIMO A HOT COCOA, BARTENDER. SMELLS LIKE HE'S BEEN SPENDING TOO MUCH TIME WITH THE SEAL--
"WHAT BETTER WAY TO DO SO THAN BY BECOMING A TEACHER?"
CRNCH!

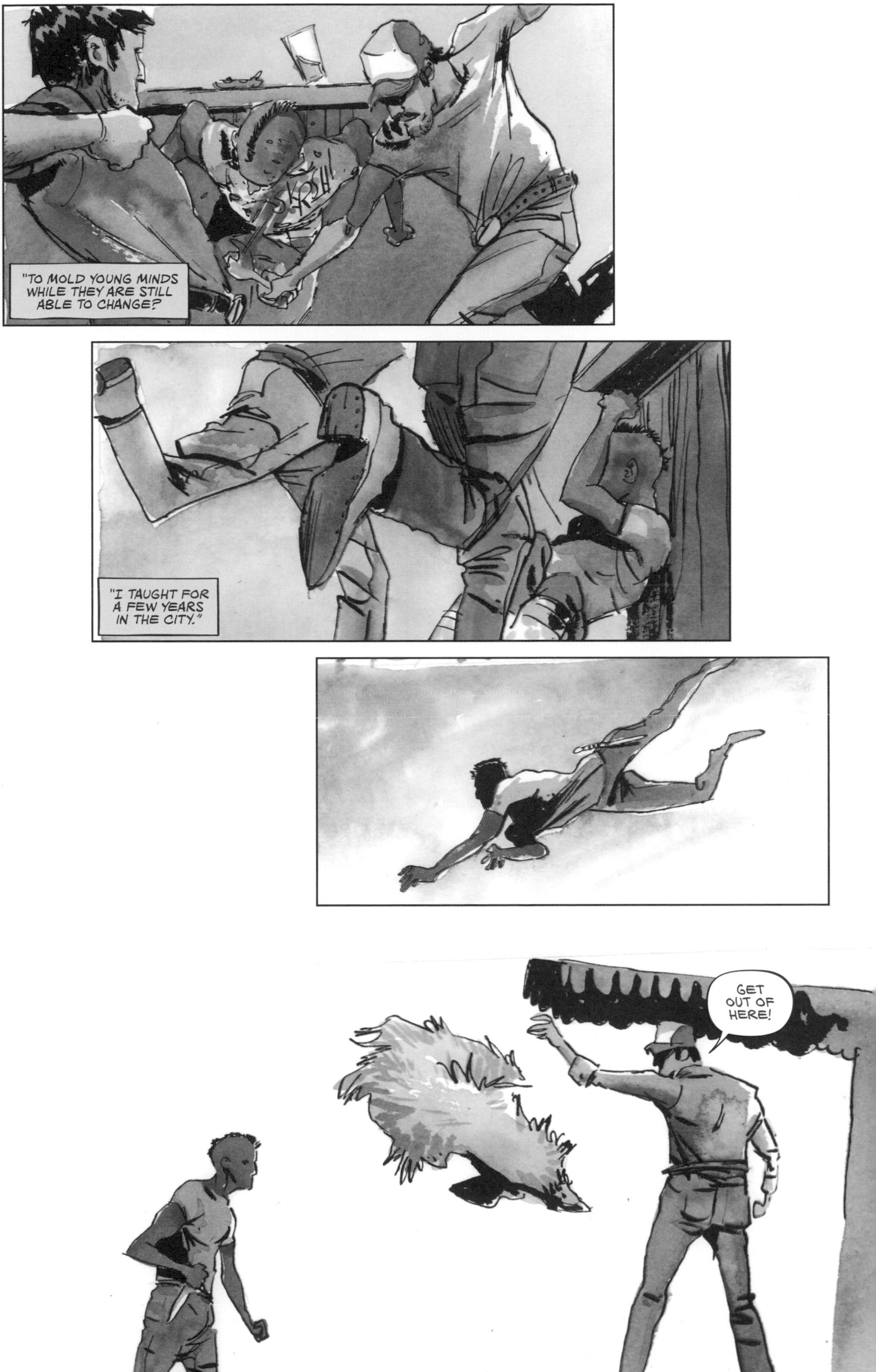
"TO MOLD YOUNG MINDS WHILE THEY ARE STILL ABLE TO CHANGE?
"I TAUGHT FOR A FEW YEARS IN THE CITY."
GET OUT OF HERE!

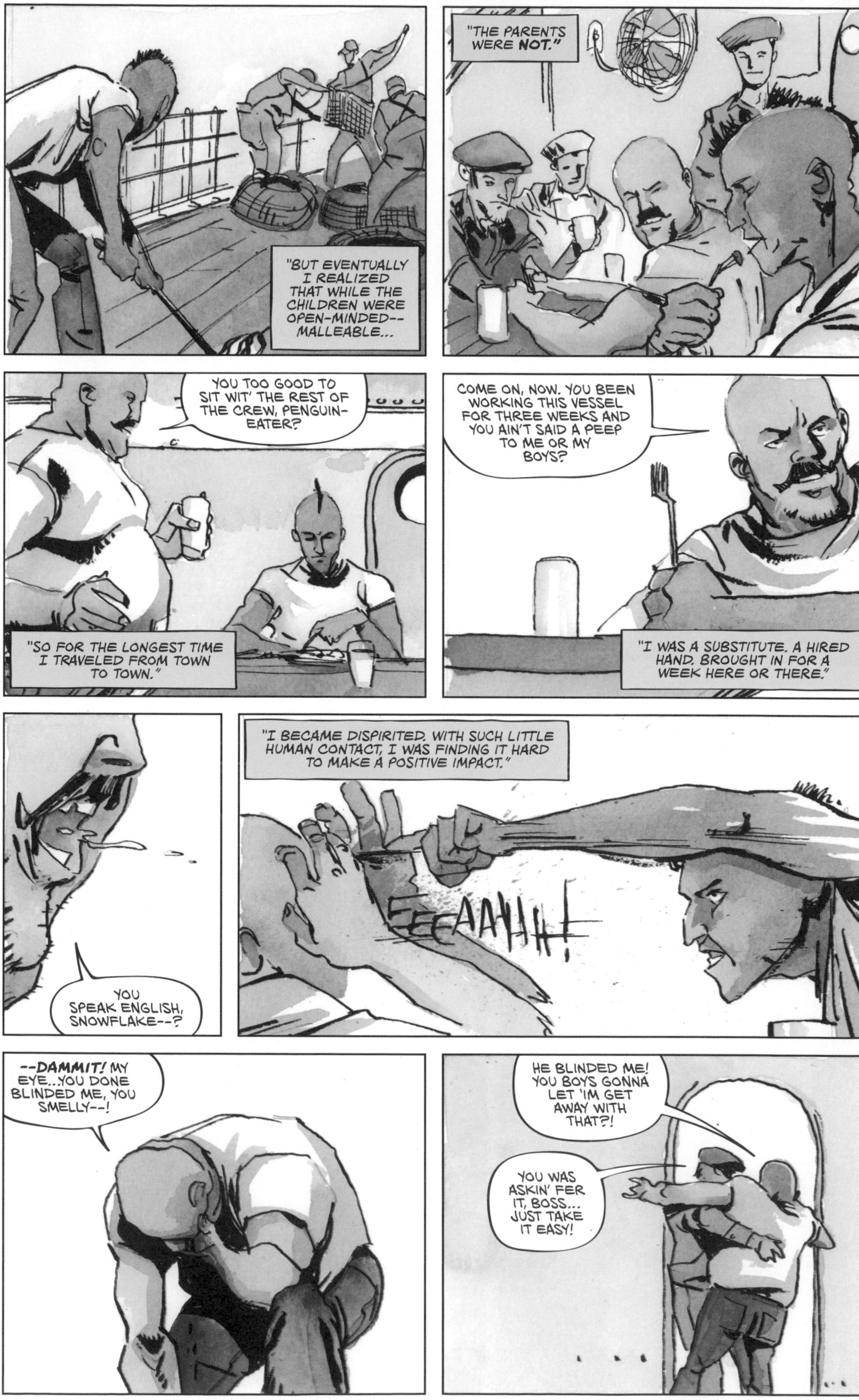
"BUT EVENTUALLY I REALIZED THAT WHILE THE CHILDREN WERE OPEN-MINDED--MALLEABLE...
"THE PARENTS WERE **NOT.**"
YOU TOO GOOD TO SIT WIT' THE REST OF THE CREW, PENGUIN-EATER?
"SO FOR THE LONGEST TIME I TRAVELED FROM TOWN TO TOWN."
COME ON, NOW. YOU BEEN WORKING THIS VESSEL FOR THREE WEEKS AND YOU AIN'T SAID A PEEP TO ME OR MY BOYS?
"I WAS A SUBSTITUTE. A HIRED HAND. BROUGHT IN FOR A WEEK HERE OR THERE."
YOU SPEAK ENGLISH, SNOWFLAKE--?
"I BECAME DISPIRITED. WITH SUCH LITTLE HUMAN CONTACT, I WAS FINDING IT HARD TO MAKE A POSITIVE IMPACT."
EEEAAHH!
--**DAMMIT!** MY EYE...YOU DONE BLINDED ME, YOU SMELLY--!
HE BLINDED ME! YOU BOYS GONNA LET 'IM GET AWAY WITH THAT?!
YOU WAS ASKIN' FER IT, BOSS... JUST TAKE IT EASY!

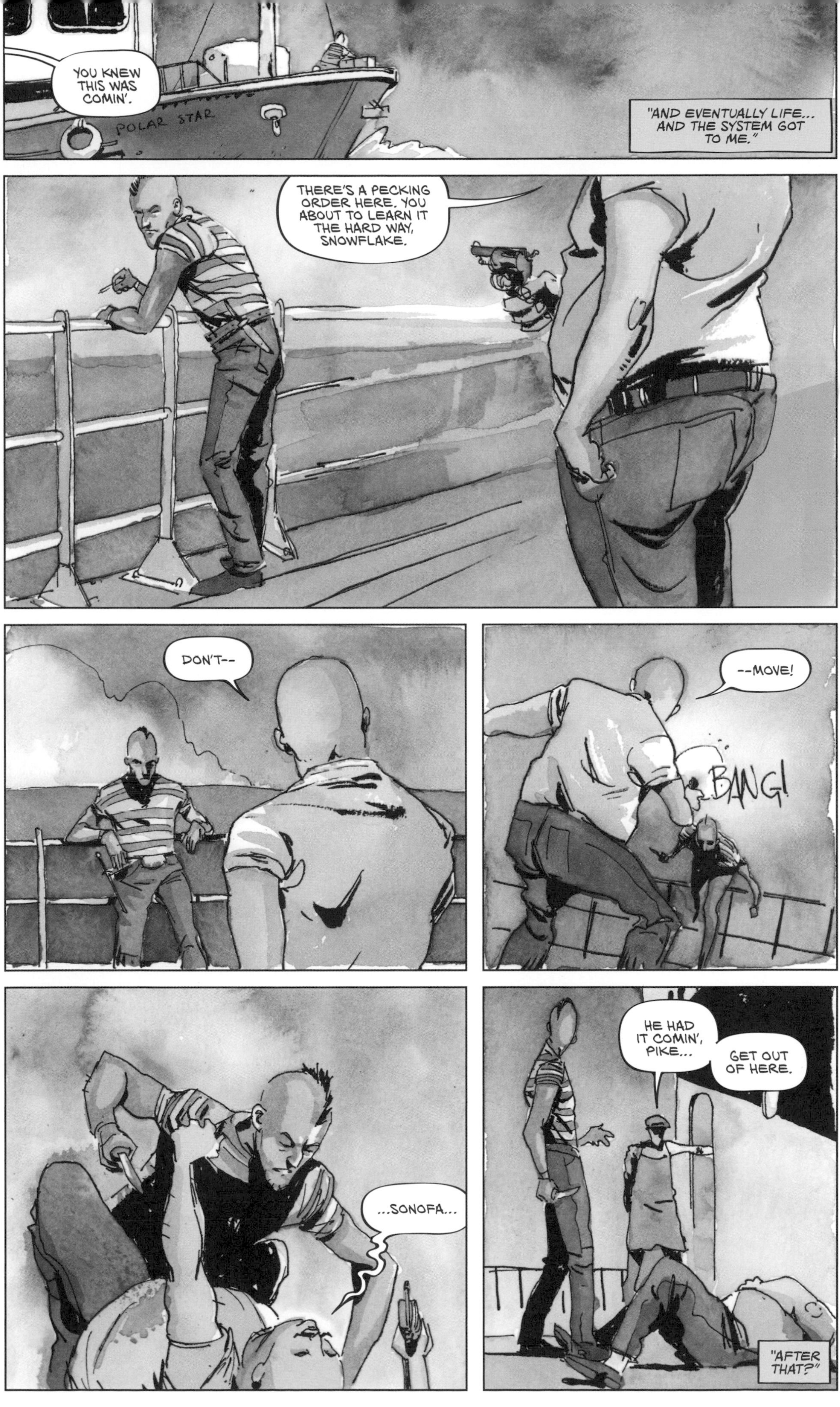
POLAR STAR
YOU KNEW THIS WAS COMIN'.
"AND EVENTUALLY LIFE... AND THE SYSTEM GOT TO ME."
THERE'S A PECKING ORDER HERE. YOU ABOUT TO LEARN IT THE HARD WAY, SNOWFLAKE.
DON'T--
--MOVE!
BANG!
...SONOFA...
HE HAD IT COMIN', PIKE...
GET OUT OF HERE.
"AFTER THAT?"

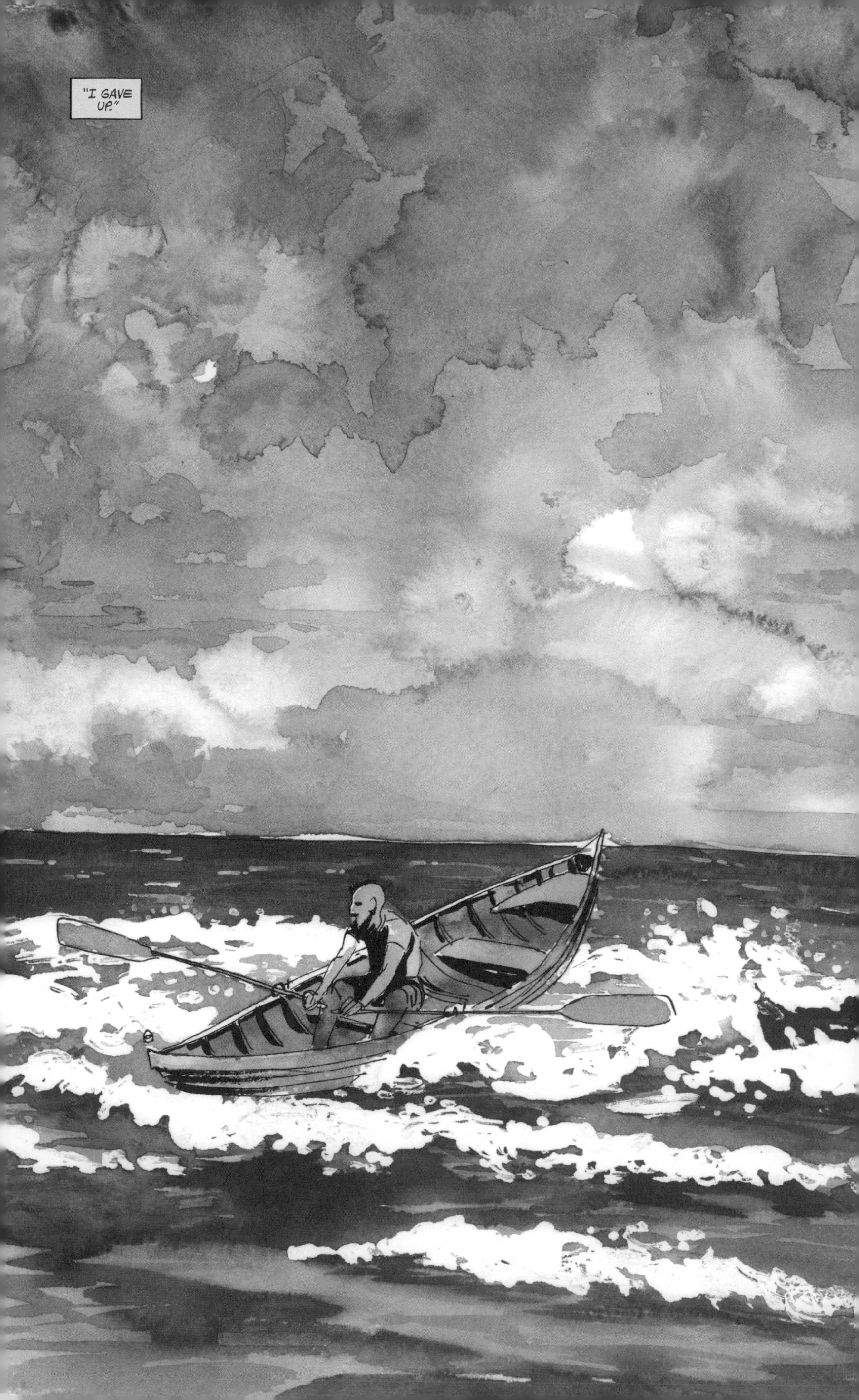
"I GAVE UP."

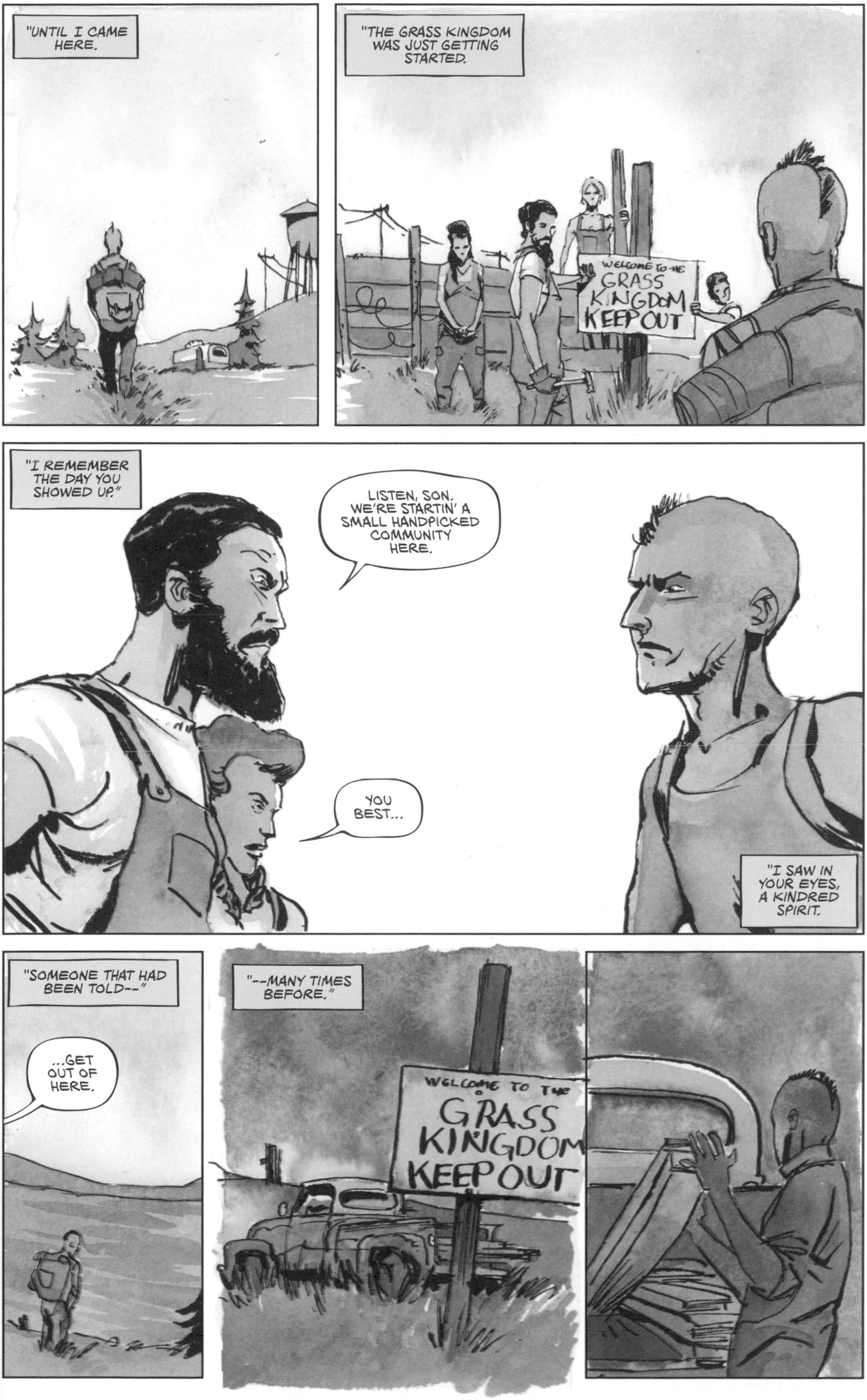
"UNTIL I CAME HERE.
"THE GRASS KINGDOM WAS JUST GETTING STARTED.
WELCOME TO THE GRASS KINGDOM KEEP OUT
"I REMEMBER THE DAY YOU SHOWED UP."
LISTEN, SON. WE'RE STARTIN' A SMALL HANDPICKED COMMUNITY HERE.
YOU BEST...
"I SAW IN YOUR EYES, A KINDRED SPIRIT.
"SOMEONE THAT HAD BEEN TOLD--"
...GET OUT OF HERE.
"--MANY TIMES BEFORE."
WELCOME TO THE GRASS KINGDOM KEEP OUT

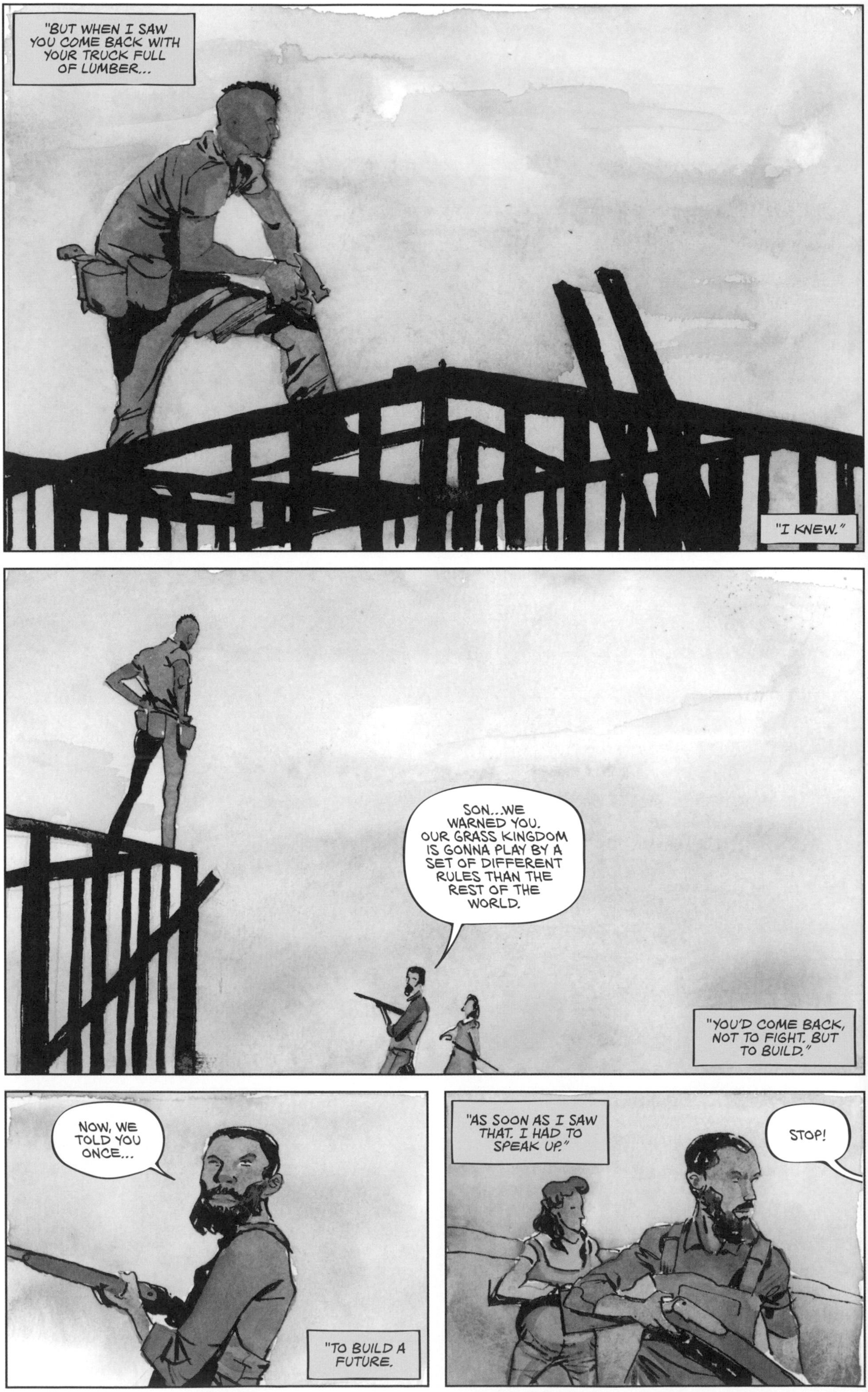
"BUT WHEN I SAW YOU COME BACK WITH YOUR TRUCK FULL OF LUMBER...
"I KNEW."
SON...WE WARNED YOU. OUR GRASS KINGDOM IS GONNA PLAY BY A SET OF DIFFERENT RULES THAN THE REST OF THE WORLD.
"YOU'D COME BACK, NOT TO FIGHT. BUT TO BUILD."
NOW, WE TOLD YOU ONCE...
"TO BUILD A FUTURE.
"AS SOON AS I SAW THAT. I HAD TO SPEAK UP."
STOP!

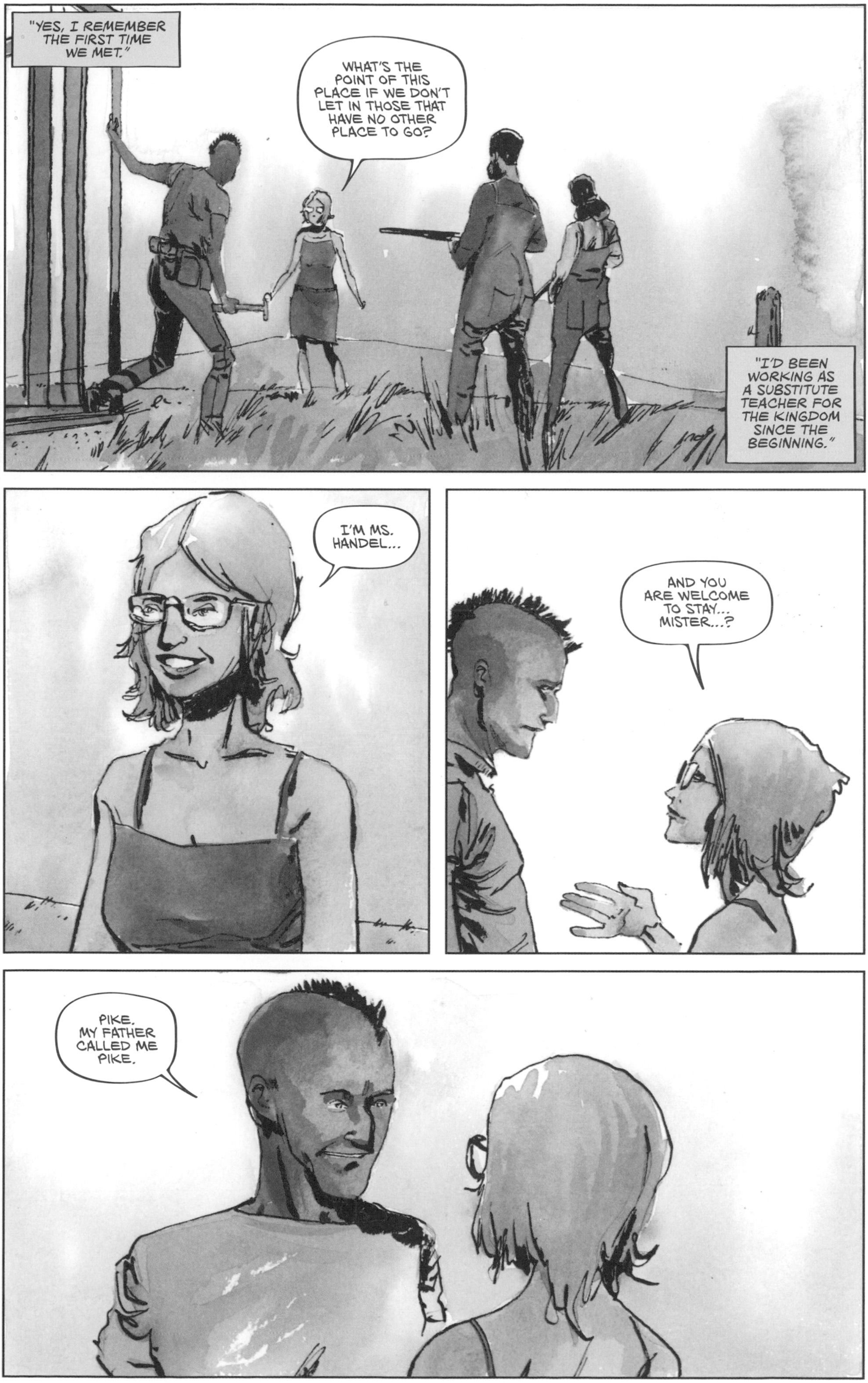
"YES, I REMEMBER THE FIRST TIME WE MET."
WHAT'S THE POINT OF THIS PLACE IF WE DON'T LET IN THOSE THAT HAVE NO OTHER PLACE TO GO?
"I'D BEEN WORKING AS A SUBSTITUTE TEACHER FOR THE KINGDOM SINCE THE BEGINNING."
I'M MS. HANDEL...
AND YOU ARE WELCOME TO STAY... MISTER...?
PIKE. MY FATHER CALLED ME PIKE.

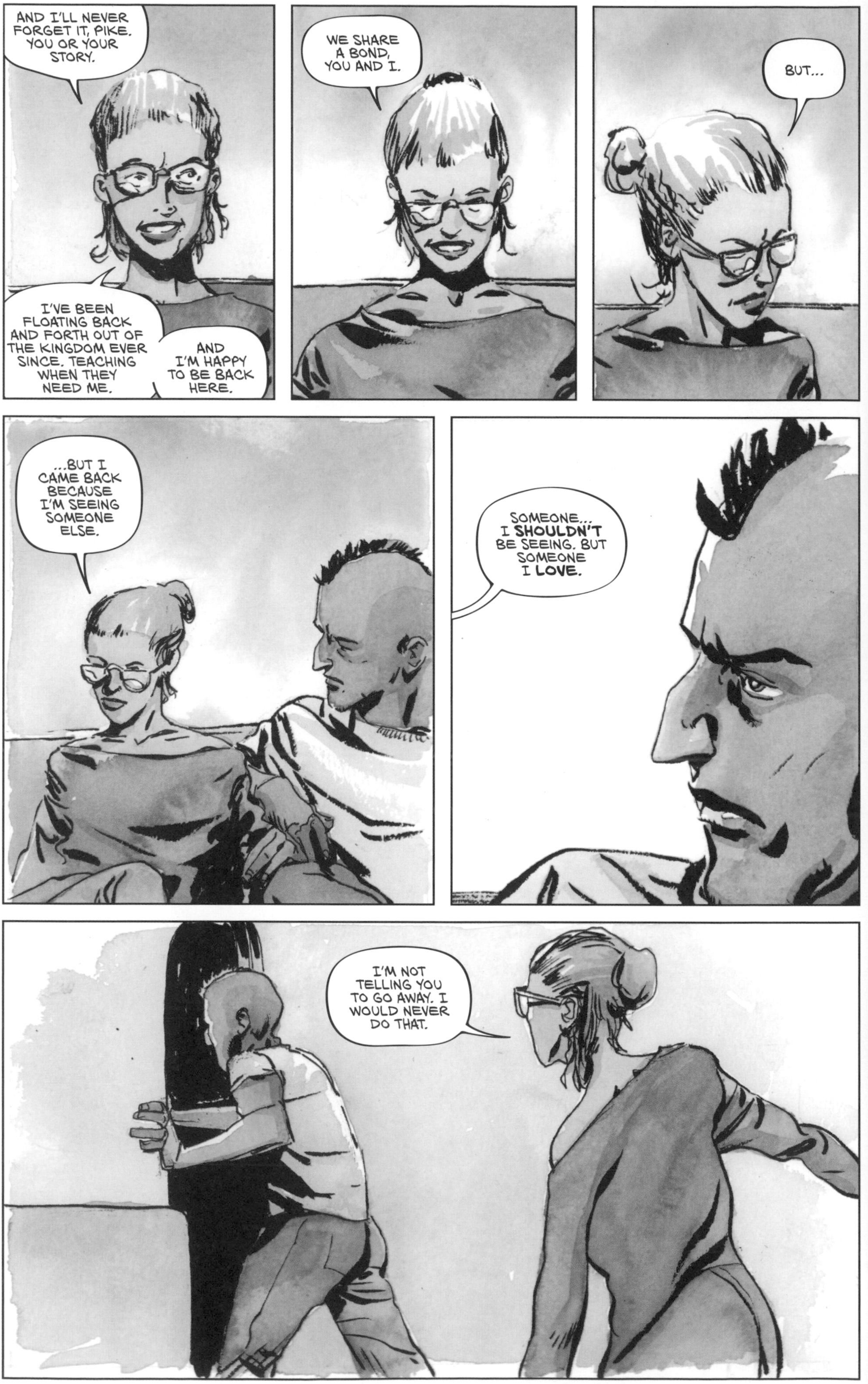
AND I'LL NEVER FORGET IT, PIKE. YOU OR YOUR STORY.
I'VE BEEN FLOATING BACK AND FORTH OUT OF THE KINGDOM EVER SINCE. TEACHING WHEN THEY NEED ME.
AND I'M HAPPY TO BE BACK HERE.
WE SHARE A BOND, YOU AND I.
BUT...
...BUT I CAME BACK BECAUSE I'M SEEING SOMEONE ELSE.
SOMEONE... I **SHOULDN'T** BE SEEING. BUT SOMEONE I **LOVE.**
I'M NOT TELLING YOU TO GO AWAY. I WOULD NEVER DO THAT.

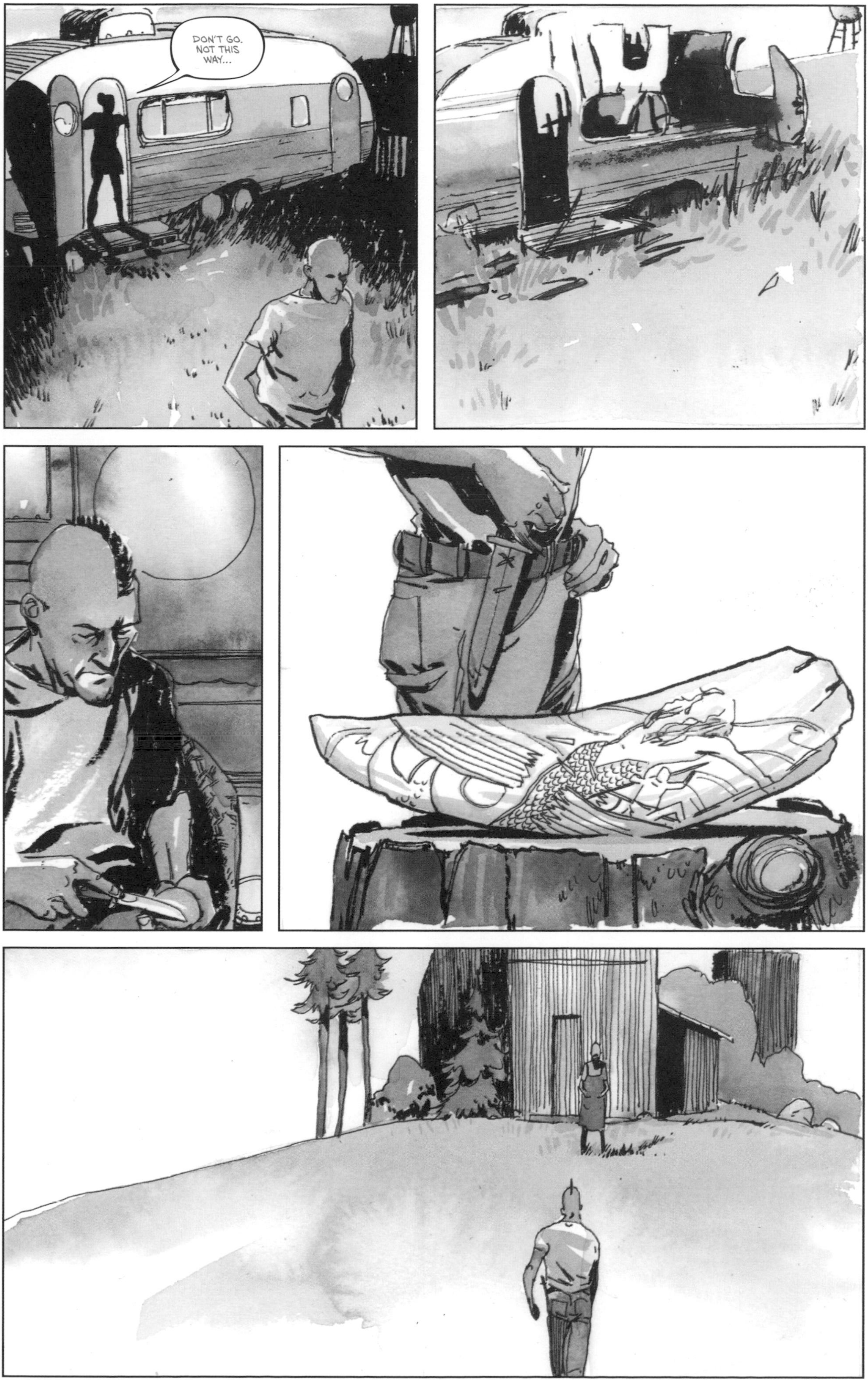
DON'T GO. NOT THIS WAY...

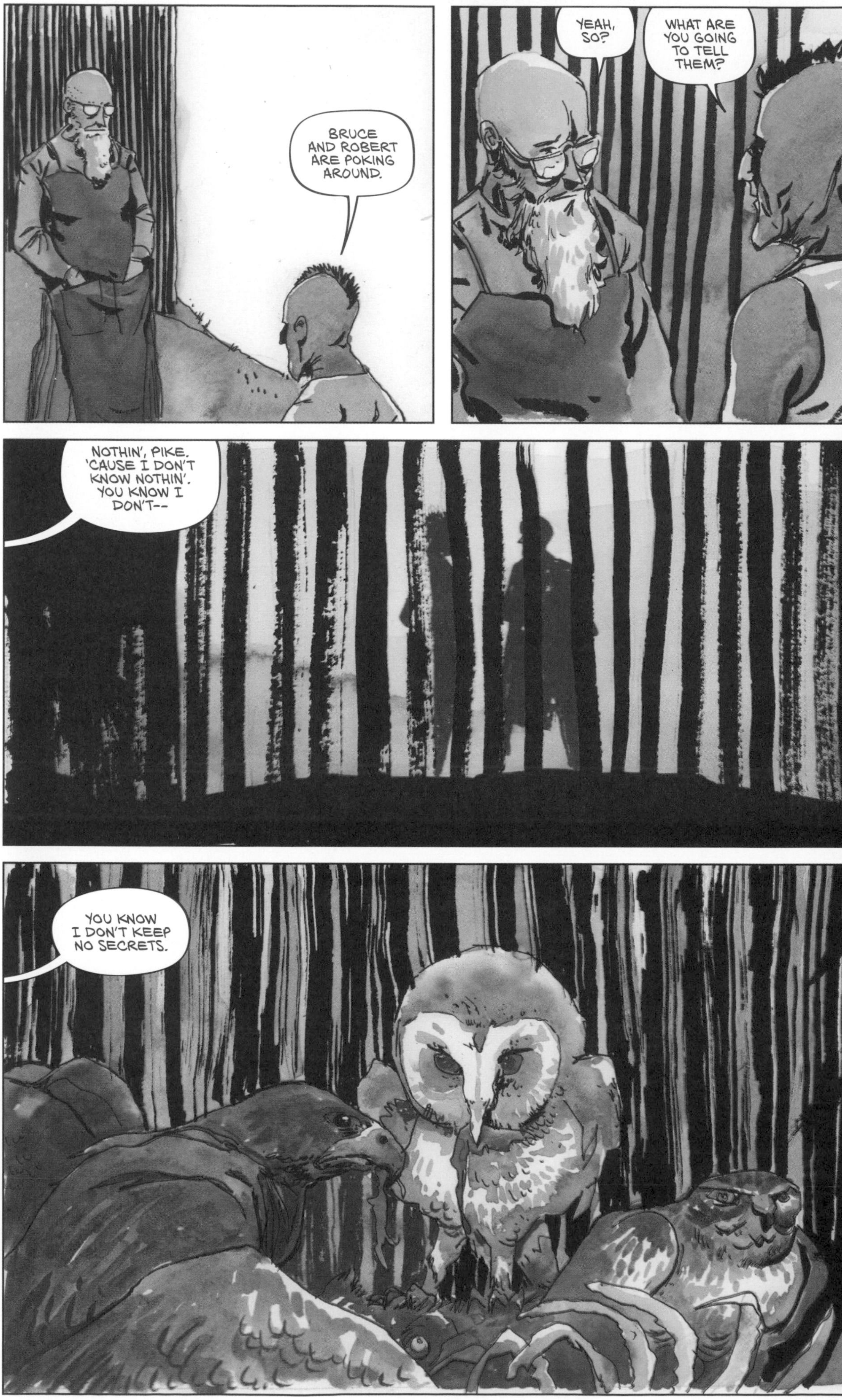
BRUCE AND ROBERT ARE POKING AROUND.
YEAH, SO?
WHAT ARE YOU GOING TO TELL THEM?
NOTHIN', PIKE. 'CAUSE I DON'T KNOW NOTHIN'. YOU KNOW I DON'T--
YOU KNOW I DON'T KEEP NO SECRETS.

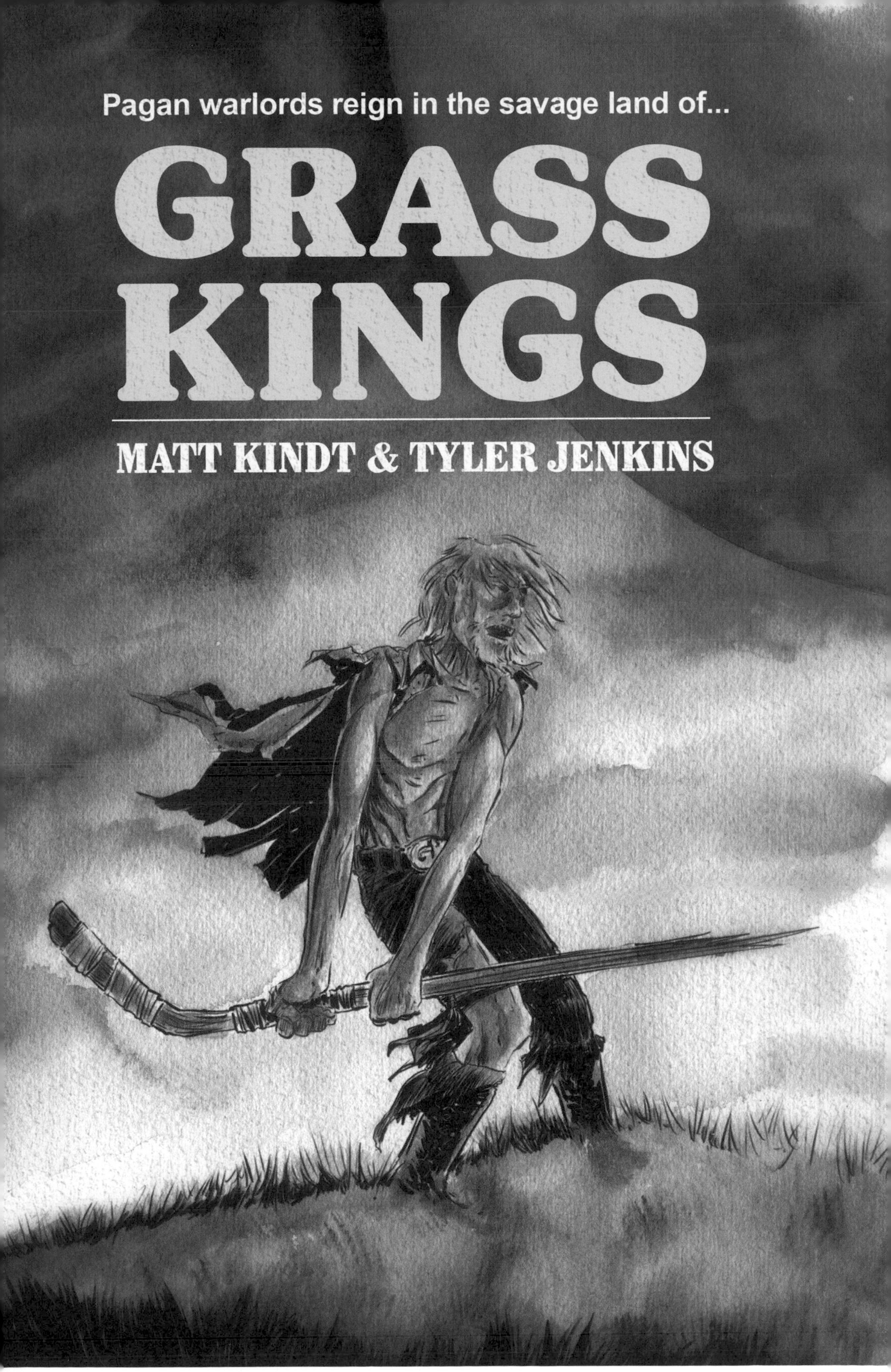
Pagan warlords reign in the savage land of...
GRASS KINGS
MATT KINDT & TYLER JENKINS

issue #8 cover by matt kindt

chapter nine

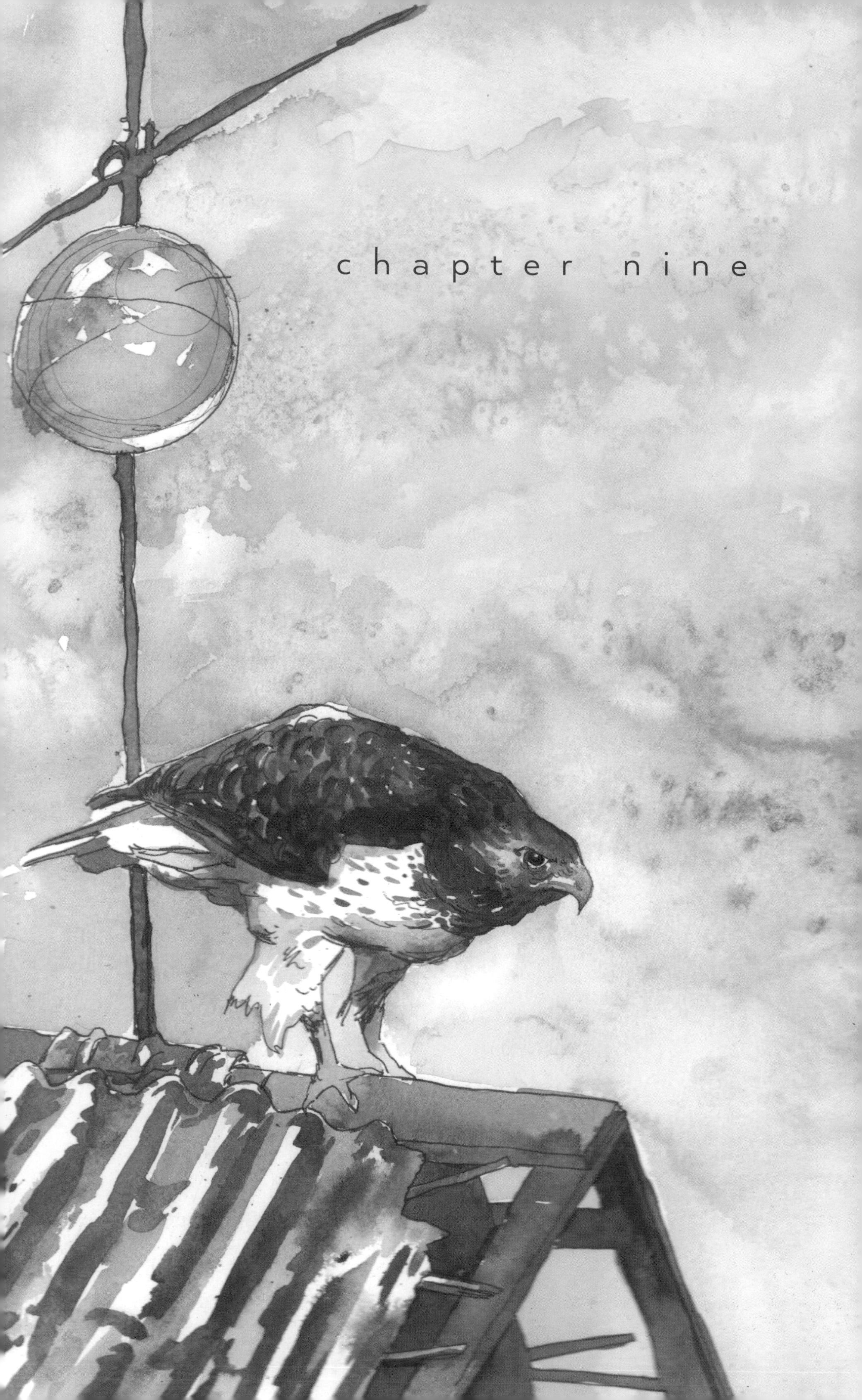

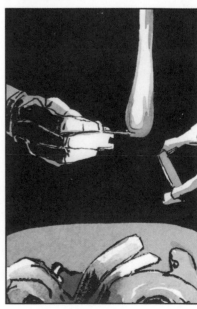

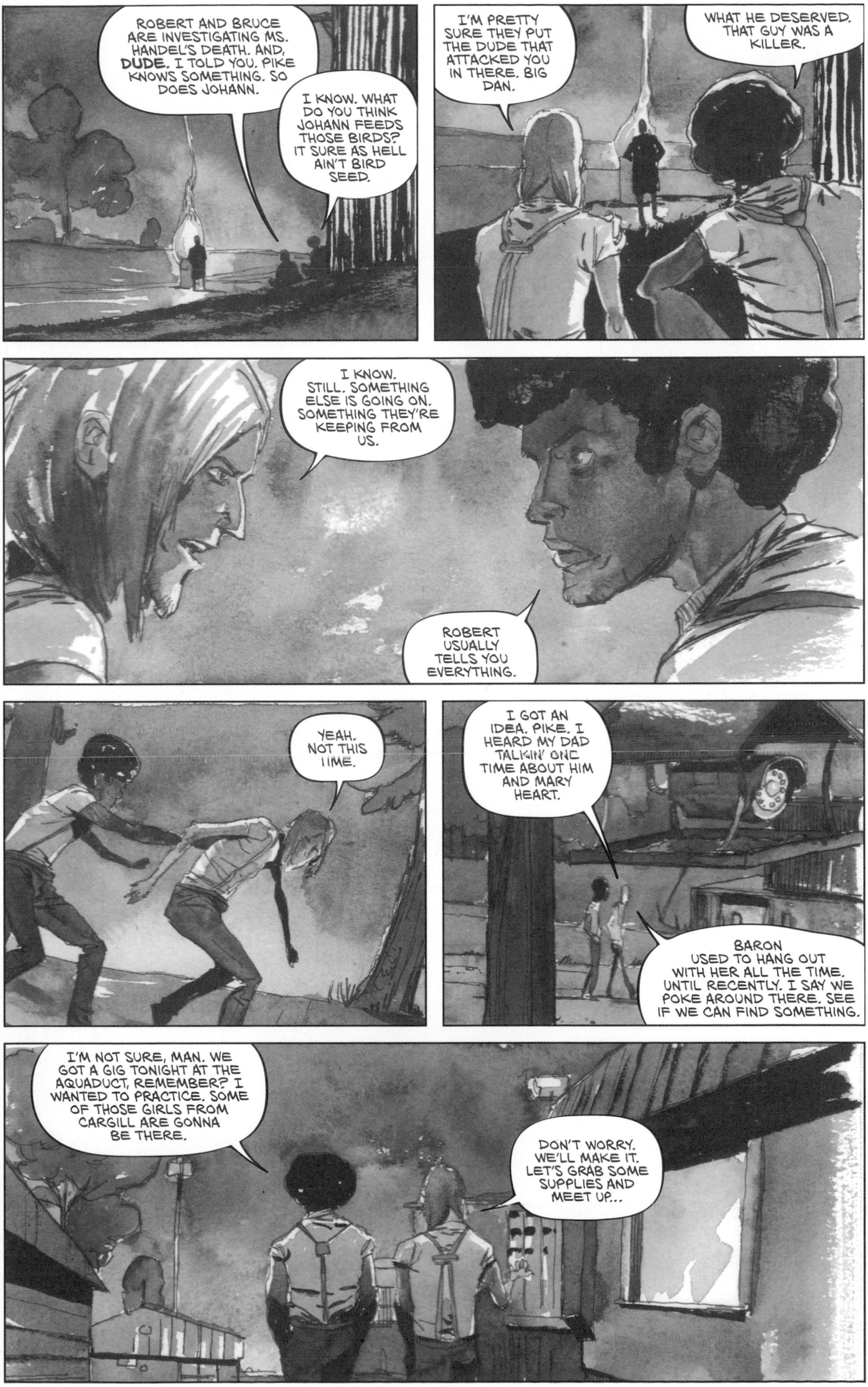
ROBERT AND BRUCE ARE INVESTIGATING MS. HANDEL'S DEATH. AND, **DUDE.** I TOLD YOU. PIKE KNOWS SOMETHING. SO DOES JOHANN.
I KNOW. WHAT DO YOU THINK JOHANN FEEDS THOSE BIRDS? IT SURE AS HELL AIN'T BIRD SEED.
I'M PRETTY SURE THEY PUT THE DUDE THAT ATTACKED YOU IN THERE. BIG DAN.
WHAT HE DESERVED. THAT GUY WAS A KILLER.
I KNOW. STILL. SOMETHING ELSE IS GOING ON. SOMETHING THEY'RE KEEPING FROM US.
ROBERT USUALLY TELLS YOU EVERYTHING.
YEAH. NOT THIS TIME.
I GOT AN IDEA. PIKE. I HEARD MY DAD TALKIN' ONE TIME ABOUT HIM AND MARY HEART.
BARON USED TO HANG OUT WITH HER ALL THE TIME. UNTIL RECENTLY. I SAY WE POKE AROUND THERE. SEE IF WE CAN FIND SOMETHING.
I'M NOT SURE, MAN. WE GOT A GIG TONIGHT AT THE AQUADUCT, REMEMBER? I WANTED TO PRACTICE. SOME OF THOSE GIRLS FROM CARGILL ARE GONNA BE THERE.
DON'T WORRY. WE'LL MAKE IT. LET'S GRAB SOME SUPPLIES AND MEET UP...

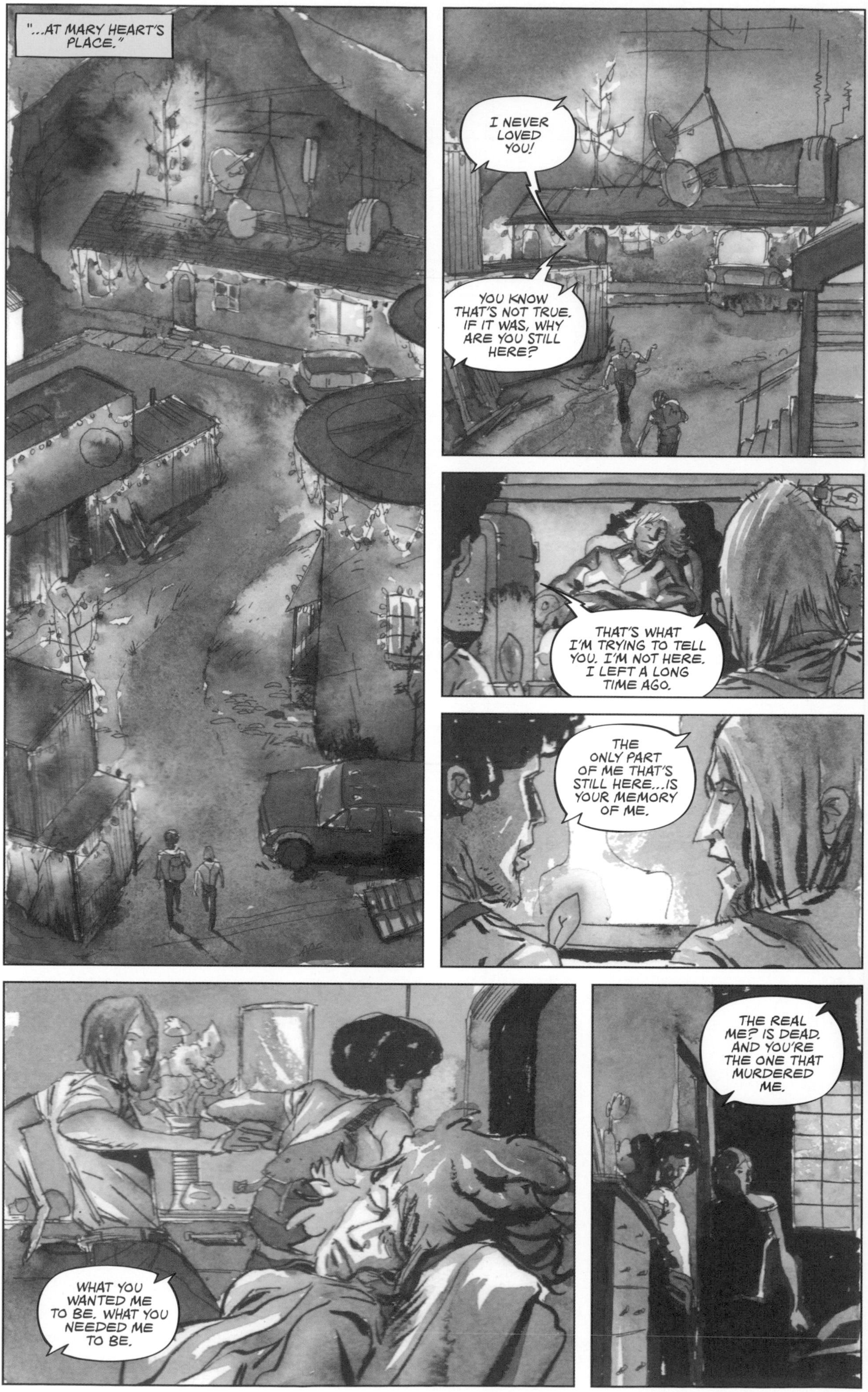
"...AT MARY HEART'S PLACE."
I NEVER LOVED YOU!
YOU KNOW THAT'S NOT TRUE. IF IT WAS, WHY ARE YOU STILL HERE?
THAT'S WHAT I'M TRYING TO TELL YOU. I'M NOT HERE. I LEFT A LONG TIME AGO.
THE ONLY PART OF ME THAT'S STILL HERE...IS YOUR MEMORY OF ME.
WHAT YOU WANTED ME TO BE. WHAT YOU NEEDED ME TO BE.
THE REAL ME? IS DEAD. AND YOU'RE THE ONE THAT MURDERED ME.

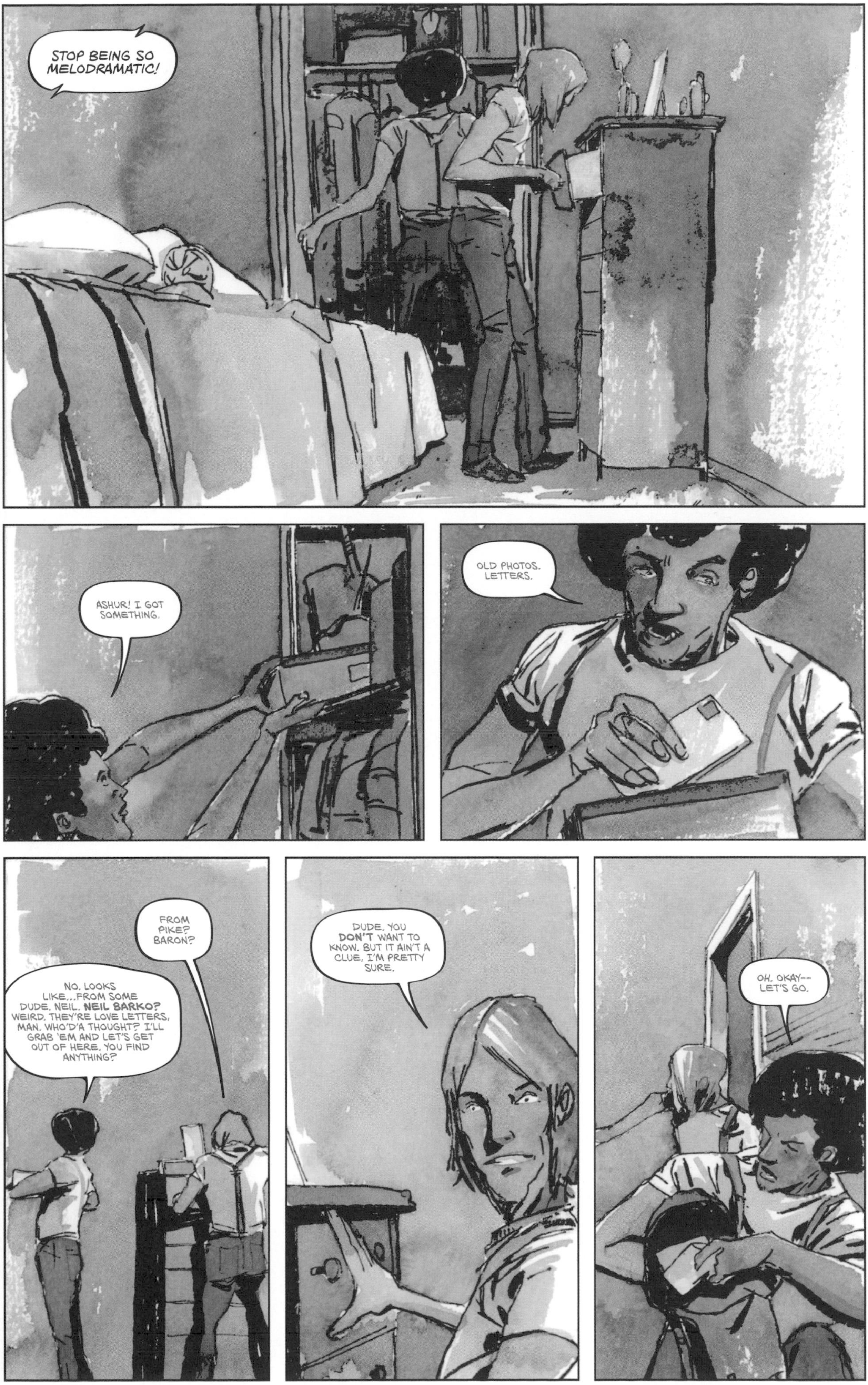
STOP BEING SO MELODRAMATIC!
ASHUR! I GOT SOMETHING.
OLD PHOTOS. LETTERS.
FROM PIKE? BARON?
NO. LOOKS LIKE...FROM SOME DUDE. NEIL. NEIL BARKO? WEIRD. THEY'RE LOVE LETTERS, MAN. WHO'D'A THOUGHT? I'LL GRAB 'EM AND LET'S GET OUT OF HERE. YOU FIND ANYTHING?
DUDE. YOU DON'T WANT TO KNOW. BUT IT AIN'T A CLUE, I'M PRETTY SURE.
OH. OKAY-- LET'S GO.

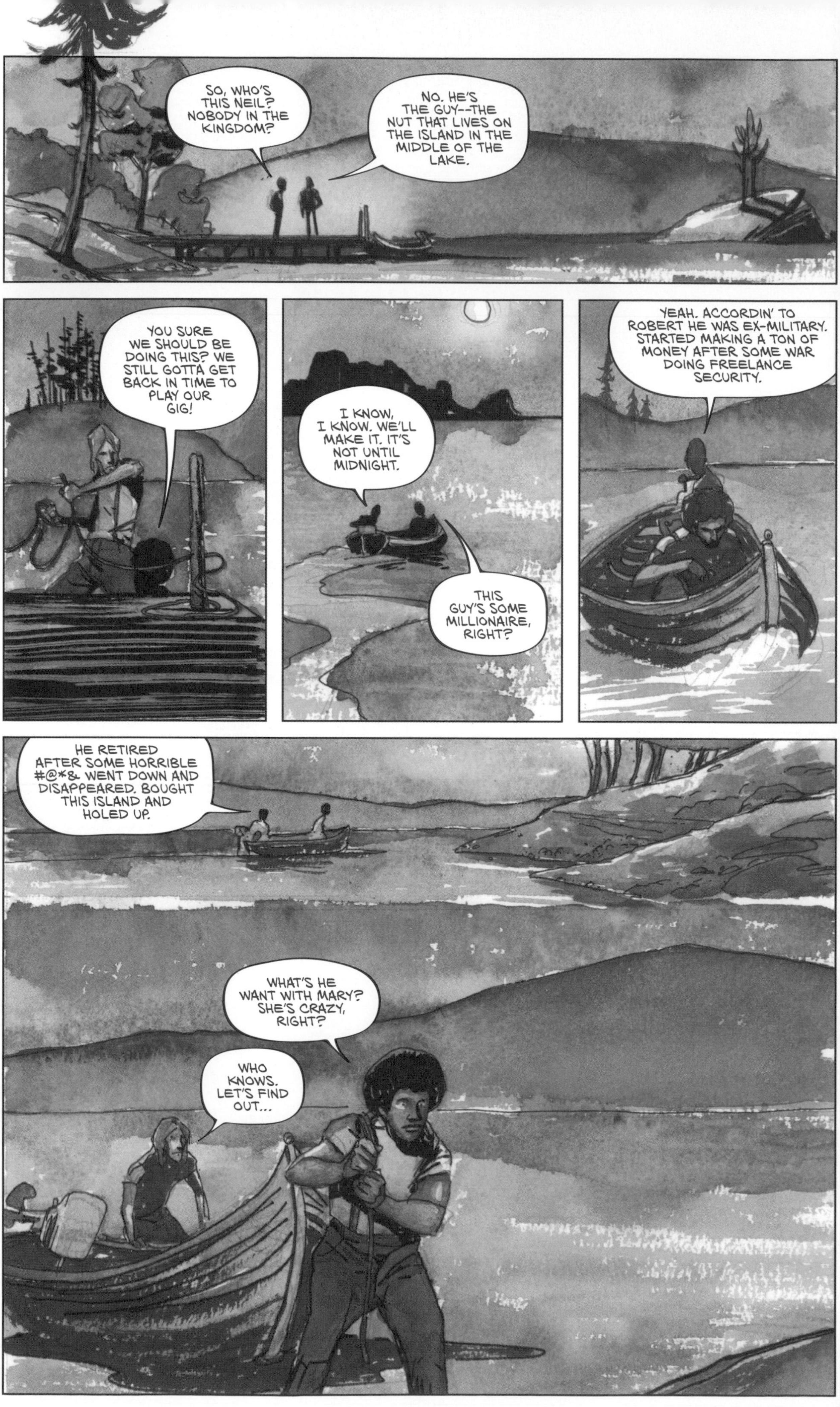
SO, WHO'S THIS NEIL? NOBODY IN THE KINGDOM?
NO. HE'S THE GUY--THE NUT THAT LIVES ON THE ISLAND IN THE MIDDLE OF THE LAKE.
YOU SURE WE SHOULD BE DOING THIS? WE STILL GOTTA GET BACK IN TIME TO PLAY OUR GIG!
I KNOW, I KNOW. WE'LL MAKE IT. IT'S NOT UNTIL MIDNIGHT.
THIS GUY'S SOME MILLIONAIRE, RIGHT?
YEAH. ACCORDIN' TO ROBERT HE WAS EX-MILITARY. STARTED MAKING A TON OF MONEY AFTER SOME WAR DOING FREELANCE SECURITY.
HE RETIRED AFTER SOME HORRIBLE #@*& WENT DOWN AND DISAPPEARED. BOUGHT THIS ISLAND AND HOLED UP.
WHAT'S HE WANT WITH MARY? SHE'S CRAZY, RIGHT?
WHO KNOWS. LET'S FIND OUT...

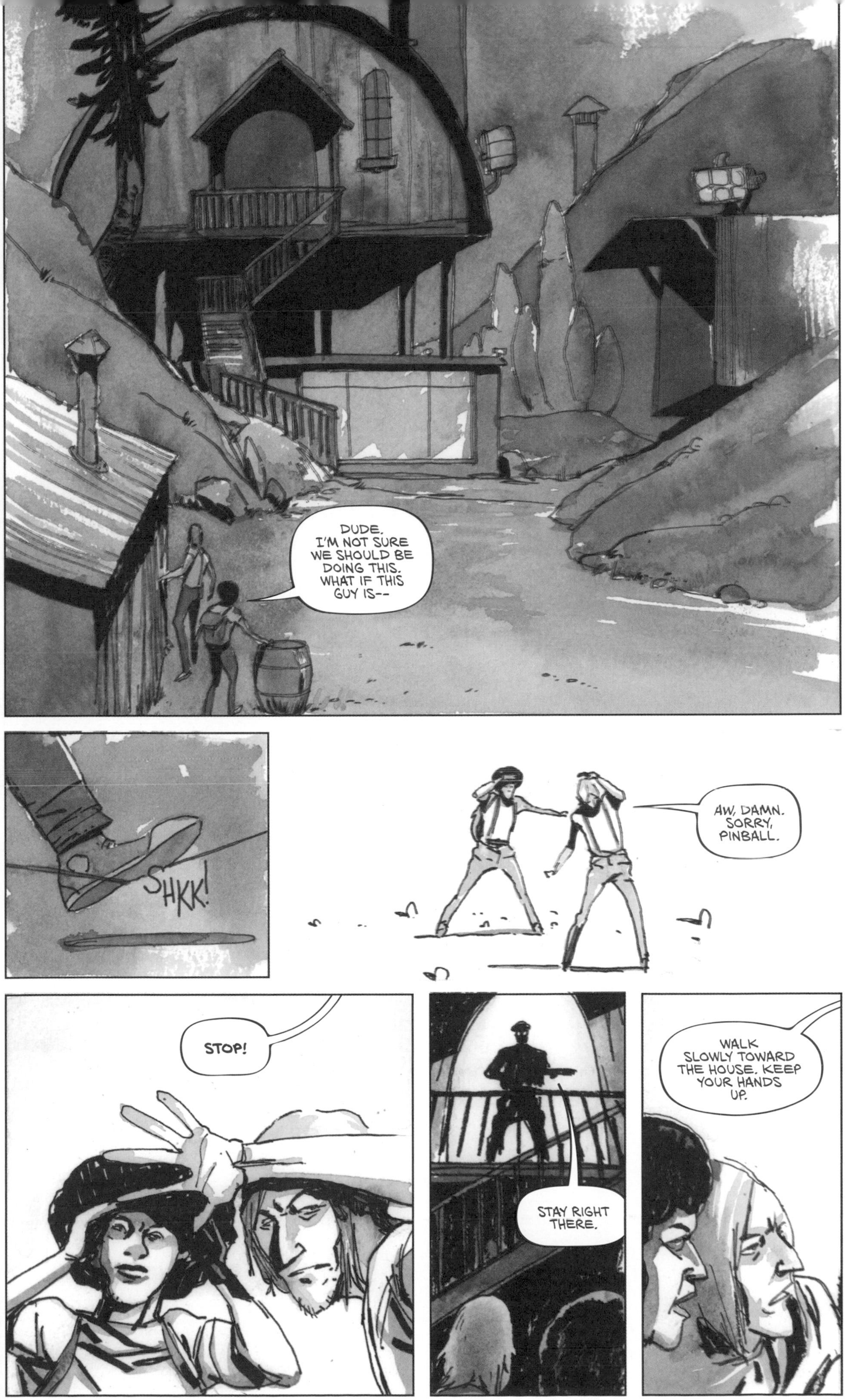
DUDE. I'M NOT SURE WE SHOULD BE DOING THIS. WHAT IF THIS GUY IS--
SHKK!
AW, DAMN. SORRY, PINBALL.
STOP!
STAY RIGHT THERE.
WALK SLOWLY TOWARD THE HOUSE. KEEP YOUR HANDS UP.

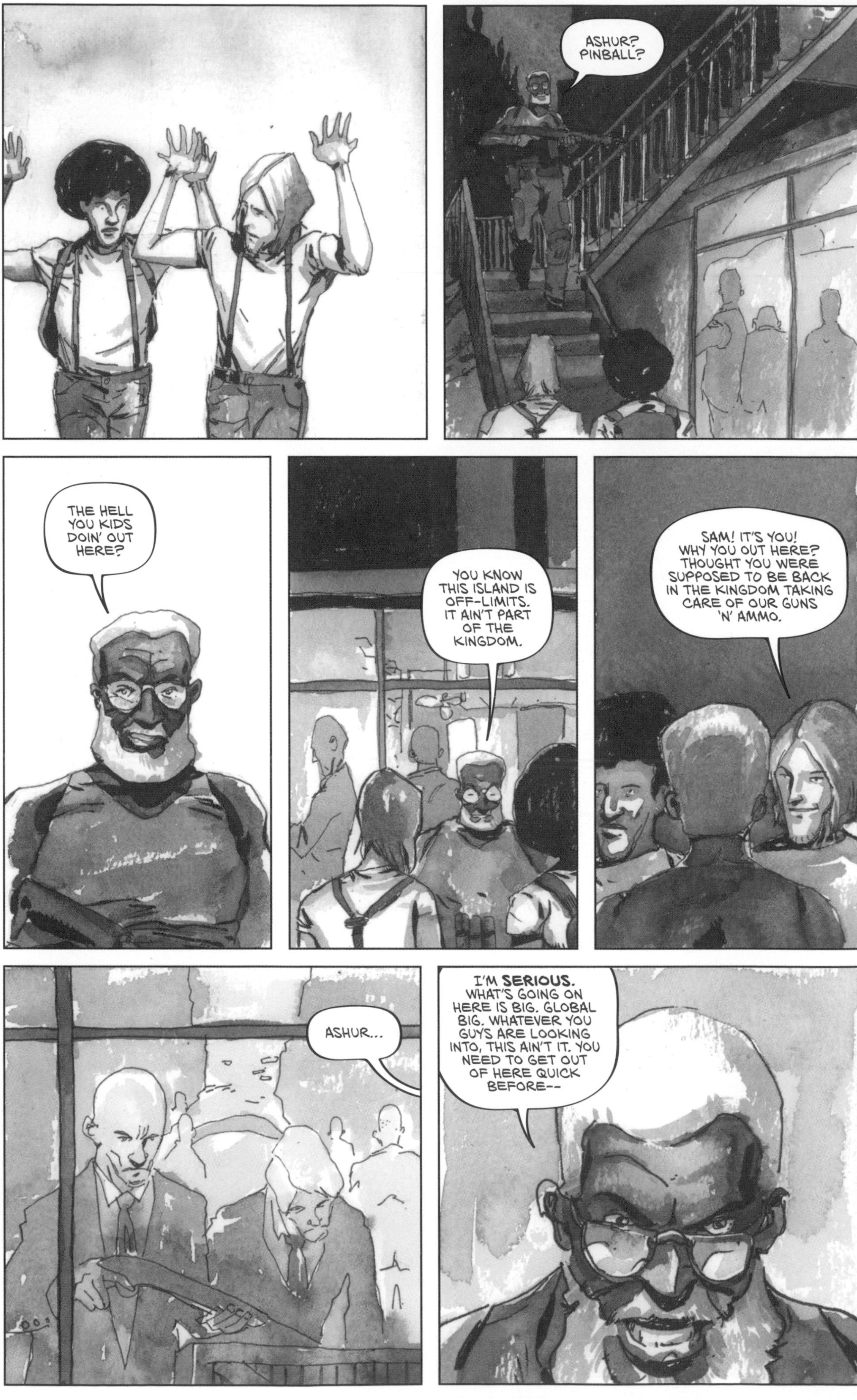
ASHUR? PINBALL?
THE HELL YOU KIDS DOIN' OUT HERE?
YOU KNOW THIS ISLAND IS OFF-LIMITS. IT AIN'T PART OF THE KINGDOM.
SAM! IT'S YOU! WHY YOU OUT HERE? THOUGHT YOU WERE SUPPOSED TO BE BACK IN THE KINGDOM TAKING CARE OF OUR GUNS 'N' AMMO.
ASHUR...
I'M **SERIOUS.** WHAT'S GOING ON HERE IS BIG. GLOBAL BIG. WHATEVER YOU GUYS ARE LOOKING INTO, THIS AIN'T IT. YOU NEED TO GET OUT OF HERE QUICK BEFORE--

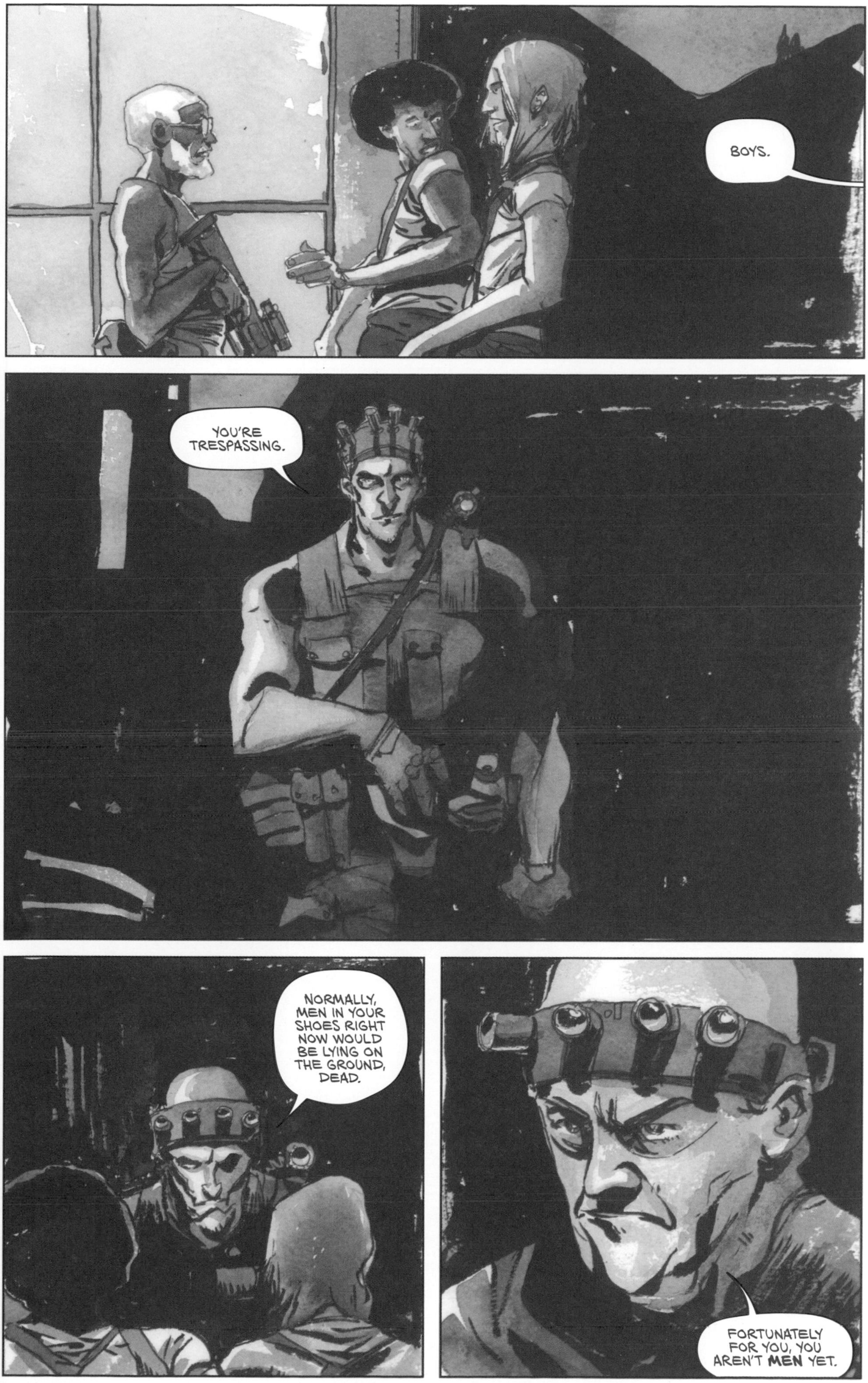
BOYS.
YOU'RE TRESPASSING.
NORMALLY, MEN IN YOUR SHOES RIGHT NOW WOULD BE LYING ON THE GROUND, DEAD.
FORTUNATELY FOR YOU, YOU AREN'T **MEN** YET.

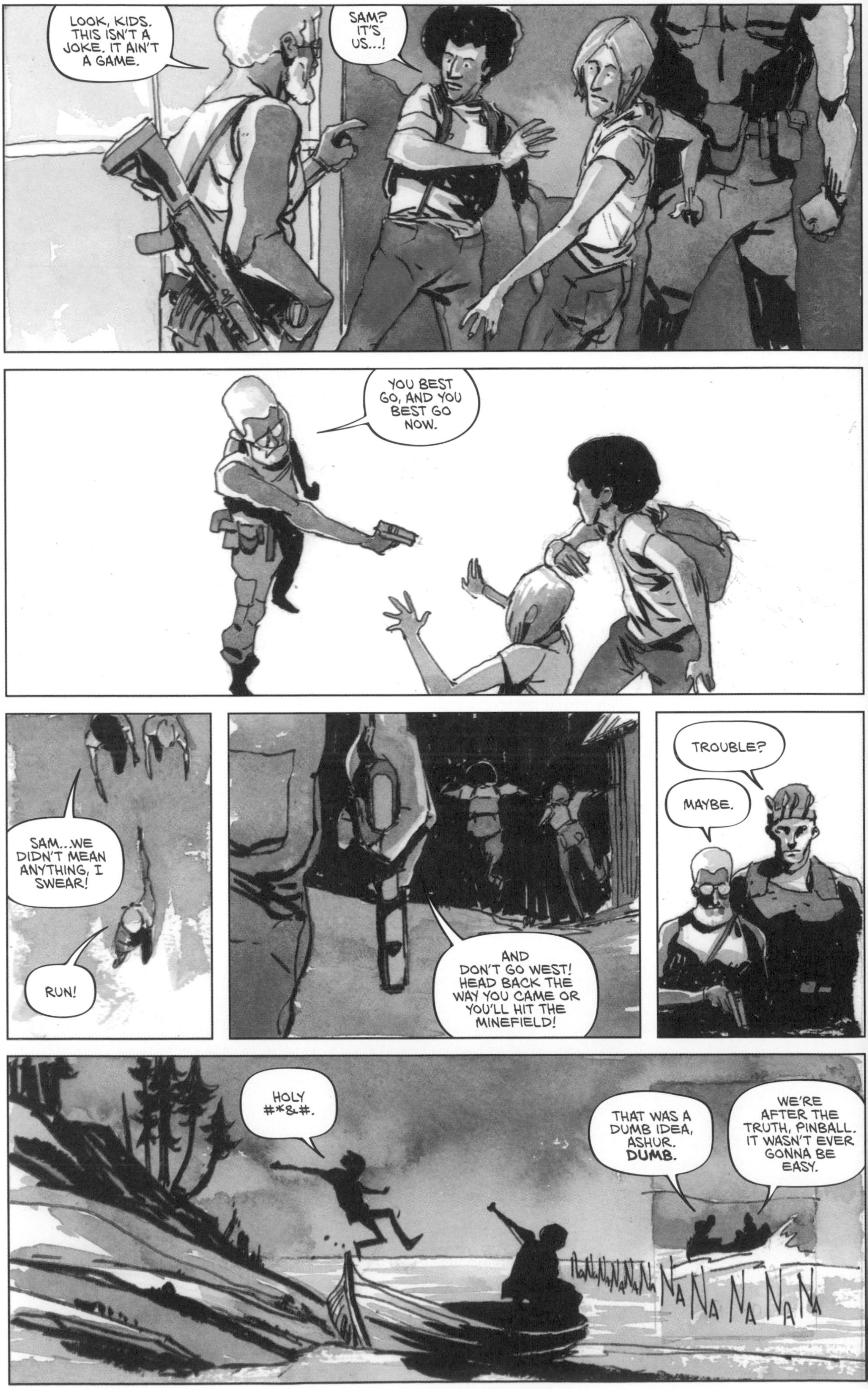
LOOK, KIDS. THIS ISN'T A JOKE. IT AIN'T A GAME.
SAM? IT'S US...!
YOU BEST GO, AND YOU BEST GO NOW.
SAM...WE DIDN'T MEAN ANYTHING, I SWEAR!
RUN!
AND DON'T GO WEST! HEAD BACK THE WAY YOU CAME OR YOU'LL HIT THE MINEFIELD!
TROUBLE?
MAYBE.
HOLY #*&#.
THAT WAS A DUMB IDEA, ASHUR. **DUMB.**
WE'RE AFTER THE TRUTH, PINBALL. IT WASN'T EVER GONNA BE EASY.
NaNaNaNaNaNaNa Na Na Na Na Na

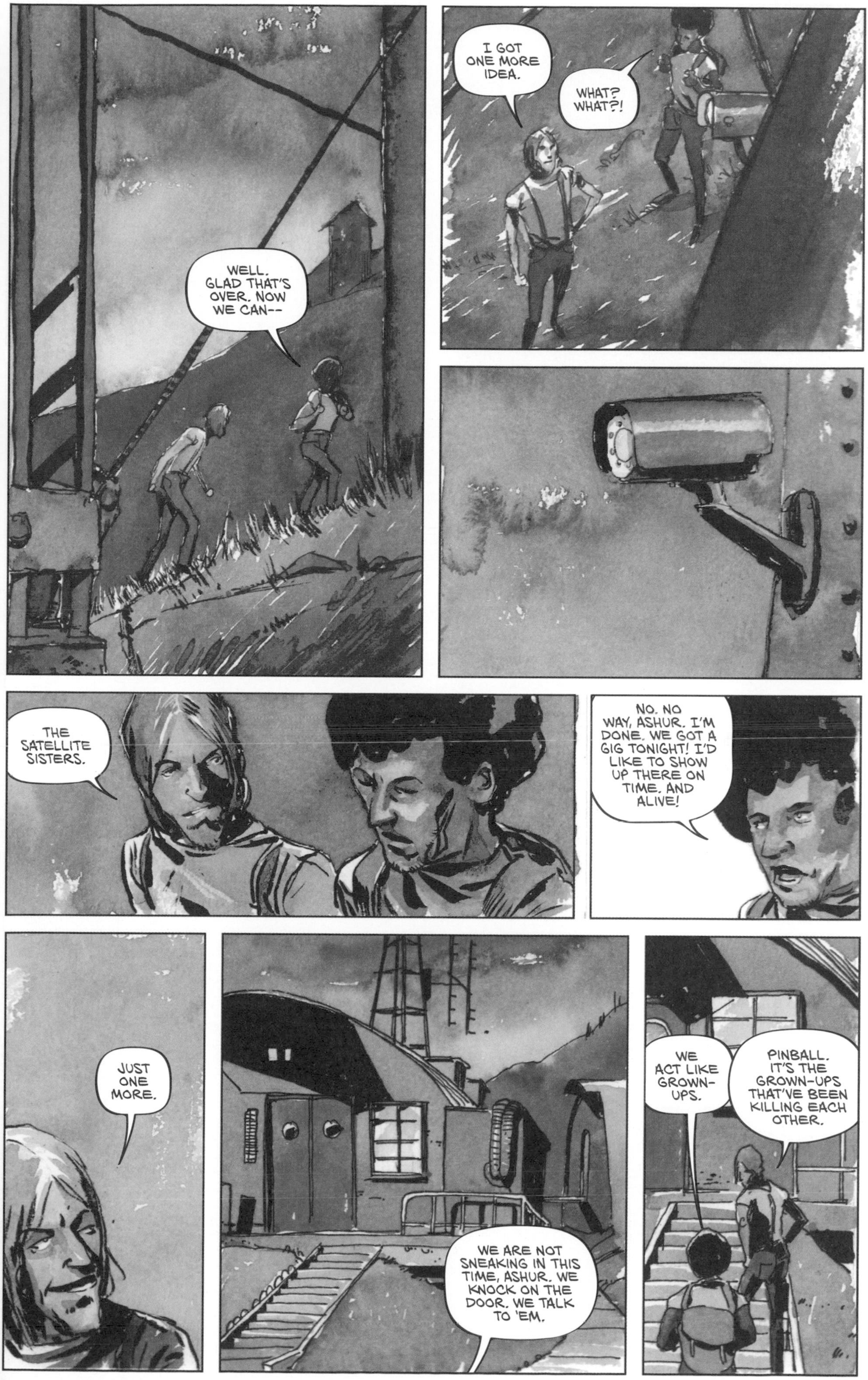
WELL. GLAD THAT'S OVER. NOW WE CAN--
I GOT ONE MORE IDEA.
WHAT? WHAT?!
THE SATELLITE SISTERS.
NO. NO WAY, ASHUR. I'M DONE. WE GOT A GIG TONIGHT! I'D LIKE TO SHOW UP THERE ON TIME. AND ALIVE!
JUST ONE MORE.
WE ARE NOT SNEAKING IN THIS TIME, ASHUR. WE KNOCK ON THE DOOR. WE TALK TO 'EM.
WE ACT LIKE GROWN-UPS.
PINBALL. IT'S THE GROWN-UPS THAT'VE BEEN KILLING EACH OTHER.

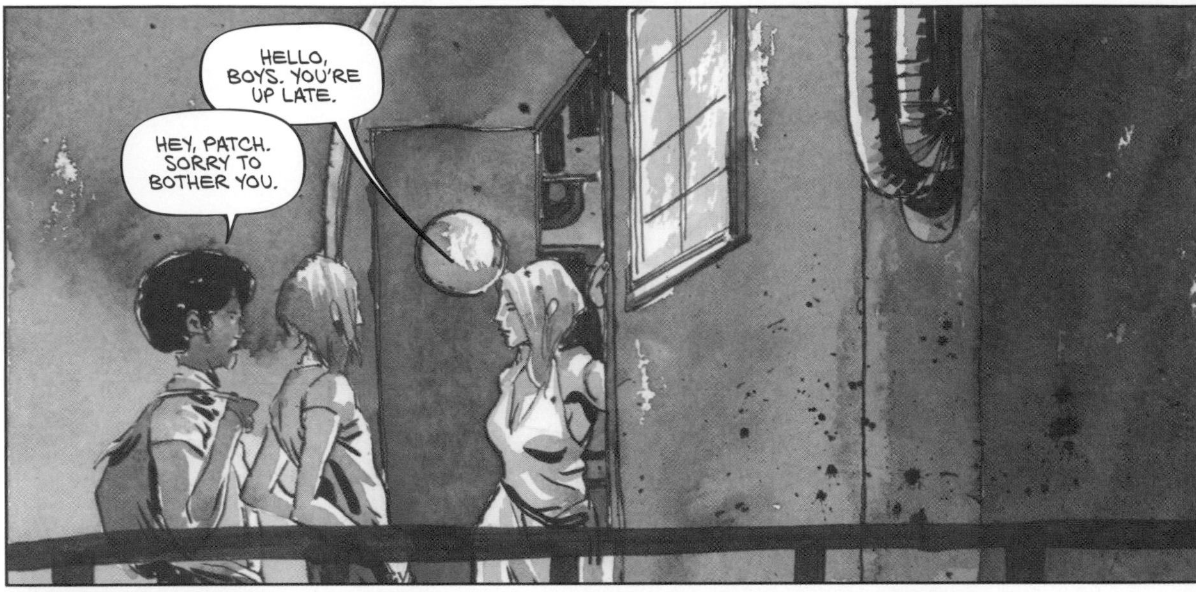
HELLO, BOYS. YOU'RE UP LATE.
HEY, PATCH. SORRY TO BOTHER YOU.

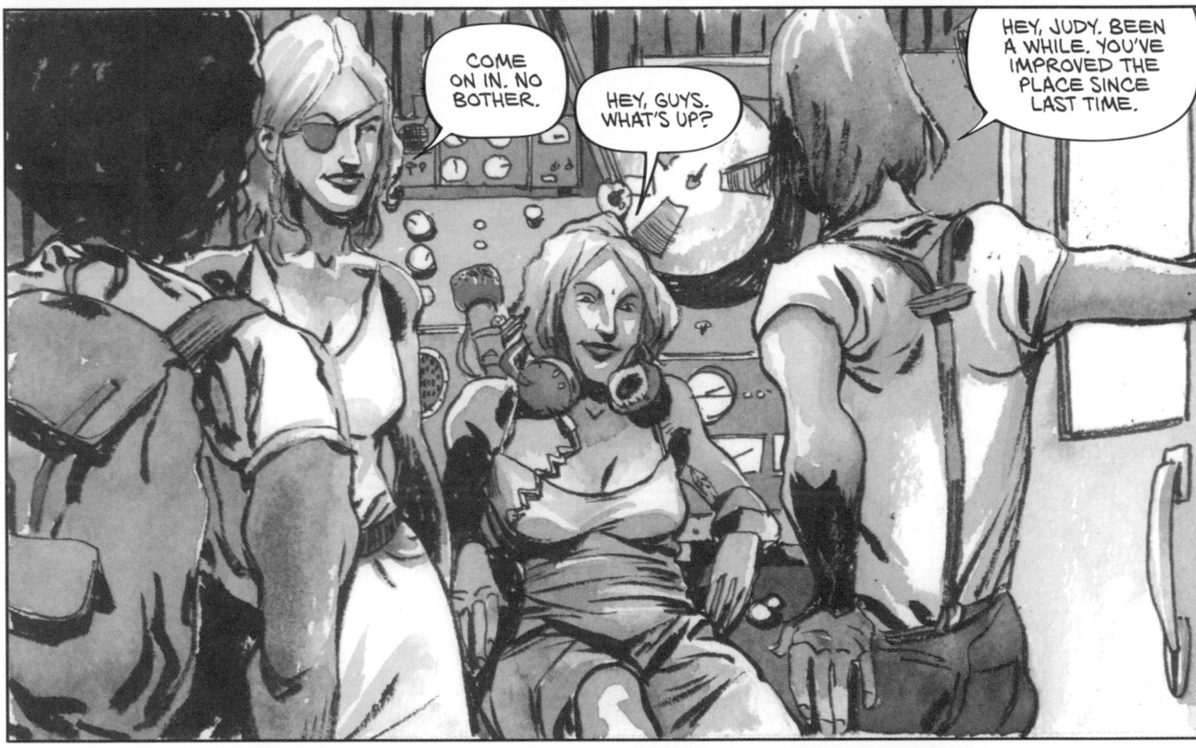
COME ON IN. NO BOTHER.
HEY, GUYS. WHAT'S UP?
HEY, JUDY. BEEN A WHILE. YOU'VE IMPROVED THE PLACE SINCE LAST TIME.

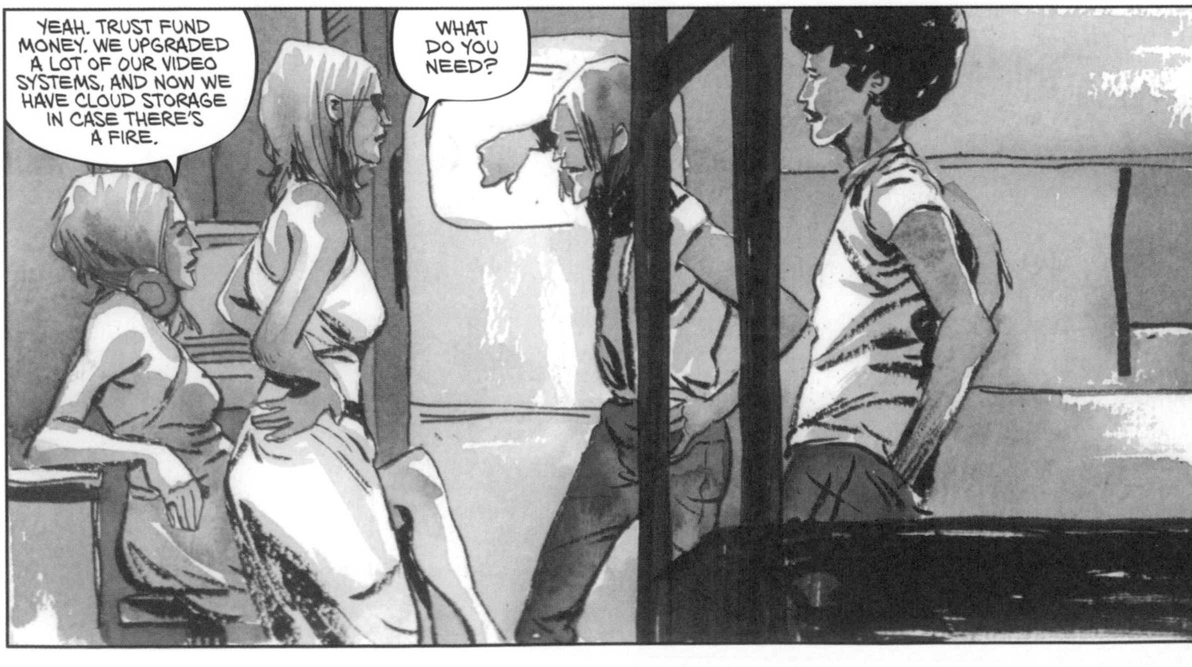
YEAH. TRUST FUND MONEY. WE UPGRADED A LOT OF OUR VIDEO SYSTEMS, AND NOW WE HAVE CLOUD STORAGE IN CASE THERE'S A FIRE.
WHAT DO YOU NEED?

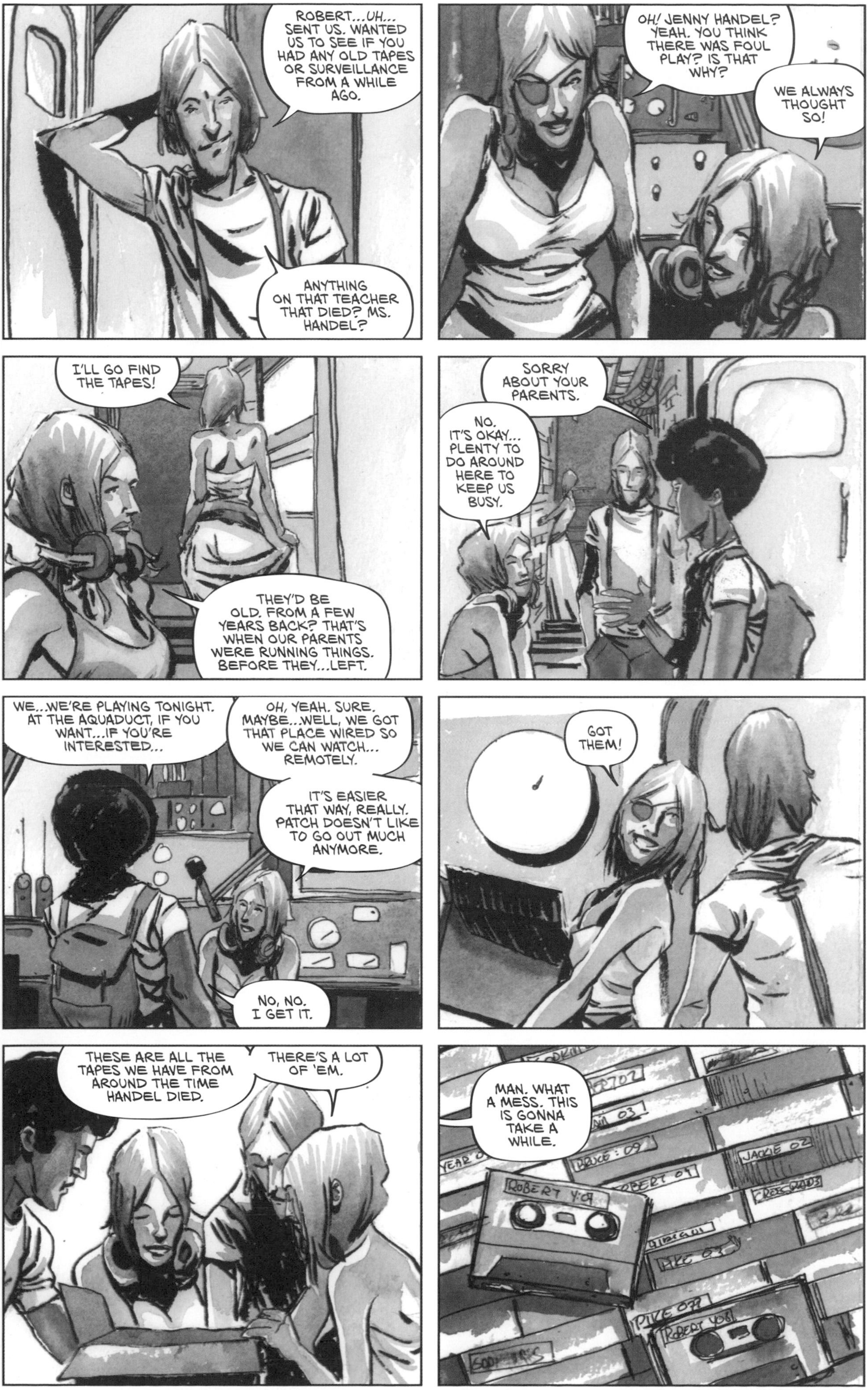
ROBERT...UH... SENT US. WANTED US TO SEE IF YOU HAD ANY OLD TAPES OR SURVEILLANCE FROM A WHILE AGO.
ANYTHING ON THAT TEACHER THAT DIED? MS. HANDEL?
OH! JENNY HANDEL? YEAH. YOU THINK THERE WAS FOUL PLAY? IS THAT WHY?
WE ALWAYS THOUGHT SO!
I'LL GO FIND THE TAPES!
THEY'D BE OLD. FROM A FEW YEARS BACK? THAT'S WHEN OUR PARENTS WERE RUNNING THINGS. BEFORE THEY...LEFT.
SORRY ABOUT YOUR PARENTS.
NO. IT'S OKAY... PLENTY TO DO AROUND HERE TO KEEP US BUSY.
WE...WE'RE PLAYING TONIGHT. AT THE AQUADUCT, IF YOU WANT...IF YOU'RE INTERESTED...
OH, YEAH. SURE. MAYBE...WELL, WE GOT THAT PLACE WIRED SO WE CAN WATCH... REMOTELY.
IT'S EASIER THAT WAY, REALLY. PATCH DOESN'T LIKE TO GO OUT MUCH ANYMORE.
NO, NO. I GET IT.
GOT THEM!
THESE ARE ALL THE TAPES WE HAVE FROM AROUND THE TIME HANDEL DIED.
THERE'S A LOT OF 'EM.
MAN. WHAT A MESS. THIS IS GONNA TAKE A WHILE.

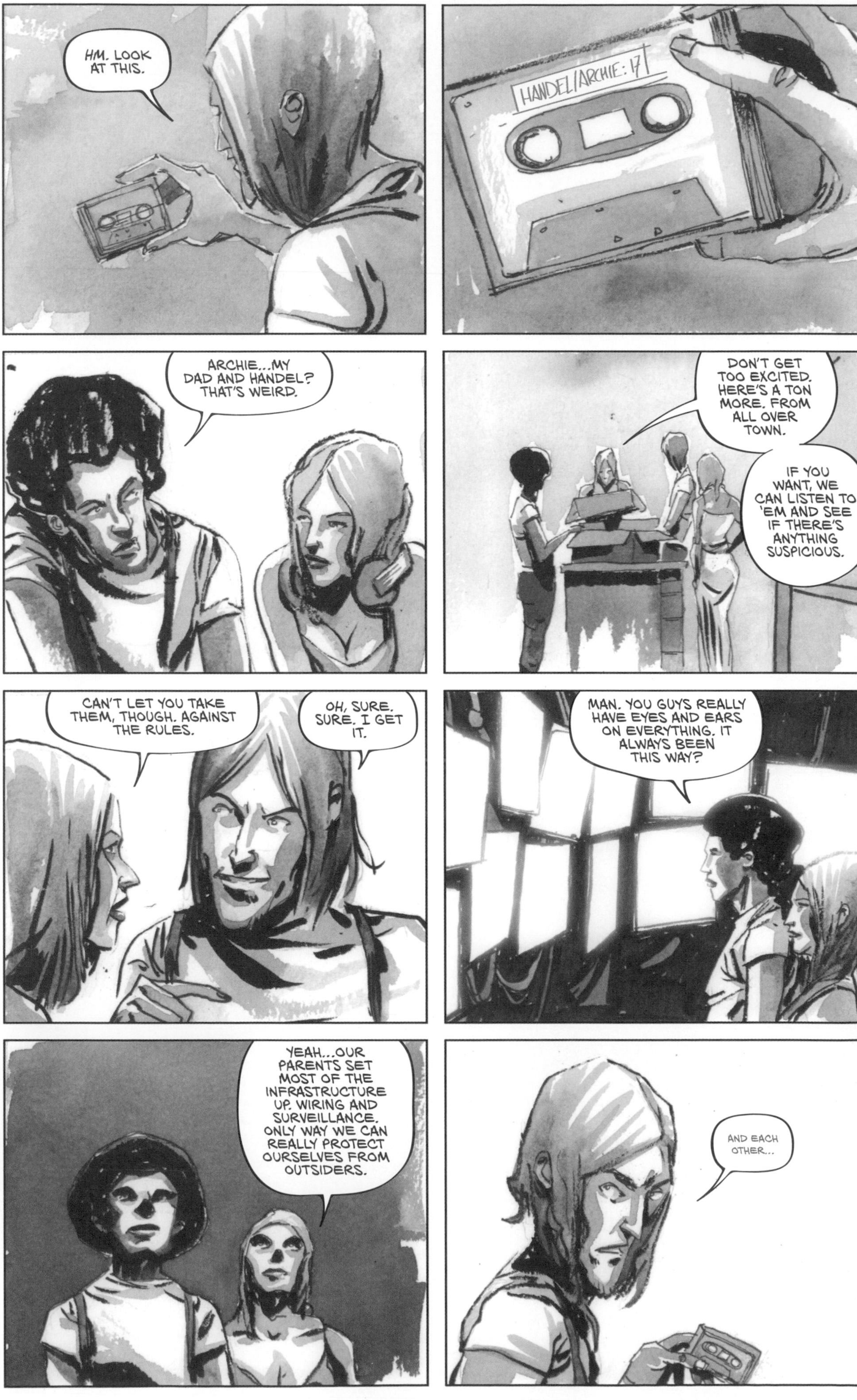
HM. LOOK AT THIS.
HANDEL/ARCHIE: 17
ARCHIE...MY DAD AND HANDEL? THAT'S WEIRD.
DON'T GET TOO EXCITED. HERE'S A TON MORE. FROM ALL OVER TOWN.
IF YOU WANT, WE CAN LISTEN TO 'EM AND SEE IF THERE'S ANYTHING SUSPICIOUS.
CAN'T LET YOU TAKE THEM, THOUGH. AGAINST THE RULES.
OH, SURE. SURE. I GET IT.
MAN. YOU GUYS REALLY HAVE EYES AND EARS ON EVERYTHING. IT ALWAYS BEEN THIS WAY?
YEAH...OUR PARENTS SET MOST OF THE INFRASTRUCTURE UP. WIRING AND SURVEILLANCE. ONLY WAY WE CAN REALLY PROTECT OURSELVES FROM OUTSIDERS.
AND EACH OTHER...

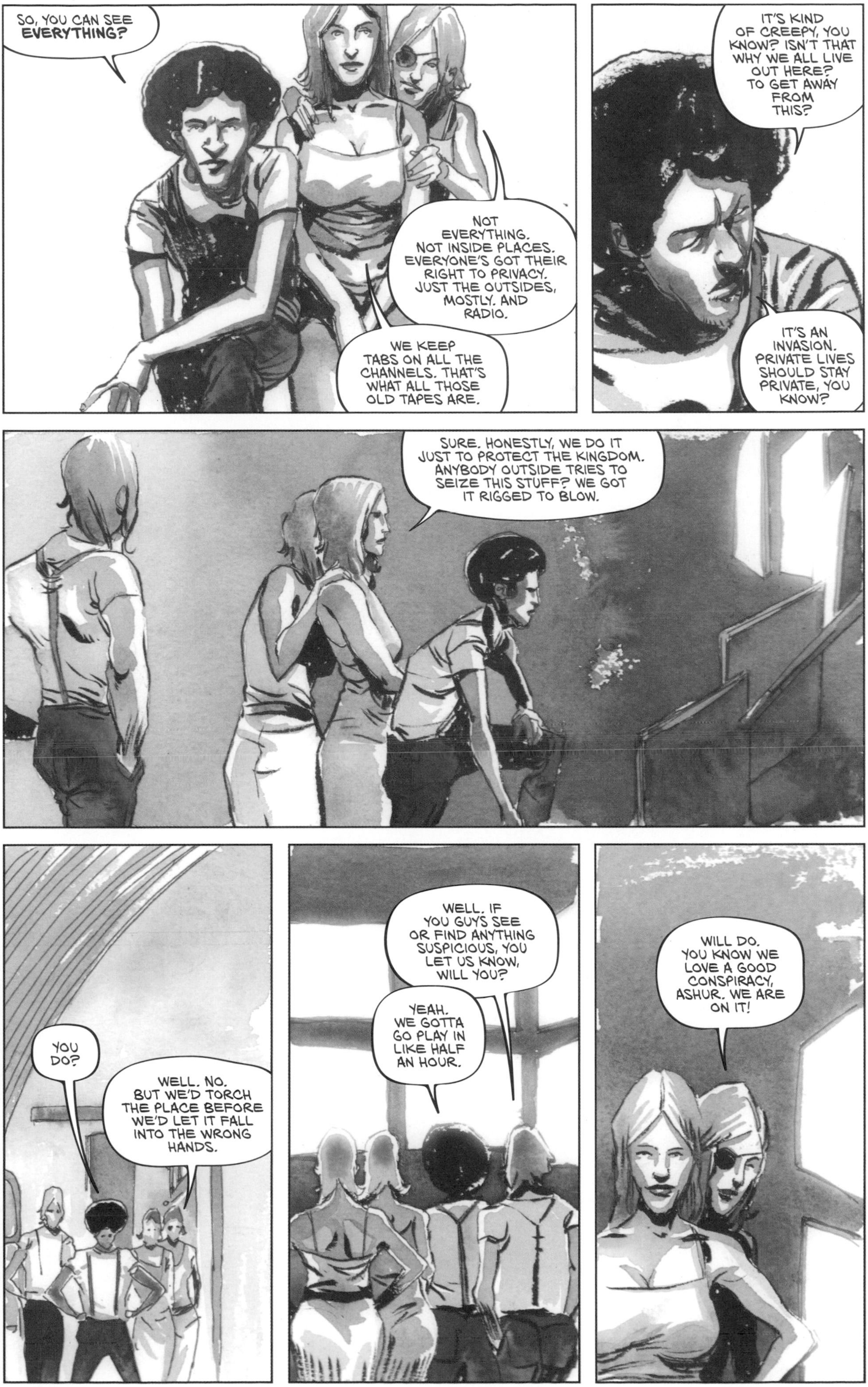
SO, YOU CAN SEE **EVERYTHING?**
NOT EVERYTHING. NOT INSIDE PLACES. EVERYONE'S GOT THEIR RIGHT TO PRIVACY. JUST THE OUTSIDES, MOSTLY. AND RADIO.
WE KEEP TABS ON ALL THE CHANNELS. THAT'S WHAT ALL THOSE OLD TAPES ARE.
IT'S KIND OF CREEPY, YOU KNOW? ISN'T THAT WHY WE ALL LIVE OUT HERE? TO GET AWAY FROM THIS?
IT'S AN INVASION. PRIVATE LIVES SHOULD STAY PRIVATE, YOU KNOW?
SURE. HONESTLY, WE DO IT JUST TO PROTECT THE KINGDOM. ANYBODY OUTSIDE TRIES TO SEIZE THIS STUFF? WE GOT IT RIGGED TO BLOW.
YOU DO?
WELL. NO. BUT WE'D TORCH THE PLACE BEFORE WE'D LET IT FALL INTO THE WRONG HANDS.
WELL. IF YOU GUYS SEE OR FIND ANYTHING SUSPICIOUS, YOU LET US KNOW, WILL YOU?
YEAH. WE GOTTA GO PLAY IN LIKE HALF AN HOUR.
WILL DO. YOU KNOW WE LOVE A GOOD CONSPIRACY, ASHUR. WE ARE ON IT!

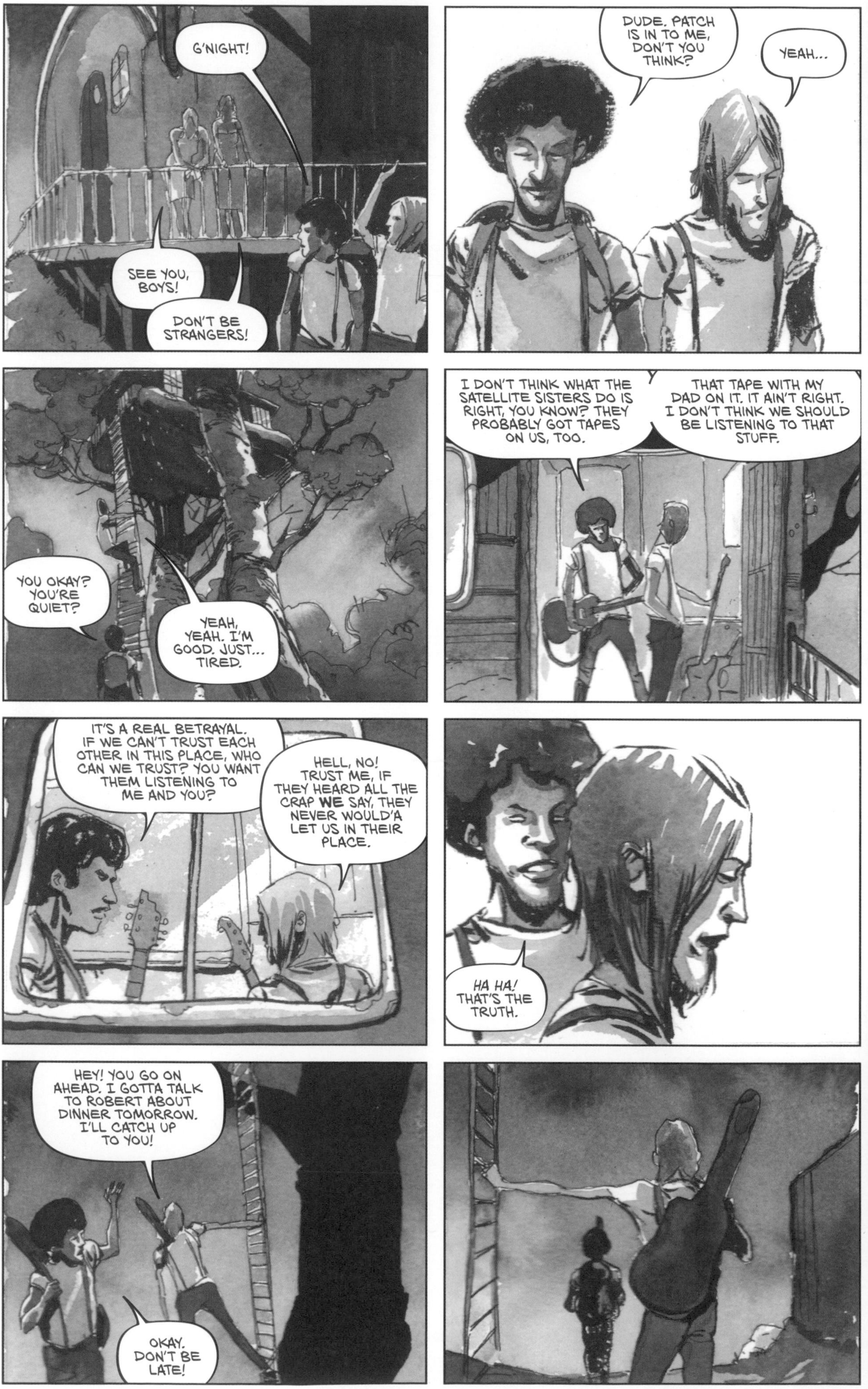
G'NIGHT!
SEE YOU, BOYS!
DON'T BE STRANGERS!
DUDE. PATCH IS IN TO ME, DON'T YOU THINK?
YEAH...
YOU OKAY? YOU'RE QUIET?
YEAH, YEAH. I'M GOOD. JUST... TIRED.
I DON'T THINK WHAT THE SATELLITE SISTERS DO IS RIGHT, YOU KNOW? THEY PROBABLY GOT TAPES ON US, TOO.
THAT TAPE WITH MY DAD ON IT. IT AIN'T RIGHT. I DON'T THINK WE SHOULD BE LISTENING TO THAT STUFF.
IT'S A REAL BETRAYAL. IF WE CAN'T TRUST EACH OTHER IN THIS PLACE, WHO CAN WE TRUST? YOU WANT THEM LISTENING TO ME AND YOU?
HELL, NO! TRUST ME, IF THEY HEARD ALL THE CRAP **WE** SAY, THEY NEVER WOULD'A LET US IN THEIR PLACE.
HA HA! THAT'S THE TRUTH.
HEY! YOU GO ON AHEAD. I GOTTA TALK TO ROBERT ABOUT DINNER TOMORROW. I'LL CATCH UP TO YOU!
OKAY. DON'T BE LATE!

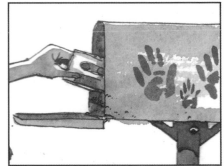

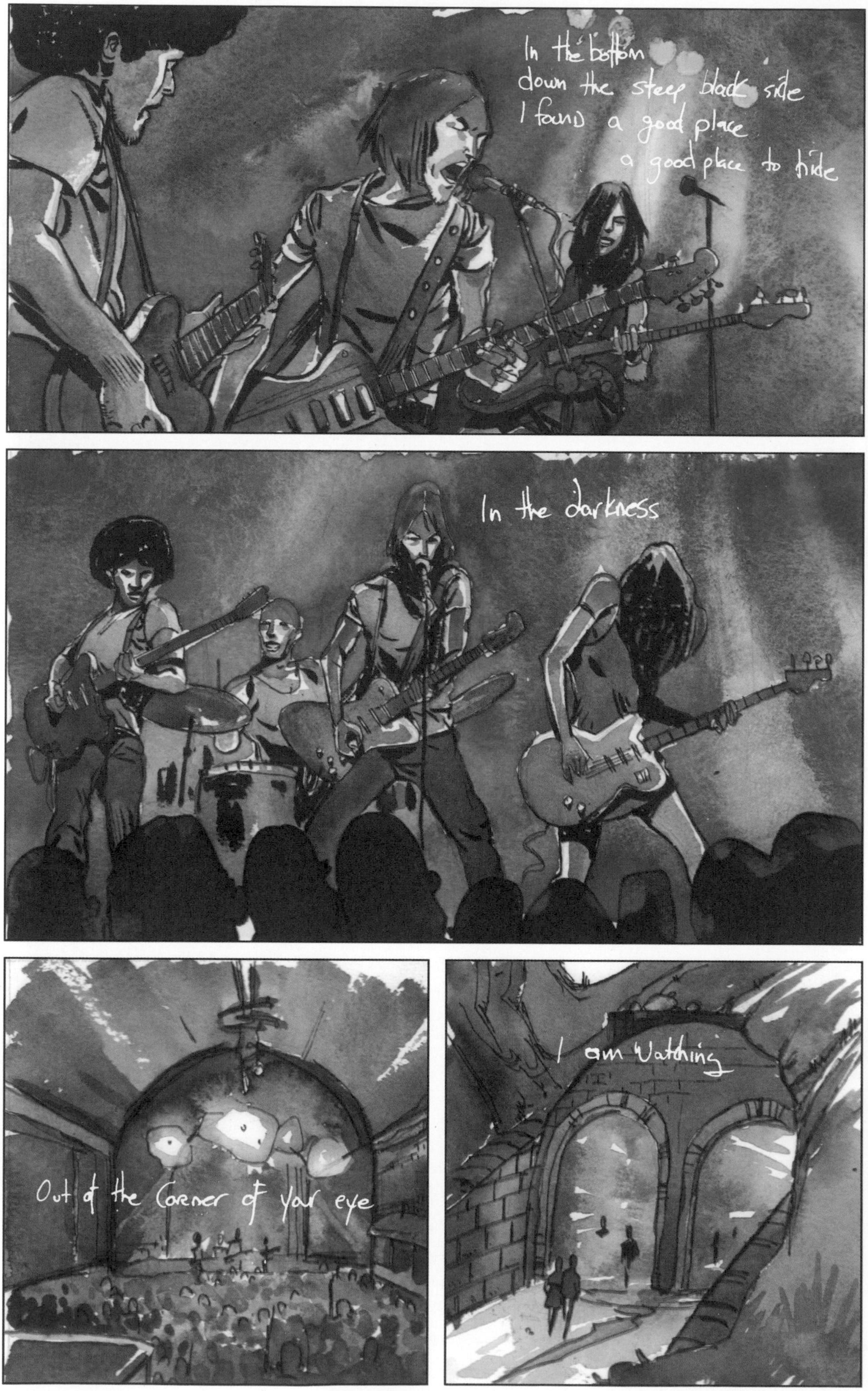
In the bottom
down the steep black side
I found a good place
a good place to hide
In the darkness
Out of the Corner of your eye
I am Watching

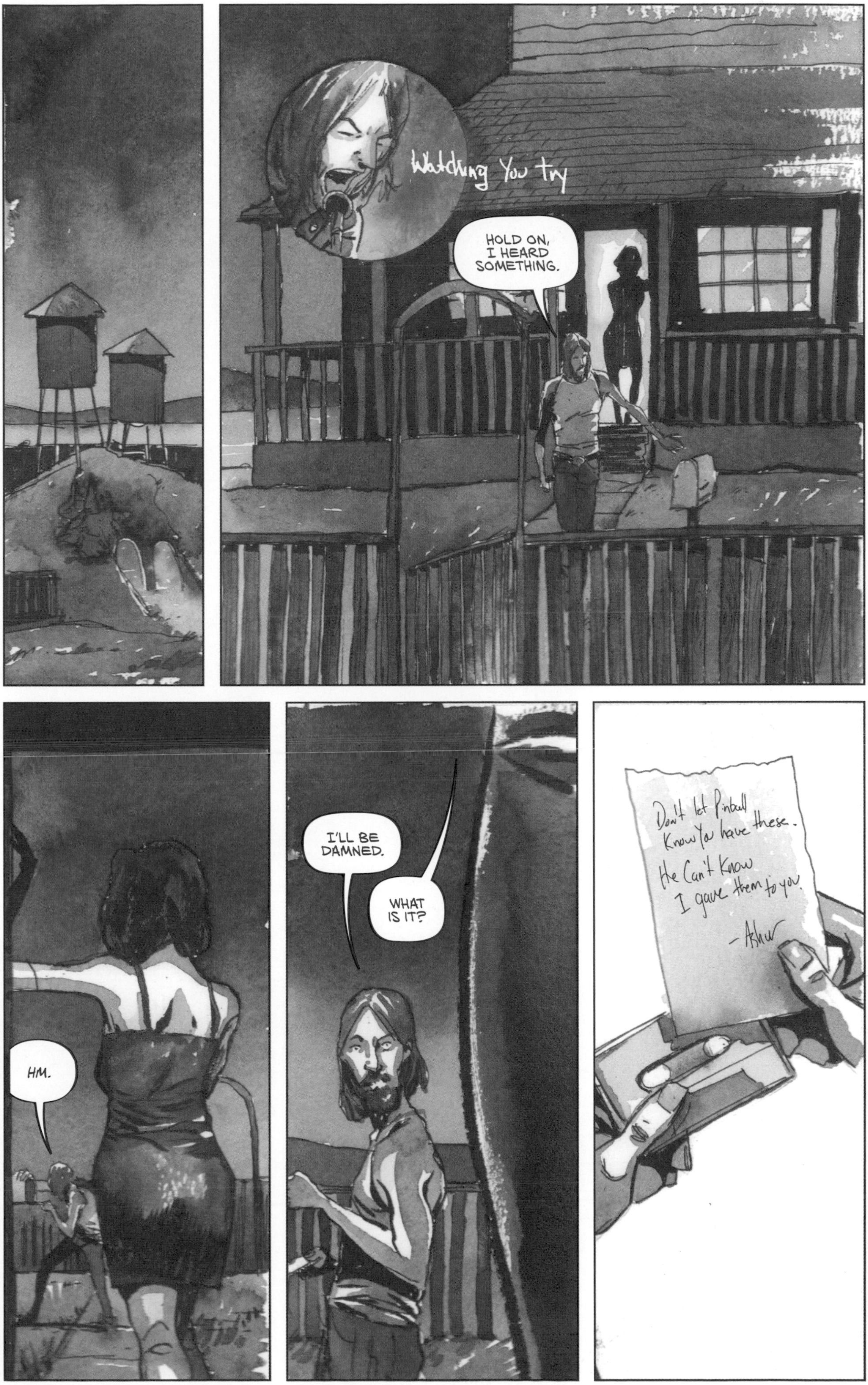
Watching You try
HOLD ON, I HEARD SOMETHING.
HM.
I'LL BE DAMNED.
WHAT IS IT?
Don't let Pinball Know You have these. He Can't Know I gave them to you.
- Arthur

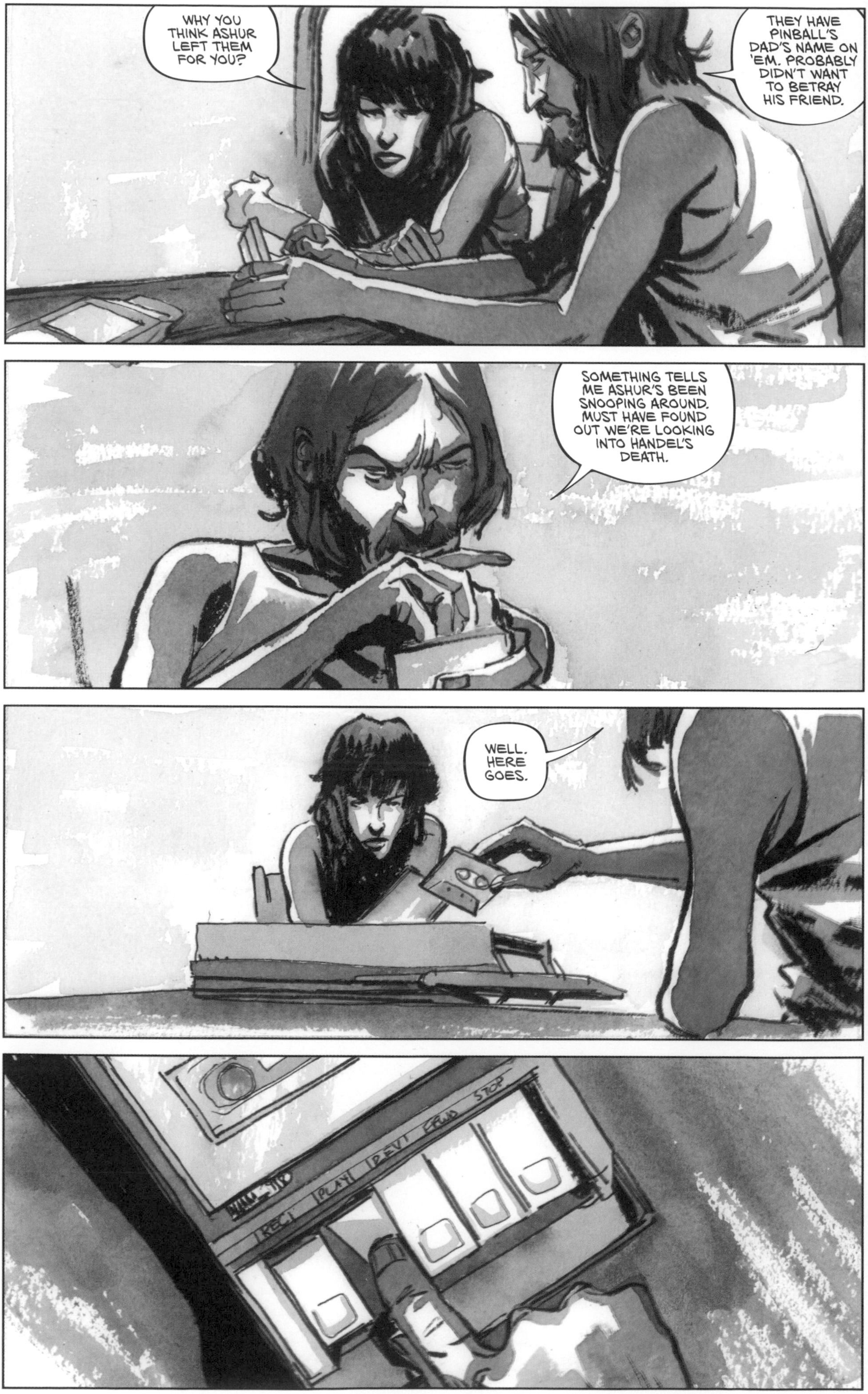
WHY YOU THINK ASHUR LEFT THEM FOR YOU?
THEY HAVE PINBALL'S DAD'S NAME ON 'EM. PROBABLY DIDN'T WANT TO BETRAY HIS FRIEND.
SOMETHING TELLS ME ASHUR'S BEEN SNOOPING AROUND. MUST HAVE FOUND OUT WE'RE LOOKING INTO HANDEL'S DEATH.
WELL. HERE GOES.

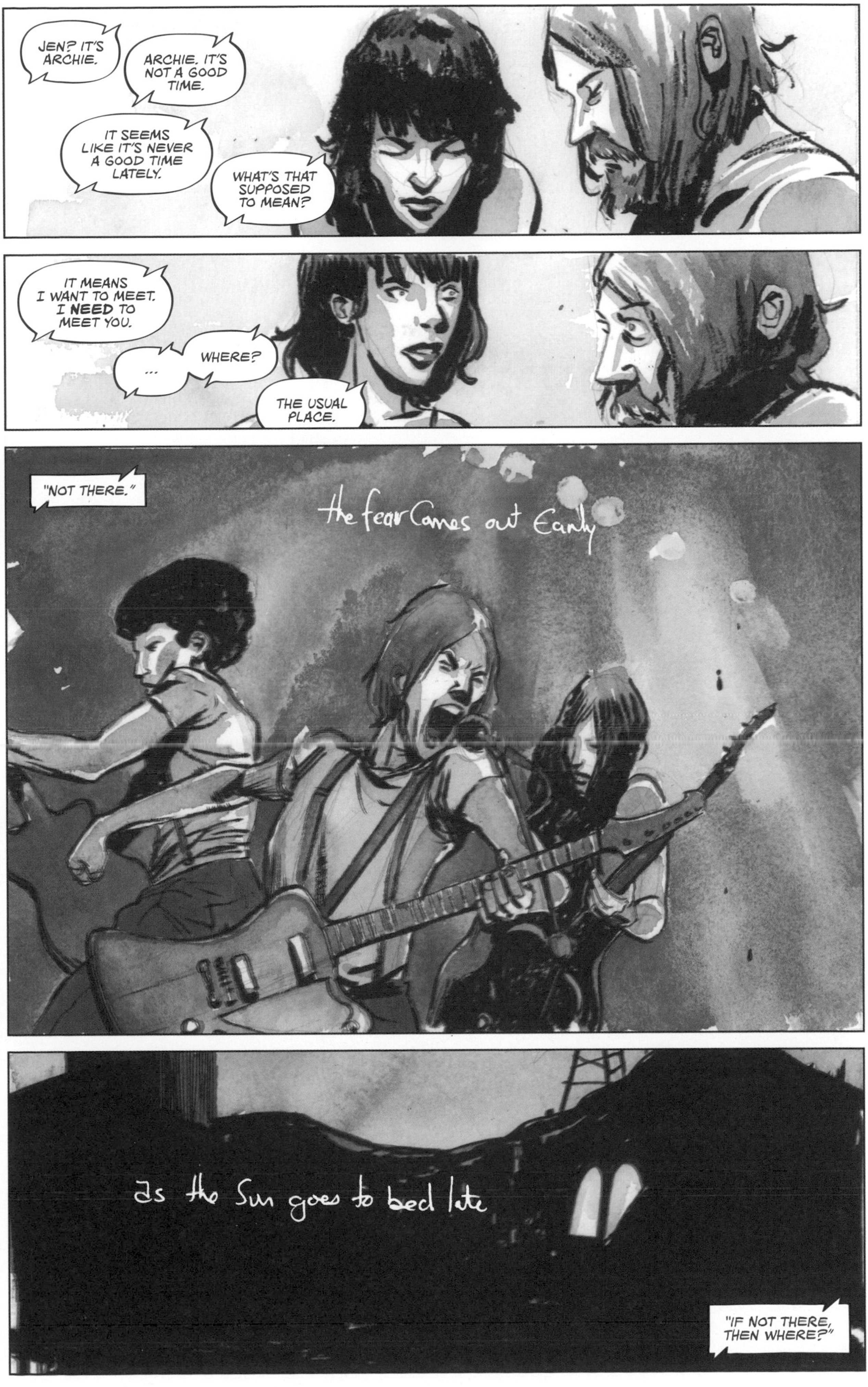
JEN? IT'S ARCHIE.
ARCHIE. IT'S NOT A GOOD TIME.
IT SEEMS LIKE IT'S NEVER A GOOD TIME LATELY.
WHAT'S THAT SUPPOSED TO MEAN?
IT MEANS I WANT TO MEET. I **NEED** TO MEET YOU.
...
WHERE?
THE USUAL PLACE.
"NOT THERE."
the fear Comes out Early
as the Sun goes to bed late
"IF NOT THERE, THEN WHERE?"

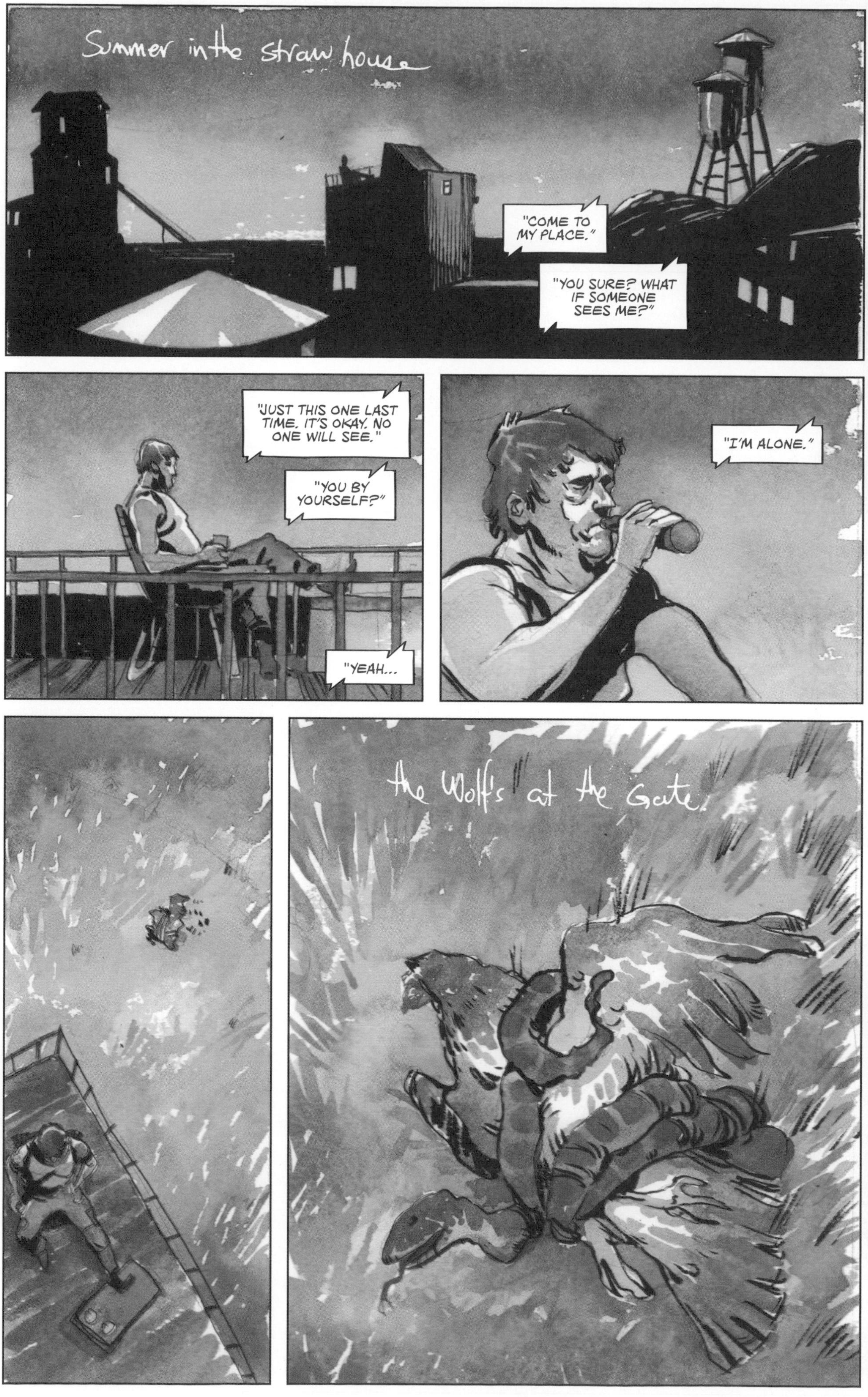
Summer in the straw house
"COME TO MY PLACE."
"YOU SURE? WHAT IF SOMEONE SEES ME?"
"JUST THIS ONE LAST TIME. IT'S OKAY. NO ONE WILL SEE."
"YOU BY YOURSELF?"
"YEAH...
"I'M ALONE."
the Wolf's at the Gate.

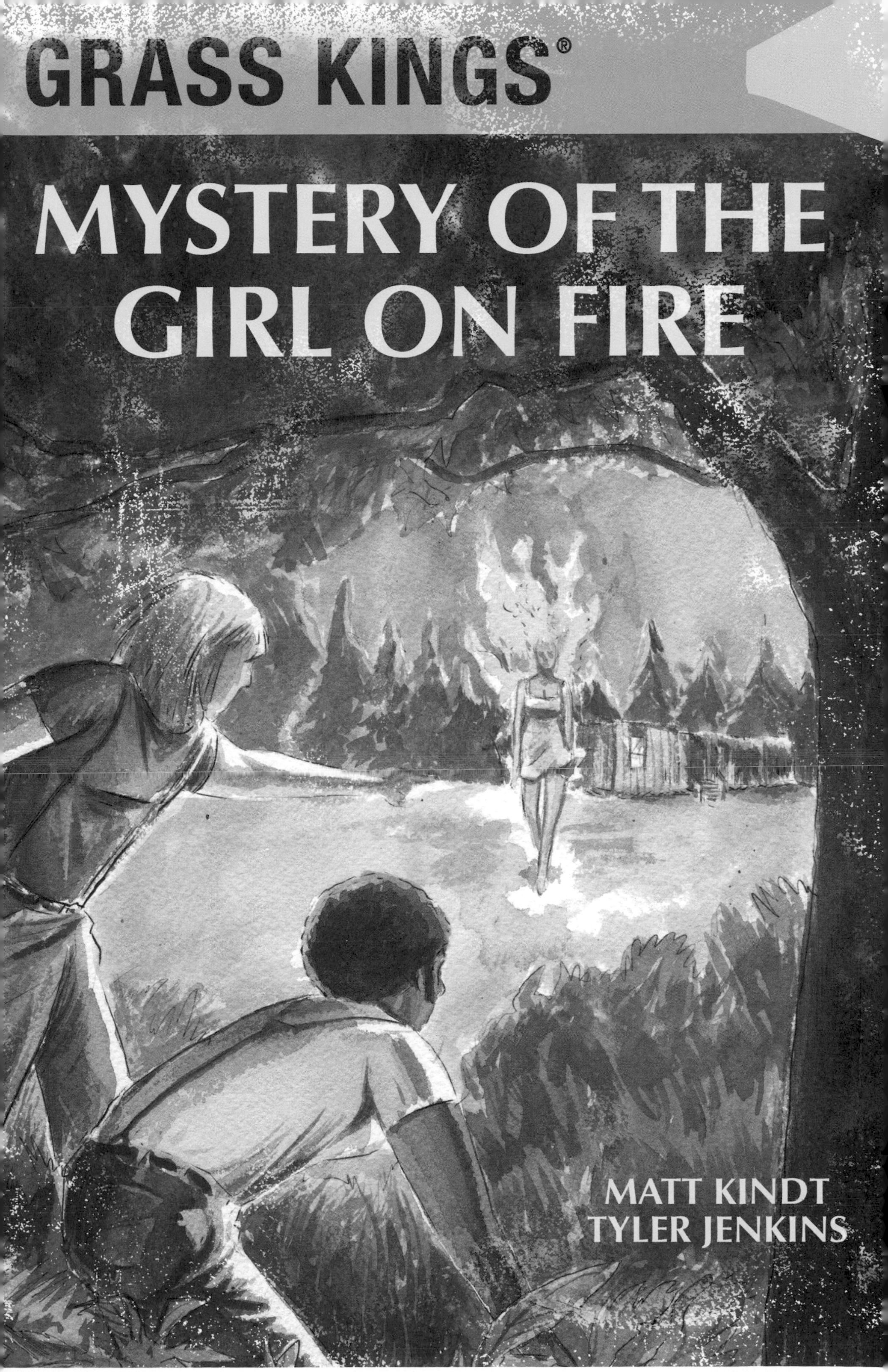
GRASS KINGS®
MYSTERY OF THE GIRL ON FIRE
MATT KINDT
TYLER JENKINS

issue #9 cover by matt kindt

chapter ten

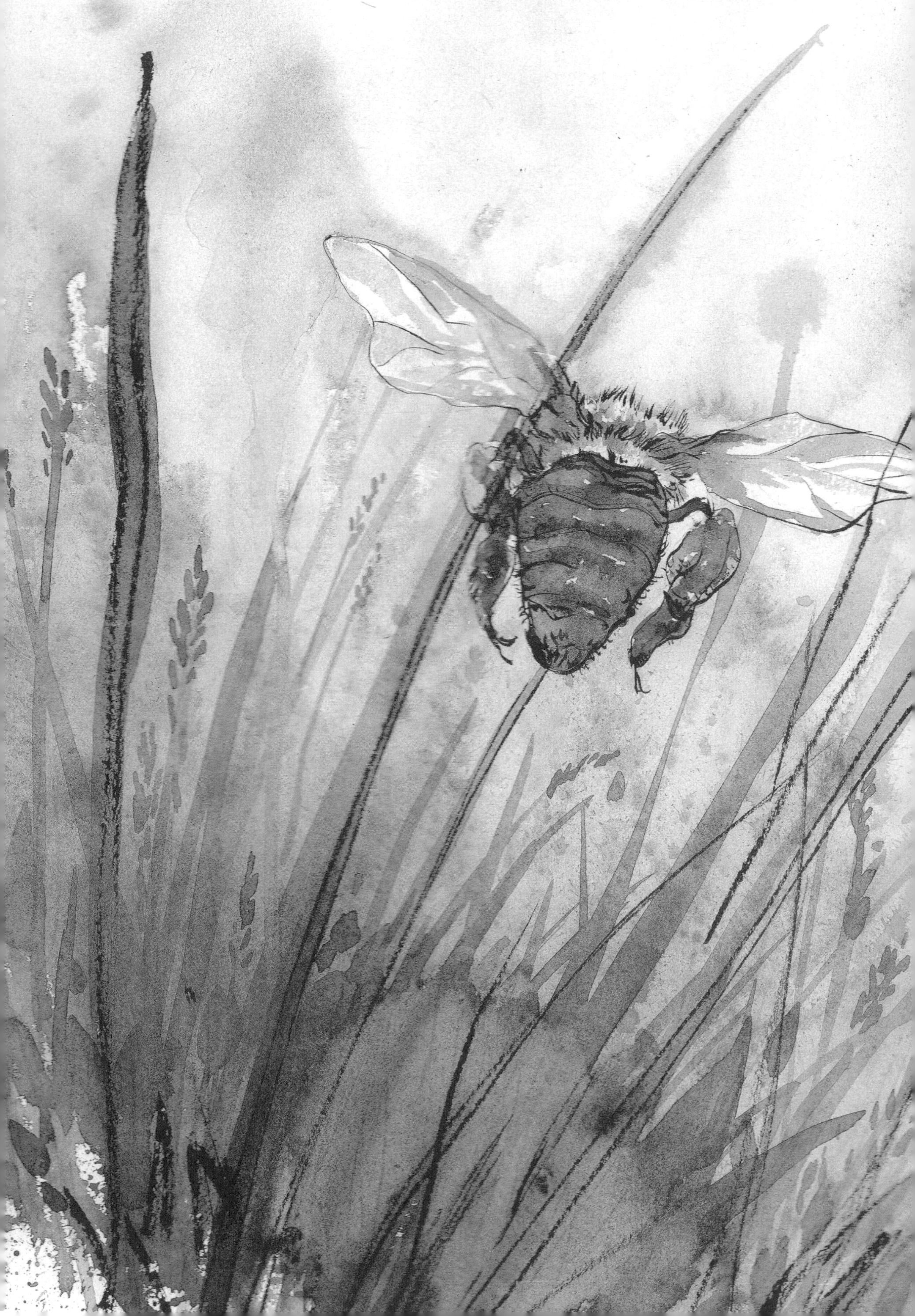

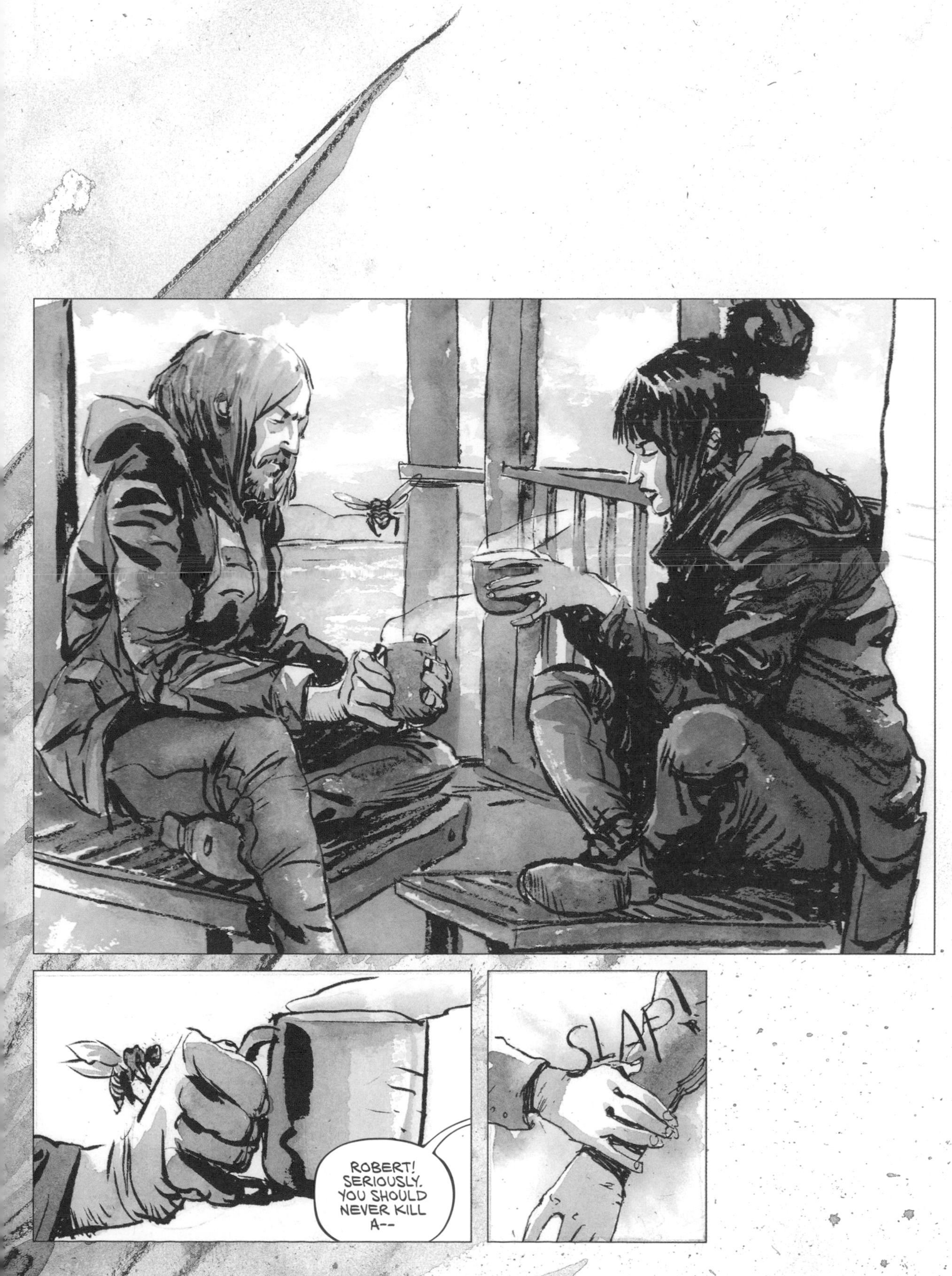
ROBERT! SERIOUSLY. YOU SHOULD NEVER KILL A--
SLAP!

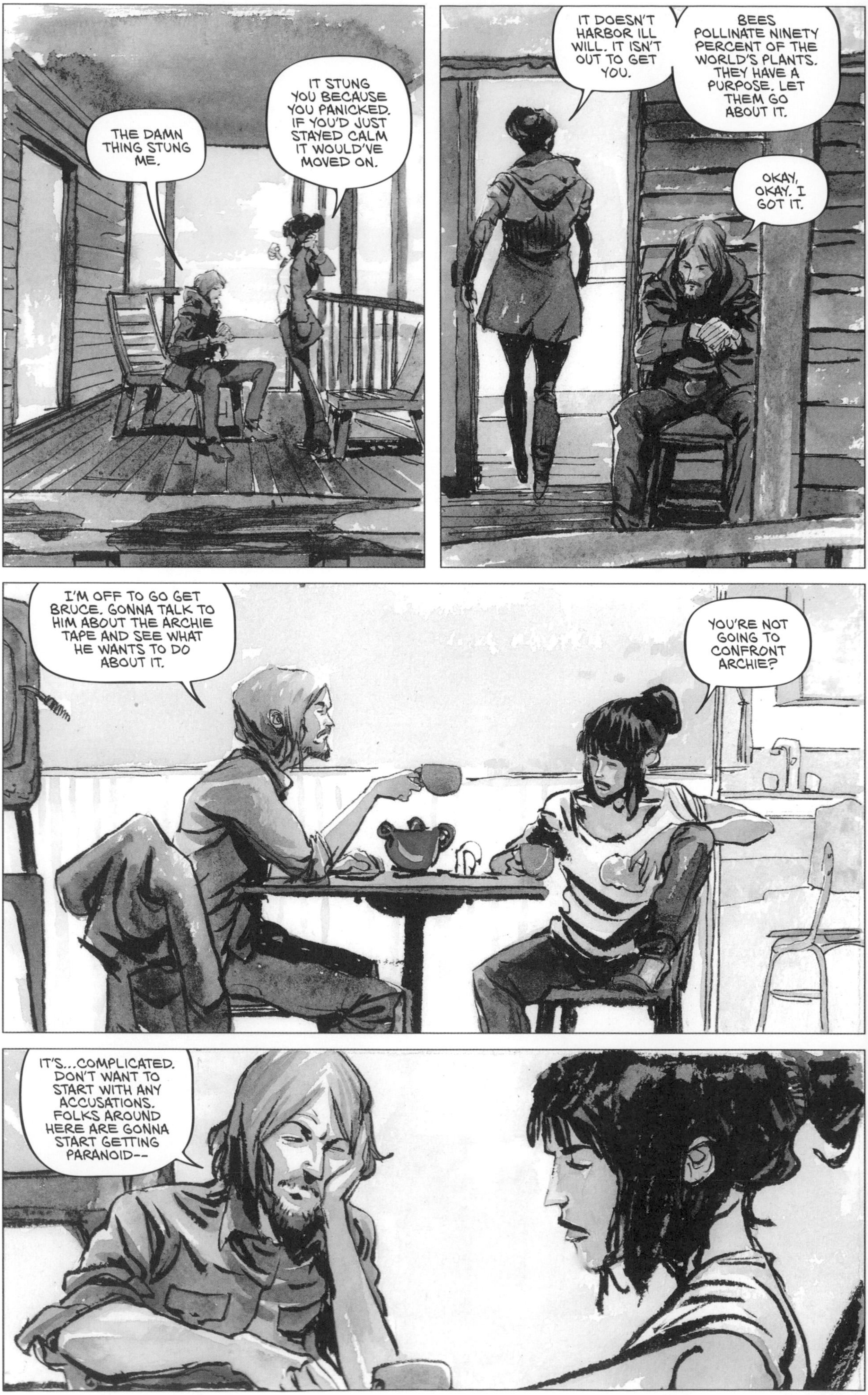
THE DAMN THING STUNG ME.
IT STUNG YOU BECAUSE YOU PANICKED. IF YOU'D JUST STAYED CALM IT WOULD'VE MOVED ON.
IT DOESN'T HARBOR ILL WILL. IT ISN'T OUT TO GET YOU.
BEES POLLINATE NINETY PERCENT OF THE WORLD'S PLANTS. THEY HAVE A PURPOSE. LET THEM GO ABOUT IT.
OKAY, OKAY. I GOT IT.
I'M OFF TO GO GET BRUCE. GONNA TALK TO HIM ABOUT THE ARCHIE TAPE AND SEE WHAT HE WANTS TO DO ABOUT IT.
YOU'RE NOT GOING TO CONFRONT ARCHIE?
IT'S...COMPLICATED. DON'T WANT TO START WITH ANY ACCUSATIONS. FOLKS AROUND HERE ARE GONNA START GETTING PARANOID--

START GETTING PARANOID? HA.

WE DON'T WANT PEOPLE FREAKING OUT ABOUT SURVEILLANCE.

THE TAPE MUST'VE COME FROM THE SATELLITE SISTERS. PROBABLY SHOULD TALK TO THEM FIRST.

DO WHAT YOU NEED TO DO. I'M HEADING TO SHELLY'S.

SOUNDS GOOD. TELL HER "HI." I'LL SEE YOU TONIGHT.

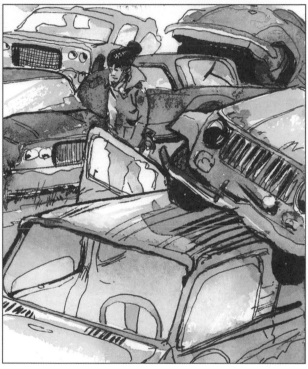

HEY, SHELLY.

HOW ARE YOU? WHAT'S UP?

CAME OVER TO TALK ABOUT JEN HANDEL.

YEAH. HEARD BRUCE AND ROBERT ARE LOOKING INTO HER DEATH. SOMETHING SUSPICIOUS ABOUT IT.

YEAH. SOMEONE DROPPED OFF A TAPE AT OUR PLACE LAST NIGHT. OLD RECORDING OF JEN AND ARCHIE TALKING. LIKE THEY HAD SOME KIND OF CONNECTION.

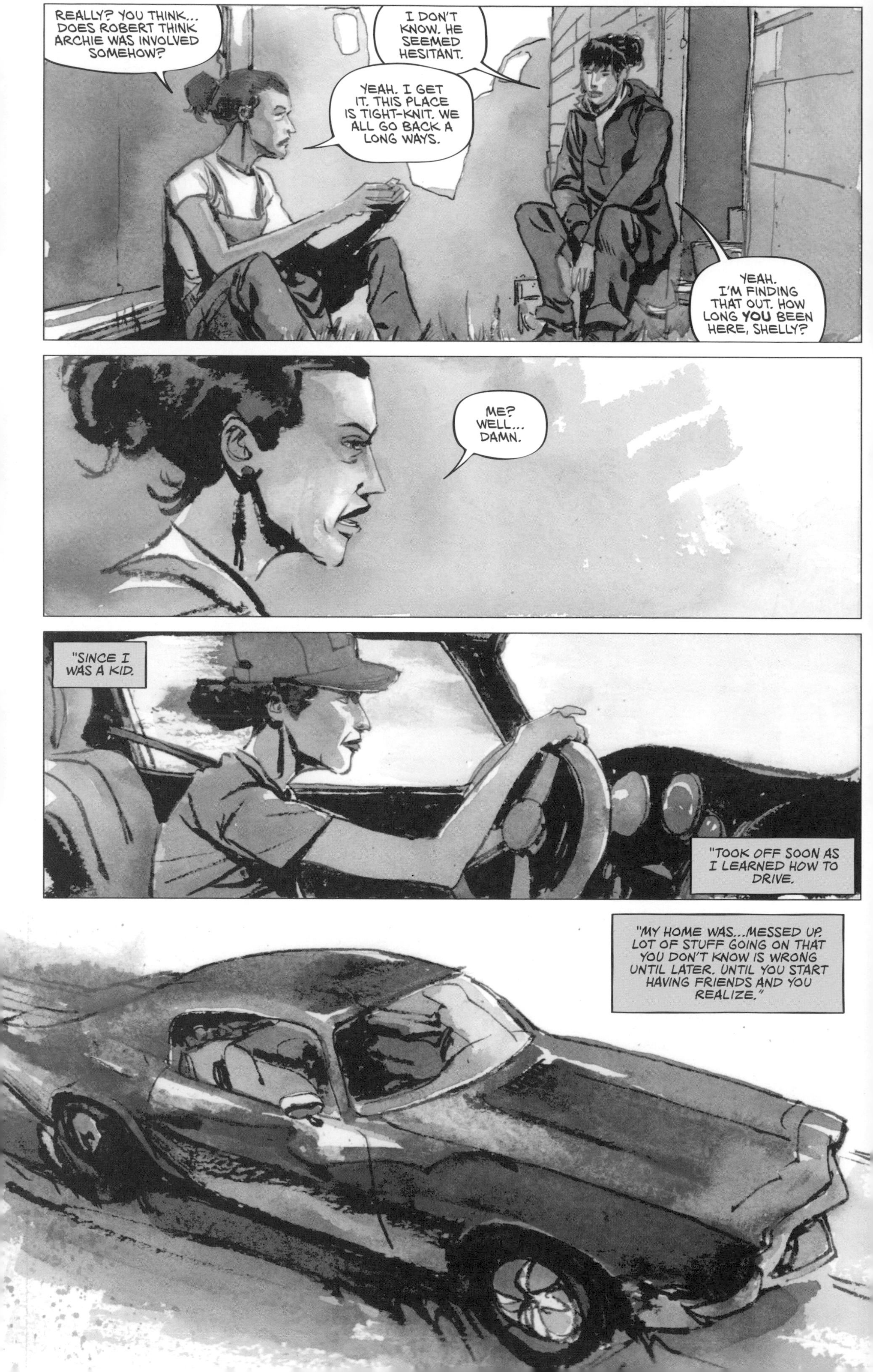
REALLY? YOU THINK... DOES ROBERT THINK ARCHIE WAS INVOLVED SOMEHOW?
I DON'T KNOW. HE SEEMED HESITANT.
YEAH. I GET IT. THIS PLACE IS TIGHT-KNIT. WE ALL GO BACK A LONG WAYS.
YEAH. I'M FINDING THAT OUT. HOW LONG **YOU** BEEN HERE, SHELLY?
ME? WELL... DAMN.
"SINCE I WAS A KID.
"TOOK OFF SOON AS I LEARNED HOW TO DRIVE.
"MY HOME WAS...MESSED UP. LOT OF STUFF GOING ON THAT YOU DON'T KNOW IS WRONG UNTIL LATER. UNTIL YOU START HAVING FRIENDS AND YOU REALIZE."

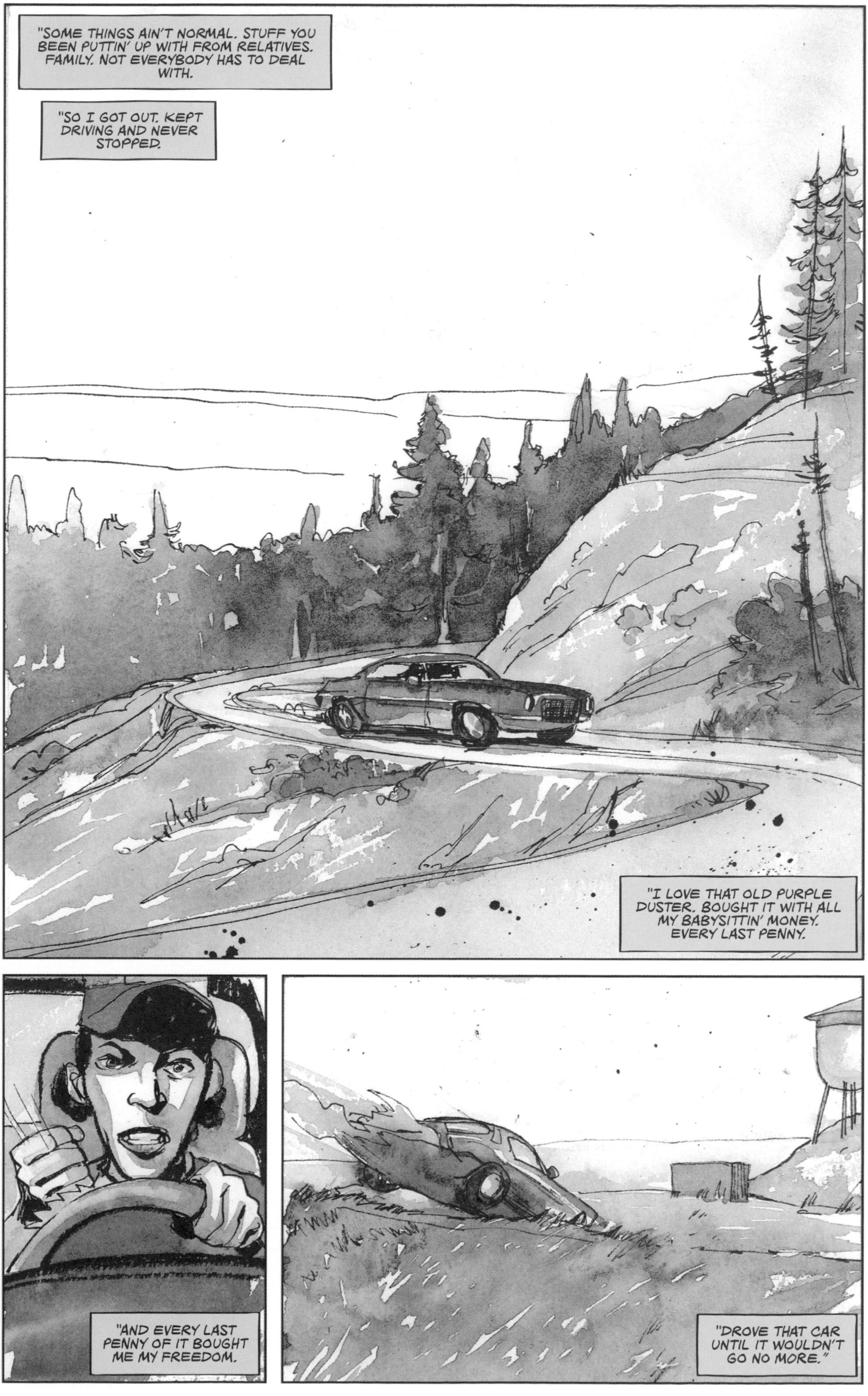
"SOME THINGS AIN'T NORMAL. STUFF YOU BEEN PUTTIN' UP WITH FROM RELATIVES. FAMILY. NOT EVERYBODY HAS TO DEAL WITH.
"SO I GOT OUT. KEPT DRIVING AND NEVER STOPPED.
"I LOVE THAT OLD PURPLE DUSTER. BOUGHT IT WITH ALL MY BABYSITTIN' MONEY. EVERY LAST PENNY.
"AND EVERY LAST PENNY OF IT BOUGHT ME MY FREEDOM.
"DROVE THAT CAR UNTIL IT WOULDN'T GO NO MORE."

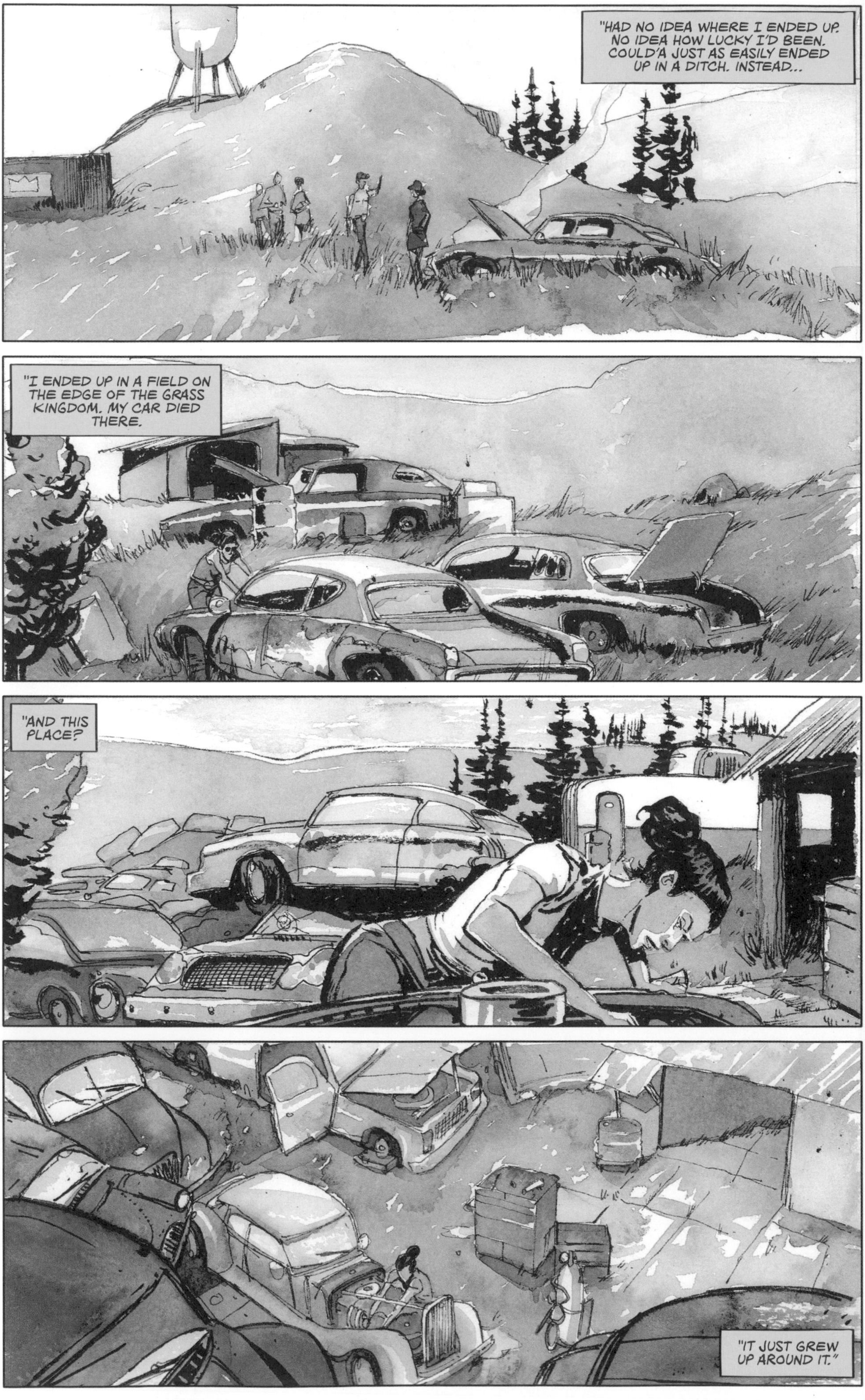
"HAD NO IDEA WHERE I ENDED UP. NO IDEA HOW LUCKY I'D BEEN. COULD'A JUST AS EASILY ENDED UP IN A DITCH. INSTEAD...
"I ENDED UP IN A FIELD ON THE EDGE OF THE GRASS KINGDOM. MY CAR DIED THERE.
"AND THIS PLACE?
"IT JUST GREW UP AROUND IT."

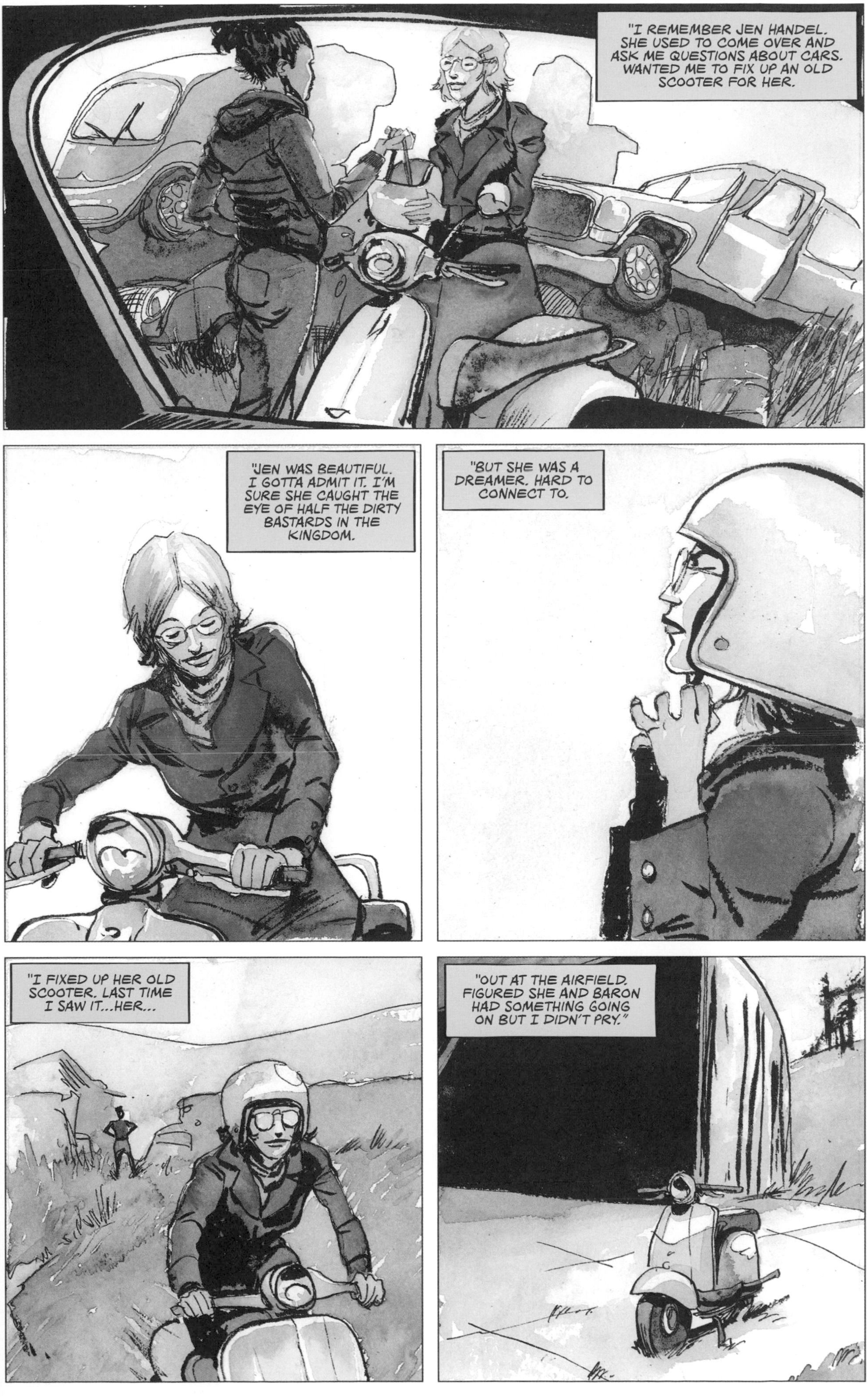
"I REMEMBER JEN HANDEL. SHE USED TO COME OVER AND ASK ME QUESTIONS ABOUT CARS. WANTED ME TO FIX UP AN OLD SCOOTER FOR HER.
"JEN WAS BEAUTIFUL. I GOTTA ADMIT IT. I'M SURE SHE CAUGHT THE EYE OF HALF THE DIRTY BASTARDS IN THE KINGDOM.
"BUT SHE WAS A DREAMER. HARD TO CONNECT TO.
"I FIXED UP HER OLD SCOOTER. LAST TIME I SAW IT...HER...
"OUT AT THE AIRFIELD. FIGURED SHE AND BARON HAD SOMETHING GOING ON BUT I DIDN'T PRY."

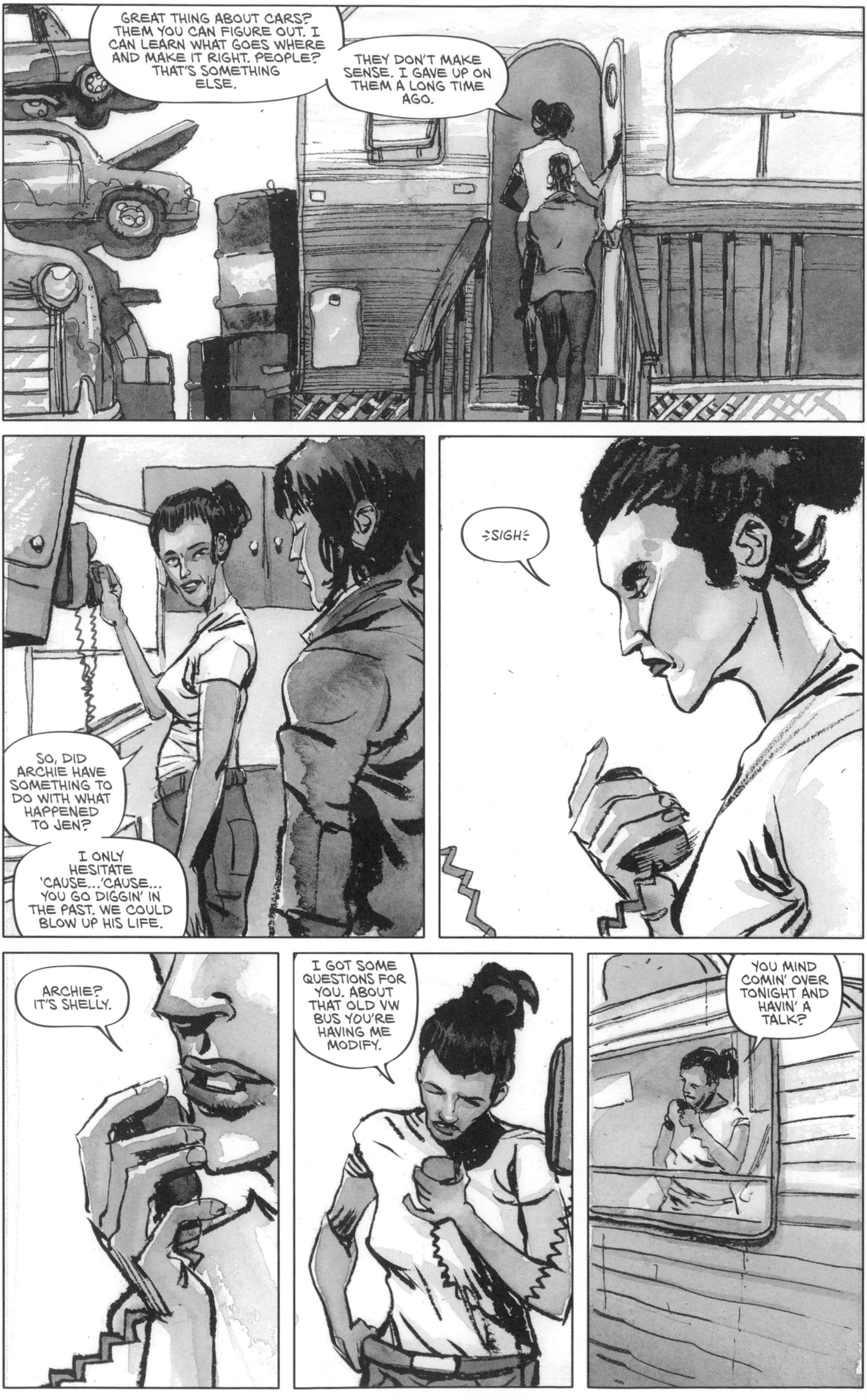
GREAT THING ABOUT CARS? THEM YOU CAN FIGURE OUT. I CAN LEARN WHAT GOES WHERE AND MAKE IT RIGHT. PEOPLE? THAT'S SOMETHING ELSE.
THEY DON'T MAKE SENSE. I GAVE UP ON THEM A LONG TIME AGO.
SO, DID ARCHIE HAVE SOMETHING TO DO WITH WHAT HAPPENED TO JEN?
I ONLY HESITATE 'CAUSE...'CAUSE... YOU GO DIGGIN' IN THE PAST. WE COULD BLOW UP HIS LIFE.
SIGH
ARCHIE? IT'S SHELLY.
I GOT SOME QUESTIONS FOR YOU. ABOUT THAT OLD VW BUS YOU'RE HAVING ME MODIFY.
YOU MIND COMIN' OVER TONIGHT AND HAVIN' A TALK?

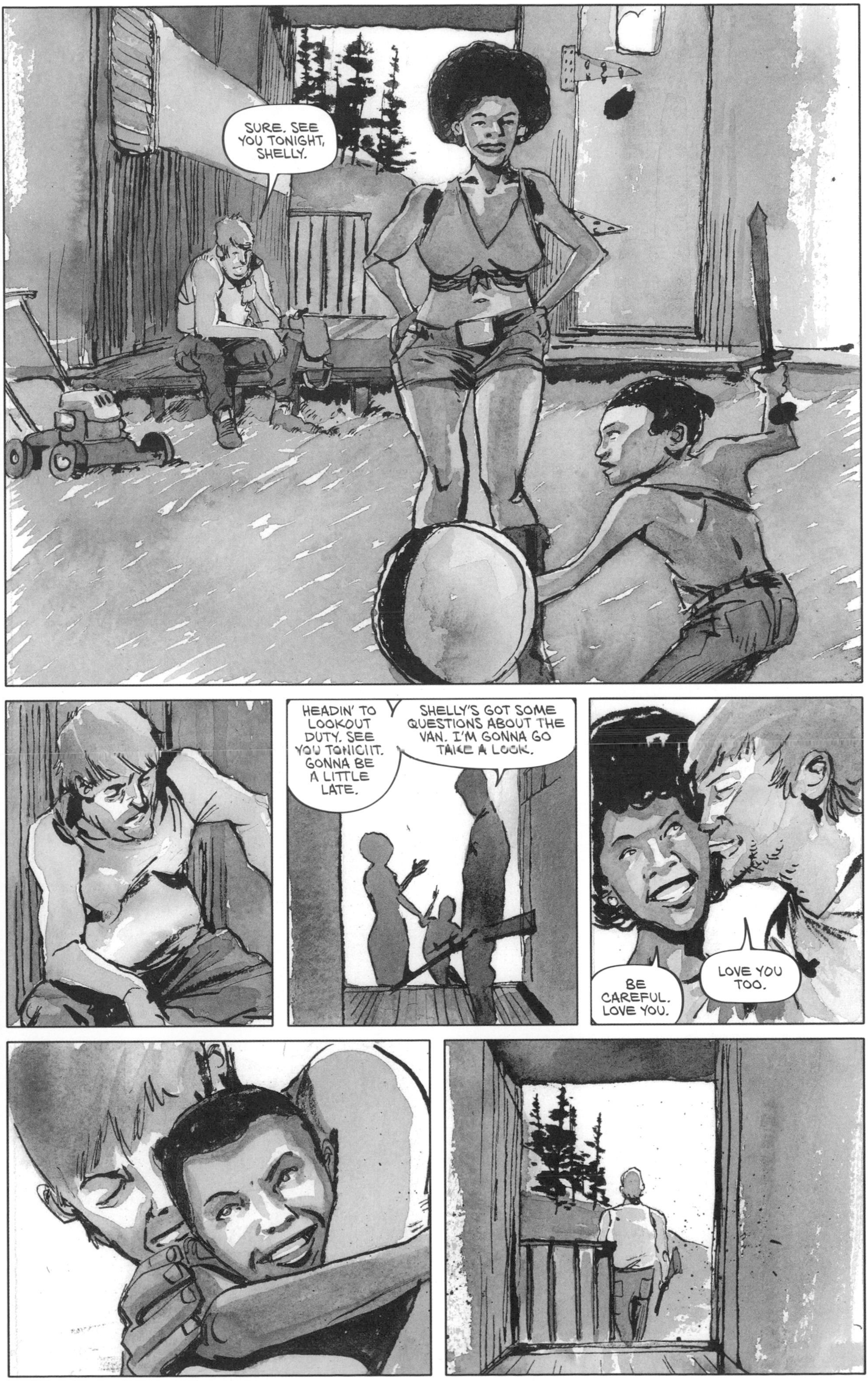
SURE. SEE YOU TONIGHT, SHELLY.
HEADIN' TO LOOKOUT DUTY. SEE YOU TONIGHT. GONNA BE A LITTLE LATE.
SHELLY'S GOT SOME QUESTIONS ABOUT THE VAN. I'M GONNA GO TAKE A LOOK.
BE CAREFUL. LOVE YOU.
LOVE YOU TOO.

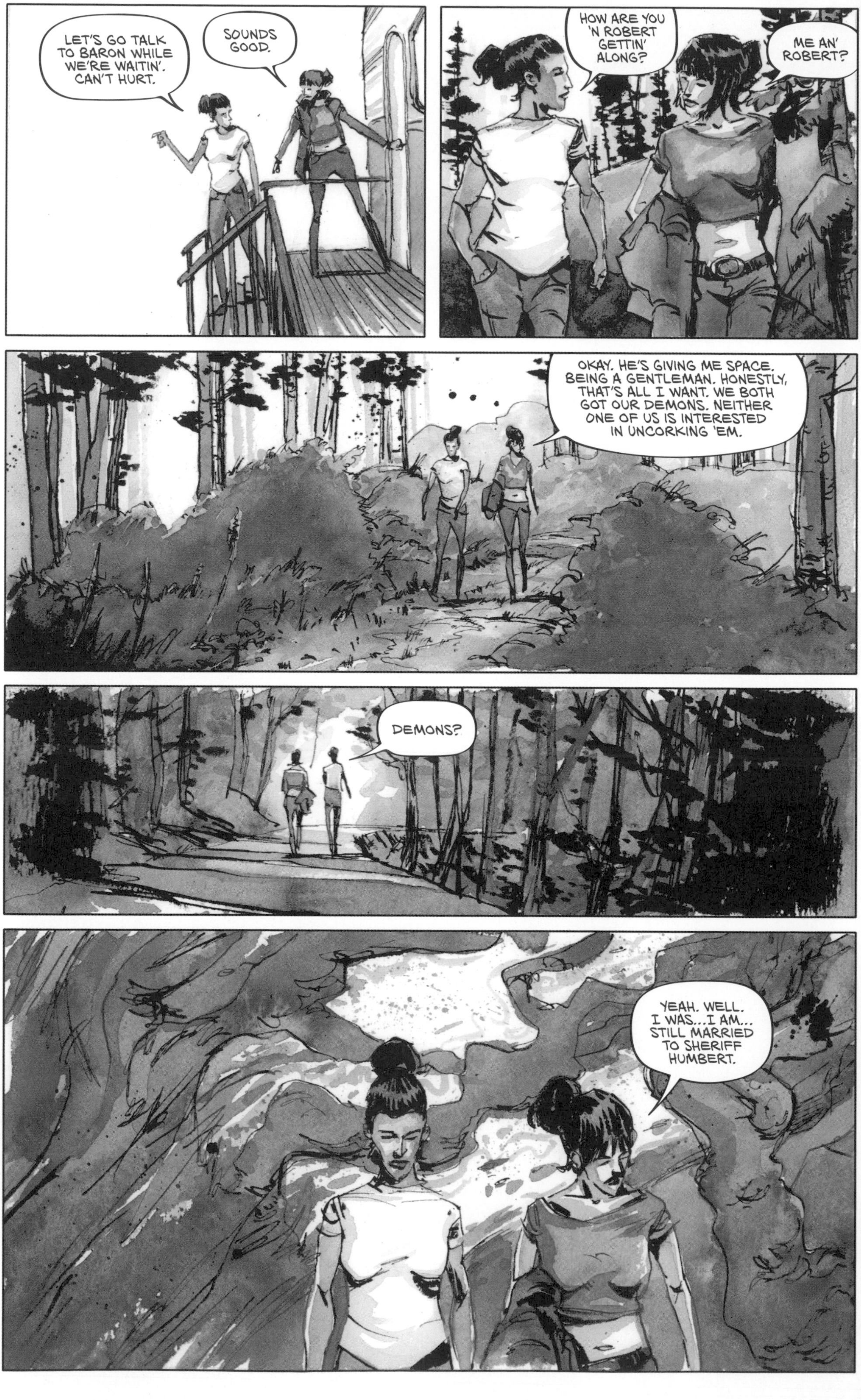
LET'S GO TALK TO BARON WHILE WE'RE WAITIN'. CAN'T HURT.
SOUNDS GOOD.
HOW ARE YOU 'N ROBERT GETTIN' ALONG?
ME AN' ROBERT?
OKAY. HE'S GIVING ME SPACE. BEING A GENTLEMAN. HONESTLY, THAT'S ALL I WANT. WE BOTH GOT OUR DEMONS. NEITHER ONE OF US IS INTERESTED IN UNCORKING 'EM.
DEMONS?
YEAH. WELL. I WAS...I AM... STILL MARRIED TO SHERIFF HUMBERT.

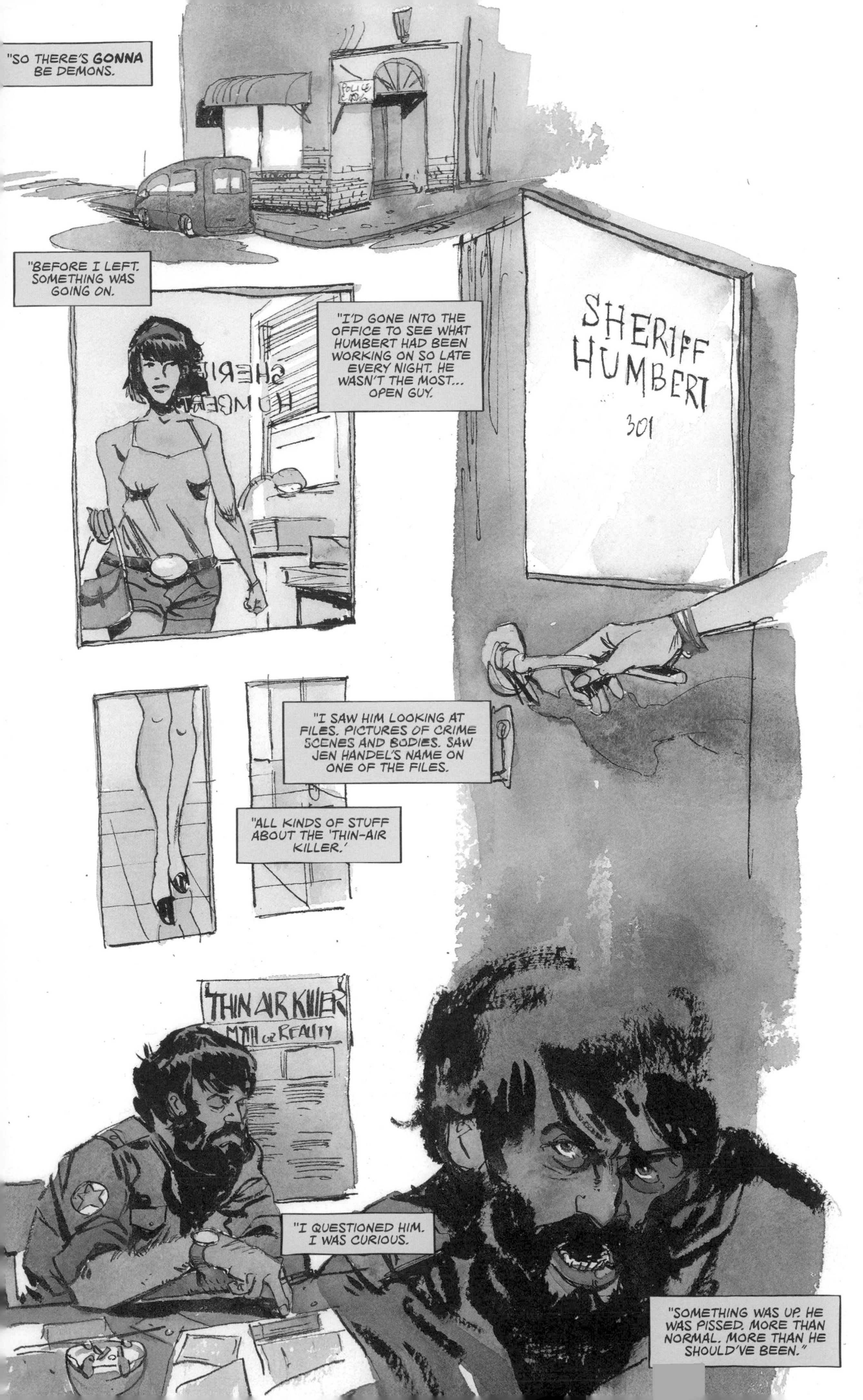
"SO THERE'S **GONNA** BE DEMONS.
"BEFORE I LEFT. SOMETHING WAS GOING ON.
"I'D GONE INTO THE OFFICE TO SEE WHAT HUMBERT HAD BEEN WORKING ON SO LATE EVERY NIGHT. HE WASN'T THE MOST... OPEN GUY.
SHERIFF HUMBERT
301
"I SAW HIM LOOKING AT FILES. PICTURES OF CRIME SCENES AND BODIES. SAW JEN HANDEL'S NAME ON ONE OF THE FILES.
"ALL KINDS OF STUFF ABOUT THE 'THIN-AIR KILLER.'
THIN AIR KILLER
MYTH or REALITY
"I QUESTIONED HIM. I WAS CURIOUS.
"SOMETHING WAS UP. HE WAS PISSED. MORE THAN NORMAL. MORE THAN HE SHOULD'VE BEEN."

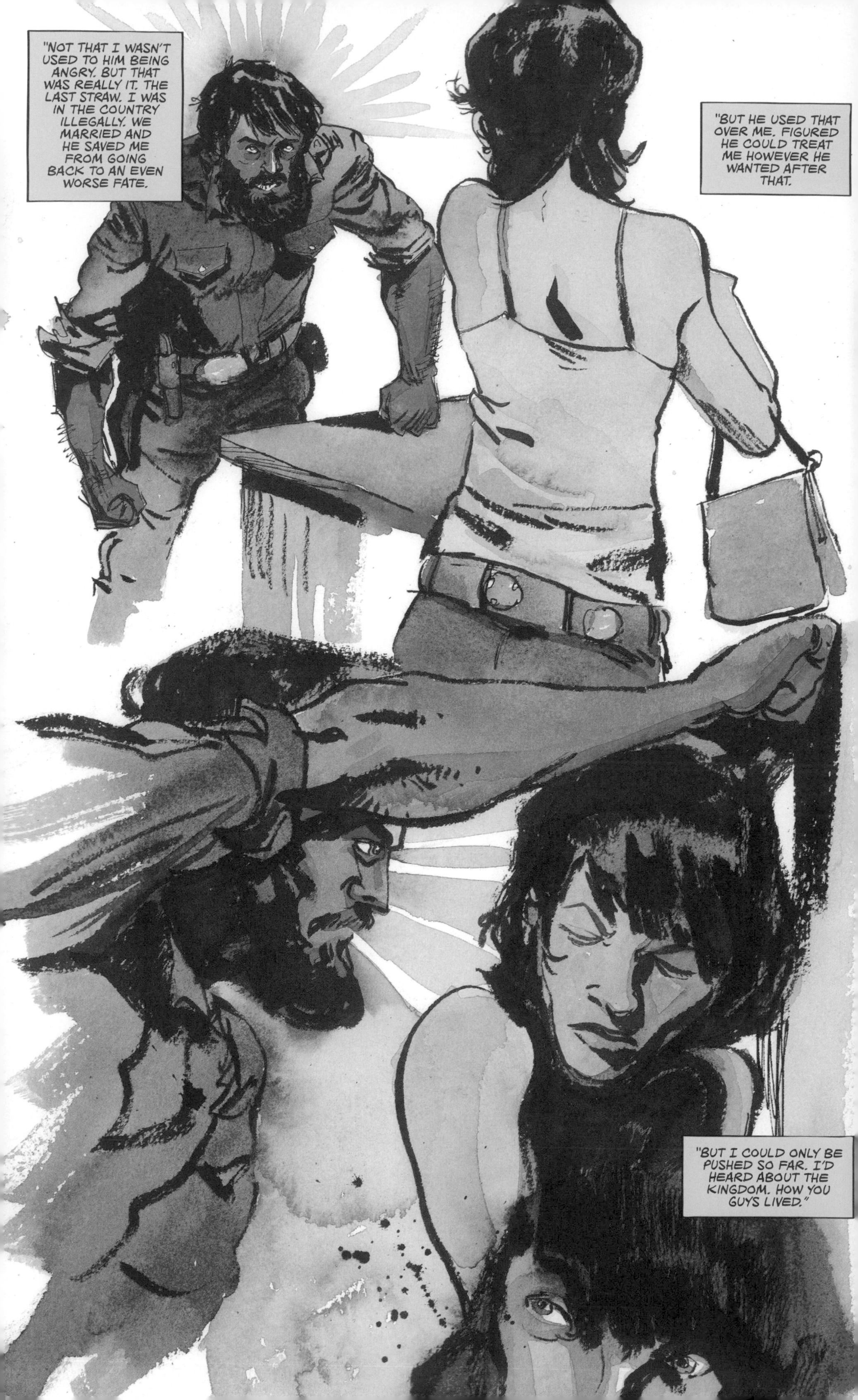
"NOT THAT I WASN'T USED TO HIM BEING ANGRY. BUT THAT WAS REALLY IT. THE LAST STRAW. I WAS IN THE COUNTRY ILLEGALLY. WE MARRIED AND HE SAVED ME FROM GOING BACK TO AN EVEN WORSE FATE.
"BUT HE USED THAT OVER ME. FIGURED HE COULD TREAT ME HOWEVER HE WANTED AFTER THAT.
"BUT I COULD ONLY BE PUSHED SO FAR. I'D HEARD ABOUT THE KINGDOM. HOW YOU GUYS LIVED."

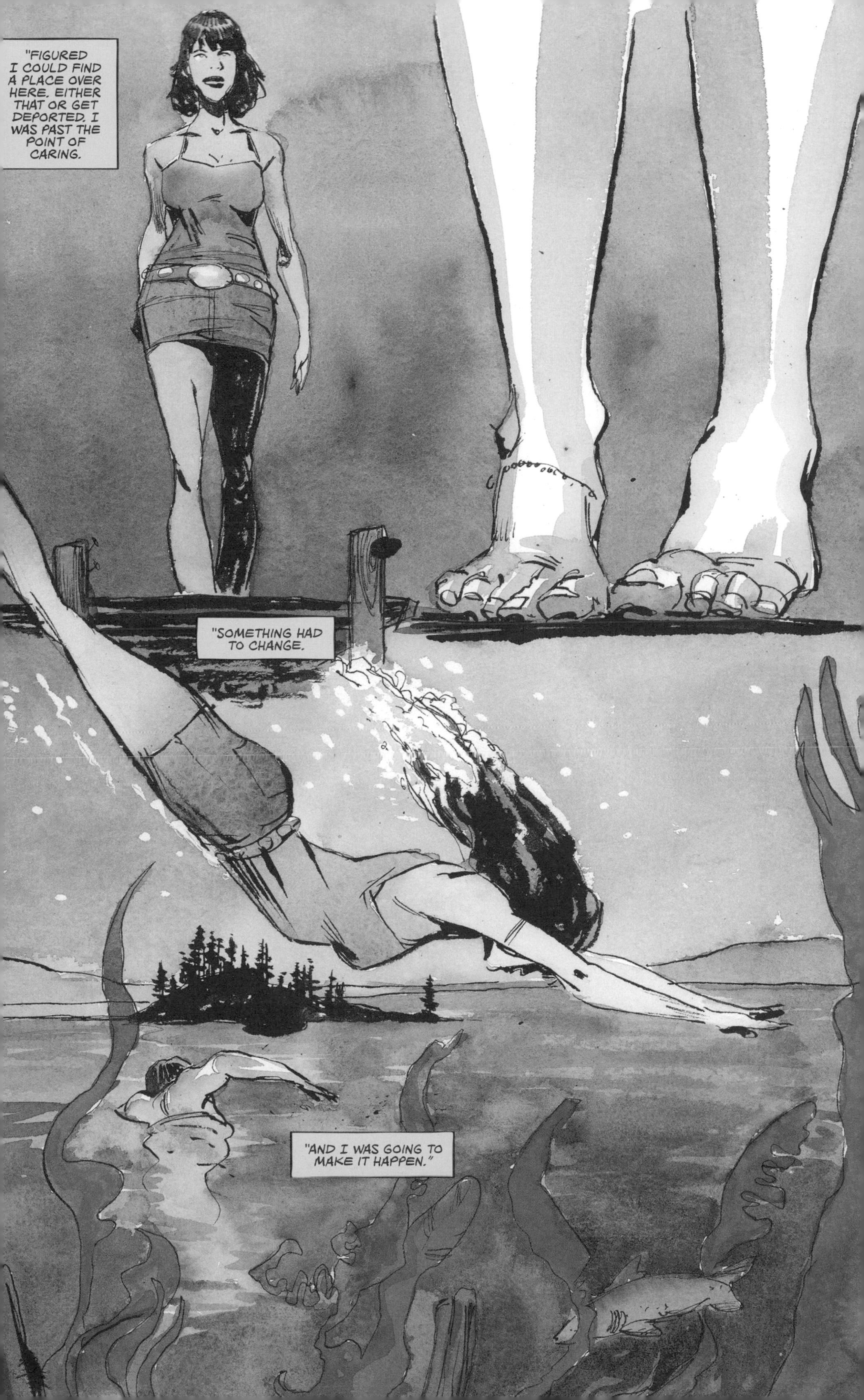
"FIGURED I COULD FIND A PLACE OVER HERE. EITHER THAT OR GET DEPORTED. I WAS PAST THE POINT OF CARING.
"SOMETHING HAD TO CHANGE.
"AND I WAS GOING TO MAKE IT HAPPEN."

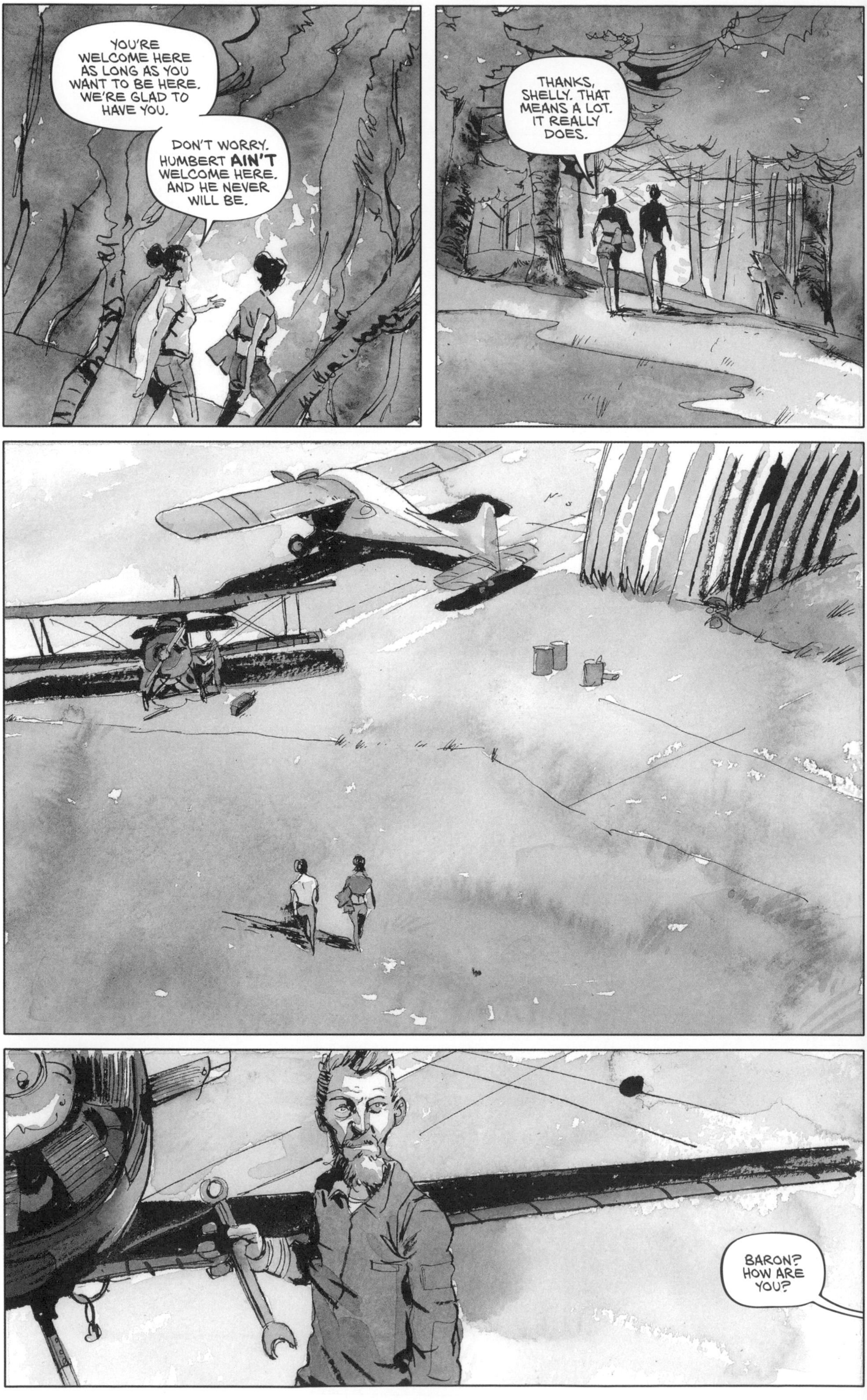
YOU'RE WELCOME HERE AS LONG AS YOU WANT TO BE HERE. WE'RE GLAD TO HAVE YOU.
DON'T WORRY. HUMBERT **AIN'T** WELCOME HERE. AND HE NEVER WILL BE.
THANKS, SHELLY. THAT MEANS A LOT. IT REALLY DOES.
BARON? HOW ARE YOU?

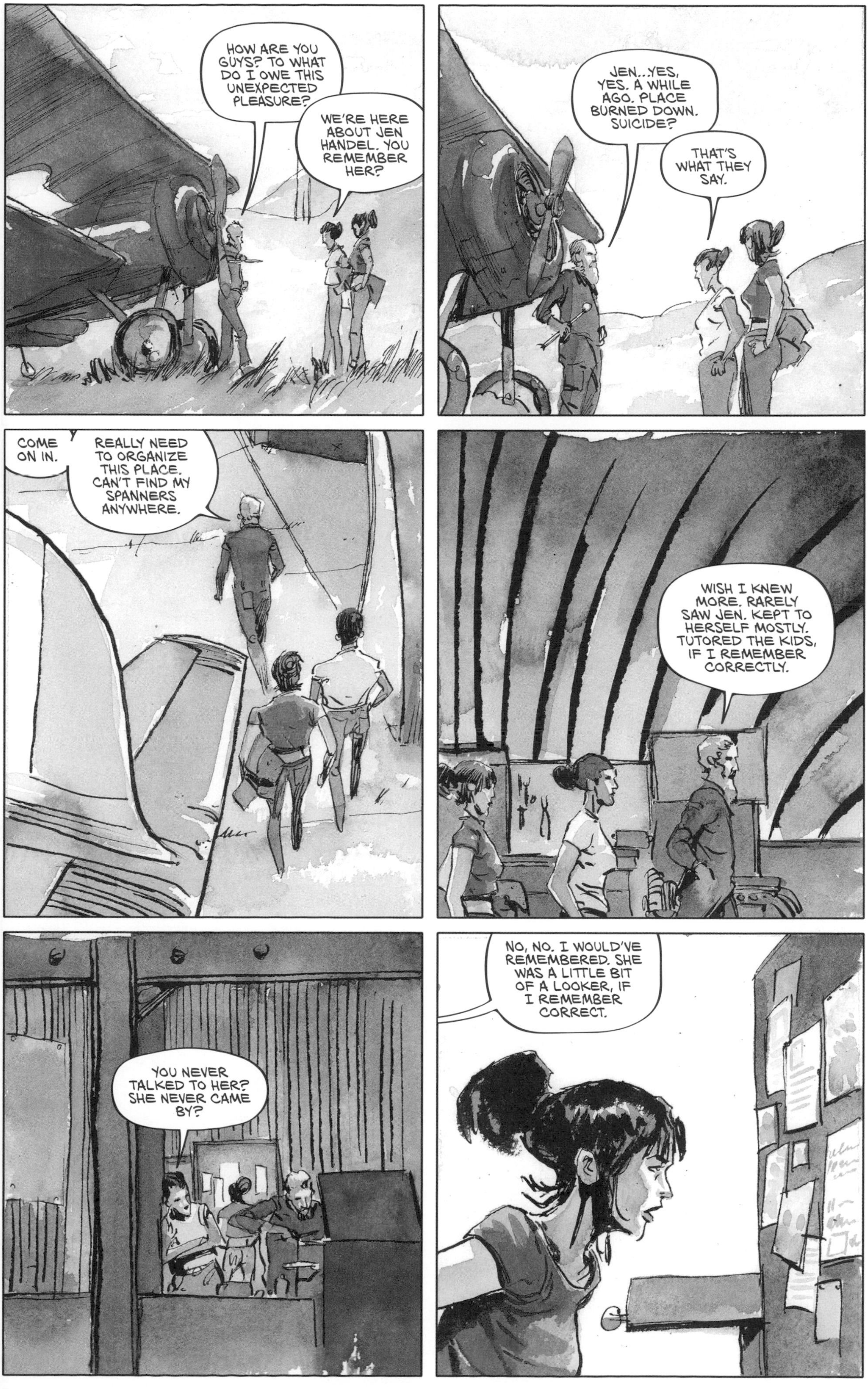
HOW ARE YOU GUYS? TO WHAT DO I OWE THIS UNEXPECTED PLEASURE?
WE'RE HERE ABOUT JEN HANDEL. YOU REMEMBER HER?
JEN...YES, YES. A WHILE AGO. PLACE BURNED DOWN. SUICIDE?
THAT'S WHAT THEY SAY.
COME ON IN.
REALLY NEED TO ORGANIZE THIS PLACE. CAN'T FIND MY SPANNERS ANYWHERE.
WISH I KNEW MORE. RARELY SAW JEN. KEPT TO HERSELF MOSTLY. TUTORED THE KIDS, IF I REMEMBER CORRECTLY.
YOU NEVER TALKED TO HER? SHE NEVER CAME BY?
NO, NO. I WOULD'VE REMEMBERED. SHE WAS A LITTLE BIT OF A LOOKER, IF I REMEMBER CORRECT.

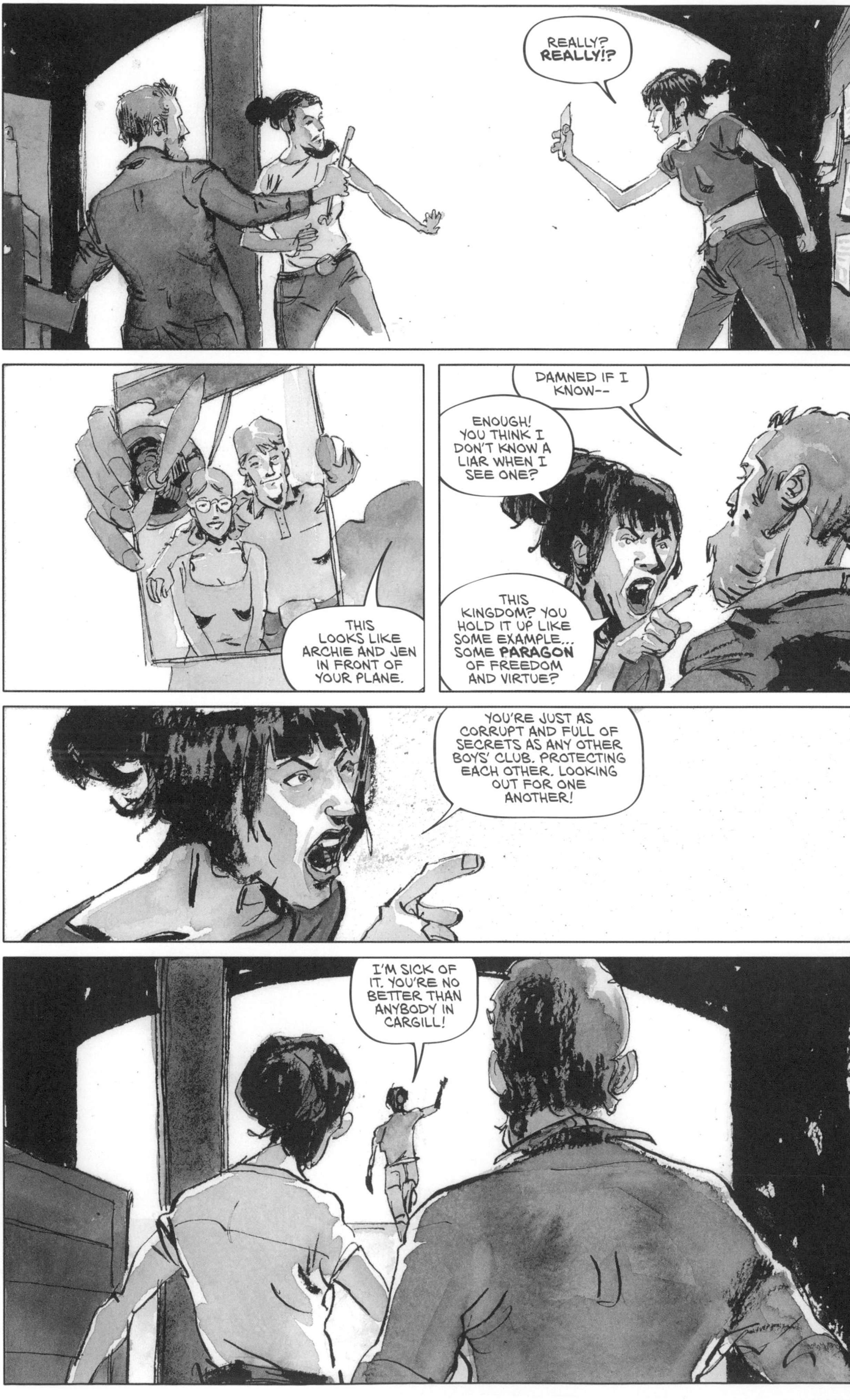
REALLY? **REALLY!?**
THIS LOOKS LIKE ARCHIE AND JEN IN FRONT OF YOUR PLANE.
DAMNED IF I KNOW--
ENOUGH! YOU THINK I DON'T KNOW A LIAR WHEN I SEE ONE?
THIS KINGDOM? YOU HOLD IT UP LIKE SOME EXAMPLE... SOME **PARAGON** OF FREEDOM AND VIRTUE?
YOU'RE JUST AS CORRUPT AND FULL OF SECRETS AS ANY OTHER BOYS' CLUB. PROTECTING EACH OTHER. LOOKING OUT FOR ONE ANOTHER!
I'M SICK OF IT. YOU'RE NO BETTER THAN ANYBODY IN CARGILL!

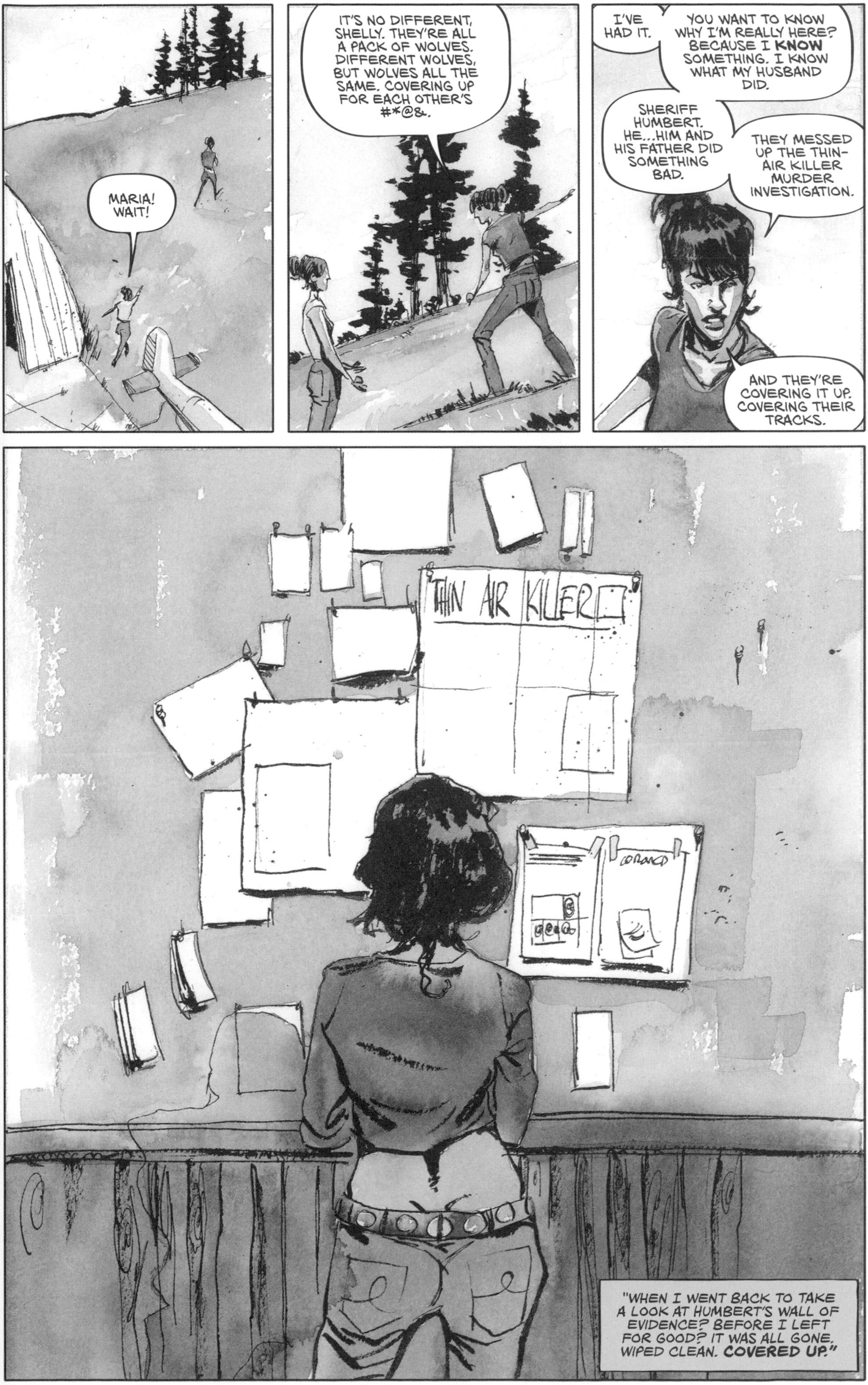
MARIA! WAIT!
IT'S NO DIFFERENT, SHELLY. THEY'RE ALL A PACK OF WOLVES. DIFFERENT WOLVES, BUT WOLVES ALL THE SAME. COVERING UP FOR EACH OTHER'S #*@&.
I'VE HAD IT.
YOU WANT TO KNOW WHY I'M REALLY HERE? BECAUSE I **KNOW** SOMETHING. I KNOW WHAT MY HUSBAND DID.
SHERIFF HUMBERT. HE...HIM AND HIS FATHER DID SOMETHING BAD.
THEY MESSED UP THE THIN-AIR KILLER MURDER INVESTIGATION.
AND THEY'RE COVERING IT UP. COVERING THEIR TRACKS.
THIN AIR KILLER
"WHEN I WENT BACK TO TAKE A LOOK AT HUMBERT'S WALL OF EVIDENCE? BEFORE I LEFT FOR GOOD? IT WAS ALL GONE. WIPED CLEAN. **COVERED UP.**"

I CAME HERE WITH A PURPOSE. TO USE THE GRASS KINGDOM AS A WEAPON TO TAKE DOWN HUMBERT. BUT NOW I SEE--YOU'RE ALL JUST AS CORRUPT.

YOU JUST LIVE ON A DIFFERENT SIDE OF THE LAKE. TRYING TO PROTECT WHAT'S YOURS AT ALL COSTS.

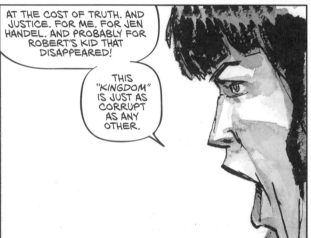

AT THE COST OF TRUTH. AND JUSTICE. FOR ME. FOR JEN HANDEL. AND PROBABLY FOR ROBERT'S KID THAT DISAPPEARED!

THIS "KINGDOM" IS JUST AS CORRUPT AS ANY OTHER.

MARIA! **LISTEN** TO ME. I'M NOT IN ON ANY OF THIS. THIS ISN'T ME! YOU HAVE TO BELIEVE THAT. COME ON.

I'M WITH YOU. WE'RE GONNA DO RIGHT HERE. WE'RE GONNA DO RIGHT BY JEN HANDEL.

AND WE'RE GONNA DO RIGHT BY YOU.

STARTING TONIGHT.

STARTING WITH ARCHIE. TONIGHT WE'RE GONNA GET TO THE BOTTOM OF IT. AND I NEED YOU AS BACKUP.

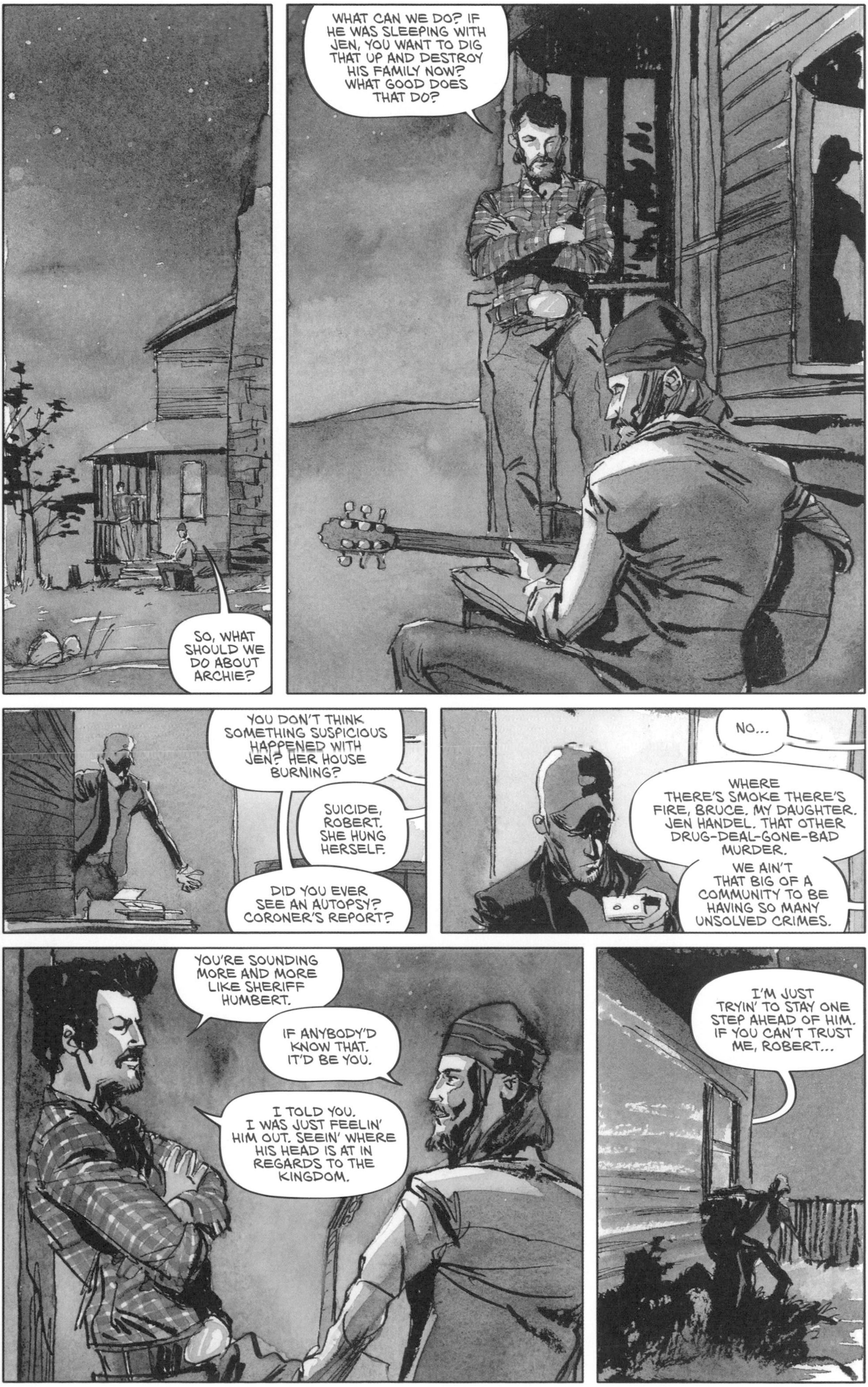
SO, WHAT SHOULD WE DO ABOUT ARCHIE?
WHAT CAN WE DO? IF HE WAS SLEEPING WITH JEN, YOU WANT TO DIG THAT UP AND DESTROY HIS FAMILY NOW? WHAT GOOD DOES THAT DO?
YOU DON'T THINK SOMETHING SUSPICIOUS HAPPENED WITH JEN? HER HOUSE BURNING?
SUICIDE, ROBERT. SHE HUNG HERSELF.
DID YOU EVER SEE AN AUTOPSY? CORONER'S REPORT?
NO...
WHERE THERE'S SMOKE THERE'S FIRE, BRUCE. MY DAUGHTER. JEN HANDEL. THAT OTHER DRUG-DEAL-GONE-BAD MURDER.
WE AIN'T THAT BIG OF A COMMUNITY TO BE HAVING SO MANY UNSOLVED CRIMES.
YOU'RE SOUNDING MORE AND MORE LIKE SHERIFF HUMBERT.
IF ANYBODY'D KNOW THAT, IT'D BE YOU.
I TOLD YOU. I WAS JUST FEELIN' HIM OUT. SEEIN' WHERE HIS HEAD IS AT IN REGARDS TO THE KINGDOM.
I'M JUST TRYIN' TO STAY ONE STEP AHEAD OF HIM. IF YOU CAN'T TRUST ME, ROBERT...

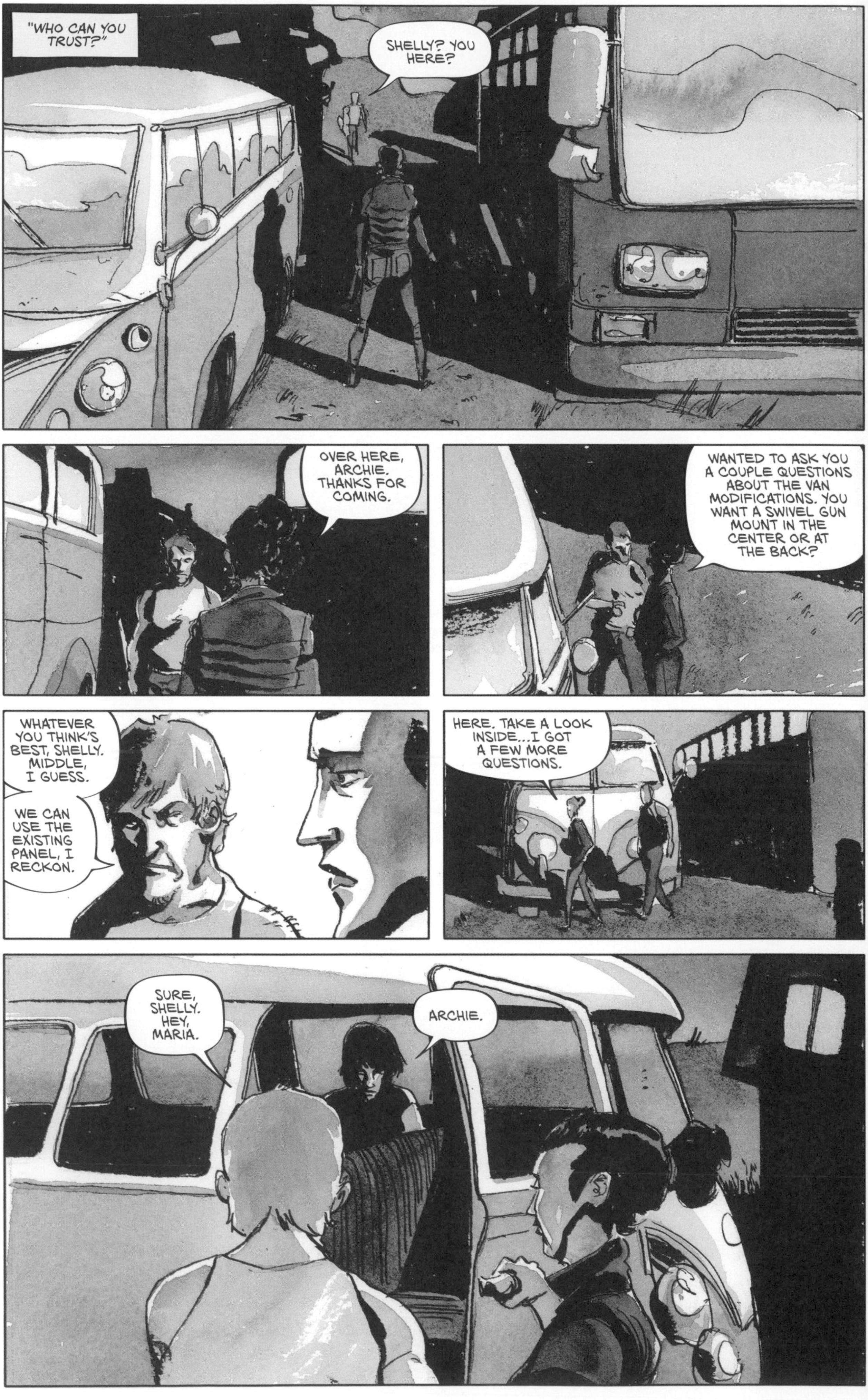
"WHO CAN YOU TRUST?"
SHELLY? YOU HERE?
OVER HERE, ARCHIE. THANKS FOR COMING.
WANTED TO ASK YOU A COUPLE QUESTIONS ABOUT THE VAN MODIFICATIONS. YOU WANT A SWIVEL GUN MOUNT IN THE CENTER OR AT THE BACK?
WHATEVER YOU THINK'S BEST, SHELLY. MIDDLE, I GUESS.
WE CAN USE THE EXISTING PANEL, I RECKON.
HERE. TAKE A LOOK INSIDE... I GOT A FEW MORE QUESTIONS.
SURE, SHELLY. HEY, MARIA.
ARCHIE.

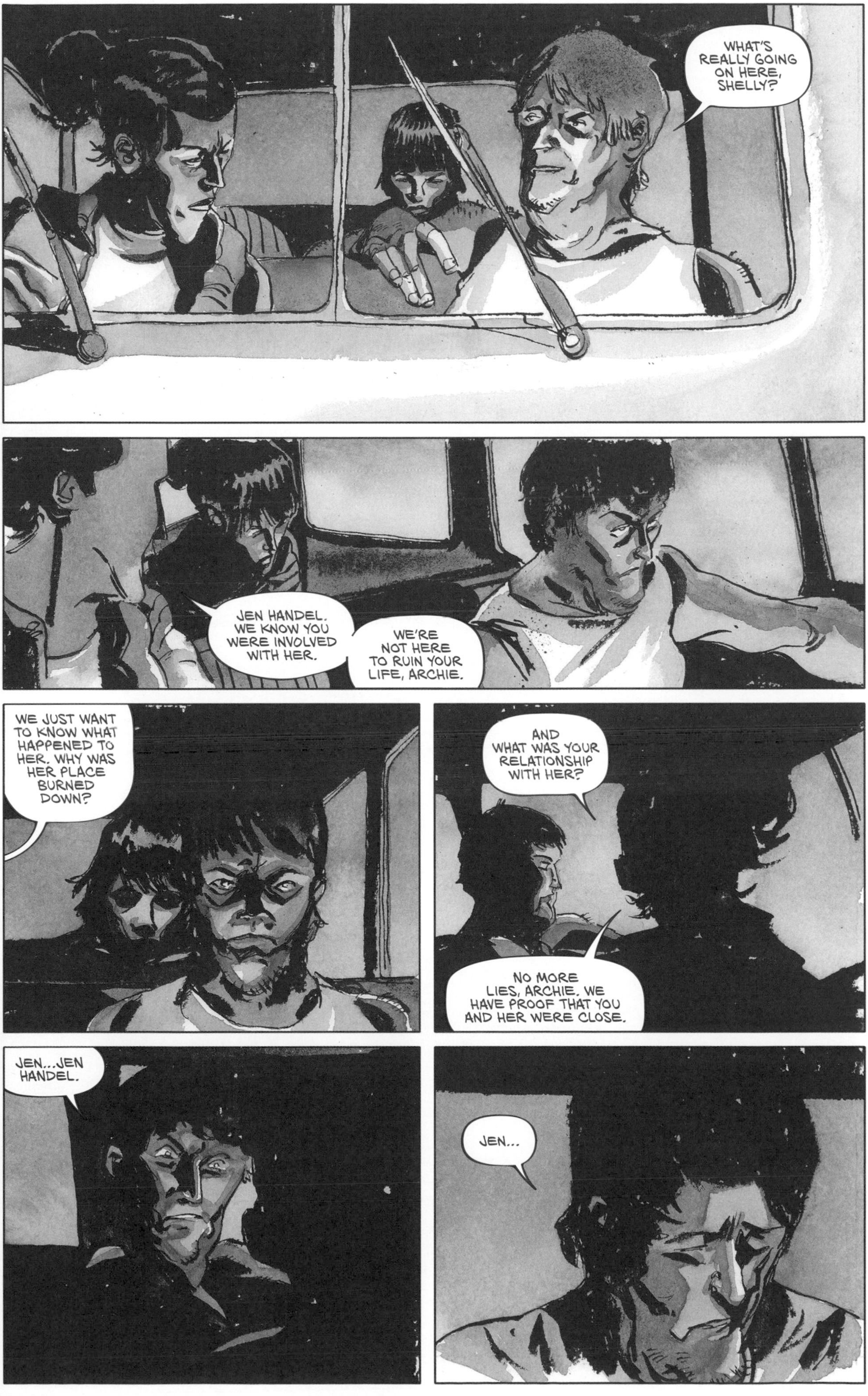
WHAT'S REALLY GOING ON HERE, SHELLY?
JEN HANDEL. WE KNOW YOU WERE INVOLVED WITH HER.
WE'RE NOT HERE TO RUIN YOUR LIFE, ARCHIE.
WE JUST WANT TO KNOW WHAT HAPPENED TO HER. WHY WAS HER PLACE BURNED DOWN?
AND WHAT WAS YOUR RELATIONSHIP WITH HER?
NO MORE LIES, ARCHIE. WE HAVE PROOF THAT YOU AND HER WERE CLOSE.
JEN...JEN HANDEL.
JEN...

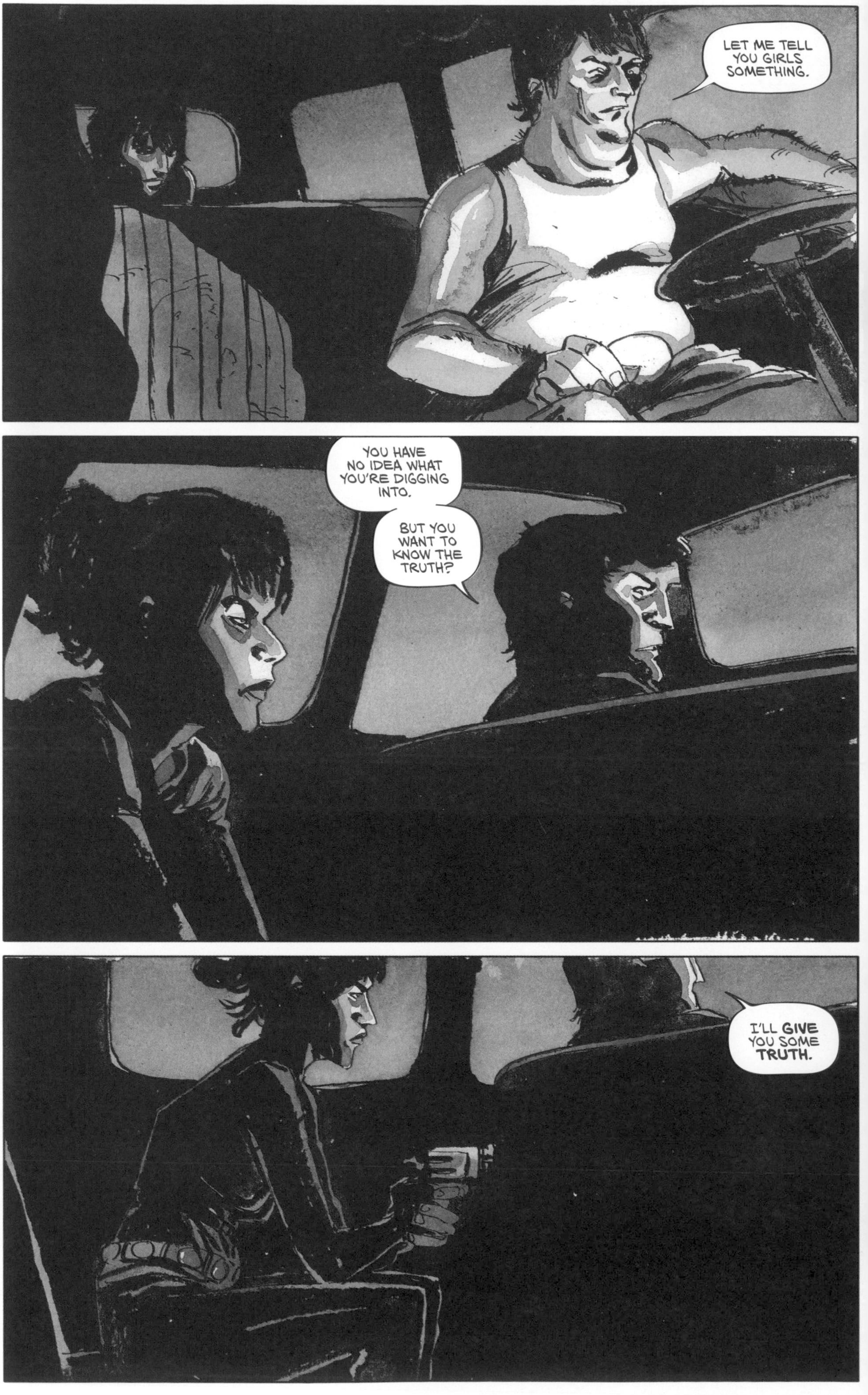
LET ME TELL YOU GIRLS SOMETHING.
YOU HAVE NO IDEA WHAT YOU'RE DIGGING INTO.
BUT YOU WANT TO KNOW THE TRUTH?
I'LL **GIVE** YOU SOME **TRUTH.**

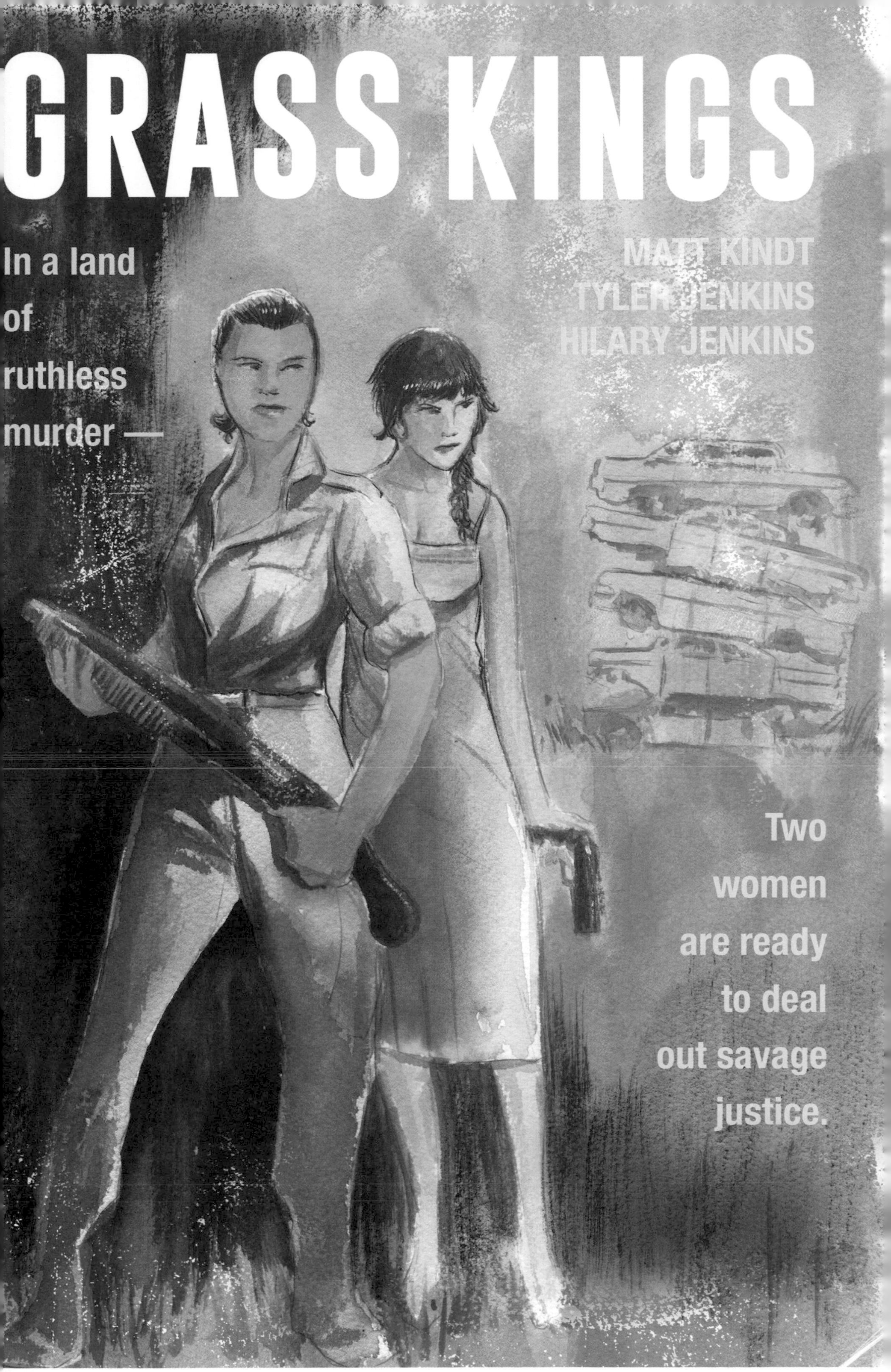
GRASS KINGS
In a land of ruthless murder —
MATT KINDT
TYLER JENKINS
HILARY JENKINS
Two women are ready to deal out savage justice.

issue #10 cover by matt kindt

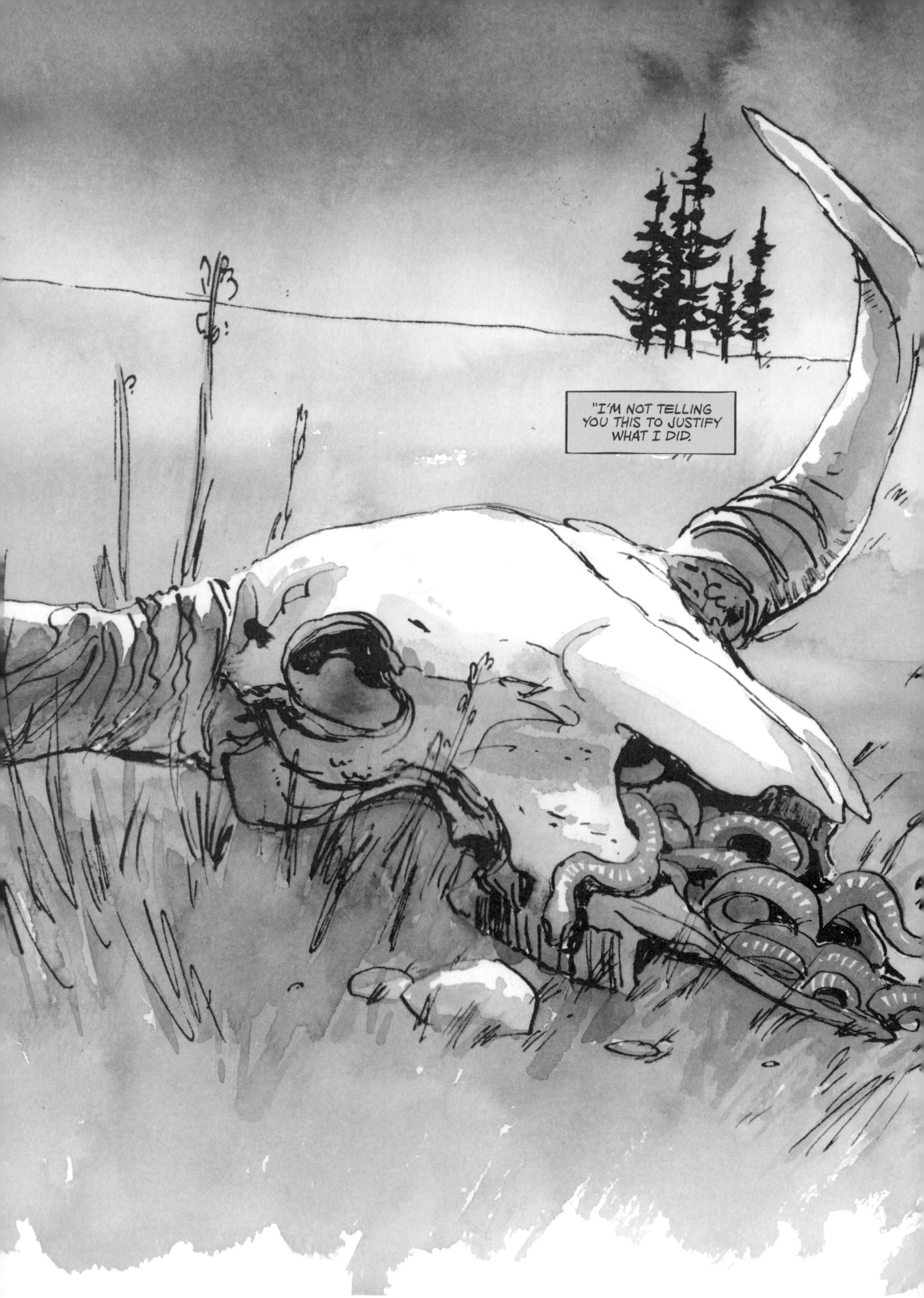
"I'M NOT TELLING YOU THIS TO JUSTIFY WHAT I DID.

chapter eleven

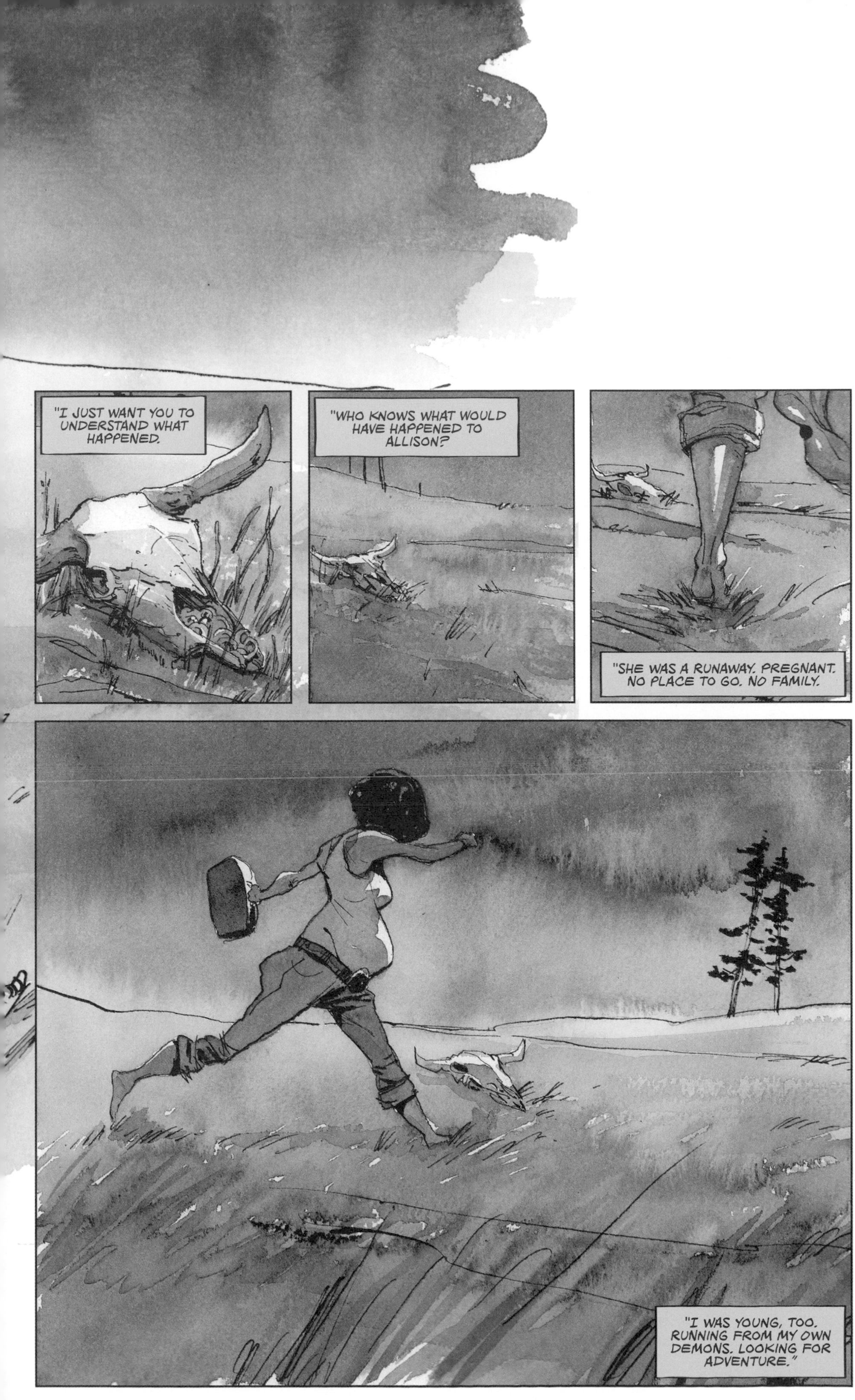
"I JUST WANT YOU TO UNDERSTAND WHAT HAPPENED.
"WHO KNOWS WHAT WOULD HAVE HAPPENED TO ALLISON?
"SHE WAS A RUNAWAY. PREGNANT. NO PLACE TO GO. NO FAMILY.
"I WAS YOUNG, TOO. RUNNING FROM MY OWN DEMONS. LOOKING FOR ADVENTURE."

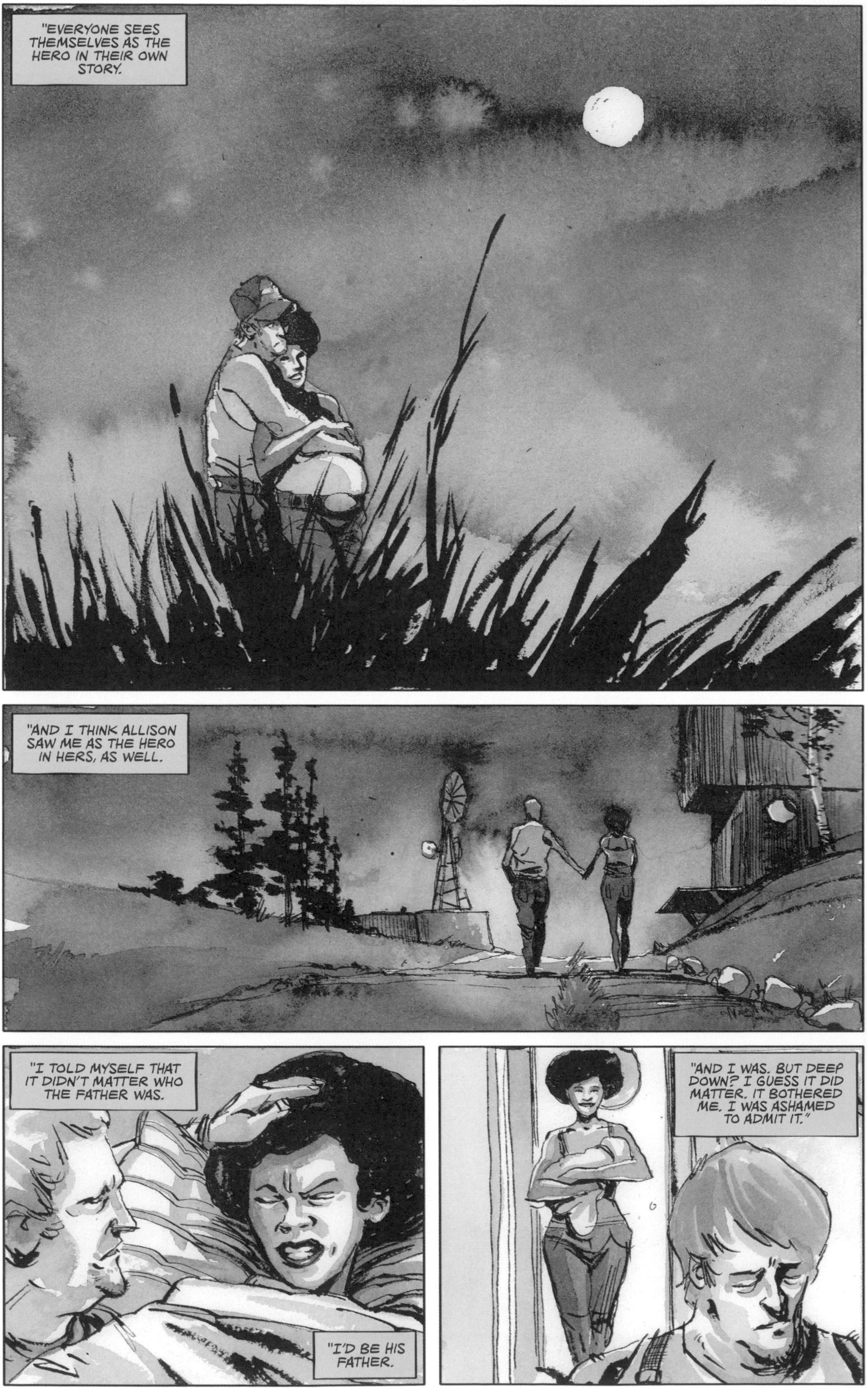
"EVERYONE SEES THEMSELVES AS THE HERO IN THEIR OWN STORY.
"AND I THINK ALLISON SAW ME AS THE HERO IN HERS, AS WELL.
"I TOLD MYSELF THAT IT DIDN'T MATTER WHO THE FATHER WAS.
"I'D BE HIS FATHER.
"AND I WAS. BUT DEEP DOWN? I GUESS IT DID MATTER. IT BOTHERED ME. I WAS ASHAMED TO ADMIT IT."

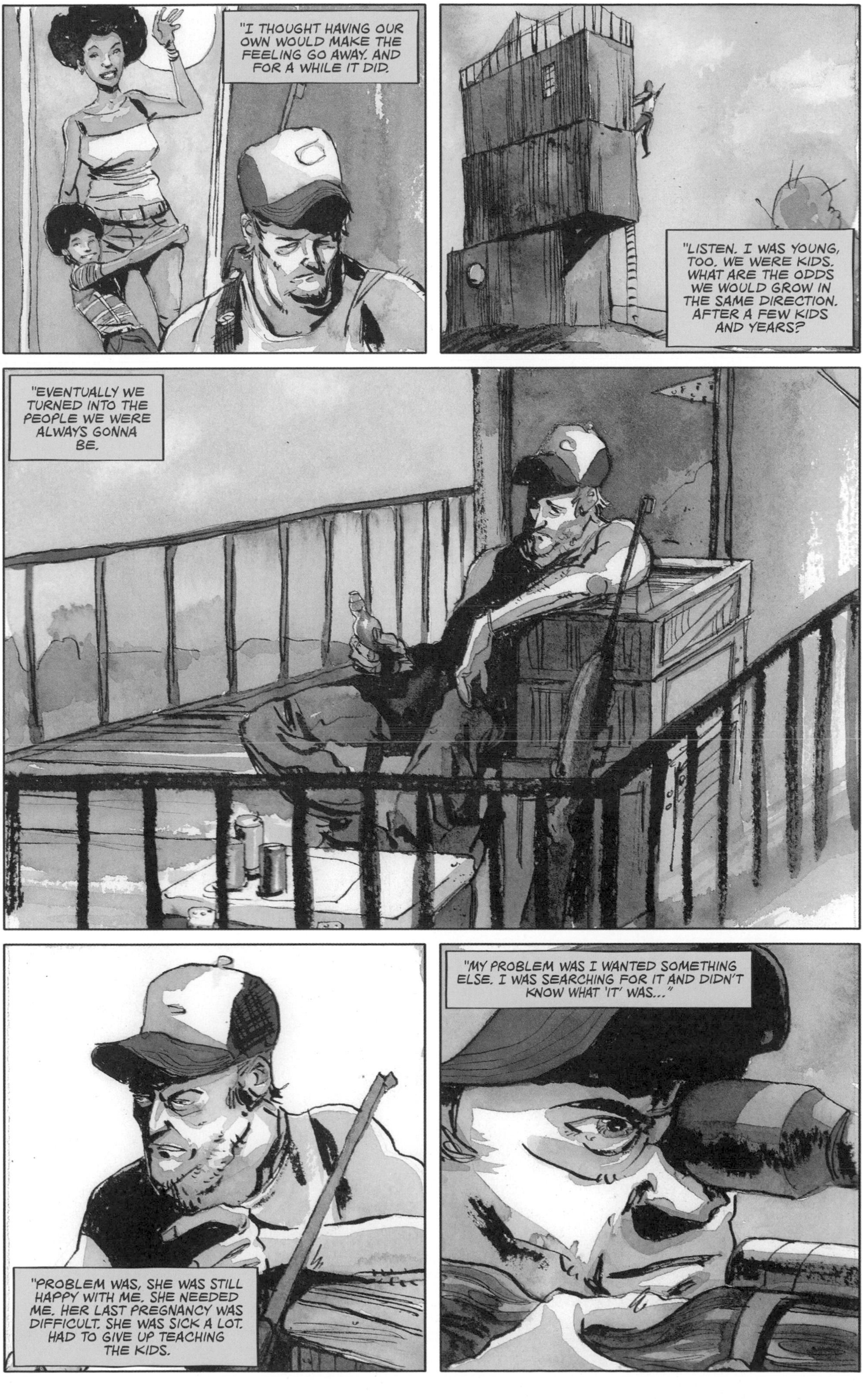
"I THOUGHT HAVING OUR OWN WOULD MAKE THE FEELING GO AWAY. AND FOR A WHILE IT DID.
"LISTEN. I WAS YOUNG, TOO. WE WERE KIDS. WHAT ARE THE ODDS WE WOULD GROW IN THE SAME DIRECTION. AFTER A FEW KIDS AND YEARS?
"EVENTUALLY WE TURNED INTO THE PEOPLE WE WERE ALWAYS GONNA BE.
"PROBLEM WAS, SHE WAS STILL HAPPY WITH ME. SHE NEEDED ME. HER LAST PREGNANCY WAS DIFFICULT. SHE WAS SICK A LOT. HAD TO GIVE UP TEACHING THE KIDS.
"MY PROBLEM WAS I WANTED SOMETHING ELSE. I WAS SEARCHING FOR IT AND DIDN'T KNOW WHAT 'IT' WAS..."

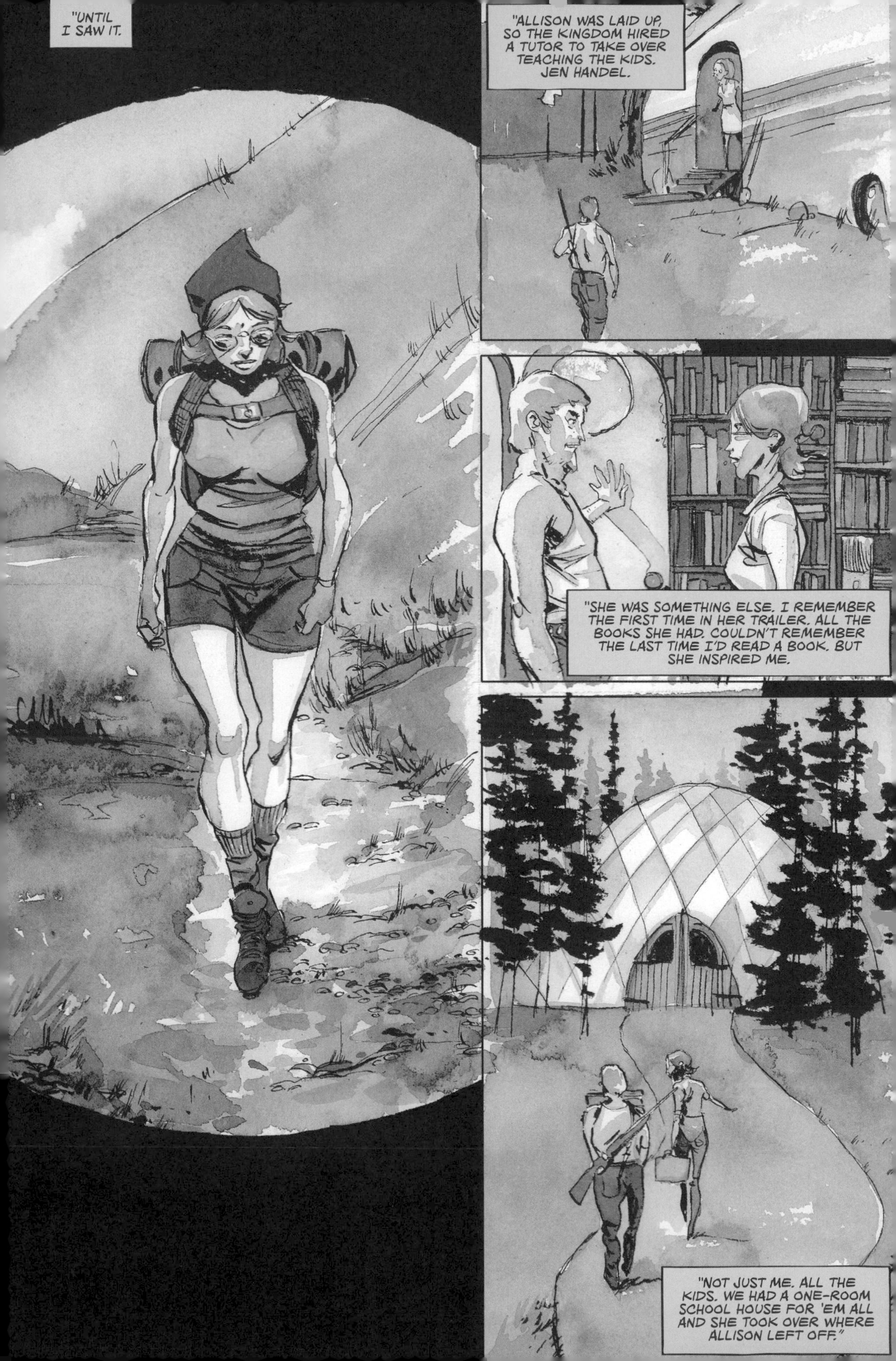
"UNTIL I SAW IT.
"ALLISON WAS LAID UP, SO THE KINGDOM HIRED A TUTOR TO TAKE OVER TEACHING THE KIDS. JEN HANDEL.
"SHE WAS SOMETHING ELSE. I REMEMBER THE FIRST TIME IN HER TRAILER. ALL THE BOOKS SHE HAD. COULDN'T REMEMBER THE LAST TIME I'D READ A BOOK. BUT SHE INSPIRED ME.
"NOT JUST ME. ALL THE KIDS. WE HAD A ONE-ROOM SCHOOL HOUSE FOR 'EM ALL AND SHE TOOK OVER WHERE ALLISON LEFT OFF."

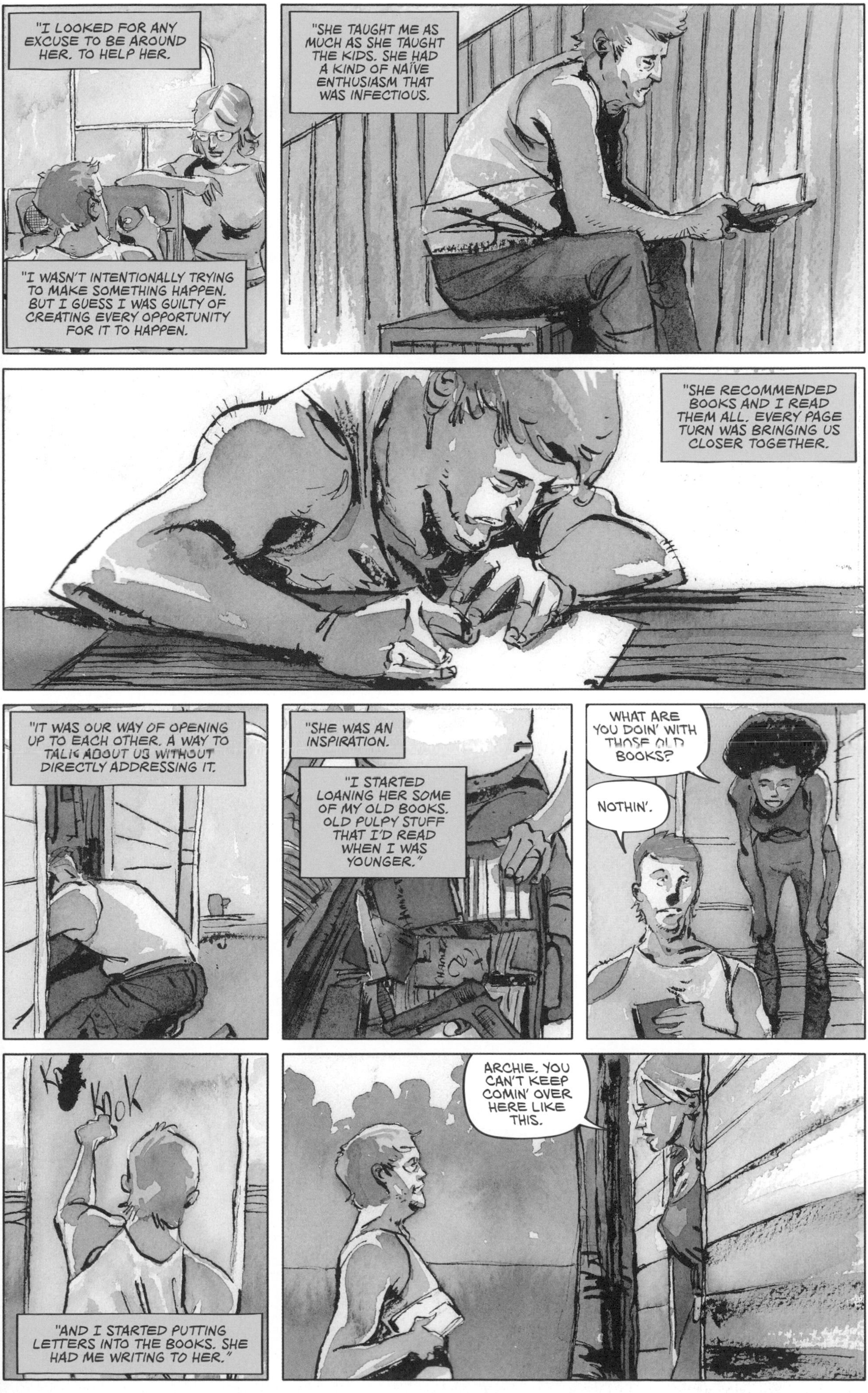
"I LOOKED FOR ANY EXCUSE TO BE AROUND HER. TO HELP HER.
"I WASN'T INTENTIONALLY TRYING TO MAKE SOMETHING HAPPEN. BUT I GUESS I WAS GUILTY OF CREATING EVERY OPPORTUNITY FOR IT TO HAPPEN.
"SHE TAUGHT ME AS MUCH AS SHE TAUGHT THE KIDS. SHE HAD A KIND OF NAÏVE ENTHUSIASM THAT WAS INFECTIOUS.
"SHE RECOMMENDED BOOKS AND I READ THEM ALL. EVERY PAGE TURN WAS BRINGING US CLOSER TOGETHER.
"IT WAS OUR WAY OF OPENING UP TO EACH OTHER. A WAY TO TALK ABOUT US WITHOUT DIRECTLY ADDRESSING IT.
"SHE WAS AN INSPIRATION.
"I STARTED LOANING HER SOME OF MY OLD BOOKS. OLD PULPY STUFF THAT I'D READ WHEN I WAS YOUNGER."
WHAT ARE YOU DOIN' WITH THOSE OLD BOOKS?
NOTHIN'.
KNOK
"AND I STARTED PUTTING LETTERS INTO THE BOOKS. SHE HAD ME WRITING TO HER."
ARCHIE. YOU CAN'T KEEP COMIN' OVER HERE LIKE THIS.

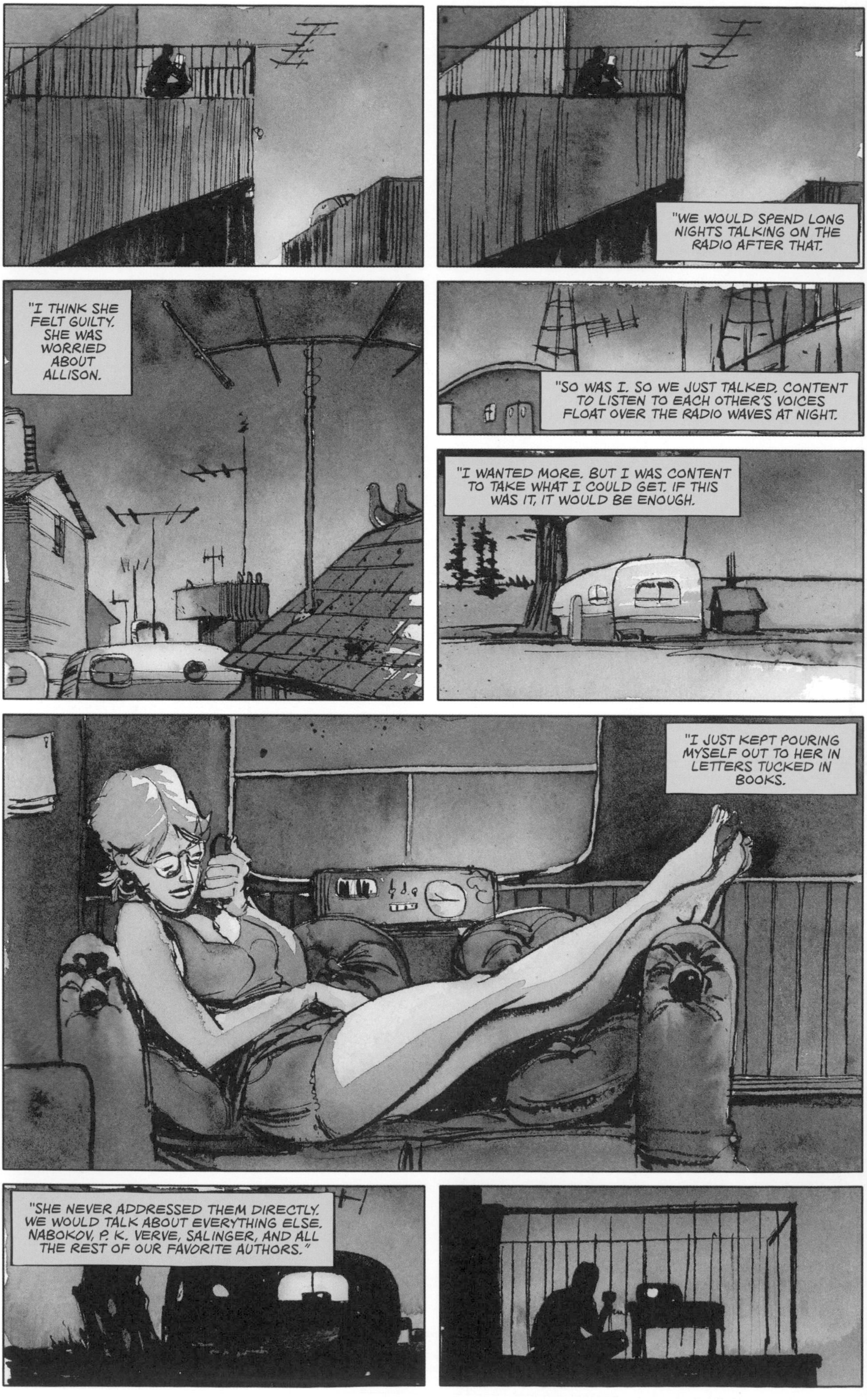
"WE WOULD SPEND LONG NIGHTS TALKING ON THE RADIO AFTER THAT.
"I THINK SHE FELT GUILTY. SHE WAS WORRIED ABOUT ALLISON.
"SO WAS I. SO WE JUST TALKED. CONTENT TO LISTEN TO EACH OTHER'S VOICES FLOAT OVER THE RADIO WAVES AT NIGHT.
"I WANTED MORE. BUT I WAS CONTENT TO TAKE WHAT I COULD GET. IF THIS WAS IT, IT WOULD BE ENOUGH.
"I JUST KEPT POURING MYSELF OUT TO HER IN LETTERS TUCKED IN BOOKS.
"SHE NEVER ADDRESSED THEM DIRECTLY. WE WOULD TALK ABOUT EVERYTHING ELSE. NABOKOV, P. K. VERVE, SALINGER, AND ALL THE REST OF OUR FAVORITE AUTHORS."

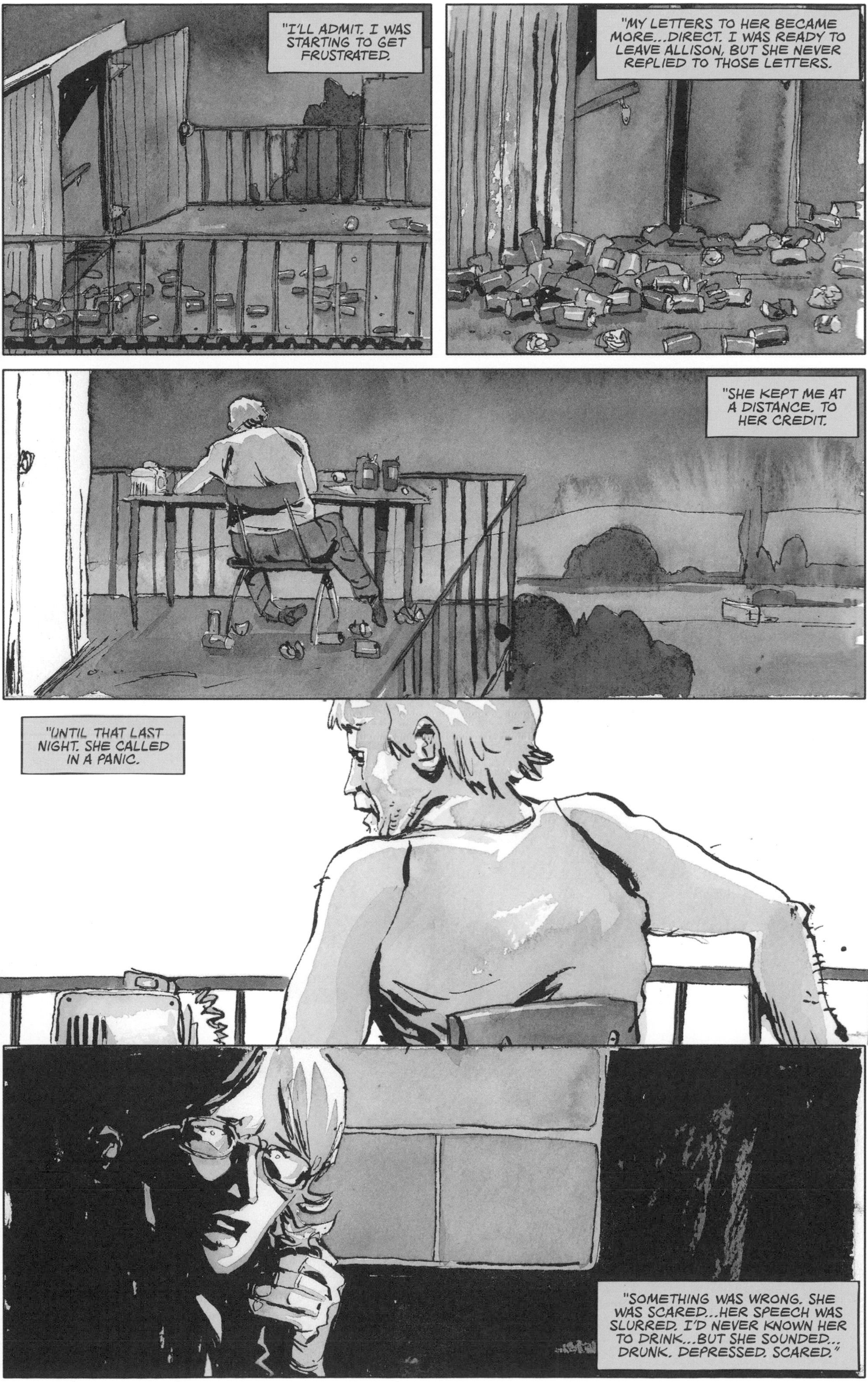
"I'LL ADMIT. I WAS STARTING TO GET FRUSTRATED.
"MY LETTERS TO HER BECAME MORE...DIRECT. I WAS READY TO LEAVE ALLISON, BUT SHE NEVER REPLIED TO THOSE LETTERS.
"SHE KEPT ME AT A DISTANCE. TO HER CREDIT.
"UNTIL THAT LAST NIGHT. SHE CALLED IN A PANIC.
"SOMETHING WAS WRONG. SHE WAS SCARED...HER SPEECH WAS SLURRED. I'D NEVER KNOWN HER TO DRINK...BUT SHE SOUNDED... DRUNK. DEPRESSED. SCARED."

"I WAS DRUNK OFF MY ASS ALREADY. BARELY REMEMBER THAT NIGHT AT ALL.

"NOT SURE HOW LONG I BLACKED OUT FOR..."

"I WAS DRUNK OFF MY ASS ALREADY. BARELY REMEMBER THAT NIGHT AT ALL.

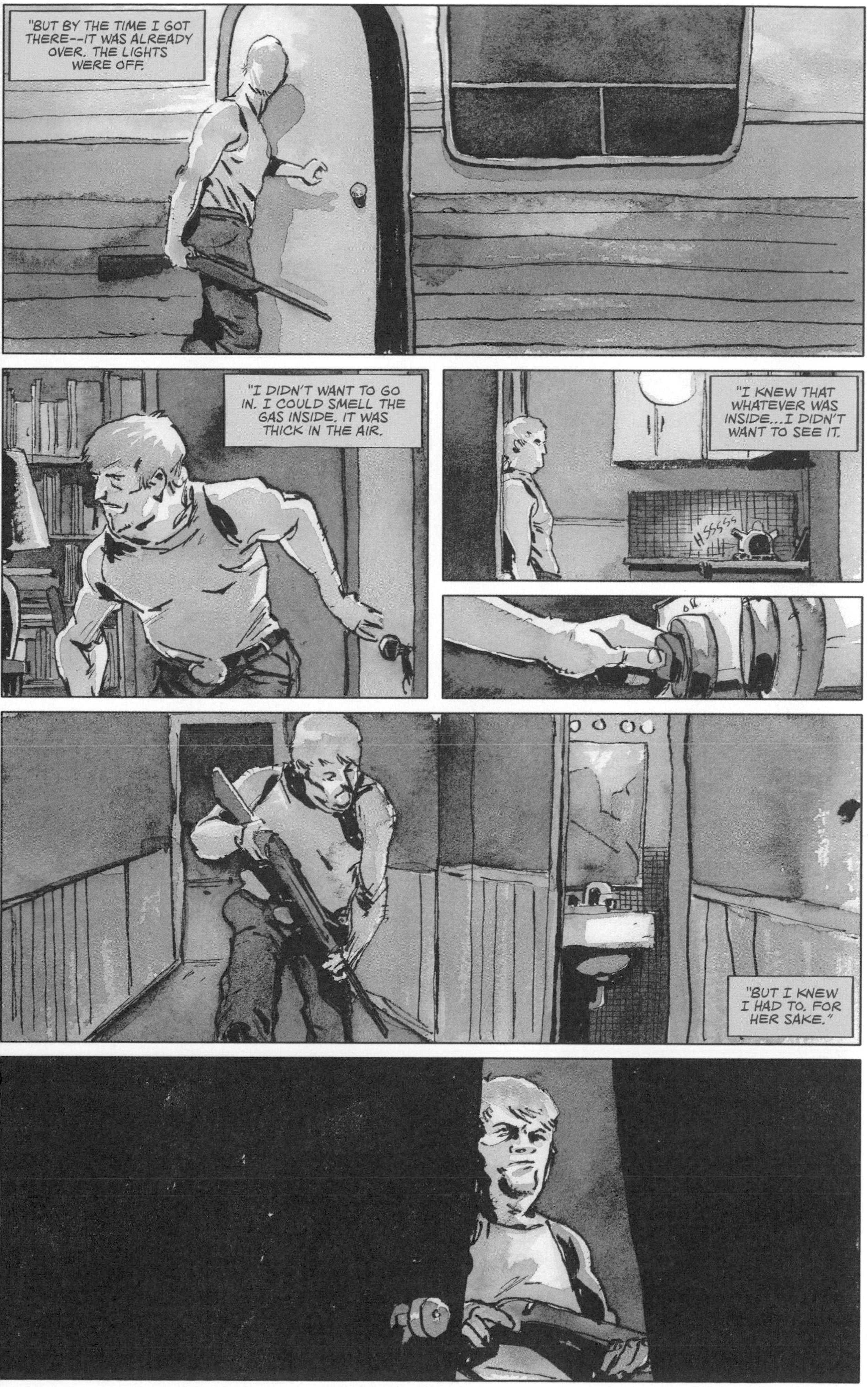
"BUT BY THE TIME I GOT THERE--IT WAS ALREADY OVER. THE LIGHTS WERE OFF.
"I DIDN'T WANT TO GO IN. I COULD SMELL THE GAS INSIDE. IT WAS THICK IN THE AIR.
"I KNEW THAT WHATEVER WAS INSIDE...I DIDN'T WANT TO SEE IT.
HSSSSS
"BUT I KNEW I HAD TO. FOR HER SAKE."

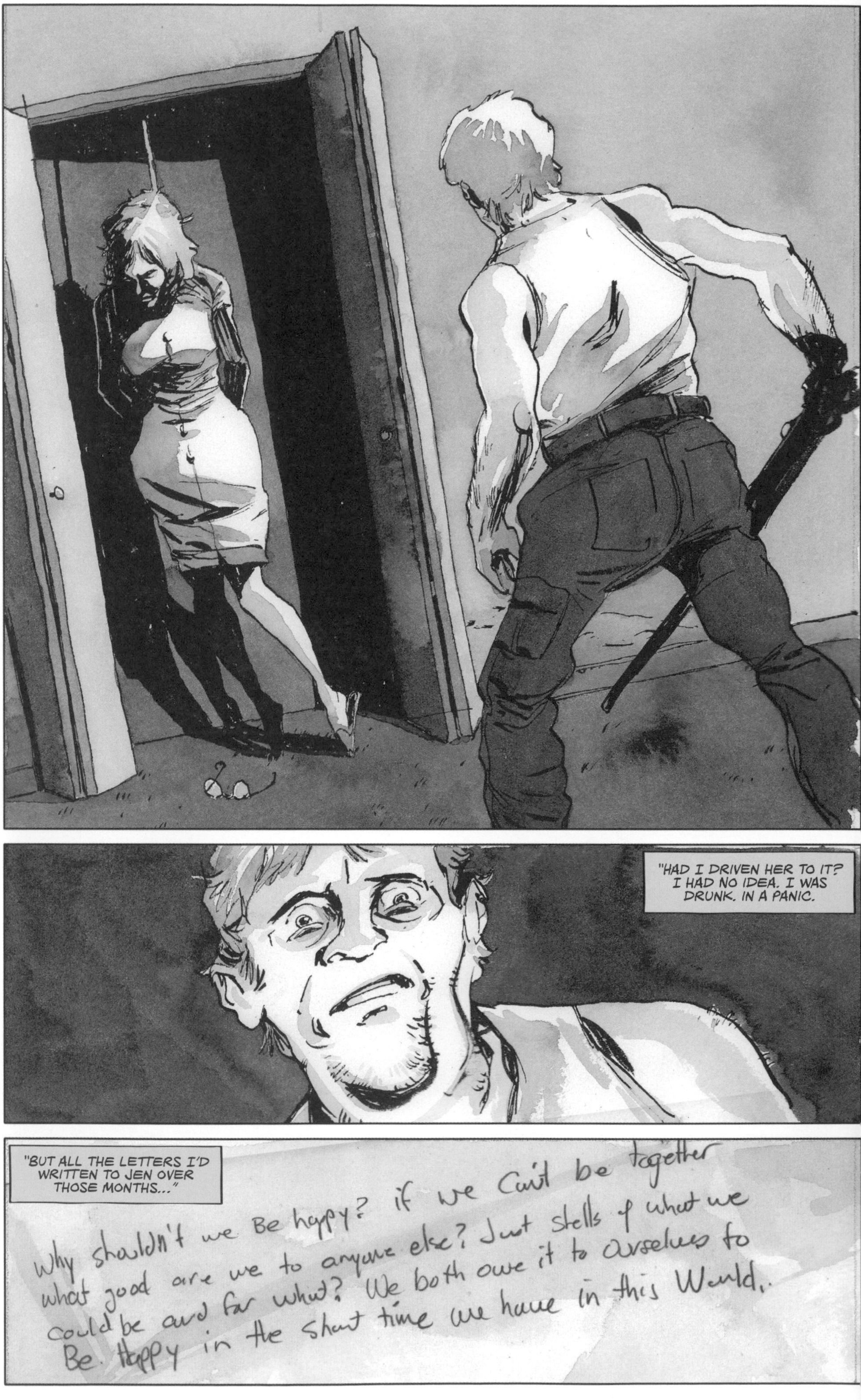
"HAD I DRIVEN HER TO IT? I HAD NO IDEA. I WAS DRUNK. IN A PANIC.
"BUT ALL THE LETTERS I'D WRITTEN TO JEN OVER THOSE MONTHS..."
if we Can't be together
why shouldn't we Be happy? Just shells of what we
what good are we to anyone else? We both owe it to ourselves to
could be and for what? in this World..
Be. Happy in the short time we have

"I SAW THE DOOR OF OUR LIVES TOGETHER SLAMMED SHUT. AND THE ONLY PATH LEFT FOR ME WAS ALLISON.

"WHAT HAD SHE DONE WITH THEM?

"I'D WRITTEN HUNDREDS OF LETTERS.

"IF ANYONE FOUND OUT, IT WOULD WRECK ALLISON. OUR LIFE. OUR KIDS.

"I PANICKED. I WAS DRUNK. I..."

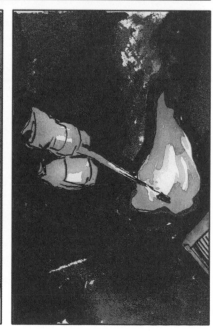

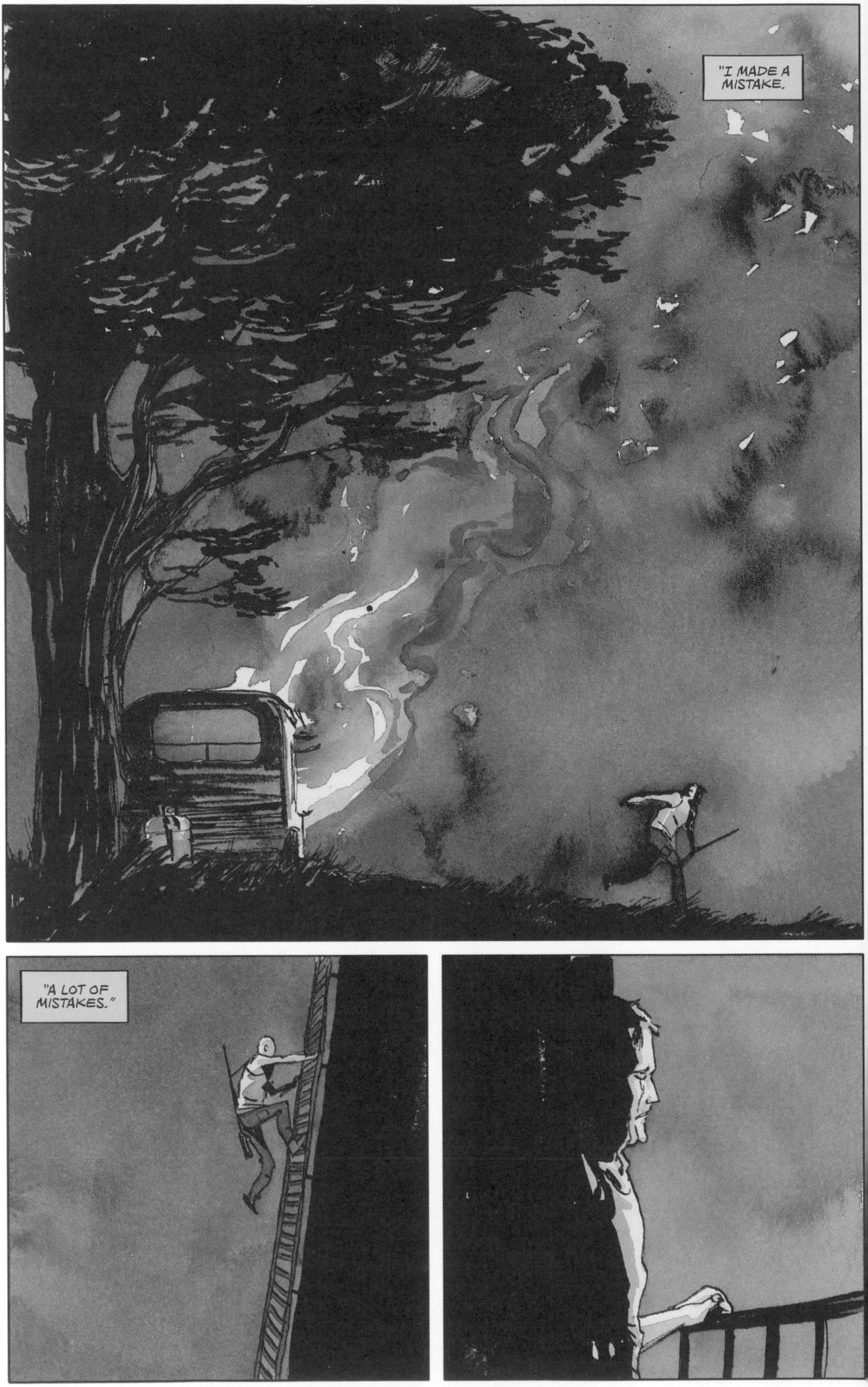
"I MADE A MISTAKE.
"A LOT OF MISTAKES."

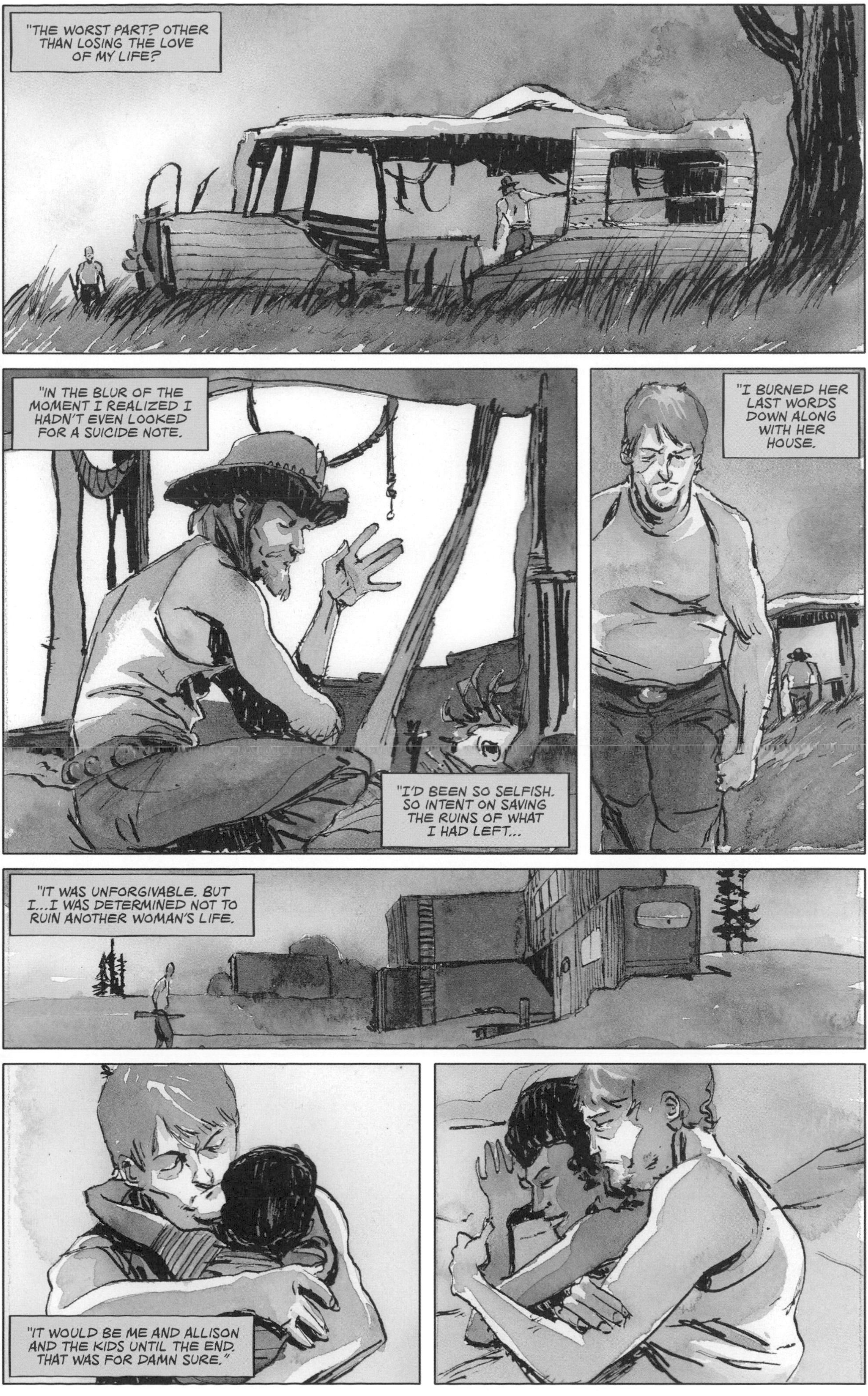
"THE WORST PART? OTHER THAN LOSING THE LOVE OF MY LIFE?
"IN THE BLUR OF THE MOMENT I REALIZED I HADN'T EVEN LOOKED FOR A SUICIDE NOTE.
"I'D BEEN SO SELFISH. SO INTENT ON SAVING THE RUINS OF WHAT I HAD LEFT...
"I BURNED HER LAST WORDS DOWN ALONG WITH HER HOUSE.
"IT WAS UNFORGIVABLE. BUT I...I WAS DETERMINED NOT TO RUIN ANOTHER WOMAN'S LIFE.
"IT WOULD BE ME AND ALLISON AND THE KIDS UNTIL THE END. THAT WAS FOR DAMN SURE."

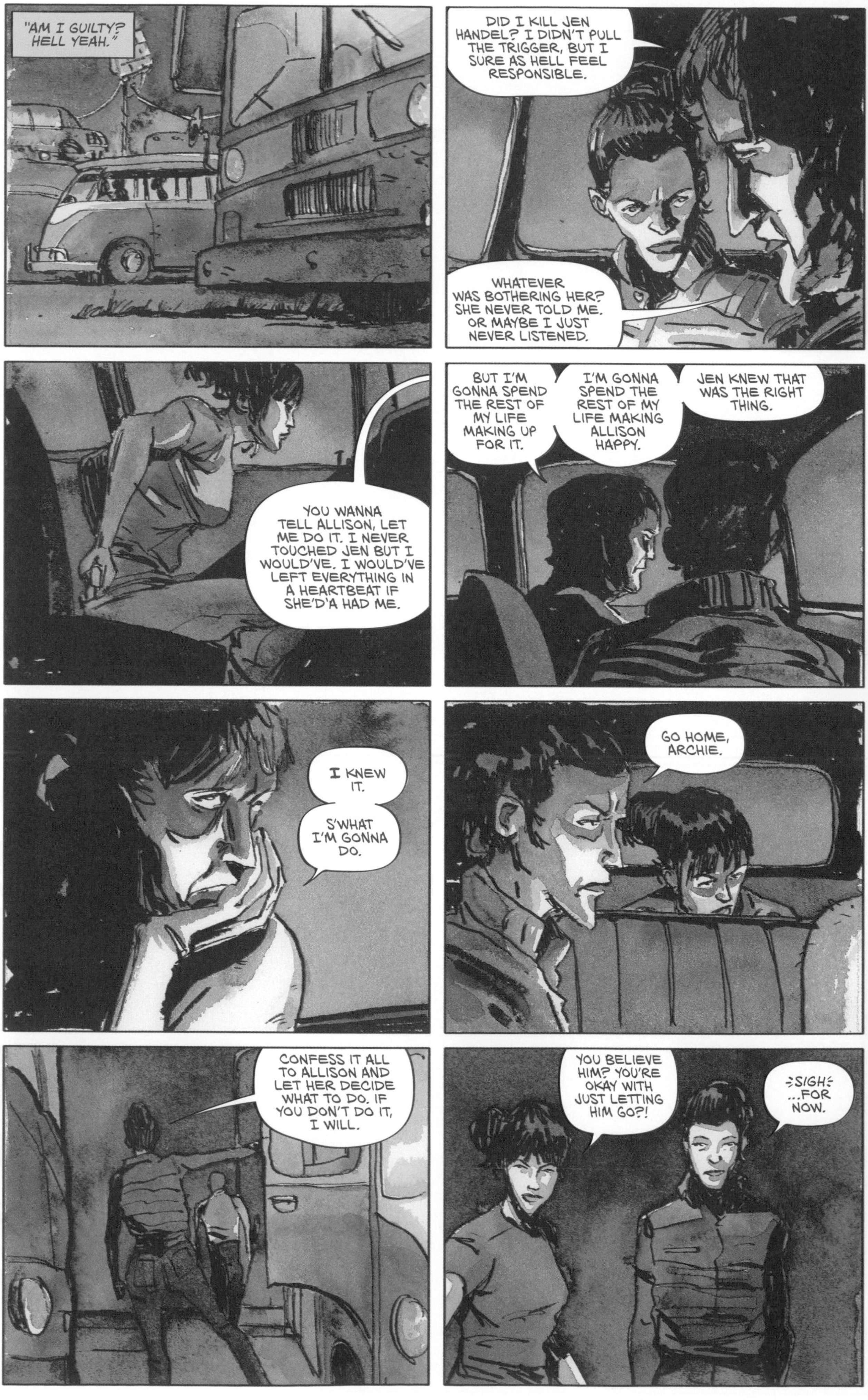
"AM I GUILTY? HELL YEAH."
DID I KILL JEN HANDEL? I DIDN'T PULL THE TRIGGER, BUT I SURE AS HELL FEEL RESPONSIBLE.
WHATEVER WAS BOTHERING HER? SHE NEVER TOLD ME. OR MAYBE I JUST NEVER LISTENED.
YOU WANNA TELL ALLISON, LET ME DO IT. I NEVER TOUCHED JEN BUT I WOULD'VE. I WOULD'VE LEFT EVERYTHING IN A HEARTBEAT IF SHE'D'A HAD ME.
BUT I'M GONNA SPEND THE REST OF MY LIFE MAKING UP FOR IT.
I'M GONNA SPEND THE REST OF MY LIFE MAKING ALLISON HAPPY.
JEN KNEW THAT WAS THE RIGHT THING.
I KNEW IT.
S'WHAT I'M GONNA DO.
GO HOME, ARCHIE.
CONFESS IT ALL TO ALLISON AND LET HER DECIDE WHAT TO DO. IF YOU DON'T DO IT, I WILL.
YOU BELIEVE HIM? YOU'RE OKAY WITH JUST LETTING HIM GO?!
SIGH ...FOR NOW.

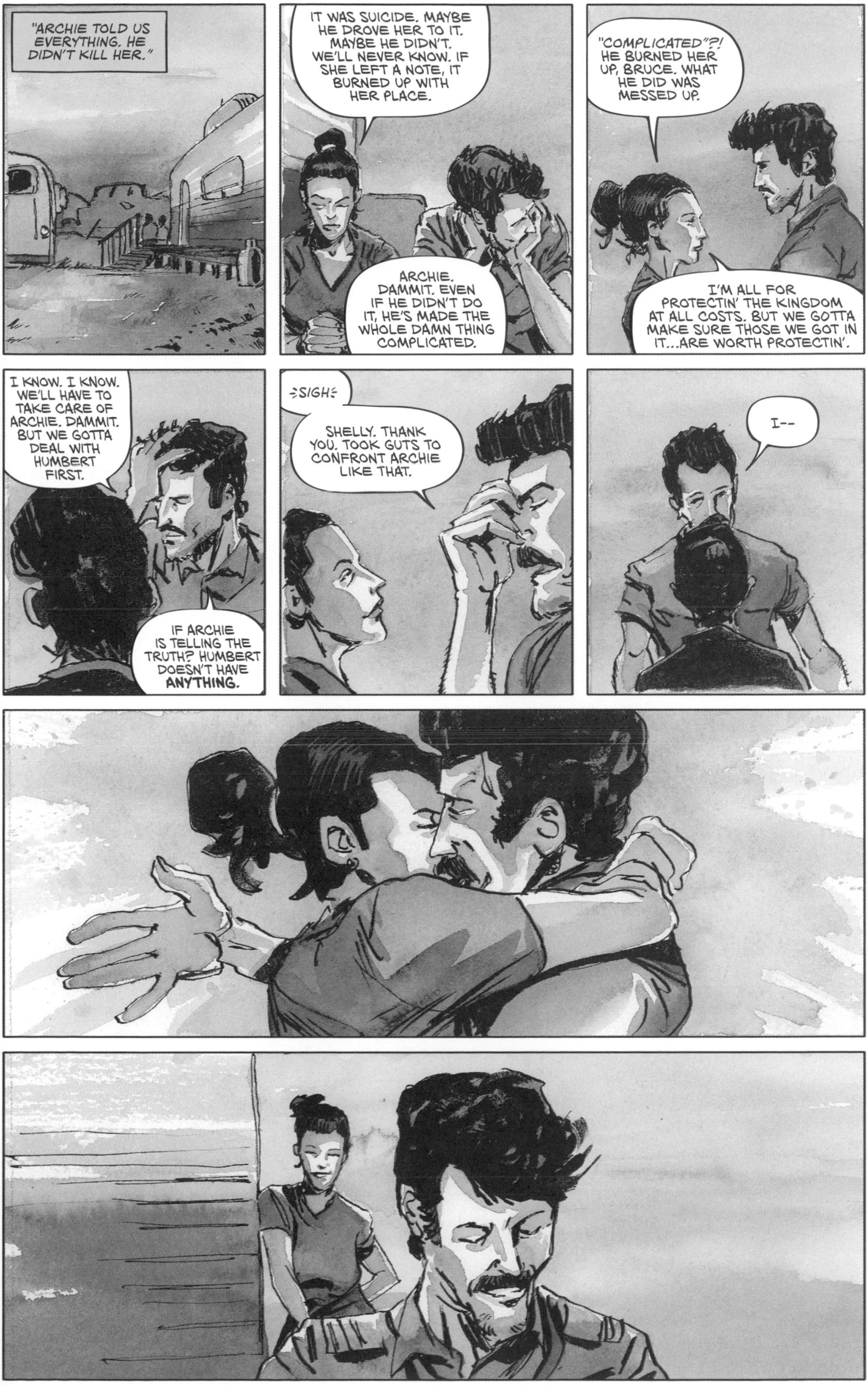
"ARCHIE TOLD US EVERYTHING. HE DIDN'T KILL HER."
IT WAS SUICIDE. MAYBE HE DROVE HER TO IT. MAYBE HE DIDN'T. WE'LL NEVER KNOW. IF SHE LEFT A NOTE, IT BURNED UP WITH HER PLACE.
ARCHIE. DAMMIT. EVEN IF HE DIDN'T DO IT, HE'S MADE THE WHOLE DAMN THING COMPLICATED.
"COMPLICATED"?! HE BURNED HER UP, BRUCE. WHAT HE DID WAS MESSED UP.
I'M ALL FOR PROTECTIN' THE KINGDOM AT ALL COSTS. BUT WE GOTTA MAKE SURE THOSE WE GOT IN IT...ARE WORTH PROTECTIN'.
I KNOW. I KNOW. WE'LL HAVE TO TAKE CARE OF ARCHIE. DAMMIT. BUT WE GOTTA DEAL WITH HUMBERT FIRST.
IF ARCHIE IS TELLING THE TRUTH? HUMBERT DOESN'T HAVE **ANYTHING.**
SIGH
SHELLY. THANK YOU. TOOK GUTS TO CONFRONT ARCHIE LIKE THAT.
I--

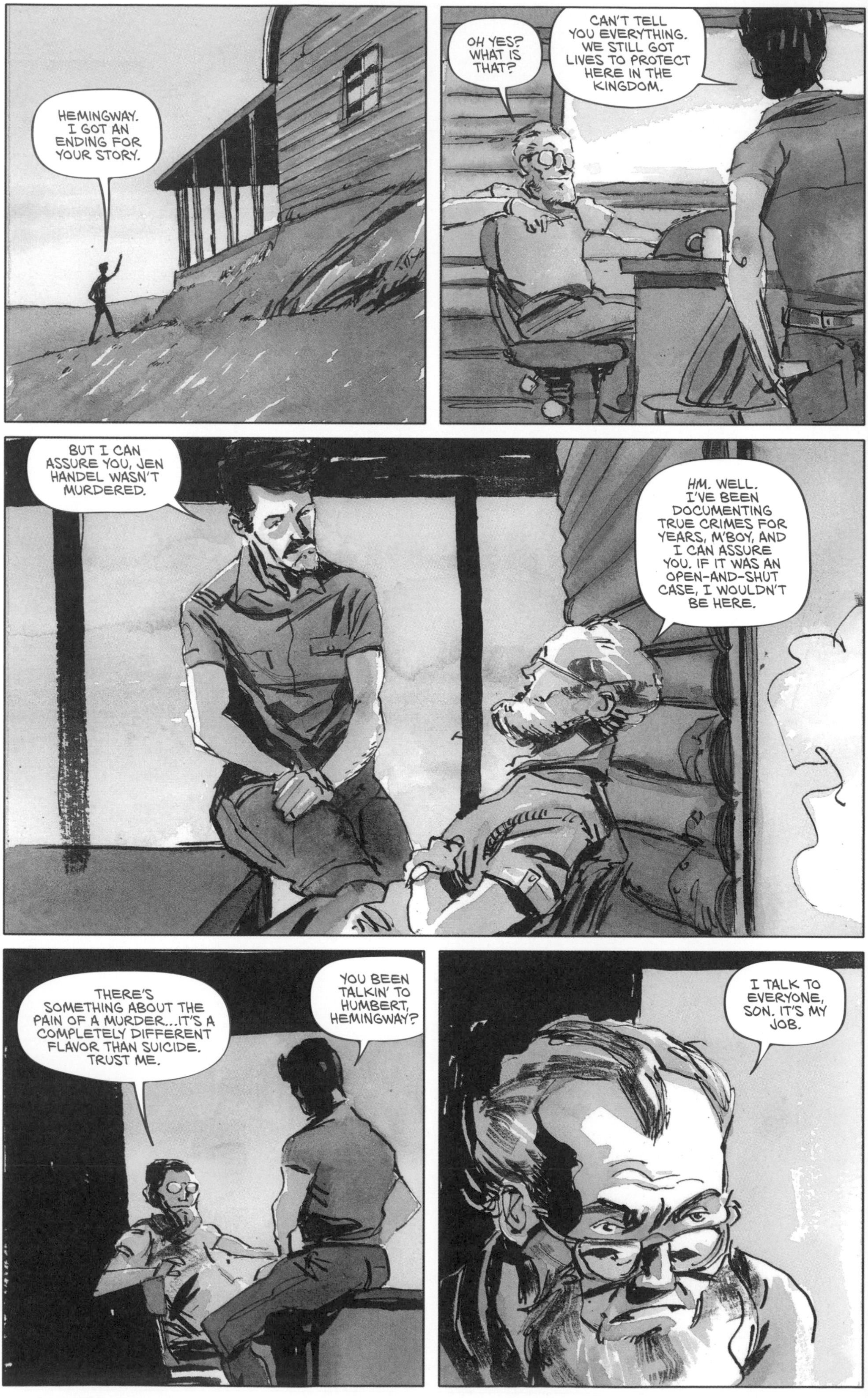
HEMINGWAY. I GOT AN ENDING FOR YOUR STORY.
OH YES? WHAT IS THAT?
CAN'T TELL YOU EVERYTHING. WE STILL GOT LIVES TO PROTECT HERE IN THE KINGDOM.
BUT I CAN ASSURE YOU, JEN HANDEL WASN'T MURDERED.
HM. WELL. I'VE BEEN DOCUMENTING TRUE CRIMES FOR YEARS, M'BOY, AND I CAN ASSURE YOU. IF IT WAS AN OPEN-AND-SHUT CASE, I WOULDN'T BE HERE.
THERE'S SOMETHING ABOUT THE PAIN OF A MURDER...IT'S A COMPLETELY DIFFERENT FLAVOR THAN SUICIDE. TRUST ME.
YOU BEEN TALKIN' TO HUMBERT, HEMINGWAY?
I TALK TO EVERYONE, SON. IT'S MY JOB.

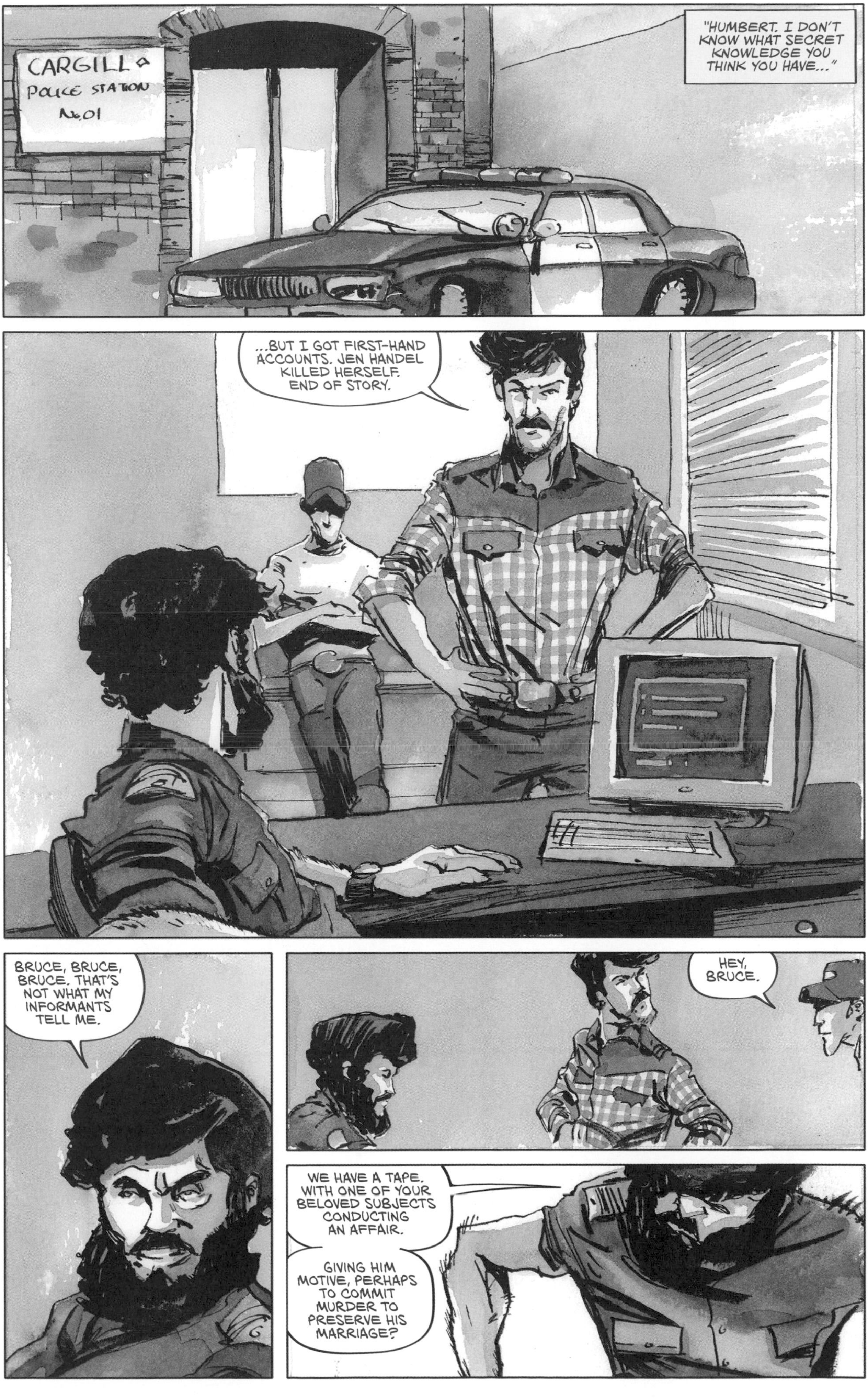
CARGILL
POLICE STATION
No.01
"HUMBERT. I DON'T KNOW WHAT SECRET KNOWLEDGE YOU THINK YOU HAVE..."
...BUT I GOT FIRST-HAND ACCOUNTS. JEN HANDEL KILLED HERSELF. END OF STORY.
BRUCE, BRUCE, BRUCE. THAT'S NOT WHAT MY INFORMANTS TELL ME.
HEY, BRUCE.
WE HAVE A TAPE. WITH ONE OF YOUR BELOVED SUBJECTS CONDUCTING AN AFFAIR.
GIVING HIM MOTIVE, PERHAPS TO COMMIT MURDER TO PRESERVE HIS MARRIAGE?

YOU'RE TALKING ABOUT ARCHIE? WE KNEW ABOUT THAT, HUMBERT. **HOWEVER** YOU GOT THAT TAPE, IT DOESN'T MATTER.

HE WENT OVER THERE TO HELP HER. SHE WAS UPSET. SHE WAS DEAD WHEN HE GOT THERE.

HE PANICKED. THOUGHT SOME OF HIS LETTERS HE WROTE HER MIGHT BE FOUND, SO HE COVERED IT UP.

HA. HA. HA.

LET ME STOP YOU RIGHT THERE. YOU EVER SEE THE **CORONER'S** REPORT?

OF COURSE YOU DIDN'T. YOU DON'T **HAVE** A CORONER. BUT CARGILL DOES. AND WE CONDUCTED AN AUTOPSY.

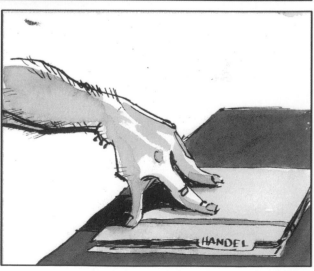

HANDEL

JEN HANDEL'S BODY WAS BURNED.
CAUSE OF DEATH WAS PROBABLY STRANGULATION. BUT TELL ME THIS...
...HOW YOU GONNA EXPLAIN THE **PLASTIC ZIP-TIES** THAT WERE MELTED INTO HER WRISTS? HOW SHE KILL HERSELF WITH HER HANDS TIED BEHIND HER BACK?

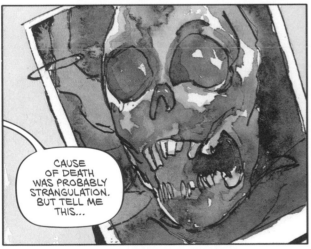

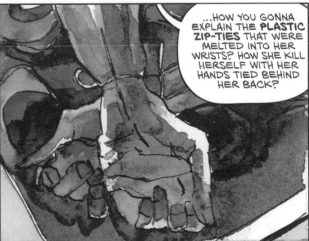

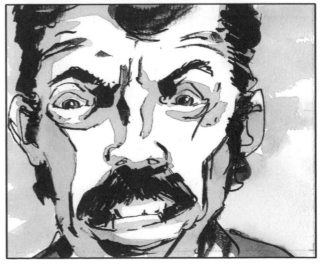

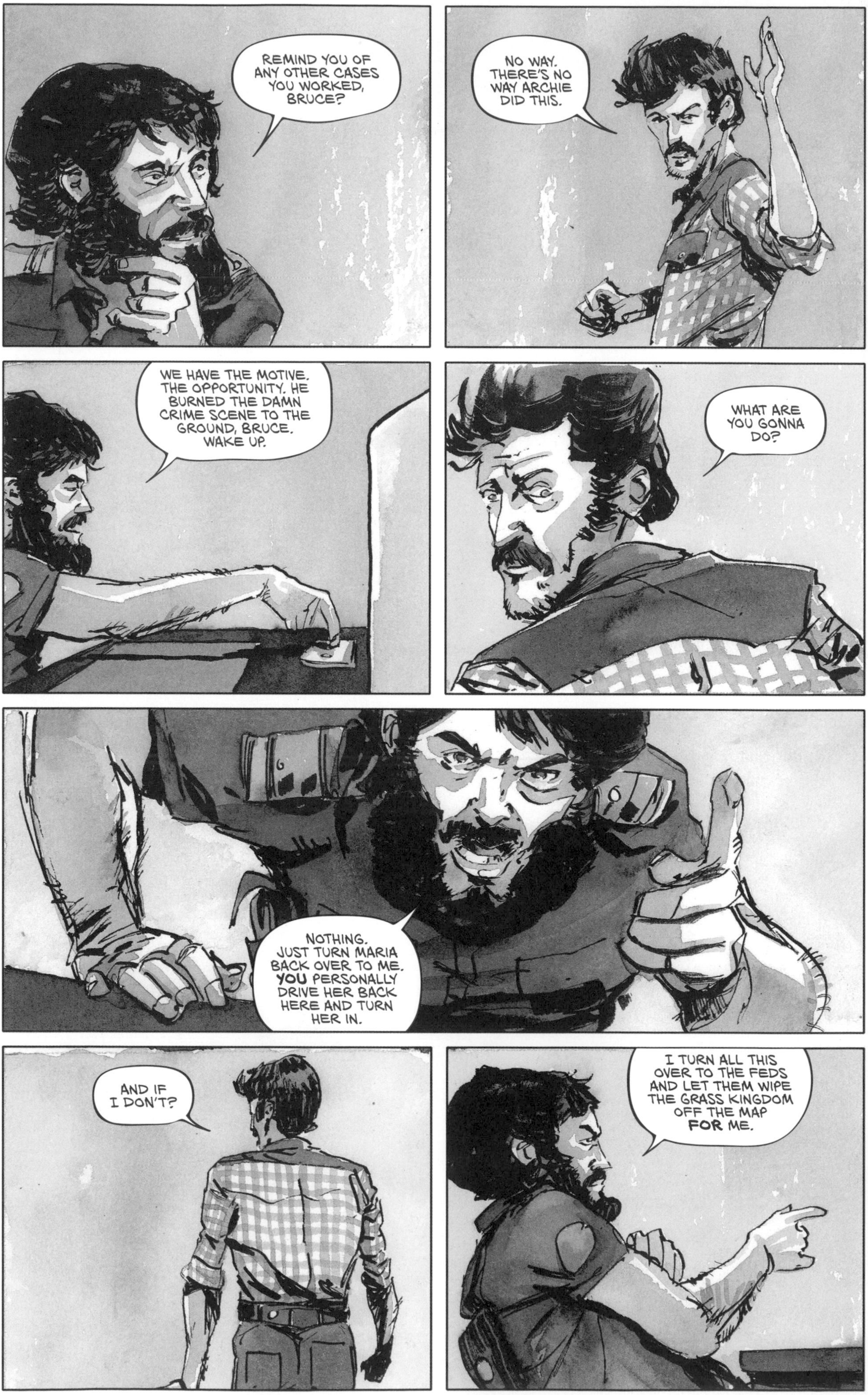
REMIND YOU OF ANY OTHER CASES YOU WORKED, BRUCE?
NO WAY. THERE'S NO WAY ARCHIE DID THIS.
WE HAVE THE MOTIVE. THE OPPORTUNITY. HE BURNED THE DAMN CRIME SCENE TO THE GROUND, BRUCE. WAKE UP.
WHAT ARE YOU GONNA DO?
NOTHING. JUST TURN MARIA BACK OVER TO ME. **YOU** PERSONALLY DRIVE HER BACK HERE AND TURN HER IN.
AND IF I DON'T?
I TURN ALL THIS OVER TO THE FEDS AND LET THEM WIPE THE GRASS KINGDOM OFF THE MAP **FOR** ME.

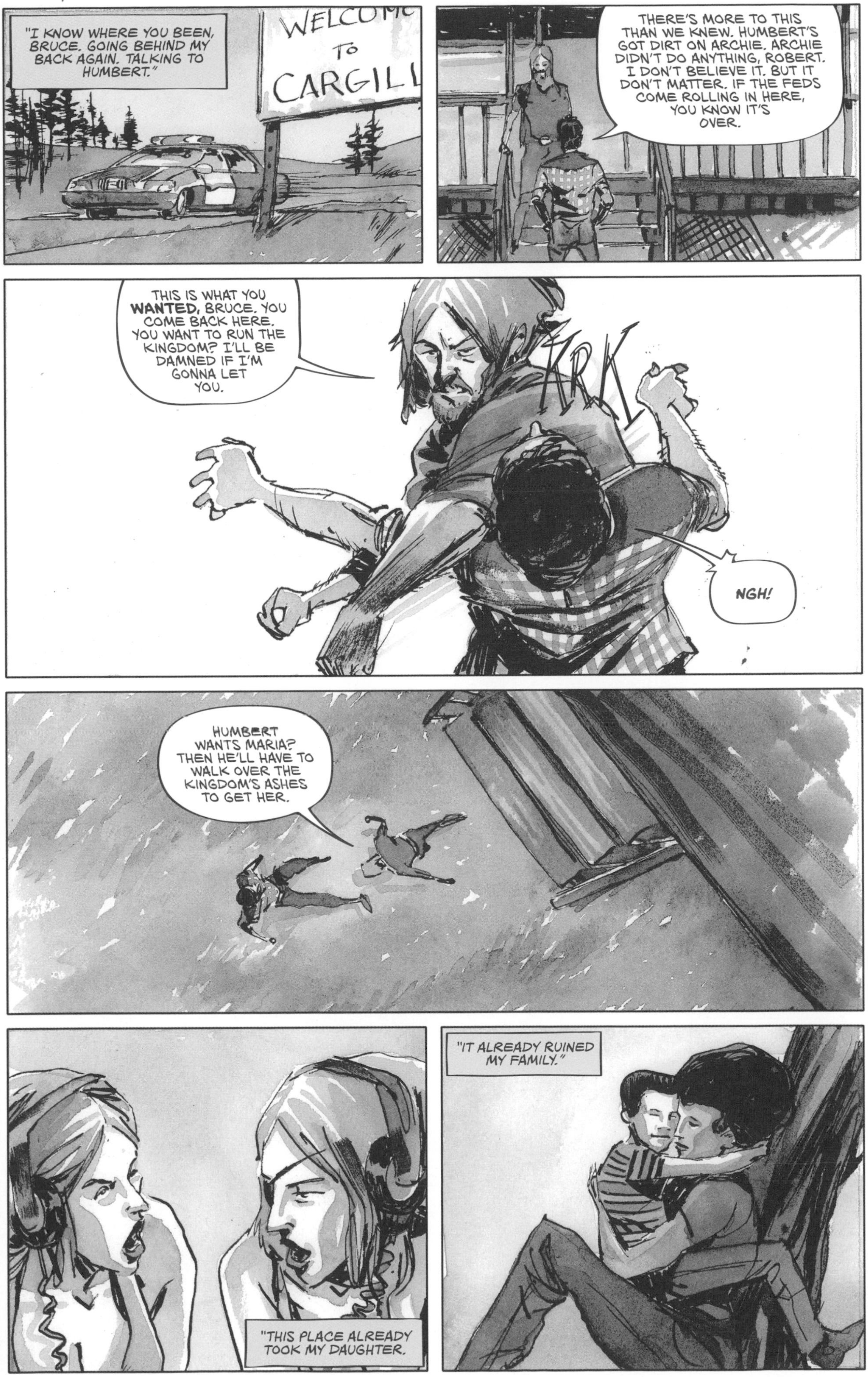
"I KNOW WHERE YOU BEEN, BRUCE. GOING BEHIND MY BACK AGAIN. TALKING TO HUMBERT."
WELCOME TO CARGILL
THERE'S MORE TO THIS THAN WE KNEW. HUMBERT'S GOT DIRT ON ARCHIE. ARCHIE DIDN'T DO ANYTHING, ROBERT. I DON'T BELIEVE IT. BUT IT DON'T MATTER. IF THE FEDS COME ROLLING IN HERE, YOU KNOW IT'S OVER.
THIS IS WHAT YOU WANTED, BRUCE. YOU COME BACK HERE. YOU WANT TO RUN THE KINGDOM? I'LL BE DAMNED IF I'M GONNA LET YOU.
KRK
NGH!
HUMBERT WANTS MARIA? THEN HE'LL HAVE TO WALK OVER THE KINGDOM'S ASHES TO GET HER.
"THIS PLACE ALREADY TOOK MY DAUGHTER.
"IT ALREADY RUINED MY FAMILY."

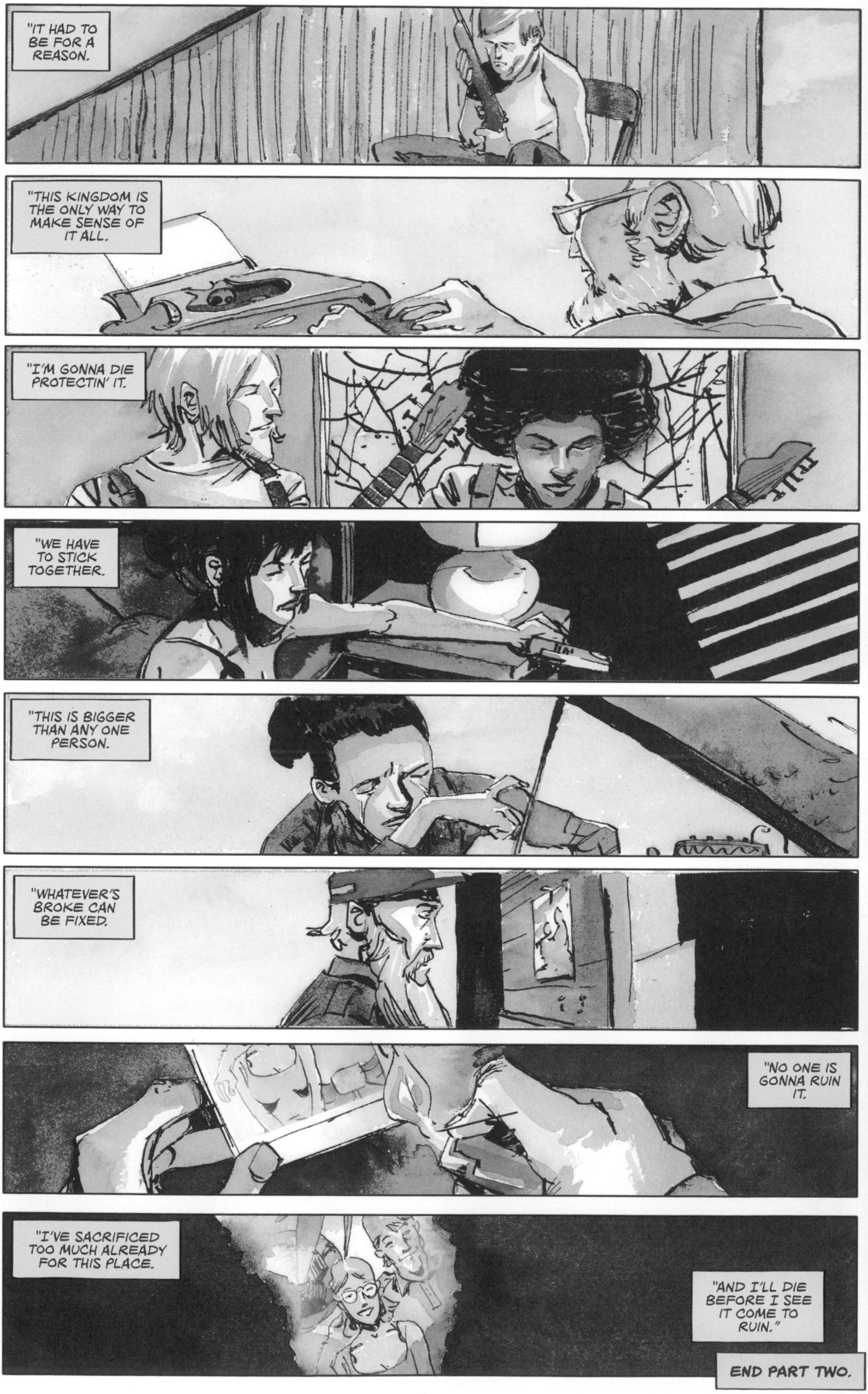
"IT HAD TO BE FOR A REASON.
"THIS KINGDOM IS THE ONLY WAY TO MAKE SENSE OF IT ALL.
"I'M GONNA DIE PROTECTIN' IT.
"WE HAVE TO STICK TOGETHER.
"THIS IS BIGGER THAN ANY ONE PERSON.
"WHATEVER'S BROKE CAN BE FIXED.
"NO ONE IS GONNA RUIN IT.
"I'VE SACRIFICED TOO MUCH ALREADY FOR THIS PLACE.
"AND I'LL DIE BEFORE I SEE IT COME TO RUIN."
END PART TWO.

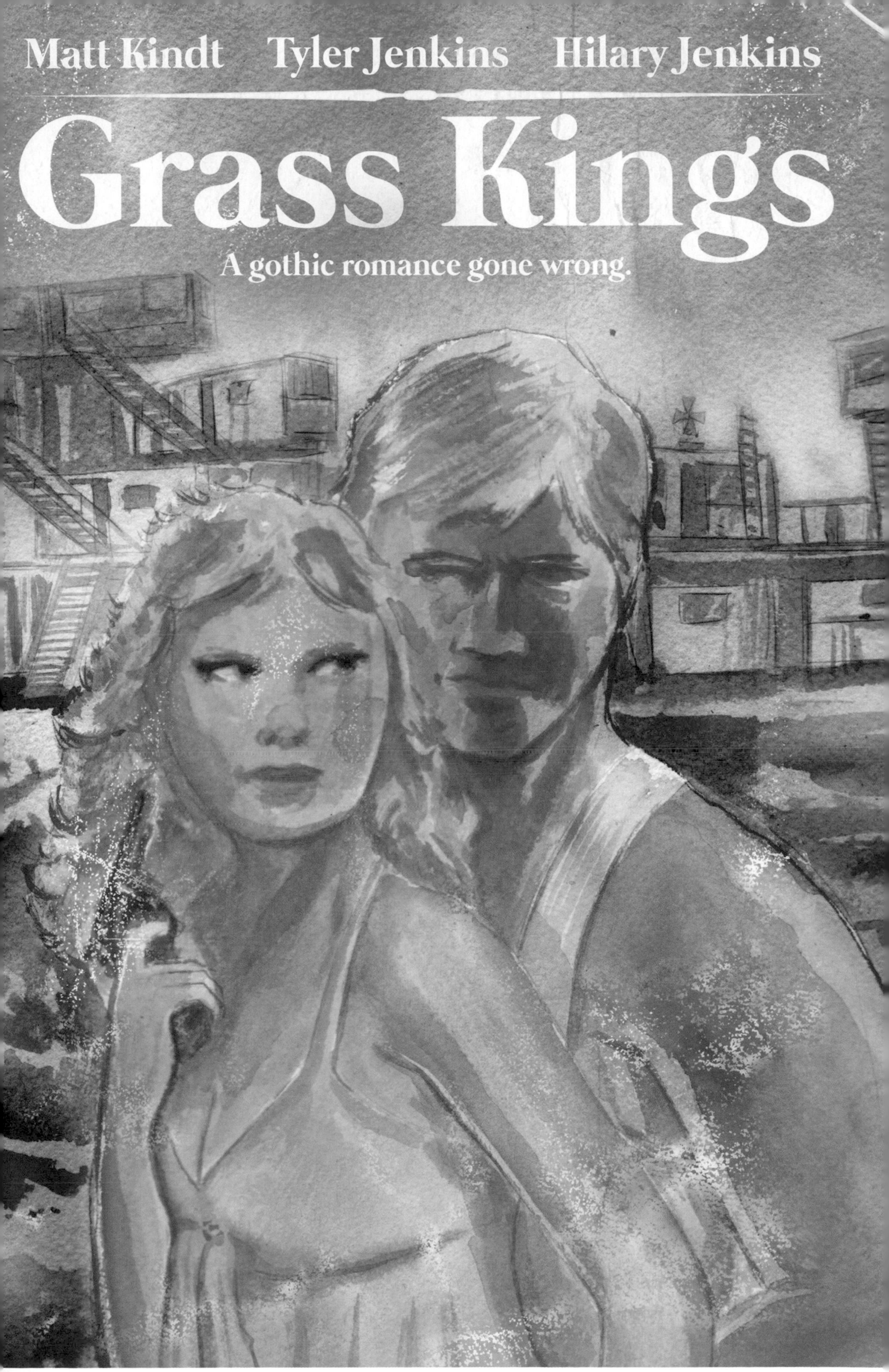
Matt Kindt Tyler Jenkins Hilary Jenkins
Grass Kings
A gothic romance gone wrong.

issue #11 cover by matt kindt

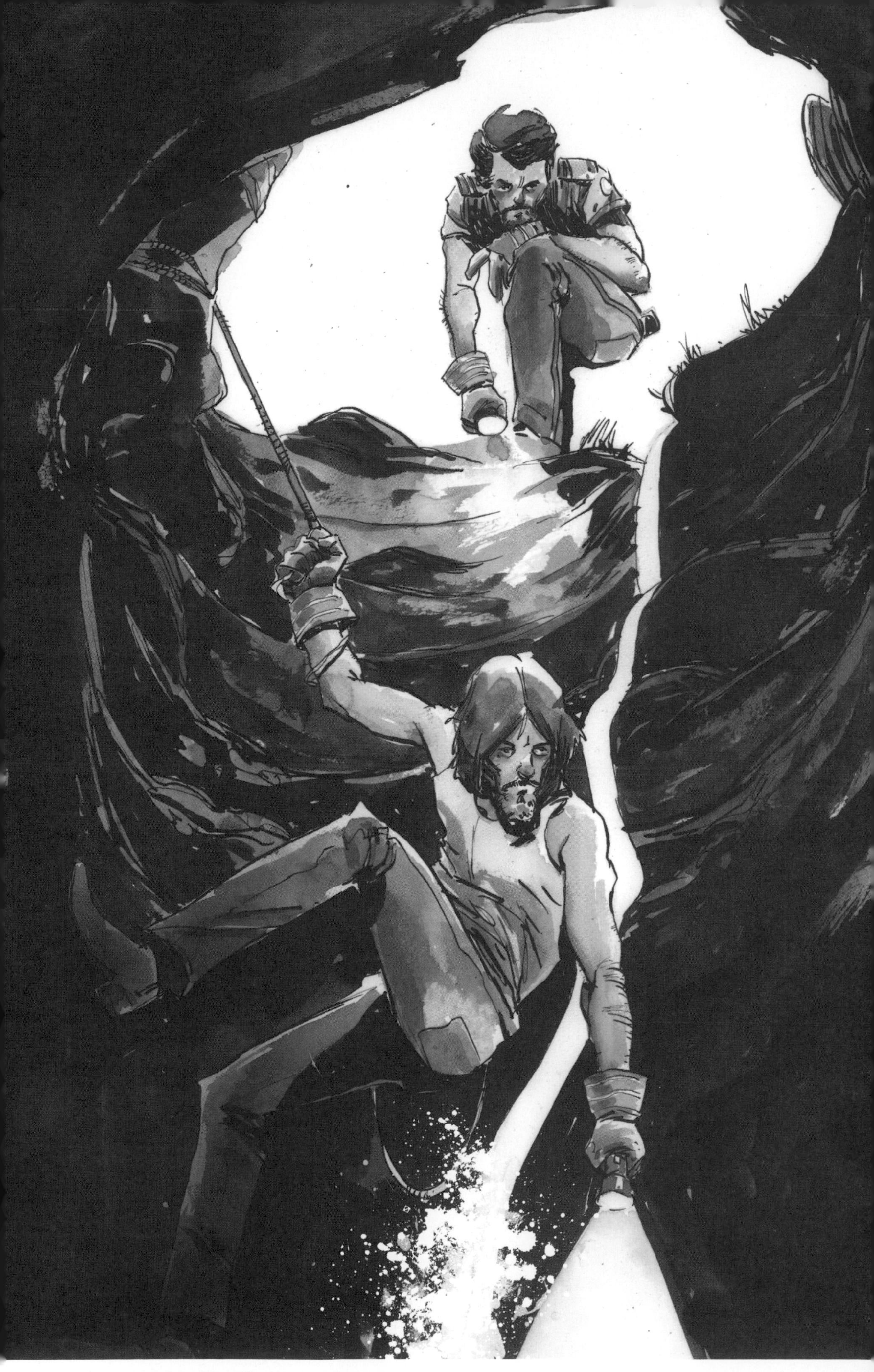

issue #7 cover by tyler jenkins

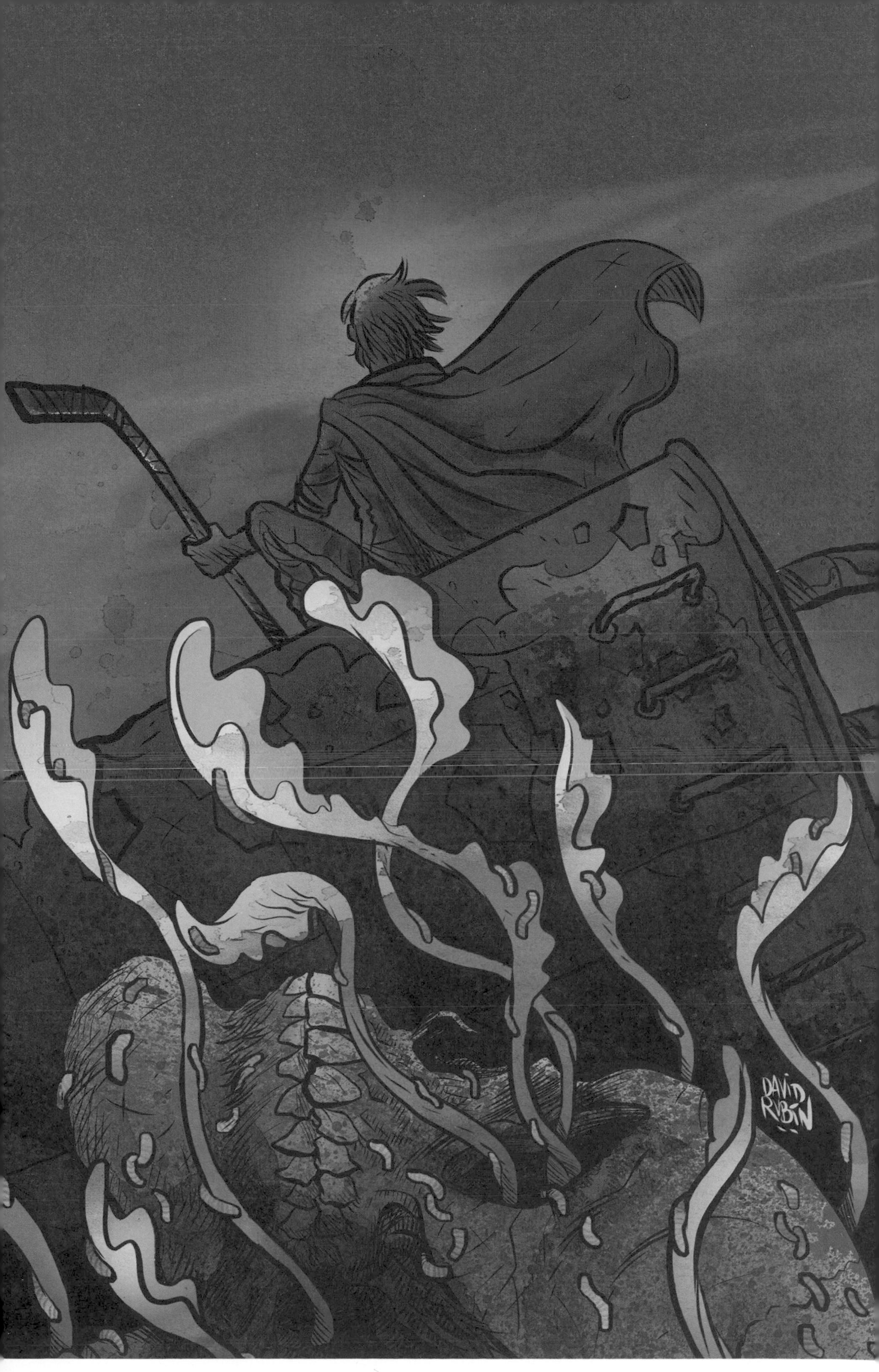
DAVID RUBÍN

issue #7 unlocked retailer variant cover by david rubín

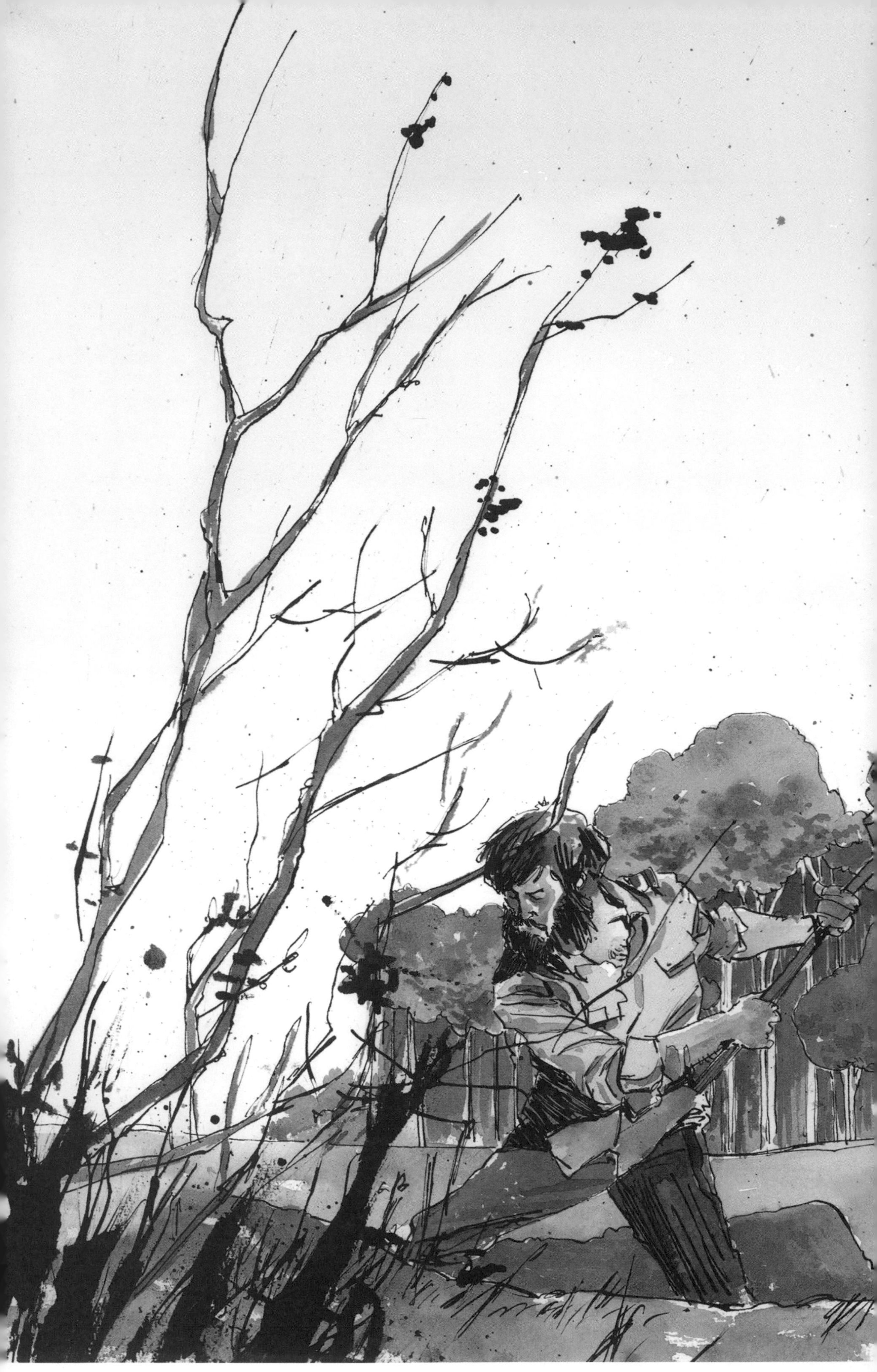

issue #8 cover by tyler jenkins

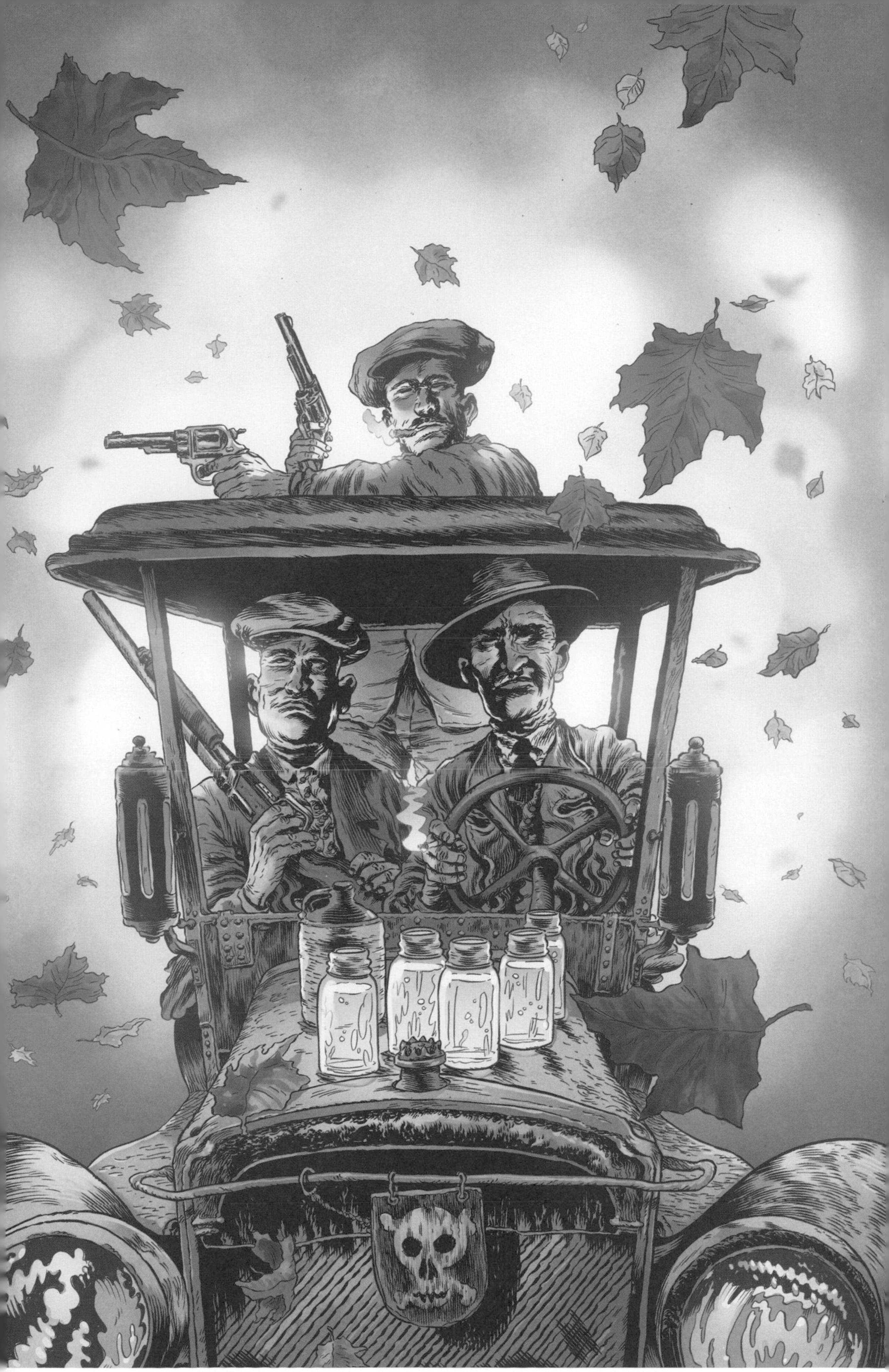

issue #8 unlocked retailer variant cover by troy nixey with colors by michael spicer

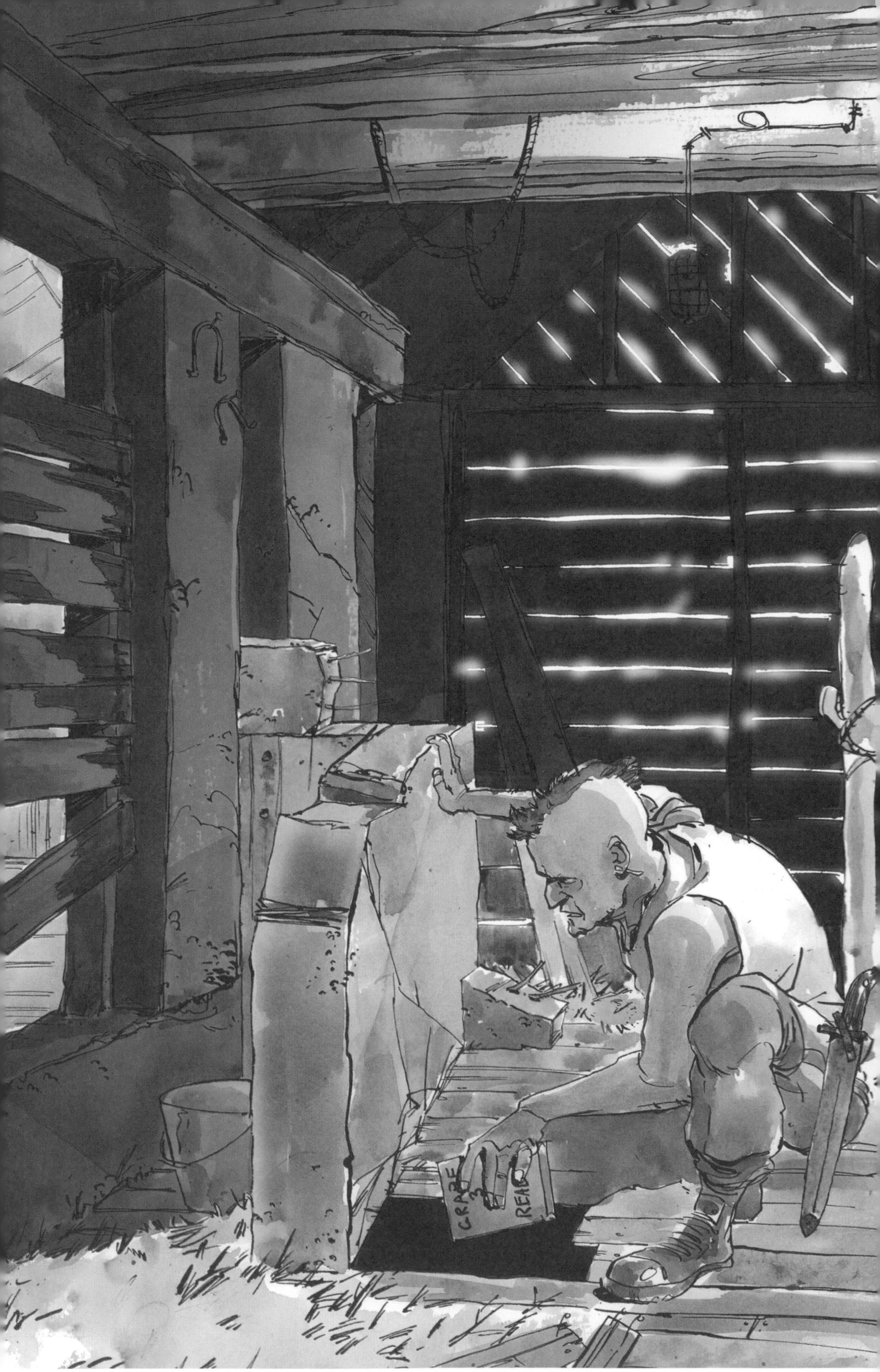
GRADE 3
READ

issue #9 cover by tyler jenkins

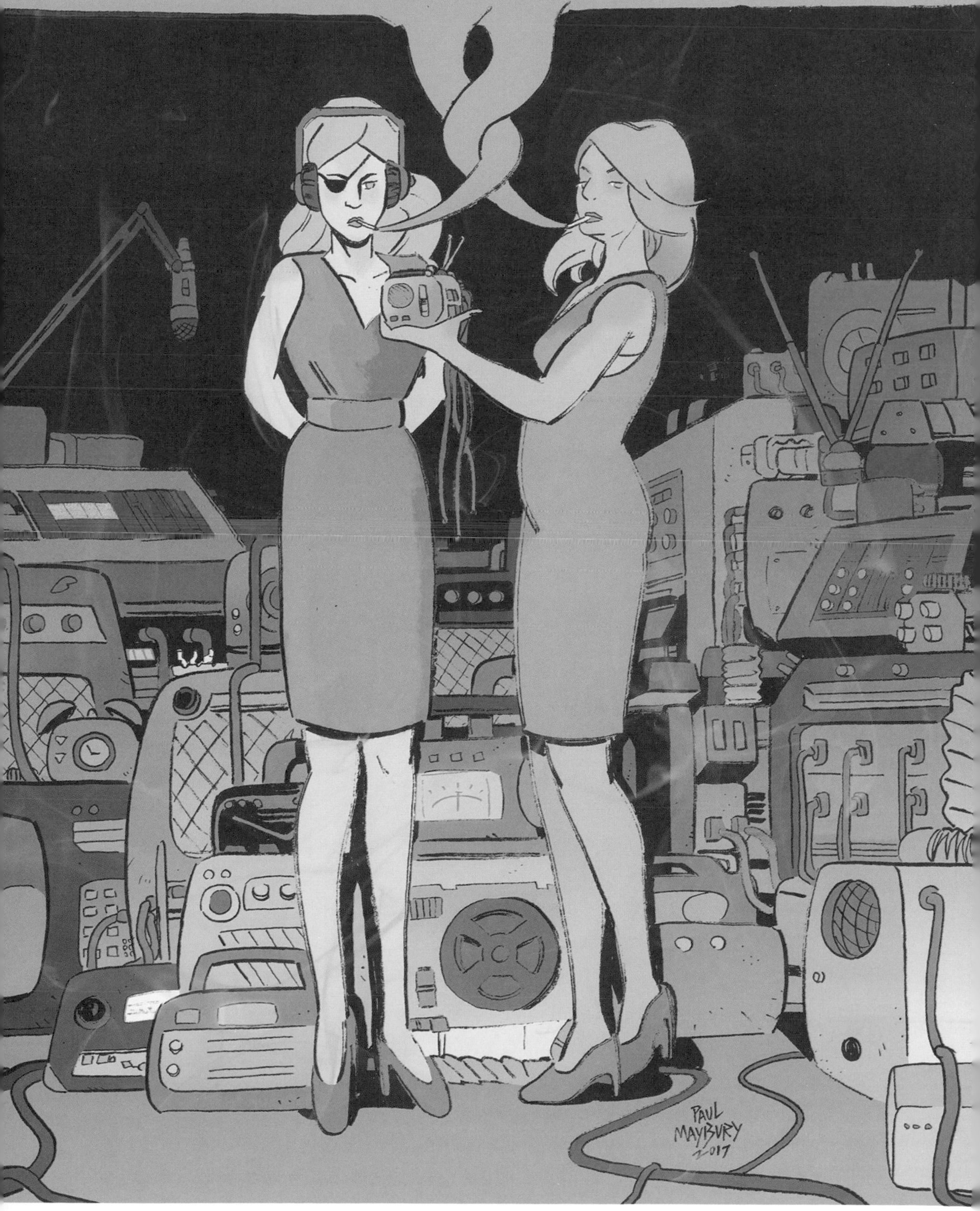
PAUL
MAYBURY
2017

issue #9 unlocked retailer variant cover by paul maybury

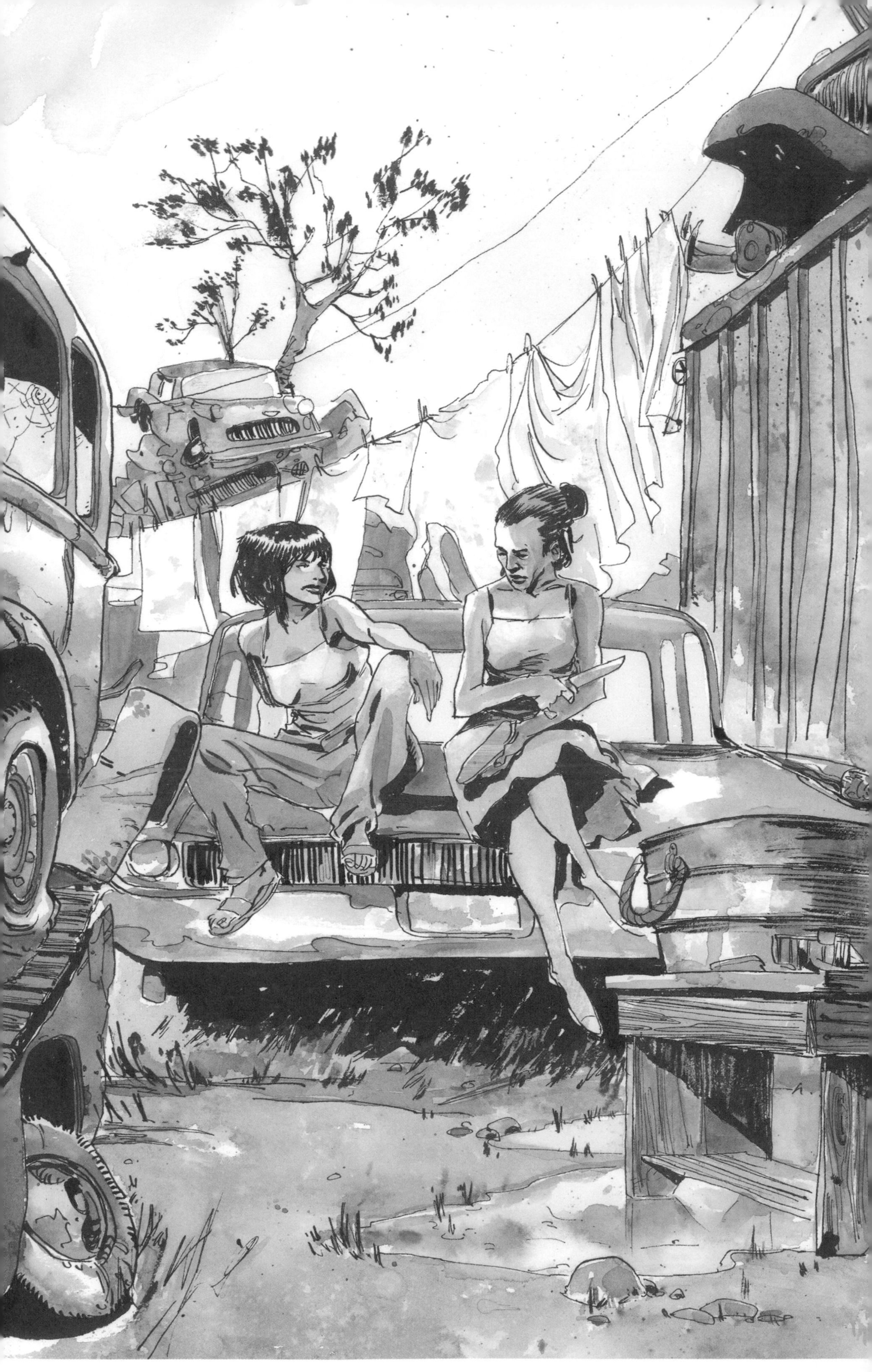

issue #10 cover by tyler jenkins

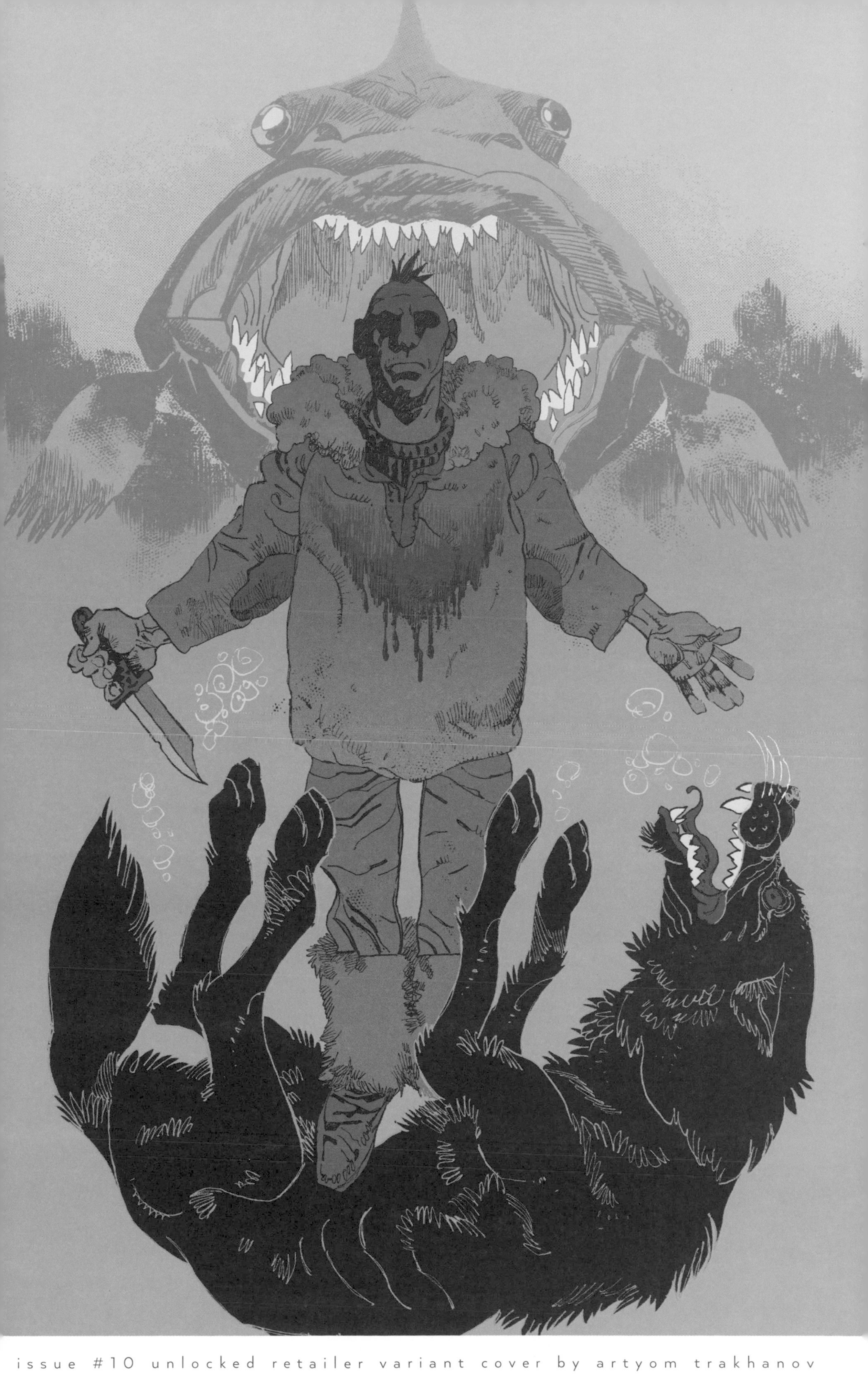

issue #10 unlocked retailer variant cover by artyom trakhanov

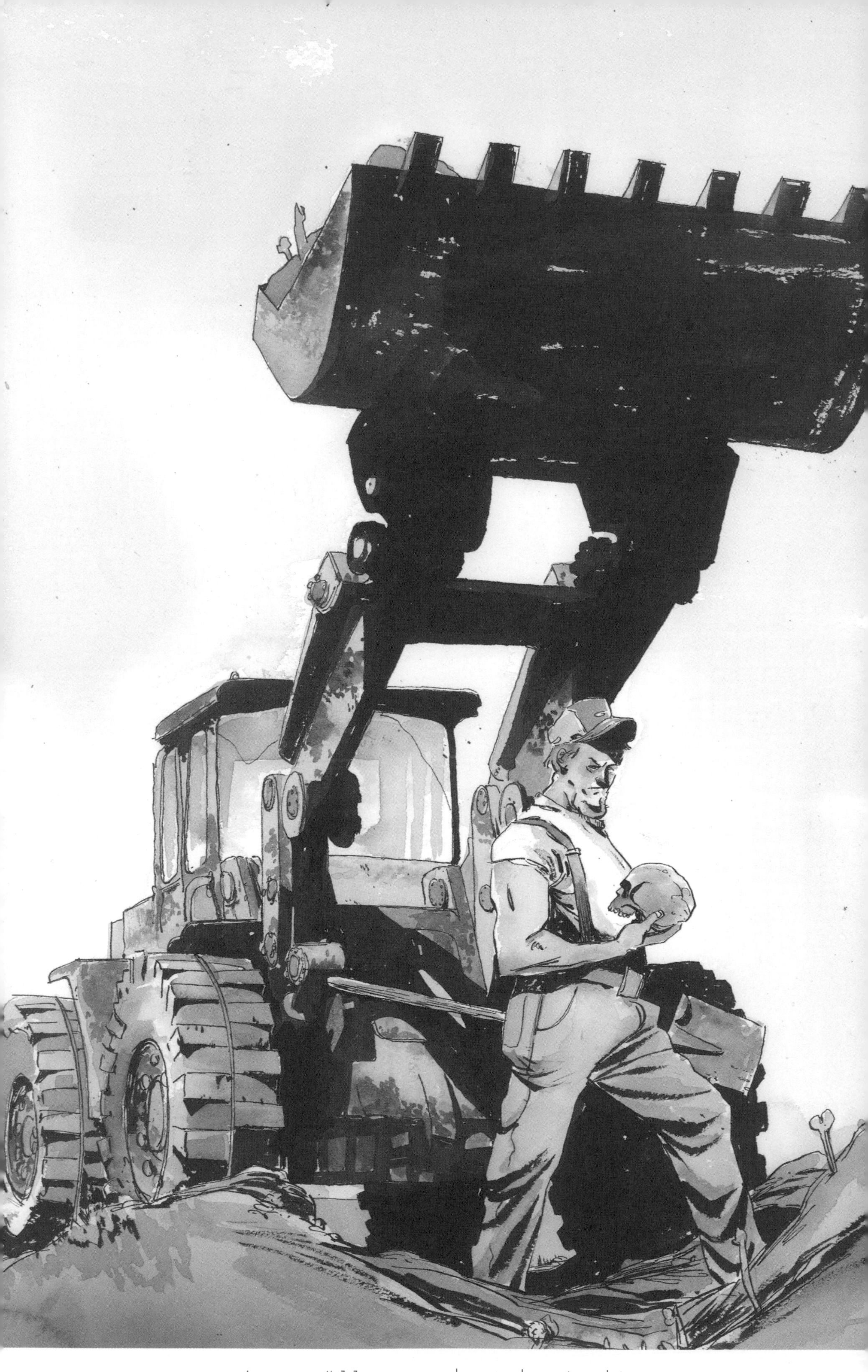

issue #11 cover by tyler jenkins

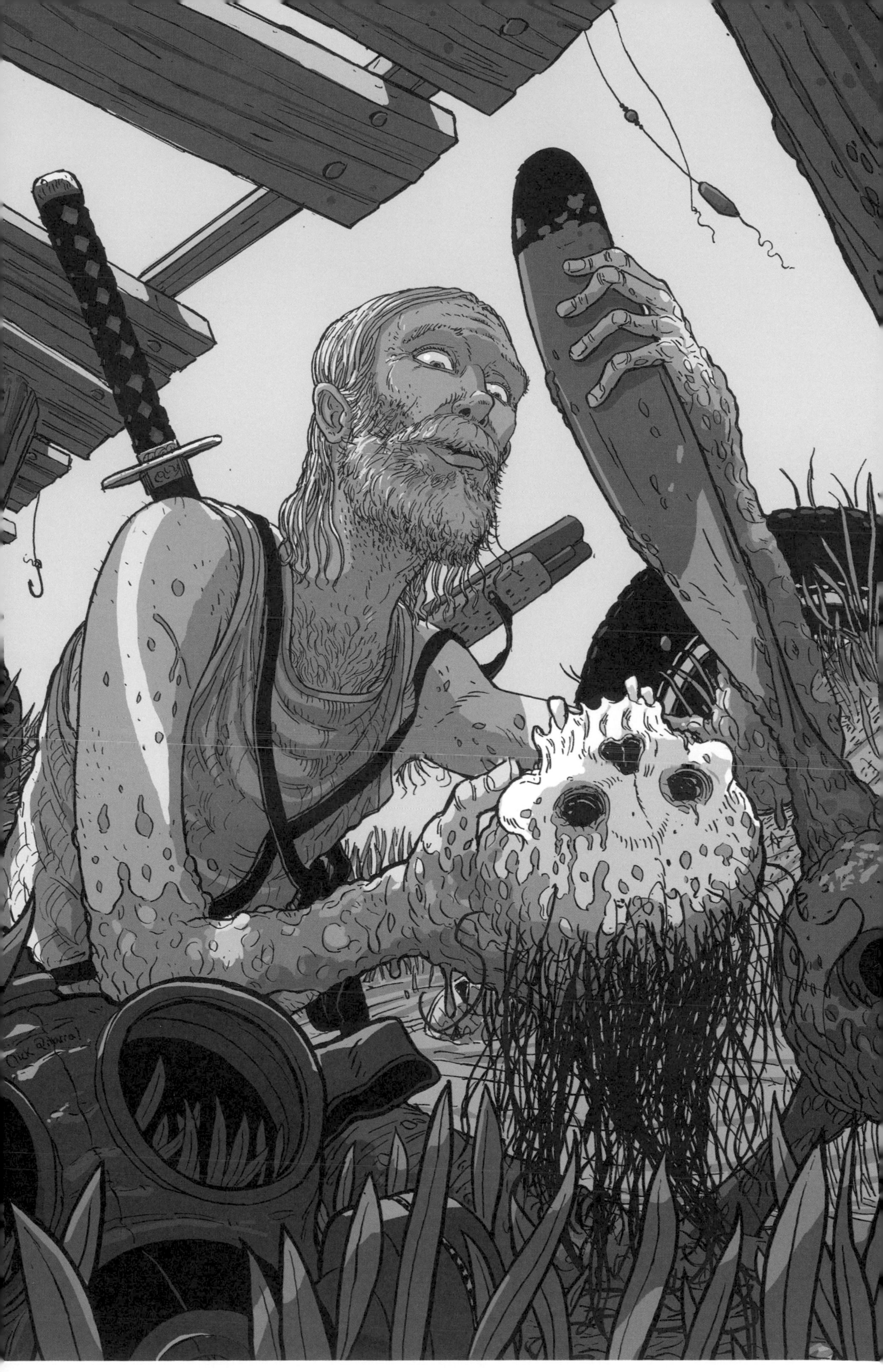

issue #11 unlocked retailer variant cover by nick pitarra

in the studio with tyler jenkins

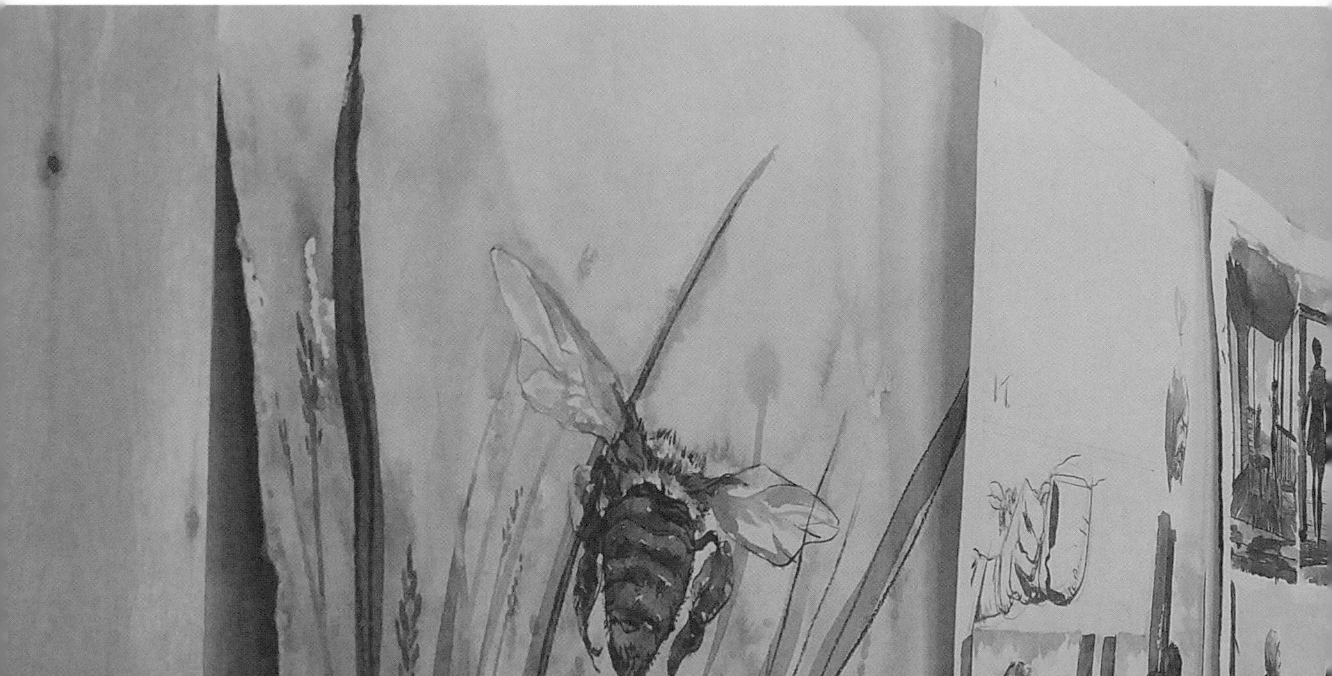

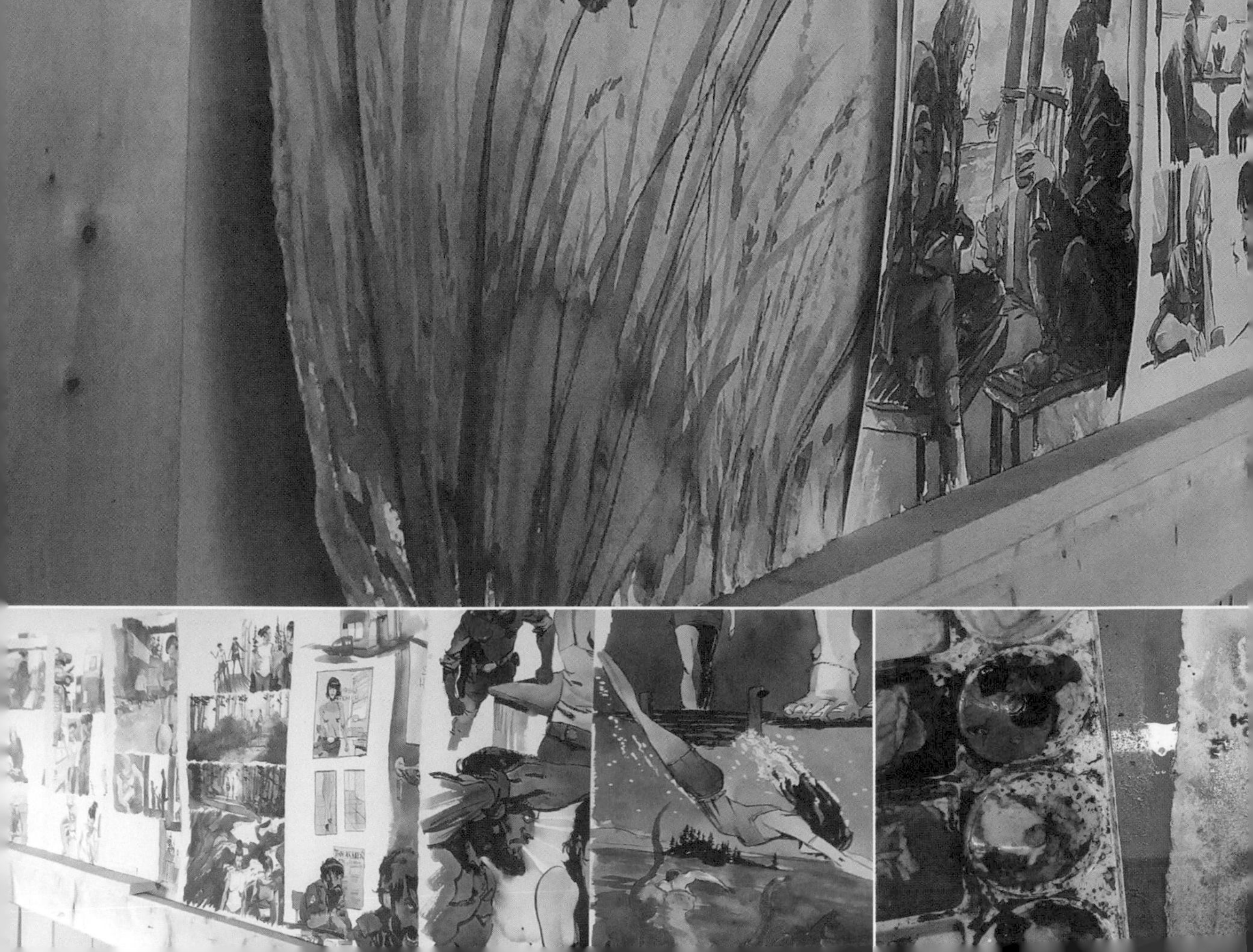

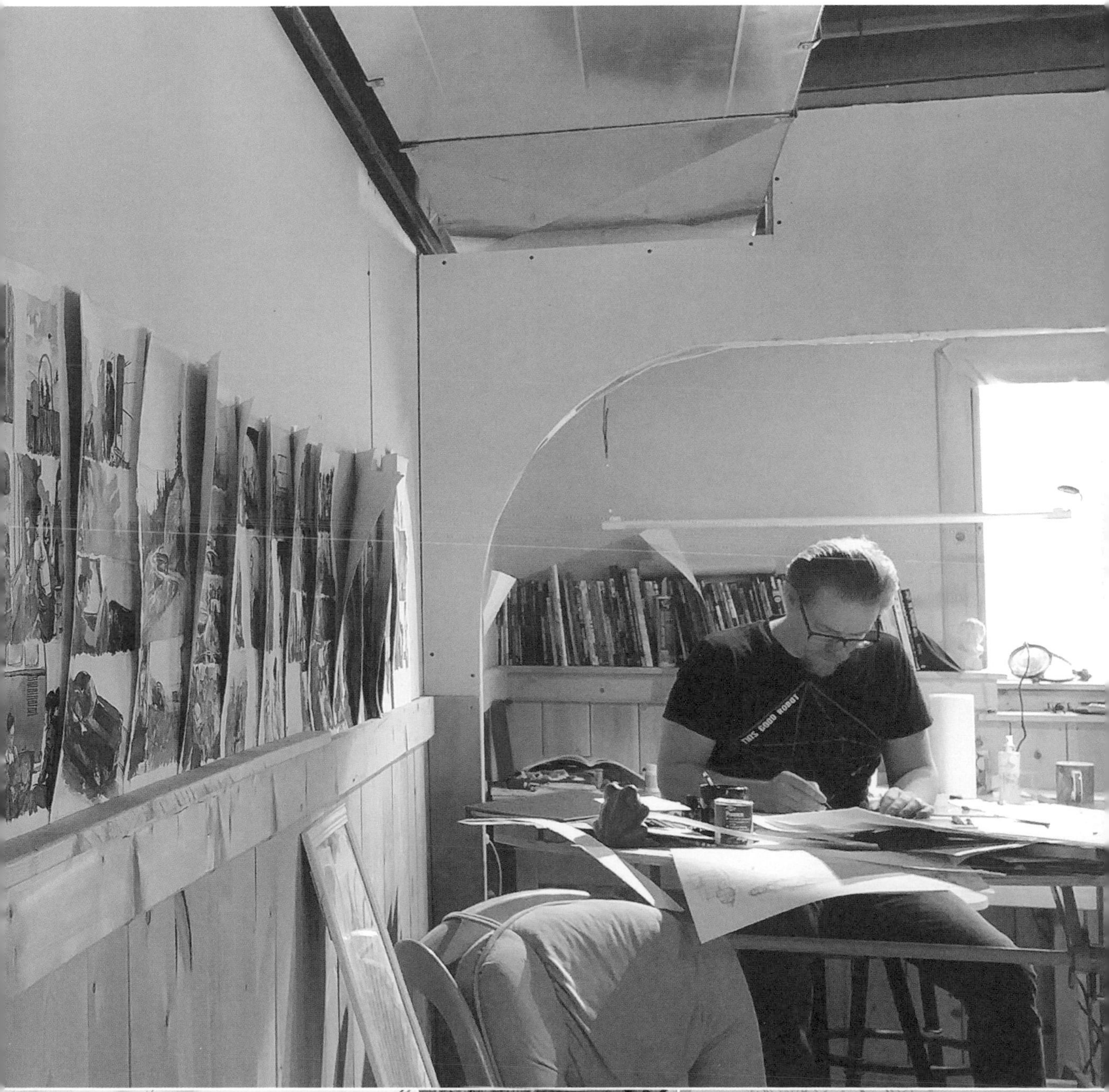
THIS GOOD ROBOT

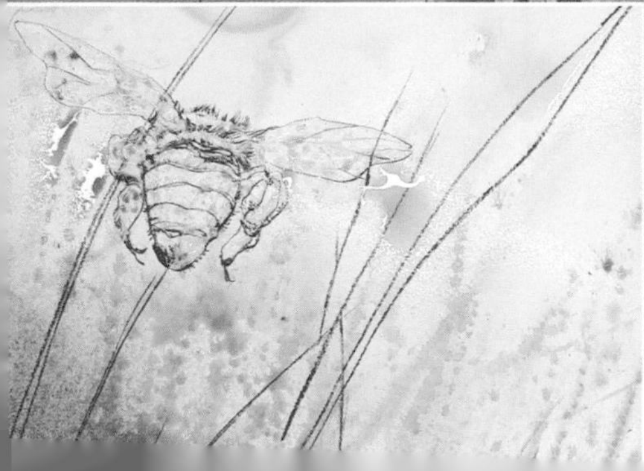

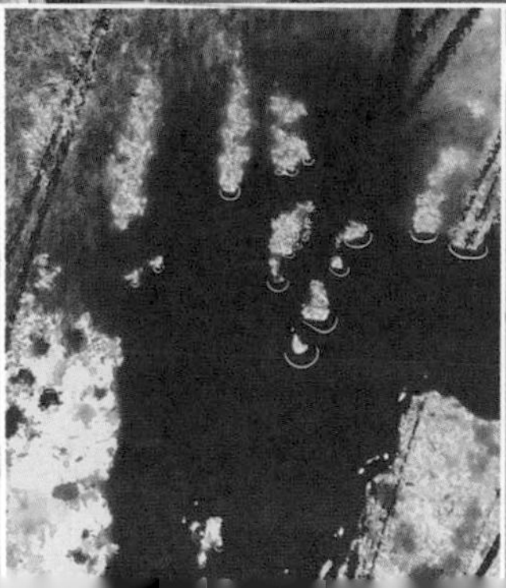

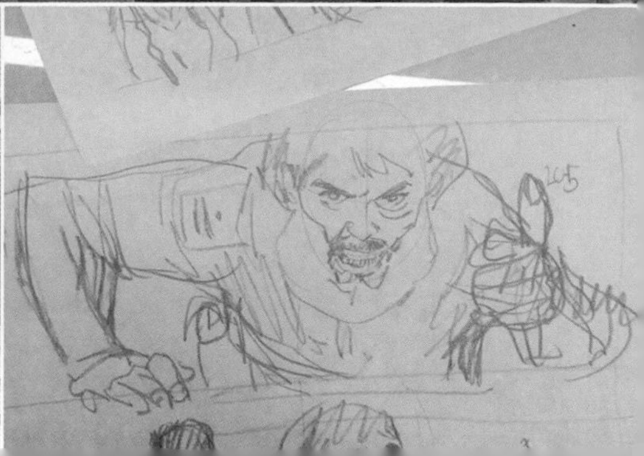

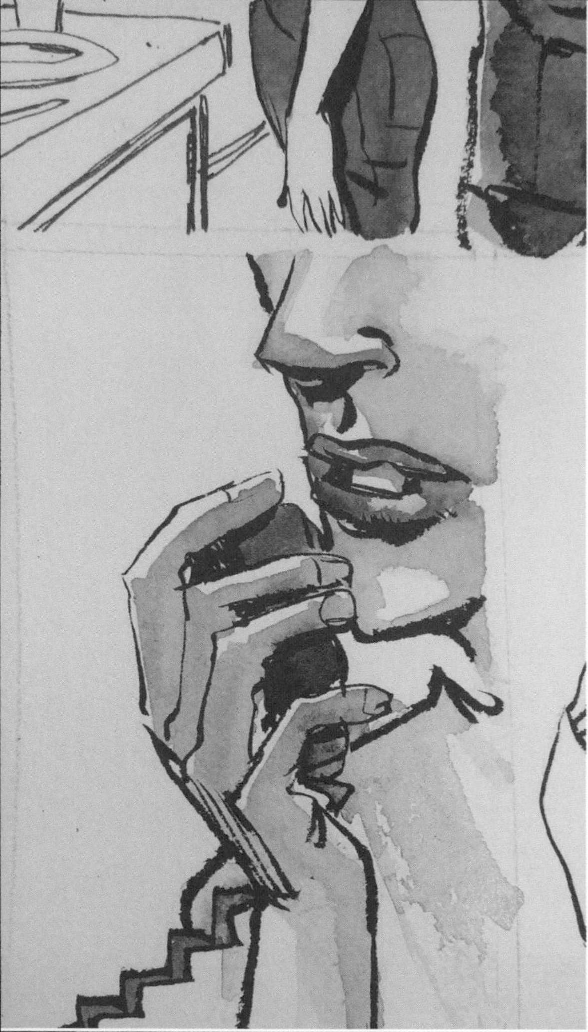
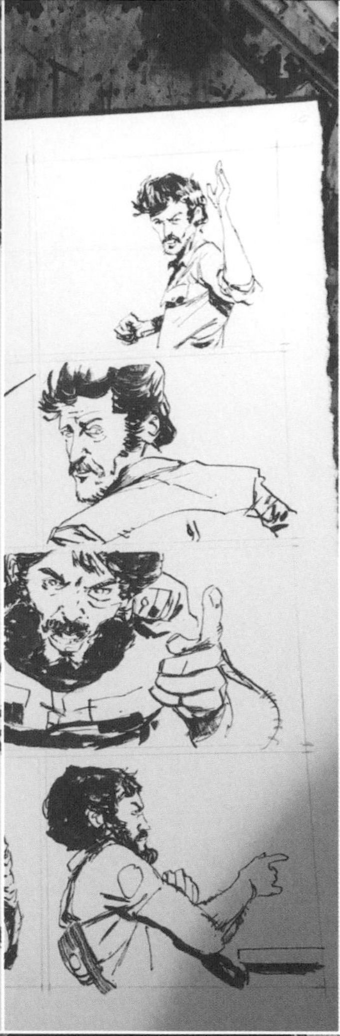
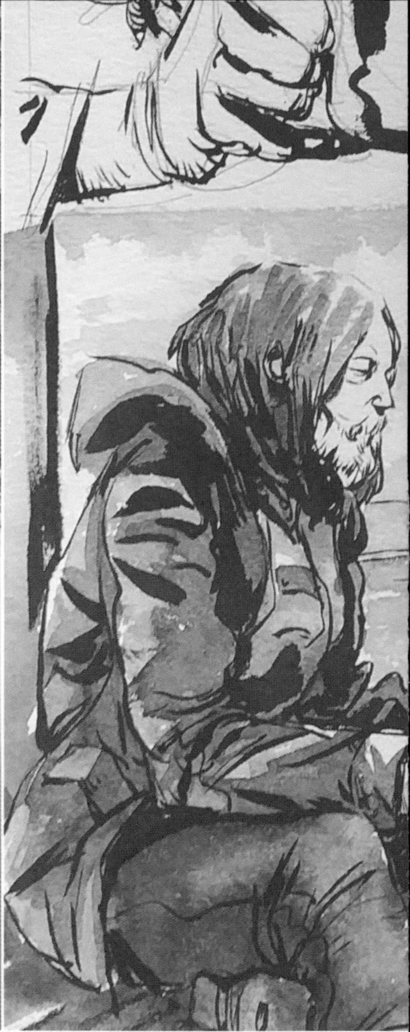
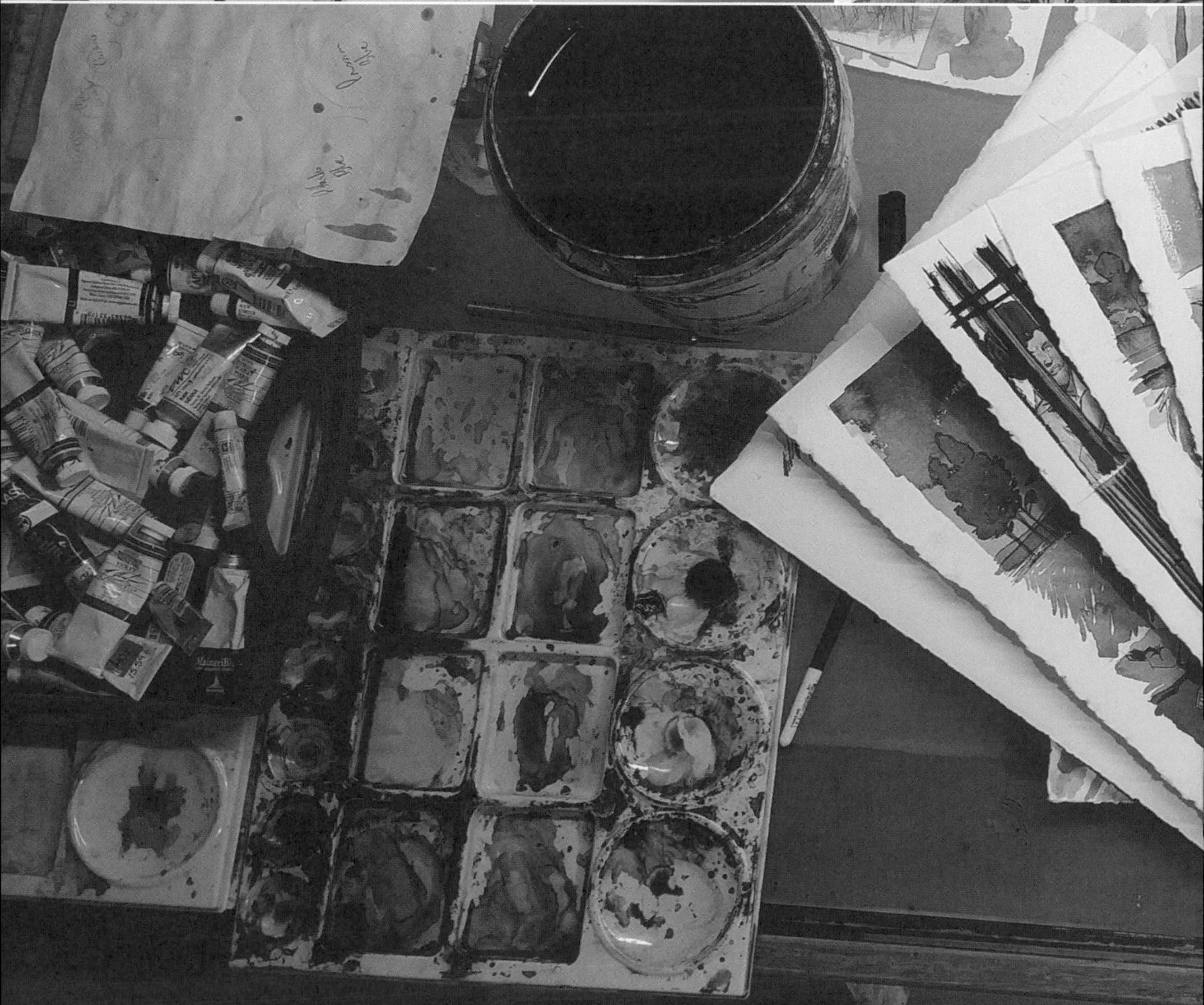

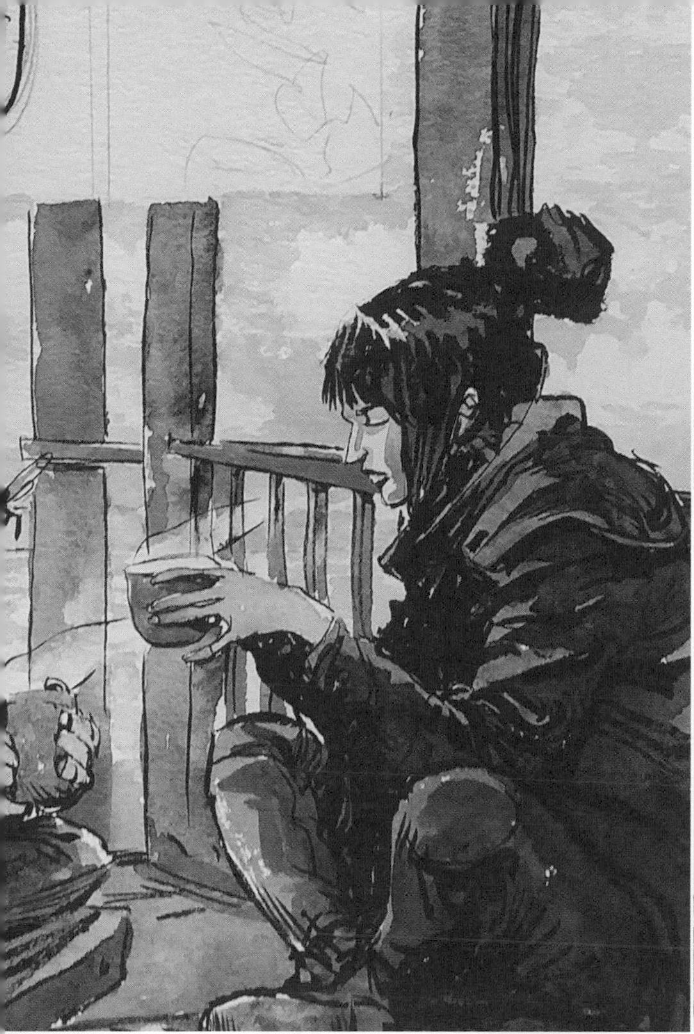

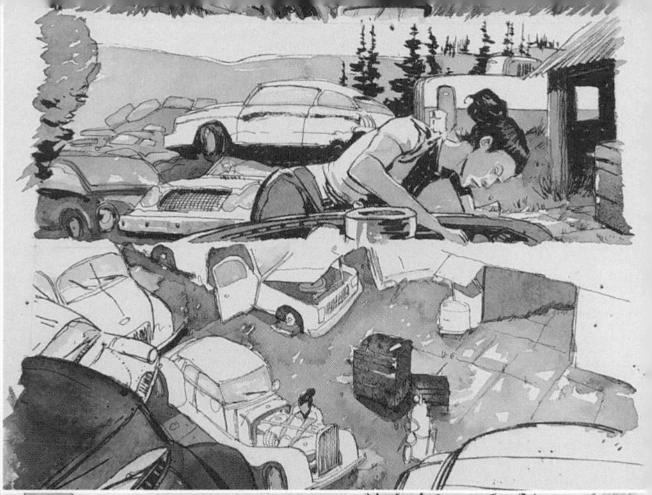

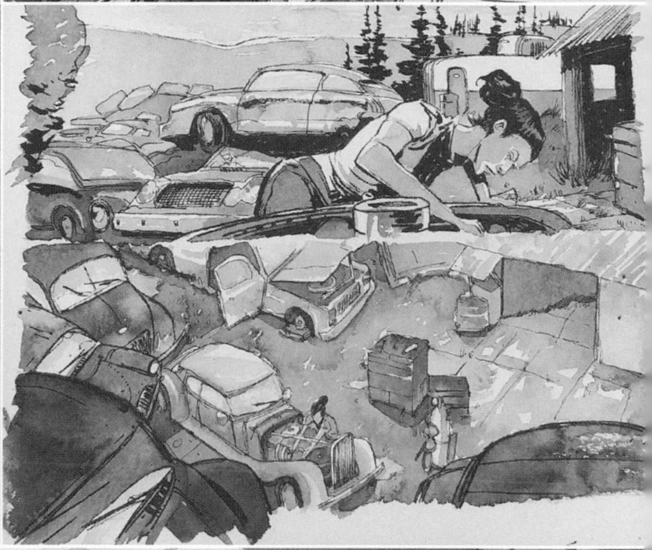

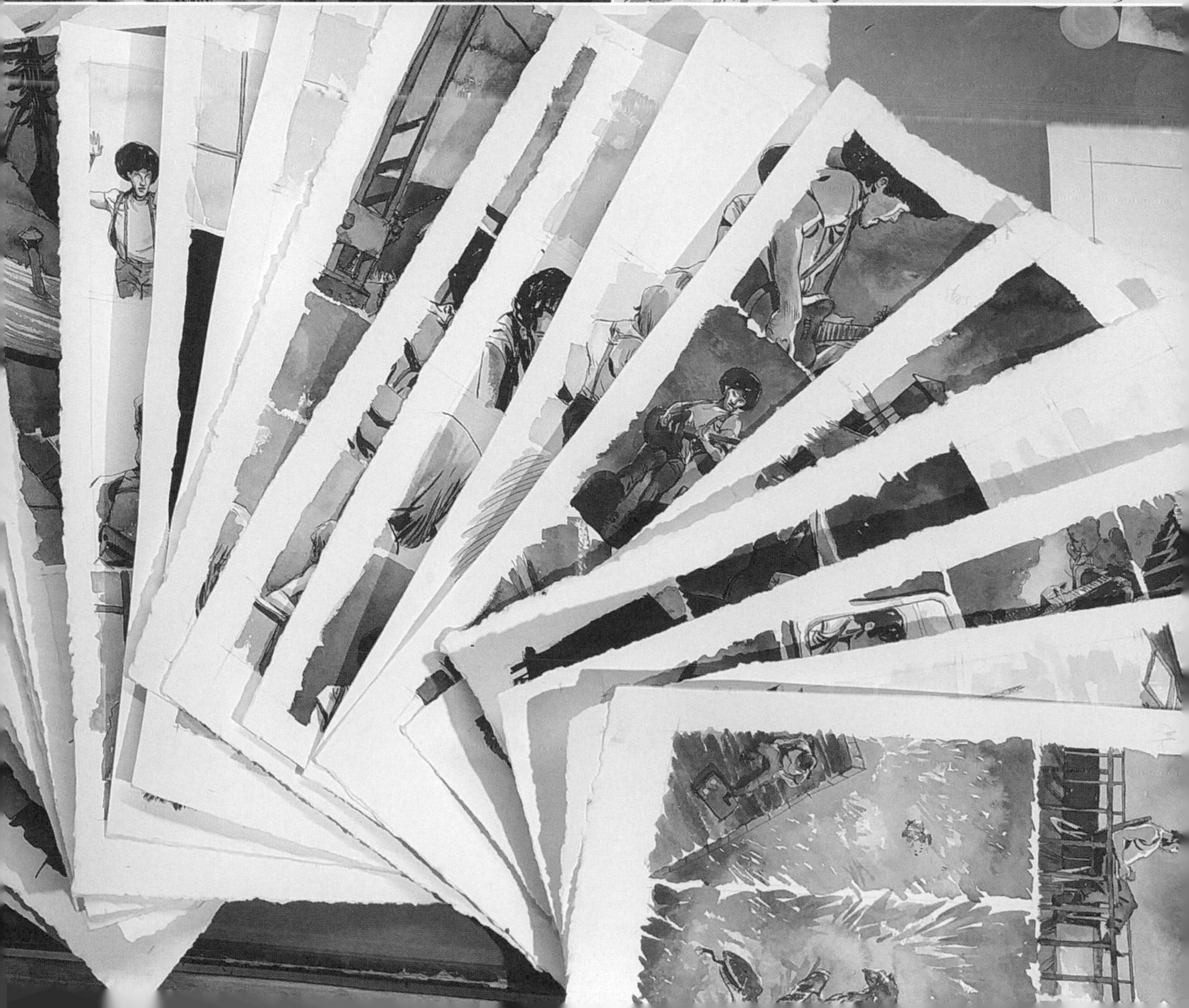

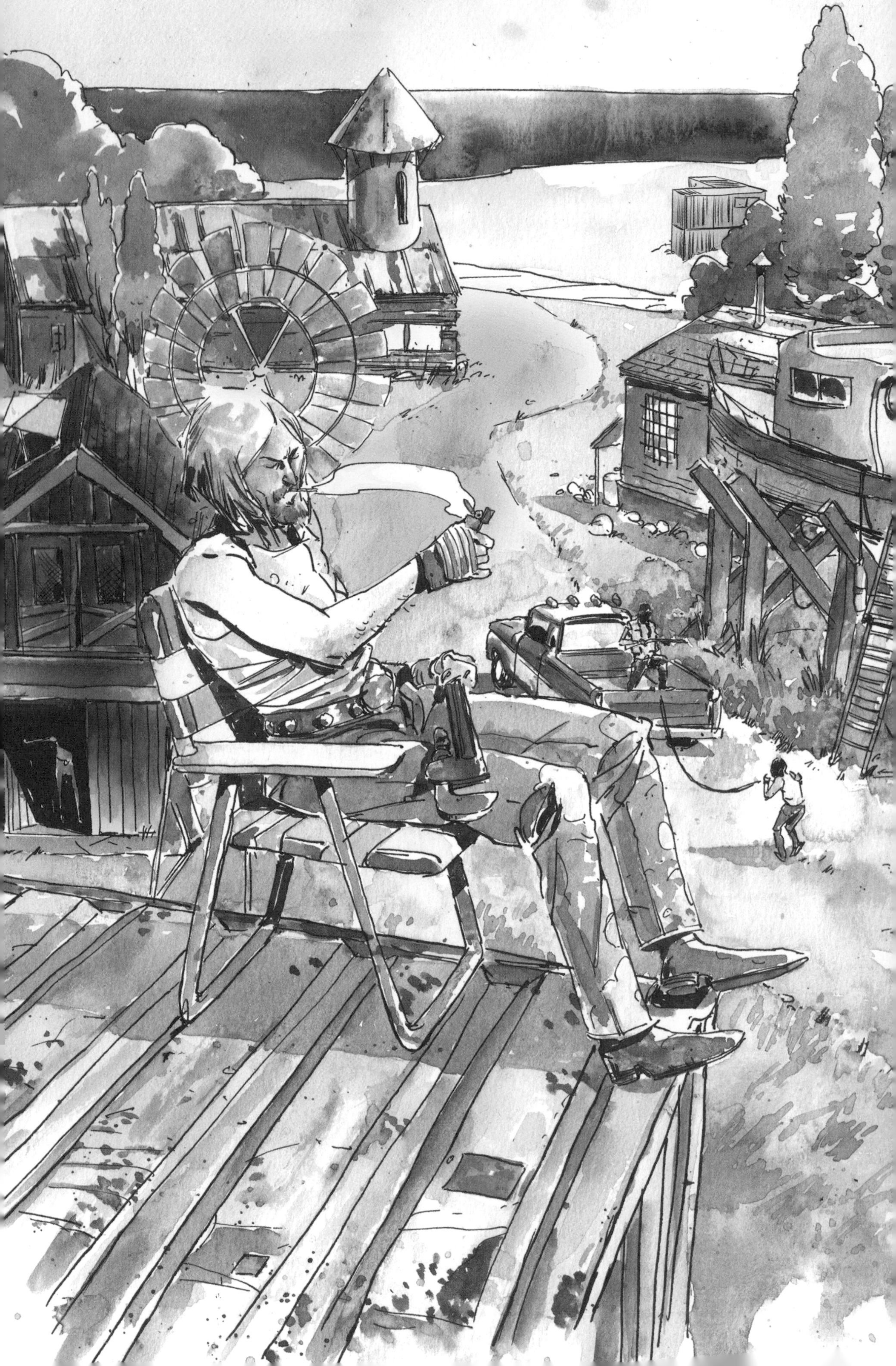

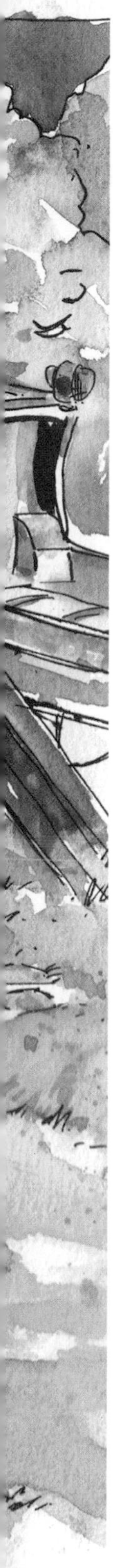

about the authors

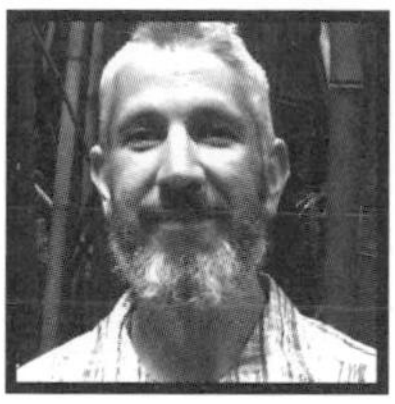

Matt Kindt is the *New York Times* best-selling writer and artist of the comics and graphic novels *Dept. H, Mind MGMT, Revolver, 3 Story, Super Spy, 2 Sisters,* and *Pistolwhip,* as well as the writer of *Grass Kings, Ether, Justice League of America* (DC), *Spider-Man* (Marvel), *Unity, Ninjak, Rai,* and *Divinity* (Valiant). He has been nominated for four Eisner and six Harvey Awards (and won once). His work has been published in French, Spanish, Italian, German and Korean.

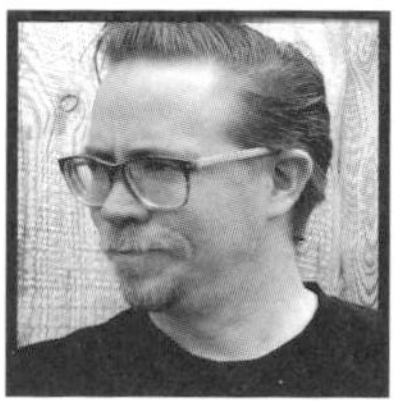

Tyler Jenkins is a dude who draws comics, makes art and music, and on occasion barbecues a mean back of ribs. Tyler is best known for creating *Grass Kings* with Matt Kindt and *Peter Panzerfaust* with Kurtis Wiebe, and handling art duties on *Snow Blind* with Ollie Masters and *Neverboy* with Shaun Simon. Tyler lives in rural Alberta, Canada, with his wife, three small child-like creatures, and more gophers than you can shove in a tin pail. Find him at tylerjenkinsprojects on Instagram.

DISCOVER VISIONARY CREATORS

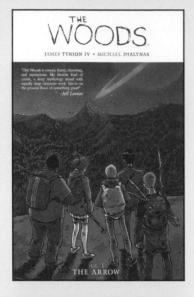

The chansons of the troubadours and trouvères

1800 mnf

The chansons of the troubadours and trouvères

HENDRIK VAN DER WERF

A study of the melodies and their relation to the poems

1972   A. Oosthoek's Uitgeversmaatschappij NV   Utrecht

Designed by Alje Olthof GVN

Printed by Hooiberg NV, Epe, The Netherlands

ISBN 90 6046 069 3

Contents

Acknowledgements

It is a pleasant duty to thank here and now the students, professors, librarians, mailmen, typists, and many others who, each in his own way, have contributed to this book. My appreciation goes in the first instance to those who read some of my former publications on this topic—including my dissertation, which this book replaces—and who commented upon them. Of those who helped me so generously at Columbia University in the earliest stages of my research I thank especially Professors Lawton Peckham, William T. Jackson, and Edward A. Lippman. I also want to give special credit to two groups of persons who read the last drafts of the present book: firstly, those graduate students at the University of Rochester's Eastman School of Music who read the draft when taking my course on medieval music and whose subsequent questions revealed certain weak spots in my explanations which, I hope, have been remedied; secondly, the colleagues who read the draft or parts of it and gave valuable criticism and advice, namely Bruce Beatie, Horst Brunner, Ralph Lane, Bruno Stäblein, Bruce Whisler, and David R. Williams.

I also want to express my gratitude to the National Endowment for the Humanities, which granted me a fellowship and thus enabled me to concentrate for eight months on research and writing. *Current Musicology* generously gave permission to quote here from my articles published in 1965 and 1970 respectively.

I thank two persons in a very special way: first, Dr. F. R. P. Akehurst, of the University of Minnesota, who very willingly provided translations for all of the Old Provençal and Old French poems included in this study. I am sure that his translations will contribute to the reader's understanding of the poetic style of the troubadours and trouvères. Secondly, I thank my wife, who more than anyone else influenced the style, the organization, and even the contents of this book with her advice, questions, and criticism, and who especially helped me by listening patiently to my endless monologues on the topic.

Finally, I thank in advance those who are going to help me with correcting the proofs as well as those who will read this book and send me their commentary.

H. V. D. W.

List of the manuscripts referred to in this study, with their symbols

TROUVÈRE MANUSCRIPTS[1]

A

Arras, Bibl. Munic. 657 (olim 139). Published by Alfred Jeanroy, *Le Chansonnier d'Arras*. Reproduction en phototypie. Vol. LXXVII of *Sociétés des anciens Textes français*. Paris 1925.

D

Frankfurt, Stadtbibliothek, olim 29 (at present without a number).

K

Paris, Bibliothèque de l'Arsenal 5198. Published by Pierre Aubry, *Le Chansonnier de l'Arsenal*. Reproduction phototypique. Transcription du texte musical en notation moderne. Paris 1909-1910.

L

Paris, Bibl. Nat., fr. 765.

M

Paris, Bibl. Nat., fr. 844. Published by Jean Baptiste Beck, *Le Manuscrit du Roi*, Facsimile. Ser. 2, Vol. 1 of *Corpus Cantilenarum Medii Aevi*. Philadelphia 1938.

Mt

Paris, Bibl. Nat., fr. 844 (a collection of chansons of Thibaud de Navarre, inserted in the preceding manuscript), published with preceding manuscript.

N

Paris, Bibl. Nat., fr. 845.

O

Paris, Bibl. Nat., fr. 846. Published by Jean Baptiste Beck, *Le Chansonnier Cangé*, Facsimile. Ser. 1, Vol. 1 of *Corpus Cantilenarum Medii Aevi*. Paris 1927.

P

Paris, Bibl. Nat., fr. 847.

Q

Paris, Bibl. Nat., fr. 1109.

R

Paris, Bibl. Nat., fr. 1591.

T

Paris, Bibl. Nat., fr. 12615.

U

Paris, Bibl. Nat., fr. 20050. Published by P. Meyer and G. Raynaud, *Le Chansonnier français de Saint-Germain-des-Près*. Vol. XXXI of *Société des anciens Textes français*. Paris 1892.

V

Paris, Bibl. Nat., fr. 24406.

W

Paris, Bibl. Nat., fr. 25566.

X

Paris, Bibl. Nat., nouv. acq. fr. 1050.

a

Rome, Bibl. Vat., Reg. 1490.

TROUBADOUR MANUSCRIPTS[2]

G

Milan, Biblioteca Ambrosiana R 71 sup.

R

Paris, Bibl. Nat., fr. 22543

W

Paris, Bibl. Nat., fr. 844; see trouvère manuscript M.

X

Paris, Bibl. Nat., fr. 20050; see trouvère manuscript U.

1. Symbols taken from Raynaud-Spanke, see page 15, footnote 1; see Raynaud-Spanke for trouvère manuscripts not listed here.

2. Symbols taken from Pillet-Carstens, see page 15, footnote 3; see Pillet-Carstens for troubadour manuscripts not listed here.

Part 1

Introduction

Written and oral traditions

Rhythm and meter

Melodic characteristics

Elements of form

1 Introduction

PRELIMINARIES

For more than seven centuries the troubadours and trouvères have fascinated lovers of poetry and music alike. In some highly romanticized representations they have been considered as perpetually enamoured young men who performed songs for beautiful young women on balconies, while accompanying themselves on a lute or other esoteric instrument. There is little evidence for this vision. In fact the scarcity of information about the personalities of these poet-composers and about the circumstances that prompted them to compose their songs is a source of real frustration for anyone who would like to find unambiguous evidence for the colorful surroundings suggested by some of the miniatures in the medieval manuscripts in which these songs are preserved. However, romantic surroundings dispelled, there still remain the many truly fascinating poetic and melodic characteristics of the songs themselves.

According to tradition the troubadours and trouvères were both poets and composers. No reasons have been found to reject this notion, although many questions remain regarding the importance of one creative activity in relation to the other. There are many excellent studies dealing with the form and content of the poem, but almost all of the studies dealing with the music are only for the highly specialized medievalists among the musicologists, and, in an often forbidding terminology, they deal primarily with minute technical problems of rhythm and meter. Furthermore, most of these musicological studies are based upon principles that are no longer prevalent among the philologists who occupy themselves with medieval literature. In the last half century, the latter have increased markedly their knowledge of the circumstances under which poetry was created and disseminated in the Middle Ages. It may still be too soon for the dual task of bridging the gap between musicological and philological studies and of writing a general study about the most important aspects of the relation between text and melody in medieval song, but this book is intended as an attempt to make a real contribution in both areas.

For a study of this nature it was considered unnecessary and impractical to examine all the preserved poems and melodies in detail; instead a careful attempt was made to evaluate a truly representative cross section of the total repertory. Thus the conclusions drawn are general ones, which do not necessarily take into consideration all of the stylistic differences that may exist between chansons of individual authors. Discussion of such details belongs in monographs concerned with specific authors or certain groups of chansons.

Despite their differences in language and location, the troubadours and trouvères left us songs that have so many characteristics in common that it is quite logical to discuss them in one study. The texts of almost 5000 songs have been preserved. But unfortunately the melodies for only one-third of them have come down to us. A truly large number of melodies composed by trouvères is found in the manuscripts; these melodies cover a long time-span and a broad geographical area, and are the work of many different men. Although the number of troubadour melodies is regrettably small, it is still large enough to warrant the conclusion that the melodies of the troubadours are very similar to those of the trouvères. From historical and literary points of view the songs of the German Minnesinger could be included in this study, but too few melodies of German songs have been preserved to justify making general conclusions about them similar to those given here about the chansons of the troubadours and trouvères. Thus for circumstantial reasons I have decided to reserve for a future monograph the discussion of those Minnesinger songs that have been preserved with music.[1]

It is rather difficult, perhaps even impossible, to give a precise description of the songs of the troubadours and the trouvères because of their diversity in form and content. However, for a general delineation of our subject we may take the medieval manuscripts as guides. A large number of them contain almost exclusively one fairly unified type of song consisting of several stanzas; a stanza may contain from seven to twelve lines, but all stanzas of a given song are of exactly the same form and are

---

1. A number of selected works about the Minnesinger are included in the Bibliography.

sung to the same melody. It is to this type of song, wherever it occurs and regardless of its subject, that this study is devoted.

Now, as well as in the 12th and 13th centuries, there is some divergence in the terminology used to designate these songs. Some authors divide them into many different groups, usually upon the basis of only one of several important criteria, such as the nature of the subject, the form of the poem, or the form of the melody. And usually each group bears a label that was already used in the Middle Ages. Other authors, however, have found that one can neither be consistent in drawing the lines between such groups nor take into consideration all important criteria at once. It is perhaps for this reason that they use only one general term, such as 'song', or even more often the French word '*chanson*'. In addition, when restricting their discussion to the content of the poem only, these authors may use other appropriate terms, such as *pastorelle* and *alba*; we will follow this system.

When, in the middle of the 13th century, these songs began to be written down, the area which now constitutes France did not yet have one official and codified language with a standard orthography, but rather a number of regional and local dialects with no uniformity in spelling whatsoever. Nevertheless we find just enough similarities among the preserved literary works of the 12th and 13th centuries to justify speaking of two languages: Provençal, or better, Old Provençal, for roughly the southern half of present-day France, and Old French for the northern half.[1] Neither seems to have been the exclusive dialect of one certain area; both seem to have been literary languages to some extent based upon the local dialects of Toulouse for Old Provençal and of Paris for Old French, as well as upon the common elements in several dialects of the surrounding areas. Neither was codified or unified, and in both the more specific dialect of the author or of the scribe shines through these somewhat artificial languages.

Obviously the Provençal term 'troubadour' is used for authors of the songs in Old Provençal and the French term 'trouvère' for authors of songs in Old French. Beyond this simple distinction there is some

divergence among present-day authors regarding the usage of these two terms. Some authors apply them indiscriminately to the authors of practically any form of medieval French and Provençal poetry, regardless of whether it has been preserved with or without music, while others prefer to restrict their reference to the poet-composers of songs about courtly love. Some, in an attempt to prevent confusion, avoid the terms altogether. In this study, following many studies in medieval literature, we shall apply these terms to all poet-composers from the 12th and 13th centuries in their capacity as authors of the lyric songs briefly described above. Thus the terms do not refer to the performers of these songs, although many of the troubadours and trouvères may have been performers as well, much the same as many present-day composers are also performers, and many poets are quite proficient in reciting poetry to an audience.

There is still some difference of opinion regarding the exact meaning of the terms 'troubadour' and 'trouvère' and of the related verbs '*trobar*' and '*trouver*'. Not being an etymologist, I restrict myself to the remark that taking the verbs 'trobar' and 'trouver' in the meaning of 'to find', 'to invent', or 'to make up' fits extremely well in the observations made in the last section of Chapter 5.

THE MANUSCRIPTS

From the 13th century on, each century saw new handwritten collections or printed editions of poems by troubadours and trouvères, and Dante was only one in a long line of distinguished authors who have written about the art of the troubadours and trouvères. The number of primary sources dating from the 13th and early 14th centuries, the number of chansons contained in them, and the number of authors named in them is so enormous that detailed catalogues have been compiled to make possible the exhaustive research required by responsible scholarship.

In 1884 Gaston Raynaud published a bibliography of all trouvère chansons known to him, indicating for each chanson in which manuscripts it occurred and where it could be found in modern editions.[2] Recently

---

1. Old Provençal was used also by some authors from Italy and Spain; and, judging by their names, some of the poets writing in Old French stemmed from the Dutch-speaking areas of present France and Belgium.

2. Gaston Raynaud, *Bibliographie des chansonniers français des* XIIIe *et* XIVe *siècles, comprenant la description de tous les manuscrits, la table des chansons classées par ordre alphabétique de rimes et la liste des trouvères.* 2 vols. Paris 1884.

a partial second edition appeared, revised by Hans Spanke.[1] In this catalogue, hereafter referred to as Raynaud-Spanke, we find a list of over 2000[2] chansons–approximately three-fourths of them preserved with their melodies–by more than 200 different trouvères. In the list of manuscripts we find reference to some 20 large collections, each containing from 50 to over 500 chansons, and numerous smaller and fragmentary sources.

It was not until 1933 that a bibliography of the troubadours and their chansons appeared, compiled by Alfred Pillet and Henry Carstens.[3] From this catalogue, usually referred to as Pillet-Carstens, we learn that the chansons in Old Provençal outnumber those in Old French by about 500 and that the list of troubadours is more than twice as long as that of the trouvères. Unfortunately, however, only about 250 melodies have been preserved; compared with the wealth of preserved trouvère melodies this is a meager harvest indeed.

In both bibliographies the chansons are numbered and it is a rather general habit to use these numbers whenever discussing a particular chanson. Although it tends to bring down a chanson's identity to a mere number, this practice facilitates further research and therefore will be followed here. In Raynaud-Spanke the chansons are ordered alphabetically and numbered consecutively according to the rhyme syllable of the first line. In Pillet-Carstens, however, the names of the authors are ordered alphabetically and numbered consecutively; in addition the chansons of each troubadour are numbered separately, thus giving each chanson two numbers.

Similarly, I will use the letters occurring in the two bibliographies and listed on page 9 to identify the manuscripts, rather than the complete signatures, and by applying them logically I hope to avoid any confusion that conceivably could result from the circumstance that some of the manuscripts concerned contain both Old Provençal and Old French chansons and therefore occur in both bibliographies, but with different identi-

fication letters. For example, *Le Manuscrit du Roi* (Paris, Bibliothèque Nationale, f.fr. 844) occurs in Raynaud-Spanke with M as siglum, while it bears the siglum W in Pillet-Carstens. In addition the same manuscript occurs in Ludwig's *Repertorium* of motets with the letter R.[4] To compound the confusion the siglum Mt is used in Raynaud-Spanke to identify the pages of a smaller collection with some 60 chansons by Thibaud de Navarre which erroneously were inserted in different parts of this manuscript.

The collections with Old Provençal and Old French chansons have all the appeal, beauty and loveliness so typical of the medieval manuscripts. The elegantly ornamented capitals, so unlike the compact minuscules, and the irregularities of the small details are combined with the orderliness and regularity of the page in its entirety. Some manuscripts even give us 'portraits' of troubadours and trouvères; at least one would assume that the little man depicted at the beginning of a group of chansons is supposed to be the troubadour or trouvère whose chansons follow. The one collection which may have been the most beautiful and most luxurious of them all, *Le Manuscrit du Roi*, has been robbed of many of its miniatures, probably by some pilferer who was after the gold used in them and who in this process mutilated many chansons and tore out whole pages.

In general these collections, or *chansonniers* as they often are called, are neatly executed and well organized. The chansons are most often grouped according to author, with chansons by unknown authors often in a special section. In a few manuscripts the chansons are given in alphabetical order according to the first letter of the poem. Interestingly, for this alphabetizing only the first letter is taken into consideration; thus all the poems beginning with a certain letter occur as one group, while there is no alphabetical order within such a group.

In the cases where music is provided, notes appear only above the first stanza of the text, which is understandable, since the melody was to be repeated for all stanzas. There are indications, to be discussed in the following chapter, that very often the text was copied first and the melody was entered afterwards, sometimes by a different scribe. Unfortunately, for some chansons

---

1. G. Raynauds *Bibliographie des altfranzösischen Liedes, neu bearbeitet und ergänzt von Hans Spanke, erster Teil*. Leiden 1955.

2. Among them are approximately 300 chansons of the sequence and the rondel types which are not discussed in the present study.

3. Alfred Pillet and Henry Carstens, *Bibliographie der Troubadours*. Halle 1933.

4. Friedrich Ludwig, *Repertorium organorum recentioris et motetorum vetustissimi stili*. Halle 1910.

this second scribe never had a chance to do his part of the work; the staffs are there, but the notes were never filled in. There are even some entire manuscripts in which space is provided for all the melodies and in which all the staffs are drawn, but the notes were never entered. In other chansonniers there is music for some, but not all, chansons. Actually there are only a few manuscripts in which the music is entered for all chansons. In others, especially several of those with Old Provençal chansons, no space is provided for the music.

Several of the small chansonniers are parts of much larger collections of literary and musical creations of the 12th and 13th centuries; conversely, a few of the chansonniers have small sections with works other than the usual troubadour and trouvère chansons. But almost always the different genres of musical and literary works are kept separate, and often the scribe neatly indicates at the beginning of each section what is to follow.

Le Manuscrit du Roi for example, originally opened with four chansons devoted to the Virgin Mary–three of them now lost–followed by over 400 chansons by various trouvères, grouped by composer; interestingly, noblemen come first and the poets without title follow. The next section contains some 60 chansons by various troubadours, followed by a section containing motets and chansons of the rondel type, and finally there are three songs of the *lai* type. One manuscript devoted solely to the works of Adam de la Halle (ms. W) gives Adam's musical works in the following order: chansons, jeux-partis (which are discussed in this study under the general heading 'chansons'), rondels, and motets. All of these are followed by works of primarily literary nature, including two plays, *Le jeu d'Adan* and *Le jeu de Robin et Marion*, which are interspersed with some short monophonic refrains.★1

If the number of preserved sources is any indication, the fashion of collecting chansons with their melodies must have been very strong and widespread in certain French circles, and this gives us the inestimable advantage that there is enormous multiplication in these collections. Many a chanson occurs in more than one source, some of them in more than ten different manuscripts. Although there are often considerable discrepancies among such multiple versions of a given chanson, there are also remarkable similarities. Both these

similarities and dissimilarities provide us with valuable information. In this aspect it is especially regrettable that so few of the troubadour chansons have been preserved with their melodies. Whereas we have a dozen versions of many trouvère melodies, we have at most four versions–excluding contrafacts★–of only a few troubadour melodies. It is for this reason that the chansons of the trouvères occupy the first and the largest place in almost all chapters of this study.

The discrepancies among the sources concern virtually every aspect of the chansons, including the names of their authors. There are instances in which a chanson with multiple versions is attributed to as many different authors as there are sources for it. If, in such cases, there is no other information, we are unable to determine the true author of the chanson. Consequently, we know that the attributions in the manuscripts are not always reliable and we have no certainty at all about the authorship of chansons for which the name of the author is given in only one or two sources. Fortunately, for an abundant number of chansons the information regarding the authorship seems very reliable, either because all or many manuscripts agree upon the attribution or because–in a very few instances–we have other reliable information.

It is virtually impossible to determine accurate dates of compilation for the chansonniers. We have to reckon with the possibility that more medieval manuscripts were lost than were preserved, and some of the preserved manuscripts may be faithful copies of older, now lost collections. Therefore it is impossible to answer a number of interesting and important questions about those chansonniers which happen to have been preserved. For example, we cannot determine which manuscript actually contains the oldest reading of a given chanson either by virtue of its own date or by virtue of the date of its model. But it is of importance for this study to note that, according to expert estimates based upon the study of handwriting and upon the probable date of the chansons included, the oldest sources with music date from the middle of the 13th century at the earliest.[2]

---

1. ★ Refers to the glossary where an explanation is given.

2. For detailed discussion of individual manuscripts see: Alfred Jeanroy, *Bibliographie sommaire des chansonniers provençaux*, Paris 1916; Jeanroy, *Bibliographie sommaire des chansonniers français du moyen âge*, Paris 1918; Eduard Schwan, *Die altfranzösischen Liederhandschriften*, Berlin 1886; Clovis Brunel, *Bibliogra-→*

THE AUTHORS

Regrettably the sources of biographical information about the troubadours and trouvères are very scant indeed and the little there is must be studied closely to separate fact from fancy. We can glean some information from the poems themselves, but we have to realize that then, just as now, a poet writing in the first person is not necessarily narrating his own personal experiences. Some of the troubadours and trouvères were important persons in fields other than poetry, and thus we may find their names in chronicles and especially in ecclesiastic, financial, political, or legal records which, by their nature, usually do not give us much more than the minimal information about a person's social status and an approximate date.[1]

The most curious and amusing, but also the least reliable, information comes from the *vidas* and *razos*, concerning approximately 100 troubadours, which are preserved in some 13th and 14th century manuscripts.[2] The vidas, which are short biographies, and the razos, which are introductory remarks to certain chansons, were once considered completely reliable; however, especially since the beginning of this century, it has been recognized that there is a strong legendary element in many of them. This is particularly true of the razos, which often draw upon the poem itself to provide the audience with an elaborate and fanciful backdrop for the chanson to come and which take almost every word in the poem quite literally, thus ignoring all consequences of poetic license. Nevertheless, neither the vidas nor the razos should be ignored, first of all because in a number of instances they provide the link between a name in a song collection and a name in some official or semi-official medieval record or document. And al-

---

phie des manuscrits littéraires en ancien provençal, Paris 1935; D'Arco Silvio Avalle, *La letteratura medievale in lingua d'oc nella sua tradizione manoscritta*, Torino 1961; and Adolf Lang, *Die musikalische Überlieferung des Provenzalischen Minnesangs: Quellen und Repertoire*; dissertation for the University of Erlangen-Nürnberg, in preparation. Unfortunately only the last work gives extensive consideration to the music. Further discussion of individual manuscripts may be found in various editions of the poems and in studies listed in Pillet-Carstens and Raynaud-Spanke.

1. For biographic sketches of selected troubadours, see James J. Wilhelm, *Seven Troubadours: The Creators of Modern Verse*. University Park, Pa. and London 1970.

2. Jean Boutière and A.-H. Schutz, *Biographies des Troubadours*, revised edition by Jean Boutière. Paris 1964.

---

though the vidas may give the impression of providing primarily social gossip in addition to rather glib musical and literary criticism, they also reveal what was considered to be typical, exceptional, or just worth mentioning about a certain troubadour or about troubadours in general during the 13th and 14th centuries.

Taken together these sources of biographical information make it possible to determine the general period during which the troubadours and trouvères created their chansons. The period of the troubadours covers approximately the entire 12th and 13th centuries, while that of the trouvères covers only the last third of the 12th and the entire 13th centuries. The earliest known troubadour whose dates have been determined with reasonable dependability is probably none other than Guillaume, known both as Guillaume VII, Count of Poitou, and as Guillaume IX, Duke of Aquitaine. In addition to the provinces of Poitou and Aquitaine, Guillaume inherited several other fiefdoms. Thus he was the ruler of a large and culturally advanced area of France; for this reason there is quite reliable information about his life, including exact dates of birth and death, 1071-1126.

We find that the position of the troubadours in the social hierarchy differs widely. To the authors of the vidas, noble status was neither a requirement nor a guarantee for receiving high praise as a troubadour. Of the approximately 100 troubadours about whom vidas have been preserved, at least seven were women and only half of them appear to have been noblemen. Information about the educational level of the troubadours is very scarce. In a very few instances there are references in the vidas to a certain troubadour's ability to read or write, perhaps implying that this was something exceptional. This seems to be in keeping with the general situation in Europe of the 12th and 13th centuries; although education was expanding rapidly, those who could read and write were few in number and the majority of them were members of the clergy. Although a few troubadours are recorded as having been clergymen at one time or another, it appears that in most cases these men wrote their songs before they entered the monastery or after they left it. The most famous person in this group is undoubtedly Folquet de Marseille, who is said to have been the son of a wealthy merchant. After having gained great fame as a troubadour he abandoned the world, entered a Cistercian monastery, became its abbot, and subsequently was bishop of Toulouse. Apparently in this case the biographer's remarks are based upon facts.[1] It is unknown how trustworthy the biographer is when relating that a papal legate forced Gui d'Ussel, canon of Brioude and Montferrand, to give up writing songs.[2]

It may be true that Guillaume of Aquitaine and Poitou is the first *known* troubadour whose poems have been preserved–unfortunately without melodies–but he certainly was not the only troubadour of his time, neither was he the author of the oldest songs preserved in Old Provençal. Among the manuscripts originating from southern France, perhaps from the abbey of St. Martial in Limoges, there is one from the 11th century which contains, among many Latin entries, two songs in Old Provençal and one using Latin for some of its stanzas and Old Provençal for the rest.[3] The melodies are notated for all three, but for several reasons transcription is rather problematic. Documents tell us that Eblon, Viscount of Ventadour, was contemporary to Guillaume as a poet-composer of songs in Provençal, but none of his songs seems to have been preserved. In addition there is probably no way of determining whether or not any of the anonymously preserved songs predate those of Guillaume.

Turning to the authors of chansons in Old French, we find a similar dearth of biographical information and there are no Old French counterparts to the Provençal vidas and razos. Nevertheless, whatever information there is points to a diversity in social and intellectual background similar to that found for the troubadours.[4] But it is impossible to make any reasonable assumptions about the question of who may have been the earliest known trouvère, because among the trouvères whose activity falls before the year 1200 there is not one for whom we have reliable dates; none of them was remotely as important in political life as Guillaume of Aquitaine and Poitou. Among those who could qualify as earliest known trouvère is Chrétien de Troyes, who

seems to have been already active as a poet in the 1160's. Chrétien is also the author of several long narrative poems, such as *Erec et Enide*, *Lancelot*, and *Perceval*; as such he is one of the very few troubadours and trouvères whose major fame lies outside the area of lyric poetry. Among other trouvères whose chansons may have been the earliest preserved there are Richard the Lionhearted (who was a great-grandson of Guillaume of Aquitaine), Blondel de Nesle, Gace Brulé, le Chastelain de Coucy, and certainly Huon d'Oisi.

Thus no one among the trouvères may be Guillaume's counterpart as earliest known troubadour, but Thibaud de Champagne certainly was his equal from a political point of view. Because of his ancestry Thibaud was almost destined to become important both in politics and in poetry. He was the grandson of Marie de Champagne, who herself was the daughter of King Louis VII and Eleanor of Aquitaine; the latter was in turn the granddaughter of Guillaume of Aquitaine and Poitou. From his father Thibaud inherited the counties of Champagne and Brie; in addition to his countdoms, he inherited, later in his life, an even loftier title as King of Navarre, and it is under this title that he is usually referred to in the chansonniers, even though Navarre itself (within the borders of present-day Spain) was a relatively unimportant little kingdom in the Pyrenees. Consequently there is an unusual amount of precise information about Thibaud; he was born in 1201, probably on May 30, and he died in 1253, probably on July 7.[5]

Thibaud de Champagne is also somewhat exceptional as a trouvère in having left us one religious *lai*; he is one of only a dozen trouvères who wrote one or two songs in that form. There are a few trouvères who are much more exceptional than Thibaud in writing poetry other than the usual chanson. One of them, Chrétien de Troyes, has already been mentioned. Two other notable exceptions are Jean Bodel, who is primarily known for his *Jeu de St. Nicholas*, and Richard de Fournival, who is perhaps best known for his *Traité des quatre nécessaires* and *Bestiaire d'amour*. Most exceptional of all is certainly Adam de la Halle, who left not only chansons and jeux partis in the usual style of the trouvères, but who also left polyphonic motets and rondels as well as

1. Ibidem, 470.

2. Ibidem, 202.

3. Friedrich Gennrich, nos. 1, 2, and 3 in *Der Musikalische Nachlass der Troubadours*. 2 vols, Darmstadt 1958, 1960.

4. Roger Dragonetti, *La technique poétique des trouvères dans la chanson courtoise*, Bruges 1960; contains an appendix, pp. 651-698, comprising brief biographical information concerning many trouvères as well as references to more detailed studies.

5. See A. Wallensköld, *Les chansons de Thibaut de Champagne, Roi de Navarre*. Paris 1925. XI-XXVII.

several other works of primarily literary interest, including two plays.

THE PERFORMERS

It is difficult to determine now who were the usual performers of the chansons of troubadours and trouvères and under what circumstances the chansons were performed. It seems fairly certain, however, that performing in public and for remuneration was considered a very base occupation and that no person of high position or of good means would do such a thing. We also know that not all troubadours and trouvères were of high position or well-to-do; thus some of them may well have made a living, at least in part, by reciting their own chansons and those of others. Furthermore, not all performances for an audience were necessarily 'public performances' in the usual meaning of the word nor was remuneration necessarily one of the aims of each performance. Thus it seems quite conceivable that even some of the highest-placed troubadours and trouvères recited chansons to their friends and equals without debasing themselves thereby to the level of public performers. These assumptions appear to be corroborated by what we read in the Old Provençal vidas. Approximately one-third of the men discussed in them are said to have been *jongleurs* as well as troubadours. Some, among them Guillaume of Aquitaine, are said to have been very able singers, whereas others are noted for their inability to sing.

It is known that contests were held in Northern France as early as the 13th century in which trouvères could win a prize for their chansons. These were similar to the contests held for French *rhetoriciens*, Dutch *rederijkers*, and the German *Meistersinger* during the 14th century and later. We know of some trouvères who won prizes and even some individual songs that were 'crowned' and were marked as such in the manuscripts. There is at least one song (R 865) from a disappointed contestant who proved to be a poor loser and who accused the judge of favoritism, and there is another song (R 1612) from a winner who felt compelled to say something nasty about envious losers. It appears that the contesting trouvère could either appear in person and perform his own song or ask someone else to do so for him. We know the name given to such contests, 'Puy' or 'Pui', but we have no information about the musical or poetic criteria.[1]

Nowadays the public performer of the Middle Ages is designated with the term 'jongleur', which is an old term and which was already used to some extent in the Middle Ages for all kinds of public performers, regardless of their artistic and social level. Thus the term 'jongleur' is applicable to anyone who juggled, danced, did animal shows, played on instruments or told stories, as well as to those who performed the chansons of troubadours and trouvères. It may be that the ideal–and most affluent–jongleur was the one who could do all these things and still more, but we also have to realize that many of the chansons of the troubadours and trouvères were sophisticated and rather esoteric songs which were probably appreciated only in certain limited circles. The wide usage of the term 'jongleur' should not be taken as an indication that the connoisseurs considered a performance of these chansons as an amusement on the same level as a dancing bear or a dressed-up monkey. It is certainly noteworthy that whenever in the vidas and razos the term 'joglar' occurs there is never any reference to forms of public entertainment other than singing chansons.

Next to nothing is known about the circumstances under which the chansons were performed, yet there is a persistent theory that the chansons were always performed to instrumental accompaniment. I have been able to find neither the origin of this theory nor any substantial evidence for it.[2] It may be true that 'the jongleur' could both play on instruments and perform chansons, but assuming on this basis that the chansons were accompanied is scarcely logical; one may just as well assume that the jongleur did a juggling act when reciting a chanson, or that his bear danced to it and his monkey climbed a tree.

It seems that those who believe that the chansons were accompanied base their belief in part on some of the miniatures found in the chansonniers. Proper eval-

1. For more detailed discussions of the pui, see Henry Guy, *Adan de la Hale*, Paris 1898, XXVII-LVIII; Margarete Rösler, 'Der Londoner Pui' in *Zeitschrift für romanische Philologie*, XLI, 1921; Dragonetti, 371-378; and 'Cantus Coronatus' in the glossary.

2. In the treatise by Grocheo there are two puzzling remarks on this subject. Both remarks probably refer to the possibility of *playing* trouvère chansons on the viella, not necessarily to *accompanying* them. For further discussion of these and other remarks by Grocheo, see 'Cantus Coronatus' in the glossary.

uation of medieval miniatures is a special discipline and no thorough iconographical study of the illustrations in the chansonniers has been made so far. Without being an expert in that field I can safely point out a few characteristics of the illuminations in the chansonniers.

The most outstanding group is formed by those which may be called 'portraits' of a certain troubadour or trouvère. Among them there are a few which portray the author with a musical instrument, especially one which looks like a lyre or a harp. But to consider these illustrations as evidence for instrumental accompaniment would be to ignore the medieval penchant for portraying a person with the clearly recognizable attributes of his specialty, and it is well-known that the harp and the lyre are the age-old symbols of the poet. Sometimes an author is presented in full armor and on horseback in such a portrait. We can conclude from this only that the author concerned was a knight, and no one would conclude that he wrote or performed his chansons on horseback and dressed in full armor or that the meter of his poems was inspired by his horse's gallop. Among the miniatures there are dozens of such portraits of troubadours and trouvères in full armor and on horseback; judging from their titles, they were all noblemen.

Besides the 'portraits' there are a few other illustrations of people with instruments among the numerous miniatures which appear in the margins and around the initials in some of the manuscripts, but there are also miniatures portraying men who appear to be singing or declaiming without instruments.[1] There are many other miniatures which have nothing to do with either singing or playing instruments; some of them illustrate matters mentioned in the poem which is ornamented by that picture, but others appear to have nothing to do with the poem. Thus basing theories upon these few miniatures with instruments appears inadvisable.

It is striking that numerous discussions and modern editions of chansons of troubadours and trouvères contain reproductions of medieval miniatures, including 'portraits' of King David, taken from liturgical books containing psalms or dealing with psalmody and from commentaries on psalms which obviously have nothing to do with these chansons and which, as is well-known,

abound with allegorical pictures of musical instruments.[2] The pictures are certainly attractive, but they are irrelevant to the chansons.

The central question is not whether medieval singers ever sang to instrumental accompaniment. In some of the narrative literature of the Middle Ages we find clear indications that this was done, but that does not prove that the chansons of the troubadours and trouvères were accompanied, too. After all, in presently existing primitive and high cultures all kinds of songs are found, and we have to reckon with the possibility that medieval western Europe also knew many kinds of songs, popular as well as esoteric ones; some of these may habitually have been accompanied, but not necessarily all of them.

Furthermore, if instrumental accompaniment of the chansons under discussion was indeed as common as some want us to believe, some reference is likely to have been made to this practice either within the songs or elsewhere. In some *envoys** we find reference to nameless messengers who were to convey the chanson to the addressee, but nothing is ever said about instrumental accompaniment. Colin Muset began one of his chansons (R 476) with the statement *Sire Cuens, j'ai vielé devant vous en vostre ostel*, with which Colin may have said that he played a fiddle or some such instrument in the count's castle. But we do not know whether he used the instrument for accompaniment, for a prelude, or a postlude to his chansons, or whether it was used for purely instrumental performance, for example to play dance tunes. We do not even know whether we should take this statement literally or allegorically. In the Old Provençal vidas and razos we find ample reference to singing and to performers who sang on behalf of certain troubadours, but again we find nothing about instrumental accompaniment, although of one troubadour, Perdigo, who was also a jongleur, it is said that he could play an instrument and 'find' very well ('saup ben violar e trobar').[3] Neither is there any reference to the use of instruments by those who, in many aspects, appear to be the cultural heirs of the troubadours and trouvères, namely the French *rhétoriciens* of the 14th century, the Dutch *rederijkers*, and the German *Meistersinger*; in fact it is well known that the Meister-

1. Two such miniatures occur in trouvère manuscript O (see Plates I and II).

2. James W. McKinnon, 'Musical Instruments in Medieval Psalm Commentaries and Psalters' in *Journal of the American Musicological Society*, XXI, 3-20. 1968.
3. Boutière and Schutz, 407.

singer were opposed to instrumental music in general and the matter of accompanying their songs does not even seem to arise.[1]

Considering the complete absence of documentary evidence of instrumental accompaniment, it seems unwise to maintain that as a rule the chansons were accompanied. Perhaps the chansons were accompanied but, in all truth, we can find no reason for this assumption other than our own wishful thinking.

THE CONTENTS OF THE POEMS

Several problems concerning the chansons, especially those relating to their performance, could conceivably be solved if there were unambiguous information about the origin of the art of the troubadours and trouvères or if the chansons could be divided into clearly distinguishable groups, each perhaps with its own history and its own performance practices. Unfortunately, however, the numerous expert studies concerning these questions, especially those about the contents of the poems, have demonstrated clearly that the chansons can not be divided into neat categories and that the origin of French lyric poetry is a very elusive problem, especially so since virtually nothing is known about those secular songs that are likely to have existed in France throughout the Middle Ages. For it is difficult to believe that there were no secular songs in France before the earliest troubadours and that during the 12th and 13th centuries there were no secular songs other than those of the troubadours and trouvères.

In various forms of the literature of the 12th and 13th centuries we frequently encounter a somewhat unusual concept, long referred to as 'courtly love'.[2] Even within the poetry of the troubadours and trouvères this concept fluctuates in meaning and defies all attempts at a generally valid definition. Thus, rather than make a

futile attempt at doing what others, more competent in these matters than I, have failed to do, I shall restrict myself to mentioning some recurring aspects of the songs devoted to courtly love.

The most realistic, albeit unromantic, starting point may well be the observation that in many of their poems the troubadours and trouvères strove to rise above the level of the ordinary everyday love songs. It is difficult to determine how conscious the authors were of this endeavor, but it appears that their motivations to do so ranged from a genuine desire to write about the beauty of love to a pedantic or fashionable attempt at being different, at appearing sophisticated and esoteric. In most poems about courtly love, one gets the impression that the authors wanted to see love not only as a completely natural compulsion but also as some noble and rational obligation to love itself. Accordingly, the poet, almost always singing of his own love, would not immediately give in to all natural inclinations; he would rather cultivate his feelings in secrecy and he would seek to behave in a manner which elevated him above the ordinary lover. Instead of going directly to the woman and blurting out that he had fallen in love with her, he would react with a fascinating combination of self-control and abandon. He was completely lost in his feelings for his lady, he might profess to have lost all control over himself, but he was unlikely to go to her and indicate in a direct manner that he loved her. A really courtly lover would not speak of his feelings with ordinary human words, neither to his friends nor to the lady herself. Instead, he would wait and try to conceal his love, but of course his love was so great and he suffered so much under it that it did not go unnoticed. In fact, usually the poet knew that it was noticeable, or at least hoped that it was, because only in this way could a true lover communicate his feelings.

The questions of whether and when to speak of one's love are discussed in a rather amusing way in the jeu-parti between Thibaud de Navarre–at that time still only a count–and an unnamed, perhaps imaginary, clerk (see Part 2, No. 11). It is certainly not accidental that the nobleman rules out any attempt at expressing one's feelings with words, while the clerk, who of course is less courtly than a count, admits that he can no longer endure the pains of silence. The obvious implication of this discussion, as well as of many other poems, is the theory that suffering and pain make one's

1. See Archer Taylor, *The Literary History of Meistergesang*, New York-London 1937. It is probably significant that elaborate instructions have been preserved for the usage of instruments before and during some Meistersinger productions of religious plays; see Fritz Schnell, *Zur Geschichte der Augsburger Meistersingerschule*. Augsburg 1958.

2. For two recent and considerably different discussions of courtly love, see Moshé Lazar, *Amour courtois et fin' amors dans la littérature du XIIe siècle*, Paris 1964; and Leo Pollmann, *Die Liebe in der Hochmittelalterlichen Literatur Frankreichs: Versuch einer historischen Phänomenologie*, Frankfurt 1966.

love more endurable and that easily divulged feelings will not last.

Emphasizing the almost super-human behavior of the man is the high praise bestowed upon the lady. Of course she is incomparably beautiful and courtly, but in addition she is of such high standing that the poet is thrown back and forth between despair of ever attracting her attention and conviction that his love is great and noble enough to overcome all obstacles and to convince her that he is worthy of her attention. Another great obstacle is formed by the slander of envious rivals who surround her continuously. Their attempts to ridicule the suffering poet in the eyes of her, whom he wants to please most, often have a double effect: they make him fear that she may feel contempt for him, and they add to her noble character and high standing because he does not expect her to be misled by such evil and uncourtly characters. Thus in both ways the lady becomes ever more unattainable and ever more desirable. It is stated repeatedly in the poems that all the author wants is a little attention from his sweet lady; but in a number of instances a cynical analyst may come to the conclusion that all the poet wants and delights in, is the suffering and the great pains he endures in the service of love.

Not only the man was required to behave in a courtly manner, but since it is almost always the man who is speaking in the poems, we can not glean much information about the lady's obligations. However, despite numerous expressions of despair, the poets make it rather clear that the lady had the duty to respond to true love, and that she should do so with benevolence and selfcontrol rather than with passion.

Whether any carnal desires were connected with courtly love depends entirely upon one's definitions of these two concepts. But this much is true: one expels some of the most famous authors of medieval lyric poetry from the circle of troubadours and trouvères if one excludes all those who, in their poems, expressed a desire for physical pleasure. It is noteworthy, however, that in poems devoted to courtly love one is not likely to encounter any references to physical pleasures that have been obtained already, whereas hints and direct remarks about future or hoped-for pleasures are not rare.

Much has been written about the origin of courtly love and some scholars have surmised that it was in-spired by the Christian's love and respect for the Virgin Mary. But this would in no way explain the secrecy or the suffering one endured because of one's love. Other historians have assumed that the whole concept of courtly love was imported from somewhere outside of France. Some refer to the literature of classical antiquity, and others point to the Arab world as a likely source, since the Christians had so much contact with it, both in the Middle East through the crusades and in Spain where Moslems, Christians and Jews were neighbors and are known to have had considerable cultural intercourse. All of these theories have, undoubtedly, certain validity, but they do not explain the peculiarity that concepts quite similar to that of courtly love occur in other cultures, both present and past.[1] Yet there is no reason to assume that all or most of these cultures have copied this phenomenon from one another. Thus, to understand the emergence of courtly love we need the help of cultural anthropologists as much as that of experts on medieval culture in general.

Courtly love was such a favorite topic that by some it is considered the typical or even the exclusive subject of the chansons of troubadours and trouvères. Those holding the latter view admit to the circles of troubadours and trouvères only those who wrote chansons about courtly love. Although there may be some merit to this approach, in this study we take a considerably wider circle of poems into consideration, entirely in keeping with the interests shown by the chanson collectors of the 13th and 14th centuries and by many of the troubadours and trouvères themselves. With considerable justification we may say that the troubadours and trouvères wrote not only chansons about courtly love, often called 'courtly chansons', but also many other chansons about all kinds of subjects, including religious, political and satirical ones, that are very similar in form and style to the courtly chansons. To a large extent these chansons were written by the same persons, they were sung to the same type of melody, and all of them were collected in the same chansonniers in which the courtly chansons occur.

Among the songs devoted to love other than the courtly variety, we find almost any subject one en-

1. See also Theodor Frings, 'Minnesinger und Troubadours', in *Der Deutsche Minnesang*, ed. Hans Fromm, Darmstadt 1963, 1-57; and Peter Dronke, *Medieval Latin and the Rise of European Love-Lyric*, 2 vols. Oxford 1965, 1966.

counters in love songs of later periods. Whether one finds songs of unrequited love, so popular in the 15th and 16th centuries, depends somewhat upon one's definition of courtly love; since the troubadours and trouvères dwelt so much upon the sufferings and pains preceding the lady's first response, it is difficult to distinguish consistently between the two varieties (e.g., Part 2, No. 7).

Perhaps the most amusing genre of love songs is formed by the *pastourelles*. Their main characters are an innocent or sometimes not so innocent, young shepherdess (pastourelle) and the author, who almost invariably arrives on the scene on horseback, which usually is a sign of nobility. Sometimes the poet remains merely a spectator watching the amorous plays of the shepherdess and her friend. At other times the author is a participant and makes overtures to the beautiful country girl who feels flattered by the interest shown by such a great and noble gentleman and who sometimes marvels at the difference in behavior between a nobleman and a country boy. It happens also, however, that the poet is rejected and driven away by the girl's friend, by a whole troupe of shepherds armed with sticks and pitchforks, or, and this must have been the ultimate in humiliation, singlehandedly by the little shepherdess herself.

The problem of establishing distinct groups in the repertoire of the troubadours and trouvères is convincingly shown in Karl Bartsch's exquisite collection of Old French *romances* and *pastourelles*.[1] Bartsch himself stated that it was impossible to distinguish clearly and consistently between these two forms[2] and his selection of poems shows that it is also impossible to describe or define them unequivocally. In Bartsch's collection there is a small number of poems taken from the motet and rondeau repertoire. On the basis of content their inclusion is completely justified, although they differ considerably from the rest of the songs in stanzaic form and melodic style. For many of his selections Bartsch drew upon the well-known trouvère manuscripts. Most of his selections differ in content from the other chansons in the same manuscripts, but they are indistinguishable from them in melodic style and stanzaic form, except

for the following peculiarities: some of them have considerably more stanzas than the average trouvère chanson and among them there are more chansons with refrain*—including chansons with multiple refrains—than in the trouvère repertoire in general. However, it is impossible to recognize pastourelles by their form only and it is noteworthy that most of the romances and pastourelles with attribution in the manuscripts are assigned to authors to whom other chansons are also attributed.

The *alba* was considerably more serious in nature; and the main characters are usually one another's equals in social standing. In most albas the poet sings of the great sorrows of departure at *dawn* (alba) and about the woman's concern for the man's safe return home. Sometimes this is done in the form of a dialogue between the young lovers and sometimes it is a night watchman, or some other sympathetic person, who announces the end of the joyful night and the disappearance of the safe cloak of darkness, and who warns of the coming of dawn and the danger of discovery which comes with it (see Part 2, No. 3).

In a recently published collection of dawn songs from all over the world and from past and present cultures, B. Woledge, who contributed the section on Old Provençal and Old French dawn songs, found it 'difficult to choose a definition of the Provençal dawn songs, because the genre shades off into other genres, and critics do not always agree which poems are *albas* and which are not'.[3] Apparently the origin of this specific genre was also unclear to this author, but regarding the manner of performance he sees a link between the alba and dancing songs.[4] Perhaps Woledge is correct in considering a certain alba as a dancing song, but in my estimate this is insufficient reason for assuming that all albas were connected with dancing.

A large number of religious songs, in form and style very similar to other troubadour and trouvère chansons, have come to us from the 12th, 13th, and early 14th centuries. This similarity extends so far that in the religious songs we encounter expressions, and even entire sentences, that are commonplace in love poetry. It is known that many of the religious songs are contra-

---

1. Karl Bartsch, *Altfranzösische Romanzen und Pastorellen*. Leipzig 1870.

2. Ibidem, pp. X–XI.

3. B. Woledge, in *Eos: An Enquiry into the Theme of Lovers' Meetings and Partings at Dawn in Poetry*, ed. Arthur T. Hatto. The Hague 1965. p. 345.

4. Ibidem, 347.

facts* of secular songs, but even though the religious songs can not be distinguished from the secular ones in stanzaic form and melodic characteristics, there is no reason to assume that all of them are contrafacts. It would demonstrate a misunderstanding of the medieval religious attitude to assume that none of the troubadours and trouvères would use his creative talents to praise God or the Virgin Mary and that only second-rate imitators would write religious songs.

The song by Thibaud de Navarre included in Part 2 (No. 10) is one of several songs that are both religious and political in content. Other examples of such a mixture may be found among the songs related to crusades, but some love songs can also be found among the crusade songs.

In some discussions of the chansons, especially in histories of music, we find occasionally the theory that the chansons of the troubadours and trouvères are dancing songs or that there are many dancing songs among them. Nothing is less true, but few things are as difficult to prove as the proposition that there is no evidence for a certain theory which has taken hold. It seems that there are two partly interconnected sources for this theory: a book on the origin of French lyric poetry by Alfred Jeanroy[1], and a lengthy review of this book by Gaston Paris.[2]

In the study by Jeanroy it is primarily his discussion of the so-called 'refrains'* that may have been the cause of the notion that there are many dancing songs among our chansons. Jeanroy contends that all chansons of the rondel type, comprising supposedly the rondeau*, virelai*, and ballade*, are dancing songs in origin. Jeanroy's reasoning on this subject is extremely weak; however, even if it is correct, it still does not prove much about the chansons of the troubadours and trouvères. No troubadour and only two trouvères are known to have written rondeaux. Whether they wrote virelais and ballades depends entirely upon one's definition of those forms; but it certainly would be erroneous to consider all chansons with refrains as dancing songs, regardless of the name one gives to them.[3] Very few of the rondeaux that have been preserved occur in collections containing

the chansons of the troubadours and trouvères, and almost all of those which do occur in them appear in separate sections, often mingled with polyphonic compositions. In fact, almost all of the chansons in fixed form from the 13th century have been preserved either without music or with a polyphonic setting.

Gaston Paris, in his review, went even further than Jeanroy and came to the sweeping conclusion that 'the poetry which we see unfold itself in the South during the 12th century... seems to originate essentially from dancing songs used for the May celebrations'.[4] And he suggested that at some special point these songs were transformed into a poetry of the aristocratic society. Paris gives many reasons for his conclusions; among them are the frequent references to May and spring in general, the fact that there are indeed some songs–very few–in the chansonniers which seem to be dancing songs, and the fact that there is some evidence of the existence of dancing songs and May celebrations in Western Europe predating the 12th century. Neither individually nor collectively do these reasons carry much weight. Perhaps no one has ever refuted them, but they have been quietly set aside.

To the best of my knowledge, Paris never posed explicitly the theory that the chansons of the troubadours and trouvères in fact were dancing songs. I do not know who came to this conclusion, but it may have been based upon the above theory of Paris, which means that we face the curious situation that the theory itself collapsed but that one of its conclusions is still with us.

Whatever may be the origin of the misunderstanding under discussion, the most convincing argument against it comes from the very few chansons which probably

1. Alfred Jeanroy, *Les origines de la poésie lyrique en France au moyen âge*. 111-113. Paris 1925.
2. Gaston Paris, 'Les origines de la poésie lyrique en France' in *Journal des Savants*. Nov. 1891, 674-688; Déc. 1891, 729-742; Mars 1892, 155-167; Juillet 1892, 407-429.

3. In many history of music textbooks, including some of the most recent ones, we find the erroneous statement that the troubadours and trouvères wrote rondeaux*, virelais*, and ballades*. One notable exception is *A History of Western Music*, by Donald J. Grout. New York 1960, 62-63. It should also be noted that in 'Rondeaux, Virelais, and Ballades in French 13th-Century Song' in *Journal of the American Musicological Society* VII, 1954, 121-130, Willi Apel retracted and apologized for the statements he had made on this subject in the *Harvard Dictionary of Music*, Cambridge, Mass. 1944, p. 769, and in the *Historical Anthology of Music*, Cambridge, Mass. 1962, p. 216. In the second edition of the *Harvard Dictionary of Music* Cambridge, Mass. 1969, this misrepresentation was corrected, but the retention of the name 'ballade'* for chansons of a certain form is not in keeping with medieval practice and is very confusing.
4. Gaston Paris, Juillet 1892, 426.

were dancing songs. (One of these songs is given as Number 4 in Part 2 of this study.) Comparison of these poems with the thousands of other poems demonstrates convincingly that dancing songs form an insignificant minority in the total preserved medieval repertory.

Practically all modern editions of specific genres from among the troubadour and trouvère poems demonstrate that is very difficult to delineate such genres, even if one takes into consideration the contents only. Categorizing the chansons on the basis of either stanzaic form or melodic style is even more difficult. Taking into consideration contents as well as stanzaic form and melodic style, all attempts at meaningful categorization fail and there remains only one large group of chansons, which vary widely in contents, stanzaic form, and melodic style.

2 Written and oral traditions

THE DISCREPANCIES AMONG MULTIPLE VERSIONS

It is a requirement of all scholarly discussion that unambiguous evidence be given for any theory presented. In this aspect, the person writing about medieval melodies has serious problems, for there is very little unambiguous evidence. The main sources of information, the manuscripts containing the music, appear to contradict one another in so many instances that one wonders whether they can be trusted at all. There are multiple versions of many trouvère chansons and, when comparing the different versions of almost any given chanson, one is struck by the many discrepancies that occur among them. These discrepancies are manifold and concern almost any aspect of the chanson. In fact, among those chansons with two or more versions which I have examined, I have not encountered one in which both text and melody are completely identical in more than two manuscripts.

The customary explanation for the many discrepancies among the melodies is very simple: the scribes, human beings as they were, made scores of errors when they wrote thousands of notes, and therefore the music in the manuscripts does not give a reliable representation of what actually was sung. A precarious situation, however, is created by this seemingly valid and simple assumption. The researcher cannot determine which notes are correct so long as he knows neither the meter nor the scale in which a given song was conceived; at the same time, he cannot determine the scale or the meter in which the song was conceived so long as he does not know which notes in the medieval sources are correct.

This circle could be broken if one were able to determine the nature of the scales and meters in medieval song from sources other than the music in the manuscripts. Consequently in most discussions of medieval song it is assumed that the songs make use only of the scales and meters discussed by the learned writers of the Middle Ages, even though these authors rarely mention the songs of the troubadours and trouvères. Accordingly, a number of theories about meters and scales of medieval song have been developed and, although they have not remained entirely unchallenged, they are widely accepted and we can find them now in most textbooks on medieval music.

However, a large-scale investigation of many melodies in all available versions has led me to the striking conclusion that, if all the usual theories about medieval song are valid, the scribes of the preserved chansonniers wrote more wrong notes than correct ones! Rather than try to refute all the existing theories regarding scales and meters in the songs of the troubadours and trouvères, I will suggest another approach which, in my opinion, fits the music as found in the medieval sources and which is largely modeled after the one prevailing in recent decades in the study of medieval literature in general.

We find that in the text of chansons with multiple versions all sorts of discrepancies occur, from the omission of one word to the omission of a whole line or even an entire stanza, and from differences in spelling to differences in word order or even in choice of words. Usually these differences in wording are insignificant, but sometimes they constitute a difference in meaning. For many chansons the sources disagree upon the order in which the stanzas are to be sung, and in some cases there is even disagreement as to which stanza is the opening stanza of the song (e.g. R 1420, Part 2, No. 8). For a few chansons there is such confusion in order and choice of stanzas that it seems impossible to determine which stem from the original author and which may have been added by others. This problem is aggravated by the fact that in these chansons the stanzas are often self-contained units, and omission or addition of one or more stanzas does not substantially alter the meaning or message of the poem. About the only elements in the text which rarely change from version to version are the number of lines per stanza, the number of syllables per line, and the sound of the rhyme syllables. Among those who occupy themselves primarily with the poems, it seems to be generally accepted now that these deviations are not mere scribal errors as had been believed earlier, but rather that most of them are changes or variants which originated largely during the *oral* tradition of the chansons and which appear to have been fully in accordance with medieval traditions and with the medieval approach to literature.

An examination of the music shows that the discrepancies among melodic versions are even more considerable than among textual versions. In some cases the discrepancies among preserved multiple melodic versions are almost negligible, whereas in other cases there are two or even three entirely different melodies, even though the text demonstrates that we are dealing with the same chanson. Though for most chansons there is little or no doubt about the common parentage of the preserved melodic versions, the discrepancies do cause some serious problems. In order to appraise these discrepancies properly we need to form a general notion of the circumstances under which these melodies were transmitted from the trouvère to the scribes who finally entered them in the collections which have come down to us.

THE TRANSMISSION OF THE CHANSONS

It seems certain that none of the preserved manuscripts with music dates from before the middle of the 13th century, and it seems likely that the earliest preserved chansons were originally composed long before the beginning of that century. Thus many of the chansons predate their written sources by a considerable number of years, whereas others originated during the time that the chansonniers were compiled. We have no documentary information about the process of creating and disseminating chansons nor about the way the scribes went about collecting chansons. All we can do is to form assumptions which are as reasonable as possible in order to have a basis for further study. Speaking in generalities, we have a choice of a scribal tradition, an oral tradition, or some combination of the two.

According to those who hold that there was an exclusively written tradition, a copy–or perhaps several copies–were made from the author's autograph. Such copies may have served as models for another generation of copies and this process perhaps continued for quite some time. It seems natural that the scribes involved in making all these copies made errors. To complicate matters there is the possibility that a scribe of the second or a later generation noticed an error at a certain point and tried to correct this without actually knowing the original melody, thus perhaps wandering even further away from the original. Therefore the end product, the preserved chansonniers, would contain many compounded errors and wrong 'corrections'.

In an exclusively oral tradition, on the other hand, the trouvère, having made a chanson, would teach this *by rote* to one or more performers. These performers in turn would teach the chanson *by rote* to the next generation of performers and this transmission may have continued for several generations. Whether second or third generation performers would learn a chanson simply from listening to someone else's public performances or in deliberate teaching and learning sessions is of minor importance. The important aspect of the process is the fact that variants could develop very easily. It is understandable that not everyone would remember a chanson equally well, and it is also very likely that each performer, whether professional or amateur, would develop his own way of performing a certain chanson and perhaps would vary it from performance to performance.

At first glance the difference between these manners of dissemination may appear inconsequential, but there is a substantial difference between changes caused by scribal inaccuracy and those caused by the freedom of interpretation taken by the performers. The former are outspoken errors and are likely to result in a distortion of the melody up to the point of becoming nonsensical. If this is the case we can determine the character of trouvère melodies only if we are able to eliminate the errors and somehow reconstruct the original with reasonable certainty. If, on the other hand, the deviations among versions are primarily variations made by performers, they are likely to be in keeping with the tradition and the style of performing this type of chanson and with the individual character and meaning of the chanson under consideration. The most important and the most characteristic features of the original may well have been preserved despite these variations. And thus the similarities and the dissimilarities can become an abundant source of information about the many features of the individual chanson and of this type of song in general.

As has been pointed out, no documentary evidence, other than the preserved manuscripts, can be brought forth in favor of either theory. But a number of observations make the theory of an exclusively written transmission very unsatisfactory.

If we accept an exclusively, or even a primarily, written transmission of the melodies of the trouvères,

we must also accept the fact that we seem unable to
locate any of the autographs or to find any reference to
them; on the other hand, Gennrich had singled out
several *envoys*★ that state or imply that the chanson was
orally delivered to the addressee.[1] We must also accept
the fact that we cannot find any of the intermediate
copies that once must have existed between autograph
and preserved manuscripts. In the 19th century and in
the beginning of this century, when most philologists
still believed in the written transmission, several of
them tried to determine the order in which the preserved trouvère chansonniers were compiled. Sometimes they came to quite different conclusions[2], but on
one point they agreed: no preserved manuscript from
the 13th or 14th centuries was a copy of any other preserved manuscript.

Since so many medieval artifacts have been lost over
the ensuing six or seven centuries, the above observations may not be of great importance. But the quantity as well as the nature of the discrepancies among the
multiple versions make it extremely difficult to believe that all or most of the deviations from the original
were caused by mere ignorance, oversight or sloppiness
on the part of the copyists.

There are two more curious phenomena regarding
the nature and the quantity of the discrepancies among
multiple versions. The first has to do with the time
which elapsed between the moment of creating a chanson and the moment of its being entered in the preserved sources. One would assume that, in general, the
shorter the period between the moment of creation and
that of preservation, the more faithful the final reading
is likely to be. Yet if we compare many chansons with
multiple versions by trouvères of different generations,
we find that there is no relation between the similarity
of the versions and the age of the chanson.

The second curious phenomenon and certainly the
most important one is the fact that in many chansons
the first four lines of the melody are preserved much
more uniformly than the following lines. In case of
scribal transmission this could only be explained by
assuming that almost invariably the persons copying

the music got tired and sloppy exactly at the beginning
of the fifth line, unlike the scribes copying the text who
were either accurate or inaccurate throughout the poem.
If, however, we assume that the chansons were disseminated in an oral tradition there is a very normal explanation for this phenomenon. Since in these chansons the melodies of the first and second lines of text
were used also for the third and fourth lines of text,
resulting for those lines in an ABAB form, the person
listening to such a chanson would hear the first part of
the melody twice in every strophe and would therefore
remember those lines better than the following lines
which usually occur only once per strophe.

Thus the theory that the chansons were either exclusively or primarily disseminated in writing does not
stand up under close scrutiny. But, as will become clear
later in this chapter, there are also objections to the
theory that the dissemination was an exclusively oral
one. The manner of organizing the chansons as described in Chapter 1 suggests that very often, before the
work on the actual chansonnier was started, the scribe
knew exactly which chansons were going to be included. Furthermore, the presumably high cost of the
material used for the chansonniers and the neatness
with which the manuscripts are executed force us to
assume that a scribe would rarely enter a chanson without first making a 'draft', probably on some inexpensive
or reusable material like a wax tablet or a slate. The
recognition of this practice leads us to some important
considerations: first, some dissemination could easily
have occurred in writing because one 'draft' may have
been used for two or more of the preserved manuscripts,
and secondly there were still at least two occasions for
scribal errors to occur, at the moment of making the
first notation and at the moment of copying from this
draft onto the valuable material for the actual chansonnier. But these two possible occasions for making
errors explain neither the nature nor the high number
of the deviations that do occur; very few of the discrepancies are clearly recognizable as being caused by
scribal inaccuracy.

All of this leads to the assumption that initially most
or all chansons were transmitted in an exclusively oral
tradition and that from about the middle of the 13th
century on there was dissemination in writing parallel
to the continuing oral tradition.

---

1. Friedrich Gennrich, 'Die Repertoire-Theorie' in *Zeitschrift für
französische Sprache und Literatur*, LXVI, 1956; 81-108.
    2. For example, Joseph Bédier and Pierre Aubry, *Les chansons
de croisade*, Paris 1909. 28-30.

THE COMBINED INFLUENCE OF ORAL AND WRITTEN TRADITIONS

The conclusion reached above has far-reaching consequences. Above all it means that we may not have any chanson in its original form; instead, in many cases we have several versions which all share the basic characteristics of that original and which probably are entirely in accordance with the traditions of the times. Thus, even if the original happens to be among the preserved versions of a given chanson, we might not be able to single it out. Above all we must discontinue the habit of assuming that what *we* in the 20th century consider the *best* version is likely to be the original, because several generations of performers and scribes may well have improved upon the original. More important yet, even if we are able to recognize the original, we should not discard the other versions, because it is from the similarities and dissimilarities among the versions that we receive our most valuable insights into the attitudes and habits of trouvères, performers, and scribes.

It can easily be recognized that in this form of dissemination and preservation there were, in principle, three opportunities for deviations to occur: variations made by the participants in the oral tradition, outright errors made by the scribes in the process of notating and copying the melodies and, finally, the possibility that the scribes made some variations and perhaps some deliberate changes of their own. In practice, however, it is often impossible to determine exactly, note by note, how certain deviations were caused. Nevertheless, in a large-scale examination of trouvère chansons certain general patterns become apparent.

For a proper evaluation of the melodies as they occur in the manuscripts it is mandatory that we first try to understand the performers' and the scribes' attitudes towards the chansons. We cannot simply assume that, in the 12th century, a performer approached a chanson with the same attitude with which present-day musicians approach a Mozart sonata. Similarly we should not *a priori* expect a scribe in the 13th century to copy a chanson with the same intentions as a present-day typographer.

A pertinent study presenting a philologist's point of view cautions us that our opinions of medieval literature are influenced by our 'prejudices and prepossessions which years of association with printed matter have made habitual... If a fair judgment is to be passed upon literary works belonging to the centuries before printing was invented, some effort must be made to realise the extent of the prejudices under which we have grown up, and to resist the involuntary demand that medieval literature must conform to our standards of taste'.[1] H.J.Chaytor, in the book from which this quote is taken, points out a number of truly fascinating and very important differences between the medieval world and ours in regard to creating, disseminating, and appreciating literature. He makes the reader realize how familiar the well-educated person of this century is with words and thoughts expressed in writing, how much he relies on the written rather than the sounded word for his information and for learning new words and foreign languages, and how much even his memory depends on how and where a certain thought or information was printed.

Very different was the case of the medieval reader. Of the few who could read, few were habitual readers; in any case, the ordinary man of our own times probably sees more printed and written matter in a week than the medieval scholar saw in a year. Nothing is more alien to medievalism than the modern reader, skimming the headlines of a newspaper and glancing down its columns to glean any point of interest, racing through the pages of some dissertation to discover whether it is worth his more careful consideration, and pausing to gather the argument of a page in a few swift glances. Nor is anything more alien to modernity than the capacious medieval memory which, untrammelled by the associations of print, could learn a strange language with ease and by the methods of a child, and could retain in memory and reproduce lengthy epic and elaborate lyric poems. Two points, therefore, must be emphasized at the outset. The medieval reader, with few exceptions, did not read as we do; he was in the stage of our muttering childhood learner; each word was for him a separate entity and at times a problem, which he whispered to himself when he had found the solution; this fact is a matter of interest to those who edit the writings which he produced. Further, as readers were few and hearers numerous, literature in its early days was produced very largely for public recitation; hence it was rhetorical rather than literary in character, and rules of rhetoric governed its composition.[2]

1. H.J.Chaytor, *From Script to Print, An Introduction to Medieval Vernacular Literature*. Cambridge, England 1945.
  2. Chaytor, 10.

A large-scale examination of trouvère chansons with multiple versions makes us realize that also in regard to music the attitude of the medieval performer and copyist must have been quite different from that which we have come to expect of our performers and printers. At that time it was apparently not compulsory for a performer always to sing a chanson with exactly the same melody. For him a chanson was not an unalterable entity with a sacred 'original form' to be respected and preserved. It was normal for a medieval performer to sing a certain melody with the notes *he* thought were the appropriate ones and we should not pass judgement on a performer who invented part of a melody or even an entire one. Thus the differences in the versions are not necessarily infractions of the rules for performing someone else's composition, as present-day audiences would be inclined to think; neither should they be considered as conscious improvisations upon a given theme in the modern sense of the word. On the contrary, according to the performer's concept, he was singing the trouvère's melody even though, according to our concept, he was varying it. The difference between these two concepts reflects the fact that our attitude towards printed music differs markedly from the medieval attitude towards the poetry and melody of a chanson learned by rote.

During the period in which it was fashionable in certain circles to collect chansons in writing, a chanson may have been notated on different occasions and as it was sung by different performers; therefore we find differing versions in the manuscripts. How much these versions differed from one another must have depended upon several factors, among them the ability of the performers to remember and, above all, the freedom they allowed themselves in making variants. Another important factor is the nature of the trouvère's original; in general we may assume that the more coherent the text and melody of the original the more uniform the versions would be.

We may safely assume that the scribes also made some changes in the chansons, but that only a very small number of these were caused by inaccuracy; instead they are the consequence of the attitude towards a chanson transmitted by oral tradition and of the medieval methods of copying. I do not wish to imply that medieval methods of copying were primitive, only that, in several respects, circumstances were quite different from those of today. There was no one prescribed way of performing a certain chanson, nor was there the uniformity in musical notation that we know now. Furthermore, we may conclude that the scribes did not copy at sight symbol for symbol. Instead, the differences between certain manuscripts suggest that a scribe may have sung to himself a section from the draft in front of him–not necessarily the melody of exactly one entire line–and then copied from memory what he had *heard* rather than what he had *seen*. Consequently he put himself in the position of a performer notating his own performance. In this process he could make deliberate changes and corrections, but he may also have unconsciously varied the melody more or less extensively by changing the distribution of the melody over the text, by ornamenting the melody, or by simplifying it, exactly the way the performers must have done.

Furthermore, it may be assumed that many of the notators and copyists had respectable educations and knew more about the theory of music and the rules of rhetoric than many a trouvère or performer. Thus in some cases the changes made by the scribes are in accordance with the performance practices, but in other cases the scribe's objective may have been to make the chanson conform to the theories.

CHARACTERISTICS OF SOME CHANSONNIERS

Beyond these general conclusions, the examination of chansons with multiple versions reveals a number of characteristic differences and similarities among individual chansonniers. The notion that large sections of the manuscripts K, L, N, P, and X are closely related is nothing new, and some researchers may already have come to the conclusion that in all probability the scribes involved in compiling these five manuscripts had at their disposal a large number of 'drafts' which, in some as yet undiscovered order, circulated among them. If this is the case it is certainly reassuring to notice how accurate these scribes actually could be. Granted, they made some real errors, such as skipping a whole line, but in general the text and the melody of a given chanson is the same for all manuscripts involved, although in the text there is no complete uniformity in spelling, and here and there the scribes used different symbols and even different clefs for a given melody. Within this group of manuscripts there are also several instances of discrepancies which may have been caused by a conscious or unconscious inclination to make variants. The basic character of the melody remains unchanged and the variant concerns only a very short passage, usually less than a line, but the discrepancies are there, and even within this group of closely related manuscripts it is very difficult to find two readings which are identical in all aspects, including the usage of notational symbols.

It has also been known for a long time that there is a close relationship between the readings of many chansons in the manuscripts T and M. However, this relationship is considerably more complex than that among the above five chansonniers. First of all the two do not have as many chansons in common as originally seems to have been the case for the K L N P X group. Secondly, there are quite a few poems which occur in both manuscripts, while the music for them occurs in only one. Then there are many chansons which are very similar in both text and melody in the two sources, but the similarity is not as close as is the case within the K group. Perhaps the two scribes of T and M derived their versions of these chansons from the same performer but on different occasions. An alternate explanation might be that the two versions came from different performers who learned the chansons from the same teacher. Obviously it is impossible to determine now which one of these hypotheses, if either, is more likely, but it seems rather certain that the versions concerned are not mere copies from one model; neither can they come from two entirely unrelated performers.

The two manuscripts also share a number of chansons related only in the text. First we may consider the chansons by Audefroy le Bastard, whose chansons occur almost exclusively in M and T.[1] The two chansonniers present the songs in exactly the same order, although the series of songs by Audefroy in M is longer by three items than that in T. The readings for the texts in both sources are so similar that both may well have been copied from one model. However, for the melodies the situation is markedly different. For one of the chansons the original scribe of M did not write in the notes; instead a melody, unrelated to the one in T, was entered

by a later hand. For the other melodies there is no doubt about their common parentage, but it seems unlikely that they were copied from one common source. (One of these melodies is given in Part 2, No. 9, and discussed in Chapter 4, p. 51.)

Determining whether or not two versions of a given melody were copied from one written model solely by evaluating the similarities and discrepancies among them may involve some rather subjective judgement; therefore it is of great value that in some instances there are also a few objective criteria. A group of 13 chansons attributed to Moniot d'Arras occur in exactly the same order in chansonniers M and T; the readings of the texts are sufficiently similar to surmise that all poems were copied from one common source.[2] However, the discrepancies among the melodies make it difficult to believe that the music was transmitted in writing. The assumption that the music was not copied along with the text is strengthened by two interesting peculiarities. Manuscript M gives the music for all of Moniot's chansons, while in T the notes are lacking for the first three – the staffs were drawn but they remained empty. The second peculiarity occurs in a chanson with multiple refrains★ (R 503). Each such multiple refrain has its own melody, and it is for these melodies that we find discrepancies which seem to point more to an oral than a written transmission of the music. In chansonnier T the melody for the first three refrains was entered, while the staffs above the last two remained empty. In manuscript M the transmission is almost the reverse: there is music for the first and fourth refrains only, while the staffs above the second, the third, and the fifth refrains are empty.

Similar evidence for a combination of oral and written tradition is found in a group of 24 chansons by Guillaume le Vinier. These chansons, like the ones by Moniot d'Arras, occur in various manuscripts, but in M and T they occur in exactly the same order and the texts appear in basically the same reading. But there are again considerable differences in the music between the versions in M and T, so many that one would be inclined to assume that these melodies differ from one another

---

1. For a discussion and modern edition of the poems by Audefroy le Bastard, see Arthur Cullmann, *Die Lieder und Romanzen des Audefroi le Bastard*. Halle 1914.

2. For a discussion and modern edition of the poems by Moniot d'Arras, see Holger Petersen Dyggve, *Moniot d'Arras et Moniot de Paris, trouvères du* XIIIe *siècle, Édition des chansons et étude historique*. Helsinki 1938.

because of variants made by performers. This is again corroborated by a chanson with multiple refrains (R 1192): manuscript M gives the melodies for all five of the refrains, but the scribe of T entered the music for the first, the third, and the fourth ones only. Furthermore, for the eighteenth and the nineteenth chansons in this group M has empty staffs, while T gives complete melodies. Only for the twenty-second chanson did neither one of the original scribes enter any music; the staffs in T remained empty, whereas in M a melody was entered by someone who obviously came after the principle scribe of that manuscript.

Of the many other chansons with multiple refrains (e.g., R 145, R 839, and R 1660) which strengthen the above observations, I will mention only the one by Pierre le Corbie (R 2041), because here it is manuscript T which gives the melodies for all the refrains, while the scribe of M entered the notes for only three of the seven refrains. Yet this chanson is the second in a group of six attributed to Pierre le Corbie occurring in the same order in M and T.

Among the manuscripts which are only rarely members of a group, chansonnier O (published by Beck as *Le Chansonnier Cangé*) is probably the most remarkable. Editors of trouvère poems have considered manuscript O to be a close relative of the KLNPX group and for a limited number of the melodies this opinion is acceptable, but for many others it is not. This manuscript gives these latter melodies in readings which differ in a peculiar way from those in the KLNPX group. One would be inclined to assume that these differences are not variants made by performers, but rather changes made by someone who could oversee an entire melody and who made it more balanced and more regular. This all seems to be the work of an *editor*. In the following chapters we will have several opportunities to show specific examples of such editorial changes, and one might surmise that these changes were made by someone with extensive experience in copying, and perhaps in composing, motets and rondeaux, which have considerably more complicated music than that found in a typical trouvère melody.

The examination of chansons with multiple versions reveals a strange peculiarity regarding the manuscripts V and R.[1] These two chansonniers give readings of the poems which are usually quite similar to those in the other sources, and editors of the poems usually consider manuscript V as closely related to the KLNPX group. For a large number of the melodies, however, these sources give readings which appear to have nothing in common either with one another or with the rest of the chansonniers. In these cases we may never know for certain which version is the one provided by the trouvère himself, but it seems reasonable to assume that the melody preserved in several manuscripts, even though in differing versions, is more likely to be the original one than the melody which occurs in only one manuscript and which has nothing in common with the versions presented in the majority of the manuscripts. However, there is the following unambiguous indication that the scribes who copied the melodies for these two manuscripts were not as reliable as most other scribes: manuscripts V and R, unlike other chansonniers, contain many entries in which the number of notes and groups of notes does not match the number of syllables per line, eventhough there is obviously nothing wrong with the metric scheme of the poems concerned.

Although we may be able to pinpoint peculiarities in certain manuscripts, we usually have no way of knowing who is responsible for them. For example, the person who actually copied the music onto the pages of chansonnier O may not have made any of the editorial changes; instead he may have had several batches of drafts coming from different notators who obtained their melodies from different performers. Perhaps it was one of these notators who did all the editing, and the only work of the final copyist was to put all the available chansons in alphabetical order and to copy faithfully what was given to him. Similarly we have no way of knowing who provided the questionable melodies in manuscripts R and V; it could have been a singer and it could have been a scribe. In those cases where the members of the KLNPX group contain different versions, we do not know who made the actual changes either. To avoid unwarranted conjectures, in all such doubtful cases the term 'the scribe of...' will be used as a collective name for all those responsible for what we find in that particular manuscript.

The preceding discussion of the probable dissemina-

---

1. For a discussion of manuscript R, see Johann Schubert, *Die* *Handschrift Paris, Bibl. Nat. Fr. 1591: Kritische Untersuchung der Trouvèrehandschrift R.* Frankfurt 1963.

tion is based upon and concerned with the trouvère chansons which have been preserved in multiple versions. However, there is no reason to believe that the chansons which have been preserved only in single versions were disseminated in a different way. In general, the only difference between chansons with multiple versions and chansons with single versions seems to be that the latter were known to fewer people and were therefore less often included in collections than the former. However, in the following chapters we shall draw attention to some chansons which occur in manuscript O only and which differ in important aspects from the rest of the trouvère repertoire; perhaps there was never any oral tradition for these chansons, and it is tempting to surmise that the person who did so much editorial work on a number of melodies in that manuscript was the composer of these anonymous songs.

The lapse of time between the creation of the earliest troubadour chansons and the compilation of the earliest chansonniers is even greater than in the case of the trouvère chansons. As far as the text is concerned, the discrepancies among the sources are similar to those for the chansons of the trouvères. Similarly, in the relatively few cases in which we can compare different versions of melodies, we see practically the same phenomena as occur for the melodies of the trouvères. Thus although the material upon which to base our opinion is less overwhelming, there can be no doubt that the dissemination and preservation of the chansons of the troubadours were very similar to the patterns observed in chansons of the trouvères. In fact there are several sources in which we find chansons in both Old French and in Old Provençal. The only important difference lies in the sad situation that those who collected troubadour chansons seem to have had less interest in collecting the melodies along with the poems.

SUMMARY

In conclusion, both written and oral traditions seem to have played a part in the transmission of the chansons of the troubadours and trouvères. Each chanson should be studied on its own merits to determine whether there was a written tradition and, if so, whether this included both text and melody. Understandably, similarity or dissimilarity in the order in which the chansons of a

certain author are presented in the sources may be of some help in the attempt to distinguish between written and oral tradition, but this evidence is by no means unambiguous. And even the strictest similarity in order and the closest possible similarity in reading of the text are not necessarily indications that the melodies were copied along with the poems.[1] One generalization may be made here: except for the group of five manuscripts discussed above (K, L, N, P, and X), there are probably more instances of written transmission of the text only than of poem and melody together. This phenomenon together with the fact that so many manuscripts preserve only the text–some of the manuscripts were not even designed to include the melodies–prompts us to surmise not only that there was much more written transmission of the poems than of the melodies, but also that the poem was valued more highly than the melody.

Thus to some extent we may be able to determine the roles of oral and written traditions, but we are unlikely ever to find the answer to the most intriguing question concerning the transmission of the chansons: which one of the preserved versions is closest to the original? For even in those cases where we find a written tradition we have no way of knowing whether the written model was the author's autograph or a version written down after a period of exclusively oral tradition. Consequently, we may not have any chanson in its original form nor are we likely to be able to reconstruct the original from the versions which have been preserved in the medieval manuscripts. However, it is likely that to a large extent the preserved readings are in accordance with the traditions of the period; perhaps they are fairly accurate presentations of the chansons as they once were performed by various performers at the time the manuscripts were compiled. Of course there are errors in the manuscripts, and there may well be changes, made consciously or unconsciously by performer or scribe, that violate the character of the original chanson, although it may often be impossible to distinguish with certainty between acceptable variants and outright errors. I hope, however, that my examination of a large

1. A convincing illustration of this statement is found for the chansons of Thibaud de Navarre. With only two exceptions, manuscripts V and K give 55 chansons by Thibaud in exactly the same order, yet for at least 16 of them the melodies in V have nothing in common with those for the same chansons in K. (See also Part 2, No. 10.)

number of chansons with multiple versions has shed at least some light onto this matter.

The discussions in the next two chapters will bring out what to some may be the weakness of the above theory, because we cannot reconcile the usual theories regarding meter and tonal organization of medieval songs with the hypothesis that the vast majority of the discrepancies are variants which leave the rhythmic character and the tonal organization of the original melody intact. Needless to say, the basis of the discussion in the following chapters will be the opinion that, in the absence of any documentary evidence, it seems reasonable to assume that in those versions which obviously all derive from one prototype there is more correct than wrong material, regardless of whether the changes were made by scribes or by performers.

3 Rhythm and meter

Over the centuries the meanings of the terms 'rhythm' and 'meter' have varied so much that we may never again be able to untangle the resulting confusion. Consequently, any author using these terms must state the meaning he intends them to carry, even though, whatever he decides, his usage of the terms will come into conflict with widely used and generally accepted technical terms. In this study, the word 'meter', deriving from a Greek word concerning measurement, will be used to denote the really measurable elements of poem and melody, notably any regular alternation of accented and unaccented, or long and short, units, such as duple or triple meter in music and iambic or dactylic meter in poetry. The term 'rhythm', deriving from a Greek word concerning flow or stream, such as the flow of a river, will be used for the more freely flowing and less measurable aspects of melody and poem, despite the fact that this will clash with the widely used terms 'modal rhythm' and 'rhythmic modes'.

In certain aspects the chansons of the troubadours and trouvères resemble the strophic songs we know in the English tradition. In both, rhyme usually plays an important role, and all stanzas are identical (or at least very similar) in form so that all stanzas can be sung to the same melody. However, we find decisive differences regarding the meter. Whereas a line of an English poem has, in general, a predetermined number of stressed and unstressed syllables, in a Provençal or French poem only the total number of syllables per line is predetermined; an accented syllable is required, in general, only in the rhyme, and other accented syllables may come at any place in the line.

Thus in the famous chanson *Can vei la lauzeta mover*, by the troubadour Bernard de Ventadorn (see Part 2, No. 2), all lines have eight syllables and end with a masculine rhyme. This means that word accents can come anywhere in the line and that the rhyme consists of only one syllable, which is either a word of one syllable or the last, accented syllable of a word of two or more syllables. In the chanson *Bons rois Thiebaut, sire consoilliez moi* (Part 2, No. 11) all lines are considered to have ten syllables, although it would seem that three

lines in each stanza have eleven syllables because of the feminine rhyme. It is traditional, however, in analysis of French poems, to leave the second and unaccented syllable of the feminine rhyme uncounted.

As in the majority of ten-syllable lines, we find a caesura after the fourth syllable in many lines of this poem.[1] The exact nature of a caesura is rather unclear, but in regard to the structure of the line it means that the fourth syllable is often either an accented last syllable of a word or a word of only one syllable, but with no rhyme at that point. In the rest of the ten-syllable line the distribution of accented syllables is entirely free and differs from stanza to stanza.

Poems with lines of equal length, such as the two discussed above, may be in the majority in the repertoire of the troubadours and trouvères, but we also find many chansons of complicated and sophisticated form in which there is an interesting play involving both rhyme and number of syllables, as will be discussed in Chapter 5.

Both French and English poetry use *elision*. In both, an unaccented final syllable of a word may be elided, or left unpronounced, if it is followed by a word beginning with a vowel. In Old French and Old Provençal poetry, however, elision is applied rather loosely; it may be present or absent according to need.[2] The scribes of the text were very inconsistent in their treatment of elision. Sometimes they omitted the vowel to be elided, but in other instances they wrote it out. To complicate matters there are cases in which the scribe of the music wrote a note above the vowel to be elided or even above the remnants of the syllable elided by the textual scribe. The opposite error is made too, although less often; there are cases of unwarranted elision when the scribe of the music neglected to write a note above an unaccented syllable preceding a vowel even though this syllable was needed to give the line the required number of syllables.

The poems of the troubadours and trouvères were

---

1. For an extensive discussion of the caesura in trouvère chansons, see Dragonetti, 489–499. See also Chapter 5, p. 66.
2. For the treatment of syllables, including elision in trouvère poetry, see Dragonetti, 483–489.

traditionally performed to a melody. In those cases in which the melody has been preserved, its pitches are, in general, indicated with sufficient clarity. Serious problems arise, however, when the researcher attempts to determine the rhythm or meter in which these chansons were performed, because the symbols employed to notate these melodies usually do not indicate either accent or duration. Basically we can choose between two possibilities. First, the chansons may have been performed in a fixed and clearly measurable meter which can be expressed adequately in modern musical notation with whole notes, half notes, quarter notes, etc. As such the chansons would be very similar to many folk songs and all art songs, including those of more recent French composers such as Gabriel Fauré and Henri Duparc. Secondly, the chansons may have been performed in some kind of 'free' and unmeasurable rhythm, here called 'declamatory' rhythm, similar to that used in speech and poetry recitations.

Some authors of studies about medieval song have expressed their belief that most of these songs originally were performed in some form of free rhythm. But advocates of performance in fixed meter appear to have been more numerous and, judging from presently standard histories of music, they have gained the upper hand, without much discussion of the primary question of whether the songs were intended to be performed in free rhythm or in fixed meter.[1]

There has been an enormous and really bewildering controversy regarding the exact nature of the fixed meter in which the chansons were supposed to have been performed. No scholar, it seems, has been able to formulate an answer that was acceptable to any other scholar, and some form of meter – usually triple meter – has been arbitrarily superimposed upon the melodies presented in modern editions. Donald Grout characterized this situation very aptly as follows: 'It is generally agreed that these songs were sung in some fairly regular rhythm and that the melody was rather strictly measured by long and short notes in regular patterns according to the rhythm of the poetry. However, there is considerable divergence of opinion on matters of detail'.[2] Grout illustrated the last remark by presenting

five different rhythmizations of Guiraut de Borneill's chanson, *Reis glorios* (see Part 2, No. 3). Similarly Burkhard Kippenberg showed ten transcriptions (by eight different experts) of Walther von der Vogelweide's *Palästinalied*[3] (Part 2, No. 1). With little effort one could find similar divergences in the transcriptions of many other medieval songs.

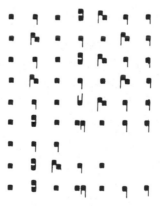

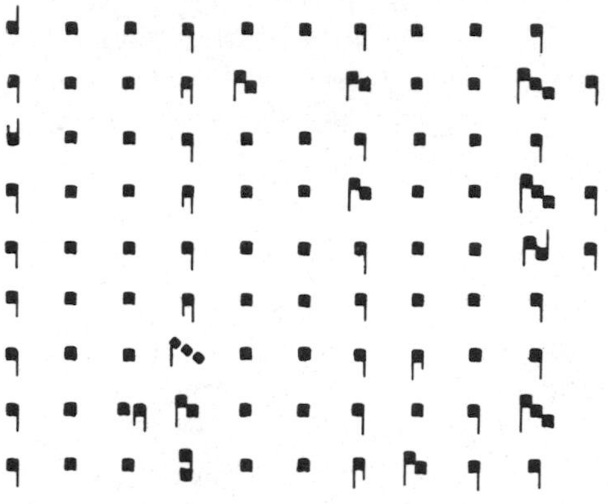

Synoptic chart of the notational symbols used in manuscript O, fo. 14, for the *jeu parti, Bons rois Thibaud, sire, consoilliez moi* (R 1666). For transcription of the entire chanson see Part 2, No. 11.

N.B. In the second line there is no notational symbol above the sixth syllable; comparison with the repetition of this melody for the fourth line shows that the missing note is connected with the note of the preceding syllable, thus erroneously making two single notes into a group of two.

Synoptic chart of the notational symbols used in manuscript O, fo. 11, for the anonymous chanson, *A l'entrant dou temps nouvel* (R 581). For transcription of the complete chanson see Part 2, No. 15.

At the beginning of this century certain scholars discovered melodies in some trouvère sources which had a

1. For a very extensive discussion of various theories on this topic, see Burkhard Kippenberg, *Der Rhythmus im Minnesang*. München 1957.

2. Donald J. Grout, *A History of Western Music*, 62.

3. Kippenberg, 226-227.

peculiar alternation of stemmed and unstemmed notes (as shown in the above charts), indicating that in these melodies certain durational patterns, known as *rhythmic modes*⋆, were repeated over and over. It appears to me that with undue haste they accepted the rhythmic modes as the key with which to solve all problems at once. At least two scholars concluded that all trouvère chansons must have been performed originally in modal rhythm, that is, each trouvère melody was based upon one of three rhythmic modes.[1] This conclusion was drawn with such haste that an additional controversy arose, and still exists, concerning who was the first to discover this so-called 'modal theory[2]'. Whoever made the discovery, the modal theory itself is rather surprising, since in its most rudimentary form it states that *all* chansons of *all* trouvères were originally performed in modal rhythm *because* in the chansonniers–together containing several thousand entries with music–a *few* melodies are found for which the scribe indicated modal rhythm; no mention is made of the fact that in most cases those indications are rather ambiguous. Subsequently the controversy about rhythm and meter gained in vehemence and was directed primarily to the problem of how to determine the proper rhythmic mode for any given chanson. Some scholars have extended this theory and have assumed that not only all the chansons of the trouvères but also those of all troubadours were in modal rhythm. Some even go so far as to assume that almost all medieval secular songs, whatever the date and place of origin, were originally performed in modal rhythm.[3]

That such enormous controversy could arise is probably largely due to the preconceived notions with which different scholars approached the basic problem. Thus, rather than examining all theories advanced

during the 19th and 20th centuries, we shall direct our attention to whatever evidence has come down to us from the Middle Ages.

THE SOURCES OF INFORMATION

Our information regarding rhythm and meter in the chansons of the troubadours and trouvères is tucked away in the rather oblique remarks made in one medieval treatise, in the peculiarities of the notation in which the chansons have been preserved, in the metric scheme of the poems, in the nature of the melodies, and, finally, but most importantly, in the nature of the variants we find for chansons with multiple versions.

It is unlikely that even the most exhaustive study of these sources of information will ever enable us to determine exactly how a certain singer performed a given chanson seven or eight centuries ago. But if we approach all available information without prejudice and if we examine many chansons, we can shed considerably more light on the problem than has been done so far, and in doing so we may be able to form a general opinion of how the majority of these chansons may have been performed.

In order to evaluate properly the information given in medieval treatises dealing with *Musica*, we must first realize that the Latin word 'Musica' is not always synonymous with our word 'music', a fact which often makes the theorists' discussions very confusing. Originally, medieval treatises about Musica were speculative discussions of numerical laws, largely inherited from the Greeks, which were supposed to govern all movements and functions of the universe, of human beings, and of what we call 'music' (the latter seems to include poetry).[4] Beginning with the Carolingian period theorists began to show an interest in discussing music, in our sense, for its own sake.

Thus, for the sake of discussion, we can distinguish between two opposing approaches in the medieval treatises, one which is primarily concerned with what learned authors in the Middle Ages called 'Musica' and the other which is primarily concerned with what we

---

1. Aubry's final exposé on this theory may be found in *Trouvères et troubadours*, Paris 1910, 188-204; Beck's survey on this matter may be found in *La musique des troubadours*, 2nd (?) ed. Paris, 1928. 44-60.

2. For a discussion of this controversy, see Jacques Chailley, 'Quel est l'auteur de la ‹théorie modale› dite de Beck-Aubry?' in *Archiv für Musikwissenschaft* x, 1953; 213-222; Friedrich Gennrich, 'Suum cuique. Wer war der Initiator der Modaltheorie?' in *Miscelánea en homenaje a Mons. Higinio Anglés*, 2 vols., Barcelona 1958, 1961; 315-330; Heinrich Husmann, 'Minnesang', in *Die Musik in Geschichte und Gegenwart*, vol. 9, 1961, col. 359; and Kippenberg, p. 105, footnote 2.

3. For example, Gennrich, *Troubadours, Trouvères, Minne- und Meistergesang*. Köln 1951.

4. See also Edward A.Lippman, 'The Place of Music in the System of Liberal Arts', in *Aspects of Medieval and Renaissance Music, A Birthday Offering to Gustave Reese*, ed. Jan LaRue. New York 1966. 545-559.

call 'music'. In treatises with the former approach music is either omitted or it occupies a very subordinate position, and it seems that music owes the privilege of being discussed exclusively to its property of being a ready example, in fact the only readily measurable element, in the entire realm of Musica. In such treatises we find discussions about scales, about the ratio of intervals, about the intricacies of modal and mensural notation, and about verse-feet in classical Latin poetry. The last aspect was extremely interesting to the theorists because classical poetry was based upon an alternation of short and long syllables in a ratio of 1 : 2. Thus in one of the most famous treatises about Musica, by St. Augustine, we find nothing at all about what we would call 'music'. The first five books deal with ratio and balance in Latin poetry, culminating in the fifth book with a fascinating discussion of hidden equality between two unequal parts of a verse. These discussions about numerical laws, or 'numbers', as they were usually called, served merely as a preparation for the sixth and final book 'in which the mind is raised from the consideration of changeable numbers in inferior things to unchangeable numbers in unchangeable truth itself'.[1] Thus for St. Augustine, who obviously loved and admired poetry, the overt and hidden 'numbers' of poetry were means that could raise the thoughts of man to the life hereafter and to God. In other treatises with the same approach the discussion of music in our sense serves as an introduction to the contemplation of other parts of the realm of Musica, and understandably only the really measurable elements of music are discussed. This is usually done in a manner which makes it obvious that, even if all medieval music had been performed in free rhythm, it is unlikely that there would have been a place in discussions about Musica for something as unmeasurable as free rhythm.

In the second group of treatises the primary purpose may be to further the understanding of what we would call music, but the concept that music is part of Musica very often makes the authors prejudiced; they insist upon taking it for granted that music has all the properties of Musica and that therefore music must be measurable in all aspects, regardless of whether they can discern this measure. Thus free rhythm was something

they would naturally try to circumvent, or at best they might mention it without giving it the proper name. One of the most striking examples of the latter attitude is found in a treatise written (ca. 1300) by Johannes de Grocheo[2]; interestingly, this treatise may also be the only one in which a few remarks about the chansons of the trouvères occur. In the first section that concerns us here, the distinction between Musica and music is so blurred that it is impossible to distinguish clearly and consistently between the two.

Grocheo wrote that some people divide music into two sections: unmeasurable music (*musica plana, sive immensurabilis*) and measurable music (*musica mensurabilis*); by the former they mean the chant of the church, and by the latter they mean polyphonic music such as conductus and motet. It was Grocheo's opinion that this division is wrong if these people mean that unmeasurable music is in no way measurable and is performed entirely at will, because any action in music must be measured according to the rules of the art. However, he added, if they mean that unmeasurable music is not so precisely measured, then this division is all right.[3] Thus it seems to be a matter of terminology. Comparison with motets must have convinced Grocheo that plain chant was not measurable, yet it would have been contrary to all medieval concepts of Musica to say so; therefore Grocheo circumvented the problem by saying that of course plain chant is measurable, otherwise it could not come under the heading of music as it should, but one must realize that chant is not measured as precisely as a motet. Grocheo also suggested his own division of the music used by Parisians: there is vulgar music, meaning music with French text and instrumental music (*musica vulgaris*), measured music (*musica mensurata*), and church music (*musica ecclesiastica*).[4] This division seems to imply that neither plain chant nor trouvère chansons are measured. Thus the description which Grocheo rejected for theoretical reasons may well be a realistic but rare evaluation given by a

---

1. R.Catesby Taliaferro, trans., *St. Augustine on Music. Books I-VI*, 1939, heading of Book VI.

2. For a modern edition with German translation, see Ernst Rohloff, *Media Latinitatis Musica* II, *Der Musiktraktat des Johannes de Grocheo*. Leipzig 1943. For an English translation, see Albert Seay, *Johannes de Grocheo, Concerning Music (De Musica)*. Colorado Springs 1967. The latter translation, however, is rather questionable in certain instances which are relevant to this study.

3. Rohloff, 47.

4. Loc. cit.

medieval theorist of the actual rhythm of plain chant and of secular chansons: they were in no way measurable, and indeed the performance was entirely at the discretion of the singer.

A little later, in very ambiguous wording, Grocheo appears to give his opinion on the performance of some trouvère chansons. When writing about the 'cantus coronatus*,... which is a song that has been awarded a crown because of its merits in words and melody',

1. Lan - quan li jorn son lonc en may
2. M'es belhs dous chans d'au - zelhs de lonh,

However, the musical and poetic characteristics found in the chansons, especially in those with multiple versions, do not at all support this idea. If Grocheo's remark has a kernel of truth in it, it is more likely to mean that these songs were performed rather slowly and that the notes, both single notes and notes in a group, were of the same length, *as long as one did not measure too precisely*.

Summarizing briefly the information gained from the treatises, we may say in the first place that the absence of free rhythm from all discussions does not prove that free rhythm did not exist in the Middle Ages. Actually it may be more appropriate to say that, if all the chansons of the troubadours and trouvères had been in any beautifully regular alternation of long and short tones or syllables, Grocheo and other theorists would have discussed them aptly and elaborately. Finally, Grocheo's circuitous discussion of unmeasurable music in combination with his own threefold division of music may not supply us with unambiguous evidence that the chansons of the trouvères were performed in free rhythm, but at least he implies with considerable clarity that not all medieval music was as clearly measurable as he would like it to be.

Turning to medieval notation of music as our second source of information about rhythm and meter, we find that the indications given by the notation are prob-

Grocheo made the statement that this song 'ex omnibus longis et perfectibus efficitur'.[1] This statement has sometimes been considered to mean that the songs concerned were to be 'performed in long and perfect notes only' and that therefore all syllables were of equal length regardless of the number of notes sung to a syllable.[2] According to this explanation the opening lines of the first chanson in Part 2 should be performed more or less as follows:

ably as circuitous as those in the treatises. Although the Greeks had an adequate system of notating music and although the West inherited many elements of Greek culture, including the concept of Musica discussed above, the West did not take over the Greek notational system. Instead it gradually developed its own notation, which was a *non-mensural notation*★ for the first few centuries of its existence; it indicated pitch with increasing clarity, but it did not indicate duration.

The oldest type of notation capable of indicating both duration and pitch seems to have been *modal notation*, i.e., the notation which specified the rhythmic mode★ of a melody.[3] The earliest descriptions of it have come to us in treatises which date from approximately the middle of the 13th century, but it is difficult to determine how and when this notation originated. We do not know whether the modes existed long before the scribes found a way of notating them or whether the modes were contrived by scribes for the sake of indicating duration. Consequently estimates regarding the date of origin differ widely. Many experts are inclined to believe that modal rhythm was in existence, or was in the process of emerging, when the earliest trouvères created their songs, but there is considerable doubt that it was available to the composers of the earliest preserved chansons in Old Provençal. Thus the whole question of modal rhythm in the chansons of troubadours and trouvères becomes very problematic,

---

1. Rohloff, 50.

2. For an extensive evaluation of Grocheo's remarks on this subject and their modern interpretations, see Kippenberg, 123-132, and my discussion of 'Cantus Coronatus' in the Glossary.

3. For further discussions of modal rhythm, see Kippenberg, 99-152, and Carl Parrish, *The Notation of Medieval Music*, New York 1957. 41-52, 73-106.

especially so if we keep in mind that, in general, we cannot find any principal stylistic differences between troubadour and trouvère melodies, and that perhaps even the earliest troubadour melodies are not in a newly created style but in a very old and traditional vein.[1] An additional problem for this study is the disturbing fact that the medieval theorists discuss modal rhythm and modal notation only in connection with purely melismatic* melodies, which occur frequently in certain forms of polyphony of the 12th and 13th centuries but not in the chansons of the troubadours and trouvères.

Thus there is great doubt about whether all of the troubadours and trouvères could have been familiar with modal rhythm, but there is little doubt that the scribes compiling the chansonniers had modal notation at their disposal. Moreover, in their time there existed also a fairly well developed form of *mensural notation** which was capable of indicating many more forms of fixed and measurable meters than modal notation. Nevertheless the scribes used the older non-mensural notation–which also continued to be used for plain chant–for the vast majority of the troubadour and trouvère chansons.

There are some curious exceptions to this general situation, especially in the Chansonnier Cangé (manuscript O). The notation in this chansonnier varies widely; at one extreme there are many melodies in the same non-mensural notation as is used in the other sources, and at the other extreme there are a very few melodies in a semi-mensural notation which clearly and faultlessly indicates modal rhythm. (This notation is called semi-mensural because only the single notes, not the ligatures, are mensural.) See examples on p. 36 and Plate 2. The notation of the rest of the chansons is between the two extremes, ranging from a notation in which the alternation of stemmed and unstemmed notes is not entirely consistent (e.g., R 787, Part 2, No. 6) to a notation in which the alternation is too inconsistent to be taken as an unequivocal indication for modal rhythm, and at the most we can say that it bears some suggestion of a modal rhythm (e.g. R 1420, Part 2, No. 8). Thus the question of how many chansons in modal rhythm there are in this collection is subject to discussion and arbitrary decision. The situation becomes

even more disconcerting when we consider the one instance in which the scribe demonstrated his ability to write in a fully mensural notation. In the only two-part motet included in this chansonnier, the scribe switched on the second staff of the motetus from non-mensural to mensural notation.[2] Furthermore, in some otherwise semi-mensurally notated chansons the same scribe wrote a few mensural ligatures (e.g. see Part 2, No. 15) and even some *semibreves*.

The manuscript giving the works of Adam de la Halle (manuscript W) is even more remarkable. As pointed out in Chapter 1, this manuscript gives Adam's musical creations in four separate groups and it is important to notice that all but one (R 658) of the chansons and jeux partis are notated in the usual non-mensural notation of the trouvère manuscripts, whereas the motets and the rondeaux are given in a very clear mensural notation. This difference in notation is not incidental; several of Adam's chansons in trouvère style (including R 658) occur in other sources and a few of the rondeaux have been preserved in a small fragment of a manuscript. It is certainly noteworthy that in these sources the notation is the same as in manuscript W: the chansons are given in non-mensural notation and the rondeaux in mensural notation.

Thus, it appears, at least some of the scribes were familiar with the rhythmic modes or even with mensural notation,[3] yet they gave the vast majority of the chansons in non-mensural notation. The explanation for this curious situation may be sought either in the chansons themselves or in the abilities and attitudes of the scribes, and the answer may be different from chanson to chanson. In the former case we may assume that the vast majority of the chansons were notated in a non-mensural notation simply because the melodies were unmeasurable, while the few that were measurable were the proverbial exceptions that prove the rule. In the latter case we have to seek the answer in a complex written tradition in which not all the scribes were suf-

---

1. See the discussion of melodic characteristics in Chapter 4.

2. Folio 21ro.

3. For some chansons in semi-mensural notation in chansonniers other than manuscript O, see R 237 in manuscript T, fo. 4; and R 238 in manuscript D (for all available melodic versions, see my study, 'Deklamatorischer Rhythmus in den Chansons der Trouvères' in *Die Musikforschung*, XX, 1967. 136-139). In manuscript M several melodies in mensural notation were entered on staffs which had been left empty by the principle scribe(s) of that collection.

ficiently familiar with mensural or semi-mensural notation and thus only a few of the melodies were notated
in their proper meter.

In order to evaluate the information imparted by certain textual and melodic characteristics, the proponents
of modal rhythm have devised two methods for determining the correct rhythmic mode of any chanson
preserved in a non-mensural notation.[1] The best known
and also the most controversial one is concerned with
the relation between the rhythmic mode and the verse
meter. The second deals with the relation between the
rhythmic mode and the melody. The reasoning behind
the latter is that single notes are likely to come on the
short units of the mode while groups of notes, or ligatures, are likely to come on the long units, because the
longer the duration of a unit the more opportunity
there is for singing several tones to that unit. Although
this method, taking into consideration the influence
which modal rhythm must have had upon the melody,
seems very sensible, only rarely does it reveal a certain
rhythmic mode (see Part 2, No. 13). Most often there
simply are not enough ligatures to be of any help and
for the rest the distribution of ligatures is so irregular
that it seems to preclude any regular alternation of long
and short syllables. Apparently proponents of modal
rhythm are inclined to consider such irregular distribution of ligatures as one of the many consequences of
scribal inaccuracy. Accordingly they take it upon themselves to correct the scribe's work and redistribute the
melody over the text in such a way that it fits the
rhythmic mode selected by the editor.[2]

The other method is summarized by Gustave Reese
as follows: 'Old Provençal and Old French had accentu-
ations such as modern French almost completely lacks,
and advocates of the modal theory claim that the music
must have been stressed in accordance with the stresses
in the words, and that the absence of time-value indications in the notation did not greatly matter since a
singer would know by observing the distribution of
accents in a line what rhythmic mode to use'.[3] Whether

the statement regarding the nature of the accents is correct or not is of minor importance for the present discussion, since we know from motets with French texts
and from the semi-mensurally notated chansons that
modal rhythm and French poetry were not considered
mutually exclusive. These same compositions show
that the statement regarding the agreement between
the two types of accents is a case of highly unrealistic
oversimplification. Although there are motets and chansons in which the word accents coincide with musical
accents more often than not, there are at least as many
others in which one cannot find any systematic agreement between the accents. In *Chascun qui de bien amer*
(R 759, see Part 2, No. 12), by Richard de Fournival,
for example, the notation is almost entirely mensural
and so clear that the rhythmic mode is obvious. But it is
also very clear that the word accents are almost equally
distributed over the units of the mode. On the other
hand we find a striking, although not complete, agreement between the two types of accents in the anonymous chanson *Li joliz temps d'estey* (R 452, see Part 2,
No. 14). Chansons such as the latter lead to the cautious
conclusion that in some chansons prominent places in
the melody appear to coincide with word accents more
often than other places; perhaps those chansons were
performed in some regular alternation of long and short
or of accented and unaccented syllables even if the notation does not indicate this.

In general, however, the distribution of word accents
in the chansons of troubadours and trouvères is very
irregular and differs from stanza to stanza.[4] Thus if
agreement of textual and musical accents had been required for all stanzas, modal rhythm would be highly
inappropriate in most instances, but a performance in a
free, declamatory rhythm would provide the optimum
relation between word and melody as advocated by the
proponents of modal rhythm. As the chanson by Richard
de Fournival (Part 2, No. 12) and many motets show,
however, such agreement was not always sought.

Finally, perhaps the most revealing but certainly the
least-used source of information about rhythm and meter lies in the differences and similarities among the
various readings of chansons with multiple versions. In
general, the persons for whom the preserved chanson-

1. See footnote 1 on p. 37.
2. For an example of such a procedure, see the reconstruction
of trouvère chanson R 1223 by Werner Bittinger in *Studien zur
musikalischen Textkritik des mittelalterlichen Liedes*, Würzburg
1953, 69-83 and Anhang, 7-12; see also my commentary upon
this in 'Deklamatorischer Rhythmus', 130.
3. Gustave Reese, *Music in the Middle Ages*, New York 1940.
207-208.

4. See charts of accented and otherwise emphasized syllables
in Carl Appel, *Die Singweisen Bernarts von Ventadorn*. Halle 1934.

niers were compiled probably were connoisseurs who were aware of the diversity among the different performances of a chanson. Therefore it must have been a matter of primary concern to them to find performers and especially notators who were completely familiar with the style of these chansons. If indeed all chansons were meant to be performed in modal rhythm or in any other kind of regular alternation of long and short syllables, or accented and unaccented tones, most of these performers and notators must have known about it.

Consequently, if a certain chanson was always performed in the same meter, one would expect not only that the variations would have remained within the possibilities of the meter but also that the meter must have prompted the performer to make certain types of variants in certain places. One could also expect that the fixed meter must have made it easy to remember the pitch of a metrically prominent place in the melody. Moreover, even though there is good reason to believe that words and melody preserved in a certain chansonnier did not always come from the same performer, the influence of the fixed meter on the variations in word order and in the choice of words should be noticeable.

Perhaps the most advantageous way to begin the evaluation of chansons with multiple versions is to consider first one of those chansons for which the choice of a certain fixed meter seems fairly convincing, namely *L'amour dont sui espris* (R 1545), by Blondel de Nesle (see Part 2, No. 5). In many aspects this chanson differs markedly from the majority of trouvère chansons. It differs particularly from most other chansons with multiple versions in that there is an unusual uniformity among the versions of this chanson regarding the distribution of word accents and of ligatures; there is an even more unusual similarity among the individual lines of the melody.[1]

Of all the preserved versions only the one in manuscript O contains indications regarding a rhythmic mode. Although the alternation of Longae and Breves is somewhat inconsistent–nine out of forty-six single notes are 'wrong'–it appears to prescribe the following modal rhythm: ♩ ♩ ♩ ♩ ♩ ♩. However, the clues gained from the distribution of word accents and ligatures

point to a different alternation: in all versions the third syllable, which is supposed to be short according to the notation in O, very often has a ligature of three or four notes; the fourth syllable, supposedly long, seldom has a ligature; and the fifth syllable, short again according to O, nearly always has a group of two or three notes. Furthermore, the examination of the distribution of word accents reveals that the third syllable is considerably more often accentuated than any of the other syllables–excluding of course the rhyme syllable.

In summary, it seems that these peculiarities weigh more heavily than the indications given in the notation of manuscript O, and that they are sufficient reason to conclude that, *if* this chanson was meant to be performed in one of the rhythmic modes known to us, it probably was performed in the following alternation: ♩ ♩ ♩. ♩ ♩ ♩.. This gives the longest duration to the syllable with the longest ligatures and with the largest number of word accents, while it gives the shortest duration to the syllables with the least ligatures.

This chanson differs from most other chansons in one other important aspect: it is known to share its melody with two polyphonic compositions which were exhaustively discussed by Heinrich Husmann. I deliberately examined this chanson before consulting Husmann's conclusion regarding the meter of the polyphonic pieces, and I consider it significant that on the basis of the characteristics of the chanson I came to the same alternation of long and short notes as Husmann did on the basis of all the information he could gather regarding the polyphonic compositions.[2]

In a large-scale examination of chansons with multiple versions one encounters very, very few chansons for which the choice of a rhythmic mode is as easy and as convincing as it is in the above chanson by Blondel de Nesle. In fact the problems and the findings differ from case to case. For example, if one deals with a chanson that is very syllabic, one may not have any difficulty in finding a meter that fits the chanson in all its versions, but rarely can one find a good reason for believing that the chanson was conceived and always performed in

---

1. For the comparison of versions of this and most other chansons, the KLNPX group is considered to contribute only one version.

2. Heinrich Husmann, 'Zur Rhythmik des Trouvèregesanges' in *Die Musikforschung*, v, 1952. 110-131. Regarding the choice of rhythmic mode, see Gennrich, 'Grundsätzliches zur Rhythmik der mittelalterlichen Monodie', *Die Musikforschung*, VII, 1954. 150-176.

that meter. If, on the other hand, one deals with a chanson that is not so syllabic, one may not even be able to find a rhythmic mode, or any other fixed meter, that fits the chanson in all its versions because of the irregular distribution of ligatures which, furthermore, may vary from version to version. In both these categories there are many chansons which have basically the same melody in all versions, but the distribution of the melodic line over the text differs from version to version. These differences are such that we may conclude that it must have been relatively easy for the performers to remember the melodic curve for each line, but that either it must have been extremely difficult or unnecessary always to remember on which word of the verse the summit of the melody was to come. Furthermore, the variants in the text, especially the variants in the word order, stand in no relation whatsoever to either a fixed meter or to the variants occurring in the melodic versions. These phenomena make it very difficult to believe that the melody had a meter of its own; instead they argue forcefully for a performance in a declamatory rhythm, not only for the chansons for which multiple versions happen to have been preserved, but also for most of the other ones, since in general the latter do not differ as a group in any important stylistic aspect from the former.

Understandably, in the course of my research I have paid considerable attention to those chansons for which modal rhythm appears to be indicated in the notation, with the following results. First of all, among the chansons which are preserved in multiple versions I did not encounter one single chanson that occurs in semi-mensural notation in all of its sources. Even more surprising may be the fact that so far I have discovered only one chanson for which the notation of two versions–out of a total of five–suggests modal rhythm.[1] However, in neither one of these versions is the alternation of stemmed and unstemmed notes entirely consistent; in fact, in one of them the alternation is far from consistent.

Secondly, in many cases, including the chanson just mentioned and example 11 in Part 2, a careful analysis of poem and melody, especially the examination of multiple versions, makes it difficult to believe that these chansons were indeed meant to be performed as in-

dicated by the scribe of the version in semi-mensural notation, regardless of whether the alternation of stemmed und unstemmed notes is consistent. And, as we have seen in the discussion of R 1545, by Blondel de Nesle, there is at least one chanson for which a scribe indicated a certain mode while all other indications point to an entirely different mode. Most of the chansons which are notated in modal rhythm appear in manuscript O, and this may be one form of the earlier mentioned *editorial* changes made in this collection (see Chapter 2, p. 32). Perhaps under influence of his knowledge of and interest in polyphonic music and chansons of the rondel* type, the scribe superimposed a rhythmic mode upon chansons which were not composed in modal rhythm and which perhaps never were performed that way.

Further research will probably uncover evidence of fixed meter in more chansons, and a re-examination of all this material may clarify the question of whether or not modal rhythm is the only form of fixed meter in the chansons. Subsequently we may also be able to form a better opinion about the origin of these fixed meters; for at this stage of the research it is impossible to determine whether they were taken over from polyphonic music, from dancing songs, or from some source outside of France such as, for example, Arab lyric poetry. For the moment it should be pointed out that thus far most of the chansons with convincing evidence of fixed meter are related in some way to polyphonic music (e.g., Part 2, Nos. 5 and 12) or occur in manuscript O only and are anonymous (e.g., Part 2, Nos. 14 and 15).

The discussion of rhythm and meter has been primarily concerned with the chansons of the trouvères for the simple reason that the melodies of so many of them have been preserved in multiple versions. But whatever research we can do on troubadour chansons reveals the same characteristics. The distribution of word accents, the distribution of ligatures, the differences and similarities among versions of the same melody, and the notation of the troubadour chansons are very similar to those of the trouvère chansons. Furthermore, it is unlikely that the earliest troubadours whose melodies have been preserved could have used modal rhythm, because it is very doubtful that it existed in their time. Yet in the aspects under discussion these early melodies

---

1. See my discussion of this chanson in 'Deklamatorischer Rhythmus', 132, footnote 34.

as a group do not differ from later ones, whereas it seems likely that introduction of modal rhythm would have had a profound effect upon the melodic contour.

CONCLUSION

Cumulatively, the aspects of poem and melody discussed heretofore, as well as those to be discussed in the following chapters, mount up to present convincing justification for rejecting the usual unproven and ineffective theory that all chansons of the troubadours and trouvères were meant to be performed in some form of fixed and regular meter, and we have found an abundance of reasons for assuming that the vast majority of the chansons were performed in what may be called a *free rhythm* largely dictated by the flow and the meaning of the text. Somewhat more specific might be the term '*declamatory rhythm*' indicating that these songs were sung, or *recited*, in the rhythm in which one might *declaim* the poem without the music. Thus in order to determine how, in general, these chansons may have been performed, one should study numerous chansons in as many versions as possible. One should study first and foremost the text and one should develop a rendition designed not so much to sing a song but rather to recite, or declaim, a poem to an audience while freely making many nuances in stress and duration. Needless to say, such a rendition will differ from performer to performer, from chanson to chanson, and from stanza to stanza, as must have been the case in the Middle Ages. Nevertheless, there may be agreement in some important aspects. For example, in such a rendition syllabic passages (that is, passages in which each syllable is sung to one note) are likely to be performed so that most syllables will be more or less equal in length. This concept of approximate equality must be taken very freely, because some sentences or phrases may be said much faster or much more slowly than others, and towards the end of a line, especially towards the end of a stanza, the singer is likely to slow down. It should be kept in mind that such differences in tempo do not have to be in a ratio of 1:2 or 1:3. In chansons in non-mensural notation this slowing down towards the end of the stanza is often indicated by a drawn-out note (resembling the *Maxima* in mensural notation) on the last or penultimate syllable; in mensural or semi-mensural notation it is often indicated by notating a

Longa above the penultimate syllable in cases where the regular alternation would have required a Brevis.

The performance of groups of two or more notes over one syllable will be most vexing. At this moment it seems to me that there is no way of determining with any semblance of certainty whether notes in a group were sung faster or more slowly than single notes, nor whether all notes in a group were of more or less equal length. Grocheo's remark about 'long notes' in the cantus coronatus, discussed earlier in this chapter, is too ambiguous and too sweeping to be of much help either. Thus the performance of such groups will have to be determined from case to case and one performer's opinion seems to be as good as another's.

I realize fully that the above observations solve neither the problem of how each individual chanson was performed seven or eight centuries ago nor of how it should be performed now. But I trust that the preceding discussions have made it abundantly clear that we must examine each chanson on its own merits and that each performer and each editor is likely to come to his own conclusions regarding the choice of *preferable* version, regarding the choice of rhythm and tempo, and, in the case of editors, regarding the way of indicating or not indicating such rhythm in notation. The choice of the first two aspects is by nature a very subjective one which cannot and need not be defended. But I would like to make some remarks concerning the notation in which the chansons should be published. It certainly seems desirable that an expert editing medieval songs which are to be performed in a free rhythm should notate these songs in such a way that the non-expert also may know how to perform them. Thus there is some reason to publish such songs in modern notation with notes of different lengths and even with barlines. An editor who does this should provide an appropriate rhythmization not only for the first stanza, but for all subsequent stanzas as well; and he should also make an emphatic statement that all these indications for duration and accentuation should be taken very freely.

Although much may be said in favor of this way of editing, for various reasons I prefer giving the melodies in a somewhat modernized form of the medieval non-mensural notation. The mere conclusion that the chansons were performed in a declamatory rhythm is not sufficient to present a scholarly reconstruction of the way in which a given chanson was performed in the time of its author. Although this should not prevent us from singing the chansons, I dislike trying to approximate the subtleties of a declamatory rhythm in a mensural notation, and thus to impose my subjective interpretation upon others. The first requirement for a convincing performance of a chanson is a clear and perfect understanding of the text. A performer fulfilling these requirements would certainly find an editor's rhythmizations superfluous; he might even find them cumbersome. By presenting the melody of a chanson as rigidly as our notational system requires, one risks directing too much attention towards the melody, and one may well obscure one of the most important characteristics of a chanson: it is a poem performed to a simple and unobtrusive melody in such a way that the text receives the almost undivided attention of performer and listener alike.

4 Melodic characteristics

When discussing music of a certain period it is usually advisable to hark back to what existed before and to look ahead to what followed. For the study of the music of the troubadours and trouvères this is no easy task. We know almost none of the secular music that must have preceded the first extant troubadour chansons, and we do not know what happened to the musical style of the troubadours and trouvères in the 14th century; their poetic style maintains itself to a limited extent, but no music has been preserved with the later poems. This lack of information makes it difficult to determine the validity and value of the melodies notated in the preserved sources, especially since the trouvère chansons with multiple versions make it very clear that many, or perhaps all, melodies were altered and varied to some extent between the moment of being created and that of being preserved.

Nevertheless the following axiom seems to have been the point of departure for nearly all discussions and modern editions of the chansons: all music of medieval Western Europe makes use of certain well-defined scales in which the octave is the main organizational phenomenon and in which certain tones perform certain functions according to their place in that scale, such as tonic or finalis, dominant or tenor, and leading tone. Since in medieval treatises on music only the so-called 'church modes' are discussed, it is widely accepted that all medieval music, whether sacred or secular, was based upon these modes. Consequently melodies that do not fulfill the basic requirements of the theories about the church modes are considered to be corrupted and such melodies either are eliminated from discussion and publication or they are 'corrected' *before* publication or discussion. Sometimes the latter procedure is acknowledged and the reasons for it are given, sometimes not, but too often, in either case, the final conclusions are based upon 'corrected' versions of medieval melodies or upon carefully selected ones.

In some studies on medieval music we find a slightly different theory: several melodies are found in the preserved repertoire of troubadours and trouvères which obviously were based upon Ionian and Aeolian scales; thus the troubadours and trouvères are sometimes considered as the first composers to have used these scales

which were to become the solely acceptable scales several centuries later. However, if one takes the church modes, or any other form of clearly defined scales, as the sole criterion for judging the authenticity and the character of medieval melodies, the result may be rather disconcerting. Many incomprehensible, incoherent passages and many bewildering deviations will be encountered, and the conclusion will doubtlessly be that the scribes were extremely negligent and inconsistent in regard to the notation of sharps and flats.

The weakness of this approach lies in the foregone conclusion that the troubadours and trouvères, like the composers of more recent centuries, were fully aware of the existence of clearly defined scales and that they made a deliberate choice of scale before composing a melody. It seems to me more realistic to assume that there was a time in the early history of music when people sang songs without having clearly defined scales, and that perhaps the scales we know were developed gradually. Thus the problem facing us here is to determine which stage of this development was reached by the troubadours and trouvères; more specifically, we want to know whether their music was in accordance with what was written in treatises of their times. Although descriptions of complex scalar systems are found in treatises predating even the earliest troubadours, we can not simply presuppose that the troubadours were as familiar with them as were the learned authors of their times. Such an assumption would be of very dubious value, since it appears that not even all plain chant was clearly and exclusively based upon these modes.

Since we may not have the original melodies as composed by the troubadours and trouvères themselves, we may not be able to determine exactly how familiar they were with the scales described in the treatises of their time. However, it seems reasonable to assume that the most remarkable and most characteristic aspects of a given melody would be remembered by most, if not all, performers, and therefore the multiple versions of a melody should reveal the most important characteristics of the original melody. It would also be reasonable to assume that the degree of uniformity among the preserved versions would be commensurate with the coherence of the original melody, since one may expect singers to have little trouble remembering well-con-structed melodies and to falter on those that do not seem to cohere. Similarly we may assume, as has been pointed out before, that the changes made consciously or unconsciously by the scribes were in keeping with the traditions of the times, although one scribe may have gone further in altering the original character of a melody than another. With these assumptions in mind I have examined in detail several hundred arbitrarily chosen melodies, paying special attention to more than 200 trouvère melodies with multiple versions. This examination, especially the analysis of the multiple versions, reveals that the scales as used by the troubadours and trouvères were not as clearly defined and as fully developed as is usually assumed. At the same time it shows that certain melodic structures provided the melodies with at least as much coherence as these 'underdeveloped' scales, and thus made it possible for whole generations of performers to remember these melodies as well as they did.

Discussion of melodic characteristics and of organizing phenomena found in medieval melodies has some inherent risks, however. First there is the problem that all analysis, whether it concerns harmony or melody, is to a certain extent subjective. Secondly, we in the 20th century are burdened with certain prejudices about music caused by our almost exclusive familiarity with music in which scales and certain traditional chord sequences play predominant roles. We have become so accustomed to these conventions that we assume certain characteristics to be objective criteria for analysis, perhaps ignoring the fact that at one time these characteristics were neither required nor widespread. Nevertheless, we can find some objective criteria for the existence of certain organizing phenomena in medieval melodies, and melodies with multiple versions show that these same phenomena were a help to many medieval performers in remembering these melodies. However, it is doubtful that the medieval performer and listener were as conscious of these phenomena as we are conscious, for example, of tonics and leading tones in Baroque choral settings.

It is probably significant that for my study of the medieval melodies I found little helpful information either in medieval treatises or in recent standard works about medieval music. Instead, I found a sound approach, valuable guidance, and many useful terms in certain ethno-

musicological studies, even though they rarely mention the troubadours and trouvères. Especially helpful was Curt Sachs' posthumously published book, *The Wellsprings of Music*.[1] In this work Curt Sachs gives a systematic account of many organizing phenomena he and other researchers before him had found in various kinds of melodies from primitive and high cultures all over the world. This does not mean that we find in this book all the criteria necessary to analyze and classify all medieval melodies. The latter was never Curt Sachs' intention. He was of the opinion that 'detailed classifications are ... impractical and useless in the immaterial world of human expression'.[2] Thus, even with the information from this book, it is often difficult to discern clearly the organizing phenomena of a certain melody, and it is still impossible to determine the function of each individual note as is often done in harmonic analysis of music from later centuries. But, thanks to Curt Sachs and his predecessors, and through the examination of the discrepancies and similarities found in melodies preserved in multiple versions, we can at least begin to recover the concepts of melody and the compositional methods of the medieval song composers. Consequently, no attempt will be made in this book to classify the chansons according to melodic characteristics. Instead, purely for the sake of discussion, I will first attempt to isolate, categorize, and discuss the organizing or structural phenomena by themselves. In addition, both in this chapter and in Part 2, I will endeavor to discuss the various ways in which these phenomena manifest themselves in some specific chansons. Therefore, the remarks made in Part 2 are at least as pertinent as the discussion on the following pages, and perhaps the melodies included are more eloquent than any verbalization ever can be.

RECITATION

The most elementary melodic structure, recitation on one tone, does not occur in the preserved repertoire of the troubadours in as simple and monotonous a form as the term suggests.[3] Instead, it occurs in a manner which suggests that here we are dealing with a remnant or,

1. Curt Sachs, *The Wellsprings of Music*. The Hague 1962.
2. Ibidem, 173.
3. Ibidem, 70.

more likely, with a varied form of a tradition of reciting long passages to one tone as we know to have been done in liturgical prayers and readings from scriptures, and as may have been done during the entire Middle Ages in other types of song and in story telling. The similarity between recitation in the chansons and in liturgical psalmody is so striking that for the following discussion we shall borrow from plain chant terminology, without intending to imply that recitation in medieval song was derived from the manner in which psalms were sung in churches.[1]

The recitation proper is usually preceded by an *intonation* and followed by a *termination*, both of which apparently could be varied rather freely by individual performers. The intonation may be of varying length, from one to several syllables; it may be a straight or a curved line; and usually it is ascending. The termination also may be of varying length and either a curved or a straight line, but in general it is longer than the intonation; it is often neumatic*, or even melismatic*, rather than syllabic*; and usually it is descending.

The possibilities for composing terminations and for varying them seem to have been endless but, taking into consideration the transposition as explained on page 36, it is possible to deduce from the preserved repertory, especially from the melodies with multiple versions, certain groups of intonations which occur very often and which appear to be interchangeable within each group. Thus for recitation leading up to *D* as recitation tone we find the following frequently occurring intonations[2]:

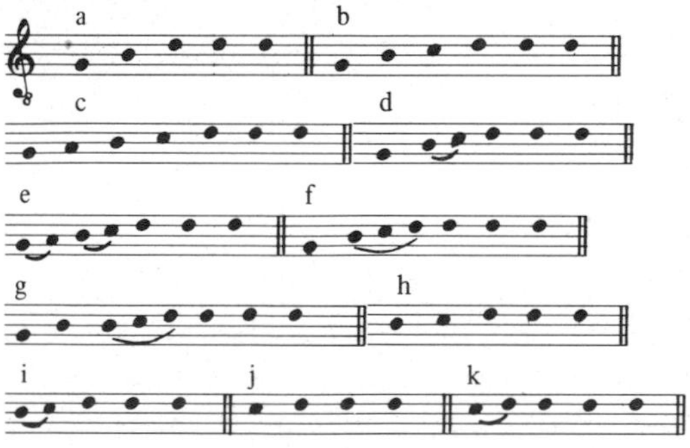
a
b
c
d
e
f
g
h
i
j
k

We find the following intonations leading up to *A* as recitation tone:

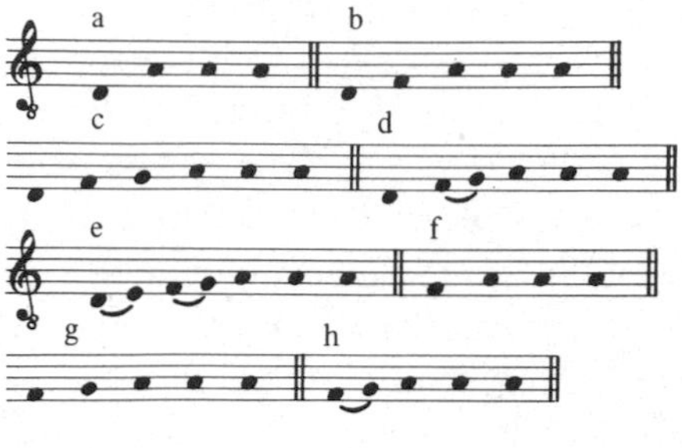
a
b
c
d
e
f
g
h

the following leading up to *F*:

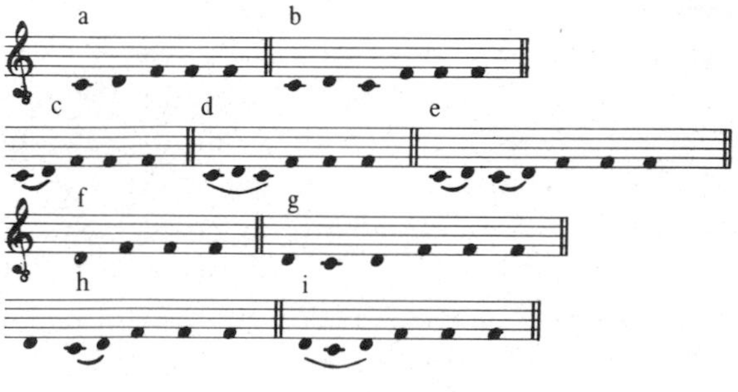
a
b
c
d
e
f
g
h
i

and the following up to *C*:

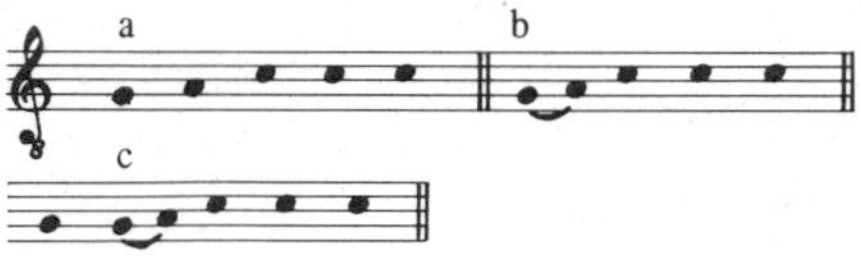
a
b
c

In addition we find the following two figures leading up to recitation on almost any tone, although they occur only rarely at the beginning of a song:

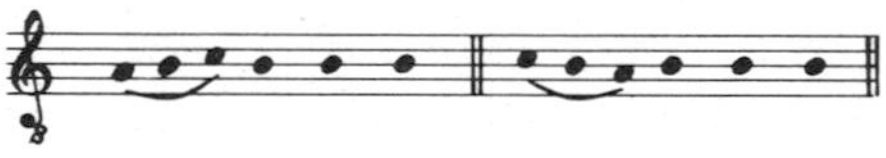

It was not only customary for the performers to vary intonation and termination, but apparently even the recitation section itself could be varied or ornamented and, conversely, sections that originally had the appearance of ornamented recitation could be reduced by

1. The present study departs from discussions of psalmody in that all endings of lines with recitation are called 'termination' merely to avoid endless discussion of the question whether a certain ending should be called 'termination', 'flexa', or 'mediant'.

2. For examples taken from the trouvère repertoire, see Hendrik van der Werf, 'Recitative Melodies in Trouvère Chansons' in *Festschrift für Walter Wiora*, Ludwig Finscher and Christoph-Helmut Mahling, eds., Kassel 1967. 231–240.

performers to real recitation as shown in the following[1]:

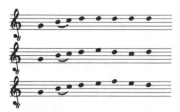

Furthermore we may conclude from the preserved melodies that when the troubadours and trouvères used recitation they rarely extended it over an entire chanson; instead it is often restricted to the opening line of a song, the melody of which is often repeated for the third line. In such cases the subsequent line serves more or less as a very ornamented and elongated termination. If the recitation extends over more than one line, however, we usually find that not all lines are recited to the same tone.

The above observations lead inevitably to the question of whether, during the trouvère period, there is perhaps a gradual development from recitation towards arioso, that is, towards singing without one-tone recitation. At this moment it is impossible to make any conjectures about such evolution because the comparative study of the melodies has not progressed sufficiently to allow the evaluation of all datable chansons. Furthermore, in the case of melodies with multiple versions it is impossible to determine which version is the oldest one. The only conclusion we can safely draw is that apparently recitation and arioso were not two rigorously separated styles for the jongleurs, notators, and scribes of the end of the thirteenth century, as they may have been in earlier times or as they may have been elsewhere. Thus, although there are many melodies clearly in recitation style and others clearly in arioso style, it should be borne in mind how closely recitation-like performance can approach arioso-like singing and how much one style must have influenced the other.

STEP-WISE STRUCTURE

A one-step melody 'in its most rudimentary form consists of only two pitches sung in alternation... Sometimes the upper and sometimes the lower note is struck more often and assumes the role of principal, starter, or final. This makes the melody either ‹hanging› or ‹standing›'.[1] Step-wise structure in this elementary form does not occur in the preserved repertory of the troubadours and trouvères, but it appears to have been used during the Middle Ages and long beyond in the liturgy, for prayers, readings, and salutations. For an example we may draw upon a modern plain chant edition[2]:

Do - mi - nus vo - bis - cum. Et cum spi - ri - tu tu - o.

In many one-step melodies from all over the world, the singers or composers are inclined to use other tones in addition to the ones of the structural steps. 'As long as the nucleus is clearly recognizable as such, any additional note in the melody is an *affix* if it joins the nucleus outside and, when the specification is necessary, more distinctly, a *suprafix* added above or an *infrafix* added below. Secondal melodies can be adorned with affixes only. Tertial, quartal, and quintal patterns, on the contrary, have had a growing tendency towards resolution into smaller steps. The filling notes within a third, a fourth, or a fifth are called *infixes*'.[3] The following Dutch children's song illustrates how the third *G-B* serves as an underlying structure for an entire melody, while the *A* provides a strong contrast and strengthens the tertial structure.

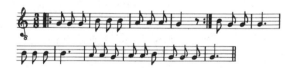

One-step structures appear to have been expanded also by linking several small steps, making the total structure resemble a chain of several conjunct intervals.[4] Consequently, in a number of instances it is difficult to distinguish between the two expanded forms of the rudimentary one-step melody. For one example we may refer to the Agnus Dei of the Requiem Mass as it

1. See also the first line of R 1125, given on p. 69.

1. Curt Sachs, 59.

2. *Liber Usualis Missae et Officii pro Dominicis et Festis cum Cantu Gregoriano*, ed. by the Monks of Solesmes, Tournai 1934. 100.

3. Curt Sachs, 64.

4. Ibidem, 143.

occurs in the modern sources of plain chant.[1] This melody may be considered as a secondal one-step melody with *F* and *B* as affixes and, with almost equal justice, as a chain of four seconds *F-G-A-B*. Somewhat less convincing to me would be its evaluation as a one-step tertial melody on the thirt *G-B* with *A* as an infix and *F* as an affix.

Ag - nus De - i, qui tol - lis pec - ca - ta mun - di,
do - na e - is re - qui - em

Secondal one-step structure rarely occurs in the preserved melodies of the troubadours and trouvères, and then only in individual lines along with other melodic characteristics. The following line taken from R 787 (Part 2, No. 6) may give a rare example of such secondal one-step motion:

Whether there are melodies built upon a *chain of seconds* is subject to discussion; the melodies which I prefer to consider freely structured, and which are discussed in the next section of this chapter, could perhaps be considered as such.

A very elementary form of *tertial one-step structure* occurs in a melodic pattern used widely in Western culture for children's songs:

It is perhaps typical that even this simple pattern can cause considerable difference of opinion among analysts. One can easily consider it as a tertial one-step pattern, *E-G*, with the tone *A* as its only 'affix' but, with almost equal justice, one can include the *A* among the structural tones and consequently consider the entire melody as based upon the combined tertial-secondal chain *E-G-A*. It may be of minor consequence which position one finally takes, but it seems difficult to consider the *E* as a non-structural tone, since it obviously is the resting point of the pattern.

In the melodies of the troubadours and trouvères, tertial one-step structures occur only in individual lines of certain songs and as such they are usually part of a larger structure. *Chains of thirds*, however, occur in abundance and range from chains of only two thirds to chains of four and sometimes even five thirds. The clearest examples of such tertial chains that I have encountered occur in the German repertory contemporary to the troubadours and trouvères. And although the tertial structure in Provençal and French melodies is considerably less obvious (e.g., Part 2, Nos. 1, 3, 6, and especially No. 13), the excerpt from a medieval German song, attributed to Meister Stolle, may serve to introduce the chain of three thirds[2]:

Lob al - ler en - gel un - de lob der rech - ten kris - ten - heit.
Und wer daz lob mit rech - ter vûge Tzû ey - me lobe ge - leit.
Den-noch wer sie me lobes ge - wert.
Die sû - ze mû - ter un - de ma - get rey - ne.

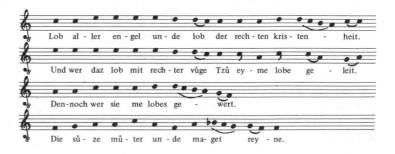

1. *Liber Usualis*, 1815

2. Jena manuscript, fo. 1, facsimile edition by Friedrich Gennrich, *Die Jenaer Liederhandschrift*, 1. Langen 1963.

A quartal one-step structure occurs only rarely by itself in the melodies of the troubadours and trouvères (a rare example of it may be seen in R 223, Part 2, No. 9), but it occurs frequently in combination with tertial structures. There are many melodies in which the interval of the fourth occurs as a structural link on top of a chain of two thirds, thus constituting a *combined tertial-quartal chain* exactly one octave wide (e.g., the Ṭ version of the jeu parti, R 2063, Part 2, No. 11). In a few instances, more often among the German than among the French and Provençal songs, there may be one or two additional tertial links above the quartal one.

In many instances it is relatively easy to distinguish between an exclusively tertial chain and a combined tertial-quartal one, but we also encounter a number of melodies in which the structure of the upper part of the melody is too faint to allow an unequivocal analysis (e.g., Part 2, No. 6). Perhaps because of such a weakness in the original, we find instances in which a melody appears in some versions to be based upon an exclusively tertial chain and in others on a combined tertial-quartal chain. In still other instances we find melodies apparently based upon a chain of thirds which have discrepancies among the multiple versions regarding the exact place of the fourth structural tone, that is, the tone a seventh above the basis tone of the chain. The latter type of discrepancy, however, is found only in melodies with a major third at the basis of the chain.

It is impossible to determine now whether there is indeed a development from exclusively tertial chains to combined tertial-quartal ones as one would expect. But it is obvious that there is a preferential relationship between the character of the lower part of the chain and the choice of structure for the upper part. In melodies with clear step-wise motion over the entire range of the melody, we find a combined tertial-quartal chain more often than an exclusively tertial one if there is a major third as the lowest link of the chain. If, however, there is a minor third in that position we may find either an exclusively tertial chain or a combined tertial-quartal one, but it seems to me that the former was preferred.

To the best of my knowledge there are no songs in the preserved medieval repertory that could be considered as being based unequivocally upon a chain of two or more fifths. Whether *quintal one-step structures* occur is subject to discussion, because there are indeed a few melodies, or better, melody sections, which appear to be one-step quintal melodies with three infixes. However, the middle one of the infixes is usually somewhat more important than the other two, thus making it virtually impossible to distinguish between a quintal one-step structure and a chain of two thirds in which the two outer tones are predominant (see also Part 2, No. 3). Furthermore, if one-step melodies based upon a step of a fifth as well as those based upon a step larger than a fifth do occur in the preserved medieval repertory, they are indistinguishable from melodies moving freely between two tones, which are to be discussed in the next section of this chapter. And although such melodies certainly could come under either heading, I would prefer to consider them as moving freely between two tones, because in general they do not have much in common with the step-wise structured melodies.

The most outspoken evidence of step-wise structure is presented in those syllabic passages which use structural tones by preference, and in those neumatic passages in which the syllables begin by preference on structural tones. Step-wise structure manifests itself also by the choice of structural tones as recitation tones, as beginning and ending tones of individual lines, and especially as ending tone of the last line. Accordingly, in such lines the structural tones outnumber by far the non-structural ones.

Understandably, in a melody constructed on a chain, not all structural tones are of equal importance and not all perform the same function. Recitation, for example, rarely takes place upon the basis tone of the chain, but rather almost always on the second or third structural tone, that is, a third or a fifth above the basis tone. In melodies based upon a chain of three or more thirds or upon a combined tertial-quartal chain, the two outer structural tones sometimes serve as two opposite poles which give direction to the interior tones and organization to the entire melody. They often serve as starting tones of individual lines; and the lower one, usually the stronger one, very often serves as the ending tone of lines, almost always as the final tone for the entire melody, and in case the melody is divided into three distinct parts, as discussed in the next chapter, often all three parts end on it. The term 'basis tone', used above for the lowest tone of the chain, was chosen very deliberately for several reasons. For the present it seems advisable to avoid the usual terms 'finalis' and 'final', partly because of their strong association with the theory of the eight church modes, but mainly because there are many songs that do not end on the basis tone. Although the basis tone performs to a limited extent the same functions as the tonic in later music, the term 'tonic' is for most of us too closely associated with harmony, and especially with leading tones, to make it acceptable in discussion of medieval melodies which are so devoid of harmony, in which we find no leading tones, and in which the tone an octave above the basis tone may not have the same function as the basis tone itself. The term 'basis tone', on the other hand, seems very appropriate because the basis tone indeed provides some kind of basis; the melody appears to 'gravitate' towards it, or to 'stand' on it, even though occasionally the melody may dip under it, especially just before the end of a line.

Among step-wise structured melodies we find many that make use of two *contrasting chains*. In a few songs the total melody is divided almost evenly between the two contrasting chains: the first part may be based upon the chain *G-B-D* and the rest based upon the chain *F-A-C*, but the melody is likely to end on *G*, thus returning to its original basis tone.[1] Usually, however, the contrast between the two chains is less outspoken and the first chain remains prevalent throughout the song, to be replaced only occasionally by another chain which perhaps should be called a *secondary chain* rather than a contrasting one (e.g. Part 2, Nos. 7 and 8). It must be emphasized however, that there are often discrepancies among multiple versions regarding the interval between the tones of the contrasting or secondary chains (e.g., Part 2, No. 8). In addition, we find melodies that are only partly based upon a certain chain. To begin with, a certain chain may impart considerable coherence to a melody and then gradually fade away, leaving as structure for the end of the song nothing but the memory of the earlier chain. Interestingly, these contrasting and interrupted step-wise structures appear to have caused occasional problems during the oral tradition, for we find instances in which the versions of a melody disagree upon the extent to which a certain chain exerts its organizing influence.

In the majority of melodies with step-wise structures, the most stable tone, the tone on which the melody comes to rest, is at the bottom of the melodic range, but there are also a number of melodies in which this tone is somewhere in the middle of the melodic compass. In such *centric melodies*, as Curt Sachs called them,[1] step-wise structure, if it occurs, is likely to be tertial above the center tone and quartal under it, although it is remarkable that this quartal structure is often rather faint. In principle, I presume, centric melodies can be based upon an exclusively tertial chain, but it is difficult to find unequivocal examples of such a structure in the preserved repertory of the troubadours and trouvères. However, one does find a limited number of tertial melodies in which the tone a third or a fifth above the basis tone takes on an importance more or less equal to that of the basis tone itself, and the melody may even end on it. This peculiarity makes it difficult to determine whether one is dealing here with a centric tertial melody or with a standing tertial one that ends on a structural tone other than the basis tone. Similarly, contrasting chains within a centric melody tend to obscure the overall structure if the tone a fourth under the center tone becomes the basis tone of the contrasting chain, as often happens (e.g., in R 1420, Part 2, No. 8).

MELODIES WITH EITHER ONE OR TWO STRUCTURAL TONES

If it were possible to categorize all medieval melodies according to the coherence imparted by tonal centers and tonal structures, we would have at one end the melodies with an outspoken tertial or combined tertial-quartal chain and at the other extreme melodies that move freely up and down without any apparent structure and without any limitations other than those dictated by the confines of an average human voice. However, for most such freely moving melodies in the preserved troubadour and trouvère repertory, we find remarkable similarities among the preserved versions. Not only is the melodic contour of most lines the same in all versions, but several of the individual lines, especially the last one, end on the same tone in all versions. Thus it would seem that the medieval singer found more structure in them than we can find in them on first hearing,

---

1. For example, R 1402, published as Example 2 in my study on recitative melodies in *Festschrift für Walter Wiora*, 237.

1. Curt Sachs, 168.

preconditioned as we are by outspoken tonics and do-
minants. Indeed, many of these freely moving melodies
share some characteristics with the step-wise structured
ones. Close scrutiny reveals that in most, but not all, of
these melodies one tone appears to perform with varying degrees of clarity the same function as the center
or the basis tone performs in melodies clearly based upon a chain. The centric songs among them fit almost
perfectly Curt Sach's description of centric melodies
from all over the world: 'The melody, freely moving
upward and downward, returns again and again to the
same note in the middle, which is often starter and final
as well as an ever recurring nucleus in the course of the
tune'.[1] Only a few changes are required to make this
description also fit the melodies that appear to be moving freely above a basis tone or between a basis tone and
its opposite pole, since these also often serve as starter
and final of individual melodic lines and the basis tone
serves as the tone upon which the entire melody seems
to rest and upon which it usually ends. There are also a
number of instances in which the place of the basis or
center tone appears to shift much the same as it does in
melodies with contrasting chains. In one important
aspect, however, the freely moving melodies differ from
the ones with step-wise structure: there are many more
instances in which it is difficult or impossible to determine the exact place of the basis or center tone. In most
such cases it is still possible to determine which tones
certainly do not serve as basis or center tone, but there
are two or three tones which appear to perform that
function equally well or equally poorly (e.g., Part 2,
No. 1).

All in all, there may not be many melodies of the
chansons of the troubadours and trouvères that move
up and down really freely, but there are many *centric*
melodies that move freely around the center tone (e.g.,
R 273, Part 2, No. 10), many *standing* ones that move
freely above a basis tone or between a basis tone and its
opposite pole,[2] and there are some *hanging* ones, most
of them containing one-tone recitation, that move freely up and down with a recitation tone near or at the
top of the melodic range as their main focus[3].

1. Loc. cit.
2. For example, R 1010, published in my study on declamatory rhythm in *Die Musikforschung*, XX, 1967. 140-144.
3. For example, R 21, published in my study on recitative
melodies in *Festschrift für Walter Wiora*, 236.

The above discussion may give a clear picture of the
organizing phenomena by themselves, but the manner
in which they actually function may be best understood
by assuming that before the earliest troubadours and
trouvères made their songs, perhaps long before, people
in France had at least three types of melodies: one-tone
recitations, freely moving melodies without any structure, and modular melodies formed primarily by linking
certain small steps. By the time of the first troubadours
and trouvères, these types had merged almost completely. Melodies that are descendants of the freely moving ones derive organization from one tone near the
top, the bottom, or the center of the melodic range or
from two tones near the top and the bottom of the melody; some such songs even derive organization for part
of the melody from several tones at intervals of a third
or a fourth from one another. The descendants of the
modular melodies cover such a wide range and use infixes and affixes so freely that they share many features
with the freely moving ones. Recitation still occurs in
the melodies of the troubadours and trouvères, but
usually in a very adorned and almost unrecognizable
form, and what little recitation there is seems to increase the coherence of the descendants of the other
two types.

SCALES

The study of scales in medieval music is beset with many
problems. First there is the question of whether the
term 'scale' is even appropriate in discussions of medieval music. Yet in the following discussion we shall
use that term, partly to avoid introducing yet another
new term and partly for reasons to be explained later,
after we shall have determined the nature of the scales
used by the troubadours and trouvères.

Determining the scale used for a given melody is
another problem; already in the Middle Ages some-
not all!-theorists settled for the rather arbitrary solution
of considering the last tone of a melody as the prime indicator of tonality; a piece ending on G, for example,
was considered to use the scale of G regardless of the
character of the melody in its entirety. This procedure
may be acceptable if tonality has to be determined only
for the sake of selecting an appropriate psalm tone, but
it hardly suffices for a scholarly discussion of scales used
in medieval music. Therefore, whenever it is possible

to determine the place of the basis or center tone with reasonable certainty, we shall take that tone as the primary indicator of the scale, as has been done by others.[1] Thus a melody clearly having G as basis or center tone will be considered to use a scale of G regardless of its ending tone. By implication the basis or center tone, unlike any other structural tone, is considered an integral part of that scale.[2]

A third problem is caused by a discrepancy between medieval theory and the music as it appears in the manuscripts: the former admits only four different scales, namely those on D, E, F, and G, while in the manuscripts we find music based upon the scales of C and A in addition to the four admitted by the theorists. Apparently the medieval theorists themselves felt troubled by this discrepancy, and in a typical medieval fashion they explained the problem away by giving the two problematic scales acceptable names. Their practice unfortunately found its way into modern studies of medieval music. Melodies based upon the scale of C are considered as transposed Mixolydian, that is, transposed G-melodies; melodies using the scale of A are considered to use the transposed Dorian, that is, D scale. Such an unrealistic approach makes discussion of the melodies concerned unnecessarily circuitous, and it does not correspond to the present-day interpretation of the word 'transposed'; therefore it will not be followed here, especially since further findings regarding medieval scales reveal that there is little reason to assume that the scribes erred in notating these melodies as using the scales of C and A.

A final problem, which so far has not received proper attention, is caused by the numerous discrepancies one finds among multiple versions concerning the use of sharps[3] or flats and the choice of scale. In fact, I found such discrepancies for approximately three-fourths of the trouvère melodies preserved in multiple versions, excluding of course those occurring only in the manuscripts K, L, N, P, and X which, as was pointed out in Chapter 2, were largely copied from one common source.

A detailed examination of these discrepancies makes it unmistakably clear that there is no ground whatsoever for the usual assumption that all of them were caused by scribal inaccuracy and inconsistency. If we hold that the discrepancies under discussion are caused by mere scribal inaccuracy and inconsistency, we also have to be willing to accept that the scribes, when choosing scales and when writing or omitting sharps and flats, were as often wrong as they were right. This seems rather incongruous, since it is clear that the scribes of all chansonniers knew perfectly well how to be consistent in the notation of B-flats – other signs do not occur with sufficient frequency to provide a basis for a detailed study. We find many melodies in all chansonniers for which the scribes indicated that all B's were to be flatted, either by writing a B-flat sign immediately following the clef on all staffs of the melody (or on all staffs on which a B occurred), or by writing a flat sign in front of the first B of every staff, thus suggesting that subsequent B's were to be flatted, too. Obviously, we may take it for granted that both the scribes who wrote down the melodies upon hearing them and those who copied the melodies from the drafts onto the pages of the preserved sources made some errors concerning choice of scale and notating or omitting sharp and flat signs. The problem is, however, to determine whether apparent inconsistencies are intentional or erroneous and this problem is seriously aggravated by the obvious lack of rules regarding the durational effectiveness of sharp and flat signs. To realize the scope of the problem, we only have to imagine the results of a scribe's copying the accidentals exactly as notated in his draft even when the distribution of the melody over the staffs in his copy differed from that in his model. Although sharp and flat signs for notes other than the B occur only infrequently, there is no reason to assume that the scribes were more inaccurate or inconsistent with them than with those for the B.

Despite all these problems, the study of scales and accidentals in trouvère melodies with multiple versions yields at least two important conclusions.

---

1. To some extent this approach was followed already in Georg Holz, Franz Saran, and Eduard Bernoulli, *Die Jenaer Liederchandshrift*, Vol. II. Leipzig 1901.

2. For an evaluation of medieval scales in general, the roles of basis tones and center tones do not differ from one another to such an extent that it is necessary to include both continually. In the following discussion, therefore, whatever is said about the basis tone holds true also for the center tone unless indicated differently.

3. The modern sharp sign (♯) does not occur in the medieval manuscripts; instead the sign (♮), which we now know exclusively as a natural sign, served also as a sharp sign. To prevent confusion in my transcription, the sharp and natural signs are used according to present practices.

Firstly, the similarities among the versions give us sufficient reason to assume that the performers of the preserved melodies divided the octave approximately as is indicated in the medieval treatises and as is done now, perhaps with one or two important exceptions. The discussion of these exceptions, which will come shortly, makes it clear that there would have been more discrepancies if the division of the octave had been substantially different.

Most important, however, is the revelation that, with few exceptions, there is a clear pattern to the alleged inconsistencies in the melodies for which we can determine the basis tone with reasonable certainty. On the basis of the discrepancies under discussion these melodies fall into two groups. One group of melodies uses the Ionian scale in one version but the Mixolydian or Lydian scale in another version (e.g., Part 2, Nos. 8 and 10); the other group consists of melodies which are Dorian in one version but Aeolian or perhaps Phrygian in another version (e.g., Part 2, Nos. 2, 6, and 7). Thus we notice two groups of three scales each; the distance between the basis tone and the tone a third above it is a major third in the former group and a minor third in the latter; and it appears that within each group the scales were more or less interchangeable. Thus we may conclude that the performers distinguished between only two scales in which the exact position of most tones had been fixed by tradition and which differed from one another primarily on one crucial interval: the distance between the basis or center tone and the tone a third above it. In one scale this interval is a major* third and in the other a minor* third, thus, to use modern terminology, making one scale 'major' and the other 'minor' in character.

In order to illustrate this phenomenon, the chart on this page presents these two scales in their various forms. In the upper left quarter of the chart the three untransposed forms of the medieval major scale are given. The second of these occurs either with C as basis tone or in a transposed form, with F as basis tone and with continuous flatting of the B. In the upper right quarter, the three forms of the untransposed medieval minor scale are given. Two points should be made in relation to these minor scales: the Phrygian scale occurs very rarely in the preserved repertory of the troubadours and trouvères, and the Dorian scale occurs very often in a transposed form, namely with G as basis tone and with continuous flatting of the B.

In order to illustrate more clearly the differences within each group, the same scales are given in a transposed form on the lower half of the chart so that the three forms of the medieval minor scale have D, and those of the major scale have G as basis tone. These transposed scales show a number of peculiarities. In the minor scale

The medieval scales untransposed

medieval major

Mixolydian	Ionian	Lydian
G	C	F
	B	E
F		
E	A	D
D	G	C
		B
C	F	A
B	E	A
A	D	G
G	C	F

(left bracket: perfect fifth; right bracket: major third)

medieval minor

Dorian	Aeolian	Phrygian
D	A	E
C	G	D
B		
	F	C
A	E	B
G	D	A
F	C	G
E	B	
		F
D	A	E

(left bracket: minor third; right bracket: perfect fifth)

The medieval scales transposed

Mixolydian	Ionian	Lydian
G	G	G
	F♯	F♯
F		
E	E	E
D	D	D
		C♯
C	C	
B	B	B
A	A	A
G	G	G

Dorian	Aeolian	Phrygian
D	D	D
C	C	C
B		
	B♭	B♭
A	A	A
G	G	G
	F	F
E	E	
		E♭
D	D	D

the second tone is usually E, rarely E-flat, but there seems to have been considerable confusion, or freedom, regarding the position of the sixth tone, for in the sources we find discrepancies more often than not regarding the choice of B or B-flat. The very frequent discrepancies found for the place of the sixth tone in the minor scale raise a fascinating question: did the singers indeed sing either B or B-flat, as the manuscripts suggest? Or did they perhaps sing a pitch somewhere in between these two, thus forcing the scribes to make rather arbitrary decisions which in turn caused the many discrepancies among their notations? We can do no more than raise the question; its answer is not provided by the extant evidence.

Turning to the major scale, we find the first disagreement among multiple versions in the choice of the fourth tone: it could be either C or C-sharp, but it appears that C was preferred. The position of the seventh, F or F-sharp, is often affected by the discrepancies among multiple versions; however, these discrepancies are certainly less frequent than those for the position of the sixth in the minor scale, probably because the seventh, unlike the sixth, was often a structural tone. For perhaps the same reason we often find accidental sharp signs for the seventh tone above the basis tone whereas this occurs only rarely for the tone immediately under the basis or center tone. This may indicate that the exact position of the latter was of very slight importance, and it is noteworthy that most accidentals for the tone under the basis tone occur in Ms. O and in the melodies of Adam de la Halle in Mss. P, Q, and W. The discrepancies regarding the place of the seventh raise questions similar to those raised about the sixth tone in the minor scale: did the singers always sing either F or F-sharp or did they perhaps sing a tone in between F and F-sharp? Similarly, one may question whether they always sang either C or C-sharp or did they perhaps sing a tone in between?

The above conclusions are based primarily upon melodies for which we can determine the place of the basis or center tone with reasonable certainty, but they are also supported by a large number of the melodies with ambiguous basis or center tones. As has been pointed out before, we can often determine in such melodies the tones which do not serve as basis or center. Consequently, we can determine that in a number of cases the discrepancies regarding the choice of scale and the no-

tation of accidentals do not affect the third tone of the scale.

However, we cannot ignore those melodies that differ from the majority by displaying discrepancies among their multiple versions concerning the exact place of the third tone above the basis tone, even though most of these discrepancies occur under such circumstances that only very cautious conclusions are justified. The discrepancies of this nature that may occur in melodies with ambiguous basis tones (e.g., Part 2, No. 1) pose a very elusive problem, and most of those occurring in melodies with reasonably clear basis tones fall into three categories. A small group of them is caused by some scribes who, perhaps during a few moments of inaccuracy, omitted one or two flat-signs from their versions of melodies basically notated in G-minor, while other scribes notated their versions of these melodies entirely in medieval minor. Other discrepancies are caused solely by the occurrence of accidentals in manuscript O. This manuscript probably contains more accidentals than any of the other manuscripts, and most likely these accidentals should be considered as 'editorial' idiosyncrasies of this particular chansonnier. As such they contribute little to our understanding of the usage of scales by the troubadours, trouvères, and the usual performers of their chansons. Another small but remarkable group of discrepancies among multiple versions is found in some chansons by Adam de la Halle. The study of stylistic characteristics of melodies of individual composers has certainly not progressed far enough yet to evaluate the position of Adam in comparison to other troubadours and trouvères, but the overall spectrum of his creative activity–including polyphonic music–suggests that he was a rather unusual trouvère with more than the common knowledge of music. Thus, at least at this moment, the discrepancies concerned in the melodies of Adam contribute as little to our present discussion as do those in manuscript O.

Although the above types of discrepancies, as well as the ones that cannot be categorized (e.g., R 2063, Part 2, No. 11), raise many questions and although all of them may have occurred during transmission, they force us to reckon with the possibility that at least some composers included in their melodies 'modulations' from major to minor or vice-versa. However, thus far I have not encountered a single melody in which such a change occurs in all sources at the same place and in the same way. This may suggest that *if* indeed some composers switched back and forth between major and minor in some of their songs, it was difficult for the performers to execute these changes as intended. This in turn leads to the question of whether the composers concerned made these changes knowingly and deliberately or whether they were caused merely by the uncertainties concerning the subdivision of the minor third.

It is impossible to indicate in percentages the number of melodies in which we find the discrepancies concerning the position of the third because, as has been pointed out, very few of them occur in melodies for which we can determine the place of basis or center tone with reasonable certainty. But they certainly form a small minority and, in any case, the number of melodies with possible modulations between major and minor which have been studied so far is too low for a final evaluation.

Our conclusions regarding the nature of the scales were based primarily upon multiple versions of trouvère melodies. There are too few multiple versions of melodies by troubadours to form the basis for a similar study of troubadour melodies alone. But what little material there is, supports rather than contradicts the assumption that, in this aspect as in so many others, the melodies of the troubadours are very similar to those of the trouvères.

The inconsistencies and discrepancies regarding choice of scale and the notation or omission of sharps and flats that occur frequently in the sources of all kinds of music from the Middle Ages and the Renaissance are usually explained with the theory that all persons owning manuscripts as well as all persons singing the music contained in them knew exactly when to sing *B* or *B*-flat, when to sing *F* or *F*-sharp and so forth, and that therefore the scribes did not bother to notate all sharp and flat signs required. It is highly questionable whether this theory holds true for music other than that of the troubadours and trouvères, but it is certain that there is no ground for it whatsoever in relation to the melodies of the troubadours and trouvères. The numerous melodies by troubadours and trouvères that have *G* as basis illustrate the actual situation very clearly. Some of the melodies with *G* as basis tone use the medieval major and others the medieval minor scale. The latter, unlike the former, require continuous flatting of the *B*; thus, if

the above theory held true, a couple of *B*-flat signs in the beginning of the melody would have sufficed and everyone would have known that from there on all *B*'s were to be flatted unless indicated otherwise.[1] Instead the scribes were remarkably consistent in notating *B*-flats for melodies using the *G* minor scale and in notating *B*-natural for melodies using the *G* major scale, whereas they were often inconsistent in notating *B*-flats for melodies in the *D* minor scale as well as for melodies in the *F* and *C* major scales. Thus the scribes were remarkably consistent in marking and omitting sharp and flat signs when these signs meant a difference between major and minor scales, and they were inconsistent when these signs did not affect the difference between major and minor.

Obviously conclusions based solely upon the discrepancies among multiple versions are based upon changes made by performers and scribes and as such do not justify any conclusions about the composers' attitudes toward scales. However, there is no indication that the composers' understanding of scales was more developed than that of the performers. And all we can do on this subject is to raise some intriguing questions. Is it perhaps possible that a composer or a performer made use of only one specific major and one specific minor scale? Did, for example, a certain composer or performer always use Mixolydian as his major and Dorian as his minor scale, while another would always use only Ionian and Dorian, and a third always Mixolydian and Aeolian? Or was there perhaps a regional difference and did the exact position of the sixth tone in the minor scale and the seventh tone in the major scale differ from locale to locale? Or did the scales used for the melodies of the troubadours and trouvères contain some intervals that were larger than a minor second but smaller than a major second?

Equally intriguing, although not directly related to the present study, is the question of whether the feeling for scale among the singers and composers of Old

---

1. I have encountered this very situation only once, namely for one of five versions of a chanson (R 620) by Blondel de Nesle. The same melody occurs also with two contrafacts for which we have one version each. In manuscript a the melody is given with *G* as basis tone, but the *B* is flatted on the first staff only, comprising less than the first melodic line. In all other versions the melody is minor in character throughout, although in manuscript T there are flat signs on the first two of a total of three staffs only.

French and Old Provençal chansons differed much from that of the composers and singers of the liturgical music of the Middle Ages. As is well known, the quantity of preserved plaint chant melodies and the quantity of multiple versions for them is so enormous that at this moment no one can survey the repertory sufficiently to reach specific conclusions. Nevertheless one can safely say that also in plain chant scales play only a very limited role in giving structure and coherence to the melodies. Thus, although the nomenclature of the church modes is certainly valid in discussion of certain melodic characteristics, it is unrealistic to maintain that all of plain chant is *based upon* the four scales discussed by medieval theorists. Instead, it appears that tertial, quartal, and combined tertial-quartal structures occur frequently and that, to a very large extent, the singers of plain chant distinguished only between the same two 'underdeveloped' scales which I found in the trouvère repertory and which, for lack of a better term, I have been calling 'medieval major' and 'medieval minor'. And here a question occurs very similar to the one raised above regarding the preference for certain major and minor scales? Did the singers in a certain church or region prefer certain scales? For example, did the singers in one abbey use only the Dorian and the Mixolydian scales while the singers of another church always used Ionian and Dorian, and those in a third church Lydian and Phrygian? Or did those church modes perhaps exist only in purely theoretical works while in actual music the octave was not yet divided into twelve minor seconds of substantially the same size?

The terms 'major' and 'minor' as well as the term 'scale' are used here with some hesitation because of the difference between the way in which the medieval performers made use of them and the way *we* know them. The examination of the melodies shows that the similarities between their scales and our scales are restricted to the distinction between major and minor and to the basis or center tone which in the medieval songs performs a function similar to that of the tonic in later music, albeit to a considerably smaller extent. The modern phenomena most conspicuous through their absence from the medieval melodies are the leading tone and the subdominant. Furthermore, the tone an octave above the basis tone is frequently a non-structural tone and in that case does not have the same function as the basis tone itself. The tone a fifth above the basis tone,

which is to become the 'dominant' in later music, is often second in importance after the basis tone, but just as often the third is of equal or greater importance; sometimes neither one plays a role in giving structure to the melody.

The term 'mode' has been avoided deliberately in favor of the term 'scale' because there is only a gradual difference between the way in which scales impart structure to medieval melodies and to music of more recent centuries. Thus we have to conclude that there is a wide dichotomy between the writings about scales by the learned authors of the Middle Ages and the way in which scales occur in the melodies of the troubadours and trouvères and, perhaps, even in plain chant. First of all it appears unrealistic that in the treatises there is no mention of the scales on *C* and *A*, while even plain chant manuscripts abound with melodies that make use of these scales. Perhaps this omission was prompted by the functions *D*, *E*, *F*, and *G* played in the theories of the Greek tonal system, which seem to have been known to some extent to the medieval theorists. Secondly, the distinctions between *authentic* and *plagal* scales which some medieval authors accepted appears somewhat farfetched to us; there does not seem to be much sense in distinguishing between two types of scales where in fact we only encounter two ways of using the available scales. It is also completely in accordance with the tradition of treatises about Musica that the authors rarely even attempted to describe actual practices; it was their aim to uncover the beauty of rational division, even where a listener untrained in the secrets of Musica noticed only chaos.

Considering, however, the limited role the scales actually played in the music of the Middle Ages, the learned authors may have been quite forward-looking in their discussion of scales as the primary source for melodic organization and in taking the last tone as prime criterion for a melody's tonality, because in these aspects the theorists either foresaw or influenced the actual development of the music. On one major point their forecast was wrong: not the scales on *D*, *E*, *F*, and *G* but rather the ones on *C* and *A* became the solely accepted scales in later centuries.

Whatever the actual nature of the scales and whatever the precise subdivision of the two controversial minor thirds, our conclusions so far explain satisfactorily why the teachers and singers of plain chant could be content for such a long time with using the hexachord system to learn a melody at sight. First of all the lack of the octave in their sightsinging method was no great obstacle because the tone an octave above the basis tone was often a non-structural one; this is probably more often so in plain chant than in melodies of troubadours and trouvères. Furthermore, the hexachord ends exactly before the point where the medieval scales became unstable: the seventh tone in the major scale and the sixth tone in minor.

Finally we return to the vexing problem of how to distinguish between correct and incorrect notes in the manuscripts. At the root of that problem lies the question: what makes a note incorrect? If we consider every note that deviates from the composer's 'original' as incorrect, we may well have more incorrect notes than correct ones, and we will be unable to distinguish one from the other. But this approach would violate one of the most characteristic aspects of medieval performance. If we take a more flexible approach and accept as correct every note that was sung by the performers whose renditions were notated, we will still be unable to distinguish between correct and incorrect notes and we will be ignoring one of the most characteristic aspects of the notator's and the scribe's prerogatives. We may go again one step further and consider as incorrect only those notes that are not in keeping with the style of the troubadours and trouvères as expressed by the surviving sources. In principle this may be the right attitude but in practice it hardly solves any problems because of the enormous variety in style encountered in the melodies of the troubadours and trouvères. Obviously, smoothly-flowing melodies in conjunct motion are prevalent, but it is equally obvious that large leaps were not avoided. A large-scale examination of

the preserved melodies shows that what strikes us as an incoherent passage is not necessarily a corrupted passage. Perhaps the most elusive problems are related to the tertial structure of many melodies and of the staffs; on the latter the distance from one line to another or from one space to another represents an interval of a third. The tertial structure of a melody may prompt a performer to sing a certain passage a third higher or lower than intended without violating the character of the melody, but the tertial structure of the staff may cause a scribe to notate a note or even an entire passage exactly one third higher or lower than intended. Such scribal errors can be distinguished with certainty only if the tertial misplacement causes uncharacteristic connections with the preceding or following passages.

All in all there are very few instances in which we can be reasonably sure that we have found a scribal error. I am convinced that the occasional errors that actually do occur cause few serious problems for the study of the songs in general, and that we can safely make a large number of general observations. But where publication or performance of individual chansons is concerned, we still have serious problems. One can give all the preserved versions exactly as they are given in the chansonniers, as it done in Part 2 of this study, but one can also take the same liberty as the medieval performers and scribes, and present a song as one thinks it should be performed. Neither extreme may be ideal, but the former is certainly acceptable for a study which has its primary goal to make the preserved versions of chansons accessible in modern editions to scholarly readers, and the latter approach should be equally acceptable for an actual performance of chansons which has the entertainment of a general audience as its primary goal.

5 Elements of form

The poems of the troubadours and trouvères show an interesting array of originality and conventionality in versification.[1] The conventionality is most apparent in the strong preference shown for a stereotyped form in which the stanza is divided into two parts. The first part, called *frons*, is itself subdivided into two identical sections, called *pedes* (singular *pes*), usually of two lines each. The second part, called *cauda*, varies in most aspects from poem to poem, but usually it is from three to six lines long. Ideally, this form is attested by content and syntax of the text as well as by such external elements as rhyme pattern, number of syllables per line, and number of lines per stanza. Accordingly, discussions of content and syntax occupy an important position in the analysis of individual poems, but, inevitably in a general evaluation of troubadour and trouvère chansons, primary attention is directed towards the external elements of form. Together these external elements are usually referred to as the *metric scheme* of the poem and they may be represented graphically as follows:

a	*b*˘	*a*	*b*˘	*b*˘	*c*	*c*	*d*	*d*
10	10	10	10	10	10	10	10	10

(R 1666; see Part 2, No. 11)

a	*b*	*a*	*b*	*c*˘	*b*	*c*˘	*b*
10	7	10	7	10	7	10	7

(R 1420; see Part 2, No. 8)

In these and the following graphic representations each letter of the alphabet stands for a new rhyme sound; the sign ˘ indicates a feminine rhyme; and the figures indicate the number of syllables in a given line.

The individual lines of a pes may be of equal or varying length, but only rarely do they rhyme with one another. The trouvères chose an *ab ab* rhyme pattern for the frons of approximately 85 per cent of their poems, whereas the troubadours chose either *ab ba* or *ab ab* for about two-thirds of their poems, with the former pattern being slightly more common than the latter. Since the rhyme pattern, as well as the number of lines, of the cauda varies from poem to poem, the total rhyme pattern of this conventional stanza may be given graphically as *ab ab* x^2 or *ab ba x*, in which the first four letters represent the rhyme of the frons, and the letter *x* the freely composed cauda.

This conventional stanzaic structure is susceptible to a number of variations. There may be three or even four pedes in the frons, and sometimes the pes contains more than the usual two lines. But the various pedes of the stanza are still identical to one another in number of lines and in number of syllables per individual line, as is shown in the following examples: *aab aab x*, *abc abc x*, or *ab ab ab x*. However, such variants do not occur very often.

Many of the authors show preferences for certain rhyme sounds and certain rhyme patterns. This preference has led some editors of the poems to consider rhyme as an additional criterion for attribution in cases where manuscripts give conflicting information concerning the name of the author. In this study, however, it is impossible to consider such personal preferences and as in the preceding chapters we shall deal with the preserved repertory in general.

The above conventional stanza pattern, with or without variation, may have served for many chansons, but there are also chansons that are unique in almost all formal aspects, and it was possible for the troubadour Arnaut Daniel to gain great fame for his skill in versification.

'With patient careful workmanship he succeeded in mastering the art of elaborate and unusual rhymes, using at times rare words for his purpose. As a technician of verse he has no equal and it is particularly for this reason that he gained the admiration and esteem

---

1. For an extensive discussion of versification in trouvère poems, see Dragonetti; for a catalogue of metric schemes in troubadour poetry, see István Frank, *Répertoire métrique de la poésie des troubadours*, 2 vols. Paris 1953, 1957.

2. This graphic presentation was first used by Aubry, *Trouvères et Troubadours*, 29.

of Dante and Petrarch.'[1] The chanson especially praised by Dante and imitated by many poets is his *Sestina*, in which six words serve in complex alternation as rhyme for the six lines of all six stanzas of the poem.

I

Lo ferm voler qu'el cor m'intra
No·m pot jes becs escoissendre ni ongla
De lausengier, qui pert per mal dir s'arma;
E car non l'aus batr'ab ram ni ab verga,
Sivals a frau, lai on non aurai oncle,
Jauzirai joi, en vergier o dinz cambra.

II

Quan mi soven de la cambra
On a mon dan sai que nuills hom non intra
Anz me son tuich plus que fraire ni oncle,
Non ai membre no·m fremisca, neis l'ongla,
Aissi cum fai l'enfas denant la verga,
Tal paor ai que·ill sia trop de m'arma.

III

Del cors li fos, non de l'arma,
E cossentis m'a celat dins sa cambra!
Que plus mi nafra·l cor que colps de verga
Car lo sieus sers lai on ill es non intra;
Totz temps serai ab lieis cum carns et ongla,
E non creirai chastic d'amic ni d'oncle.

IV

Anc la seror de mon oncle
Non amei plus ni tant, per aquest'arma!
C'aitant vezis cum es lo detz de l'ongla,
S'a lei plagues, volgr'esser de sa cambra;
De mi pot far l'amors qu'inz el cor m'intra
Mieills a son vol c'om fortz de frevol verga.

V

Pois flori la seca verga
Ni d'en Adam mogron nebot ni oncle,
Tant fina amors cum cella qu'el cor m'intra
Non cuig qu'anc fos en cors, ni eis en arma.
On qu'ill estei, fors en plaza, o dinz cambra,
Mos cors no·is part de lieis tant cum ten l'ongla.

I

The firm desire which *enters* my heart cannot be destroyed by the beak or *nail* of the slanderer, who loses for his slander his *soul*. And since I dare not beat him with branch or *stick*, except in private, where I have no *uncle*, I will enjoy joy, in a meadow or *room*.

II

When I remember the *room*, where to my hurt I know no man *enters*, but where all are more severe to me than brother or *uncle*, I have no limb which does not tremble, even my *nail*, as does the child faced with the *switch*, so afraid am I my *soul* may be too much for her.

III

I wish my body were too much, not my *soul* and that she had thus admitted me in private to her *room*! For it hurts my heart more than a blow from a *switch* that her slave may not *enter* where she is. I shall be ever with her as the flesh with the *bone*, and listen to no remonstrances of friend or *uncle*.

IV

Never did I love my *uncle's* sister as much or more, by my *soul*! For as close as is the *nail* to the finger, so would I be, if she wished, to her *room*. Love, which *enters* my heart, can do more with me than a strong man with a *twig*.

V

Since the dry *stick* grew, or from Adam descended nephews and *uncles*, so perfect a love as *enters* my heart has never been, I think, in a body or even in a *soul*, for wherever she is, out on the square or in a *room*, my heart departs not a *nail's* breadth from her.

1. Raymond Thompson Hill and Thomas Goddard Bergin, *Anthology of the Provençal Troubadours*, New Haven 1941. 74.

VI

C'aissi s'enpren e s'enongla
Mos cors en lei cum l'escorssa en la verga;
Qu'il m'es de joi tors e palaitz e cambra,
E non am tant fraire, paren ni oncle:
Qu'en paradis n'aura doble joi m'arma,
Si ja nuills hom per ben amar lai intra.

Arnautz tramet sa chansson d'ongla e d'oncle,
A grat de lieis que de sa verg'a l'arma,
Son Desirat, cui pretz en cambra intra.

As is shown in the following graphic presentation, the rhyme words–excluding those of the envoy–change position in the stanza in a pre-arranged order: the first rhyme word of each stanza moves to the second line of the following stanza; the second rhyme word moves to the fourth line; the third rhyme word moves to the sixth line; the fourth rhyme word moves to the fifth line; the fifth rhyme word moves to the third line; and, finally, the sixth rhyme word moves to the first line. The three lines of the envoy have the same rhyme words as the last three lines of the final stanza.

Stanza I	Stanza II	Stanza III	Stanza IV	Stanza V	Stanza VI
a˅	f˅	c˅	e˅	d˅	b˅
b˅	a˅	f˅	c˅	e˅	d˅
c˅	e˅	d˅	b˅	a˅	f˅
d˅	b˅	a˅	f˅	c˅	e˅
e˅	d˅	b˅	a˅	f˅	c˅
f˅	c˅	e˅	d˅	b˅	a˅

Arnaut Daniel presented in this poem an ingenious design for unifying the rhyme pattern of a long stanzaic poem, and it is certainly not the only such device developed by the troubadours and trouvères. In fact, certain intricate patterns appear over and over, and in due course appropriate names were developed for them. One of the most popular ways of unifying the rhyme

VI

For my heat roots in her and *claws* into her, as clings the bark to the *branch*, for she is for me the tower, the palace and the *room* of love, and I love not so much brother, parent or *uncle*. My *soul* will have double joy in heaven, if ever man *enters* there for having loved well.

Arnaut sends his song of the *nail* and the *uncle*, for the enjoyment of her who has the *soul* of a *stick*, to his friend Dezirat, whose reputation *enters* every *room*.

over the entire poem was the pattern known as *coblas unissonans* (*cobla* = stanza), in which all stanzas have not only the same rhyme scheme but also the same rhyme sounds, as is the case, for example, in the chanson *Lanquan li jorn son lonc en may*, by Jauffre Rudel. In this poem the troubadour goes one step further by using exactly the same word, namely the word *lonc* (which is the key word of the whole poem), as rhyme for the second and fourth lines of all stanzas (Part 2, No. 1).

In *coblas doblas* all stanzas have the same rhyme pattern and in addition two consecutive stanzas have the same rhyme sounds (e.g., R 1666, Part 2, No. 11). In *coblas ternas* three consecutive stanzas have the same rhyme sounds. Slightly different in form are *coblas alternadas*, in which all stanzas have the same rhyme scheme, but alternative rather than consecutive stanzas have the same rhyme sounds (e.g., R 787, Part 2, No. 6). Since these three forms are so similar and since the order of the stanzas was often altered during oral tradition, it is not surprising that the sources of a few chansons with multiple versions disagree as to whether a given chanson consists of coblas doblas or coblas alternadas. Usually in such cases it is difficult to determine what the original order may have been.

Two other favorite possibilities of combining stanzas are *coblas retrogradas* and *coblas capcaudadas*. In the former stanzas are paired but the rhyme pattern is reversed, and in the latter (*capcaudadas* from *cap* = head and *cauda* = tail) the end of each stanza has the same rhyme sound as the beginning of the next stanza, as is the case in Arnaut Daniel's *Sestina* given above.

Conventionality and originality manifest themselves also in the author's choice of number of syllables per line and number of lines per stanza. There are instances of completely original choice of these two elements, but in general there was an overwhelming preference for certain well-tried forms. Beginning with the number of lines per stanza, we find that the troubadours and trouvères wrote primarily poems of from seven to ten lines per stanza, with stanzas of eight lines occurring probably often as the total of stanzas with seven, nine, and ten lines. Next we notice a very strong preference for *isometric*, or *monometric*, stanzas, that is, stanzas in which all lines are of equal length, disregarding, of course, arithmetic differences caused by the occurrence of masculine and feminine rhymes within one stanza. Approximately two-thirds of all chansons have such isometric stanzas. We also find some outspoken preferences in the choice of line length, especially in isometric stanzas, approximately half of which have ten-syllable lines, and most of the others have either lines of seven syllables or lines of eight syllables.

These preferences stand out very clearly in Frank's *Répertoire métrique*, in which approximately 1000 Provençal chansons are listed as having *ab ba x* as the basic rhyme pattern.[1] Within this basic form there are about 200 different rhyme patterns, one of which, *ab ba ccdd*, is shared by slightly over 300 chansons. The difference between masculine and feminine rhyme plays a rather ambiguous role in determining the metric scheme of the poems. The last—the unaccented—syllable of the feminine rhyme is not taken into consideration in the syllable count, yet, in the final analysis, a ten-syllable line with a feminine ending is considered to be different from a ten-syllable line with a masculine ending. Because of this traditional inconsistency and the many ways of varying the number of syllables per line, we find more than fifty different metric schemes among the chansons with the *ab ba ccdd* rhyme pattern. About half of these chansons have isometric ten-syllable lines, but, because of the occurrence of feminine and masculine rhyme, there are still ten different metric schemes among them. Among all the chansons listed in Frank's *Répertoire métrique* as sharing the basic *ab ba x* form, we find almost 500 different metric schemes, and in the entire *Répertoire métrique* there are approximately 1575 different ones. More than 1200[2] of these were used only once, which is a remarkably high number, considering

1. Frank, Vol. 1, 90-147.
2. The last two figures were kindly supplied by Professor Bruce Beatie.

the preferences for certain line types, certain rhyme patterns, and the conventional stanzaic structure discussed above.

In some instances the duplication of metric scheme was intentional, for during the entire Middle Ages it was acceptable practice to make an occasional contrafact, that is, an imitation of a pre-existing chanson in which the original's melody and all or part of its metric scheme are taken over by the new chanson. Sometimes we even find allusions in the contrafact to the contents of the model. We find an intriguing example of this in relation to a chanson briefly mentioned above. The chanson, *Lanquan li jorn son lonc en may* (Part 2, No. 1), by Jauffre Rudel, is imitated in a very interesting way by the German poet Walther von der Vogelweide. Rudel's poem sings of the beloved in a far away country, emphasizing her distance from him; Walther's poem is about the joy experienced by the crusader upon entering another far away country, namely the Holy Land, 'in which God had lived as a human being'. Thus in this case the poems share not only the melody and most of the rhyme scheme (the length of the lines differs somewhat, partly because of the difference in metric principles between French and German poetry), but also related motifs.

THE FORM OF THE MELODIES

Considering the care with which the troubadours and trouvères designed the form of their poems and considering the agreement among the manuscripts regarding rhyme and stanzaic form, one would expect the authors, composers, and scribes to pay equal attention to detail regarding the musical form. But the manuscripts make it abundantly clear that the form of the poem must have been of far greater interest to everybody involved than the form of the melody. Convention and lack of sophistication in the form of the melody are typical, while originality and attention for detail are exceptional.

The conventionality manifests itself in a preference, especially strong among the trouvères, for a sequence of melodic lines which may be represented with the formula A B A B X corresponding to the frons, pedes, and cauda of the poem. (To achieve differentiation between the formulas for music and poem, capital letters are used for identification of melodic lines.) The letters

A B represent a melodic sentence consisting of two members, usually relating to one another as *antecedent* and *consequent* phrases, that is, as two connecting lines, neither one of which could satisfactorily stand by itself because the A section is a typical opening phrase to be concluded by the B section. The letter X in the formula represents a freely composed section of as many lines as required. Understandably, for the melodic form we find a few variants of the above formula similar to the variants in the stanzaic form; thus a pes may consist of three members, e.g., in the form A A B or A B C, and the frons may consist of three or more pedes, e.g., in the form A B A B A B.

The lack of attention to melodic form is especially attested by the varying relationship between the melodic lines for the pedes. One would expect the melody for the second pes to be a literal repeat of that for the first pes. Yet in reality the relation of the second melodic sentence to the first may be anything from a literal repeat to an elusive echo. To confuse matters even more we find discrepancies on this point among multiple versions of many chansons; sometimes there may be a literal repeat of the first sentence in one or more manuscripts, while in other sources the second sentence is a more or less varied version of the first. In addition there are many instances in which it is difficult to determine whether the second sentence presents a modified repeat of the first one or entirely new material. It is noteworthy that for chansons with multiple versions the scribe of manuscript O notated literal repeats of the first melodic sentence more often than the other scribes did.

Almost the only alternative to the above stereotyped melodic form used by the troubadours and trouvères is the so-called through-composed melody, that is, a melody in which there is no repetition, neither varied nor literal, of any melodic line. Because of the difficulty in distinguishing between through-composed melodies and melodies with varied repetitions, and because of discrepancies among multiple versions, it is hazardous to indicate in percentages the occurrence of either form. Yet it is certain that among the trouvère melodies the stereotyped form outnumbers the through-composed one by far; probably in a ratio of three to one. Among the preserved melodies by troubadours, however, the ratio is approximately the reverse. It should be noted, however, that the latter evaluation is not necessarily re-

presentative because of the scarcity of preserved troubadour melodies.

VERSIFICATION AND MELODY

Since the troubadours and trouvères paid so little attention to the form of the melody, it is not surprising that they showed equally little interest in the relation between the metric scheme and the sequence of melodic lines. For an estimated seventy per cent of their chansons, the trouvères combined the conventional textual form with the conventional melodic one[1]; most of the remaining chansons have the conventional textual form without the corresponding melodic form; others have neither the conventional melodic form nor the conventional textual one; and very few have the conventional melodic form but a different form for the textual stanza. Understandably we find considerably less correspondence between these two elements among the Provençal chansons that have been preserved with music; it appears that the *ab ba x* rhyme scheme is combined by preference with a through-composed melody, while the *ab ab x* sequence is matched in two out of three cases by the A B A B X melodic form. Finally we find in the sources a few—very few—melodies that have the conventional melodic form but an entirely different form for the textual stanza.

The above percentages are given with considerable hesitation not only because of the difficulties encountered in determing the exact melodic form, but also because of possible differences in opinion as to what songs should be included. And it is the latter problem that could make the greater difference in the statistics. For example, I do not take into consideration chansons of the sequence or rondel type, many of which are in-

1. The term 'canzone form' is often used for this conventional form. For several reasons I have chosen to avoid this term. There is, first, the confusion as to what the term should designate; it has been used in three different ways: referring to the textual form, to the melodic form, and to the combination of the two. Secondly, the word 'canzone' is merely the Italian version of the word 'chanson', and thus using the term 'canzone form' may be taken to imply that this is the regular form for chansons and that all other forms are exceptional; such implication would certainly misrepresent the actual situation, and, furthermore, not enough appropriate terms can be found for other forms. For similar reasons I prefer to avoid the term 'bar form' too. The word 'bar' was used by the Meistersinger for their particular type of song, which was always in the conventional form under discussion.

cluded by Pillet-Carstens, István Frank, and Raynaud-Spanke. On the other hand I include pastourelles, satirical songs, and the like, which in turn are excluded by Dragonetti, despite the close similarity in form and melodic style between many such songs and the courtly chansons.

The lack of interest in small details of melodic form and in correspondence between poem and melody manifests itself in several other respects. Within the cauda of the text there is always rhyme and often a recurrence of rhyme sounds from the frons, whereas in the cauda of the melody there is rarely repetition of earlier-heard melodies either from the frons or from within the cauda. In this aspect analysis is sometimes elusive because it is difficult to distinguish strictly between varied repetitions and presentations of new material (e.g., R 1420, Part 2, No. 8). However, the few chansons that have an interesting melodic form, to be discussed later, make the lack of it in all the other chansons so much more obvious.[1]

In the technique of versification the line, running from rhyme to rhyme, is the basic unit; correspondingly, a melodic line is that section of the total melody to which one line of the poem is sung. The question has been raised many times of how these units were treated in actual performance, specifically whether each line was sung as a separate unit ending with a ritardando* and perhaps followed by a short pause, or whether two or more lines could be combined and performed one after another without any noticeable break.

Examination of contents and syntactical structure of almost any strophe reveals unmistakably that, when conveying the content of the poem is the primary goal of the performance, a break after the rendition of each individual line is not required and that in many instances a conspicuous pause might even be a hindrance to the easy understanding of the poem (e.g., Part 2, No. 10, lines 6-7). But it is equally obvious that both to authors and performers the rhyme was a very important aspect of the text. Among multiple versions of the poems we find many discrepancies concerning choice and order of words within the line, but there is remarkable uniformity concerning the rhyme. Thus we have to reckon with the probability that the performers would give some special emphasis to the rhyme for its

own sake, although contents and sentence structure may have been the primary criteria for determining the way in which individual lines would be treated.

The analysis of the music reveals a similar situation; the shape of the melodies does not dictate a ritardando or a pause at the end of each line and in a number of cases two or more consecutive melodic lines appear to form one logical melodic sentence which would be disrupted if performed with conspicuous breaks at every rhyme word. Examination of many melodies has shown that the basis tone was the preferred ending tone for the last line; extending this finding in a logical way we may assume that, besides the basis tone, all structural tones would provide favorable resting points within the stanza. Starting from this vantage point we find that, generally, such favorable resting points occur at the end of each pes in melodies with the stereotyped stanza form. In a large number of these melodies the pes actually ends on the basis tone itself and thus we may conclude that at this point the singer would make a clearly noticeable break. Exception could perhaps be made for those instances in which the end of a pes does not mark the end of a sentence or phrase in the text. Further melodic analysis reveals little in the form of generalities. Although there are chansons in which each melodic line appears to be a self-contained melodic entity, the prevailing situation is different. Especially in through-composed melodies and in the cauda of melodies in the stereotyped stanza form the total melody is often shaped so that a performer could have stopped at the end of each line–or almost anywhere else–but he may also have sung as many lines to one breath as physically possible. In this aspect again the melodies with multiple versions and melodies that were used for more than one poem are the most revealing.

In our considerations of the rhythm we have observed that multiple versions often display discrepancies regarding the exact distribution of the melodic line over the text. There are instances in which such discrepancies straddle the ending of one and the beginning of the next line, but there are other instances in which multiple versions differ markedly from one another except for the ending tones of all or certain individual lines. The latter occurrence may be an indication that all performers made pauses or at least noticeable ritardandos at the end of the lines concerned and consequently maintained the ending tones even though

1. See especially chanson R 238, to be discussed shortly.

they varied the rest of the melody. The former instances, on the other hand, seem to suggest that the lines concerned were sung, at least by some performers, without any, or with only very slight, interruption.

An even stronger indication that a melodic line is not necessarily a separate unit comes from those instances in which two different poems are sung to the same melody even though the two differ in metric scheme in such a way that, for example, one poem has two lines of seven syllables each where the other has only one line of 14 syllables.[1] The most interesting evidence of the practice of running two lines together, however, is found in those songs which require elision of the feminine ending of a certain line before the vowel at the beginning of the next line, as shown in the following excerpt from a chanson (R 242) by Moniot d'Arras.[2]

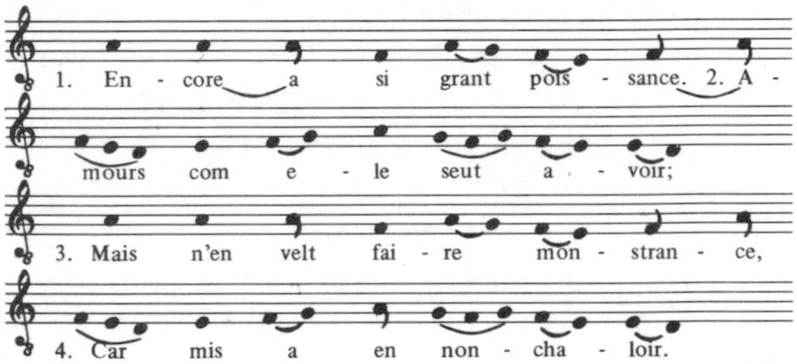
1. En - core a si grant pois - sance. 2. A -
mours com e - le seut a - voir;
3. Mais n'en velt fai - re mon - stran - ce,
4. Car mis a en non - cha - loir.

Obviously, when such elision is required, it would be against the nature of language to make a pause between the two lines; at most the performer could give relief to the rhyme by slightly lengthening the last few syllables of the first line.

In summary, it is my impression thus far that more often than not a singer would make the rhyme stand out somewhat, even if it came in the middle of a sentence; and such ways of marking the end of a line seem to have varied from a clear ritardando, followed by a pause, to a very slight lengthening or other emphasis of the rhyme. Thus for our study of performance practices we have to examine each case on its own merits, taking into consideration both text and melody and keeping in mind that there was no uniformity in the way a given chanson was performed and that the rendition of a given melody probably varied from stanza to stanza.

1. Such is the case with a chanson (R 987) by Moniot de Paris and one of its contrafacts (R 980). A large-scale examination of melodies may well reveal more cases of such partial contrafacture than presently known, because thus far most contrafacts have been discovered through the study of metric schemes.

2. Manuscript M, fo. 119. For discussion of similar cases–without reference to the music, however–see Dyggve, *Moniot*, 90; Wallensköld, *Thibaud*, XLVII, footnote 1; and Joseph Bédier, *Les Chansons de Colin Muset*, Paris 1938. 41.

Entirely in keeping with the above is the finding that, in general, the troubadours and trouvères do not appear to have made any systematic and consistent attempt to reflect in the melody the difference between masculine and feminine rhyme. Ending formulas that appear admirably suited for feminine rhymes occur probably just as often with masculine as with feminine rhymes and vice-versa (e.g., Part 2, No. 8). Any formula used in a given chanson for one type of rhyme may be heard in another chanson–or even in the same chanson–for the other type. A very outspoken example of this disregard for rhyme was noticed by Husmann in an anonymous chanson in manuscript O (R 373) in which two lines with different endings are sung to the same melody.[3] A similar case may be seen in a chanson (R 1623) by Conon de Béthune.

Similarly, the caesura after the fourth syllable in lines with ten syllables does not seem to have exercised a specific and consistent influence upon the melody. First of all it should be pointed out that, when making the poem, the troubadours and trouvères were not very consistent in regard to the caesura. Accordingly, among experts on versification there is some difference of opinion as to what exactly constitutes a caesura[4] and, consequently, in some specific cases opinions can differ about whether the poet actually made a caesura and, if so, about its exact place. Furthermore, we do not generally find such agreement among the textual versions concerning the choice of word in the caesura as we find concerning the rhyme. It is not surprising therefore that the relation between caesura and melody is difficult to fathom. In many cases one cannot find a trace of the caesura's influence upon the melody or upon the way the chanson was performed. But there are at least two ways in which the textual caesura may be reflected in the melody: one is the place where melodic ornamentations and elongations occur and the other the structure of the melody.

3. Heinrich Husmann, 'Das Prinzip der Silbenzählung im Lied des zentralen Mittelalters' in *Die Musikforschung*, VI, 1953. 9-16. See also chansons R 1059, R 1402, and R 1475, given as Example 3, p. 238, in *Festschrift für Walter Wiora*.

4. See also Dragonetti, 489-499.

In general, the melodies of the troubadours and trou-vères are fairly syllabic*, with only a sparse sprinkling of ligatures and elongated notes. It is rather remarkable that such ornamentations and elongations come by preference towards the end of the lines, especially the last line. In ten-syllable lines, however, they occur frequently over the fourth syllable also, although there are many instances in which multiple versions disagree on the exact syllable which is to be held or ornamented (e.g., R 2063, Part 2, No. 11).

The second form of the caesura's influence upon the melody – or upon the manner of performing a chanson – is found in lines in which there seems to be a break in the melody exactly at the caesura. In some of these lines multiple versions give the same note or, if there is a group of notes, the same ending note, for the fourth syllable, thus perhaps indicating that in those cases the performer would slow down noticeably or otherwise give special attention to the fourth syllable. In one specific case (see Part 2, No. 7), a melody first used for a ten-syllable line recurs later in the chanson to serve two lines of text, so that the melodic passage before the caesura is used for a four-syllable line and, at least in some versions, the rest of the melody, lenghtened by one note, is used for the subsequent line of seven syllables. Furthermore, almost all versions give the same ending tone for the four-syllable section on both its occurrences. Even though this does not prove that all performers made a clear break at the end of this passage both times, it seems likely that the fourth syllable was treated somewhat differently from the surrounding syllables.

Thus it appears that there was neither a standardized relation between caesura and melody nor a specific way of treating the caesura in the performance. In some cases the caesura seems to have been ignored completely and in other instances it seems to have received special attention, but it is difficult to determine what form such special attention could take other than a simple elongation or an ornamentation.

Chansons with multiple versions make it abundantly clear that performers could make variations that affected the correspondence between text and melody, but there is no indication that only the performers are to be blamed for the lack of interest in details of the melodic form.

One of the very few instances of ideal agreement be-tween musical and textual form appears in a chanson by Conon de Béthune (Part 2, No. 8). This agreement stands out very clearly in the following graphic representation, in which the top two lines indicate the metric scheme, as in preceding graphs; each new letter in the bottom line stands for a new melodic line, and the symbol ′ indicates a modified repeat of an earlier line:

a	b	a	b	c⌣	b	c⌣	b
10	7	10	7	10	7	10	7
A	B	A	B	C	B′	C	B′

Equally rare in accordance between melody and rhyme is *Ensi con cil qui cuevre sa pesance*, R 238, by Hugues de Berzé[1]:

a⌣	b	a⌣	b	b	a⌣	b
10	10	10	10	10	10	10
A	B	A	B	C	A	B

We can certainly find a few more chansons with comparable unity of melodic and textual form (not all of them repeat melodic lines of the frons in the cauda), but for every chanson with such carefully designed formal unity we find at least a hundred chansons that have little or no agreement between the two forms beyond the frons.

So far we have considered only stanzas which can be divided into frons and cauda, with the former subdivided into two pedes. According to Dragonetti, however, Dante in his *De Vulgari Eloquentia* recognizes three more possible divisions of the strophe. But Dragonetti adds that these occur far less often than the one discussed, and he points out that 'the metric scheme of the stanza does not necessarily correspond to the form of the melody the way Dante and his commentator Mari-

---

1. Published in *Die Musikforschung*, XX, 1967. 136-139. A chanson in which formal or musical elements from the frons recur at the end of the cauda is often called a 'Rundkanzone'. Although this designation, indicating the 'rounded' form of the chanson, has certain merits, it is not without problems because of the many ways in which the end of the cauda can resemble the frons. There are very few chansons for which the term is as appropriate as for the chanson under discussion, because in it both the complete metric scheme and the melody of the pes are repeated. In my opinion, the term becomes virtually meaningless if applied to all chansons in which any musical material or formal element from the frons is repeated.

go want us to believe.'[1] Similarly, Carl Appel, in a study of the relationship between rhyme scheme and musical forms of a number of early troubadour chansons, came to the conclusion 'that the two seem to have little to do with one another'.[2] For Gennrich, on the contrary, the relation between the two weighs heavily in the study of medieval monody. He is of the opinion 'that the strophe represents an organism born from its creator's will toward form, which was directed towards a distinct goal. It is therefore of primary concern to detect this will toward form. This manifests itself most clearly in the combination of musical structure and form of the text. The two components must interact in order to make a correct characterization of the strophe possible.'[3] This evaluation of medieval song, whatever it may mean, is far out of touch with reality. One can not deny that there existed a preferred form for the poem as well as a preferred form for the melody. Neither can one deny that both forms are combined very often, but it is obvious that the authors worried little about agreement or lack of it between the two. It is equally obvious that, in general, the melodies as they appear in the manuscripts do not do justice to the refinements of the poem. However, this is irrelevant because it was not the music per se but rather the performer who had to do justice to these refinements. And it is more important to conclude that with this type of melody, performed in a declamatory rhythm, the chansons could be performed in such a way that the melody would fit the poem perfectly.

In relation to French and Provençal song of the 12th and 13th centuries, Gennrich's evaluation is at best appropriate for certain forms that fall outside of the typical repertory of troubadours and trouvères. It pertains to the rondeau* and, to some extent, to the lai and descord, which are the French and Provençal parallels of the sequence. Basing my opinion largely on Gennrich's edition of them,[4] I would say that the virelais* and ballades* of the 13th centuries were not yet as fixed in form as Gennrich wants us to believe and that the form of the rondeau did not become fixed until the middle of the 13th century. Most of the rondeaux preserved with music have a polyphonic setting and only a few of them occur, together with other polyphonic music, in the chansonniers M, T, and a. In these rondeaux there is indeed optimal correspondence between rhyme scheme, syllable count, and melodic form. Restricting our discussion to the eight-line rondeau we find that there are only two melodic lines, used exactly in correspondence to the two rhyme sounds. Although these two melodies are not always written out completely upon their third or fifth occurrence, they are identical in all their appearances, unlike the recurring lines in the chansons, which are always written out completely and which are often varied. There is also a marked difference between the rondeaux and the chansons regarding the content; above all, the actual content of the rondeaux is very slight, which is hardly surprising since it seems to have been the goal of rondeau writers to construct a one-stanza poem in which the poet was to repeat two lines as often as possible without becoming incoherent. It is Gennrich's contention that the rondeaux are aristocratic poems dealing often with courtly love.[5] My conclusion is almost exactly the opposite: many of them are bawdy in character and full of double entendres. Obviously, there is a need for a complete re-evaluation of the origin and the nature of the rondeaux, virelais, and ballades.[6]

1. Dragonetti, 384. A unique case of careful and unusual overall design is found in a chanson (R 987) by Moniot de Paris, as shown in the following graph:

a a		b a b a		b b a b b a		b a b a
10 10		7 6 7 6		7 7 6 7 7 6		7 6 7 6
A A		B C B C'		D D E D D E		B C B C'

In R 987 the strophes are followed by multiple refrains; this is not the case in R 980 and R 2111, two anonymous chansons that have almost the same metric scheme and melody as R 987.

2. Carl Appel, 'Zur Formenlehre des provenzalischen Minnesangs' in Zeitschrift für romanische Philologie, LIII, 1933. 160.

3. Friedrich Gennrich, Grundriss einer Formenlehre des mittelalterlichen Liedes als Grundlage einer musikalischen Formenlehre des Liedes, Halle 1932. 18. ('... dass die Strophe einen Organismus darstellt der aus dem auf ein bestimmtes Ziel gerichteten Formwillen seines Schöpfers geboren ist. Es handelt sich deshalb in erster Linie darum, den Formwillen zu erkennen. Er geht am deutlichsten aus der Verbindung der musikalischen Struktur mit dem Bau des Textes hervor. Beide Komponenten müssen zusammenwirken, woll eine richtige Characteristic der Strophe möglich werden.')

4. Friedrich Gennrich, Rondeaux, Virelais und Balladen aus dem Ende des XII., dem XIII. und dem ersten Drittel des XIV. Jahrhunderts, mit den überlieferten Melodien, 2 vols. Dresden 1921, Göttingen 1927.

5. Friedrich Gennrich, 'Refrain-Studien' in Zeitschrift für romanische Philologie, LXXI, 1955. 365-390.

6. See Nico H. J. van den Boogaard, Rondeaux et refrains du XIIe siècle au début du XIVe. Paris 1969.

Finally, I will briefly turn to the question of whether the troubadours and trouvères ever attempted to achieve any relation between the melody and the *content* of the poem. Thus far my search for a relation between the character of the melody in its entirety and the general mood of the poem has been without success. But I have found many short passages in which the composer could have provided some relation between melody and text, but failed to do so, and a few passages in which the composer *may* have provided such a relation.

An informative case in which a composer could have provided a descriptive melodic passage is found in Bernard de Ventadorn's famous song of the lark (Part 2, No. 2). The opening passage, an ascending line, can easily be seen as painting the bird's soaring flight, but it can also be seen as the very conventional first line of a melody with *D* as basis tone. There are scores of first lines resembling this one; but there are also scores of first lines which rise more rapidly and higher than this one and which therefore would have been more appropriate for this particular line of text *if* the author had intended to depict the bird's flight in the melody. The third melodic line of this song in the W and R versions can be considered both as a beautiful example of tone painting and as a typical line in a troubadour melody. The ambiguity of this particular line is further manifested by the circumstance that in the G version the text under discussion occurs as the fourth, instead of as the third line, and that the third and the fourth melodic lines paint the lark's flight with equal effect.

Jaufre Rudel, in his song about the far-away beloved, also had a unique opportunity for tone painting, namely over the word 'lonh' (long, distant) at the end of the second and fourth lines of each stanza. The word 'lonh' is indeed sung to three or four notes on all its occurren-

ces, probably indicating a somewhat elongated rendition of this word in comparison to words sung to only one note; but there are many other words in this song, even in the same lines, performed to three, four, or even five notes. Thus it is difficult to determine whether or not Jaufre expressed the meaning of the word 'lonh' in the notes he chose, but we have to reckon with the possibility that the author intended this word to be performed in a somewhat drawn-out manner or that some performers at their own initiative chose to do so (see Part 2, No. 1).

A slightly different opportunity for expressing the meaning of the text in the melody is provided by the numerous exclamations that occur, such as 'Dex!' (God!) or 'Helas' (e.g., Part 2, No. 2, line 5), or the refrain to the song about the jealous husband (Part 2, No. 13). The crucial question is not whether in these passages the music fits the text, but whether the composer deliberately chose a melodic passage which by itself expressed the exclamation or at least gave the singer the optimal opportunity to render the exclamation with the desired effect. For two reasons it is extremely difficult to find an unambiguous answer to this question for the cases examined. First of all, performance in a really free rhythm gives an able singer the opportunity to make exclamations of joy as well as outcries of despair to any type of melody. Secondly, most melodic passages concerned seem as conventional and traditional as the rest of the song, and one can easily find very similar melodic passages elsewhere–often within the same song–for a text of an entirely different meaning.

The following is easily the most convincing instance of relation between an exclamation and its melody that I have noticed; yet it is not without its ambiguity.

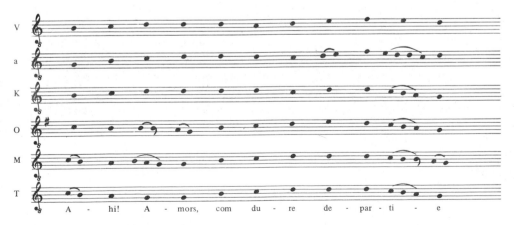

A - hi! A - mors, com du - re de - par - ti - e

The chanson (R 1125 by Conon de Béthune)[1] begins with the exclamation 'Ai! Love, how hard is the departure that I have to take from the best [woman] who ever was loved and served!' The discrepancies among the melodic versions regarding the opening passage are intriguing. In some manuscripts the song begins with stereotyped intonation formulas leading to D as recitation tone. But three sources give these intonation formulas only after the caesura and provide the preceding outcry of lament with a melodic passage which seems to be composed specifically to express the poet's misery in tones and as such it would have been an undeniable example of expressive composing if this passage had occurred in all sources and only at the outset of the poem. But the expressive wail of the opening melody is in all three sources repeated literally, or almost literally, for the third line of text, in which there is nothing resembling the exclamation of lament in the first line. For many chansons in manuscript T the melody is given for the first few words of the second strophe; in this case the notes are given for exactly the section under discussion, namely the first four syllables, and they form an almost literal repeat of the corresponding passage in the first strophe even though there is no corresponding exclamation in the text of the second, nor of any subsequent strophe. Because of the discrepancies among the versions it is impossible to determine with any semblance of certainty whether the V, a, and K versions or the O, M, and T versions retained the original character of the opening passage. However, it seems likely that all, or most, performers would have retained the latter opening *if* they had experienced it as a musical expression of the poet's feelings and *if* it had been with this chanson from its inception.

All in all, one can not prove that there is no tone painting in the melodies of the troubadours and trouvères, or that there are no other remarkable instances of intentional relation between the content of the poem and its melody. But I do not think that such cases are very numerous and it is extremely difficult to isolate them with certainty.[2]

The final conclusion is that the chansons of the troubadours and trouvères were first and foremost poems to be performed to relatively unobtrusive melodies which left the performer ample freedom for a dramatic rendition of the text. This thesis is corroborated by the fact that medieval treatises about music rarely discuss the chansons of the troubadours and trouvères, whereas the treatises on poetry discuss the versification of these chansons elaborately but hardly touch upon the melody. This also explains why some of the collectors did not even provide any space in their chansonniers for the melody; all they were interested in was the poem.

THE CHANSONS AS CREATIONS OF A NOTATIONLESS CULTURE

I pointed out in Chapter 2 that the form in which the chansons were preserved depended at least in part upon whether or not writing was involved in the dissemination, and that there probably was more written transmission for the text than for the melody. But it is also obvious that the absence or presence of writing can have a clearly distinguishable influence on the process of creating a chanson. And it is here that the explanation for the striking difference in attitude towards poem and melody may be found. The poems are sophisticated creations in carefully designed forms and it seems conceivable that some authors made their poems with the help of 'pen and ink'. Consequently it must have been relatively easy for the performers to retain the basic form of the poem and for the scribes to correct whatever errors may have occurred. The melodies, on the contrary, sound to us like remembered improvisations in a very traditional and simple fashion and it seems unlikely that notation was used in the process of making them. For with the help of notation the musician was able to compose new, artful, and complicated sentences; without notation he made up short, simple phrases, smoothly flowing and perhaps charming, but in a traditional and conventional vein. The troubadour or trouvère, as it were, made up his melody line for line while singing; the term 'composer' seems strangely out of place, while the terms 'troubadour' and 'trouvère', in the meaning of 'finder', fit quite well. Free invention guided by an enviable memory was the hallmark of the

---

1. Sources: V 74; a 23; K 93; O 90 (originally a fourth higher); M 46; T 100. Complete text and complete melodies from K and M were published in Joseph Bédier, *Les Chansons de Croisade... avec leurs mélodies publiées par Pierre Aubry*. Paris 1909. 32ff.

2. Compare Bruno Stäblein's findings in this aspect in 'Oswald von Wolkenstein, der Schöpfer des Individualliedes' in *Deutsche Vierteljahrsschrift für Literaturwissenschaft und Geistesgeschichte*, VII, 1972, 113-160.

music of the troubadours and the trouvères, both in regard to its creation and its performance. The composer, in making up the melody, had to rely upon his talent for improvisation in conjunction with his memory; the stronger and the more developed his memory, the more distinguished and the more memorable was the product of his invention. The performer of course needed a good memory, but in addition to this he needed a talent for improvisation and this not only for occasions when his memory would fail him; the better his ability to invent, the livelier and the more inspired was his performance produced from memory. Understandably, the flow of the melody was smooth, straightforward, and in conjunct motion, but it was difficult for the performers to retain it precisely as made up by the composer and, because of the lack of design, it was impossible for the notators to reconstruct the original.

The situation is very similar for plain chant–excepting of course the sequences–but it was almost completely different for the clausulae and motets, the new forms of polyphony that emerged in France around the year 1200. Compositions for two or three voices were written over a brief phrase of plain chant–hence probably the name *clausulae* (sing. *clausula*)–in which this preexisting melody served as the lowest part. The plain chant melody, appropriately called *cantus firmus*, was often carefully subdivided into small sections, as in the tenor for chanson R 759 (Part 2, No. 12). Early in their development the clausulae gained considerably in sophistication and complexity by the addition of separate texts, in Latin or French, to each of the voices so that there were as many simultaneously sounding texts as there were independent voices to the composition, the cantus firmus supposedly preserving the original liturgical text. These polytextual and often polylingual clausulae, called *motets*, became the focal point of experimentation in the area of polyphonic music. It is obvious that in the motets, despite the polytextuality, the music was of primary concern; the composers were intent upon sophisticated design and calculated construction. As such the motets would fit superbly into Erwin Panofsky's discussion of Gothic architecture and scholasticism.[1] Because of this preoccupation with design

rather than with melody or poetry the melodic flow is often chiseled and serrated in comparison to the melodies of the contemporary trouvères, and conjunct motion is not as prevalent as in the chansons.

The motets also differ from the chansons in regard to form and content of the poems. It would be an exaggeration to say that rhyme scheme and syllable count in the former are always haphazard, but it is true that only rarely in the motets is there the sophisticated and well-balanced stanzaic form that is so striking in the chansons of the troubadours and trouvères. In fact, motets of more than one stanza are exceptional and it appears that the length of the poetic line is primarily determined by the length of the melodic line. Furthermore, since there is rarely any repetition of melodic material in parts other than the cantus firmus–except in the rondeaux–there is no relation whatsoever between rhyme scheme and musical form. Gaston Raynaud, the only philologist to make an extensive study of these poems, wrote that the French motet texts were not subject to any rules of versification; instead he considered them mere accessories to the music.[2] He also found that in choice of subject matter the poets of motets were rarely inventive. They relied upon themes that abound in other forms of lyric poetry and, barring only a few exceptions, they varied these themes endlessly and without any literary sophistication.[3]

It is in the area of clausulae and motets that we find the first music that literally was 'written' with primary attention to the music; here we find the first real compositions, the first real composers, and the first unambiguous evidence of measured music. The music preserved for clausulae and motets in the manuscripts of the late 13th and early 14th centuries–that is, contemporary to the chansonniers of the troubadours and trouvères–was probably copied directly or indirectly from the composer's autograph, perhaps for the sake of performance. These copies had to be accurate, and comparison of multiple versions shows that discrepancies among them are negligible in comparison to the numerous discrepancies found among the multiple versions of trouvère melodies. Thus, despite a few occasional similarities, the chansons of the trouvères and the

1. Erwin Panofsky, *Gothic Architecture and Scholasticism.* Cleveland 1957.

2. Gaston Raynaud, *Recueil de motets français des* XIIe *et* XIIIe *siècles*, vol. I, Paris 1881. pp. XVI–XVII.
3. Ibidem.

motets differ so much from one another that there certainly is no reason to consider the chansons as monophonic motets or the motets as polyphonic chansons.

Even though the free rhythm in which the melodies of the troubadours and trouvères were performed fits the notationless character of the music very well, it is not a necessary consequence of the absence of notation. A fixed meter certainly fits in music of a notationless culture, but modal rhythm as described by the medieval theorists would be an alien occurrence there because it has all the features of a cerebral system and in origin it may have been more a notational device than a compositional one. Obviously this study is not an appropriate occasion to establish the degree of influence exercised by notation upon the entire field of medieval music, including polyphony. Be it sufficient to note that this influence grew slowly and gradually and that even polyphony did not originate and develop entirely and exclusively because of the influence of notation. Rather, as Walter Wiora has pointed out, different musical forms which had existed in the notationless realm entered at one point or another into the field of the written composition.[1] And it may not always be easy to distinguish between such a transfer and a new development. It is undeniable, however, that early in the trouvère period the influence of notation is already noticeable in the so-called Notre Dame School and that by the end of the trouvère period there are two distinct styles. From then on, the division between the two kept widening and a new era in the history of music had started. In this new era the notationless music has come to be called 'folk music' and only *compositions* have the privilege of being called 'music'.

Although the designation 'folk song' would be inappropriate for the chansons of the troubadours and trouvères with respect to the poem, it has been used with some justification in relation to the melodies. Indeed, the melodies of the chansons have many characteristics in common with folk songs collected in Western Europe over the last century and the performers of both display a similar attitude toward the songs they sing. It has long been recognized that it is normal for a folk song to be performed with varying melodies and in different rhythmizations; sometimes it is recognizable that dif-

fering melodic versions originate from one common source and on other occasions only the similarity in text makes us suspect that at some time there may also have been a melodic relationship between the versions. It is even known that folk singers (that is, the soloists among them) often vary the songs of their own repertory. Perhaps it is also significant that so many of these solo folk singers are known more for their ability to declaim a poem–to a melody–than for their musical excellence. It is equally interesting that many of these folksong singers–including several who make up their own melodies–never mastered the art of reading and writing musical notation, without any noticeable harm to their careers.

It is important to realize that during the period under discussion there was not yet an abyss between the notationless culture and the world of the written composition. Therefore many a musician could work in both realms, although his familiarity with *composition* may be evident in his *invented* music. A few times the poetic technique of the trouvères was combined with the new technique of composing, and we find some chansons in modal rhythm as well as some motets with poems in trouvère style. Moreover, in certain instances it is difficult to classify a melody in either one of the two groups; there may be many borderline cases. From the beginning until the end of their era we find trouvères who paid little attention to their melodies and others who came close to real composing; at the same time we find trouvères who obviously were much more successful as 'men of letters' than as musicians. We notice, for example, that Thibaud de Navarre ventured into more literary forms and more different subject areas than the average trouvère, while his music shows very little internal organization; on the other hand, Gace Brulé may have been an unadventuresome poet, but his melodies show more design and coherence than the average trouvère melodies.

We have observed that neither the composers nor the performers of troubadour and trouvère melodies relied on notation for their creative and recreative processes, but the collectors to whom we owe the preserved manuscripts were dependent on those who could notate and copy music. We may assume that, in the process of collecting the chansons, many a scribe was involved who had knowledge of written compositions and we may also assume that at times this knowledge

1. Walter Wiora, *The Four Ages of Music*, trans. M. D. Herter Norton, New York 1965. 130.

had influence upon the way he notated and copied a chanson. A scribe familiar with the repetition scheme of rondeaux may have been inclined to make corrections so that recurring lines in chansons became identical, even though in the performance they had only resembled each other. He may have altered the sequence of melodic lines so that a better overall form was achieved. To make melodies conform to the theoretical treatises he may have corrected several lines to make them end on the basis or center tone, he may have flatted several *B*'s, and he may even have superimposed a modal rhythm on melodies which originally were free of any meter. The scribe of the *Chansonnier Cangé*, manuscript O, appears to have pressed his personal stamp upon the chansons and the entire chansonnier more than any other scribe.

Thus a vague and meandering imaginary line runs through Western culture dividing literary and muscial creations into two realms, one relying on notation and script for its tendency towards over-all design and structure, the other kept alive and vivid by free invention and memory. The troubadours and trouvères, interestingly and revealingly, seem to straddle this line and therefore we know more about them than we do about those working exclusively in the realm of notationless and scriptless culture. Unlike other musicians of their time, many troubadours and trouvères are known by name, which was normal for men of letters. And unlike most other music produced in the notationless realm, their melodies were notated, although they did not belong to the liturgical repertoire for which notation seems to have been developed in the first place.

Notes to the reproductions

In manuscript O the chansons are grouped alphabetically and the first chanson of almost every group is adorned with a miniature comprising the opening capital. Within each group the chansons of Thibaud de Navarre come first if there are any of his chansons beginning with the letter concerned; next follow those of Gace Brulé. This explains why so many of the miniatures in O illuminate chansons by these two authors.

Some of the miniatures in manuscript O bear an obvious relationship to the first strophe of the poem they adorn. In the very first chanson, for example, the poet compares himself to a captured unicorn and, appropriately, a captured unicorn is pictured in the miniature. The chanson beginning with: *L'autre nuit en mon dormant* (The other night, while I was sleeping), is of course illuminated with a portrait of a sleeping man. If the four miniatures reproduced here are similarly inspired by a thought expressed in the poem, the first two may refer to actual performance and the others to the process of making a chanson.

The first miniature may have been inspired by the opening line of the chanson: *Hear, why I complain and sigh!* The second miniature presents a crowned person speaking, preaching, or perhaps singing to an audience of two and as such may portray the author, Thibaud, King of Navarre, performing this chanson about the virtues of going on a crusade. Although neither of these miniatures, nor any others in manuscript O, show musical instruments, they do not provide evidence that the chansons concerned were performed without instrumental accompaniment. But, coming from an actual trouvère manuscript, they form a welcome counterbalance to the illuminations with instruments which so often illustrate discussions of the troubadours and trouvères and which are not taken from an actual chansonnier.

The miniatures in Plates 3 and 4 may both have been inspired by the reference occurring in both poems to 'making' a chanson. However, I would hesitate to consider these illuminations as evidence that the troubadours and trouvères as a matter of course used writing gear when making a chanson. In manuscript O there are altogether six such miniatures of a man with a scroll and, in some instances, with a 'pen', and in two of them

there is no reference in the poem to either 'making' or 'singing' a chanson. (One of these is R 1954, included as No. 13 in Part 2 of this study.) It is obvious from medieval literature in general that the verb 'to sing' may refer to actual singing as well as to the act of making a poem. Furthermore, miniatures of persons either writing or reading occur in other chansonniers (e.g., ms. A, fo. 131ro and 133vo) as portraits of authors other than noblemen; obviously, these are symbolic portrayals of authors and, although they strengthen my discussion presented at the end of Part 1, they do not prove that the majority of the troubadours and trouvères could read and write.

The four plates also serve to illustrate what may well be the most peculiar aspect of manuscript O. As pointed out in Chapter 3, this manuscript differs from the other chansonniers in presenting many melodies in a semi-mensural notation, that is, a notation in which the single notes have mensural meaning in that the stemmed notes represent longer notes than the unstemmed ones, while the ligatures, or groups of notes, have no mensural meaning whatsoever. Only in Plate 2 do we encounter examples of very consistent alternation of long and short notes. In the first song there all even-numbered notes and the last note of each seven-syllable line are given either as stemmed notes or as ligatures, except for the sixth note of the first line which should have been long and which is indeed long on the second occurrence of that melodic line. The second song is given in a completely regular alternation of one long and two short notes with each line ending on a long note or, in case of feminine endings, two long ones, thus recommending a performance in the third rhythmic mode.

Plate 1 presents perhaps the typical notation of manuscript O in that the alternation of stemmed and unstemmed notes is far from regular. In the first song[1] at least six or seven notes should have had a different shape to make the alternation completely consistent. The melody in the right column of Plate 1 has only four stem-

1. Concerning the author of this chanson, see Dyggve, 'Personnages historiques figurant dans la poésie lyrique française des XIIe et XIIIe siècles; VIII' in *Neuphilologische Mitteilungen*, XLI, 1940. 57f.

med notes, strewn in an apparently haphazard manner. The notation of the melodies in the other plates too is such that opinions can easily differ as to whether it is semi-mensural or non-mensural.

PLATE 1

Manuscript O, fo. 89vo; left column:
Ne sui pas esbahiz (R 1538), of unknown authorship; right column: *Oez, por quoi plaing et sopir* (R 1465), by Gace Brulé.

PLATE 2

Manuscript O, fo. 127ro; left column:
Robert, veez de Perron (R 1878), jeu-parti with Thibaud de Navarre as first speaker; right column: *Signor, sachiez qui or ne s'en ira* (R 1239), by Thibaud de Navarre.

PLATE 3

Manuscript O, fo. 94ro; left column:
last two-thirds of *Onques ne me poi parcevoir* (R 1803), anonymous; right column: beginning of *Pour froidure ne pour yver felon* (R 1865), by Thibaud de Navarre.

PLATE 4

Manuscript O, fo. 140ro; left column:
all except first six words of *Trop m'a belit quant j'oi au point du jour* (R 1993), anonymous; right column: *Une chanson encor vuil* (R 1002), by Thibaud de Navarre.

PLATE I

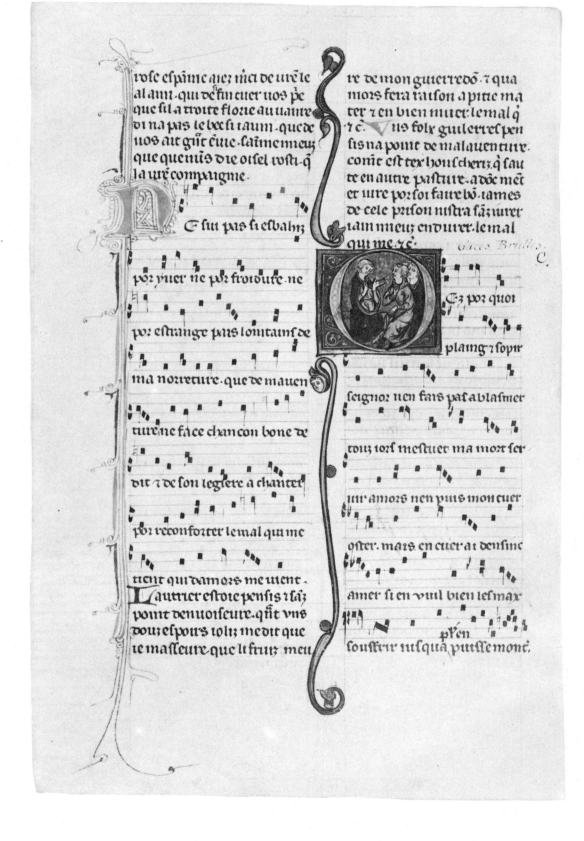

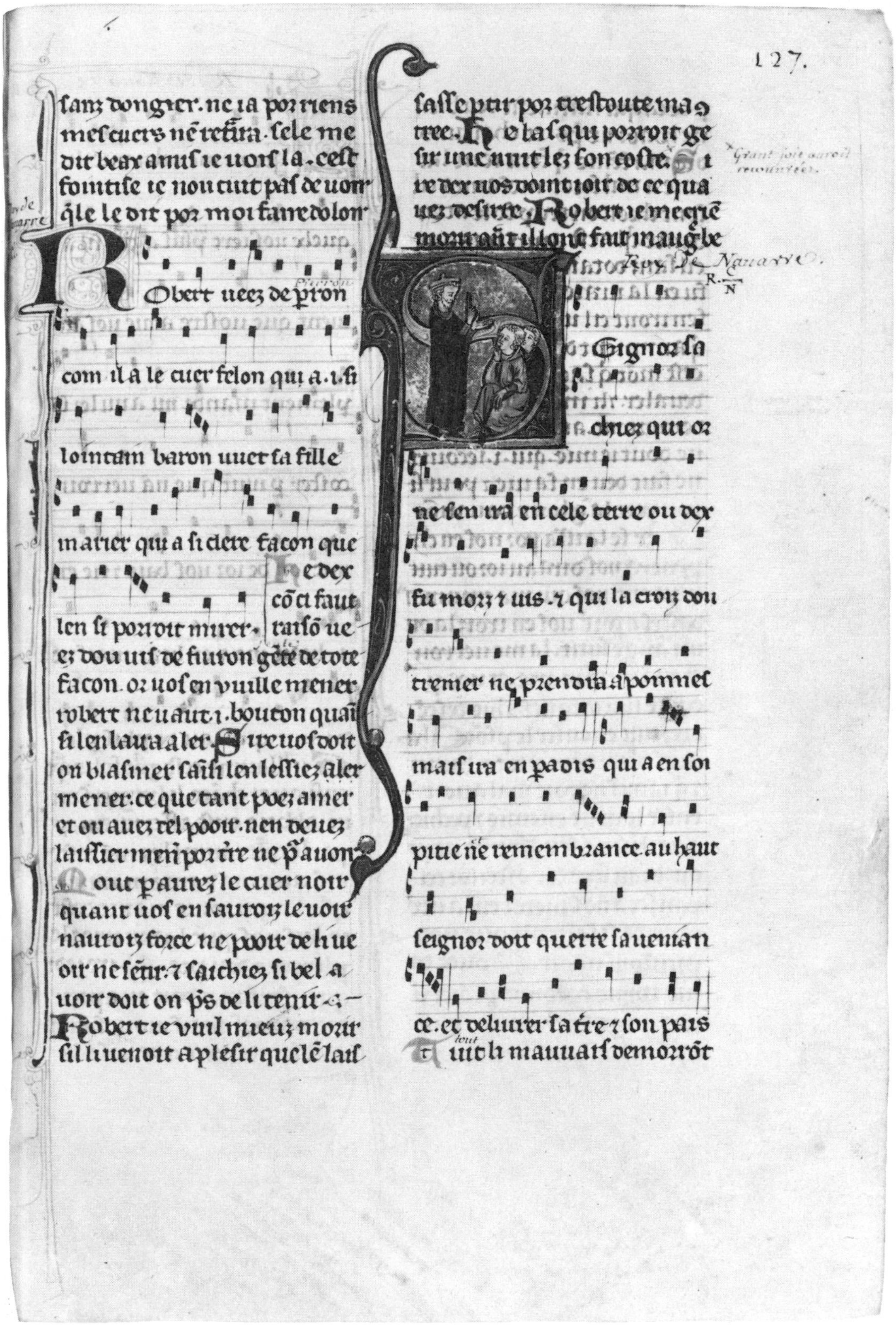
127.
sanz dongier. ne ia por riens
mes cuers ne retira. se le me
dit beax amis ie uoil la. cest
fointise ie non cuit pas de uoir
qle le dit por moi faire dolor
Robert ueez de pieron
com il a le cuer felon qui a .i. si
lointain baron uuet sa fille
marier qui a si clere facon que
len si porroit mirer.
He dex co ci faut raiso ue
ez dou uis de fiuron gēte de tote
facon. or uos en uuille mener
robert ne uaut .i. bouton quāt
si len laira aler. Sire uos doit
on blasmer s'ainsi len lessiez aler
mener ce que tant poez amer
et ou auez tel pooir. nen deuez
laissier men por tre ne p auon.
Mout pauez le cuer noir
quant uos en sauroiz le uoir
nauroiz force ne pooir de li ue
oir ne sentir t saichiez si bel a
uoir doit on pis de li tenir.
Robert ie uuil mieuz morir
sil li uenoit a plesir que le lais
sasse plir por trestoute ma co
tree. He las qui porroit ge
sir une nuit lez son coste. Si
te dex nos doint ioir de ce qua
uez desirre. Robert ie me qre
morrant il lont fait maugre
Roy de Navarre
Seignor sa
chiez qui or
ne sen ira en cele terre ou dex
fu morz t uis .t qui la croiz dou
tremer ne prendra a poinnes
mais ira en paris qui a en soi
pitie ne remembrance au haut
seignor doit querre sa ueniance.
ce. et deliurer sa tre t son pais
Tuit li mauuais demorront

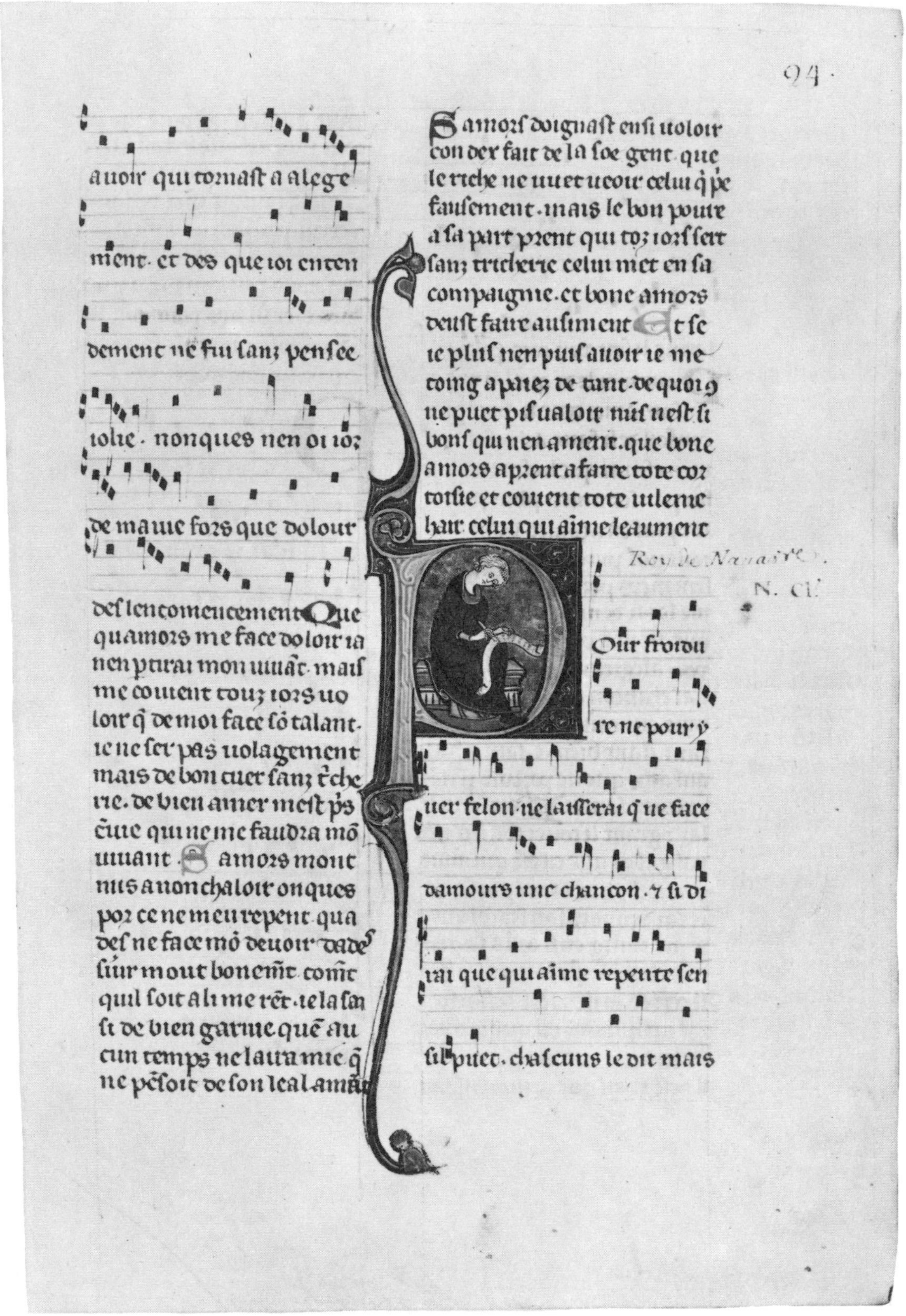

PLATE 3 78

94·

auoir qui tornast a alegre

ment. et des que ioi enten

dement ne fui sanz pensee

iolie. nonques nen oi ioz

de ma uie fors que dolour

des lencomencement Que
quamors me face doloir ia
nen ptirai mon uiuat. mais
me couient touz iors uo
loir q de moi face so talant
ie ne ser pas uolagement
mais de bon cuer sanz reche
rie. de bien amer meist ps
cure qui ne me faudra mo
uiuant ꟺ amors mont
niis a nonchaloir onques
por ce ne meu repent qua
des ne face mo deuoir dades
sur mout bonemt comt
quil soit ali me ret. iela san
si de bien garnie que au
cun temps ne laura mie q
ne pesoit de son leal ama

S amors doignast ensi uoloir
con der fait de la soe gent. que
le riche ne uuet ueoir celui q pe
fausement. mais le bon poure
a sa part prent qui toz iors sert
sanz tricherie celui met en sa
compaignie. et bone amors
deust faire ausiment Et se
ie plus nen puis auoir ie me
coing a paiez de tant de quoi g
ne puet pis ualoir nuf nest si
bons qui nen aiment. que bone
amors aprent a faire tote cor
toisie et couient tote uilenie
hair celui qui aime leaument

Rou de Nauarre

N. CI.

Our froidu

re ne pour y

uer felon ne laisserai q ue face

damours une chancon. 7 si di

rai que qui aime repente sen

sil puet. chascuns le dit mais

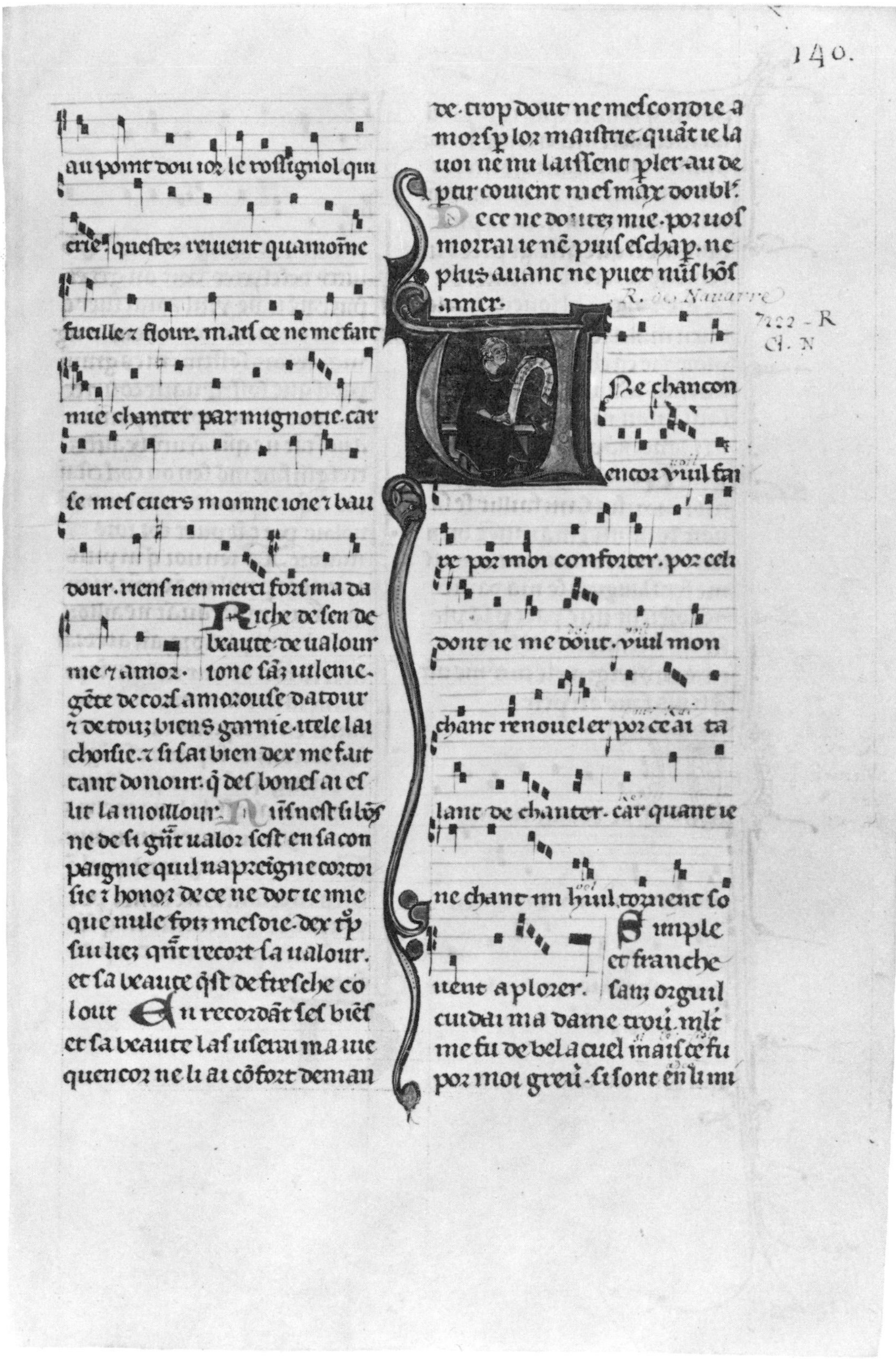
140.

Part 2

Prolegomena

Troubadour chansons

Trouvère chansons

Prolegomena

Order of presentation of individual chansons:

1 First line of the poem, followed by its number either in Pillet Carstens (P.C.) or Raynaud Spanke (R.), and name of author, if known.

2 Commentary, beginning with the indication of sources with music.

3 The melody with text of the first strophe. Where multiple versions are given, the presentation begins with all versions of the first line, then all versions of the second line, etc.

4 Complete poem, repeating the first strophe.

5 Translation by Dr. F. R. P. Akehurst.

The chansons included in Part 2 were chosen primarily to illustrate certain melodic and metric characteristics; therefore the texts are only to a limited extent representative of the contents of the total repertory. Since beauty and originality in thought and expression were not the primary criteria for inclusion, this selection presents poems which are among the best next to those which are trivial and full of clichés; as such it perhaps gives a more honest representation of the variety in poetic quality of the chansons in general than do some anthologies of selected poems by the most talented troubadours and trouvères. However, the present selection does not present poems about a sufficiently wide variety of subjects, although it shows correctly that courtly love was an often recurring subject.

Presentation of the texts has been influenced by several principles. Above all, I wanted to include the entire poem rather than the minimum required, namely the presentation of the first strophe only. When possible, this text was taken from what appeared to me the best edition of that individual poem; in other cases a text was taken from one carefully selected manuscript and given here with slight modernization of the spelling and some other adjustments in order to improve its comprehensibility to modern readers. Consequently, the poems included in the following pages have been modernized in spelling according to as many different principles as there are different editors involved. But presenting the poems as published by recognized experts in the field of medieval poetry was considered preferable to aiming at uniformity in spelling where there was no uniformity in spelling in the manuscripts.

Secondly, I wanted at least the first strophe to be presented essentially as it occurs in a manuscript whose melodic version was to be included, too. In a few instances this meant that an existing modern edition could not be used for the first strophe or that it needed some readjustments.

Thirdly, it is my experience that presentation of all textual versions along with the melodic ones hampers the comparison of the latter, especially when many versions are included. Furthermore, most modern editions indicate in footnotes all important textual variants. Therefore, in order to avoid unnecessary duplication and to facilitate comparison of the melodies, textual variants are given only for the first strophe and only when specifically desirable.

Paradoxical as it may seem, the melodies given here are not representative of the melodic and rhythmic aspects of the melodies in general, because those given here were chosen to illustrate rhythmic and melodic characteristics. There is a disproportionate selection of chansons with specific rhythmic or metric peculiarities and there is an understandable emphasis upon the melodic characteristics discussed in Chapter 4, even though some of them—for example, the quartal one-step structure in No. 9—occur very rarely. I trust, however, that forthcoming publications of many medieval songs will provide the reader with a better presentation of the medieval repertoire in general than is possible in this study.

As explained at the end of Chapter 3, the melodies are given here in a non-mensural notation, except in those cases where a mensural transcription seemed justifiable or desirable for the sake of discussion. Each square note in the manuscripts is represented here by an oval note, and all notes sung to one syllable are tied together with a bow over or under the notes. Real or apparent mensural indications occurring in the manuscripts are discussed in the commentary or indicated in square notes above the modern notation. However, these square notes are intended to indicate only the difference between long and short, and are not photographic reproductions of the original notes.

By and large I was able to avoid illegible passages that occur in almost any manuscript. Thus the only serious problem in the transcription was caused by the *nota plicata*, which in the manuscripts occurs in various shapes; for example: ⊓, Γ, and ⌐ transcribed here as ♩; and ⊔, ⊔, and ⌐ transcribed here as ♪.

The exact meaning of these notational symbols in relation to the melodies of the troubadours and trouvères is still unclear and may never be completely clarified. Nevertheless, a limited investigation of their occurrence in the chansons, and especially in melodies with multiple versions, has revealed some important peculiarities. Although the scribes used various forms of the nota plicata, no evidence was found that they consistently attached special meaning to these various shapes, as is the case in mensural notation, other than either an ascending or a descending motion.[1] The nota plicata is either the only note or the last in a group of notes over a syllable; yet there is no indication that it occurs only in relation to a specific sequence of consonants as is the case in certain plain chant manuscripts. It seems reasonably certain that, in general, the nota plicata represents two tones: the tone indicated by the note itself and the neighboring higher or lower tone, according to the direction indicated by the stem. This conclusion seems justified by numerous discrepancies concerning the nota plicata among multiple versions. For there are many instances in which we find a nota plicata in some versions of a certain melody where in the corresponding passage in other versions there is a group of two consecutive notes moving in the direction indicated by the stem of the nota plicata (e.g., Part 2, Nos. 5 and 7). We even find similar discrepancies among recurring melodic lines within a song (e.g., Part 2, No. 8, lines 2 and 4 in manuscript O; No. 12, same lines and source). Another indication for this conclusion comes from the occurrence of an accidental flat sign in the *B* space preceding either an ascending nota plicata *A* or a descending nota plicata *C*, while no note *B* follows, other than the one implied by the nota plicata (e.g., Part 2, No. 5, line 8 in manuscript M; No. 6, line 6 in manuscript O; and No. 11, lines 2 and 4 in manuscript M). Whether the performance of the two tones represented by the nota plicata differed in any way from the performance of two tones represented by the usual groups of two notes is unclear, but we cannot take it for granted that two different ways of notating a group of two tones represent by necessity two different ways of performing them.

My efforts to present the synoptic charts as clearly as possible have had some consequences that need to be mentioned. In most cases the melodic versions in the K N L P X group are so similar that only one of them is included and only important variants are indicated above the version represented. Wherever there is a discrepancy among the versions concerning the number of syllables or notes, these are presented as clearly as possible so that comparison of the melodies remains easy.

In some instances individual versions have been transposed; resulting sharping or flatting is indicated in the usual manner, namely immediately after the clef.

In those cases where there is a *B*-flat sign at the beginning of each staff in the manuscript, I notate a *B*-flat sign at the beginning of each line. But because of the lack of rules governing the effectiveness of accidentals, i.e., sharp or flat signs occurring in places other than the beginning of the staff, these signs are given in the transcription as they appear in the manuscript. Since there is some indication that the effectiveness of accidentals often ceases at the end of the staff on which they appear, I indicate, when desirable, the beginning of a new staff in the manuscript with a little arrow above the staff in the transcription.

The sign ♮, having two meanings in the manuscripts, is transcribed here either as ♮ or as ♯ according to present usage of these signs.

---

1. For a different—and in my estimate unproven—point of view, see Higinio Anglés, 'Die Bedeutung der Plika in der mittelalterlichen Musik', *Festschrift für Karl Gustav Fellerer*, Kassel 1962. 28-39.

Troubadour chansons

I

Lanquan li jorn son lonc en may (P.-C. 262.2), BY JAUFRE
RUDEL

Sources with music: X 81; R 63; W 189. The first
stanza in W is somewhat mutilated; some words, notes,
and clefs are torn out. The brackets in our transcription
mark the missing sections of the melody, and the position of the wanting clefs has been reconstructed in analogy with the following lines and with the corresponding
lines in the remaining versions. The melody in W is a
fifth higher than in the other sources and has been
transposed here to facilitate comparison.

Jeanroy, who published all of Jaufre's poems, drew
for this particular text upon a manuscript which does
not contain the music.[1] Nevertheless, for the present
edition the text has been taken from Jeanroy's collection, because the reading of the first stanza in the source
used by Jeanroy is very similar to those in the three
manuscripts containing the music.

It was Husmann's discovery that the melody of Walther von der Vogelweide's *Palästinalied* strongly resembled the melody of Jaufre's *Lanquan li jorn son lonc
en may*.[2] Since Jaufre lived approximately half a century
before Walther and since there is some motific relationship between the two poems, as pointed out on page
63, it seems justified to assume that Walther made his
song to Jaufre's melody, even though there are some
differences in the rhyme patterns and in the meters of
the two poems.

Despite the undeniable similarity there are some remarkable structural differences between the melody

preserved with Walther's poem and those preserved
with Jaufre's text. Lines one and three of the latter have
all the characteristics of a rather ornate recitation on F
with D as ending tone; lines two and four, while perhaps retaining the F as structural tone, end on C in all
versions. The recitation patterns of the first and third
lines are more or less repeated at a higher level in the
fifth line with the high C as recitation tone and A or G
as ending tone. The sixth line is certainly the line with
the most serious discrepancies among the three versions
and, not coincidentally, it is also the line with the
weakest structure. In the last line the melody is restricted again to the lower part of the melodic range, as
in the beginning of the song; in fact, in versions X and
R the last line is a literal repeat of the second and fourth
lines, while in the W version, as far as can be discerned,
it only resembles those lines. In its entirety the melody
of Jaufre's chanson has a rather ambiguous structure:
most lines have F and one line has the high C as the
most important structural tone; only one line, the sixth,
encompasses the entire range of the melody; and although the low C is not very pronounced as structural
tone, it serves in all versions as ending tone of both pedes and of the entire chanson. Thus, in my estimate, it is
difficult to determine whether this melody is a centric
one, moving around F, or a standing one with C or
perhaps even D as basis tone.

It is interesting to compare this rather loose organization with the strong tertial structure in the melody preserved with Walther's poem. The melody in its entirety
is based upon the chain D-F-A-C with perhaps C-E-G
as a contrasting or secondary chain in the transition
from the first to the second, from the third to the
fourth, and from the sixth to the seventh line. Especially noteworthy are the differences in ending tones:
the first and third lines end on C, while the second,
fourth, and last lines end on D, rather than on C as in
the three Provençal melodies.

Certainly the most serious discrepancy among the
three Provençal versions is the occurrence of the two
E-flats (B-flats in the original) in the last two lines of the
W version. The importance of these accidentals becomes very clear if we assume, for the sake of discussion
only, that the C is the basis tone in the three Provençal

---

1. Alfred Jeanroy, *Les chansons de Jaufré Rudel*, Paris 1915. 28.

2. Heinrich Husmann, 'Das Prinzip der Silbenzählung', 8-23.
For a facsimile edition and description of the manuscript fragment containing Walther's song with music, see Raphael Molitor, 'Die Lieder des Münsterischen Fragmentes' in *Sammelbände
der Internationalen Musikgesellschaft*, XII, 1910-1911. 475-500. For
a presentation of contrafacts to Walther's song, see Anna A. Abert,
'Das Nachleben des Minnesangs im liturgischen Spiel' in *Die
Musikforschung* I, 1948. 95-105. Lines 3 and 4 of Walther's melody are difficult to read; it is especially difficult to decipher
whether the notes above the fourth syllable of the third line and
the fifth syllable of the fourth line are as given here or whether
they are as the corresponding notes in the first and second lines,
as preceding editors have assumed.

versions. With *C* as basis tone these accidentals not only form a discrepancy among the Provençal versions concerning the usage of medieval major or minor, but they also make the ending of the W version resemble the melody for Walther's poem by being minor in character rather than major. Thus, rather than merely dismissing these accidentals as scribal errors–as seems to have been done thus far–we have to raise a serious question about the tonal character of the original melody. Of the many possible answers to that question the following are worth mentioning. It is possible that in the original melody there was either some tonal ambiguity or some modulation between major and minor which disappeared from Walther's and from two of the preserved Provençal versions, but which in its original or in some modified form remained in the W version. However, it is also possible that the two *E*'s were flatted by a performer or scribe who was familiar both with the Provençal melody as preserved in manuscripts X and R and with Walther's melody–or another version similar to it–and confused the two near the end.

Scholarly opinion on the original meter of the songs under discussion has varied considerably, so much so that it was possible for Kippenberg to append to his study a synoptic chart of ten different metrizations, by eight different scholars, of the melody preserved with Walther's poem.[1] However, there are no indications for any form of fixed meter in Jaufre Rudel's chanson; instead, the discrepancies among the three melodic versions concerning the way in which the melody is distributed over the text suggest a performance in declamatory rhythm rather than one in a fixed meter. This conclusion is in no way contradicted by the fact that Jaufre's melody–if indeed this melody originated with him–was also used for a German poem. Even though the meter of German lyric poetry of the period concerned was based upon a predetermined number of stressed syllables per line, there is no evidence that this poetry was by tradition performed to a melody in fixed meter. Unfortunately, the melody used for Walther's song has been preserved in only one manuscript, depriving us of any information that might have been gleaned from a comparison of melodic versions. But the preserved textual versions reveal many discrepancies in choice of words and word order, including some discrepancies concerning the number of unstressed syllables in a given line. By themselves these discrepancies may not provide unambiguous evidence either for or against declamatory rhythm; but lack of such discrepancies would certainly have been a strong point in favor of fixed meter, since a melody with fixed meter would have made it relatively easy for the performers to retain the original wording even during an oral tradition of an entire century, whereas a performance in declamatory rhythm might prompt the performers to make the changes that actually are found.[2]

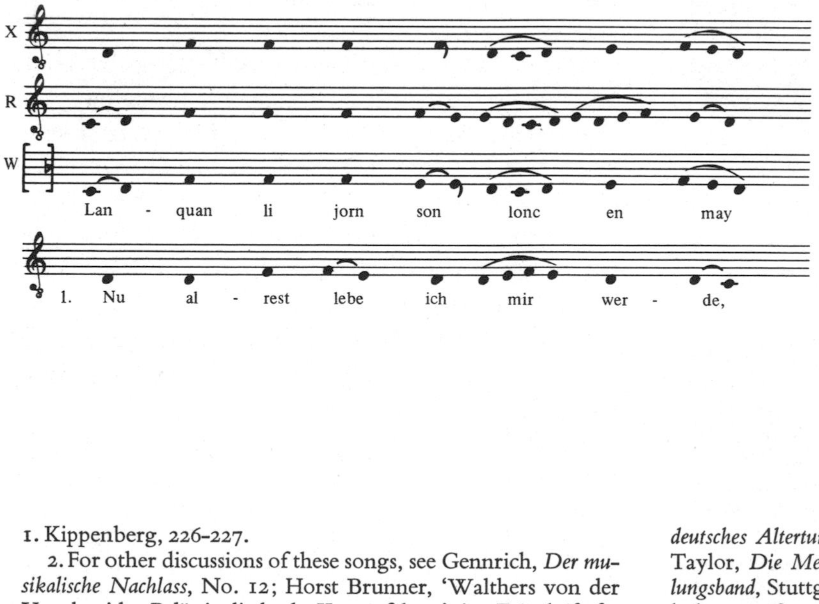
X
R
W
Lan - quan li jorn son lonc en may
1. Nu al - rest lebe ich mir wer - de,

1. Kippenberg, 226–227.

2. For other discussions of these songs, see Gennrich, *Der musikalische Nachlass*, No. 12; Horst Brunner, 'Walthers von der Vogelweide Palästinalied als Kontrafaktur' in *Zeitschrift für deutsches Altertum und Literatur*, XCII, 1963, 195–211; Ronald J. Taylor, *Die Melodien weltlichen Lieder des Mittelalters; Darstellungsband*, Stuttgart 1964, 44; and James J. Wilhelm, *Seven Troubadours*, 89ff.

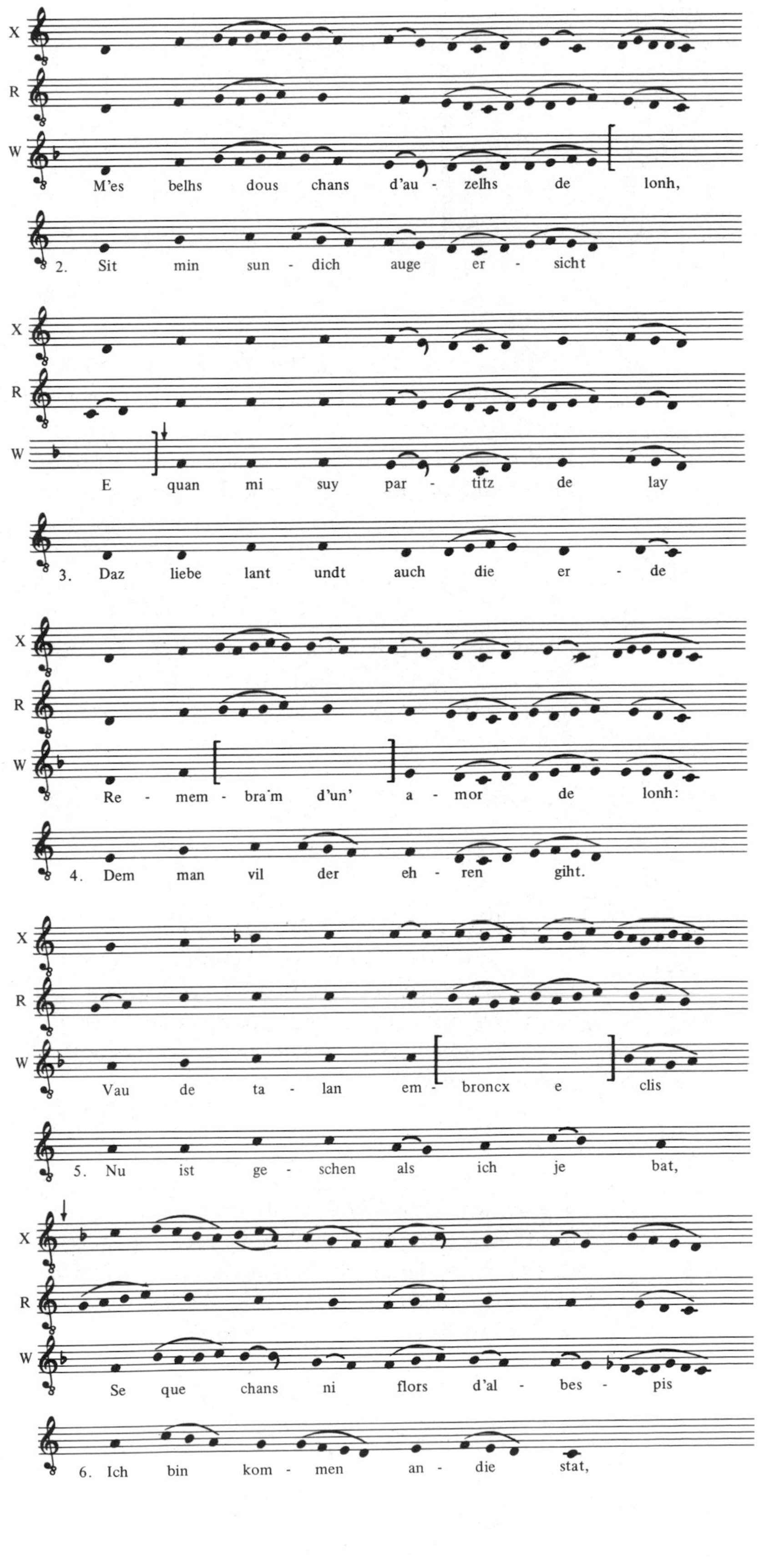
X
R
W
M'es belhs dous chans d'au - zelhs de lonh,
2. Sit min sun - dich auge er - sicht
X
R
W
E quan mi suy par - titz de lay
3. Daz liebe lant undt auch die er - de
X
R
W
Re - mem - bra'm d'un' a - mor de lonh:
4. Dem man vil der eh - ren giht.
X
R
W
Vau de ta - lan em - broncx e clis
5. Nu ist ge - schen als ich je bat,
X
R
W
Se que chans ni flors d'al - bes - pis
6. Ich bin kom - men an - die stat,

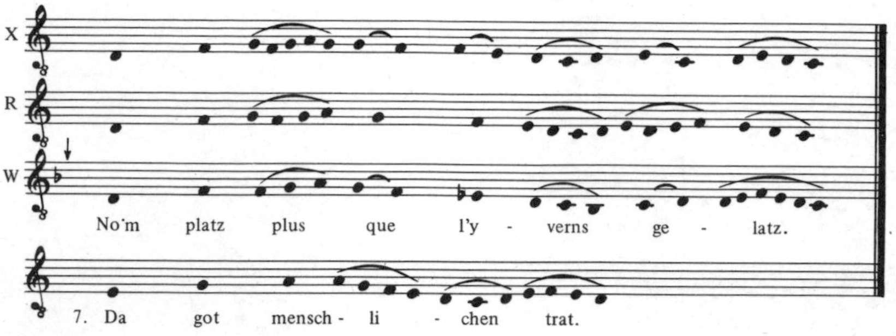
X
R
W
No·m platz plus que l'y - verns ge - latz.
7. Da got mensch - li - chen trat.

I

Lanquan li jorn son lonc en may
M'es belhs dous chans d'auzelhs de lonh,
E quan mi suy partitz de lay
Remembra·m d'un amor de lonh:
Vau de talan embroncx e clis
Se que chans ni flors d'albespis
No·m platz plus que l'yverns gelatz.

I

When the days are long in May, the sweet song of birds in the distance is beautiful to me. And when I have left there, I remember a distant love. I go on with head bowed with desire, so that a song and the flower of the hawthorn please me no more than the icy winter.

II

Be tenc lo Senhor per veray
Per qu'ieu veirai l'amor de lonh;
Mas per un ben que m'en eschay
N'ai dos mals, quar tan m'es de lonh.
Ai! car me fos lai pelegris,
Si que mos fustz e mos tapis
Fos pels sieus belhs huelhs remiratz!

II

I hold him my true lord by whom I shall see the distant love. But for one good I have two ills, for she is so far distant from me. Oh! if I were a pilgrim, so that my staff and cloak could be seen by her beautiful eyes.

III

Be·m parra joys quan li querray,
Per amor Dieu, l'alberc de lonh:
E, s'a lieys platz, alberguarai
Pres de lieys, si be·m suy de lonh:
Adoncs parra·l parlamens fis
Quan drutz lonhdas er tan vezis
Qu'ab bels digz jauzira solatz.

III

Joy will surely come to me when I ask her to shelter her guest from afar, for the love of God. And if it pleases her, I shall rest near her, for I come from afar. Then will begin the elegant conversation when the distant lover will be so close, that he will enjoy comfort with good words.

IV

Iratz e gauzens m'en partray,
S'ieu ja la vey, l'amor de lonh:
Mas non sai quoras la veyrai,
Car trop son nostras terras lonh:
Assatz hi a pas e camis,
E per aisso no·n suy devis...
Mas tot sia cum a Dieu platz!

IV

Sad and joyful shall I return, if I see that distant love. But I know not when I shall see her, for our lands are very far apart. There are many passes and many roads, and for that reason I cannot be sure. But let everything be as God wills.

V

Ja mais d'amor no·m jauziray
Si no·m jau d'est'amor de lonh,
Que gensor ni melhor no·n sai
Ves nulha part, ni pres ni lonh;
Tant es sos pretz verais e fis
Que lay el reng dels Sarrazis
Fos hieu per lieys chaitius clamatz!

VI

Dieus que fetz tot quant ve ni vai
E formet sest'amor de lonh
Mi don poder, que cor ieu n'ai,
Qu'ieu veya sest'amor de lonh,
Verayamen, en tals aizis,
Si que la cambra e·l jardis
Mi resembles tos temps palatz!

VII

Ver ditz qui m'apella lechay
Ni deziron d'amor de lonh,
Car nulhs autres joys tan no·m play
Cum jauzimens d'amor de lonh.
Mas so qu'ieu vuelh m'es atahis,
Qu'enaissi·m fadet mos pairis
Qu'ieu ames e no fos amatz.

Mas so q'ieu vuoill m'es atahis.
Totz sia mauditz lo pairis
Qe'm fadet q'ieu non fos amatz!

V

I shall never enjoy love again, unless it be that distant love. For I know none finer nor more beautiful anywhere, near or far. So true and fine is her worth, that I wish I might be declared a captive for her sake in the land of the Saracen.

VI

God, who made everything that comes or goes and who formed this distant love, give me the possibility soon truly to see this distant love, for such is my desire, in so pleasant a place that the room or garden seems to me always a palace.

VII

He speaks truly who calls me eager or desirous of a distant love. For no other joy pleases me as much as the enjoyment of a distant love. But there is an obstacle to what I want! For my guardian angel thus ruled: that I should love and be not loved.

But there is an obstacle to what I want! May my guardian angel be cursed, who ruled that I should not be loved!

2

Can vei la lauzeta mover (P.-C. 70.43), by BERNARD DE
VENTADORN

Sources with music: W 190; G 10; R 56. Because of
the many textual discrepancies among these three sources, the text of the first stanza has been copied in full
from each manuscript along with the music. The text of
the full poem is taken from the edition by Moshé
Lazar.[1]

Besides Bernard's chanson the following five songs
are known to use the melody presented here: *1.* R 1934
in U 47; *2.* R 365 in O 13; *3.* the Latin song, *Quisquis
cordis et oculi*, in Florence, Bibl. Laur. plut. 29, 1 fo. 437vo
(facsimile edition by Luther Dittmer, Brooklyn, 1960),
and in London, Brit. Mus. Egerton 274 (trouvère manuscript F), fo. 24vo; *4.* R 349 (Old French translation
of the Latin song) in X 191 and P 181; *5. Sener, milas
gracias* (an Old Provençal song inserted in the mystery
play of St. Agnes and, as indicated in the rubrics,
modeled after the Latin song), in Rome, Bibl. Vat.
Chigi C. V. 151 fo. 74.[2]

Bernard's song is probably the oldest troubadour or
trouvère melody which has been preserved in so many
and such varied sources. Therefore it is very remarkable
that the melody has been preserved with such uniformity as far as the melodic contour is concerned. Comparison of the versions as well as examination of textual
and melodic characteristics make it rather clear that this
uniformity is neither the consequence of a written tradition nor of strong metric features, but rather of a
strong melodic structure.

The melody opens with a frequently occurring intonation formula leading up to *A* as recitation tone,
even though there is little actual recitation. This formula must have established the *D, F,* and *A* as structural

tones in the mind of the medieval performer and perhaps even the medieval listener. The second line, rea-
ching up to the high *C* and ending on *A* in all versions,
added the *C* as structural note and made the chain *D-
F-A-C* the basic structure of the melody. This chain
was contrasted and probably strengthened by the occurrence of *D* and *G* in a crucial position as the last two
notes of the fifth line, and the occurrence of the notes *C,
E,* and *G* in the last two lines. If these elements were
with this melody from its conception, the uniformity
among the preserved versions is scarcely surprising.

The usage of *B*-flat in some of the versions should be
noted. The French chanson, *Plaine d'ire et de desconfort,*
notated in U on three-and-a-half staffs, has a *B*-flat sign
at the beginning of each of the first three staffs; on the
last staff no such signs was needed because no *B* occurs
in the final passage. The other French chanson and the
melody for Bernard's poem in manuscript W have occasional *B*-flat signs. Since there were no general rules
for the durational effect of such signs, they are given in
the transcription in the exact place in which they occur
in the manuscript, while the little arrows above the
staff indicate the place where a new staff begins in the
manuscript.

Restricting ourselves to the three songs presented
here we find that the two anonymous trouvère chansons are partial contrafacts of Bernard's famous song;
they take over the melody and the eight-syllable line of
the model, but the rhyme patterns differ slightly, as
shown in the following graphs:

Bernard de Ventadorn	*a*	*b*	*a*	*b*	*c*	*d*	*c*	*d*
R 1934			*a*	*b*	*a*	*b*	*b*	*a*	*a*	*b*
R 365			*a*	*b*	*b*	*a*	*a*	*b*	*a*	*b*

1. Moshé Lazar, *Bernard de Ventadour, troubadour du* XIIe *siècle:
Chansons d'amour*, Paris 1966. 180.

2. Since all versions are very similar in melodic contour and
in order not to overcrowd the synoptic chart, the Latin song and
its contrafacts have been omitted. These versions were published
by Gennrich–in two different metrizations–in 'Internationale
mittelalterliche Melodien' in *Zeitschrift für Musikwissenschaft,*
XI, 1929. 322-324; and in *Der musikalische Nachlass,* No. 33 and
No. 277.

W Quan vei l'a - lo - e - te mo - der
G Quan vei la lau - de - ta mo - ver
R Can vei la lau - ze - ta mo - ver

R 1934 Plai - ne d'ire et de des - con - fort
R 365   1. A - mis quelx est li mieuz vail - lanz,

W De joi ses a - les contre al rai,
G De joi sas a - las con - tral rai,
R De joi sas a - las con - tral rai,

R 1934 Plor en chan - tant m'en re - de - dui
R 365   2. Ou cil qui gist to - te la nuit

W Que s'ou - blide et lais - se ca - der
G Per la dol - cor qu'al cor li vai
R Que s'o - bli - da lais - sa.s cha - zer

R 1934 Sa - chiez de fi que j'ai grant tort
R 365   3. A - vec s'a - mie a grant des - duit

W Per la dou - cor qu'el cor li vai,

G S'o - bli - da e.s lais - sa ca - der,

R Per la dos - sor c'al cor li vay,

R 1934   Car as - sez trop c'ha io - e fui.

R 365   4. Et sanz fai - re tous ses ta - lanz

W He tan granz en - vi - de m'en pren

G He las com grand en - ve - ia.m ve

R Ai las cal en - ve - ia m'en ve

R 1934   Quant mon cuer ne ma boi - che mui

R 365   5. Ou cil qui tost vient et tost prent

W De co qu'est si en jau - si - on,

G De cui que ve - ia jau - ci - on,

R De qui q'eu ve - ya jau - zi - on,

R 1934   A rien qui te - nist a de - port

R 365   6. Et, quant il a fait, si s'en fuit,

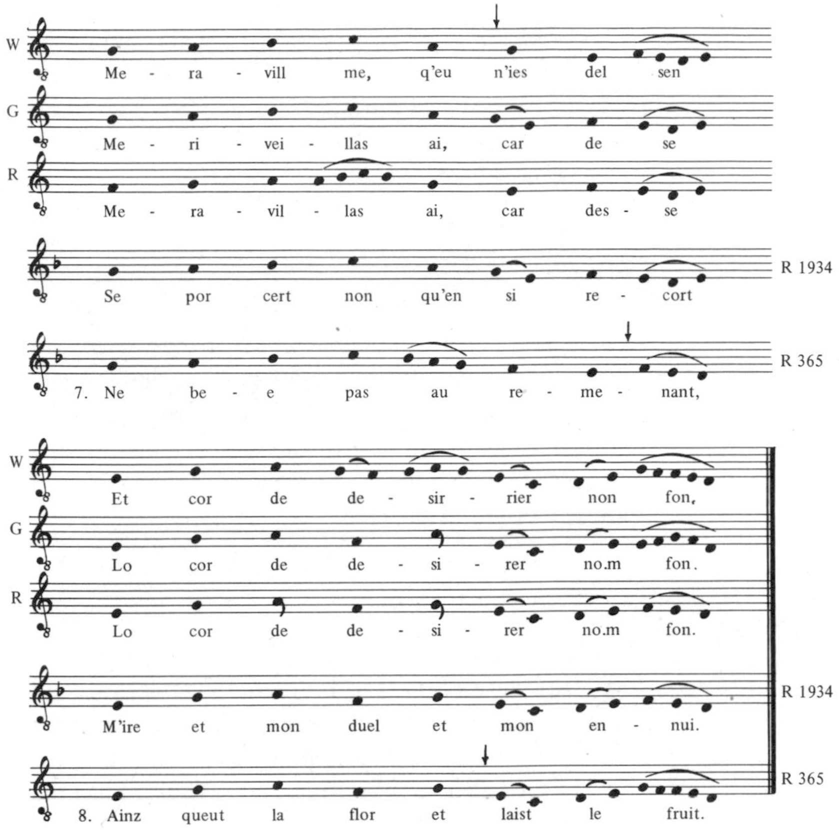
W
Me - ra - vill me, q'eu n'ies del sen
G
Me - ri - vei - llas ai, car de se
R
Me - ra - vil - las ai, car des - se
Se por cert non qu'en si re - cort
R 1934
7. Ne be - e pas au re - me - nant,
R 365
W
Et cor de de - sir - rier non fon,
G
Lo cor de de - si - rer no.m fon.
R
Lo cor de de - si - rer no.m fon.
M'ire et mon duel et mon en - nui.
R 1934
8. Ainz queut la flor et laist le fruit.
R 365

I

Can vei la lauzeta mover
de joi sas alas contral rai,
que s'oblid' e·s laissa chazer
per la doussor c'al cor li vai,
ai! tan grans enveya m'en ve
de cui qu'eu veya jauzion,
meravilhas ai, car desse
lo cor de dezirer no·m fon.

I

When I see the lark beating its wings joyfully against the sun's rays, which then swoons and swoops down, because of the joy in its heart, oh! I feel such jealousy for all those who have the joy of love, that I am astonished that my heart does not immediately melt with desire!

II

Ai, las! tan cuidava saber
d'amor, e tan petit en sai,
car eu d'amar no·m posc tener
celeis don ja pro non aurai.
Tout m'a mo cor, e tout m'a me,
e se mezeis e tot lo mon;
e can se·m tolc, no·m laisset re
mas dezirer e cor volon.

II

Alas! I thought I knew so much of love, and I know so little; for I cannot help loving a lady from whom I shall never obtain any favour. She has taken away my heart and my self, and herself and the whole world; and when she left me, I had nothing left but desire and a yearning heart.

III

Anc non agui de me poder

III

I have no power over myself, and have not had posses-

ni no fui meus de l'or' en sai
que·m laisset en sos olhs vezer
en un miralh que mout me plai.
Miralhs, pus me mirei en te,
m'an mort li sospir de preon,
c'aissi·m perdei com perdet se
lo bels Narcisus en la fon.

sion of myself since the time when she allowed me to look into her eyes, in a mirror which I like very much. Mirror, since I was reflected in you, deep sighs have killed me, for I caused my own ruin, just as fair Narcissus caused his by looking in the fountain.

IV

De las domnas me dezesper;
ja mais en lor no·m fiarai;
c'aissi com las solh chaptener,
enaissi las deschaptenrai.
Pois vei c'una pro no m'en te
vas leis que·m destrui e·m cofon,
totas las dopt' e las mescre,
car be sai c'atretals se son.

IV

I despair of ladies: I shall not trust them ever again; just as I used to defend them, now I shall condemn them. Since I see that *one* of them does not help me against her who is ruining and destroying me [i.e. the goddess Love?] I fear them all and have no faith in them, for I know they are all the same.

V

D'aisso's fa be femna parer
ma domna, par qu'e·lh o retrai,
car no vol so c'om deu voler,
e so c'om li deveda, fai.
Chazutz sui en mala merce,
et ai be faih co·l fols en pon;
e no sai per que m'esdeve,
mas car trop puyei contra mon.

V

My lady shows herself to be [merely] a woman (and that is why I reproach her) in that she does not want what one should want, and she does what is forbidden her. I have fallen out of favour, and have acted like the fool on the bridge[1]; and I do not know why this has happened to me, unless it was because I tried to climb too high.

VI

Merces es perduda, per ver,
et eu non o saubi anc mai,
car cilh qui plus en degr'aver
no·n a ges, et on la querrai?
A! can mal sembla, qui la ve,
qued aquest chaitiu deziron
que ja ses leis non aura be,
laisse morir, que no l'aon!

VI

Mercy is gone, that is sure, and I never received any of it, for she who should have the most mercy has none, and where else should I seek it? Oh! how difficult it is for a person who sees her to imagine that she would allow to die this poor yearning wretch, and would not help the man who can have no help but her!

VII

Pus ab midons no·m pot valer
precs ni merces ni·l dreihz qu'eu ai,
ni a leis no ven a plazer
qu'eu l'am, ja mais no·lh o dirai.

VII

Since pleas and mercy and my rights cannot help me to win my lady, and since it does not please her that I love her, I shall speak to her about it no more. So I am leaving her and her service; she has killed me, and I re-

1. This line is obscure. Perhaps there is an allusion here to an Old French proverb which states that a wise man does not fall down on a bridge, because he gets off his horse. Bernart would

thus be saying that he has come to grief because he was not circumspect. (Transl.)

Aissi·m part de leis e·m recre;
mort m'a, e per mort li respon,
e vau m'en, pus ilh no·m rete,
chaitius, en issilh, no sai on.

Tristans, ges no·n auretz de me,
qu'eu m'en vau, chaitius, no sai on.
De chantar me gic e·m recre,
e de joi e d'amor m'escon.

ply with death, and I am going sadly away, since she will not accept my service, into exile, I do not know where.

Tristan, you will hear no more of me, for I am going sadly away, I do not know where. I am going to stop singing, and I flee from love and joy.

3
Reis glorios, verais lums e clartatz (P.-C. 242, 64), BY GUIRAUT DE BORNEILL

Only source with music: R 8. The text of the first stanza as given by Adolf Kolsen differs somewhat from the one in R; therefore the text from R is given along with the music, and Kolsen's edition follows in its entirety.[1]

It is difficult to imagine a better way than the opening of this song to establish the *D* and the *A* as structural notes. Apparently the *C* is the upper limit and upper pole of the melody. The melody in its entirety may be based upon the chain *D-F-A-C*, but obviously the tone *F* is the least influential in giving coherence to this very attractive melody. According to Gennrich it has been preserved with one other Provençal text outside of the troubadour repertoire and, judging from Gennrich's transcription, the two melodies are very similar.[2] However, one of the most striking features of the above song does not occur in the contrafact: the first melodic line is not repeated; instead the third melody, used in Guiraut's song for the fourth line of text, is heard twice in a row, in almost literal repetition, giving it the form *ABCCD*.

This song may not be very typical for the melodic style of the troubadours in that it is so short – only five lines, including the refrain – but it is very typical in that its structure is clearest in the beginning of the melody, while the rest of the melody moves more freely.[3]

Rei glo - ri - os, ve - ray lums e clar - tatz,
Totz po - de - ros, Sen - her, si a vos platz,
Al mieu com - paynh si - as fi - zels a - ju - da;
Qu'ieu non lo vi, pus la nuech fo ven - gu - da,
Et a - des se - ra l'al - ba!

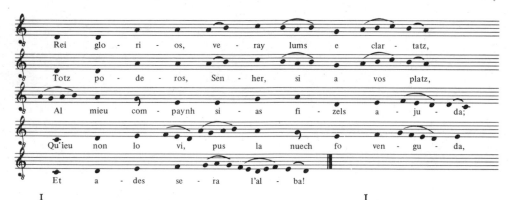

I

Reis glorios, verais lums e clartatz,
Deus poderos, Senher, si a vos platz,
Al meu companh siatz fizels aiuda;
Qu'eu no lo vi, pos la nochs fo venguda,
  Et ades sera l'alba!

I

Glorious King, true shining light, almighty God, Lord, if it please you, be of good help to my companion; for I have not seen him since it was dark, and soon it will be dawn!

II

Bel companho, si dormetz o velhatz,
No dormatz plus, suau vos ressidatz;
Qu'en orien vei l'estela creguda
C'amena·l jorn, qu'eu l'ai be conoguda
  Et ades sera l'alba!

II

Dear companion, if you are asleep or awake, sleep no more, but softly rise; for I have seen rising in the east the star which brings on the dawn; I have recognized it, and soon it will be dawn!

III

Bel companho, en chantan vos apel;
No dormatz plus, qu'eu auch chantar l'auzel

III

Dear companion, in song I call you; sleep no more, for I hear singing the bird which is seeking the daylight in

1. Adolf Kolsen, *Sämtliche Lieder des Trobadors Giraut de Bornelh*, Vol. 1, Halle, 1910. 342–347.

2. Gennrich, *Der musikalische Nachlass*, No. 58.

3. For five different rhythmizations of the first line, see Grout, *A History of Western Music*, 62. See also Bruno Stäblein, 'Eine Hymnusmelodie als Vorlage einer provenzalischen Alba', Miscelánea en homenaje a Mons. Higinio Anglés, Barcelona 1958–1961. 889–894.

Que vai queren lo jorn per lo boschatge
Et ai paor que·l gilos vos assatge
  Et ades sera l'alba!

IV

Bel companho, issetz al fenestrel
E regardatz las estelas del cel!
Conoisseretz si·us sui fizels messatge;
Si non o faitz, vostres n'er lo damnatge
  Et ades sera l'alba!

V

Bel companho, pos me parti de vos,
Eu no·m dormi ni·m moc de genolhos,
Ans priei Deu, lo filh Santa Maria,
Que·us me rendes per leial companhia,
  Et ades sera l'alba!

VI

Bel companho, la foras als peiros
Me preiavatz qu'eu no fos dormilhos,
Enans velhes tota noch tro al dia.
Era no·us platz mos chans ni ma paria
  Et ades sera l'alba!

the wood, and I am afraid the jealous husband will catch you, and soon it will be dawn!

IV

Dear companion, go to the window and look at the stars! You will know if I am a faithful messenger. If you do not, it will be the worse for you, and soon it will be dawn!

V

Dear companion, since I left you I have not slept or left my knees; I have been praying to God, the son of Mary, to give you back to me in true friendship, and soon it will be dawn!

VI

Dear companion, out on the steps you asked me not to be sleepy, but to stay awake all night until it was light; now you do not like my song or my company, and soon it will be dawn!

4

A l'entrada del tens clar (P.-C. 461, 12), ANONYMOUS

This chanson occurs in manuscript X, fo. 82, only and has been included primarily to show the difference in poetic style between a dancing song and the vast majority of the songs in the Old Provençal and Old French chansonniers.

In modern editions this song is usually given in a ternary meter. Although the various metrizations in which this song has been presented fit the first line of the text fairly well, they do not fit all lines. In fact neither the melody nor the text contain any indication for a specific meter. Furthermore, since nothing is known about the meter of medieval dances, there is no reason to take it for granted that all dancing songs were performed in a ternary meter. Thus I can do no better than follow the example of the medieval scribe and present the melody here in a non-mensural notation.

The melody is somewhat atypical for the repertory of the troubadours and trouvères. The first four lines have clear recitation on *D*, but there is no clear basis tone; the fifth line forms a vague transition to the second part of the melody, the refrain, which has no clear structure, but which may be considered as being constructed upon the chain *C-E-G*. Since the tone *G* occurs only once in the first four lines, the two sections of the melody are rather disjoint. Not surprisingly, some have assumed that there is an error in the notation and that the melody from the middle of the fifth line should be raised by one step in accordance with a three-part setting of this tune.[1] In my opinion, however, this does not take away the disjoint character of the two sections.

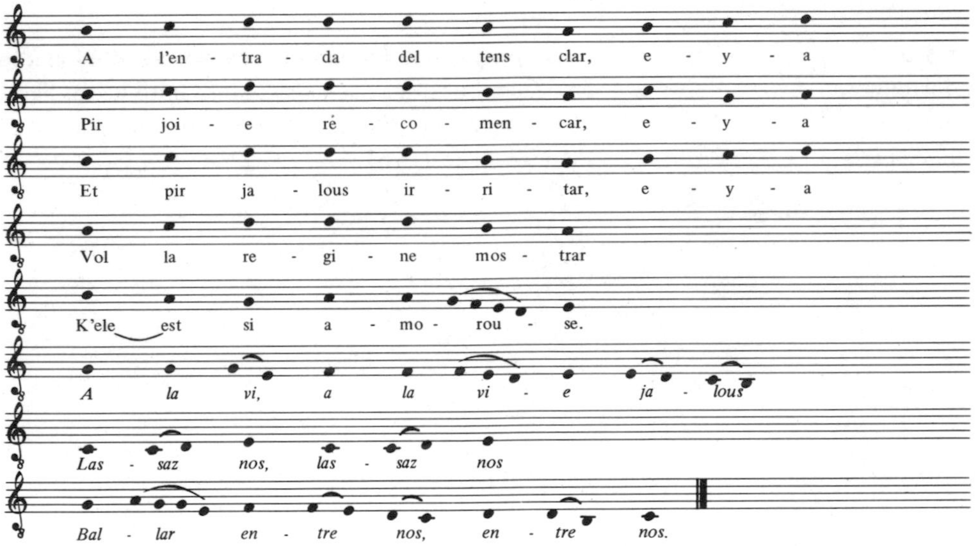
A l'en - tra - da del tens clar, e - y - a
Pir joi - e rė - co - men - car, e - y - a
Et pir ja - lous ir - ri - tar, e - y - a
Vol la re - gi - ne mos - trar
K'ele est si a - mo - rou - se.
A la vi, a la vi - e ja - lous
Las - saz nos, las - saz nos
Bal - lar en - tre nos, en - tre nos.

I

A l'entrada del tens clar, eya
Pir joie recomencar, eya
Et pir jalous irritar, eya
Vol la regine mostrar
K'ele est si amorouse.
A la vi, a la vie jalous
Lassaz nos, lassaz nos
Ballar entre nos, entre nos.

I

At the beginning of the good weather, to begin again the good times, and to annoy the jealous husband, the queen [of April] wants to show that she is in love! *On your way, jealous husband, let us dance by ourselves*!

1. Jack Westrup, *New Oxford History of Music*, Vol. II, London 1956. 241. See also Gennrich, *Der musikalische Nachlass*, No. 244.

II

Ele a fait per tot mandar, eya,
Non sie jusq'a la mar, eya,
Pucele ni bachelar, eya,
Que tuit non venguent dancar
En la dance joiouse.
A la vi, a la vie jalous
Lassaz nos, lassaz nos
Ballar entre nos, entre nos.

III

Lo reis i vent d'autre part, eya,
Pir la dance destorbar, eya,
Que il est en cremerar, eya,
Que on ne li vuelle emblar
La regine avrillouse!
A la vi a la vie

IV

Mais pir neient lo vol far, eya,
K'ele n'a soig de viellart, eya,
Mais d'un legeir bachelar, eya,
Ki ben sache solacar
La donne savourouse!
A la vi a la vie jalous

V

Qui donc la veist dancar, eya,
Et son gent cors deportar, eya,
Ben puist dire de verrar, eya,
K'el mont non sie sa part
La regine joiouse,
A la vi a la vie jalous

II

She has invited everybody, there is not a youth nor maiden from here to the sea who will not come and dance here the joyous dance. *On your way,* etc.

III

The king came from the other direction to disturb the dance, for he is afraid somebody will steal away his April queen! *On your way,* etc.

IV

But is no use his wishing, for she does not care for old men, but for a young man, who knows how to console the sweet lady! *On your way,* etc.

V

Anyone who sees her dance and enjoy herself could truly say that in all the world there is not her equal, the joyous queen! *On your way,* etc.

Trouvère chansons

5

L'amours dont sui espris (R 1545), BY BLONDEL DE NESLE

Sources with music: K 114; N 42; P 41; X 80; O 79; M 143; T 92. The text is taken from manuscripts T and O. In rare unanimity, this chanson is attributed to Blondel in all sources that give an author's name. The version in M is somewhat mutilated; the brackets in our transcription mark the torn-out sections. The K, N, P, and X versions are so similar to one another that only one version is given here.

As pointed out in Chapter 3, pp. 42-43, this chanson is one of the very few for which we find considerable internal evidence concerning its meter. The distribution of ligatures and word accents, as well as the remarkable uniformity among the preserved versions regarding the distribution of those elements, makes a convincing argument for some form of fixed meter. It may be impossible to determine with certainty the exact form of that meter, but *if* this chanson was performed in modal rhythm, the one indicated at the top of the synoptic chart may be close to the original. In principle this meter was first established by Husmann on the basis of his analysis of two motets which used the present melody for their upper part, but, as explained in Chapter 3, in our transcription the bar lines are given in a different manner in analogy to the rhythmic mode chosen for chanson R 452 (see No. 14).

Although many questions remain about this chanson and its meter, a few conclusions may be drawn. The most important observation probably concerns the difference between this chanson and the vast majority of troubadour and trouvère songs regarding the distribution of word accents and ligatures. There are a few other chansons with similar characteristics, but their absence from the vast majority of the Old Provençal and Old French repertoire strengthens the theory that *in general* the chansons of the troubadours and trouvères were performed in a declamatory rhythm. Secondly, this chanson shows that it was possible to combine some stylistic elements of the trouvère chansons with some typical characteristics of the motet. Motets are almost always in a fixed meter, often in modal rhythm, but they rarely have a tertial structure and rarely repeated lines, except in rondeaux; thus the melody of Blondel's chanson is typical for a motet in its meter and distribution of ligatures, but it is typical for a trouvère chanson in its form and structure. The rhyme pattern of the poem may be somewhat atypical for a trouvère poem in that it uses only two rhyme sounds for so many lines, but the regular alternation of them is considerably more sophisticated than one may find in a typical motet. The manuscripts give either four or five stanzas in coblas doblas, and stanzas three and four occur in reverse order in several of the sources, which is all very typical for a trouvère chanson. Furthermore, the quality and the content of the poem are similar to many trouvère chansons.

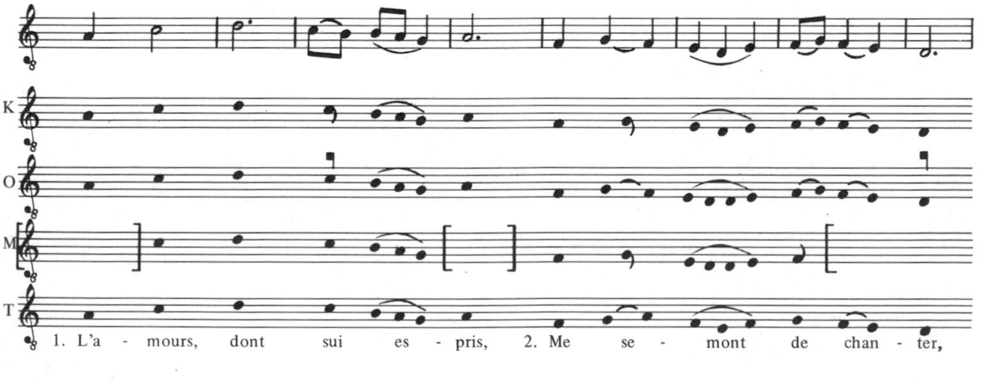
K
O
M
T
1. L'a - mours, dont sui es - pris, 2. Me se - mont de chan - ter,

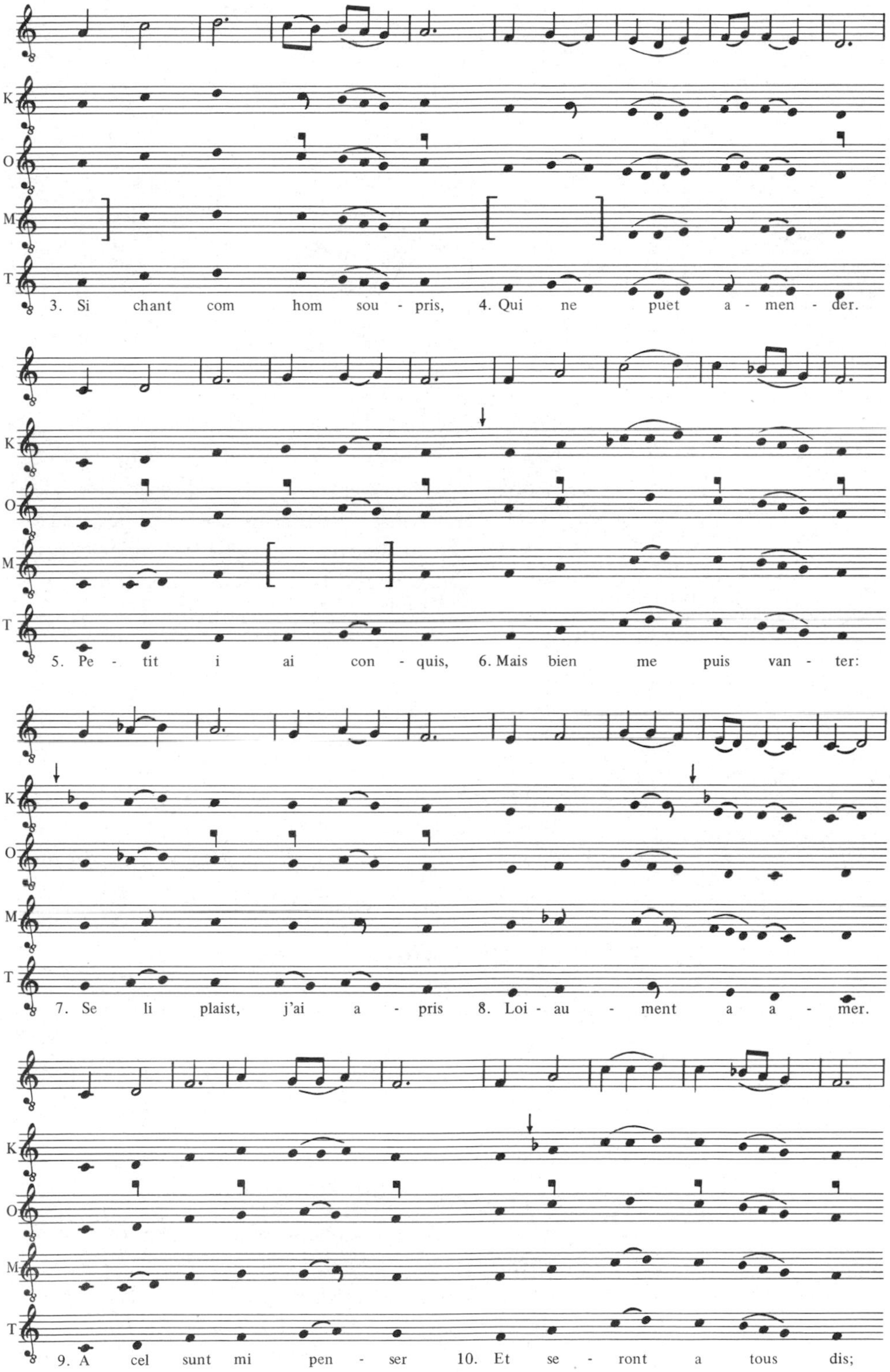
K
O
M
T
3. Si chant com hom sou - pris, 4. Qui ne puet a - men - der.
K
O
M
T
5. Pe - tit i ai con - quis, 6. Mais bien me puis van - ter:
K
O
M
T
7. Se li plaist, j'ai a - pris 8. Loi - au - ment a a - mer.
K
O
M
T
9. A cel sunt mi pen - ser 10. Et se - ront a tous dis;

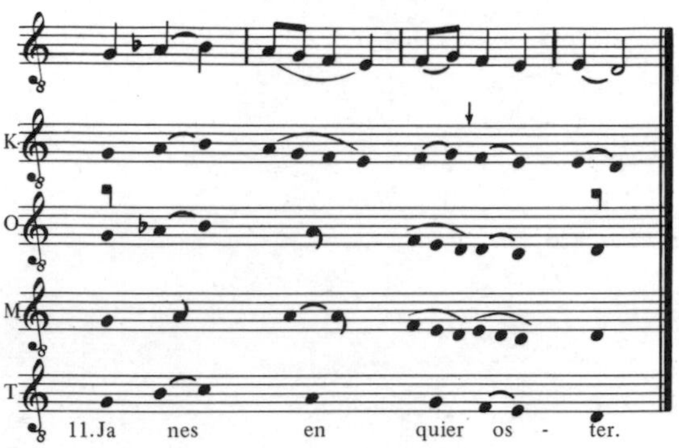
K
O
M
T
11. Ja nes en quier os - ter.

I

L'amours dont sui espris
Me semont de chanter;
Si fais con hons sopris,
Qui ne puet endurer.
Et s'ai je tant conquis
Que bien me puis venter:
Que j'ai piec'a apris
Leaument a amer.
A li sont mi penser
Et seront a touz dis,
Ja nes en quier oster.

I

The love I feel compels me to sing; and I am like a man taken by surprise, who cannot resist. Yet I have gained so much that I can be proud of it: for I learned long ago to love loyally. My thoughts are always of her, and always will be, for I never wish to have them elsewhere.

II

Remembrance dou vis
Qu'il a vermoil et cler
A mon cuer a ce mis
Que ne l'en puis oster.
Et se j'ai les maus quis,
Bien les doi endurer.
Or ai je trop mespris:
Ainz les doi mieuz amer.
Comment que j'os conter,
N'i a rien, ce m'est vis,
Fors que merci crier.

II

The memory of her bright, rosy face has forced my heart into a way from which I cannot divert it. And since I asked for these pains, I must endure them. Nay, in fact, I should love them better than that. Whatever I say, there is nothing to do but cry for mercy.

III

Lons travaux sanz espoir
M'eüst mort et trahi.
Mes mes cuers atendoit
Ce por qu'il a servi.
Se por li l'ai destroit,
De bon gré l'en merci.
Et sai bien que j'ai droit,
Q'ainz si bele ne vi.

III

A long service without hope would have killed and deceived me. But my heart was awaiting the reward it suffered for. If I tortured my heart for her sake, I thank her for it. And I know that I am right, for I never saw such a beautiful lady. My heart and I have acted so well that nothing we have done has been in vain.

Entre mon cuer et li
Avons fait si adroit
Qu'ainz de rien n'i failli.

IV

Dex, pourquoi m'ocirroit,
Car ainz ne li menti,
Se ja joianz en soit
Li cuers donc je la pri.
Je l'aing tant et covoit
Et cuit por voir de li
Que chacuns qui la voit
La doie amer ausi.
Que fox di. Non feroit,
Nuns avoir ne porroit
Cuer qui l'amast ensi.

V

Plus bele ne vit nuns
Ne de cors ne de vis;
Nature ne mist plus
De beaute en nul pris.
Por li maintendrai l'us
D'Eneas et Paris,
Tristan et Pyramus,
Qui amerent jadis.
Or serai ses amis,
Or pri Deu de la sus,
Qu'a lor fin soie pris.

IV

God, why should she kill me, for I never lied to her, however joyous it might have made the heart that now prays to her. I love and desire her so much, and I truly think that everyone who sees her must love her too. No, they could not, I am foolish to say so. Nobody could have a heart that would love her as much as mine.

V

No one ever saw a more beautiful lady, both of face and figure. Nature did not put more beauty in any other. For her I shall continue the tradition of Aeneas, Paris, Tristan and Pyramus, who were lovers of old. I shall be her lover; I pray to God above that I may be considered their equal.

6

Ne me sont pas achoison de chanter (R 787), BY GACE
BRULÉ

Sources with music: K 66; N 22; P 8; X 51; O 86; a 33.
The most recent edition and discussion of the poem is
found in Dyggve's complete edition of the poems by
Gace Brulé, from which the poem is copied here.[1] Concerning the rhyme in this poem, Dyggve remarks that
the scribe of O, whose version Dyggve took as the basis
for his reading, wrote the rhyme sound *-eie* as *-oie*, and
that apparently Gace Brulé considered the sounds *-eie*
and *-aie* as rhyming with one another. Consequently
Gace presents in this poem an interesting combination
of coblas unissonans and coblas alternadas by using the
same rhyme sounds throughout the poem, while in-
verting *a* and *b* rhymes in alternate stanzas in the following order[2]:

Stanzas I, III, and V   *a*   *b*   *a*   *b*   *c*˘ *c*˘ *a* *a*

Stanzas II and IV   *b*   *a*   *b*   *a*   *c*˘ *c*˘ *b* *b*

The overall structure of the melody can probably be
best characterized as based upon the tertial chain *D-F-
A-C*, even though there are some ambiguous passages.
One may question, for example, whether the short excursion to the high *F* in the first and third lines of some
of the versions is important enough to include the high
F among the structural tones. Of more relevance, however, is the question of whether in the first line in the O
and K versions the *C* or the *D* is the structural tone. In
the discussion of melodic characteristics (p. 50) I suggested that perhaps this line is a rare example of a
secondal one-step melody based upon the notes *C* and
D and ending with a flourish descending to *F*. Although
I have some reservations about this analysis, it seems
plausible because in my estimate the *C* and not the *D*
serves as primary structural tone.

Some of the discrepancies in this melody within the
K L N P X group are more significant than usual and are
therefore indicated in the synoptic chart above the K

version. The interesting aspect of the discrepancies for
the first and third lines is the curious fact that the
K L N P X group presents two versions which are both
supported by sources outside the group in such a way
that one can present an abundance of hypotheses explaining these discrepancies. Some of these explanations
will be presented here to demonstrate how tenuous attempts to reconstruct the original melody can become.

One can hold, for example, that both versions were
part of the original in the order in which they are preserved in the P and X versions. This A B C B, or
A B A′ B, order was changed in all other versions to the
more usual A B A B form, in which the singers or
scribes of the O, K, L, and N versions simply made the
first melodic line serve twice, whereas the singer or
scribe of the a version anticipated the C melody for the
opening line.

In another explanation one may defend the hypothesis that both lines are ornamented recitations on *C* with
F as basis tone, and that both versions are traditional
forms of such recitation. Two different hypotheses are
open from here on: either the excursion to the high *F*
was in the original as first or third line, but was omitted
by some singers; or this excursion did not occur in the
original, but was so much a part of the general tradition
of this type of melody that different singers or scribes
happened upon it independently of one another.[3]

Obviously there is no dearth of hypotheses explaining
the discrepancies under discussion, but only one observation is paramount: the two versions resemble one
another strongly and to the medieval singer, scribe, and
listener the differences among them were probably of
little consequence.

Of somewhat more relevance than the above discrepancies is the one concerning the ending of the first
line in manuscript a. With some justification one may
doubt the validity of the upward leap on the last syllable. Comparison with the O version suggests that
perhaps the scribe of a erred and somehow shortened
the first line so that the first note of the second line was
given as the last note of the first line. However, in the
third line the scribe gave exactly the same melody, except for the omission of the flat sign, and this duplication makes me hesitate to take it for granted that the
scribe of manuscript a did indeed make an error.

1. Holger Petersen Dyggve, *Gace Brulé, trouvère champenois*,
Helsinki 1951. 359.
   2. However, there are discrepancies among the preserved versions concerning the order in which the stanzas are presented;
see Dyggve, loc. cit.

3. See also the first line of R 1125 on page 69.

The scribe of O gave this melody in a somewhat inconsistent alternation of one stemmed and two unstemmed notes, suggesting a performance in the third rhythmic mode. Even though the discrepancies regarding the distribution of the melody over the text are not as numerous and as significant as those found for the chanson by Jaufre Rudel (No. 1), there are considerably more such discrepancies than found for the preceding chanson by Blondel de Nesle. Since there are no internal indications of any form of fixed meter, it is difficult to believe that the melody was transmitted in the meter suggested in such an ambiguous manner by the scribe of O.

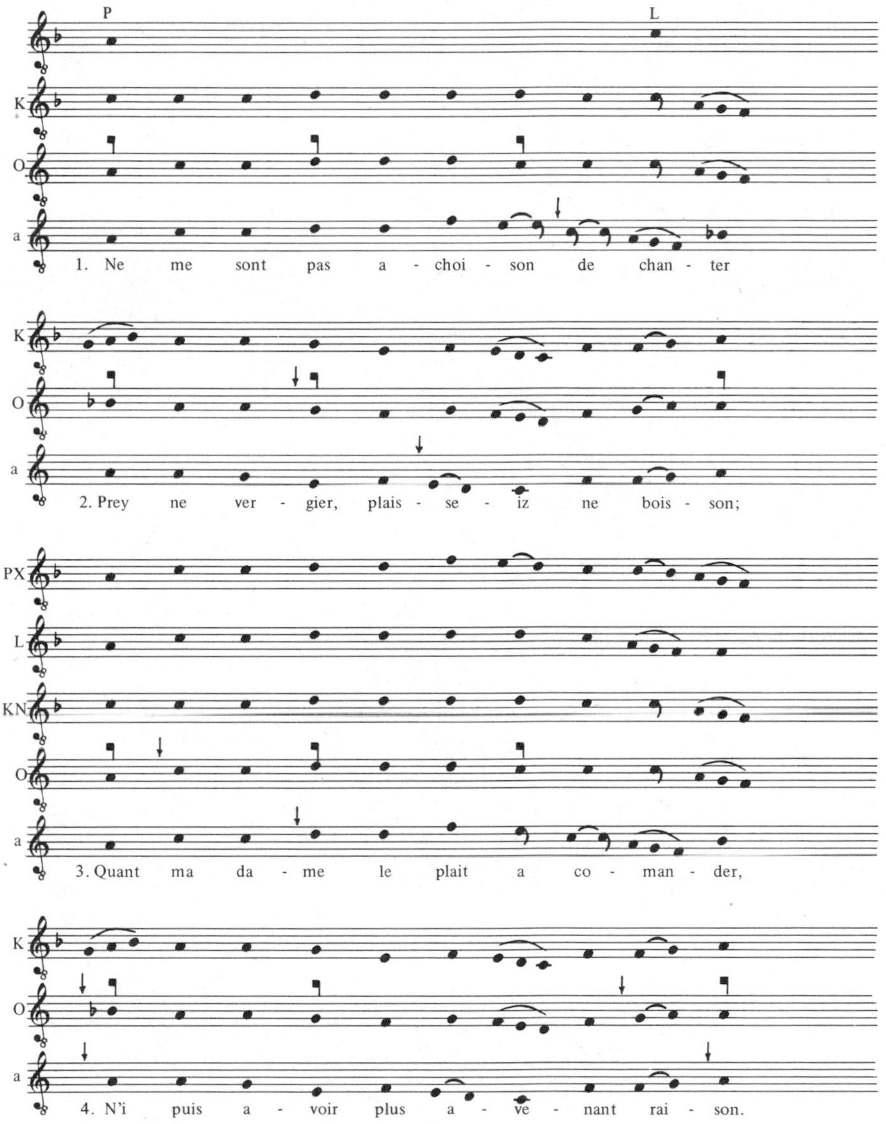
1. Ne me sont pas a - choi - son de chan - ter
2. Prey ne ver - gier, plais - se - iz ne bois - son;
3. Quant ma da - me le plait a co - man - der,
4. N'i puis a - voir plus a - ve - nant rai - son.

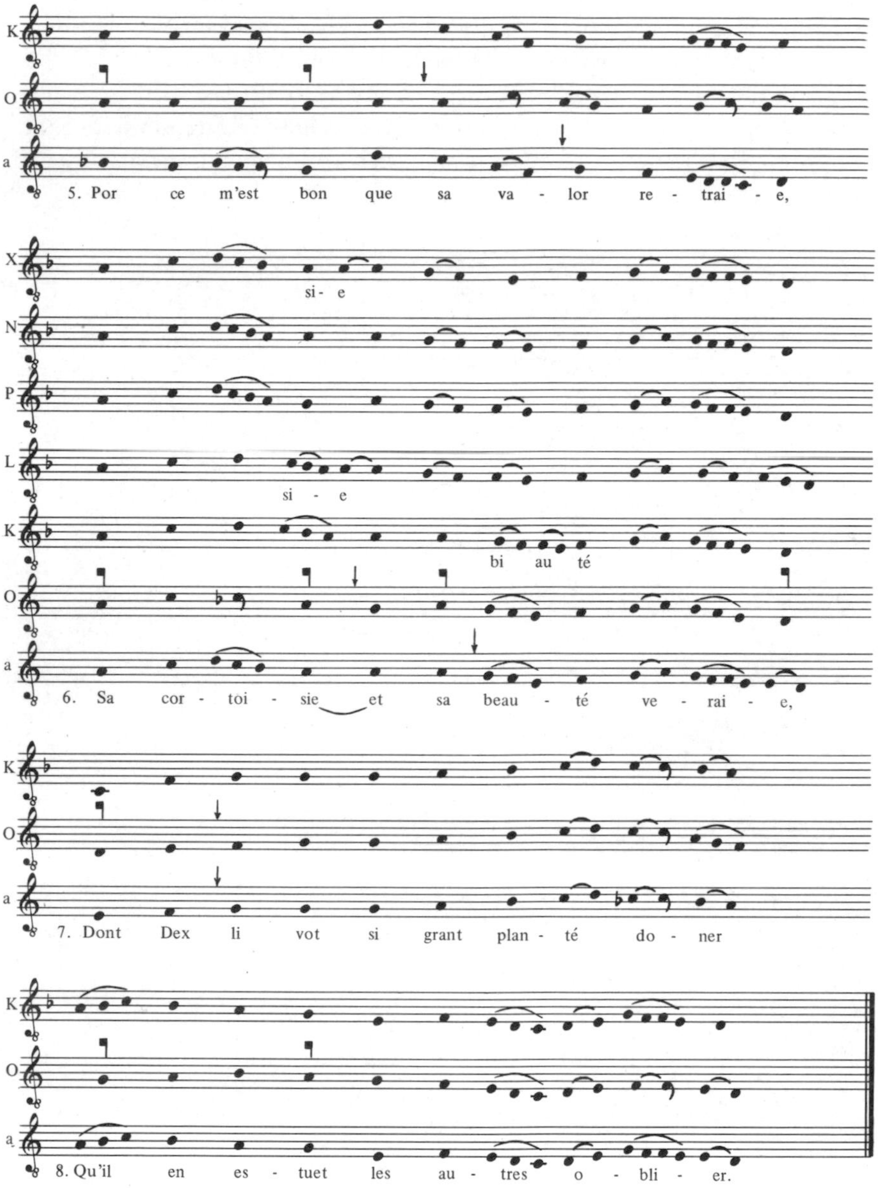
K
O
a
5. Por ce m'est bon que sa va - lor re - trai - e,
X
si - e
N
P
L
si - e
K
bi au té
O
a
6. Sa cor - toi - sie et sa beau - té ve - rai - e,
K
O
a
7. Dont Dex li vot si grant plan - té do - ner
K
O
a
8. Qu'il en es - tuet les au - tres o - bli - er.

I

Ne me sont pas achoison de chanter
Prey ne vergier, plaisseïz ne boisson;
Quant ma dame le plait a comander,
N'i puis avoir plus avenant raison.
Por ce m'est bon que sa valor retraie,
Sa cortoisie et sa beauté veraie,
Dont Dex li vot si grant planté doner
Qu'il en estuet les autres oblïer.

I

Meadows and gardens, parks and groves are for me no reason to sing. I can have no more fitting reason than when my lady wishes to command me. I am happy to talk of her worth, her courtesy and her true beauty, which God gave her in such abundance that all other [ladies] must be forgotten.

II

Et nonporquant, mout dout l'emprision
Qu'ai en mon cuer faite de li amer.
Bien sai de voir qu'anbedui en morron,
Mais nus ne doit si bele mort douter.
De ce me vant qu'autres senz me desvoie
Tres granz amors, qui m'enseingne tel voie
Qu'a mon voloir moi et mon cuer tendron,
Mais, par mon chief, ja n'en retorneron.

III

Ja ne porrai ma grant joie achever,
Morir m'estuet en lieu de guierredon.
Soëf trait mal qui en cuide eschaper;
Beaus conforz est d'atendre garison.
Mais sanz espoir me tormente et esmaie
Iceste amors qui m'ocit et apaie;
Merci me fait en ma dame cuider
Tel que Raisons n'oseroit creanter.

IV

Biens et beautez sont en li compaignon,
Sens et valors les i fist assambler;
Et cil qui voit son cors et sa façon,
Quant plus a sens, plus i covient penser.
Quant ainz la vi, bien soi que j'en morroie:
Plus m'ocirroit, quant je plus la verroie,
Mis granz desirs par si bele achoison,
Dont ja n'avrai sanz joie reançon.

V

Touz jors cuidai ceste dolor celer,
Que nou scüst la bele o le douz non,
N'el nou savra. Qui li doit donc conter
Quant nuns ne set m'angoisse se je non?
Dit ai que fox: ja nuns hons qui la voie
Si nices n'est que bien ne saiche et croie
Que j'aing cele que tant m'oez loer,
A ce qu'ele est bele et bone sanz per.

Fins amorous, touz jors di et diroie
Nuns n'est amis qui contre Amor guerroie:
Puis qu'ele vuet dedans son cuer entrer,
Vers sa vertu ne puet sens foisoner.

II

Nevertheless, I am afraid of the decision I made in my heart to love her. I know my heart and I will perish because of it, but nobody should fear such a fine death. Great Love, who shows me the road by which my heart and I willingly travel, boasts that I shall be led astray by other advice, but, I swear it, we shall never leave the pathway!

III

I shall never achieve great joy, I must die instead of being rewarded. He who foresees the end of his distress bears it lightly–it is such a great consolation [merely] to be expecting relief. But this love which kills and soothes me torments and dismays me without hope. It makes me believe my lady will have mercy, and Reason would never permit such a thought.

IV

Good and beauty are together found in her, put there by wisdom and worth. And if a man sees her body and face, the more wisdom he has, the more he must think of her. When I first saw her, I knew I should die of it: the more I saw her the more my great desire would kill me, and with good cause; and unless I have joy of her I shall never be set free.

V

I always expected to keep this pain a secret, so that the beautiful lady with the sweet name would not learn of it, nor shall she learn of it. Who should tell her, since I alone know of my anguish? I am foolish to say that: no man who ever saw her, however stupid he might be, would fail to see and realize that I love the lady you hear me praise so much, for no lady equals her in beauty and goodness.

True lovers, I say now and shall always say that no man is a lover who struggles against love; if she wishes to enter his heart, wisdom cannot equal her strength.

7

Desconfortez, plains d'ire et de pesance (R 233), BY GACE
BRULÉ

Sources: X 219; N 161; K 333; M 36; T 47; U 63. The
chanson is attributed to Gace Brulé in M and in one
manuscript without music; in T it is attributed to Vielart
de Corbie; and it is anonymous in the other sources.
Dyggve, whose edition is followed here, considers the
chanson as having been written by Gace.[1] Two chansons were conceived in imitation of the above one,
namely *Tout soit mes cuers en grant desperance* (R 215) and
Desconfortes com cil qui est sans joie (1740); the former
chanson occurs in K 201, N 96, and P 174; the latter in
K 203 and N 98. Both chansons are attributed to Oede
de la Courroierie, a clerk in the service of Count Robert II of Artois in the last quarter of the 13th century.[2]

Altogether seven stanzas have been preserved for the
chanson attributed to Gace Brulé, although no single
source contains more than five stanzas. All sources have
the first three stanzas in common, in the order in which
they are presented here; the fourth stanza occurs in
K N X only; the fifth occurs in T only; the sixth in U
and in a manuscript without music; and the seventh
stanza occurs only in U and K N X. The first six stanzas
printed here have coblas unissonans; the last stanza differs slightly from the others. Apparently there is no way
of determining whether all stanzas originated with Gace
Brulé.

This chanson has been included to illustrate several
aspects, one of them being the clear occurrence of contrasting chains in its melody. The primary chain, without any doubt, is formed by the tones *D*, *F*, *A*, and *C*,
while in several passages, among them the beginning of
lines two and four, the tones *C*, *E*, and *G* provide a contrasting structure. Apparently this structure was with
the melody from its beginning in such a clearly recognizable way that it was easily retained during the
oral tradition. It is noteworthy that a large percentage
of the chansons attributed to Gace Brulé have melodies
with *D* as basis tone and that many of these have been
preserved with more than average uniformity among
the versions, but there is no evidence of a written tra-

dition as there is for the chansons of Thibaud de Navarre.

Because of the two contrafacts, altogether eight different versions are found for this melody within the
KNPX group. This provides a rather unique opportunity to show the similarities and discrepancies among
readings of a given melody within this group of closely
related manuscripts. The most important, and also the
most unusual, discrepancy among the melodic versions
within this group concerns the ending formula. Manuscripts K and N, each of which gives all three chansons,
present the melody as ending on *F* in a manner similar
to the first and third lines. Manuscripts P and X, however, each giving only one of the three chansons, agree
with manuscripts M, T, and U in giving an ending on
D. Although the ending on *D* is given in four different
sources, and even though the *D* is the more usual ending
tone of melodies of this type, there is no certainty that
the ending in K and N is the consequence of inaccuracy
and should therefore be rejected; it is possible that in the
area in which the manuscripts of the KNPX group
were compiled both endings were considered equally
suited for the melody concerned.

Two other aspects of this melody are worthy of
special attention. First, the discrepancies regarding the
usage of *B*-flat or *B*-natural are emphasized by the
occurrence of a *B*-natural sign in manuscript T, by
the complete absence of flat signs in M, and by the inconsistency with which the flat signs occur in the various
versions within the KNPX group. Secondly, there is
the interesting aspect that the melody for the fifth line
resembles the melody given for the eighth and ninth
lines. The KNPX versions agree in giving the fifth
melodic line almost literally for the combined eighth
and ninth lines, even though the latter two, when taken
together, have one syllable more than the former line;
the difference is simply made up by repeating the penultimate note. In the other three versions the part of the
melody coming before the caesura of line five is repeated for line eight, but the part after the caesura differs both from the corresponding melodic section in the
KNPX group and from the melody given for line
nine.[3]

1. Dyggve, *Gace Brulé*, 319.
2. Dragonetti, 685.

3. See also Chapter 5, p. 67.

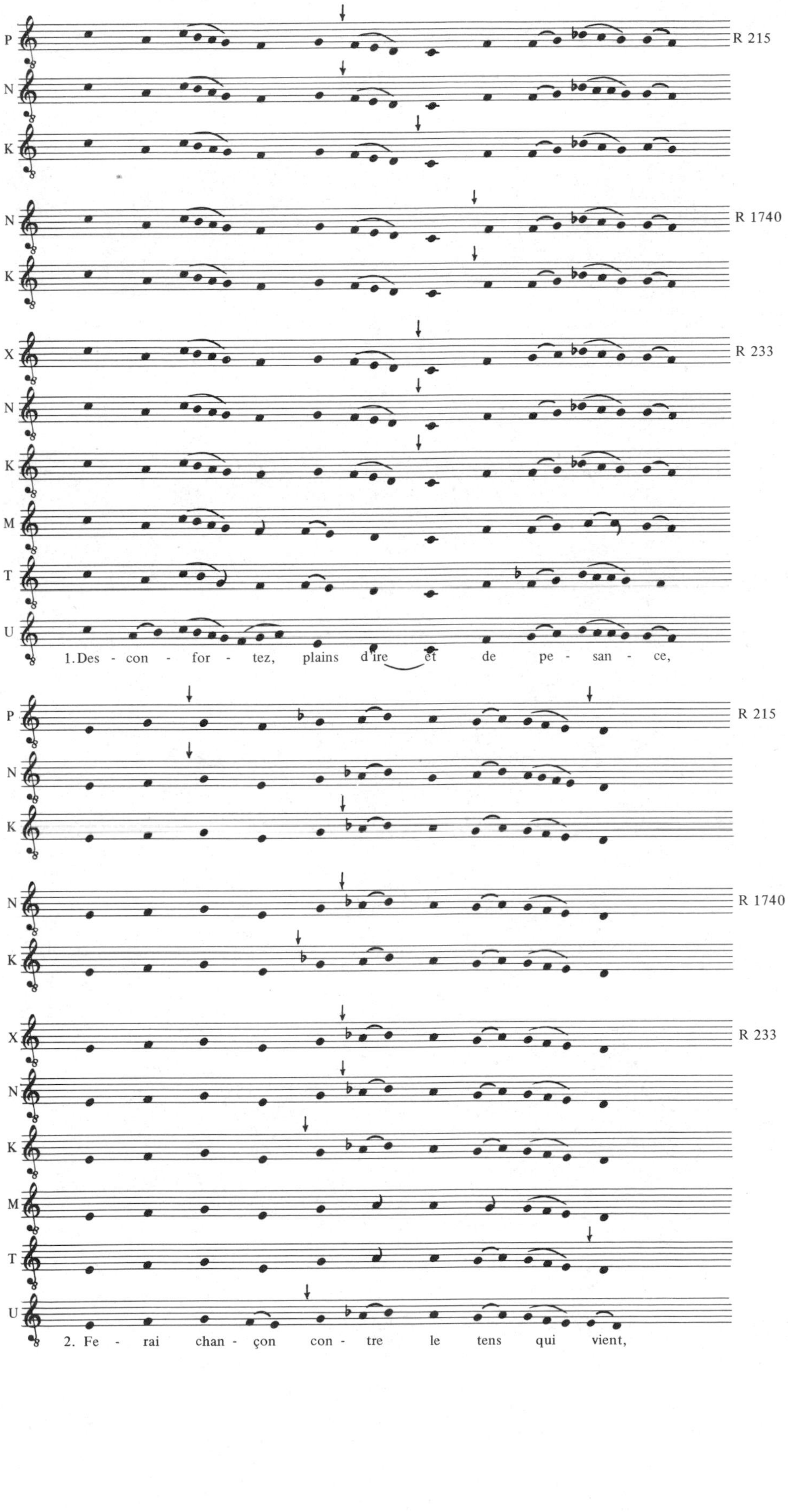
P
N
K
R 215
N
K
R 1740
X
N
K
M
T
U
R 233
1. Des - con - for - tez, plains d'ire et de pe - san - ce,
P
N
K
R 215
N
K
R 1740
X
N
K
M
T
U
R 233
2. Fe - rai chan - çon con - tre le tens qui vient,

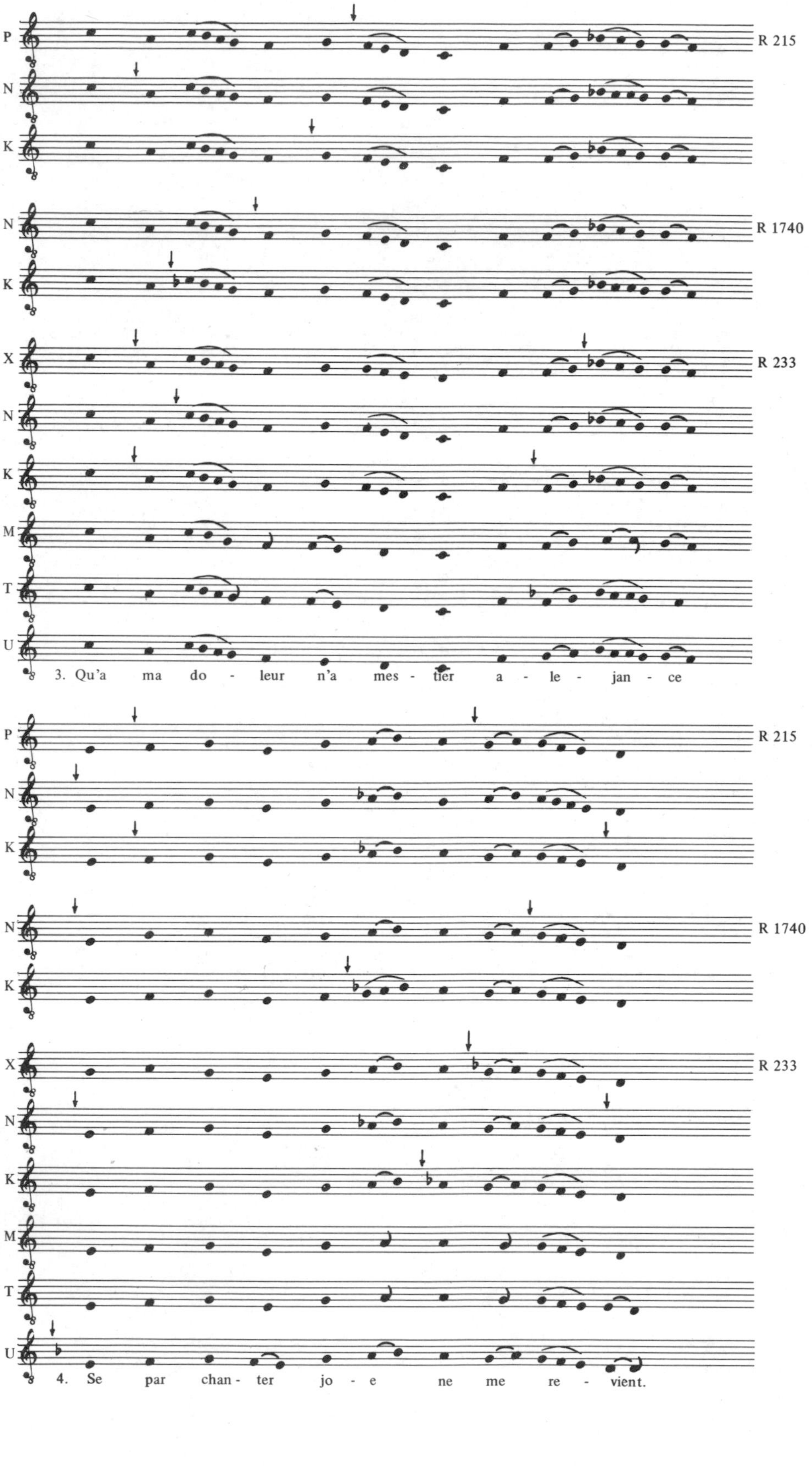
P
N
K
R 215
N
K
R 1740
X
N
K
M
T
U
R 233
3. Qu'a ma do - leur n'a mes - tier a - le - jan - ce
P
N
K
R 215
N
K
R 1740
X
N
K
M
T
U
R 233
4. Se par chan - ter jo - e ne me re - vient.

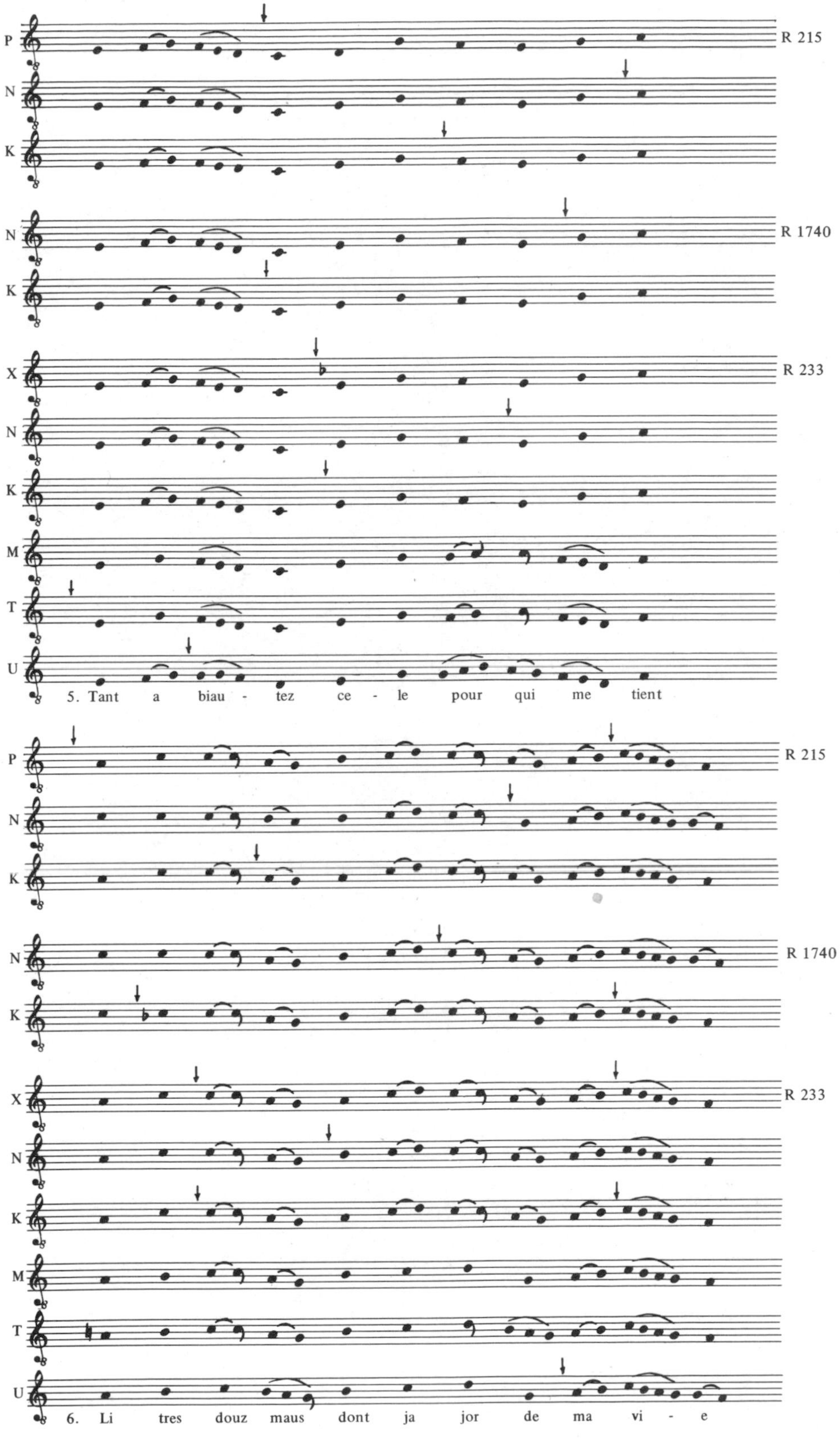
P
R 215
N
K
N
R 1740
K
X
R 233
N
K
M
T
U
5. Tant a biau - tez ce - le pour qui me tient
P
R 215
N
K
N
R 1740
K
X
R 233
N
K
M
T
U
6. Li tres douz maus dont ja jor de ma vi - e

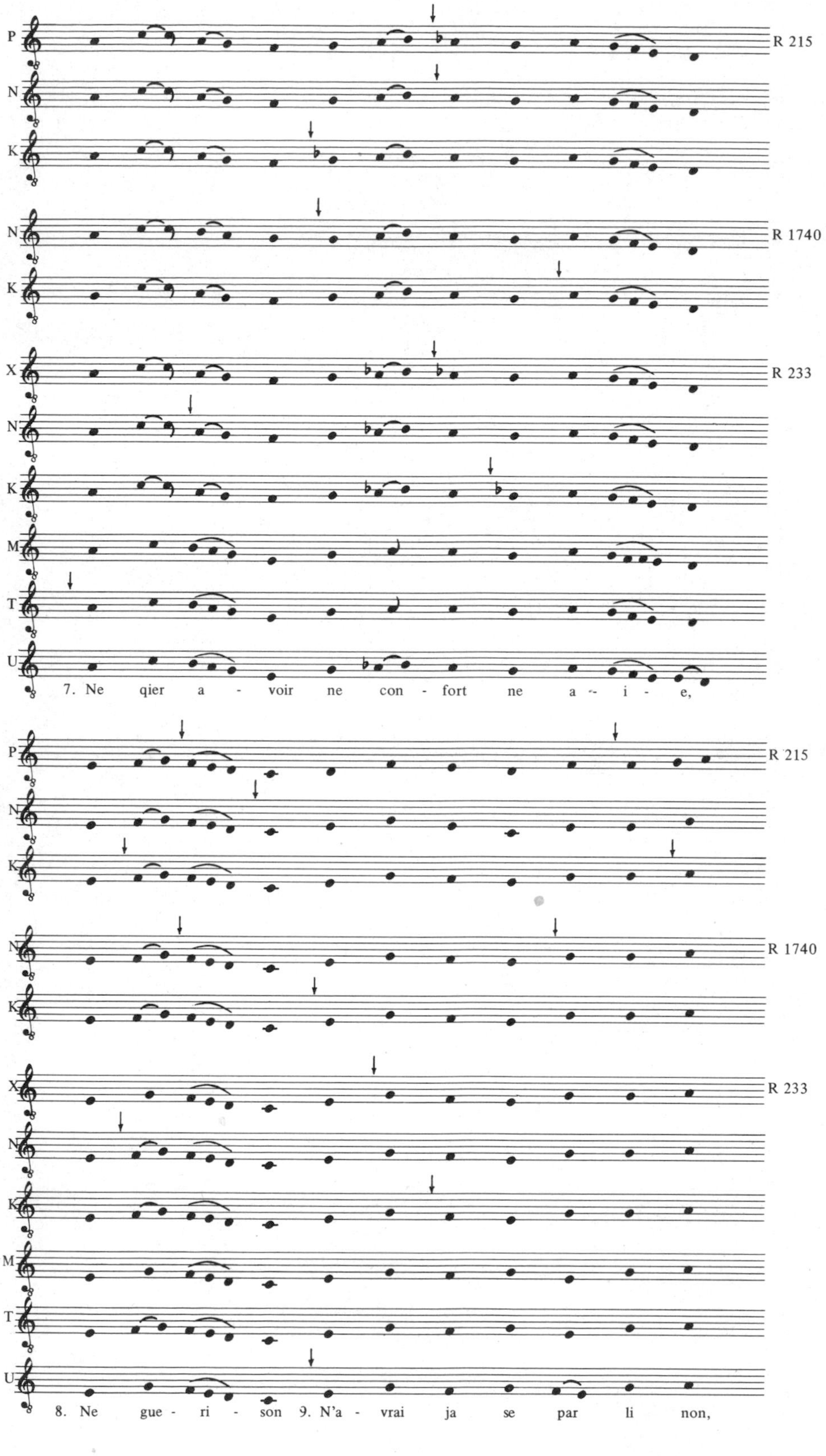
R 215
R 1740
R 233
7. Ne qier a - voir ne con - fort ne a - i - e,
R 215
R 1740
R 233
8. Ne gue - ri - son 9. N'a - vrai ja se par li non,

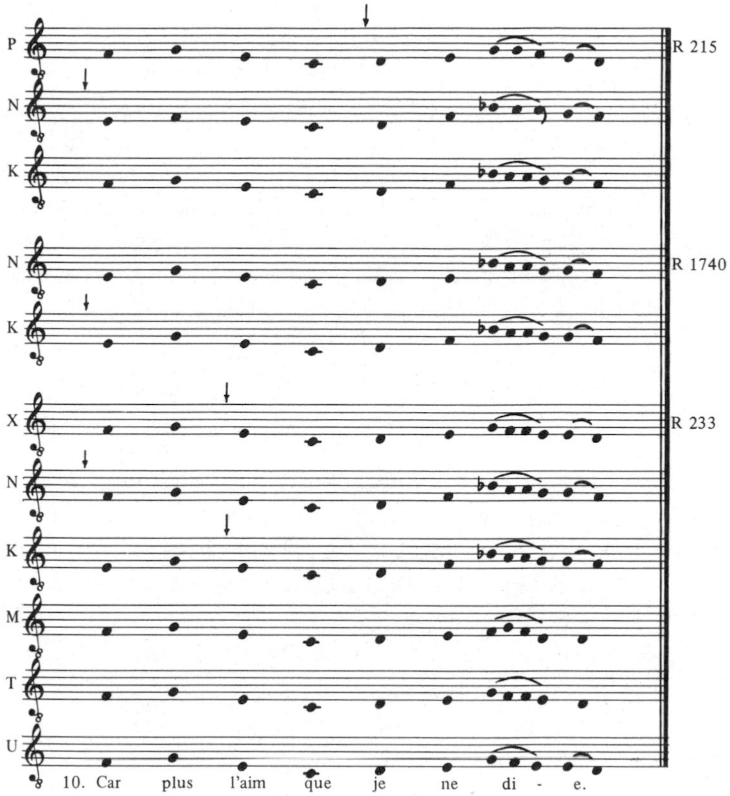
P
N
K
R 215
N
K
R 1740
X
N
K
M
T
U
R 233
10. Car plus l'aim que je ne di - e.

I

Desconfortez, plains d'ire et de pesance,
Ferai chançon contre le tens qui vient,
Qu'a ma doleur n'a mestier alejance
Se par chanter joie ne me revient.
Tant a biautez cele pour qui me tient
Li tres douz maus dont ja jor de ma vie
Ne qier avoir ne confort ne aïe,
Ne guerison
N'avrai ja se par li non,
Car plus l'aim que je ne die.

I

Dejected and full of woe and sorrow, I shall write a song in spite of the approaching bad weather; for there is no comfort for my ills unless joy comes back to me by my singing. The lady is very beautiful for whose sake I suffer this sweet pain, for which I do not in the least seek relief or advice, nor shall I be healed except by her alone, for I love her more than I can say.

II

Mult a en li courtoisie et vaillance,
Simple resgart qui trop bien li avient;
Ses biaus parlers, sa simple contenance
Me fet penser plus qu'a moi ne couvient.
Dex, que ferai? S'ele ne me retient
A son ami, trop iert mal conseillie,
Qu'ainz par autrui ne fu si bien servie
Sanz traïson;
Trop fera grant mesprison,
Quant je l'aim, s'ele m'oublie.

II

She has great courtliness and worth, a simple expression which becomes her very well. Her beautiful speech, her simple face make me think thoughts above my station. God, what am I to do? If she does not make me her friend, she will be ill-advised, for she would never be served as well and unfailingly by another. Since I love her, she would be very wrong to ignore me.

III

Nus me porroit contre sa mescheance
Si biau servir que ja li vausist nient
Més ja pour ce ne doit avoir doutance
Fins cuers loiax qui bone amor maintient,
Car loiautez le destraint tant qu'il crient
A mesprendre envers sa douce amie;
Ne je de ce ne me desconois mie,
    Ainz m'abandon
    A fere sanz ochoison
    Quanqu'Amors conmande et prie.

III

Nobody could serve his lady so well, when luck was not on his side, for it to be of any use; nevertheless, a man of true, loyal heart who keeps to love should not be afraid; although to remain loyal is such a torture to him that he is afraid he may be unfaithful to his sweet lady. I make no secret of my actions: I declare freely that I will do immediately whatever Love commands or asks me to do.

IV

'Douce dame, la plus bele de France',
Dire puis bien, 'de moi ne vous souvient',
Car des l'eure que g'estoie en enfance,
Li donai je mon cuer qu'ele tant tient,
Si sai de voir qu'a morir me couvient,
S'el ne m'envoie du sien une partie;
Se je l'avoie, je n'en morroie mie,
    Més guerison
    Avroie et trestout son bon
    Feroie et sa conmandie.

IV

'Sweet lady, the most beautiful in France', may I well say, 'you do not remember me'. For since I was a child I gave her my heart which she possesses so surely. And I know very well that I must die if she does not give me a part of her heart. If I had it, I should not die, but I should be healed, and would do all her will and whatever she commanded.

V

Bele vaillans, doulce, cortoise et franche,
De qui valour nuit et jour me sovient,
Alegiés moi pour Dieu la mesestance
Que li miens cuers pour vostre amor soustient,
C'a vostre honour certes pas n'apartient
Que vos faciés a nului vilonie,
Et je vos sent de tele conpaignie,
    De si douç non,
    Que j'arai mon guerredon,
    S'en vos n'est pitiés faillie.

V

Beautiful lady, sweet, courtly, noble lady, whose excellence I remember night and day, for God's sake ease the pain which I feel on account of your love; for it is unfitting to your high rank that you should do harm to anybody, and I know you are so kind, and with such a sweet name, that I shall have my reward, unless pity has altogether forsaken you.

VI

Por moi lo di, qui sui en tel balance
Por la bele qui trop bel se maintient;
Mi conpaignon, ou j'avoie fiance,
Mi ont grevé, ne sai dont ce lor vient.
Mult me mervoil de coi lor resovient,
N'en i at nul qui sor moi n'ait envie;
Al moins font il pechié et vilonie,
    Que senz raison
    Vont querant tel mesprison
    Par koi je perde m'amie.

VI

I say this for myself, who am in such torment over the beauty who behaves so beautifully. My companions, whom I trusted, have harmed me, and I do not know why. I marvel at their resentment, for there's none but envies me. At any rate, they are committing a sin and a base act in that they are seeking without cause some misunderstanding which will lose me my lady.

VII

Chançon, va t'en sanz nule demorance
As fins amanz, si leur di de par moi:
Des mesdisanz vos envoit Dex venjance,
Qui vos heent, si ne sevent pour quoi;
Trop sont vilain et de mauvaise loi,
S'en prïerai Jhesus le filz Marie
Que tel mehaig leur envoit en l'oïe,
    Qu'el front en haut
  Soient seignié d'un fer chaut,
  Qu'i pere toute lor vie.

VII

Song, go without waiting to true lovers, and tell them from me: God send you vengeance on slanderers who hate you and do not know why. They are base and impious, and I shall pray to Jesus son of Mary to wound them in the ear [?], and to see they are marked on their forehead with a red-hot iron, so that it shows all their life long.

8

Tant ai amé c'or me convient haïr (R 1420), BY CONON
DE BÉTHUNE

Sources: O 117; M 45; T 99. Both M and T attribute
the chanson to Conon de Béthune, who was an important nobleman in northern France and who died in
1219 or 1220. In manuscript O the melody is a fourth
higher than in M and T; here it is transposed down to
facilitate comparison.

The poems of Conon were published twice by the
same editor, Axel Wallensköld, in 1891 and in 1921.[1]
In a footnote on the first page of the latter edition
Wallensköld gave his reasons for presenting a completely new edition of the poems, the most noteworthy
one being his admission that his earlier attempts to reconstruct the original language of the poem were completely arbitrary. In the second edition he gave the text
according to a carefully chosen manuscript.

Of the four stanzas given by Wallensköld,[2] and copied here, manuscripts M and T give only the first
three (the scribe of M left sufficient space for a fourth
stanza); manuscript O preserves only the second and
third stanzas; and the fourth stanza occurs only in a
source that does not give the music. Nevertheless the
four stanzas are neatly united in their rhyme pattern
by forming a combination of coblas doblas and coblas
alternadas.

Each pair of stanzas forms coblas doblas by having
the same rhyme sounds, but within each pair the *a* and

b rhymes are inverted as follows:

| Stanzas I and III | *a* | *b* | *a* | *b* | *c*˘ | *b* | *c*˘ | *b* |
| Stanzas II and IV | *b* | *a* | *b* | *a* | *c*˘ | *a* | *c*˘ | *a* |

This chanson has been included to present a centric melody with contrasting chains. The first and third melodic lines have the basic characteristics of a melody
based upon the chain *G-B-D*, in which the *D* serves as
recitation tone. The second and fourth lines serve more
or less as an extended termination which emphasizes the
function of *G* as the most important tonal center. Lines
five and seven are clearly based upon the chain *D-F-A*,
even though there is disagreement on whether the *F*
should be sharped, while lines six and eight are modified repeats of lines two and four, and return firmly to
the *G*. Thus in its entirety this melody may be said to
be constructed around *G* as center tone, even though
the centric character of the melody does not become
apparent until the beginning of the cauda.

Probably the most remarkable aspect of this chanson,
however, is the agreement between rhyme pattern and
melodic form of each individual stanza, as shown in the
following graphic representation:

a	*b*	*a*	*b*	*c*˘	*b*	*c*˘	*b*
10	7	10	7	10	7	10	7
A	B	A	B	C	B′	C	B′

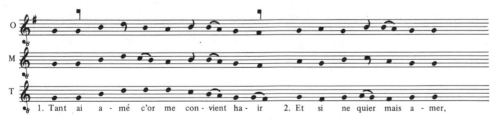

1. Tant ai a - mé c'or me con - vient ha - ïr 2. Et si ne quier mais a - mer,

1. Axel Wallensköld, *Chansons de Conon de Bethune*, Helsingfors 1891; and *Les Chansons de Conon de Bethune*, Paris 1921.

2. 1921 edition, 13.

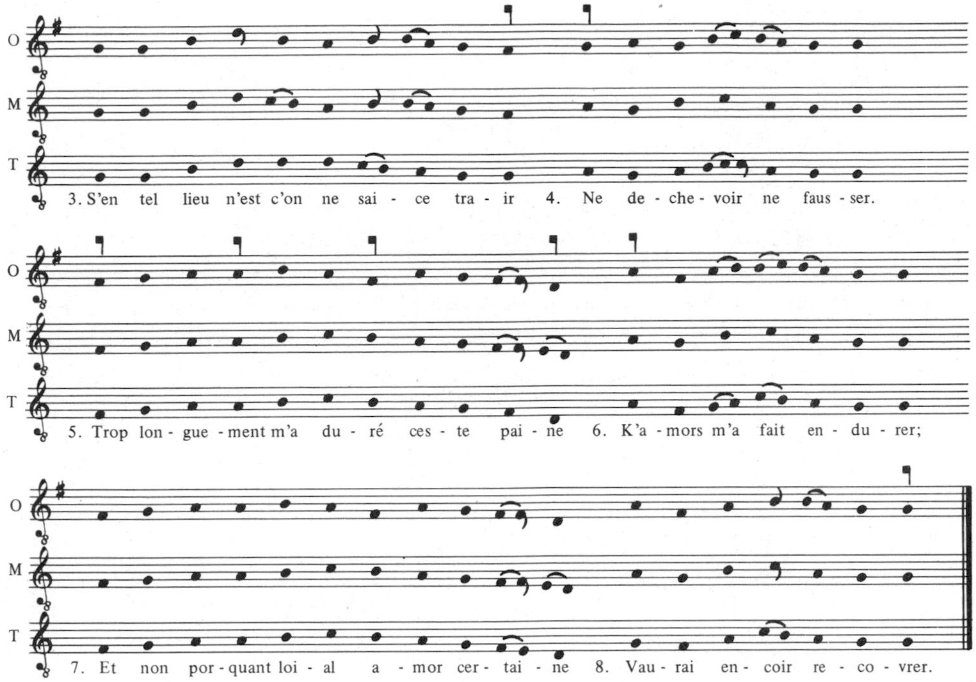
O
M
T
3. S'en tel lieu n'est c'on ne sai - ce tra - ir 4. Ne de - che - voir ne faus - ser.
O
M
T
5. Trop lon - gue - ment m'a du - ré ces - te pai - ne 6. K'a - mors m'a fait en - du - rer;
O
M
T
7. Et non por - quant loi - al a - mor cer - tai - ne 8. Vau - rai en - coir re - co - vrer.

I

Tant ai amé c'or me convient haïr
Et si ne quier mais amer,
S'en tel lieu n'est c'on ne saice traïr
Ne dechevoir ne fausser.
Trop longuement m'a duré ceste paine
K'amors m'a fait endurer;
Et non por quant loial amor certaine
Vaurai encoir recovrer.

I

So long have I loved that now I must hate, and I no longer wish to love, unless it is someone who does not know how to betray and deceive and play false. The pain that Love makes me endure has lasted too long; and yet I would still like to win true, certain love.

II

Ki or vauroit loial amor trover
Si viegne a moi por coisir!
Mais bien se doit belle dame garder
K'ele ne m'aint pour traïr,
K'ele feroit ke fole et ke vilaine,
S'em porroit tost mal oïr,
Ausi com fist la fause Chapelaine,
Cui tos li mons doit haïr.

II

She who wishes to find true love should come to me for it! But a beautiful lady must beware of loving me in order to betray me, for she would be wrong and uncourtly to do that, and would soon hear evil words about it, as did false Chapelaine, whom everybody should abhor.

III

Assés i a de celes et de ceaus
Ki dient ke j'ai mespris
De çou ke fis covreture de saus,
Mais mout a boin droit le fis,
Et de l'anel ki fu mis en traïne,

III

There are many men and ladies who say I made a mistake when I put pennies on my head (but I was quite right to do it) and concerning the ring which was put on in treachery (but it was put on in honour) since it was by that ring that I made my feudal surrender, and

Mais a boin droit i fu mis,
Car par l'anel fu faite la saisine
    Dont je sui mors et traïs.

now I am betrayed and slain.[1]

IV

A moult boen droit en fix ceu ke j'en fix,
    Se Deus me doinst boens chevals!
Et cil ki dient ke i ai mespris
    Sont perjuré et tuit fauls.
Por ceu dechiet bone amor et descline
    Que on lor souffre les mals,
Et cil ki cellent lor faulse covine
    Font les pluxors deloiauls.

IV

I was quite right to do what I did, and may God at least make it profitable to me. And those who say that I did wrong are all perjured and liars. Because their evil sayings are tolerated, True Love is declining and cast down; and those who hide their false conduct make many others disloyal too.

1. Axel Wallensköld, who has twice edited Conon de Béthune, has not been able to elucidate completely this poem. The third strophe in particular is obscure. The word *saus* may mean 'willows' and the *couverture de saus* would thus mean figuratively 'a whipping'. However, *saus* may be a variant of *sous*, 'pennies', and in my opinion it may refer to a feudal custom of putting pennies on the head before laying them on the altar in submission. This would accord with the mention of a ring, *anel*, and the *saisine*, which both might refer to such a ceremony. Perhaps such a ceremony is referred to by Bernart de Ventadorn who says: 'qu'eu sui sos om liges on que m'esteya/si que de sus del chap li ren mo gatge;...' (see *The Songs of Bernart de Ventadorn*, ed. Stephen G. Nichols, Jr., Chapel Hill 1962) which Nichols translates: 'I am her liegeman wherever I may be, and I give her my pledge from the crown of my head.' (Pp. 164-165.) (Transl.)

9

Fine amours en esperance (R 223), BY AUDEFROY LE BASTARD

Sources with music: O 55; M 146; T 55. Text taken from Cullmann.[1] This chanson provides us with a somewhat unusual example of a melody moving freely between two poles. For the first six lines the three preserved versions are rather similar, but from the seventh line on the T version is radically different from the other two and ends on *C*, while the other two end on *G*. However, these same tones also form the two poles between which this melody moves, and the entire difference between the versions may be reduced to the difference in importance between the two poles. In most troubadour and trouvère melodies the lower pole is the more important one; it usually occurs more often than the higher one and usually serves as ending tone for the pedes and for the entire song. Here, the lower pole indeed serves as ending tone for the pedes and as final ending tone for two of the versions. It seems unlikely that the discrepancy is caused by mere scribal inaccuracy; thus it is more likely to be a change made consciously by a performer. One might argue that the ending on *G* was intended by the composer and that one of the three performers whose versions were preserved erred and made a different ending. It is equally possible, however, that the composer intended the unusual ending, which somewhere in the process of the oral tradition was changed by one or more performers. The whole situation is made more complicated because it is the T version that differs here, while usually the melodies in T are closely related to those in M and it is the scribe of O who gives the divergent versions.

Whatever the original ending may have been, this melody is rather unusual, because of the small range between the two poles; in the repertory under discussion I have encountered only very few songs in which the two poles are a fourth part. There are several with a fifth or a sixth between them, and there are many with an octave in between. Although the *C* is quite obviously the upper pole, its function is somewhat obscured because the third *G–B* plays a rather important role in some of the lines. In this aspect this melody is an eloquent illustration of my earlier remark that different modes of organization are encountered very often within one song.

Another noteworthy aspect of this chanson is the lack of correspondence between the ending of the melodic line and the nature of the rhyme. The melodies for lines one, three, and six have endings which seem extremely well suited for their feminine rhymes; yet the same melodic pattern occurs at the end of line five, which has a masculine rhyme.

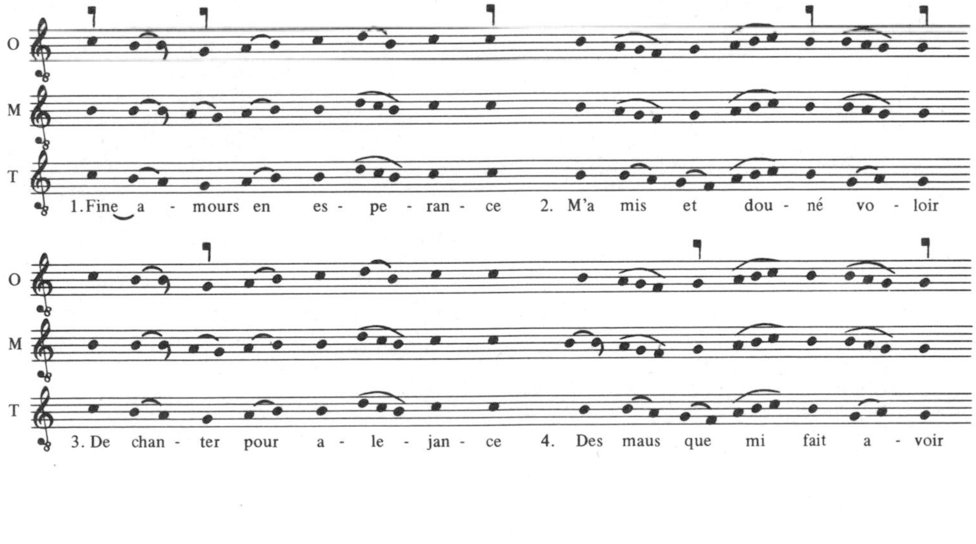
O
M
T
1. Fine a - mours en es - pe - ran - ce 2. M'a mis et dou - né vo - loir
O
M
T
3. De chan - ter pour a - le - jan - ce 4. Des maus que mi fait a - voir

1. Arthur Cullman, *Die Lieder und Romanzen des Audefroi le Bastard*. Halle, 1914. 91.

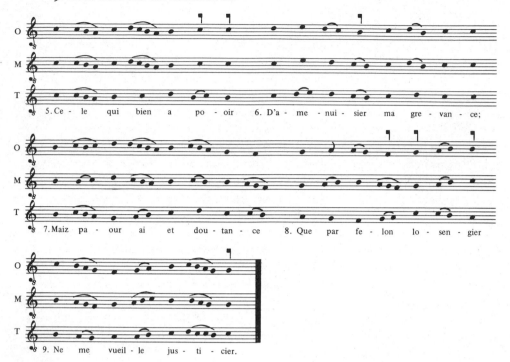

5. Ce - le qui bien a po - oir 6. D'a - me - nui - sier ma gre - van - ce;

7. Maiz pa - our ai et dou - tan - ce 8. Que par fe - lon lo - sen - gier

9. Ne me vueil - le jus - ti - cier.

I

Fine amours en esperance
M'a mis et douné voloir
De chanter pour alejance
Des maus que mi fait avoir
Cele qui bien a pooir
D'amenuisier ma grevance;
Maiz paour ai et doutance
Que par felon losengier
Ne me vueille justicier.

II

Tant me plaist sa contenance
Et ses gens cors a veoir
Et sa tresdouce samblance,
Que vueill en gré recevoir
Que que me face doloir;
Qu'adés ai en ramembrance
Que biaus servirs et soufrance
Fair fin ami avancier
Et s'onor croistre et haucier.

III

Par sa tresdouce acointance
Et par son bel decevoir
Fist mes cuers de moi sevrance

I

True Love has given me hope and a desire to sing in order to lighten the woes which I am forced to suffer by the lady who would certainly be able to reduce my pain; but I am much afraid she wants to punish me because of a vile slanderer.

II

It pleases me so much to see her face and body and expression, that I will welcome whatever causes me pain; for I always remember that good service and suffering advance the cause of the true lover and increase and heighten his honour.

III

Because of her sweet friendship and her beautiful deceit my heart left me and went to be with hers. It is very happy to stay with her, but it is not accepted complete-

Et prist lez le suen manoir;
Tant li plaist a remanoir
Qu'il aimme la demourance;
Mais pou i a retenance,
Ainz trueve orgueill et dangier
Qui me fait coulour changier.

IV

Souvent ai ire et pesance
D'amor qui tant seut valoir.
Or a tourné en enfance
Sa cointise et son savoir,
Quant ceus met en nonchaloir
Qui pour li ont mesestance,
Et ceus doune recovrance
Qui se painnent de boisier
Et de faus cuers renvoisier.

V

Dame debonaire et franche,
Bien me faites persevoir
Ke fins cuers sens repentence
Ne mi puet maix riens valoir.
Vostres seus, saichiés de voir,
. . . .
Se per vos n'ai delivrance
Cui je ne puis eslongier,
Ne ma dolour aligier.

VI

Chançons, va ramentevoir
A la pluz bele de France,
De par moi li fai moustrance
Que ne me sai revengier
Fors que par mercit proier.

ly, but rather treated with pride and cruelty, which often causes me to change colour.

IV

I am often unhappy and downcast because of love, which used to be so great. Love has changed his knowledge and skill to foolishness if he ignores those who have pain on his account, and gives succour to those who take pains to deceive and who basely amuse themselves.

V

Noble lady, you make me see that the true heart, determined to love, can no longer be of any use to me. I am yours, you should know, ... if I do not have some help from you, which I cannot continue, nor relieve my suffering.

VI

Song, go and remind the most beautiful lady in France, show her on my account that I do not know how to take my revenge except by pleading for mercy.

IO
Dex est ausi comme li pellicans (R 273), BY THIBAUD DE
NAVARRE

Sources with music: K 34; X 29; O 37; Mt 67; V 17.
The melody in manuscript X is very similar to that in
K, and has therefore been omitted; the melody in V has
nothing in common with the melodies offered in the
other manuscripts, but in this case it has been included
for reasons given below. The text is taken from O.

The transmission of Thibaud's chansons seems to
have been very unusual, and too complex to be discussed here in detail. Sizeable collections of Thibaud's
chansons appear in several manuscripts in exactly the
same order and with largely the same reading of the
text. We may therefore assume that these groups of
chansons were circulated in written form among several collectors. However, it appears that for some chansons only the text was circulated in writing, whereas
for others both text and music seem to have been available, even though some of the scribes copied only the
text. Unfortunately, there is no unambiguous indication whether these collections were compiled under
Thibaud's supervision.[1]

One other general characteristic emerges from the
study of multiple versions of Thibaud's chansons. In
those cases where oral tradition of the music seems likely,
the melodies did not fare well; we find very serious
discrepancies, probably because of the indistinct structure of the melodies themselves.

The chanson under discussion certainly was part of a
group of chansons circulated in writing, and all four
manuscripts preserving the music along with the text—
there are also four sources preserving only the text—
seem to have used this model for the text. However, the
scribe of manuscript V either had a model without the
music or copied the text only and entered a melody that
has nothing to do with the other melodies preserved for
this chanson. Whether the scribe of manuscript O copied the music from the same model as the scribes of K
and Mt is difficult to say; the discrepancies between the
O version and the K–Mt version may have been caused
either by performers during the oral tradition or by the

person who did all the 'editorial' work on a large number of chansons entered in O. If the latter is the case, we
find among Thibaud's chansons some interesting examples of the way in which this person changed or
modified the melodies given to him.

Perhaps the only structural element we find in the
melody preserved in manuscripts K, O, and Mt is the
tone *F* functioning as the melodic center, from which
the melody starts, around which it freely moves upward and downward, and to which the melody returns
at the end. An important difference between our concept of melody and that of the trouvères comes to light
in this song. Whenever we hear or sing a tune, our
musical instinct, conditioned by centuries of melodies
with finals or tonics, selects immediately the tone on
which the melody ought to end, and in a song such as
this we expect several lines to end on this tone. Apparently the trouvères and jongleurs did not have such
expectations. Immediately the first line establishes, for
us, the *F* as final or tonic, while for the medieval singer
this *F* became the center, which could be starter and
final, but which in the first place was the gravitational
center of the melody to which it had to return a number of times. It is interesting to note that only two lines,
the third and the last, end on *F*, while six of them start
on *F*. Obviously *F* is the center tone for the entire
chanson, even though one line does not touch it at all.

In a somewhat inconsistent alternation of one Longa
and two Breves, the scribe of O suggests a performance
in the third rhythmic mode. Herein this chanson resembles many songs with ten-syllable lines for which a
performance in third rhythmic mode is suggested in the
notation. In a ten-syllable line performed in the third
rhythmic mode, the longest time units come on the
first, fourth, seventh, and tenth syllables, which fits the
poetry to some extent, because in ten-syllable lines there
is often a caesura after the fourth syllable and almost always an accent on the tenth syllable, both of which
could conceivably be expressed or emphasized by a
lengthening of those syllables. Thus the third mode
would fit the ten-syllable line reasonably well if it were
not for the fact that lengthening of the first and seventh
syllables fits only occasionally.

---

1. Concerning a written collection of Thibaud's chansons,
which perhaps was compiled at his request, see Wallensköld,
Thibaud de Champagne, p. XVII.

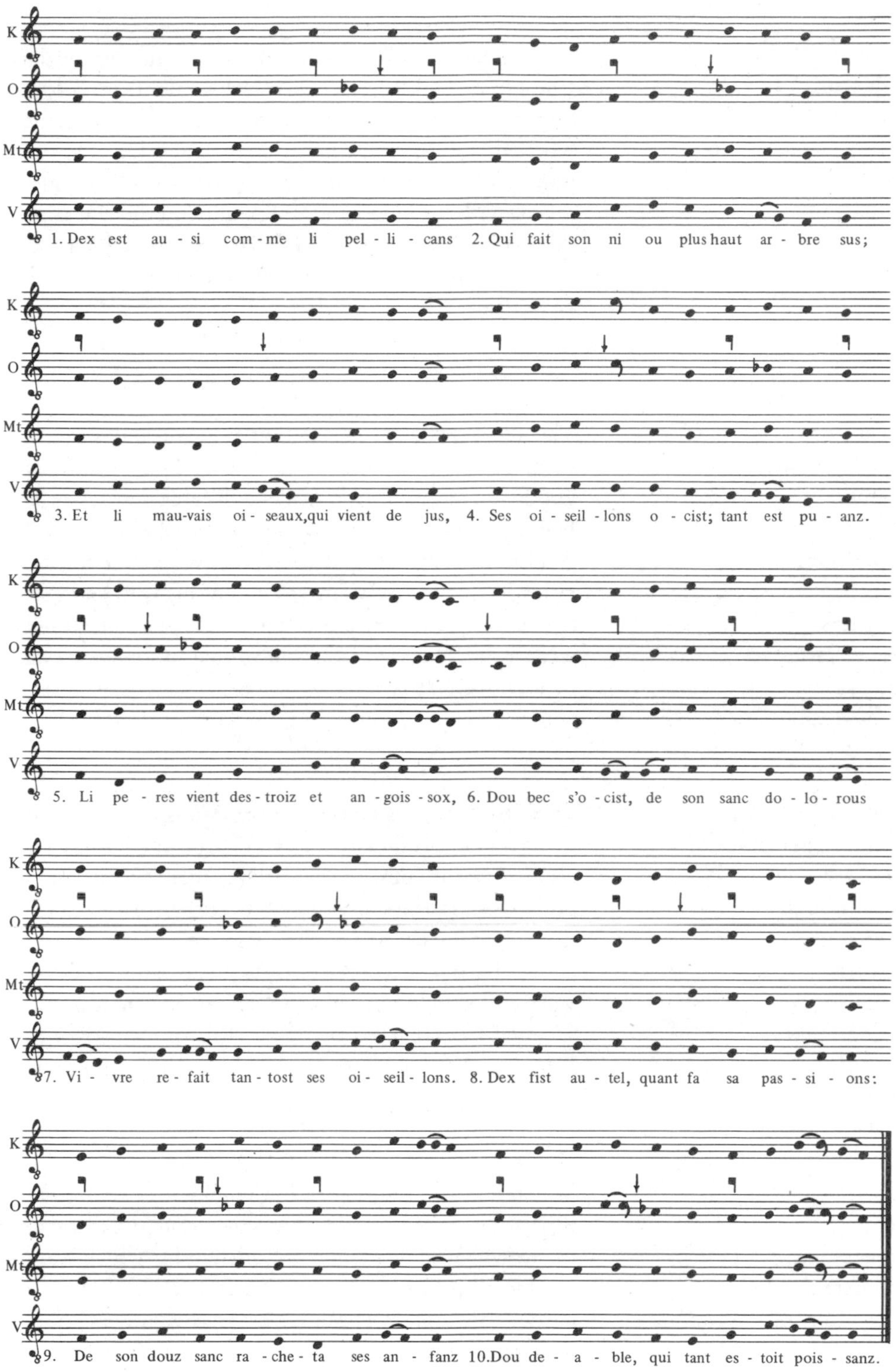
K
O
Mt
V
1. Dex est au - si com - me li pel - li - cans 2. Qui fait son ni ou plus haut ar - bre sus;
3. Et li mau-vais oi - seaux,qui vient de jus, 4. Ses oi - seil - lons o - cist; tant est pu - anz.
5. Li pe - res vient des - troiz et an - gois - sox, 6. Dou bec s'o - cist, de son sanc do - lo - rous
7. Vi - vre re - fait tan - tost ses oi - seil - lons. 8. Dex fist au - tel, quant fa sa pas - si - ons:
9. De son douz sanc ra - che - ta ses an - fanz 10.Dou de - a - ble, qui tant es - toit pois - sanz.

I

Dex est ausi comme li pellicans
Qui fait son ni ou plus haut arbre sus;
Et li mauvais oiseaux, qui vient de jus,
Ses oiseillons ocist; tant est puanz.
Li peres vient destroiz et angoissox
Dou bec s'ocist, de son sanc dolorous
Vivre refait tantost ses oiseillons.
Dex fist autel, quant fa sa passions:
De son douz sanc racheta ses anfanz
Dou deable, qui tant estoit poissanz.

II

Li guierredons en est mauvais et lenz,
Que bien ne droit ne pitié n'a mais nus:
Ainz est orguilz et baraz au desus,
Felonie, traïsons et bobanz.
Mout par est ore nostre estaz perilloux.
Et se ne fust li exemples de ceux
Qui tant aiment et noises et tençons,
–Or est des clers qui ont lessiez sarmons
Por guerroier et por tuer les gens–
Jamais en Deu ne fust nuns hons creanz.

III

Nostres chief fait toz nos membres doloir,
Por c'est bien droiz qu'a Deu nos en plaignons.
Et granz corpes ra mout sus les barons,
Cui il poise, quant aucuns vuet valoir;
Et entre genz en font mout a blasmer,
Qui tant sevent et mentir et guiler.
Le mal en font desor eus revenir,
Et, qui mal quiert, malx ne li doit faillir.
Qui petit mal porchace a son pooir,
Li granz ne doit an son cuer remenoir.

IV

Bien devriens en l'estoire veoir
La bataille qui fu des deus dragons,
Si con l'en trueve ou livre des Bretons,
Dont il covient les chasteax jus cheoir.
Ce est cist siegles cui il covient verser,
Se Dex ne fait la bataille finer.
Les jauz Mellin en covint fors issir
Por devener qu'estoit a avenir.
Mais Antecriz vient, ce poëz savoir,
Es maçues qu'Anemis fait movoir.

I

God is like the pelican, which builds his nest up in the tallest tree. And the evil bird which comes from below kills the little pelicans, because it is so wicked; the worried and distressed father arrives, and kills himself with his beak, and immediately makes his little ones revive with his blood and suffering. God did the same thing by His passion: with His sweet blood He redeemed His children from the Devil, who was so powerful.

II

The recompense of this action is small and slow in coming, for there is no longer in anybody justice or good or mercy: instead pride and deception take the first place, and felony, treason and presumption. Our condition is now one of very great peril. But for the example of those who are so fond of quarrels and battles–that is to say the clerks who have abandoned their sermons to make war and kill people–nobody would believe in God any more.

III

Our head gives us pain in all our limbs, and it is just that we complain of this to God. And the barons are also greatly at fault, since it grieves them when somebody wishes to be superior; and other persons do much that is blameworthy, who know so well how to lie and cheat. Their evil comes back to them, and whoever seeks evil should not fail to receive it. If a man is preparing to combat a small evil [scil. the Muslems in Palestine] he should not keep in his own heart a great evil [scil. hypocrisy].

IV

We should see in the story in the book of the Bretons the battle of the two dragons, which caused a castle to fall down. It is [symbolic of] this world, which must tumble if God does not put an end to the battle. It needed the wisdom of Merlin to know what was going to happen. But you may know that the Antichrist is coming, with the clubs that the Devil controls.

V

Savez qui sont li vil oisel punais[1],
Qui tuent Deu et ses enfançonnez?
Li papelars dont li nons n'est pas nèz.
Cil ort puant, ort et vil et mauvais.
Il ocient tote la simple gent
Par lor faus moz, qui sont li Deu enfant.
Papelart font le siegle chanceler.
Par saint Pere! mal les fait encontrer.
Il ont toloit joie et solaz et pès:
Cil porteront en enfer le grant fès.

Or nos doint Dex li servir et amer
Et la Dame, qu'on n'i doit oblier,
Qu'il nos vuille garder a touz jors mais
De maus oiseaus qui ont venin es bès!

V

Do you know who are the vile, stinking birds who are killing God and his children? They are *Papelards* [i.e. religious hypocrites] whose name is so filthy. They are very dirty and smelly and evil. They kill simple people by their falsehoods, people who are the children of God. *Papelards* make the world rock [on its foundations]. By St. Peter, it is a bad thing to meet them. They have taken away joy and pleasure and peace. They will carry this great burden in hell.

Now may God let us serve and love Him, and the Lady who must not be forgotten, and may He keep us forever from the evil birds, who have poison in their beaks!

1. Changed from 'puant' after M and T.

II

Bons rois Thiebaut, sire, consoilliez moi (R 1666), JEU-
PARTI BETWEEN AN UNNAMED CLERK AND THIBAUD
DE NAVARRE

Sources with music: K 42; N 9; X 41; O 14; Mt 71;
a 138. The N and X versions are so similar to the K
version that they were omitted from this synoptic chart.
The melodies given in manuscripts A and V for this
chanson have nothing in common with the other melodies or with one another. The notation in O is semi-
mensural, with rare consistency indicating the third
rhythmic mode, as shown in the synoptic chart of its
notational symbols on p. 36.

The text of this chanson was published twice within
a very short time span, and by two different editors,
perhaps independently of one another. The first, Wallensköld, gave the text according to manuscript K,
with additional stanzas from other manuscripts.[1] The
second editor, Arthur Långfors, gave the text according
to manuscript O.[2] For this edition, I have gone back
directly to manuscript O, taking from other manuscripts the following corrections, which seem to make
more sense than the reading of O: Stanza II, first word,
'Clers', rather than 'Cuens'; Stanza IV, line 2, 'qu'en
clerc n'a abstinence', instead of 'que clers ait abstinence'; Stanza IV, line 3, 's'amiez', instead of 's'envoyez';
and second envoy, line 1, 'qu'a moi', instead of
'q'amors'.

This chanson is certainly worthy of our special attention because it is one of the very few chansons for
which a scribe indicated a certain rhythmic mode in
completely consistent alternation of stemmed and unstemmed notes, and for which multiple versions of
text and melody are available. Even though the third
rhythmic mode, suggested in this case by the scribe of
O, fits all poems with ten-syllable lines to a limited extent, one has only to read the poem under discussion to
conclude that there is no indication in the text that this
poem was conceived and always performed in the meter suggested by the scribe of O. The information imparted by the melodic versions supports this conclusion.

The position of this chanson in the manuscripts suggests that the scribes of manuscripts O, T, V, K, N, X,

and Mt may have copied it directly or indirectly from
the same written model. Besides minor differences in
choice of words and spelling, there are some noteworthy discrepancies in the number of stanzas given by
the various scribes. Only the scribes of O and T entered
the stanzas and envoys as they are given here; the scribes
of K, X, and V entered only the first five stanzas;
the scribe of N entered the first five stanzas plus the two
envoys; and the scribe of Mt gave the first three stanzas
plus stanza six and the two envoys. Nevertheless, all
these variants may have crept in during the written tradition. Similarly, the discrepancies among the melodic
versions can be explained as changes made by scribes
rather than by performers. However, there is the remarkable fact that the scribe of T did not give the
music and that the scribe of V entered a melody that
has nothing in common with any of the other melodies
given for this chanson. Beyond that, the most noteworthy discrepancy occurs in the K N X version, which
gives part of the second line a third higher than the other
versions, unlike the corresponding part of the fourth
line.

The scribe of manuscript a may or may not have had
access to the same version of the text as the scribes mentioned above, but he almost certainly received his music
from a different source. As usual, the discrepancies between the a version and the other ones are more serious
and more frequent in the cauda than in the frons. If
these discrepancies occurred during the oral tradition, it
is difficult to believe that this chanson was traditionally
performed in a fixed meter. This conclusion is strengthened by the information gained from the examination of the two other chansons which have exactly the
same metric scheme and basically the same melody as
Bons rois Thiebaut. These chansons are:

1. *Rois de Navarre, sire de vertu* (R 2063), preserved
with music in M 85, T 97, K 140, N 64, P 87, and X 96.
In the manuscripts the melodies for this chanson are
notated a fourth lower than those of *Bons rois Thiebaut*;
to facilitate the comparison they are given here a fourth
higher. The melodies of K, N, P, and X are very similar
to one another and therefore only K is given here. The
melody in V has been omitted because it has nothing in
common with the other melodies for this chanson or
with the V version of *Bons rois Thiebaut*. In M, T, K, P,
and X this chanson is attributed to Raoul de Soissons,
in N to Tierri de Soissons. The latter is an unknown

1. Thibaud de Champagne, 152 ff.
2. *Recueil général des jeux-partis français*, Paris 1926. 24 ff.

person, while the former is known very well; he was a somewhat younger contemporary of Thibaud de Navarre, which makes it impossible to determine whether this song predates *Bons rois Thiebaut* or whether it was written in imitation of it.

2. *Ma derreniere veul fere en chantant* (R. 321), preserved with music in K 200 and N 96. In both sources the chanson is attributed to Oede de la Couroierie, who lived during the last third of the 13th century. In all likelihood, therefore, this chanson is the youngest of the three under discussion. Its melodic versions are very similar to the KNPX version of *Rois de Navarre* and were therefore not included in the synoptic chart.

A comparison of all melodic versions reveals some very intresting discrepancies. The T version of *Rois de Navarre* is certainly the most coherent of all versions and the clearest in structure. Except for a few passages, it is structured upon the combined tertial-quartal chain *C-E-G-C*. The M version of the same song is closely related to its T version with one important exception: there is an *E*-flat (*B*-flat in the original) near the end of both occurrences of the *B* melody, which causes ones of the most outspoken switches between major and minor that I have encountered. This switch is made even more striking by the KNPX version of the same chanson, which in the first four lines is almost exactly a second higher than the M and T versions. These lines appear to be based upon the chain *D-F-A*, which is minor in character, while the rest of the melody resembles the corresponding part of the M and T versions. In summary, the caudas of these three versions resemble one another and are based upon the chain *C-E-G-C*; their frontes resemble one another in melodic contour but not in structure, which is *C-E-G* in the T version, *C-E-G* and *C-E*-flat-*G* in the M version, and *D-F-A* in the KNPX version.

The frons of *Bons rois Thiebaut* resembles that of *Rois de Navarre* as given in manuscript T, but its cauda is considerably less coherent and narrower in range; it never comes above the tone *A* and it can only be characterized as having the *C* alternately as basis and as center tone.

As pointed out above, the melodic versions of the song by Oede de la Couroierie are almost identical to the KNPX versions of *Rois de Navarre*, but differ from the KNX versions of *Bons rois Thiebaut*. Thus the melodic versions of the frons fall into two distinct groups.

One consists of all versions of *Bons rois Thiebaut* and the T version of *Rois de Navarre*; the second group is formed by the KNPX version of *Rois de Navarre* and the chanson by Oede de la Couroierie; the M version of *Rois de Navarre* is an isolated case. For the cauda, however, the grouping is different because the versions of *Bons rois Thiebaut* form a separate group, clearly distinguished from all other versions.

Several important questions about this melody remain unanswered. First, we do not know who its composer was; it may have been invented by Thibaud de Navarre, by Raoul de Soissons, or by the clerk participating in the jeu-parti; it is also possible that it predates all of these persons. But, whoever invented it, the melody fits the general character of Thibaud's melodies very well, both in melodic style and in lack of uniformity among the preserved versions. Secondly, it is impossible to establish the original form of this melody with reasonable certainty, although one can justify a few observations on this point regardless of who composed it. Above all, it seems unlikely that the original melody had a structure as clear and coherent as is found in the T version of *Rois de Navarre*, because it would have been very easy for the performers to retain the basic characteristics of such a coherent melody. The M and KNX versions of the same song justify the supposition that the original melody had some equivocation between major and minor, which, however, was lost entirely by some performers and retained in two different forms by others. But it is equally possible that the original melody was merely very unclear in structure, especially in the frons, and that different performers stabilized the melody with various degrees of success. Nevertheless, despite the serious discrepancies, the similarities among the preserved versions are too close and too numerous to be incidental; all versions under discussion must have derived from one original.

Returning finally to the meter of the three songs, we may find it difficult to come to any positive conclusions. But, since there is no support whatsoever for the metric indications in manuscript O, I believe that originally all three chansons were intended to be performed in a declamatory rhythm. We find some support for this conclusion in manuscript M, the scribe of which wrote an extra long note over the penultimate syllable, thus suggesting, in my opinion, that the singer slowed down toward the end of the stanza. If the chanson had been performed as suggested by the scribe of O, this lengthening of the penultimate note would have been superfluous, since it would have been long in the third rhythmic mode.

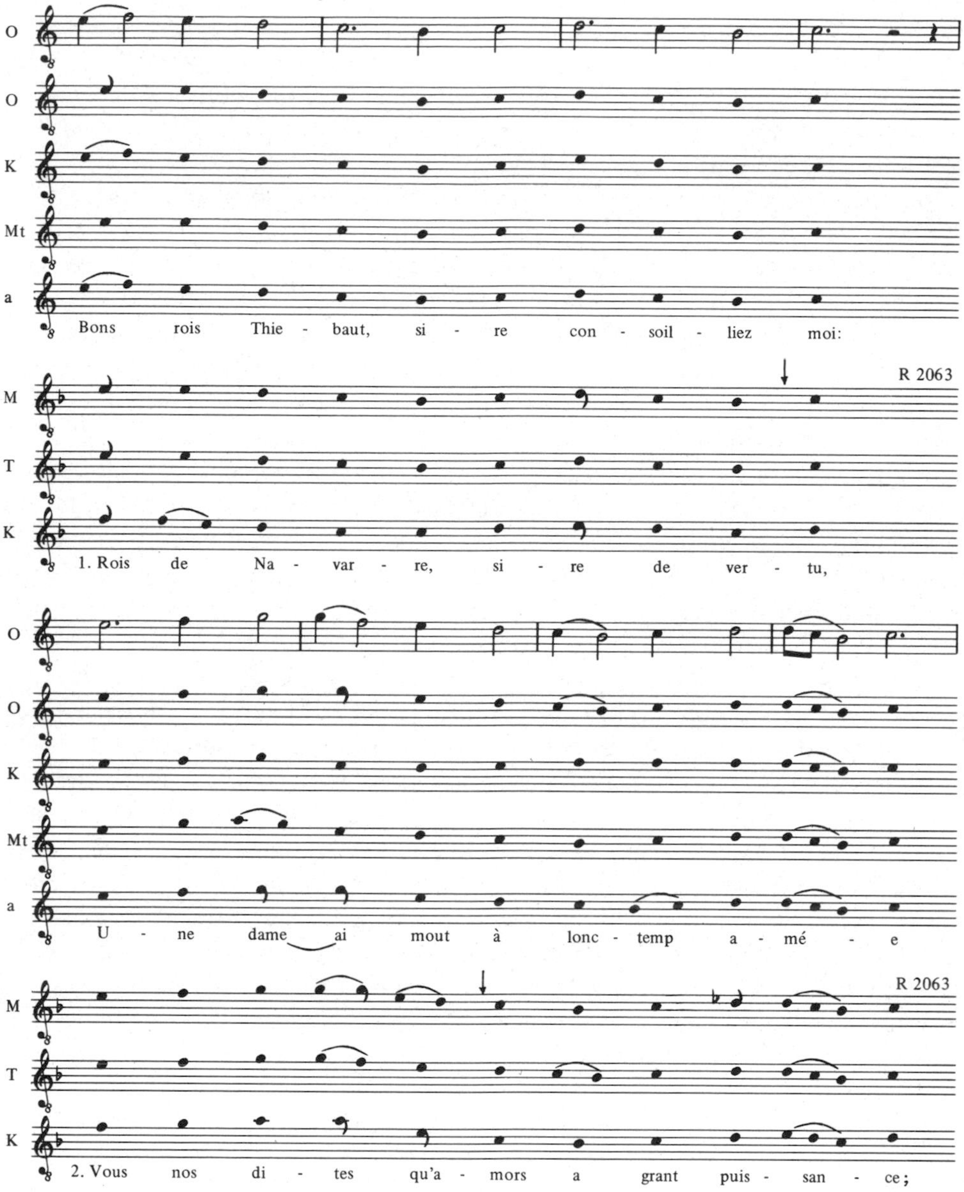
O
O
K
Mt
a
Bons rois Thie - baut, si - re con - soil - liez moi:
R 2063
M
T
K
1. Rois de Na - var - re, si - re de ver - tu,
O
O
K
Mt
a
U - ne dame ai mout à lonc - temp a - mé - e
R 2063
M
T
K
2. Vous nos di - tes qu'a - mors a grant puis - san - ce;

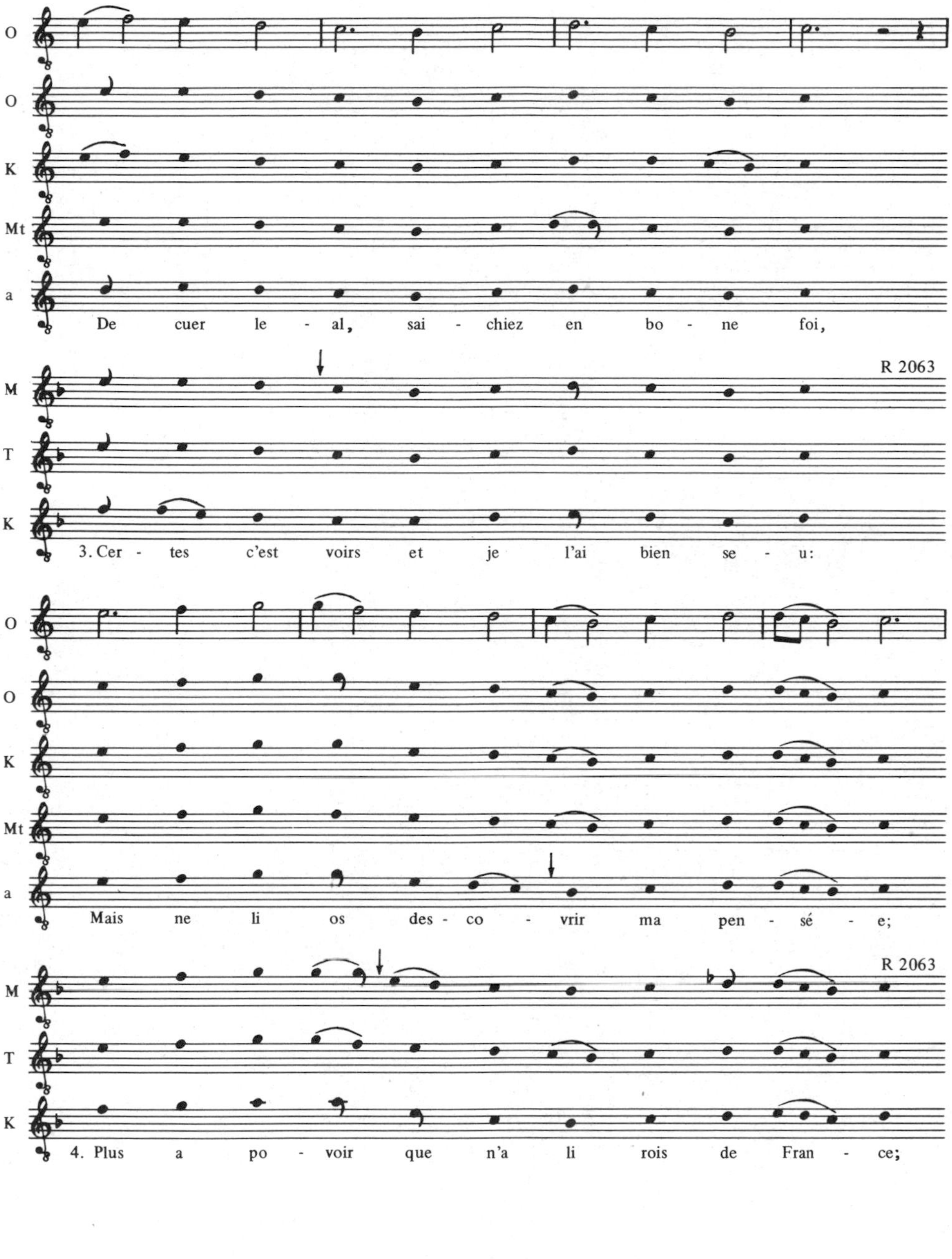
O
O
K
Mt
a
De cuer le - al, sai - chiez en bo - ne foi,
R 2063
M
T
K
3. Cer - tes c'est voirs et je l'ai bien se - u:
O
O
K
Mt
a
Mais ne li os des - co - vrir ma pen - sé - e;
R 2063
M
T
K
4. Plus a po - voir que n'a li rois de Fran - ce;

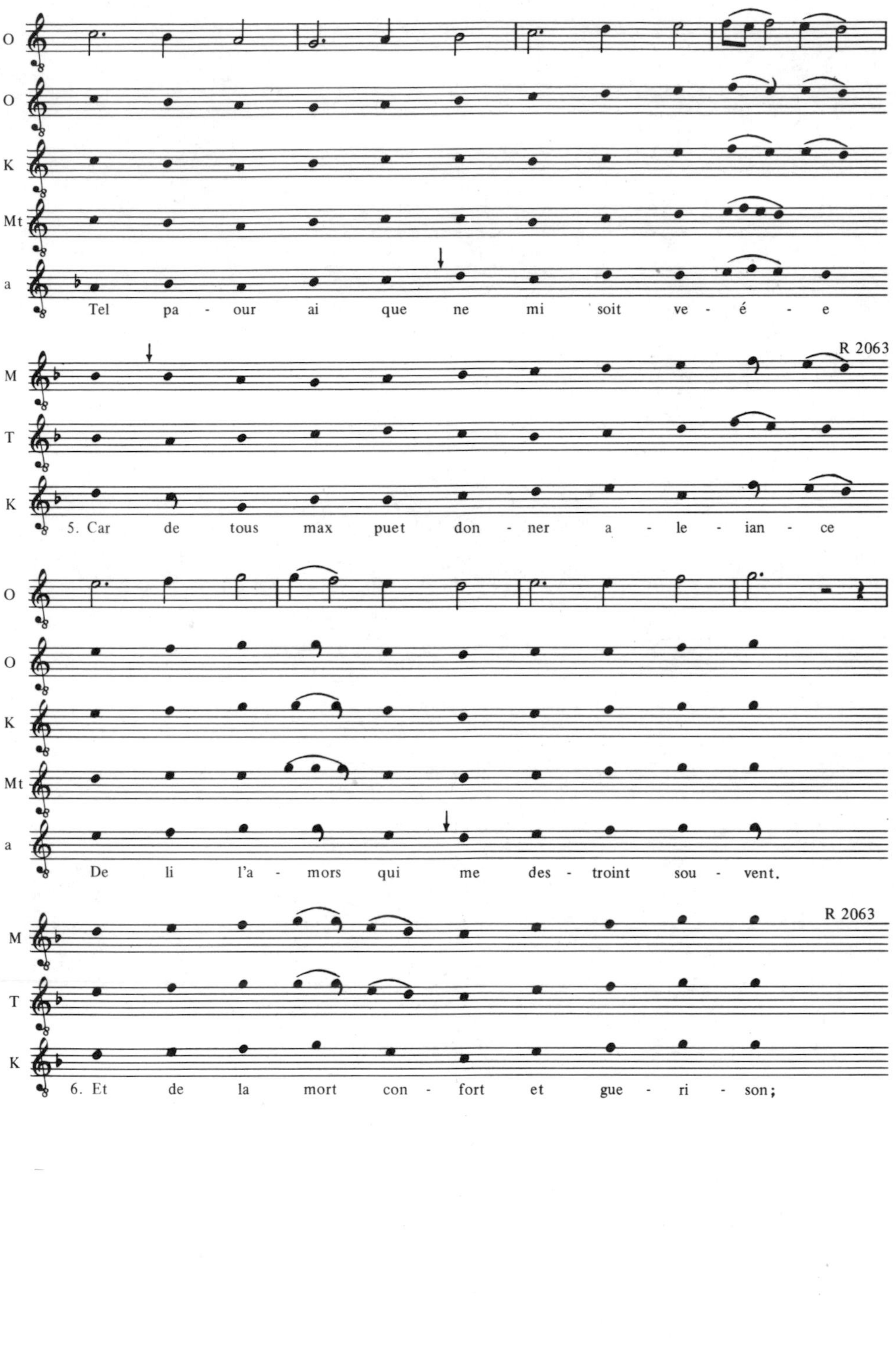
O
O
K
Mt
a
Tel pa - our ai que ne mi soit ve - é - e
R 2063
M
T
K
5. Car de tous max puet don - ner a - le - ian - ce
O
O
K
Mt
a
De li l'a - mors qui me des - troint sou - vent.
R 2063
M
T
K
6. Et de la mort con - fort et gue - ri - son;

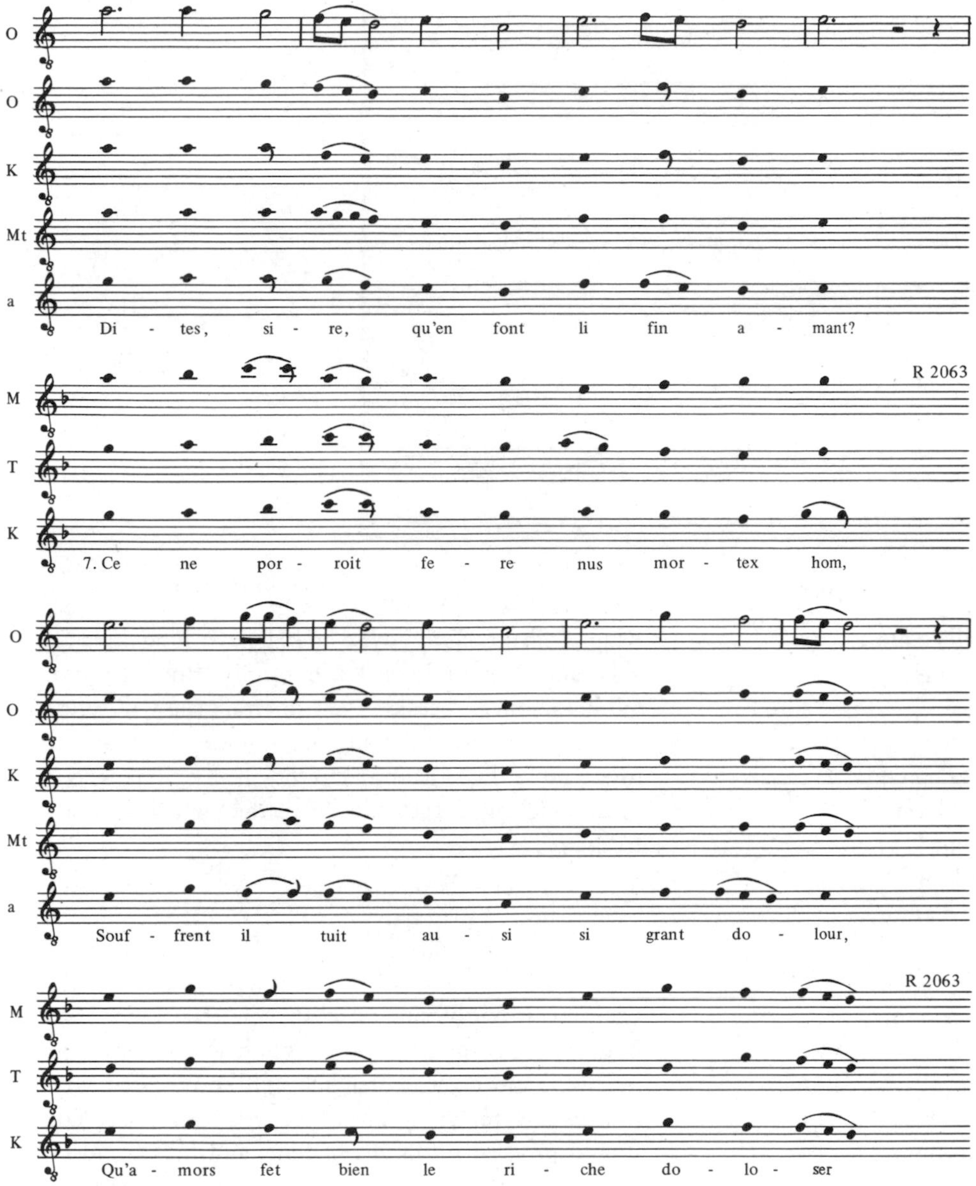
O
O
K
Mt
a
Di - tes, si - re, qu'en font li fin a - mant?
R 2063
M
T
K
7. Ce ne por - roit fe - re nus mor - tex hom,
O
O
K
Mt
a
Souf - frent il tuit au - si si grant do - lour,
R 2063
M
T
K
Qu'a - mors fet bien le ri - che do - lo - ser

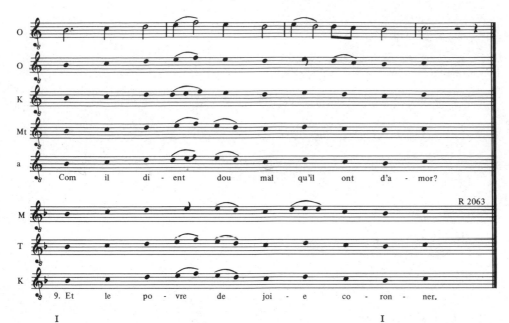

Com il di - ent dou mal qu'il ont d'a - mor?

R 2063

9. Et le po - vre de joi - e co - ron - ner.

I

Bons rois Thiebaut, sire consoilliez moi:
Une dame ai mout à lonctemp amée
De cuer leal, saichiez en bone foi,
Mais ne li os descovrir ma pensée;
Tel paour ai que ne mi soit veée
De li l'amors qui me destroint souvent,
Dites, sire, qu'en font li fin amant?
Souffrent il tuit ausi si grant dolour,
Com il dient dou mal qu'il ont d'amor?

II

Clers je vos lo et pri que toigniez quoi;
Ne dites pas por quoi ele vos hée,
Mais servez tant et faites le, porqoi
Qu'ele saiche ce que vostre cuers bée,
Que par servir est mainte amors donée.
Par moz coverz et par cointes semblanz
Et par signes doit on venir avant,
Qu'ele saiche le mal et la dolor
Que fins amis trait por li nuit et jor.

III

Per Deu, sire, tel consoil me donez
Ou ma mort gist et ma granz desestance,
Que moz coverz et signe, ce savez,
Et tel semblant vienent de decevance
Assez trueve on qui set faire semblance
De bien amer, sanz grant dolour soffrir,
Mais fins amis ne puet son mal covrir

I

King Thibaut, Sire, advise me: I have long loved a
lady, and with a loyal heart, faithfully. But I dare not
tell her about it, because I am so afraid she will refuse
me her love, which so pains me. Tell me, what do true
lovers do in this situation? Do they really all have such
great suffering as they say, from the pain that comes
from love?

II

Clerk, I strongly suggest that you stay quiet. Say
nothing to her for which she might hate you, but serve
her well, and do it so that she will know what your
heart wants, for many a heart is given for service. You
should proceed by means of hints and looks, and by
signs, so that she will know the pain and suffering that
a true lover has on her account, both day and night.

III

For God's sake, Sire, you give me advice which will
bring me death and torture, for hints and signs and
looks, as you know, come from deception. There are
many who know how to give the appearance of love,
without feeling its pangs; but the real lover cannot hide
his pain, nor fail to say what comes into his heart because of the sharpness of the pain he has to bear.

Qu'il ne die ce dont au cuer li vient
Par l'angoisse dou mal que il sostient.

IV

Clers, je voi bien que haster vos volez!
Et bien est droiz qu'en clerc n'a abstinence.
Mais, s'amoïez autant con dit avez,
Nou diroie por quanqu'il a en France.
Car quant l'on est devant li en presance,
Adonc viennent trembler et grief sopir,
Et li cuers faut, com doit la bouche ovrir.
N'est pas amis, qui sa dame ne crient,
Car la cremours de la grant dolor vient.

V

Par Deu, sire, pou sentez, ce m'est vis
La grant dolour, le mal et le joïse
Que nuit et jor trait fins leax amis.
Ne savez pas conment Amors justise
Ce que suen est et en sa conmandise!
Je sai de voir que, se le seüssiez,
Ja dou dire ne me repreïssiez;
Car por ce fait Amors ami doloir
Que de son mal regeïsse le voir.

VI

Clers, je voi bien que tant estes apris
Que la corone est bien en vos assise.
Quant dou proier par estes si haitiz,
Ce fait li max des roins qui vos atise;
Itelx amours n'est pas ou cuer assise.
Dites li tost, quant se vos angoissiez!
Ou tost l'aiez, ou vos tost la laissiez;
Que bien puet on a voz diz parcevoir
Qu'aillors volez changier vostre voloir.

Envoi 1
Par Deu, sire, j'ain de cuer sanz faintise,
Mais vos guilez Amors; por ce cuidiez
Que je soie ausincques tost changiez
Con vos estes, qui mis a non chaloir
Avez Amors, et ces de son pooir. –

Envoi 2
– Clers, puis qu'a moi avez tel guerre prise
Et vos de rien mon consoil prisiez,
Criez merci, mains jointes, a ses piez,
Et li dites tot quanque vos voudroiz.

IV

Clerk, I see very well that you are in a hurry! and it is right that a clerk has no abstinence! But, if you loved as much as you say, you would not have said so for the whole of France! For when you are before her, there come tremblings and sighs, and the heart fails just when the mouth should speak. Whoever does not fear his lady is no lover, for fear comes from the great pain of love.

V

I am sure, Sire, that you do not feel the great pain, the suffering and joy which a true lover feels night and day. You do not know how Love controls what is his to command. I know that if you knew it, you would never blame me for speaking out. For Love causes the lover to hurt in order that he will reveal the truth about his pain.

VI

Clerk, I see that you are so wise that it is right for you to wear the crown. If you are in such a hurry to woo the lady, it is because the fever in your loins drives you on. This love is not seated in the heart. If you are so concerned, tell her at once. You will either have her soon, or you will lose her soon. For it is easy to tell from what you say that you want to transfer your desire to someone else.

Envoy 1
No, Sire, I love from my heart and without guile, but you it is who deceive love. For this reason, you think I can be changed as easily as you are, who have degraded love and those in his power.

Envoy 2
Clerk, since you have engaged me in such battle, and you spurn my advice, cry for mercy at her feet with clasped hands, and tell her whatever you wish.

12

Chascuns qui de bien amer (R 759), BY RICHARD DE FOURNIVAL

Sources: O 31; K 224; N 108; P 64; first stanza as a motet in manuscript Wolfenbüttel 1099 (1206)[1], fo. 216vo. The K, N, and P versions are so similar to the O version and the upper part of the motet that they have not been included in the synoptic chart. Manuscripts K, N, and P attribute the chanson to Richard de Fournival, a clergyman and author of learned treatises, who probably lived in Amiens around the middle of the 13th century.

Manuscript O gives the melody in a mixture of mensural and semi-mensural notation; K, N, and P give it in non-mensural notation; and the Wolfenbüttel manuscript gives the tenor in clear modal notation, but the melody in non-mensural notation. The overall meter of the tenor and the melody is clearly the first rhythmic mode, although a few passages are somewhat unclear in detail. Several interruptions of the first mode pattern are suggested by the scribe of O. For the sake of the relationship between the upper part and the tenor of the motet, the first one, occurring at the beginning of line ten, is unacceptable, while those in lines 14 and 15 either are required or fit the motet, but do not significantly alter the correspondance between the two voices.

The composition in its entirety is an interesting mixture of motet and chanson elements. The contents of the poem and the number of stanzas are more or less in accordance with the trouvère literature in general, and the chansonniers attribute a few chansons in typical trouvère style to the same author. The metric scheme of the poem, graphically presented as follows:

a	*b*	*a*	*b*	*a*	*b*	*a*	*b*	*a*	*b*	*b*	*b*	*c*	*c*	*D*⌣	*C*
7	4	7	4	7	4	7	4	7	5	7	7	4	7	10	8

is somewhat atypical for a trouvère chanson, but not exceptional for a motet, although the rhyme pattern is somewhat more sophisticated than that of the average motet. The through-composed form of the melody and the character of the individual melodic lines are typical for a motet, but atypical for a trouvère chanson. The discrepancies among the melodic versions are inconsequential, as they usually are among multiple versions of motets, and they are unlike the discrepancies among multiple versions of trouvère melodies. The tenor has all the features of the 13th-century motet tenor; it is taken from a liturgical chant, namely *Alleluia Justus germinabit*; it is subdivided into groups of three notes and stated twice in such a way that the second statement differs metrically from the first.[2]

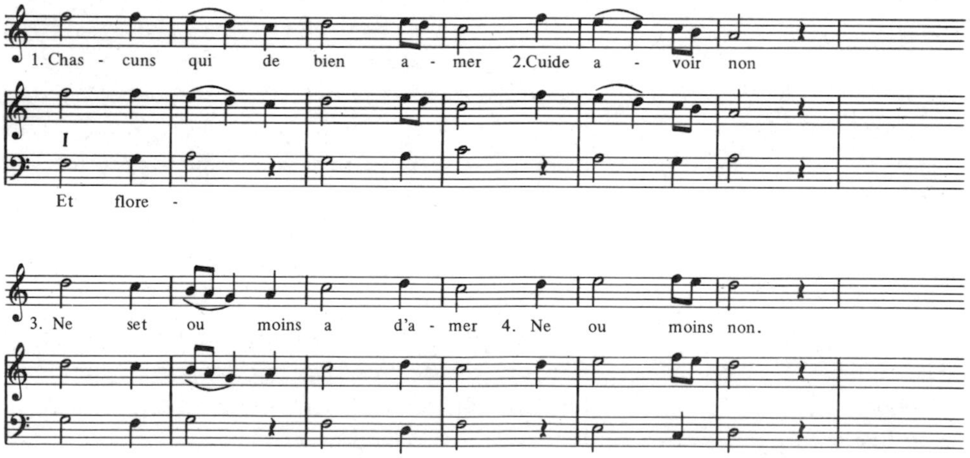
1. Chas - cuns qui de bien a - mer 2.Cuide a - voir non
I
Et flore -
3. Ne set ou moins a d'a - mer 4. Ne ou moins non.

1. Facsimile edition by Luther Dittmer, Brooklyn 1960. The motet, together with the versions from K and O, was published in slightly different metrization by Gennrich, *Zeitschrift für Musikwissenschaft*, IX, 1926-1927. 14 ff.

2. The beginnings of the first and second statement of the tenor melody are marked with I and II respectively.

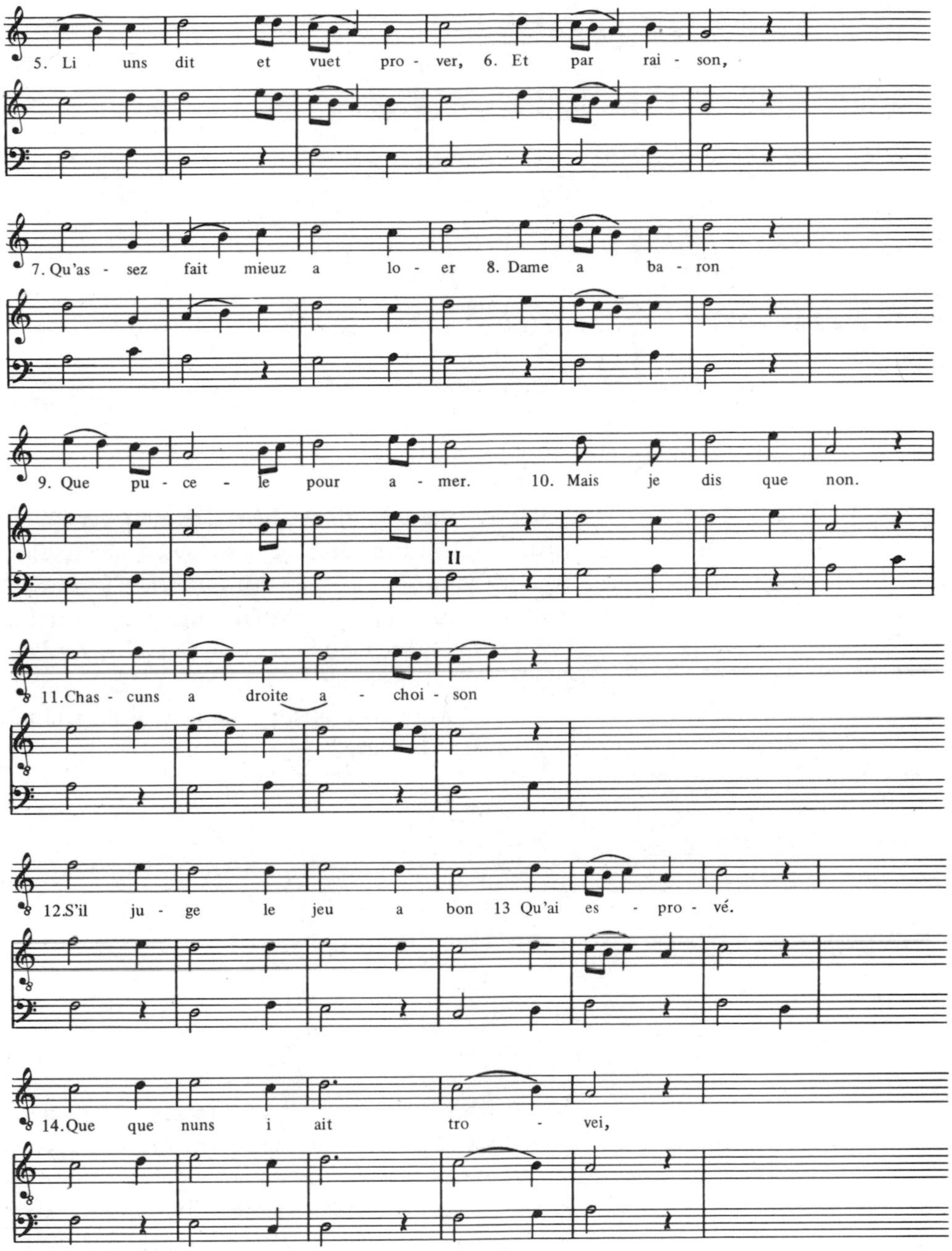
5. Li uns dit et vuet pro - ver, 6. Et par rai - son,
7. Qu'as - sez fait mieuz a lo - er 8. Dame a ba - ron
9. Que pu - ce - le pour a - mer. 10. Mais je dis que non.
II
11. Chas - cuns a droite a - choi - son
12. S'il ju - ge le jeu a bon 13 Qu'ai es - pro - vé.
14. Que que nuns i ait tro - vei,

15. J'ai mis mon cuer en jo - ne da - moi - sel - le, 16. Dont

ja ne par - ti - rai mon gré.

bit.

I

Chascuns qui de bien amer
Cuide avoir non
Ne set ou moins a d'amer
Ne ou moins non.
Li uns dit et vuet prover,
Et par raison,
Qu'assez fait mieuz a loer
Dame a baron
Que pucele, pour amer.
Mais je dis que non.
Chascuns a droite achoison
S'il juge le jeu a bon
Qu'ai esprové.
Que que nuns i ait trovei,
J'ai mis mon cuer en jone damoiselle,
Dont ja ne partirai mon gré.

I

Not everyone who thinks he is a great lover knows what kind of a woman it is best to love. Some say, and even try to prove by logic, that it is better to seek the love of a nobleman's wife than that of a young girl. But I say no. Everyone who thinks I am right to defend this argument is correct, although he may see no reason in it. I have set my heart on a young lady, from whom I wish never to be parted.

II

Celui puet on escuser
De mesprison
Qui egaument vuet donner
Selonc son bon.
Por ce vuil par droit mostrer
Et sanz tençon
Que jone dame a loer
A plus haut don
Qu'a la pucele panser;
N'i a fors le non.
Mais dame rent guierredon,
Et pucele est tost chanjanz
Et sanz bonté.
J'en ai mon voloir osté.

II

A man who gives according to his means can be freed from any accusation. In this way I wish to prove beyond any argument that to woo a noblewoman is more rewarding than to court a young lady, for that is rewarded only in name. A lady gives a reward, and a young girl is changeable and unkind. I have abandoned them, and set my heart on a beautiful young noblewoman, from whom I wish never to be parted.

S'ai mis mon cuer en jone dame et bele
Dont ja ne partirai mon gré.

III

La dame blamer ne quier,
Li ne s'amor;
Com plus l'estuet covoitier,
Plus a savour.
Auques m'en fait esloingnier
Au chief dou tor
Ce qu'il i a parcenier
Et nuit et jor.
Mais qui pucele acointier
Seit de grant valour,
Je di qu'il fait le moillor.
Qui simple et coie et taisant
La puet trover,
Mout s'i doit bien acorder.
Li noviaus tans dou tout me renovele
A vaillant damoisele amer.

III

I do not wish to condemn the lady or her love. The more she is desired the more attractive she is. But what makes me abandon her after a while is that she has a companion both day and night. But the man does best who can get to know a young girl of great worth, for he will find her simple and quiet and modest, and this is very agreeable. The new season makes me a new man, in order to love a worthy young girl.

IV

Pucele fait a prisier,
Bien m'i assent,
Mais ele me fait proier
Trop longuement;
Ne ne s'i puet nuls fier
Certeinnement,
Et, ce que vuet outroier,
Change sovant.
Mès dame ainme sanz trichier
Et bien tient covent.
Pucele est archez a vent,
Tot adés son baisier vent;
Bien l'ai provey,
Car sovent m'a escové.
Por ce ain je mieuz la jone dame et bele
Dont ja ne partirai mon grei.

IV

The young girl is worthy of praise, I admit; but she makes me woo too long. Nobody can rely on her, and she changes her mind about what she will give you. But a gentlewoman loves without falsehood and keeps her promise. The young girl bends according to the wind, and is always selling her favours. I have proved it, for many a one has robbed me. For this reason I prefer the beautiful young noblewoman, from whom I wish never to be parted.

V

Chascuns dit d'amors son bon
Et son talant,
Mais pucele a plus douz non,
Car adès rent
Miel et roses a foison,
Qui près la sent;
Mais dame, de tel poison

V

Everyone says what is good and desirable about love, but the young girl does better, for she smells of honey and roses. The gentlewoman has lost this love-potion. And thus I rightly say that the young girl is superior, just as the primrose and the first wild rose give the most pleasure. For this reason I have set my heart on a young girl, from whom I hope never to be parted.

N'a mais neant.
Por ce di, et par raison
Que, tot ausiment
Con novele flor d'ayglant
Et la prime voire rent
Plus de bonté,
A pucele sormonté.
Por quoi j'ai mis mon cuer en la pucele
Dont ja ne partirai mon gré.

VI

Des dous jeus m'estuet fenir
Le jugement.
Bele dame a maintenir
Plait voirement.
Mais ce c'on n'i puet venir
Sans partement
Me fait d'autre part tenir.
Au finement
Vuil a mon oés retenir
Touse de jovent.
Plus la voi, plus l'atalant,
Bien li ai mon mautalant
Tout pardoné.
Tel jugement ai doné:
C'on doit touz jors mieuz amer la pucele–
Dont ja ne partirai mon gré.

VI

Now I have to make a decision in this argument. It is pleasing to woo a gentlewoman, but the fact that you cannot come to her without strife makes me choose the other side of the dispute. Finally, I want to have a young girl for myself. The more I see her, the more I love her: I have forgiven her all my unhappiness. Such is my judgment: one should always prefer the young girl, from whom I hope never to be parted.

13

Haute chose a en amor (R 1954) BY GILLEBERT DE
BERNEVILLE, AND
Trop est mes maris jalos (R 2045) BY ETIENNE DE
MEAUX

Sources with music for R 1954: K 143; N 66; P 115;
X 98; R 88; O 56. In the KNPX group this chanson is
attributed to Gillebert de Berneville. The N, P, and X
versions are very similar to the K version except for
lines 10 and 11, as indicated in the synoptic chart. The
text is taken from O.

Source for R 2045: P 131. The 'Estienne de Miauz'
mentioned in the last stanza is probably the author of
this song, and it is uncertain which song is modeled
after the other. Because of the wide difference in character, both poems are included.

Form:

R 1954	*a*	*b*	*a*	*b*	*b*	*c*	*c*	D	D	A	D
	7	7	7	7	7	5	5	3	3	5	3
R 2045	*a*	*b*	*a*	*b*	*b*	*c*	*c*	D	D	D	
	7	7	7	7	7	5	5	3	3	8	
	A	B	A	B	A	C	D	E	F	G	H

There are three very striking peculiarities to this chanson: the narrow range, the strong tertial structure, and
the rather regular distribution of ligatures. Almost
every melodic line has a one-step tertial structure, with
infixes and affixes, and the melody in its entirety is
based upon a chain of only two thirds. The few Longae,
occurring in manuscript O, in combination with the
ligatures on the even numbered syllables give an almost
consistent indication of the second rhythmic mode. The
distribution of ligatures supports this rhythm in surprising fashion, but the distribution of word accents
shows no outstanding features and the comparison
of versions fails to reveal any conclusive evidence. The
relative uniformity among the preserved melodic versions may be the consequence of the regular distribution of ligatures, of the strong melodic structure, of a
written tradition, or of a short oral tradition over a
small geographic area.

It appears that four separate versions have been preserved for this melody, but in reality we may have only
one dependable and one unreliable version, which is
scant for any worthwhile conclusions about the original meter of the songs concerned. It is the general experience that manuscript O is often closely related to
the KLNPX group; in this case the textual reading of
all stanzas in O is very similar to that in KNPX and the
few discrepancies between KNPX and O may have
been caused either by a performer or a scribe. The
melody of *Trop est mon maris jalos*, preserved in P only,
may have come from the same source as the O and
KNPX versions of *Haute chose*. The discrepancies between the R version of the latter chanson and the
other versions could be a rather strong argument against
fixed meter, if it were not for the circumstance that the
scribe of R rightfully is suspected of having been unreliable and careless. Although in this case the scribe of
R preserved a melody obviously deriving from the
same prototype as the other preserved versions, his lack
of care in notating the melody seems to manifest itself
in two instances, in lines one and ten, in which he entered a note above a syllable which should be elided.
Therefore the other discrepancies between this and the
other manuscripts may also have been caused by scribal
inaccuracy and thus the comparison of versions does
not reveal sufficient information to come to a final
conclusion regarding the original rhythm or meter in
this melody. However, in this particular instance the
issue of modal versus declamatory rhythm becomes
rather academic if we state the alternatives as follows:
either the chanson was performed in a declamatory
rhythm in which most notes received approximately
equal time; or it was performed in the second rhythmic
mode, applied with great suppleness and with primary
attention to an expressive rendition of the poem. In
either performance most notes would have more or
less equal duration—except those at the end of individual
lines, which probably were held longer—and the text
could be rendered very expressively, depending upon
the performer's ability. Thus, in this case, the scribe of
O either gave the chanson in its original rhythmic mode
or he made a genuine attempt to express, with the
means available to him, how the chanson actually was
performed.

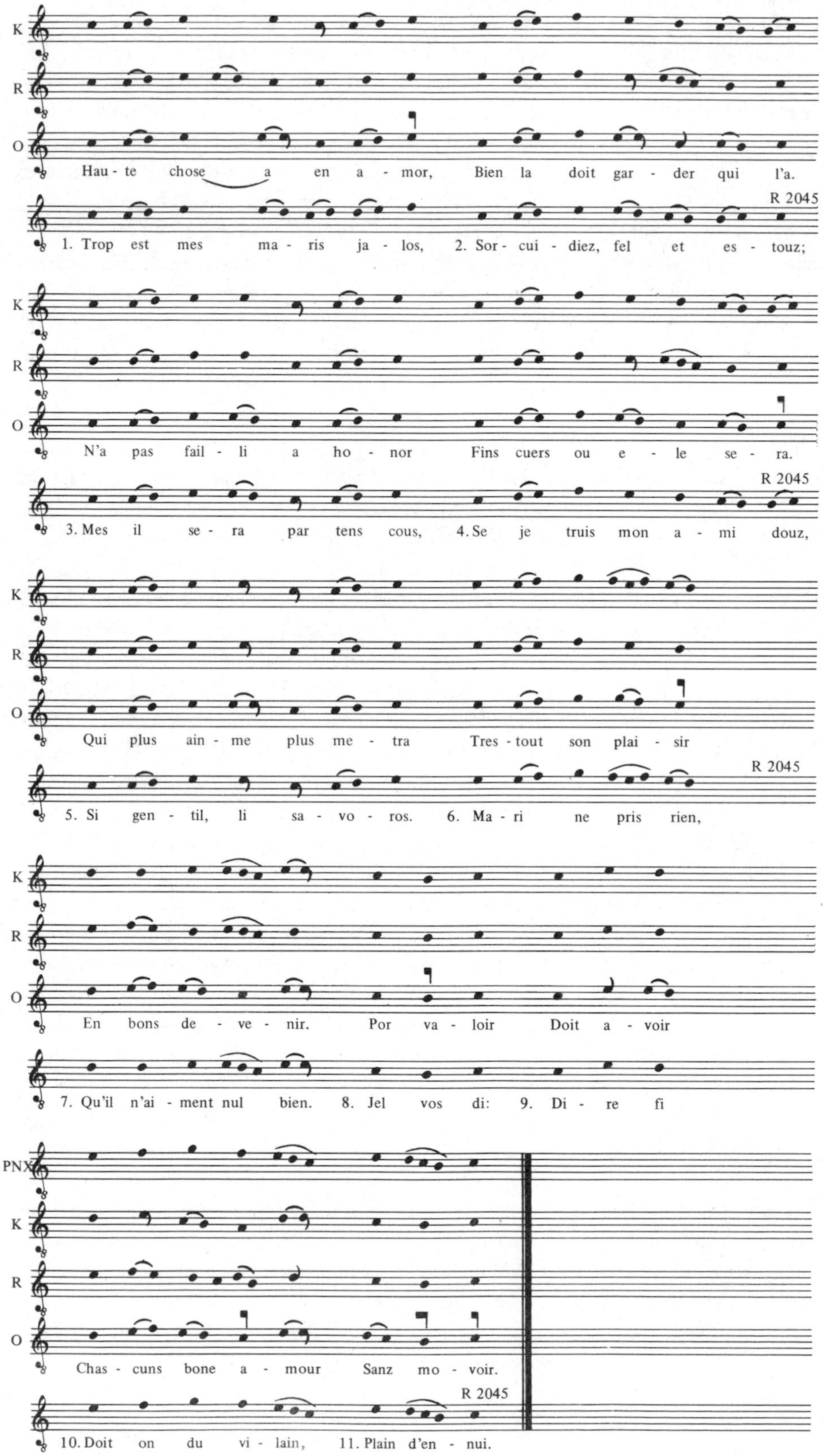
K
R
O
Hau - te chose a en a - mor, Bien la doit gar - der qui l'a.
R 2045
1. Trop est mes ma - ris ja - los, 2. Sor - cui - diez, fel et es - touz;
K
R
O
N'a pas fail - li a ho - nor Fins cuers ou e - le se - ra.
R 2045
3. Mes il se - ra par tens cous, 4. Se je truis mon a - mi douz,
K
R
O
Qui plus ain - me plus me - tra Tres - tout son plai - sir
R 2045
5. Si gen - til, li sa - vo - ros. 6. Ma - ri ne pris rien,
K
R
O
En bons de - ve - nir. Por va - loir Doit a - voir
7. Qu'il n'ai - ment nul bien. 8. Jel vos di: 9. Di - re fi
PNX
K
R
O
Chas - cuns bone a - mour Sanz mo - voir.
R 2045
10. Doit on du vi - lain, 11. Plain d'en - nui.

R 1954, BY GILLEBERT DE BERNEVILLE

I

Haute chose a en amor,
Bien la doit garder qui l'a.
N'a pas failli a honor
Fins cuers ou ele sera.
Qui plus ainme plus metra
Trestout son plaisir
En bons devenir.
Por valoir
Doit avoir
Chascuns bone amour
Sanz movoir.

II

Dame, par vostre valour
Mes fins cuers vos enama.
Car bien sai qu'il n'a moillor
Deça la mer, ne delà.
Amors pas ne m'oblia,
Quant me fist choisir
Tot a mon plaisir.
Pour valoir.

III

De trop fera son peour
Qui d'amors se partira.
Ne jamès plus vilain tour
En sa vie ne fera
D'amor, qui la laissera.
Mais sanz repantir
S'i doit on tenir.
Por valoir.

IV

Amours enseigne et aprent
Son home et le met en pris.
Por c'est fols qui ne s'i rent
Et qui son cuer n'i a mis.
Et je, cum lëaus amis
Amors servirai
Et si m'i tandrai.
Por valoir etc.

V

Mout est fox qui ne s'apent

I

Love is a great possession – whoever has it should guard it well. A true heart where love is has attained great honour. The man who loves best will take greatest pleasure in becoming the best in other ways. *To be great, everyone should have and preserve True Love.*

II

Lady, my true heart loved you for your great worth, for I know well there is none better here or beyond the sea. Love did not ignore me when he made me choose a lady who was wholly pleasing to me. *To be great*, etc.

III

The man who abandons love will be doing the worst thing possible, and whoever leaves him will do no worse thing in his whole life. One should keep to Love without regret. *To be great*, etc.

IV

Love teaches and instructs men who are his, and elevates them. For that reason it is madness not to abandon oneself to Love and give him one's heart. And I, as a true lover, will serve Love and be faithful to him. *To be great*, etc.

V

A man is mad not to resolve to serve Love always. For

A amors servir toz dis;
Qu'amors tient celui joiant
Qui a li est ententis.
Si m'a lacié et sopris,
Ses prisons serai
Et si m'i tendrai.
Por va.

Love makes joyful whoever is heedful of him. He has captured me by surprise: I shall be his prisoner and be faithful to him. *To be great*, etc.

R 2045, BY ETIENNE DE MEAUX

I

Trop est mes maris jalos,
Sorcuidiez, fel et estouz;
Mes il sera par tens cous,
Se je truis mon ami douz,
Si gentil, li savoros.
Mari ne pris rien,
Qu'il n'aiment nul bien.
Jel vos di:
Dire fi
Doit on du vilain,
Plain d'ennui.

My husband is very jealous, arrogant, evil and proud; but he will soon be a cuckold, if I can find my sweet friend, who is delightful and full of zest. I do not care at all for my husband, for husbands like nothing that is good. *I am telling you*: *one should despise the tedious, rustic fellow.*

II

Quant a la fenestre vois,
Il me guete trestoz jorz;
Sachiez qu'il vit seur mon pois,
Car por lui pert mes amors.
Il set bien que j'aime aillors:
Or se puet desver,
Car je vueil amer.
Jel vos di:
Dire fi.

When I look out of the window, he always spies on me; he is a burden to me, I can tell you, for my love suffers on his account. He knows I love someone else: now he can go mad, for I am determined to be in love. *I am telling you*, etc.

III

Cuide il por son avoir
Metre en prison cuer joli,
Nenil voir il a povoir
Que soie du tot a lui;
A m'amor a il failli.
Nus ne doit avoir
Ami por avoir.
Ce vos di:
Dire fi
Doit on.

Does he think he can capture an ardent heart because he is rich? He has certainly no power to make me his in any way. He has not won my love. Nobody should be able to buy love. *I am telling you*, etc.

IV

Hardiement li dirai:
Fol vilain malëuros,
Amer m'estuet sanz delai
Sachiez un autre que vos;
Or pöez estre jalos:
Je vos guerpirai,
Un autre amerai!
Ce vos di:
Dire fi
Doit on.

V

Por tot l'avoir de Cisteaus
Ne doit avoir cuer joli,
Ce dit Estiene de Miauz,
Jolive dame mari,
Ançois doit avoir ami.
Et je l'en crerrai
Et ami avrai.
Ce vos di:
Dire fi
Doit on du vilain,
Plain d'ennui.

IV

I shall boldly tell him: 'You stupid, evil peasant, I must
love another than you, and right away. Now you can
be jealous—I shall leave you and love another!' *I am
telling you*, etc.

V

Estienne de Meaux says that a pretty lady should not
willingly take a husband, for all the riches in Cîteaux,
but she should have a lover instead. And I shall believe him and take a lover. *I am telling you*, etc.

14
Li joliz temps d'estey (R 452), ANONYMOUS

This chanson occurs in O, fo. 76, only, and is given in a mixture of semi-mensural and mensural notation as indicated in our transcription above the staff. The transcription given here is strongly suggested by the notation and supported by the distribution of both word accents and ligatures.

When raising the question of properly identifying the mode of this chanson, Gennrich assumes that it is in the second mode, which at certain points is modified to accomodate lines of six syllables in a seven-syllable pattern.[1] This sounds very reasonable, but it is difficult to disprove that the chanson is in third mode with upbeat, which at certain points is modified to accommodate lines of seven syllables in a six-syllable pattern. Furthermore, one can easily defend the theory that in this chanson two modes, the second and the third, occur side by side. However, proper identification of the meter is of minor importance, as is the question of where to draw the barlines. What is of importance in this case is the observation that in some aspects this chanson differs from the trouvère repertoire in general. Most unusual is the distribution of ligatures and word accents, as well as the occurrence of the two *C*-sharps near the end. A more subtle difference lies in the more than average care the composer gave to the design of the individual lines, the result of which is rather appealing. At the same time the form and content of the poem, as well as the overall form and basically tertial structure of the melody, conform to the general style of the trouvères.

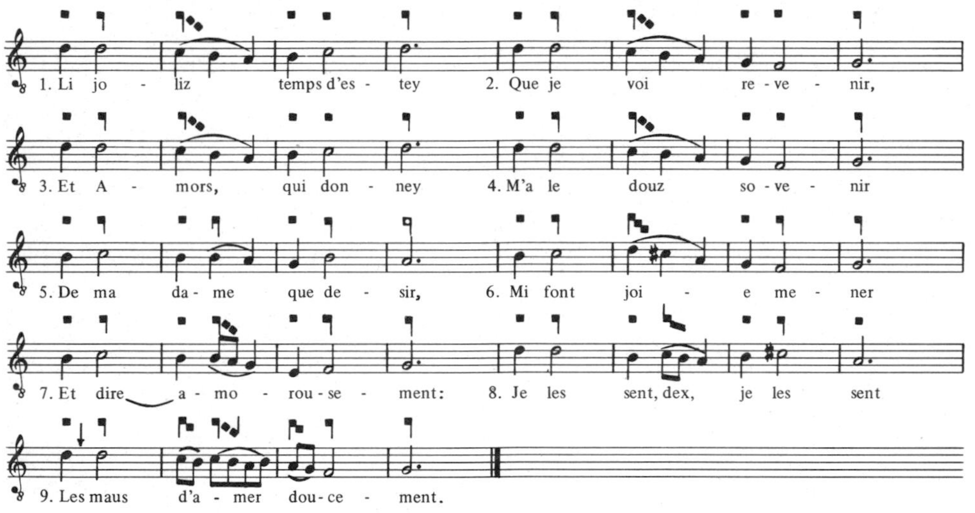
1. Li jo - liz temps d'es - tey 2. Que je voi re - ve - nir,
3. Et A - mors, qui don - ney 4. M'a le douz so - ve - nir
5. De ma da - me que de - sir, 6. Mi font joi - e me - ner
7. Et dire a - mo - rou - se - ment: 8. Je les sent, dex, je les sent
9. Les maus d'a - mer dou - ce - ment.

I

Li joliz temps d'estey
Que je voi revenir,
Et Amors, qui donney
M'a le douz sovenir
De ma dame que desir,
Mi font joie mener
Et dire amorousement:
Je les sent, dex, je les sent
Les maus d'amer doucement.

I

The pretty summer time which I see returning, and Love, who has given me the sweet memory of the lady I desire, these make me joyous, and say in my love: *I feel, God, I feel with pleasure the pains of love.*

1. 'Streifzüge durch die erweiterte Modaltheorie' in *Archiv für Musikwissenschaft*, XVIII, 1961. 127 f.

II

Ploins de joliveté
En espoir d'amanrir
Ma tres douce grietey
Dont je ne quier garir,
Tant aing si douz mal soffrir
Que ne puis oublier
Que ne die hautement:
Je les sent, Dex.

III

Trop me soi mal garder
Quant premiers l'acointai,
Quant, por li resgarder
Me prist li maus que j'ai.
Douz Dex, se je s'amor ai,
Encor porrai chanter
Et dire envoisiement:
Je les.

IV

Nuns hons ne puet durer
Sanz amors, bien le sai.
Por ce vuil endurer
Les gries max que je trai,
Et touz jors, tant con vivrai,
Servirai sanz fauser
Ma dame por cui je chant:
Je les.

V

Sentir les me covient
Les joliz maux d'amer;
Mais l'amors qui me tient
Fera trop a blasmer,
Se celi que n'ox nommer
Ne saisist et retient
Si qu'ele die en chantant:
Je les sent.

II

Full of happiness, and hopeful of seeing diminished my sweet sickness, from which I have no wish to be cured, I love so much to suffer such a sweet pain that I cannot forget to say out loud: *I feel, God,* etc.

III

I had such a poor defence when I first saw her that my sickness was caused just by looking at her. God, if I have her love, I shall still be able to sing and say joyfully: *I feel, God,* etc.

IV

No man can survive without love, well I know. For this reason I shall endure the great pains I feel. And as long as I live I shall always faithfully serve my lady, for whom I sing: *I feel, God,* etc.

V

It is right for me to feel the sweet pains of love. But Love, who has me in his power, will do wrong if he does not capture and take into his service the lady whom I dare not name, so that she too says in song: *I feel, God,* etc.

15
A l'entrant dou temps novel (R 581), ANONYMOUS

Only source: O 11. The synoptic chart of the notational symbols. given in Chapter 3, page 36 shows that the scribe of O notated the melody in a completely consistent alternation of stemmed and unstemmed notes indicating the second rhythmic mode. Although not as strongly as in the preceding chanson, the meter suggested by the scribe is supported by the distribution of ligatures and word accents. This chanson resembles the preceding one also in other aspects, and it is tempting to surmise that they were composed by the same person and that it was this composer who attempted to superimpose modal rhythm on a number of other chansons in manuscript O.

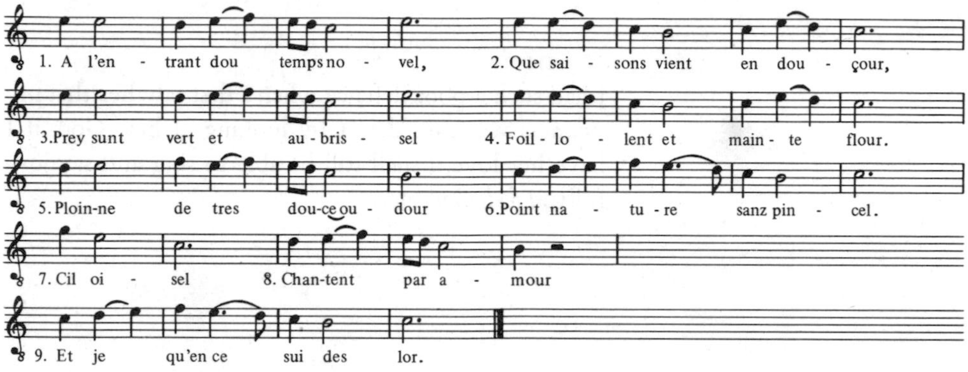
1. A l'en - trant dou temps no - vel, 2. Que sai - sons vient en dou - çour,
3. Prey sunt vert et au - bris - sel 4. Foil - lo - lent et main - te flour.
5. Ploin-ne de tres dou-ce ou - dour 6. Point na - tu - re sanz pin - cel.
7. Cil oi - sel 8. Chan-tent par a - mour
9. Et je qu'en ce sui des lor.

I

A l'entrant dou temps novel
Que saisons vient en douçour,
Prey sunt vert et aubrissel
Foillolent et mainte flour.
Ploinne de tres douce oudour
Point nature sanz pincel.
Cil oisel
Chantent par amour
Et je qu'en ce sui des lor.

I

At the beginning of the new year, when the fine weather begins, the fields are green and the bushes come into leaf. Nature paints without a brush many a flower full of sweet scent. The birds sing for love, and I do too, for in this I am one of them.

II

Quant cil fist maint bel joël
Cui je toing a Creator,
Ne fist il onques tant bel
Por faire maint ameor
Con celi qu'a tel honor
Qu'ele prent tot a ratel,
Sanz cembel,
Et cuer et seignor
Qui vers li fait de l'uel tor.

II

When He who I believe is the creator made many a beautiful jewel, he made no finer, nor more able to attract admirers, than this lady who has such worth that without any further lure she makes every man and heart her prisoner, indeed whoever turns his eyes in her direction.

III

Bone Amor m'a si navré
Enz ou cuer parfondement,
Que jamès joie n'avrey,

III

The god of love has so wounded me deep in my heart that I shall never be happy unless my beautiful lady has mercy on me. For God gave her so much beauty,

S'en sa merci ne me prent
Ma dame ou cors avenant,
Ou Dex mist tant de beauté,
De bonté,
De contenement,
Qu'en nule autre n'en a tant.

IV

De ce doi savoir bon gré
A la mal parliere gent,
Car il li ont reporté
Que je l'ain entierement.
Bien les puet croire de tant,
Sanz soirement, de vertey,
Car santé
Ne joie n'atent
Fors que de li soulement.

V

On suet dire en reprovier:
'Ce que eulx ne voit, cuers ne duet.'
Je le soloie cuidier,
Mais or voi qu'estre ne puet,
Car adès doloir estuet
Celui qu[i] ainme sanz trichier.
Jostisier
Trop forment me vuet
Li max qui dou cuer me muet.

goodness and consolation that no other lady has as much.

IV

I should be grateful to the gossip-mongers that they have let it be known that I love her completely. She can surely believe them in this, without further confirmation, for I can obtain no health or happiness save from her alone.

V

It is often said in someone's defence that 'what the eye does not see, the heart does not grieve for'. I used to believe that, but now I see that it cannot be. He who loves without guile always has to suffer. The pain which comes from my heart has too great a control over me.

Selective bibliography

Since it is impossible to present here a complete list of works concerning the art of the troubadours and trouvères, I have selected for inclusion here primarily recent studies with valuable bibliographies and studies of an introductory nature, in addition to those works quoted or referred to in the course of the present book. I have included a number of recent and general works concerning the German strophic songs contemporary to the chansons of the troubadours and trouvères.

Aarburg, Ursula, 'Melodien zum frühen deutschen Minnesang: eine kritische Bestandsaufnahme' in *Der deutsche Minnesang: Aufsätze zu seiner Erforschung*, H. Fromm, ed. Darmstadt 1961. pp. 378-423.

Abert, Anna A., 'Das Nachleben des Minnesangs im liturgischen Spiel' in *Die Musikforschung*, I, 1948. pp. 95-105.

Anglade, Jean, *Grammaire de l'ancien provençal, ou ancienne langue d'oc*. Paris 1921.

Anglés, Higinio, 'Die Bedeutung der Plika in der mittelalterlicher Musik' in *Festschrift Karl Gustav Fellerer*. Kassel 1962. pp. 28-39.

Anglés, Higinio, 'Rhythm in Medieval Lyric Monody' in *Report of the Eighth Congress of the International Musicological Society, New York 1961*, I. Kassel, 1961. pp. 3-11.

Apel, Willi, 'Rondeaux, Virelais, and Ballades in French 13th-Century Song' in *Journal of the American Musicological Society*, VII, 1954. pp. 121-130.

Apfel, Ernst, 'Spätmittelalterliche Klangstruktur und Dur-Moll-Tonalität' in *Die Musikforschung*, XVI, 1963. pp. 153-156.

Appel, Carl, 'Die Singweisen Bernarts von Ventadorn, nach den Handschriften mitgeteilt', Heft 81 in *Beihefte zur Zeitschrift für romanische Philologie*. Halle 1934.

Appel, Carl, 'Zur Formenlehre des provenzalischen Minnesangs' in *Zeitschrift für romanische Philologie*, LIII, 1933. pp. 151-171.

Aubry, Pierre, *Trouvères et Troubadours*. 2me édition, revue et corrigée. Paris 1910.

Aubry, Pierre, *See also* Bédier.

Avalle, D'Arco Silvio, *La letteratura medievale in lingua d'oc nella sua tradizione manoscritta*. Torino 1961.

Baehr, Rudolf (ed.), *Der Provenzalische Minnesang: Ein Querschnitt durch die neuere Forschungsdiskussionen*, Vol. VI in *Wege der Forschung*. Darmstadt 1967.

Bartsch, Karl, *Altfranzösische Romanzen und Pastorellen*. Leipzig 1870.

Bec, Pierre, *Petite anthologie de la lyrique occitane du moyen âge: initiation à la langue et à la poésie des troubadours*. Avignon 1961.

Beck, Jean Baptiste, *Die Melodien der Troubadours*. Strassburg 1908.

Beck, Jean Baptiste, *La Musique des Troubadours*, 2nd (?) edition. Paris 1928.

Bédier, Joseph, *Les Chansons de Croisade ... avec leurs mélodies publiées par Pierre Aubry*. Paris 1909.

Berger, Roger, *Le nécrologe de la confrérie des jongleurs et des bourgeois d'Arras (1194-1361)*, vol. II in *Mémoires de la commission départementale des monuments historiques du Pas de Calais*. Arras 1963.

Bertau, Karl Heinrich, *Sangverslyrik: Über Gestalt und Geschichtlichkeit mittelhochdeutscher Lyrik am Beispiel des Leichs*. Göttingen 1964.

Beyer, Paul, *Studien zur Vorgeschichte des Dur-Moll*. Kassel 1958.

Beyschlag, Siegfried, *Altdeutsche Verskunst in Grundzügen*, 6th ed. of *Die Metrik der mittelhochdeutschen Blütezeit in Grundzügen*. Nürnberg 1969.

Bezzola, Reto R., *Les origines et la formation de la littérature courtoise en occident (500-1200)*. 3 vols. Paris 1960.

Biber, Walter, *Das Problem der Melodieformeln in der einstimmigen Musik des Mittelalters*. Bern 1951.

Bittinger, Werner, *Studien zur musikalischen Textkritik des mittelalterlichen Liedes*. Würzburg 1953.

Boogaard, Nico H. J. van den, *Rondeaux et refrains du XIIe siècle au début du XIVe*. Paris 1969.

Bossuat, Robert, *Manuel bibliographique de la littérature française du moyen âge*. Vol. I, Melun 1951; Vol. II, Paris 1955; Vol. III, Paris 1961.

Boni, Marco, *Antologia trobadorica con traduzioni e note*, 2 vols. Bologna 1960-1962.

Boutière, Jean, and A.-H. Schutz, *Biographies des Troubadours*, revised edition by Jean Boutière. Paris 1964.

Brunel, Clovis, *Bibliographie des manuscrits littéraires en ancien provençal*. Paris 1935.

Brunner, Horst, 'Walters von der Vogelweide Palästinalied als Kontrafaktur' in *Zeitschrift für deutsches Altertum und Literatur* XCII, 1963. pp. 195-211.

Brunner, Horst, *Studien zu Überlieferung und Rezeption der mittelhochdeutschen Sangspruchdichter im Spätmittelalter und in der frühen Neuzeit*. As yet unpublished Habilitationsschrift, Universität of Erlangen-Nürnberg 1971.

Brunner, Horst, *Weltliche Lieder des Deutschen Mittelalters I. Minnesang und Sangspruchdichtung*, to be published as vol. XV in: *Monumenta Monodica Medii Aevi*, Bruno Stäblein, general editor.

Burger, Michel, *Recherches sur la structure et l'origine des vers romans*. Genève 1957.

Camproux, Charles, *Le 'Joy d'Amor' des troubadours : jeu et joie d'amour*. Montpellier 1965.

Chailley, Jacques, *Les Chansons à la Vierge de Gautier de Coincy*. Paris 1959.

Chailley, Jacques, *Précis de musicologie*. Paris 1958.

Chailley, Jacques, 'Quel est l'auteur de la ‹théorie modale› dite de Beck-Aubry?' in *Archiv für Musikwissenschaft*, X, 1953. pp. 213-222.

Chaytor, H.J., *From Script to Print, An Introduction to Medieval Vernacular Literature*. Cambridge, England 1945.

Cullmann, Arthur, *Die Lieder und Romanzen des Audefroi le Bastard*. Halle 1914.

Davenson, Henri, *Les troubadours*. Paris 1964 (?)

Davis, William M., 'Current Scholarship on the Origins of the Medieval Provencal Lyric: Some Conclusions' in *Philologia Pragensia*, X, 1967. pp. 92-96.

Dragonetti, Roger, *La technique poétique des trouvères dans la chanson courtoise*. Bruges 1960.

Del Monte, Alberto, *Storia della letteratura provenzale*. Milano 1958.

Dronke, Peter, *Medieval Latin and the Rise of European Love-Lyrics*, 2 vols. Oxford 1965-1966.

Dronke, Peter, *The Medieval Lyric*. London 1968.

Dyggve. *See* Petersen Dyggve.

Faral, E., *Les jongleurs en France au moyen âge*. Paris 1910.

Frank, Istvan, *Répertoire métrique de la poésie des troubadours*, 2 vols. Paris 1953-1957.

Frankel, Hans H., 'Poets' Biographies in Provençal and Chinese' in *Romance Philology*, XVI, 1962-1963. pp. 387-401.

Frings, Theodor, 'Minnesinger und Troubadours' in *Der deutsche Minnesang*, pp. 1-57; Vol. XV in *Wege der Forschung*. Darmstadt 1963.

Fromm, Hans (ed.), *Der deutsche Minnesang : Aufsätze zu seiner Forschung*, Vol. XV in *Wege der Forschung*. Darmstadt 1963.

Gennrich, Friedrich, *Grundriss einer Formenlehre des mittelalterlichen Liedes als Grundlage einer musikalischen Formenlehre des Liedes*. Halle 1932.

Gennrich, Friedrich, 'Grundsätzliches zur Rhythmik der mittelalterlichen Monodie' in *Die Musikforschung*, VII, 1954. pp. 150-176.

Gennrich, Friedrich, 'Internationale mittelalterliche Melodien' in *Zeitschrift für Musikwissenschaft*, XI, 1928-1929. pp. 259-296 and 321-348.

Gennrich, Friedrich, *Der musikalische Nachlass der Troubadours*. Vols. III and IV of *Summa Musicae Medii Aevi*. Darmstadt 1958-1960.

Gennrich, Friedrich, 'Refrain-Studien' in *Zeitschrift für romanische Philologie*, LXXI, 1955. pp. 365-390.

Gennrich, Friedrich, 'Die Repertoire-Theorie' in *Zeitschrift für französische Sprache und Literatur*. LXVI, 1956. pp. 81-108.

Gennrich, Friedrich, *Rondeaux, Virelais und Balladen aus dem Ende des XII., dem XIII. und dem ersten Drittel des XIV. Jahrhunderts, mit den überlieferten Melodien*. Vols. XLIII and XLVII of *Gesellschaft für romanische Literatur*. Dresden 1921, Göttingen 1927.

Gennrich, Friedrich, 'Streifzüge durch die erweiterte Modaltheorie' in *Archiv für Musikwissenschaft*, XVIII, 1961. pp. 126-140.

Gennrich, Friedrich, 'Suum cuique. Wer war der Initiator der Modaltheorie?' in *Miscelánea en homenaje a Mons. Higinio Anglés*, 2 vols., Barcelona 1958-1961. pp. 315-330.

Gennrich, Friedrich, *Troubadours, Trouvères, Minne- und Meistergesang*. Köln 1951.

Gennrich, Friedrich, *Die Jenaer Liederhandschrift*. Langen 1963.

Gerhardt, Mia L., *Essai d'analyse littéraire de la pastorale dans les littératures italienne, espagnole et française*. Leyde 1950.

Grandgent, Charles Hall, *An Outline of the Phonology and Morphology of Old Provençal*. Boston 1905.

Greimas, A.J., *Dictionnaire de l'ancien français*. Paris 1969.

Grout, Donald J., *A History of Western Music*. New York 1960.

Guy, Henri, *Adan de la Halle*. Paris 1898.

Hamlin, Frank R., Peter T. Ricketts, and John Hathaway, *Introduction à l'étude de l'ancien provençal: textes d'étude*. Genève 1967.

Handschin, Jacques, *Der Toncharakter: Eine Einführung in die Tonpsychologie*. Zürich 1948.

Harrison, Frank L., and E. Dobson, *Medieval English Lyrics*. In press.

Hatto, Arthur T., editor, *Eos: An Enquiry into the Theme of Lovers' Meetings and Partings at Dawn in Poetry*. The Hague 1965.

Hibberd, Lloyd, 'Estampie and Stantipes' in *Speculum*, XIX, 1944. pp. 222-249.

Hill, Raymond Thompson, and Thomas Goddard Bergin, *Anthology of the Provençal Troubadours*. New Haven 1941.

Hoepffner, Ernest, *Les troubadours dans leur vie et dans leurs oeuvres*. Paris 1955.

Hoepffner, Ernest, 'Virelais et ballades dans le Chansonnier d'Oxford (Douce 308)' in *Archivum Romanum*, IV, 1920. pp. 20-40.

Holmes, Urban T., *A History of Old French Literature from the Origins to 1300*. New York 1962.

Hughes, Anselm, editor, *Early Medieval Music up to 1300*, vol. II in *New Oxford History of Music*. London 1955.

Husmann, Heinrich, 'Minnesang' in *Die Musik in Geschichte und Gegenwart*, vol. IX. Kassel 1961; col. 359.

Husmann, Heinrich, 'Das Princip der Silbenzählung im Lied des zentralen Mittelalters' in *Die Musikforschung*, VI, 1953. pp. 8-23.

Husmann, Heinrich, 'Zur Rhythmik des Trouvèregesanges' in *Die Musikforschung*, V, 1952. pp. 110-131.

Jackson, W.T.H., *The Literature of the Middle Ages*. New York 1960.

Jahiel, E., 'French and Provençal Poet-Musicians of the Middle Ages: A Biblio-Discography' in *Romance Philology*, XIV, 1960-1961. pp. 200-207.

Jammers, Ewald, *Ausgewählte Melodien des Minnesangs*. Tübingen 1963.

Jeanroy, Alfred, *Bibliographie sommaire des chansonniers provençaux*. Paris 1916.

Jeanroy, Alfred, *Bibliographie sommaire des chansonniers français du moyen âge*. Paris 1918.

Jeanroy, Alfred, *Les chansons de Jaufré Rudel*. Paris 1915.

Jeanroy, Alfred, *Histoire sommaire de la poésie occitane*. Toulouse 1945.

Jeanroy, Alfred, *Les origines de la poésie lyrique en France*. Paris 1889.

Jeanroy, Alfred, *La poésie lyrique des troubadours*, 2 vols. Paris 1934.

Kippenberg, Burkhard, 'Die Melodien des Minnesangs' in *Musikalische Edition im Wandel des historischen Bewusstseins*, ed. Thrasybulos G. Georgiades, Kassel 1971. pp. 62-92.

Kippenberg, Burkhard, *Der Rhythmus im Minnesang: Eine Kritik der literar- und musikhistorischen Forschung mit einer Übersicht über die musikalischen Quellen*. München 1962.

Kolsen, Adolf, *Sämtliche Lieder des Trobadors Giraut de Bornelh*, vol. I. Halle 1910.

Kuhn, Hugo, *Minnesangs Wende*, 2nd ed. Tübingen 1967.

Lang, Adolf, *Gesamtausgabe der Troubadour-Melodien*, to be published as vol. V in *Monumenta Monodica Medii Aevi*, Bruno Stäblein, general editor.

Lang, Adolf, *Die musikalische Überlieferung des provenzalischen Minnesangs: Quellen und Repertoire*. Dissertation in preparation, Univ. of Erlangen-Nürnberg.

Långfors, Arthur, *Recueil général des jeux-partis français*. Paris 1926.

Lazar, Moshé, *Amour courtois et fin'amors dans la littérature du XIIe siècle*. Paris 1964.

Lazar, Moshé, *Bernard de Ventadour, troubadour du XIIe siècle: chansons d'amour*. Paris 1966.

Lerond, Alain, *Chansons attribuées au Chastelain de Couci (fin du XIIe-début du XIIIe siècle)*. Paris 1964.

Levy, E., *Petit dictionnaire provençal-français*, 3rd ed. Heidelberg 1961.

Linker, Robert W., *Music of the Minnesinger and Early Meistersinger; A Bibliography*. Chapel Hill 1962.

Lippman, Edward A., 'The Place of Music in the System of Liberal Arts' in *Aspects of Medieval and Renaissance Music, A Birthday Offering to Gustave Reese*, ed. Jan LaRue. New York 1966. pp. 545-559.

Lommatzsch, Erhard, *Leben und Lieder der provenzalischen Troubadours*, 2 vols. Berlin 1957-1959.

Lomnitzer, Helmut, 'Zur wechselseitigen Erhellung von Text- und Melodiekritik mittelalterlicher deutscher Lyrik' in *Probleme mittelalterlicher Überlieferung und Textkritik; Oxforder Colloquium 1966.* Berlin 1968. pp. 118-144.

Lord, Albert B., *The Singer of Tales.* Cambridge, Mass. 1960.

Macedonia, John A., *Motif-Index of the Biographies of the Troubadours.* Dissertation, Ohio State Univ., Columbus, Ohio, 1961. *Dissertation Abstracts,* XXII (1961-1962), col. 3667.

Maillard, Jean, *Evolution et esthétique du lai lyrique des origines à la fin du XIVe siècle.* Paris 1963.

McKinnon, James W., 'Musical Instruments in Medieval Psalm Commentaries and Psalters' in *Journal of the American Musicological Society,* XXI, 1968. pp. 3-20.

Mohr, Wolfgang, 'Zur Form des mittelalterlichen deutschen Strophenliedes' in *Der deutsche Minnesang,* pp. 229-254; Vol. XV in *Wege der Forschung.* Darmstadt 1963.

Molitor, Raphael, 'Die Lieder des Münsterischen Fragmentes' in *Sammelbände der Internationale Musik-Gesellschaft,* XII, 1910-1911. pp. 475-500.

Mölk, Ulrich, *Trobar clus, trobar leu: Studien zur Dichtertheorie der Trobadors.* München 1968.

Monterosso, R., *Musica e ritmica dei trovatori.* Milano 1956.

Moret, André, *Les débuts du lyrisme en Allemagne (des origines à 1350).* Lille 1951.

Moser, Hugo, and Joseph Müller-Blattau, *Deutsche Lieder des Mittelalters von Walther von der Vogelweide bis zum Lochamer Liederbuch; Texte und Melodien.* Stuttgart 1968.

Nelli, R., *L'érotique des troubadours.* Toulouse 1963.

Panofsky, Erwin, *Gothic Architecture and Scholasticism.* Cleveland 1957.

Paganuzzi, Enrico, 'Sulla notazione neumatica della monodia trobadorica' in *Rivista Musicale Italiana,* LVII, 1955. pp. 23-47.

Paris, Gaston, 'Les origines de la poésie lyrique en France' in *Journal des Savants* (Nov. 1891) pp. 674-688; (Déc. 1891) pp. 729-742; (Mars 1892) pp. 155-167; (Juillet 1892) pp. 407-429.

Parrish, Carl, *The Notation of Medieval Music.* New York 1957.

Parry, J., *The Art of Courtly Love.* New York 1941.

Petersen Dyggve, Holger, *Moniot d'Arras et Moniot de Paris,* vol. XIII in *Mémoires de la société néo-philologique de Helsinki.* Helsinki 1938.

Petersen Dyggve, Holger, *Gace Brulé, trouvère champenois,* vol. XVI in *Mémoires de la société néo-philologique de Helsinki.* Helsinki 1951.

Pillet, Alfred, and Henry Carstens, *Bibliographie der Troubadours.* Halle 1933.

Pollmann, Leo, *Die Liebe in der hochmittelalterlichen Literatur Frankreichs.* Frankfurt 1966.

Pollmann, Leo, *'Trobar clus': Bibelexegese und hispano-arabische Literatur.* Münster 1965.

Raynaud, Gaston, *Bibliographie des Chansonniers français des XIIIe et XIVe siècles.* 2 vols. Paris 1884.

Raynaud, Gaston, *Recueil de motets français des XIIe et XIIIe siècles.* 2 vols. Paris 1881.

Reese, Gustave, *Music in the Middle Ages.* New York 1940 (revised edition in preparation).

Rösler, Margarete, 'Der Londoner Pui' in *Zeitschrift für romanische Philologie,* XLI, 1921.

Rohloff, Ernst, *Media Latinitatis Musica II, Der Musiktraktat des Johannes de Grocheo.* Leipzig 1943.

Sachs, Curt, 'The Road to Major' in *Musical Quarterly,* XXIX, 1943. pp. 381-404.

Sachs, Curt, *The Wellsprings of Music,* ed. Jaap Kunst. The Hague 1961.

Salmen, Walter, *Der fahrende Musiker im europäischen Mittelalter.* Kassel 1960.

Salmen, Walter, 'Zur Geschichte der Ministriles im Dienste geistlicher Herren des Mittelalters' in *Miscelánea H. Anglés,* 2 vols., Barcelona 1958-1961. pp. 811-819.

Schnell, Fritz, *Zur Geschichte der Augsburger Meistersingerschule.* Augsburg 1958.

Schubert, Johann, *Die Handschrift Paris, Bibl. Nat. Fr. 1591: Kritische Untersuchung der Trouvèrehandschrift R.* Frankfurt 1963.

Schwan, Eduard, *Die altfranzösischen Liederhandschriften.* Berlin 1886.

Sesini, Ugo, 'Le melodie trobadoriche nel canzoniere provenzale della Biblioteca Ambrosiana' in *Studi Medievali,* XII (1939) pp. 1-101; XIII (1940) pp. 1-107; XIV (1941) pp. 31-105.

Spanke, Hans, *G. Raynauds Bibliographie des altfranzösischen Liedes, neu bearbeitet und ergänzt, erster Teil.* Leiden 1955.

Stäblein, Bruno, 'Eine Hymnusmelodie als Vorlage einer provenzalischen Alba' in *Miscelánea H. Anglés,* 2 vols., Barcelona 1958-1961. pp. 889-894.

Stäblein, Bruno, *Das Schriftbild der einstimmigen Musik,* vol. III in *Musikgeschichte in Bildern : Musik des Mittelalters und der Renaissance.* Leipzig (in preparation).

Stäblein, Bruno, 'Zur Stilistik der Troubadour-Melodien' in *Acta Musicologica,* XXXVIII, 1966. pp. 27-46.

Stäblein, Bruno, 'Oswald von Wolkenstein, der Schöpfer des Individualliedes' in *Deutsche Vierteljahrsschrift für Literaturwissenschaft und Geistesgeschichte,* VII, 1972, 1. Heft.

Taylor, Archer, *The Literary History of Meistergesang.* New York, London 1937.

Taylor, Ronald J., *The Art of the Minnesinger : Songs of the thirteenth century transcribed and edited with textual and musical commentaries,* 2 vols. Cardiff 1968.

Taylor, Ronald J., *Die Melodien weltlichen Lieder des Mittelalters,* 2 vols. Stuttgart 1964.

Taylor, Ronald J., 'The Musical Knowledge of the Middle High German Poet' in *Modern Language Review,* XLIX, 1954. pp. 331-338.

Tervooren, Helmut, *Bibliographie zum Minnesang und zu den Dichtern aus 'Des Minnesangs Frühling'.* Berlin 1969.

Thomas, John W., *Medieval German Lyric Verse; in English translation.* Chapel Hill, 1968

Thompson, Raymond, and Thomas Goddard Bergin, *Anthology of Provençal Troubadours,* New Haven 1941.

Van der Werf, Hendrik, 'Concerning the Measurability of Medieval Music' in *Current Musicology,* X, 1970. pp. 69-73.

Van der Werf, Hendrik, 'Deklamatorischer Rhyth-mus in den Chansons der Trouvères' in *Die Musikforschung,* XX, 1967. pp. 122-144.

Van der Werf, Hendrik, 'Recitative Melodies in Trouvère Chansons' in *Festschrift für Walter Wiora,* eds. Ludwig Finscher and Christoph-Helmut Mahling; Kassel 1967. pp. 231-240.

Van der Werf, Hendrik, 'The Trouvère Chansons as Creations of a Notationless Musical Culture' in *Current Musicology,* I, 1965. pp. 61-68.

Wallensköld, Axel, *Chansons de Conon de Béthune.* Helsingfors 1891.

Wallensköld, Axel, *Les Chansons de Conon de Béthune.* Paris 1921.

Wallensköld, Axel, *Les chansons de Thibaut de Champagne, roi de Navarre.* Paris 1925.

Wentzlaff-Eggebrecht, Friedrich Wilhelm, *Kreuzzugsdichtung des Mittelalters : Studien zu ihrer geschichtlichen und dichterischen Wirklichkeit.* Berlin 1960.

Wiese, Leo, *Die Lieder des Blondel de Nesles.* Dresden 1904.

Wilhelm, James J., *Seven Troubadours : The Creators of Modern Verse,* University Park, Pa. and Londen 1970.

Wiora, Walter, 'Elementare Melodietypen als Abschnitte mittelalterlicher Liedweisen' in *Miscelánea H. Anglés,* 2 vols., Barcelona 1958-1961. pp. 993-1009.

Wiora, Walter, *Das deutsche Lied,* 2 vols. Wolfenbüttel 1971.

Wiora, Walter, *Europäischer Volksgesang.* Köln 1952.

Wiora, Walter, *The Four Ages of Music.* New York 1967. English translation by M. D. Herter Norton of *Die vier Weltalter der Musik.* Stuttgart 1961.

Woledge, Brian (ed.), *The Penguin Book of French Verse,* Vol. I. Harmondsworth 1961. (Contains a number of trouvère poems with English translation.)

Wright, L.M., 'Misconceptions Concerning Troubadours, Trouvères, and Minstrels' in *Music and Letters,* XLVIII, 1967. pp. 35-39.

Glossary

Explanations of some important terms occurring without explanation in the course of this book.

BALLADE

It is difficult to define the term 'ballade' when considering songs of the 12th and 13th centuries. In discussions of 14th-century songs it is usually reserved for those songs with refrain which resemble one another so much in form that they are considered as chansons in fixed form, together with the virelai and the rondeau. This type of ballade has the conventional strophic form as described in Chapter 5, with the last one or two lines of the cauda recurring in every strophe of the song and thus forming a refrain. The authors of these ballades have shown a strong preference for writing exactly three strophes in coblas unissonans with a refrain of only one or at the most two lines; in general, this refrain is formally and musically an integral part of the cauda of the chanson, unlike the refrain of the virelai which is a section by itself.

Perhaps one can justify using a special term for songs of the above description because they share certain characteristics that are not common to all songs with refrain. But using this label for all chansons with refrain, regardless of other formal elements, seems confusing and superfluous since the term 'song with refrain' both suffices and is understandable also outside of the small circle of medievalists. Whether the troubadours and trouvères wrote ballades depends therefore upon one's definition of the term. Chansons with refrain are no exception among the chansons of the troubadours and trouvères, although they certainly form only a relatively small minority. Usually they have more than three stanzas and no specific preference is apparent for any other formal elements. Thus it seems preferable to me not to use the term 'ballade' in relation to the chansons of the troubadours and trouvères.

Special mention should be made of a large group of songs perhaps predating the 14th century and occurring anonymously in manuscript I[1] under the heading 'balette'. Some 155 of these songs–unfortunately preserved without music–have a refrain and at least some of the elements of either the ballade or the virelai*, but not all of them correspond to the description of either one. Instead these songs make it clear that their authors did not consistently distinguish between only two types of songs with refrain. Thus it seems justified to assume that these songs predate the period in which authors showed such a strong preference for combining certain formal elements with certain types of refrains that we now consider their songs as having fixed forms. (See also pp. 24-25 and 68.)

Recently Willi Apel[2] made an attempt to save the term 'ballade' for the repertoire of the troubadours and trouvères by proposing the term 'ballade' as the designation of the chansons in the conventional ab ab x form, which is already known under the terms 'canzone form' and 'bar form' (the former term is used primarily by philologists, the latter by musicologists; compare footnote 1, p. 64). It seems to me very confusing to use the label 'ballade' both for 14th-century songs of a certain strophic form *with* refrain and for 13th-century songs of the same strophic form but *without* refrain, while there actually are some troubadour and trouvère chansons that have all the characteristics of the 14th-century ballade except the preference for three strophes in coblas unissonans.

CANTUS CORONATUS

The term 'cantus coronatus' as used by Johannes de Grocheo in his treatise about Musica (written ca. 1300) is beset with many problems. In a literal translation it

anonymous Old French poems presented, without music, in six categories. Only a minority of these poems, especially those in the first and third categories (labeled 'grans chans' and 'jeus partis' respectively), resemble in style and content the trouvère chansons. Yet even most of these chansons occur exclusively in this source and only a few of them occur also in the typical trouvère manuscripts. The songs in the other categories, such as the 'balette' here under discussion, have little or nothing in common with the chansons of the trouvères. For a discussion of the balette, see Ernest Hoepffner, 'Virelais and Ballades'.

2. Apel, *Harvard Dictionary of Music*, 2nd ed. (Cambridge, Mass. 1970), articles 'Ballade' (French), p. 71, and 'Trouvère', p. 873.

1. Manuscript I (Oxford, Bodleiana, Douce 308) contains many

means 'crowned song', but it is not clear whether it refers exclusively to prize-winning songs, to trouvère chansons in general, or to a specific category of trouvère chansons. (Grocheo limits his discussion of secular songs to those of northern France; the chansons of the troubadours remain therefore outside of his scope.)

Grocheo begins his discourse on the *musica vulgaris* with a scholastic and in itself praiseworthy attempt at dividing the entire repertoire into specific categories. But in the ensuing description of these specific categories and in his comparison of them with liturgical music his dividing lines fall down almost completely. This failure is probably more due to the intractability of the material than to the author's apparent inability to deal with it. The musica vulgaris, according to Grocheo (p. 50, lines 8-17)[1], consists of music which is made with human voices and music made with 'artificial' instruments. The former can be divided into two kinds which are called '*cantus*' and '*cantilena*' respectively. Each of these has a triple subdivision: the three forms of the cantus are *cantus gestualis* (=chanson de geste), *cantus coronatus*, and *cantus versiculatus*; the three forms of the cantilena are called *rotunda*, *stantipes*, and *ductia*.

Apparently the distinction between vocal and instrumental music concerns only the manner of performance because Grocheo informs us that the instrumentalists performed, or should be able to perform, any form of cantus and cantilena (p. 52, lines 32-37). Similarly, the distinction between cantus and cantilena as well as the tripartite subdivision of the two tumbles down when Grocheo remarks that the cantus versiculatus is called a 'cantilena' by some and that there is a fourth kind of cantilena which is called *cantus insertus* or *cantilena entrata* (p. 51, lines 17-18).

In the section which concerns us most, namely the one about the cantus (p. 50, lines 18-43), we encounter such serious problems that we can determine neither the meaning of the terms 'cantus coronatus' and 'cantus versiculatus' (in the treatise the latter is also called 'cantus versicularis' and 'cantus versualis') nor the nature of the characteristics Grocheo ascribes to them. Grocheo informs us that the cantus coronatus was crowned because of its quality; that it was composed

by, and performed for, kings and noblemen; and that it contained only long and perfect [notes]. He also gives the first few words of two specific examples, namely 'Ausi com l'unicorne', which may refer to chanson R 2075 by Thibaud, King of Navarre; and 'Quant li roussignol', which may refer to chanson R 1559, in some manuscripts attributed to Raoul de Ferrieres and in others to the Chastelain de Coucy, both of whom were noblemen. Grocheo seems to be of the opinion that the cantus versicularis is of less value than the cantus coronatus, but he fails to say why; neither does he give any further description. However, again he gives the first few words of two specific examples, namely *Chanter m'estuet, quar ne m'en puis tenir*, which is probably chanson R 1476 by Thibaud, King of Navarre; and *Au repairier que ie fis de Prouvence*, which is probably the anonymous chanson R 624.

Later (p. 51, lines 32-40) Grocheo writes that the cantus coronatus must have exactly seven 'versus' and that the cantus versicularis resembles the former but that its number of 'versus' is not determined. This distinction is nullified in two ways. First, in the comparison of the hymn with the cantus coronatus (p. 62, lines 26-31) Grocheo states that the number of 'versus' of the latter is determined at seven *or thereabouts* (vel eo circa), while in the former a smaller or greater number of them may be found. Secondly, there is the peculiar situation that neither cantus coronatus cited by Grocheo has seven 'versus', regardless of whether this term means 'line', as seems most likely, or 'stanza'.

Similarly, Grocheo's observation about the long and perfect notes in the cantus coronatus loses its impact later in the treatise, where we read that the Kyrie and Gloria 'are sung »tractim« and with all long and perfect [notes] in the manner of the cantus coronatus' (p. 64, line 45; p. 65, line 3). (Concerning the ambiguous meaning of the reference to long and short [notes], see Chapter 3, p. 39.) A little further in the treatise even more doubt is cast upon Grocheo's value as reporter on contemporary musical practices. First we read: 'the Gradual and Alleluia are sung in the manner of the stantipes and the cantus coronatus ... but the sequence is sung in the manner of the ductia ...' (p. 65, lines 26-29), and then we read: the Offertory 'is sung in the manner of the ductia or the cantus coronatus ...' (p. 65, line 47; p. 66, line 1).

Of equal ambiguity are the two passages in which the

---

1. The numbers of pages and lines refers to Grocheo's treatise in the edition by Ernst Rohloff.

cantus coronatus is mentioned in relation to playing the viella. (When introducing the instruments, Grocheo gives the viella as a string instrument, without any reference as to whether it is played with a bow. See p. 52, lines 18-22.) In the first of these passages (p. 52, lines 32-37) the author seems to be discussing the repertory of the viella player and he writes: 'In general, a good performer ‹introduces› on the viella every cantus and cantilena and every musical form. Those that are commonly done for the rich people on feasts and at games are, in general, reduced to three: namely, the cantus coronatus, the ductia, and the stantipes. But we have earlier spoken of the cantus coronatus and therefore we have to speak now of the ductia and the stantipes.' The crucial point in the interpretation of this paragraph is the meaning of the word 'introduces'; it may refer to an instrumental introduction, or perhaps even accompaniment to a vocally performed cantus coronatus; but it may also refer to a *good* performer's ability to present on his viella all kinds of musical forms, including the cantus coronatus. In this respect it is perhaps important to note that in Grocheo's opinion the string instruments are preferable over all other instruments and that the viella is superior to all other string instruments (p. 52, lines 11-31).

The second passage (p. 63, lines 26-31) in which the viella and the cantus coronatus are mentioned together occurs in the discussion of plain chant where Grocheo states that a *neupma* is sometimes added to certain antiphons and explains that 'a *neupma* is like a ‹cauda› or an ending (‹exitus›) following the antiphon, much like the ending after a cantus coronatus or stantipes on the viella, which the viella players call ‹modus›'. Probably here he is writing about a melismatic ending of, or addition to, certain antiphons, the cantus coronatus, and the stantipes, but it is not clear whether he means here a purely instrumental presentation of the cantus coronatus followed by a neupma or a vocal performance followed by an instrumental postlude. Knowing Grocheo's inability to be precise, one should hesitate to conclude from these passages that as a rule the chansons of the trouvères were accompanied, preceded by a prelude, and followed by a postlude.

We know at least a dozen chansons which were awarded a crown, probably in a contest, because some scribes, namely those of manuscripts M, T, X, a, and C (the last is a manuscript without notes), marked certain chansons as crowned; not, however, the ones mentioned by Grocheo. Most pleasing among these indications are the ones by the scribe of X, who drew a little crown above the prize-winning chanson and wrote the word 'coronee' inside of this crown. Examination of these crowned chansons does not provide any help in understanding Grocheo's discussion of the cantus coronatus. It is clear that, in order to earn a crown, a chanson did not have to have exactly seven lines (and certainly not seven stanzas); nor did it have to be in any form of modal rhythm; and its author did not have to be a nobleman.

CAUDA (GERMAN: ABGESANG)

The last section of a chanson in the stereotyped strophic form discussed in Chapter 5, especially pp. 60 and 63-64.

CONTRAFACT

A poem written, or invented, in the metric scheme and sung to the melody of a pre-existing song, e.g., Part 2, Nos. 1 and 2.

It was Gennrich's habit to distinguish between *regular* and *irregular* contrafacts; in the former both the complete metric scheme and the melody of the model were taken over, whereas in the latter not all components of the metric scheme were used. When necessary to distinguish between such forms of contrafacture, I prefer to use other terms, such as *complete* and *partial*, in order to avoid the unwarranted implication either that there were regulations concerning contrafacture or that complete contrafacts were normal and partial ones exceptional.

ENVOY

Addition to a chanson in the metric scheme of the last few lines of the poem; it is usually either exactly as long as the cauda or shorter. It may contain any additional thought or message, such as a dedication, not usually expressed in the poem proper.

FRONS (GERMAN: AUFGESANG)

The first section, containing the pedes (sing.: pes*) of a

chanson in the sterotyped strophic form discussed in Chapter 5, especially pp. 60 and 63-64.

JEU-PARTI

A chanson in which two poets discuss a given topic (e.g., Part 2, No. 11). Usually the participants contribute alternate strophes. An extensive discussion of Old French jeux-partis may be found in: Artur Långfors, *Recueil général des jeux-partis français* (Paris 1926).

LIGATURE: See *Notation.*

MAJOR-MINOR

Certain intervals, or distances between two tones, may be *major* or *minor* in size. In our tonal system the octave is divided into seven consecutive intervals, called '*seconds*', five of which are large, or major, and two of which are small, or minor. The minor seconds are approximately half the size of the major ones and are therefore often referred to as 'half steps' as opposed to 'whole steps' for the major seconds. (These whole and half steps are graphically indicated in the scale charts on p. 55). The exact size of an interval may be changed by sharping or flatting, that is raising or lowering by half a step, one or both of its determining tones.

For this study the distinction between a major and a minor *third* is also important. A major third consists of two major seconds whereas a minor third consists of a major and a minor second. Finally, a *scale* is considered to be major in character if there is a major third between its tonic, or in this study its basis or center tone, and the tone a third above it; whereas a scale is considered to be minor in character if there is a minor third in that position.

MELISMATIC

A *melisma* is a group of many notes sung over one syllable. Accordingly, a *melismatic* melody contains many melismas. In the repertoire of the troubadours and trouvères melismas occur occasionally, by preference at or near the end of a line, especially the last line (e.g., R 21 published in my article on recitative melodies in the Festschrift für Walter Wiora). Whether melismatic melodies occur in the repertoire under discussion depends upon one's interpretation of that term. For example, the melody of Jaufre Rudel, presented as No. 1 in Part 2, may be called melismatic by some but neumatic* by others; in comparison with melismatic melodies in the plain chant repertoire, such as a Gradual or Alleluia, this melody is certainly not very melismatic, but it has more and longer groups of notes than the average troubadour or trouvère melody. (See also *Neumatic* and *Syllabic.*)

MENSURAL: See *Notation.*

METRIC SCHEME

The term 'metric scheme' refers usually to the combination of the number of lines per strophe, the number of syllables per line, and the rhyme pattern of the strophe.

MODAL NOTATION: See *Modal rhythm.*

MODAL RHYTHM

In *modal rhythm* certain durational patterns, known as *rhythmic modes*, are repeated over and over. Each rhythmic mode consists of either two or three durational units. In the few chansons that appear to be in modal rhythm one syllable is sung to one such durational unit of the mode, although two or more notes may be sung to one unit, as may be seen in Part 2, Nos. 11 and 15. Following are the six best known rhythmic modes given in old and present-day notation:

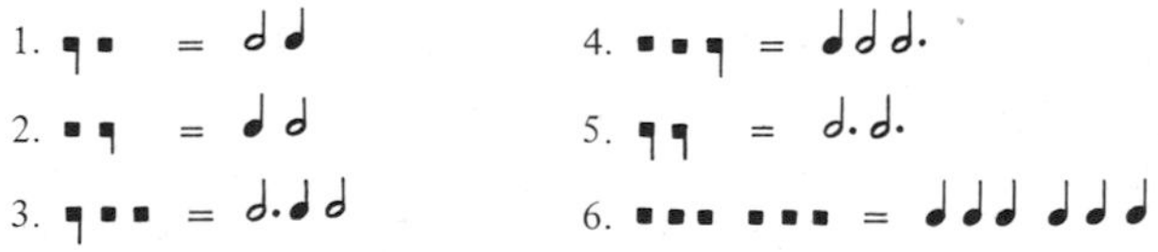
1.
2.
3.
4.
5.
6.

Although in medieval notation barlines were unknown, they are usually added in modern editions of old music. For melodies in modal rhythm each pattern, or mode, is placed between barlines. The usual method is to place a barline in front of the note for the accented rhyme syllable; other barlines are placed at appropriate distances from this one.

One of the rules which is supposed to have governed modal rhythm in the chansons of the troubadours and trouvères required that the entire chanson be in the same rhythmic mode. However, judging from a few entries in ms. O (among them Part 2, No. 14), this rule was not always applied. Accordingly some of the proponents of modal rhythm surmise that occasionally the rhythmic mode could be 'modified'. For example, it is Gennrich's opinion that Nos. 5 and 14 in Part 2 are in the second rhythmic mode, which is modified at certain points to accommodate lines of six syllables. According to others such irregular usage of the modes would be considered as *mixed modal rhythm*; in other words two rhythmic modes occur side by side in one chanson or even in one line. According to this way of reasoning the first four lines of No. 14 in Part 2 would be in either third or fourth mode, depending upon where the barlines should come, while the rest of the chanson is in normal second mode.

Whatever the proper name of the rhythmic modes used in these chansons, the occurrence of modal rhythm in irregular form raises the question as to where one should draw the line between mixed or modified modal rhythm and normal ternary meter. Furthermore, these questions are of rather minor importance for this study, since there are so few chansons in the troubadour and trouvère sources which appear to have been performed in a fixed meter.

NEUMATIC

The term *neume* has several meanings; in this context a neume is a group of a few notes sung over one syllable. Accordingly, in a *neumatic* melody neumes prevail over single notes and melismas. Whether a melody is syllabic*, neumatic, or melismatic* depends in part upon one's interpretations of those terms.

NON-MENSURAL: See *Notation*.

NOTATION

The music discussed in this study is notated in one of the following forms: non-mensural notation, semi-mensural notation, or mensural notation.

a. In *non-mensural* notation, which is commonly used for the chansons, no indications are given regarding the duration of the individual note. In this notational system basically only the following two symbols are used: ˥ (called virga) originally used for notes relatively higher than surrounding notes and ▪ (called punctum) for notes that are relatively lower than the surrounding notes. In the chansonniers no apparent attempt was made to distinguish consistently between the two. The two symbols could be combined or 'tied' together into *ligatures*; the following are the most common ligatures for the chansons of the troubadours and trouvères:

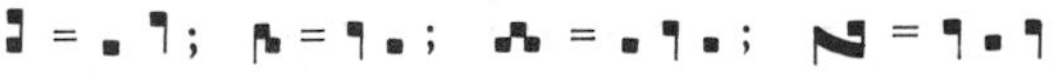

and 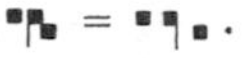.

For a discussion of the *nota plicata*, see the Prolegomena to Part 2, page 84.

b. In *semi-mensural* notation as encountered in the chansonniers the ligatures are non-mensural as above, but the single notes carry durational meaning rather than the older indication regarding relative pitch; ˥ indicates a note of long duration and ▪ a note of short duration. Since in both semi-mensural and non-mensural notation the same symbols are used for the single notes, it is sometimes difficult to determine which one of the two systems was used. Unfortunately the exact duration of the short and long notes in the semi-mensural notation depends upon circumstances, as is illustrated in the symbols used for the different rhythmic modes (see glossary section on modal rhythm).

c. In *mensural* notation, which is extremely rare in the chansonniers, complicated rules give durational meaning to both single notes and ligatures according to their shape and position; for details see Carl Parrish, *The Notation of Medieval Music*, New York 1959, chs. 5ff.

PES (GERMAN: STOLLE)

The *pedes* (sing.: pes) form together the frons of a chanson in the stereotyped strophic form discussed in Chapter 5, especially pp. 60 and 63-64.

REFRAIN

In reference to the chansons of the troubadours and trouvères the term 'refrain' is used in two related meanings. Firstly, it is used for the usual type of refrain, namely a text which in each strophe recurs in exactly the same position, usually at the end. Secondly, the term is used for certain little ditties of two to four lines which emerge in various forms of music and literature of the 12th, 13th, and early 14th centuries; they became parts of rondeaux*, virelais*, ballades*, and motets; they were strewn (with and without music) into several romans, plays, and other literary works; they occur as isolated lines in motet- and rondeau-sections of certain manuscripts; and they were rather loosely tacked onto strophes of trouvère chansons, each chanson with a different refrain and each refrain with its own melody. (To distinguish between the two types, I have referred to chansons with the latter type of refrain as *chansons with multiple refrains*.) Many of these refrains occur more than once in the literature mentioned, but it is difficult to distinguish in a meaningful way between somewhat varied multiple occurrences of the same song and two or more songs which happen to resemble one another. Jeanroy developed the theory that all of these ditties, in some instances called 'rondels', originated in those dancing songs which he considered to be the predecessors of the rondeaux, virelais, and ballades.[1] However, his evidence seems rather insufficient. (See also pp. 24-25 and 68).

RHYTHMIC MODES: See *Modal rhythm.*

RITARDANDO

A gradual slowing down.

RONDEAU

The label 'rondeau' is given to those songs with refrain in which the refrain* occurs two or three times even though the song can be said to have only one strophe. Restricting our attention to the rondeaux dating from the 13th and 14th centuries and preserved with music, we notice that the entire refrain, having at least two lines, occurs both at the beginning and at the end of the song and that in addition the first part of the refrain occurs near the middle of the song. Although the number of lines could vary somewhat, the authors maintained a rather strict parallel between the refrain and the free part of the song concerning metric scheme and melodic form, so that the form of almost any rondeau of this period can be reduced to the following formula:

1. Jeanroy, *Les origines de la poésie lyrique*, pp. 102-113.

AB a A ab AB

AB A A AB AB

(Obviously, all lines sung to a certain melody must have the same number of syllables.)

Probably from the middle of the 13th until the beginning of the 16th century the rondeau, in slightly varying forms, enjoyed considerable popularity among poets as well as among composers of polyphonic music. But only two trouvères are known to have written rondeaux, namely Guillaume d'Amiens and Adam de la Halle; only the rondeaux of the former are monophonic. The number of rondeaux written during the 13th century depends in part upon how strictly one requires songs with that name to correspond to the above formula, since many of the chansons that might be labeled 'early rondeaux' lack one or more of the elements that later became standard for the rondeau.

The origin of the rondeau is still very obscure. Partly because if its name it has often been associated with dancing, particularly with a circle dance (see also *Refrain*). But, according to Grocheo, some of his contemporaries associated the rondeau with a circle *song* because of its circular form. The latter association fits, better than the former, the form of the songs with refrain that predate the 14th century. For these songs display above all an interest in playing with recurring thoughts, words, and lines, and with pre-existing and perhaps well-known little songs or parts of songs. (See also pp. 24-25 and 68.)

SEMI-MENSURAL: See *Notation.*

SYLLABIC

In a syllabic melody most or all syllables are sung to one note each (see also *Melismatic* and *Neumatic*).

VIRELAI

The term 'virelai' usually designates a song with the following characteristics: the conventional strophic form as described in Chapter 5 (ab ab x) for melody and text, and a refrain which has the same metric scheme and the same melody as the x section of the strophe proper and which is sung at the beginning of the song as well as after each strophe. The authors of this type have shown a strong preference for writing exactly three strophes and refrains of three or four lines, so that some characteristic rhyme schemes of the virelai would be as follows:

AB AB cd cd abab AB AB cd cd abab AB AB cd cd abab AB AB
or
ABBA bc bc abba ABBA bc bc abba ABBA bc bc abba ABBA
or
ABA cd cd aba ABA cd cd aba ABA cd cd aba ABA.

Although its name varies from period to period (e.g., chanson balladée or bergerette) this type of song was popular during the 14th through 16th centuries. But in the manuscripts whose contents may predate the 14th century, other than manuscript I, to be discussed below, we find very few of them; how many there actually are depends on how strictly one requires the presence of all the above mentioned characteristics. In ms. I[1] under the heading 'balette' we find some 155 songs with refrain, which in varying combinations show the characteristics of either the ballade* or the virelai, but not all of them correspond to the description of either one. Instead these songs make it clear that their authors did not consistently distinguish between only two types of songs with refrain. Thus it seems justified to assume that these songs predate the period in which the authors showed such a strong preference for combining certain formal elements with certain types of refrains that we now consider their songs as having fixed forms. (See also pp. 24-25 and 68.)

---

1. See footnote 1 in *Ballade*, p. 153.

Index

Medieval authors are listed under their first names. The chansons are numbered in italics.